Marching With Caesar – Sacrovir's Revolt

by
R.W. Peake

Also by R.W Peake

Critical praise for the Marching with Caesar series:

Marching With Caesar-Antony and Cleopatra: Part I-Antony

"Peake has become a master of depicting Roman military life and action, and in this latest novel he proves adept at evoking the subtleties of his characters, often with an understated humour and surprising pathos. Very highly recommended."

Marching With Caesar-Civil War

"Fans of the author will be delighted that Peake's writing has gone from strength to strength in this, the second volume...Peake manages to portray Pullus and all his fellow soldiers with a marvelous feeling of reality quite apart from the star historical name... There's history here, and character, and action enough for three novels, and all of it can be enjoyed even if readers haven't seen the first volume yet. Very highly recommended."
~The Historical Novel Society

"The hinge of history pivoted on the career of Julius Caesar, as Rome's Republic became an Empire, but the muscle to swing that gateway came from soldiers like Titus Pullus. What an amazing story from a student now become the master of historical fiction at its best."
~Professor Frank Holt, University of Houston

For Ray "Titus Pullo" Stevenson

"Look here, Mars! Look here, Mars! I am Titus Pullo! These bloody men are my gift to you."

Thirteenth Forever

Foreword

With this, Volume XX of the *Marching With Caesar* series, I suppose it's natural for me to take stock of all that's taken place, but it was during my final edit of this manuscript, on May 21st, that the incomparable Ray Stevenson died. Hopefully, I don't need to tell my readers who Ray Stevenson was, but on the off chance that this is their first book in the series, or they forgot what I wrote way back in 2012, while the inspiration for the series came during my commute to my well-paying job as a VP of Product Management and Development at a software company that I absolutely loathed, when I was listening to the audio version of *Caesar's Commentaries* and I wondered what it was like for the grunts who did all the digging, fighting, and dying, it was Ray Stevenson, as Titus Pullo in the HBO series *Rome*, who provided the inspiration for the first Titus Pullus.

For those few who enjoy my books but may not have seen the HBO series (all five of you ☺) that, while it only lasted two seasons, has become revered as a classic, I can't recommend it highly enough, because in the very first scene of the very first episode, the germ of an idea for my Titus was planted, based on the idea of, during a time when your fellow countrymen averaged a height of five feet four inches, and a weight of a hundred ten pounds, what kind of advantage would it give someone to be a foot taller, and a hundred pounds heavier, in the kind of combat that was a feature of the ancient world, where killing another man was up close and personal? However, it wasn't just the size differential that made Mr. Stevenson's portrayal so inspiring and enticing as an example for my own Titus. As anyone who watched *Rome* knows, Stevenson's Pullo had an issue with anger management, and was capable of a ferocity that marked him as even more dangerous than he already was because of his size and strength.

When I first sat down and wrote, "These are the words of

Titus..." I knew that I wanted my Titus to be one of those few men (who did exist) who survived an entire career under the standard, one consisting of not just one enlistment, but two or even more, and who rose through the ranks to attain the post that had existed for centuries but was formalized by Augustus, the post of Camp Prefect. And, given the time period in which my Titus the Elder lived, starting his career with the 10th Legion, surviving a campaign in Hispania, the seven-year campaign in Gaul, and both civil wars, I knew that he would need some...edge, in both a literal and a figurative sense. I can't say there was an "Ah ha" moment when I realized that it was Mr. Stevenson's portrayal that provided the inspiration, but very quickly, when I thought of my Titus, it was Mr. Stevenson I saw. That unquenchable rage that the screen Pullo unleashes in battle was inspired by Ray Stevenson; as much as it pains me to admit it, that rage that is always present and simmering just below the surface of what is now four generations of Pullus men belongs to their creator. Whereas Mr. Stevenson's Pullo is an easygoing, affable man under other circumstances, that's where my characters diverge from his portrayal.

Up until maybe a month before I decided to publish what is now the First Edition of *Marching With Caesar-Conquest of Gaul*, which included part of Titus' origin story and the training and first campaign in Hispania, it was "These are the words of Titus Pullo...", but then I went back and reread *Caesar's Commentaries*, where I learned that the real Titus Pullo was a turncoat (or he was a patriot, depending on how you look at Caesar's actions), and there was no way I could go with the same name, because another decision I made from the beginning was that Titus the Elder was a Caesarian through and through. However, for no good reason I can articulate, I was enamored with the "Pullx" portion of the name, and I didn't want to change it to something completely different, so he became Titus Pullus.

Yet, even with a slightly different name, my Titus was and is inspired by Ray Stevenson's Titus, and for that I make no apologies, and am forever grateful. Hopefully, you, my readers, feel the same way.

As always, I want to thank my dynamic duo, my editor

Beth Lynne and my cover artist Laura Prevost, for their patience and understanding in dealing with me, but most of all, to y'all, my readers, who make this worth doing.

May 27, 2023
Semper Fidelis
R.W. Peake

Historical Notes

The Revolt of Sacrovir, led by an Aedui nobleman named Gaius Julius Sacrovir, which actually encompasses the uprising by the Treveri as well, led by a Treveri nobleman named Gaius Julius Florus, is mentioned by both Tacitus and Cassius Dio, with the former going into the most detail, devoting seven paragraphs to it, and it's Tacitus I rely on the most heavily. What I found most interesting, as readers can probably tell as they make their way through Volume XX, is the *crupellarii*, a type of gladiator that was apparently very popular in Gaul during this time period. In appearance, they are something akin in appearance to the heavily armored knights of the late Medieval Period, being armored from head to toe. However, unlike the later version that used plate armor, the *crupellarii* wore the kind of segmented armor similar to the *lorica segmentata*, but it was not limited to protecting the torso. According to the various depictions that I could find, the legs and arms were similarly covered by a series of overlapping plates, while the helmet more closely resembles the kind of helm worn by men at arms and knights of a later era, with eye slits and holes for ventilation arranged along the lower part of the helmet.

While Tacitus provides general numbers of the Aedui forces, totaling forty thousand, he only mentions specifics when it comes to the part of the force that was "armed like our legionaries," putting that number at one-fifth of the total, which would mean there was more than one Legion's worth of men equipped like their Roman foes. My number of the *crupellarii* of a bit more than a thousand is an arbitrary one, but what Tacitus also mentions was how hard it was to kill these heavily armored men, and how the Legionaries facing them were forced to resort to using axes and other heavier weapons when their *gladii* and javelins, with their slender soft iron shafts, proved inadequate to the job.

It was as I was reading this that a larger theme that is the purview of the writer of historical fiction began to form, and the result is this version of the story. Whereas Tacitus writes that, aside from the difficulty in killing the *crupellarii*, it was an easy victory for Rome, there is a maxim about history being written by the winners, and given the level of panic that Tacitus describes among the people of all classes in Rome, it got me thinking...is that really what happened? I think that it's at least within the realm of possibility that Tacitus, writing almost a century later, was availing himself of the official story, and not what really happened, because what we do know is that even with two Roman Legions, which are basically unnamed other than the reference to their being part of the Army of the Rhenus, both Upper and Lower, the Romans would be significantly outnumbered. There is a quote that has been attributed to a variety of sources; as an old Cold Warrior, I prefer the version that says it was Lenin who famously quoted, "Quantity has a quality all its own," and that is the premise of this version of the pivotal battle that takes place seventeen miles north of Augustodunum, modern-day Autun.

According to Tacitus, Sacrovir eschewed the idea of defending Augustodunum, choosing to meet the Romans some seventeen miles north of the Aedui tribal seat, who would have been approaching from the north after putting down the Treveri. Using a combination of the Barrington's Atlas, the France Outdoors series of topographical maps and Google Earth, I found a location about a kilometer west of Bard-le-Regulier and the same distance east of La Tuilerie, at 47° 8'45.84"N, 4°18'15.04"E that, if I had been Sacrovir, I would have chosen as a good place to defend. Therefore, for better or worse, that is the site of the pivotal battle between the rebel Aedui and the 1st and 2nd Legions. In my retelling, the battle is a much harder-fought affair, with the Romans incurring heavier losses than Tiberius indicated in his letter to the Senate announcing the victory. This is partially for dramatic purposes, but would it be the first time where the official version and what really happened are markedly different? Also, it's a result of these heavier losses that will end up having an even larger impact in the lives of Gnaeus and his family.

Another aspect that is of my own invention was the composition of the armor worn by the *crupellarii*, using the famous iron ore from Noricum that, while it has never been specifically mentioned by Gnaeus' forebears, going back to Titus the Elder, I think has been established is the material from which the *gladius* that cost a huge Gregarius more than a year's pay to have made some seventy years prior to this part of the story. Given how Tacitus comments on the difficulty of penetrating their armor, and the fact that there is no historical record of barbarian tribes having difficulty penetrating the *lorica segmentata*, I account for the difference by the use of better materials to make the armor. The strategic value of several hundred sets of armor composed of this high-quality metal is also my invention, although I don't think it's a huge leap to think that they would be seen as hugely valuable to a man like a certain Praetorian Prefect.

What is not an invention was the obvious discord, tension, and conflict between Gaius Silius and Lucius Visellius Varro, not to be confused with his father Gaius Visellius Varro, who was the *Praetor* of Germania Inferior (which, for continuity purposes, Gnaeus refers to as the Lower Rhenus since that was how it was referred to for many years prior to this), but as Tacitus states, was too infirm to accompany the army. I don't think it's a huge stretch to think that, first, *someone* representing the *Praetor* would accompany the army, and second, that a father would choose his son to fulfill that role, nor do I think it's a stretch that the enmity that was on display in the year 24 BCE, the year in which Varro the younger was the junior Consul, began during this period, especially given the nature of the charges Varro levies against Gaius Silius of using the revolt as a pretext to enrich himself, and secretly conspiring with Sacrovir the Aedui.

One character who receives a brief mention, Sextus Papinius Allenius, was real, and would go on to serve as Consul in 36 CE, but given the trajectory of his career, and the record indicating that he had served as a military Tribune around this period of time, he finds himself here in the pages of our story. Another is Lucius Vitellius, who would go on to be named Consul three times but whose real distinction is that he was the father of Aulus Vitellius, one of the Four Emperors of 69 CE.

Finally, as far as I, or anyone knows, Gaius Julius Sacrovir didn't have a half-brother who was a former Primus Pilus and Camp Prefect, and I freely confess that it was a happy accident when I named Tiberius Sacrovir several volumes ago. Again, that's what's great about historical fiction.

Table of Contents

Chapter 1

The front line Cohorts of the 1st Legion were ready to depart Ubiorum a day sooner than the four days that our *Praetor*, Gaius Silius, had given us Centurions to prepare our men, giving the men the opportunity for one last debauch, not the night before our scheduled departure, but the night before that. While I cannot take full credit for this, I was the first to suggest it to Macer, but the other Centurions, the Pili Priores in particular, added their weight, although it was ultimately Silius' decision, which he quickly gave, being experienced enough to know that it was expected. Alex and I had arranged for the Fifth's men to have privileges to the Dancing Faun, which was still inhabited by Vinicius and my former Fourth Cohort, the men of which had adjusted to the presence of the men of my new command. Not, it must be said, without a handful of incidents, although only one of them resulted in a brawl, but enough witnesses were honest that the Fifth man was provoked into it by a man of the Second of the Fourth; once I heard the man's name, even before I heard the witnesses' statements, I was certain I knew my Fifth ranker was not at fault. None of this was a surprise, however, and by the time we were ready to march the day after the next one, when we gathered at the Faun, not only was it packed, despite the fact that it had been expanded, the atmosphere, while raucous, was largely peaceful.

Now that Macer was Primus Pilus, he had to be even more circumspect about where he spent his off-duty hours, despite the fact that he had been a regular at the Faun ever since he had been the Quartus Pilus Prior and my father one of his Centurions. Consequently, I was sitting at my regular table, in my regular chair facing the door, along with my successor Vibius Vinicius, my former Optio and now the Pilus Posterior, Aulus Saloninus, and yet another former Optio of mine,

1

Numerius Gillo, making the fourth, when the door opened and Macer appeared. Now, he was well-known and the men all respected him, particularly in the Fourth Cohort, which was where he had gotten his start as a paid man, yet none of us were surprised when the noise suddenly subsided, as if men were embarrassed at being caught doing something they should not have been doing, although he made a point to call to one of the rankers, paying particular attention to the older veterans as he made his way towards us, and I suspect I was the only one who noticed that there was a pattern of one man per table to whom he called out. I knew that this was a trick he had been taught by my father, back when he had been Macer's Optio, who in turn had learned it by reading the Prefect's account, since I recalled reading the same thing. Or, I thought suddenly, and with a twinge of sadness that surprised me, perhaps the Prefect had even told his grandson about this back when they lived in Siscia, as my father sat there, listening with the kind of rapt attention I know I would have paid if the gods had allowed me to spend a moment with my great-grandfather. I was sufficiently distracted by this thought that, when Macer arrived at our table, I was slightly surprised, although I managed to come to my feet like the other three did, and Saloninus began to hurry off to grab a chair, but Macer stopped him.

"I can't stay," he said apologetically. "I'm making the rounds of all the places."

"No worries, Primus Pilus," Vinicius assured him, which I thought a bit superfluous, but then he pointed at me. "Pullus was just warning us about what we can expect if *Praetor* Varro is involved in any way. Although," he shook his head, "how he managed to be appointed to a post as prestigious as one of the *Praetors* for Germania proves what Pullus is saying about how he's got connections to..."

His voice trailed off, although this was not unusual then, and is not now a handful of years later, but we all knew that the person he was not naming was not our *Imperator* Tiberius, but the Praetorian Prefect, Sejanus, a man with whom I had run afoul of during my short time in the Praetorian Guard. However, what caught my eye was the way in which Macer reacted, if only because, despite our different ranks, as he is my direct superior, and has been for most of my career, I knew him well enough to see that he looked embarrassed.

I was about to learn why when Macer fumbled, "Er, yes, well about that." Looking at me directly, he continued, "I'm afraid that I owe you an apology, Titus. I assumed that it was Lucius Visellius Varro who had been named *Praetor*, but it's not. It's *Gaius* Visellius Varro, his father, who's been put in that post."

"That," I replied with a fair amount of fervency, "is a relief." Choosing to ignore his lapse in calling me by my father's name, something I had noticed he did when he was distracted or under duress, I addressed the others, saying, "You boys will never know just what a *ballista* bolt we dodged without that patrician bastard here in the province!"

The others muttered what could only be called a lukewarm agreement, but I did not begrudge them; they did not have any firsthand dealing with Lucius Visellius Varro, and while I know they trusted me, it is just not the same unless you experience something for yourself. I am afraid that my attention was on them, so I did not see Macer's expression, but then he cleared his throat in a manner I had learned long before, when I was the newly arrived and fellow paid man Gnaeus Volusenus, serving as the Quartus Hastatus Posterior, that meant that something important was coming.

"Yes, about that. It's true that it's the father, but his son came with him, and..." he closed his eyes, another habit of his when he knew the likely reaction and did not want to see it happen, "...he's coming with us as the *Praetor*'s official representative."

"Oh, *fuck* me," I breathed...or I believed I did; the laughter from the others told me differently, although Macer only smiled, and it was a faint one. A thought occurred to me, and I asked, "When you say that he's accompanying us as the Praetor's 'representative,' what does that mean, exactly? So, he's still a *Quaestor* then, yes?"

Of the other three men, I saw by the expression in Saloninus' eye, his other obscured by the patch he had worn since the Long Bridges, that, while he might not have understood exactly why I was asking, that it was not an idle question, and like me, he turned to look up at Macer, who was standing there wearing an expression that made my heart sink.

"Sometimes you ask the worst questions, Pullus," he muttered, but knowing that prevaricating would not help matters, he answered my question. "Yes, his official rank is *Quaestor*," Macer replied, but then once again closed his eyes as he said with a sigh, "but his father has officially named him as his representative."

There was a small chorus of gasps at this, but Licinius said quickly, "He wouldn't be foolish enough to try and overrule Gaius Silius, would he? Silius is the most experienced *Praetor* we've got!"

Rather than answer directly, Macer looked at me.

"Well, Gnaeus? Do you think Licinius has the right of it?"

I did not care for being put on the spot, but these were men I trusted, and I thought for a moment.

"I don't know anything about his father," I began, then in something of a small measure of revenge, I asked Macer, "Do you?"

"Only what everyone else knows," Macer replied evenly, though I could tell he understood what I was doing. "He was Consul, what, almost a decade ago, just a couple years before Augustus died, and that he was a dicing companion of the old boy. He was younger than Augustus, but I guess now he's around Augustus' age when he died."

This aligned with my own memory of the man, although I confess that I had some hard feelings towards him because of who his son was, and I did not believe that the Varro I knew simply sprang up with the character he possessed from dragon's teeth.

Knowing Macer expected an answer, I said slowly, "I think that Licinius is right that Varro the Younger isn't going to dispute with Silius openly, or use his *imperium* to try and overrule him. Still," I felt compelled to add, "Silius needs to keep an eye on him, because he's up to something, I'm certain of it. I feel it in my bones."

Macer departed a few moments later, but while I stayed a bit longer, I had lost my taste for the wine and stories swapped between men about to go on the march, my mind more occupied by the idea of someone who had been bold enough to have a man try to assassinate a King, who I had thwarted in the process. Suddenly, the prospect of facing rebelling Gauls was not as pressing a concern for me.

Our departure from Ubiorum two days later was, as always, attended by the hundreds of women and children who, by law, did not exist when it came to their attachment to the men of the first four Cohorts of the 1ˢᵗ. I was one of the few, if not the only one, whose wife and children were legitimate, thanks to the intercession of Germanicus Julius Caesar, whose death had occurred two years earlier, but with which many of us were still struggling, and I include myself in that number. Perhaps it is vanity, but I believed then, and do now, that I had more of a just cause in my grief because of my personal connection to the Roman who many, if not most of us, believed was destined to become the next Imperator once Tiberius died. As we had hoped, Piso was brought to trial on a long list of charges: insubordination, corruption, misuse of funds, abandoning and reentering Syria without the authorization of the Imperator, fomenting civil war, which I assumed was based on his attempt to rally the Legions against Germanicus, the murder of Germanicus, and violating the *Lex Iulia Maiestatis*, which I gave up trying to explain to Bronwen, not wanting to admit that I barely comprehend what it means myself, although it essentially is based in sacrilege against the Imperator or his family. To the anger and dismay of the vast majority of the Head Count, especially in Rome, and with a unanimous sentiment of anger in the Legions, Piso, while he was convicted, it was on only one charge. If that charge had been the murder of Germanicus by poisoning, the commonly held belief, that would have been enough, but he was, in fact, found innocent of that and every charge except for one we considered to be extremely minor, the violation of Germanicus' *imperium* by taking Legions he was not authorized to command out of the province to wage war.

In the days after we received the news about the verdict, the atmosphere was incredibly tense, and while I was not of the same opinion, many of us wearing the transverse crest in particular likened it to the days immediately following the death of Augustus. I cannot deny that it was close to the same, but there was not the frenetic quality that had been present the last time, when men only spoke in whispers, and rankers darted about the camp, either searching for or seeking out the latest bit of gossip about an event that would undoubtedly impact our fate. This time, while the men were angry, they seemed at a loss as to what they could do about it, which I suppose now that I think about it was why I was not as concerned as Macer and others were. In addition, even in the moment I recognized that my time in Rome with the Praetorians had rubbed off on me, because I was more aware of the undercurrent that runs through the upper reaches of our society. While I do not recall where I heard it, or from whom I heard it, I did remember hearing about the connection between the *gens* Claudii, the line of Tiberius and one of the most prestigious and ancient of our ruling families, and the *gens* Calpurnia, more specifically, the Calpurnii Pisones branch, one that dated back to well before the Punic Wars. As I had read in the Prefect's account, and learned firsthand, the leading families take care of each other, and even before the verdict, I had prepared myself for what in my bones I thought was the likely outcome. Still, when it arrived, I was surprised that I felt just as bitterly disappointed as my comrades, even given what transpired with Piso's suicide, but what was more of a shock was how Bronwen reacted.

"That *viper*, that *mentula!*" She spat the words, then added a few more in her Parisii tongue that, while impossible for me to pronounce, I at least knew was saying not very nice things about Piso's mother. She had been preparing our evening meal when I walked into our apartment, but now she stood there, waving the knife she had been using to chop some vegetables, and as riveting as her display was, I could not keep my eyes from watching the blade moving around. "He should have been staked to the ground, then had his guts pulled out so the foxes can chew on them while he watched!" she raged, but before I could comment, her eyes narrowed, the sign she was thinking, and she amended, "No! That was too good for him! He should have had each limb tied to a different horse, then sent in a different direction, but very *slowly!*"

This startled and disturbed me in equal measure, and I cut her off by exclaiming, "The Prefect actually witnessed that once. I remember reading about it. It was at..."

"Actium," Bronwen finished for me, and I felt my jaw drop in shock. "Where do you think I got the idea from, my love?" she asked with a sweetness that made the subject even more jarring, and all I could do was shake my head.

"I should have never taught you to read our tongue," I muttered, although at the time, it had seemed like a good idea. What I had not been prepared for was how quickly she took to it; within six months, she could read almost anything in our tongue with only occasional help from me or Alex. As much to change the subject as anything, I asked her, "But why are you so...upset about this? You never met Germanicus."

"So?" she countered, but she at least had stopped waving the knife about. "It is still an injustice, is it not?"

"Well, yes, it is," I agreed, yet somehow I felt certain there was something more than the idea of whether or not Piso was escaping justice for his action involved. "But I still..."

"He gave you permission to marry," Bronwen cut me off, a bit impatiently, as if it was obvious. "And you married me, so why would I not be upset about the man who murdered the Roman who made my deepest wish come true escaping the punishment he deserved? He should have been found guilty and executed, not allowed to take his own life!"

And, when she put it this way, I could understand her adamancy, and I said as much, taking her into my arms as I did, which I suppose is why she began crying.

"It is not fair, Gnaeus." Her words were muffled because her head was buried in my chest. "He was a good man, and he deserved better than your Imperator gave him."

For the first time since I heard the initial news, I felt the stinging of tears; more importantly, I felt the surge of indignant anger that I knew I had been stuffing down, fearful that it would come boiling out at the worst possible moment, or more likely, that I would say something intemperate that one of the Imperator's creatures might hear.

However, what might be called a minor miracle occurred

in Rome. When the trial concluded, apparently, the sentiment of those who had observed the proceedings was such that, according to the gossip we heard, it was extremely unlikely that Piso would be convicted of the murder of Germanicus, although the evidence was overwhelming on several lesser charges, including the only one of which he was convicted, the illegal departure from his province. However, the reaction by the Head Count was understandably virulently opposed, and while there was only minor violence in the Forum the last day of the trial, it was made clear to Piso that, acquitted or not, he would never draw a peaceful breath as long as he lived. Consequently, after making sure that his affairs were in order, which included begging Tiberius to ensure that his wife and son were not made destitute because of what he thought was coming. While I did not say as much to Bronwen, I will say that, given how he was acquitted of Germanicus' murder, he certainly did not seem to think that was happening, although I suppose it is more likely that he saw the reality for what it was; at this point, the verdict had already been decided by the true power in Rome, not Tiberius, but in the mass of humanity the patricians sneeringly call the Head Count, thinking of them as a type of humanity barely a step above livestock, whose only value lay in the ability to manipulate them to achieve a patrician's own aims. Being honest, when I was Gnaeus Volusenus, I viewed them much the same way, but I was wrong, which I now know; I suspect that most patricians will feel the same way until the day they die.

Nevertheless, even Piso's suicide did not do much to lift the pall that still clung like the wisps of a stubborn fog brought on by the death of Germanicus, but it does not stop the Legions from marching when they are given the order to do so as we were on that day. Because of the crowd, Silius had decreed that we would be wearing our armor, including decorations as we paraded out of Ubiorum, and the number of onlookers was increased by the men of the other six Cohorts, although most of them stayed in the camp.

As arranged, Bronwen, Algaia, and the children were standing at the corner where the Via Praetoria intersected with the street that led to our apartments, which placed them on my side of the formation, and I braced myself for more of the same treatment I had received that morning, not from my wife but from my son. Somehow, Titus had convinced himself that, now at almost seven, he was old enough to accompany the army, and he had not taken my refusal well at all, refusing to either kiss or hug me, or in a vain attempt to appease his growing sense of maturity, the arm I offered him as if he was a grown man, pointedly turning his back. Bronwen stood there, her eyes shining with tears, but also trying not to laugh, which was essentially what I was doing, although I was surprised at how much this rebuff hurt. Fortunately, and to my relief, Titus had clearly had second thoughts because, on seeing the Fifth approaching, he stepped away from his mother, but instead of thrusting his arms out for me to pick him up, his normal demand when he was not angry with me, he stiffened to *intente* and rendered what I could see was a heartfelt if imperfectly rendered salute.

My *Signifer,* Tiberius Lentulus, without any order from me, dipped the Century standard, whereupon I automatically barked, "Century! Eyes right!"

I did not look over my shoulder to see if my men obeyed; a Centurion can tell by the barely audible sound that is almost drowned out by the crunching of hobnails on the stone roadway when more than one hundred fifty men snap their heads to one side. Besides, I had my own part to play, acknowledging my son's salute with one of my own, my reward being the broad smile on my son's face, presumably more from the sight of all these grown men looking him in the eye as we marched past. Only when I was a pace beyond him did I break eye contact with Titus, looking up to see his mother, tears streaming down her face, but with a smile that was a perfect copy of her son's, reminding me where he got it from.

"Be safe, husband! And bring your men back to their families!"

Technically we are not allowed to make any kind of sign of acknowledgement when an onlooker calls to us, even if it is a man's wife, but there are some things where the regulations do not mean as much, while ignoring a man's wife is always a bad idea.

Judging that the last rank of the Century was passing Titus and his mother and sister, I snapped out, "Eyes front!", hearing the same slight rustling sound as the men turned their heads back to the front, whereupon I called out over my shoulder, "Thanks, boys. My son will never forget that, I promise you."

"He's almost big enough to be marching with us already, Centurion," Lentulus commented, which earned a ragged chorus of agreement from the men who heard my *Signifer*.

"He is," I agreed, then said, "but if my wife ever hears any of you say something like that, she'll probably cut your balls off. And," I added, "you're on your own."

This was met with laughter, as I hoped, although I was also serious about not being willing to step in between my Parisii wife and one of my men if they were foolish enough to suggest that our son would be under the standard. It was a fight that I had learned was impossible to win, which meant that I knew better than to fight it, and if I am being honest, back then when he was only four, it was not something that was sufficiently pressing for me to choose to fight about it.

Leaving our families and comrades behind, we made rapid progress, the weather on this early April day perfect for marching, especially once Silius gave the order to doff our armor at the first rest stop. It may seem a small thing, and it is, but it is also a sign of a veteran commander, one who knows that when it was possible to see to the comfort of the men, it would not be forgotten later, when he was unable to do so. While Varro the Younger had not been part of the Alaudae's march to Casurgis to help Catualda, staying behind in Mogontiacum, I could not imagine that it would have even occurred to him to do such a thing, and I was happy that he would not be in any position to countermand Silius' orders. His father would have been another story, but by this time, we had heard that Varro the Elder's "infirmity" was actually a case of gout, which some wags in the ranks call the "patrician's ailment," believing that it comes from eating too many oysters, or in some versions, larks' tongues. When men spoke of these things, I kept my mouth shut, because I have in fact eaten both, back when I was in the Praetorians and the Second Cohort was assigned the duty of guarding a banquet held by the Imperator.

The occasion was the sendoff for Germanicus on his embassage to the East, and he made arrangements for the Centurions to be able to sample some of the dishes, which included oysters, larks' tongues, and some sort of specially cultivated fish that was apparently prepared in such a way that it was still wriggling when it was presented, although ours had long since stopped. To my surprise, the tongues were actually quite tasty, but as my Optio Publius Sabinus, who was now serving as Optio in the First of the Seventh, had pointed out at the time, it would have taken the entire supply of larks at the banquet to sate my appetite. Despite the circumstances, basically being allowed to eat the leftovers from the banquet, I knew that if I divulged this fact to anyone other than Macer among my current comrades, it would mean I would be unmercifully teased, so whenever the topic came up, I kept my mouth shut. What mattered at this moment was that the elder Varro was not going to be there, but unlike most of my counterparts, all of whom were of the opinion that the son would not possibly be bold, or stupid enough to try and countermand any order Silius might issue, I was not so certain. Now, this did not mean I thought he would do anything so straightforward as openly challenge Silius' authority, but not even I could imagine what the sly nobleman had in mind.

It is a four-day march to Augusta Treverorum, although in this case, it depended on how long we stayed in Mogontiacum, which was where we would be meeting Varro and whichever Legion would be coming by barge from their home base in Vetera in what is now called the Province of the Lower Rhenus (Germania Inferior). This change by Tiberius had not really altered anything as far as we in the Legions were concerned, aside from adding another *Praetor* to the mix, which in our view was a headache for those two and not us, knowing as we did that it was inevitable that the "Senate" would appoint two men who were rivals, while all we could hope for was that their squabbling did not have an impact on us, while also recognizing that the Senate was only acting under the instructions provided them by Tiberius. I had already approached Macer about the possibility of visiting my mother if we were going to be in Mogontiacum for more than a watch or two, and I was only partially exaggerating when I sold my Primus Pilus on the idea that, because of her relationship with Censorinus, who was no longer the acting *Duumvir* but was still well-connected, she would be able to provide valuable information about the *Praetor* of the Lower Rhenus and his actions. Macer was not fooled about my real reason, but he also gave his permission provided that we ended up staying overnight, because he also knew that while it was not my main motivation, it was likely I would learn something valuable. As it turned out, we were in Mogontiacum for two full days, and according to Censorinus, it was because the elder Varro was listening exclusively to his son, which was why no Legion under their command was ready to march.

"Are you aware of any bad blood between Silius and either Varro?"

The question itself was not surprising; that it was from Censorinus and aimed at me was, but I could only shake my head, as did Alex.

"Nothing that filtered down to my level," I replied, which was disappointing to Censorinus, though he, wisely, did not seem to blame me for it.

We were in the *triclinium* of my mother's villa, waiting for Carissa and Grimhilt to prepare the evening meal on our first night, after we were informed by a visibly angry Sacrovir that the *Praetor* of the Lower Rhenus had not even decided which Legion would be marching with us, which meant that neither the 2nd nor the 14th, the two most logical choices since they were at Vetera, had been making preparations. Mandalonius was still serving my mother as well, and she had kept us both informed and entertained with her tales of the small dramas taking place under her roof with the two barbarian women, one Gaul and one German, as they engaged in what seemed to be a never-ending struggle for the ascendant position in my mother's service, a problem that, as amusing as it was, I place squarely at my mother's feet for causing. She had hired Grimhilt on a temporary basis when Carissa's sister had fallen ill, but when Carissa and Mandalonius had returned, she had not had the heart to dismiss Grimhilt. The result was some of the most humorous letters my mother ever wrote as she alternately laughed and complained about the antics of these two strong-willed women that, now even close to two years later, was still ongoing, with neither of them able to gain the upper hand on the other woman.

This diversion notwithstanding, I was more interested in why Censorinus was asking about any bad blood, replying to my query about why he was asking this by saying, "There's no real reason, I suppose, at least nothing substantial. There just seems to be some sort of...tension between Silius and Varro. Not," he added quickly, "the *Praetor* but his son. And, the son is the one who urged Varro not to make a decision about which Legion was going to be marching until Varro the Elder could consult with Silius, which is why you're delayed."

"I'm certainly not complaining," my mother interjected from her spot on the largest couch, which she liked to recline on, but with her feet tucked underneath her in a most unladylike fashion that I remember from my childhood, which I adored and Censorinus clearly did not mind, unlike the man I had thought was my father, Quintus Volusenus, who constantly chided her about it when he deigned to talk to her at all. "Having my son under my roof, even if it *is* for only one meal, is the nicest surprise I could have." When it was clear that I had recognized the bait and was refusing to take it, my mother's nostrils flared slightly, but she turned her mind to the topic at hand. "I keep hearing about some sort of connection that Varro the Younger has with our Praetorian Prefect. If that's true, does that change matters?"

Understanding what she meant, both Censorinus and I exchanged a glance, and despite my ambivalence towards the man, I saw that he was as appreciative of my mother's intelligence and shrewd insights as I was.

"That," I said slowly, not sure how I felt about what I was about to divulge, "is actually the truth, at least as far as the strong possibility that what the son is doing is at the behest of the Prefect and not his father."

My mother, who knows me better than anyone save Bronwen, wasted no time in pressing, "I can tell by the way you're saying that that you know more than you're letting on."

"No, I don't," I protested, yet I have always had a hard time lying to my mother, which caused me to amend, "I mean, I don't have any firm evidence, just the kind of whispers that are as substantial as smoke."

I was not at all surprised when this did not suffice, although it was Censorinus, who, perhaps wanting to take the burden on his own shoulders and spare my mother my irritation, said, a bit sharply, "You know better than I do that your mother is discreet, Gnaeus, but I would hope that I've earned your trust by now and know that I am as well."

Now, while I trusted Censorinus to a degree, I cannot say I was anywhere near as convinced about his discretion as he would have liked, but one sidelong glance at my mother told me there was one, and only one answer that would have been acceptable to either of them.

"Of course," I lied. "You've proven yourself to a degree that I don't have any doubts."

Taking a breath, I went on to explain everything I knew to that point, and while I had told my mother most of this in the immediate aftermath of the campaign to install Catualda, over the intervening time, there had been other bits of information that had reached our ears in Germania. By the time I was through, I had managed to convince myself that we at least knew the cause of the delay, but what we could not determine was why Varro the Younger was impeding Silius', and our progress in this manner.

It was actually Censorinus who mused, "I wonder if he's trying to buy some time for those rebels in Augusta Treverorum for some reason."

For the first time, Alex, who had been nursing his single cup of wine, contributed, "I was wondering that myself. But," he shook his head, "to what end? And that would be a dangerous game to play, even if it was at Sejanus' behest."

"Maybe not," my mother interjected. "Not if his goal is to make things more difficult for Silius." Addressing me, she asked, "Isn't it true that time is the most valuable asset for the commander of an army on the defensive?" I understood what she was doing, as I understood that she already knew the answer to that, and I nodded.

"Yes, generally speaking. If this Florus is even somewhat experienced, he's going to know that every day he can forestall a battle gives him the opportunity to rally more rebels to his cause, and to improve his defenses." Even as I was speaking, things were coming more into focus, and I was feeling more confident as I continued speaking. "And if you're right, Mama, Varro is putting as many obstacles in Silius' path as he can in order to trip him up. But," I almost shouted this in frustration; judging by the manner in which the others winced, I suppose I did, "to what end? Why would he be after Silius?"

"*He's* not," Alex said quietly. "I mean," he added quickly, "not for his own purposes. This is something that Sejanus wants."

"Germanicus." I was not even aware I said the name aloud except for the manner in which the others reacted. "That's what this is about. Remember, Silius was absent from his post for more than a year because he was with Germanicus. They were not only colleagues, they were friends, close friends if I'm any judge."

"But Germanicus is dead already," Censorinus objected, which was true enough, but I had this growing sense that I had stubbed my toe on the hidden cause of what was taking place, recalling everything that I had heard about Sejanus from my fellow Praetorians, and what I had observed myself.

Consequently, I had my reply ready. "Sejanus hates the *idea* of Germanicus. He hates the way that he's still loved by the people. And," I added pointedly, "loved by the Legions."

"How does destroying Silius help him destroy Germanicus?" Censorinus was still clearly skeptical, but before I could say anything, it was my mother who said, "By making an example of Silius, it will send a message to all of Germanicus' other friends who might want to continue to sing his praises. And," she concluded, "I suspect that he thinks Tiberius will be pleased to see Germanicus' *dignitas* diminished."

Thankfully, before anyone could make a comment one way or another, Carissa appeared to announce that the meal was ready, and the subject was dropped, moving on to other topics, which consisted of two proud fathers trying to outdo each other with tales of the exploits of their children. Fortunately, at least with my mother, we had a receptive audience; I did not much care whether Censorinus was interested.

The Lower Rhenus Legion, which turned out to be the 2nd , arrived in Mogontiacum two days later, but I did not actually see Varro in the flesh until the march had started, nor did I immediately recognize the Centurion wearing the white crest of Primus Pilus of the 2nd, although I was certain that he looked familiar.

"That's Lucius Carbo," Macer told me. "He replaced Quintus Mutilus when he retired this winter. I met him when we had our meeting when Sacrovir was elevated."

It was not so much what my friend and Primus Pilus said as the way he said it that made me look down at him carefully, but he was staring at the backs of some of his rankers as they chatted during our first rest stop.

"Is there anything I should know about Carbo?"

Macer shrugged, yet he did not look away from his men as he said only, "If I had to guess, there's a reason that Varro picked him and his Legion." It was when he paused, and my recalling how the Centurion looked familiar that came rushing at me, so I was at least partially prepared when he added, "He apparently came with the Varros from Rome when the Elder took the post of *Praetor*."

"He's a Praetorian," I exclaimed. "I think he was the Pilus Prior of the Fourth Praetorian Cohort. Or," I thought, "maybe the Pilus Posterior."

This surprised Macer.

"How could you not know which he was? The Praetorians don't wear different color crests between the Pili Priores and the other Centurions?"

"They do, but remember when I told you that Sejanus didn't like us wearing our uniforms?"

"Ah." He looked chagrined. "That's right. I forgot. But," he continued, "yes, he came from the Praetorians. I don't know which Cohort."

"Given what I know about the Praetorians, I think it would be a good idea for you to watch your tongue around your fellow

Primus Pilus."

Whether it was the words or my grim tone, I do not know, but he slapped me on the shoulder as he assured me, "I always do."

The command group *Cornicen* sounded the signal warning that the rest stop was ending, and I headed back to my Century, trying to quell the unsettling feeling that the young Varro was in the process of loading the dice for a throw that, despite not knowing what it might be, I did know I was not going to like.

Since we were marching into Gaul, it meant that our progress was on a good Roman road, paved, graded and measured perfectly for a Legion to march in column. Naturally, this also meant that anyone coming the other direction, or moving slower than we were in the same direction, was not just expected but required to step aside for us. This is so commonplace that we barely notice, but while it is not quite as commonplace, there are times when a merchant caravan, or a drover driving a herd of cattle to market has other ideas, refusing to cede the right of passage to us. At least, that is how it starts, but the outcome is never in doubt, and yes, sometimes blood is shed when some civilian refuses to accept the inevitability. Given that the last time we had marched through this territory was when we returned from Rome after marching in Germanicus' triumph, and while this had been more than three years earlier, it was not sufficiently in the past that we did not notice the marked difference in the attitude of the Gauls.

"If looks could kill," I remember commenting to Lentulus, "we'd all be dead men walking."

"I noticed the same thing," he agreed, using his head to indicate a small cluster of men, each of them standing next to a small cart, the sign this was a group of merchants who had been forced to give us the right of way, but it was the way they were glaring at us as we marched drag behind the 2nd that was more noticeable than the fact they were all bearded and wearing traditional tribal garb. "This lot here, for example." He laughed as we marched past, the snout of his wolf headdress turning back to the front as they left our vision. "The fact they're still glaring daggers at us even after the 2nd passed by is a sign, that's for certain."

17

It was an astute observation, one that reminded me that my *Signifer* possessed a shrewd mind, and probably more importantly to me as his Centurion, was very observant. No party that I had ever encountered had been cheerful about having their progress impeded, yet they never seemed this angry before, and while this is the first one that I remember, it was not the last. Unlike the last time I marched, with the Alaudae, we had a full complement of cavalry, but in what most of us considered to be a wise decision, Silius had left the several *turmae* comprised of Gauls behind, men of the Tungri tribe, whose lands are almost due east from Ubiorum, deeming them suspect because of the proximity to what was going on with the other tribes. I for one was happy to see the Batavians, including Herminius and his section, with us, although they were rarely around, ranging out over the countryside as they were, but it made me feel better knowing they were out there.

On our third day, a day out of Augusta Treverorum, the First of the 1ˢᵗ was actually in the vanguard, putting us at the front of the column, and there was a shout from the lead Century, Clepsina's Second as it happened, followed immediately by the *Cornu* call of a friendly rider approaching. Within a hundred heartbeats, I saw the rider, recognizing him as Wigmar, one of Herminius' men, but he only waved as he went cantering by, heading for where Silius and the rest of the command group was riding, which included Sacrovir, who, now that he was a Prefect, was not only given a horse, but was expected to ride it. I had gone on several rides with him on Latobius, who himself was part of the baggage train, where Alex alternated riding him and Lightning, he being one of three people who Latobius tolerated besides me, with Bronwen being one, and my son the other, something his mother did not know about at that time, thinking that he only rode with me and not alone. Sacrovir, however, had not taken to riding as my great-grandfather had, though both of them came to it late in life, but whereas the first Titus Pullus came to love riding Ocelus, and my father essentially grew up with the huge gray stallion, the best that could be said for Tiberius Sacrovir was that he endured riding with the same kind of grim determination that had made him a Primus Pilus. Perhaps

18

within a dozen heartbeats, the horn sounded the halt from the command group, and since my Century was immediately ahead of the First, I walked over to where Macer was taking the opportunity to suck from his flask.

"I wonder what that's about," he muttered as he corked the flask.

"I recognized Wigmar. He's in Herminius' section and they were," I pointed off in a southerly direction, "scouting in that area."

By this time, we were heading west, and Augusta Treverorum lay directly ahead of us, just a bit more than a day's march away, and the area where I was pointing was in the general direction of Divodorum (Metz), though the tribe in whose land the town was located, the Mediomatrici, had not been mentioned as one of the rebelling tribes, not that this meant anything. As the two of us knew, both from experience with Arminius, and from the knowledge gleaned from men like my great-grandfather, the barbarian tribes are quite excitable, and it does not take much to incite them to join with tribes they normally hate when the common enemy is Rome. Our conversation was interrupted when, from the command group, the sound of raised voices carried across the spring air, and while we were too far away to make out what was being said, because of my height and the fact that Silius and the other senior officers were mounted, I could see emphatic gestures being made, and it appeared that the dispute was between Prefect Sacrovir and the young Varro, who looked slightly ridiculous on horseback, and even more ridiculous wearing a muscled cuirass, although nobody was wearing their helmets. Silius had ordered us to put our armor back on that morning, in recognition of how little we actually knew of what was taking place.

"I'd love to know what that was about," Macer murmured as we two Centurions openly gawked like a pair of *Gregarii* as Sacrovir continued gesticulating at Varro, who, to my eyes, seemed cowed, while Silius watched impassively.

"If Fortuna loves us, we'll be finding out soon enough."

I made this comment because, suddenly, Sacrovir jerked his horse's head about and gave it a kick in the flanks to come bouncing in our direction, his face a study in the kind of fury that, when he was our Primus Pilus, boded ill for every man in the Legion.

As angry as he was, the Prefect had the presence of mind to beckon us with a gesture of his head to meet him where he had drawn up a couple dozen paces off of the roadway, and we trotted over to join him.

He was facing away from the men, while the *Cornicen* attached to the command group remained silent, and as soon as we reached his side, Sacrovir seethed, "That *cunnus*! That little, jumped-up piece of *cac*! Who does he think he is? *Caesar*?" Never in my association with Tiberius Sacrovir had I seen him so angry; later, Macer confirmed that it was a first for him as well. But then, Sacrovir fell silent for such a long period that I nudged my Primus Pilus, who shot me a furious glance of his own, barely moving his head in a negation of my plea. However, all the Prefect was doing was trying to regain some of his composure, and he resumed by giving a laugh, a bitter one with no humor, then he began to explain, "But, I suppose I have to hand it to him. He's put the *Praetor* in it, and done it neatly." Now, he looked down at us to ask, "Do you remember what I told you, Marcus? That the son was just here as his father's representative, and that Silius had overall authority because he's actually a *Praetor* and that turd isn't?" Macer nodded, but I had a sick feeling in my stomach, so I was not surprised when Sacrovir said, "Well, I was wrong. Guess whose Tata gave his boy a gift in the form of an ivory baton?"

Macer gasped, "*What*? Are you joking?" Then, before Sacrovir could snarl at him, he said quickly, "No, of course you're not." He hesitated, then added hopefully, "But at least that means Varro doesn't outrank Silius."

"It *wouldn't*," Sacrovir agreed, but then he looked directly at me and he gave me a grim smile, one that I knew was meant to convey a message, "but the slippery bastard has one other thing. A document...from Rome," he added meaningfully. He paused, looking from me to Macer as he said, "It's one that gives him *Propraetorial Imperium*, and it's signed by..."

"Sejanus."

Sacrovir looked at me, for I had been the one who said the

name, and nodded.

"Yes, Gnaeus. He has a scroll that gives Lucius Visellius Varro overall command of this campaign."

Now that the secret was out, it did not take long before Varro made his first move, yet as much as I wanted to, it was difficult for me to find fault with it. What Wigmar was bringing was word that the Turoni had risen up along with their neighbors to the west, the Andecavi, but whereas we were marching to subdue the Treveri, they had yet to make any kind of offensive move. Consequently, when the debate that Macer and I witnessed began, it was triggered by Varro, first producing the small ivory baton that was normally carried by a *Praetor*, claiming to be equal status with Silius. Later, we would learn that this much Silius had either deduced for himself, or had been forewarned about, because as nearly as I could tell, while Sacrovir was raging at Varro, that was when I noticed Silius sitting there without an expression on his face that gave anyone, including me, an indication of his thoughts. That, however, quickly changed when Sacrovir, acting in his capacity as Prefect, threw his weight behind Silius, telling the pasty patrician that as far as he was concerned, Gaius Silius was still the overall commander. This was the moment that Varro produced his final surprise, the scroll, complete with the seal of the Praetorian Prefect claiming that Sejanus had received instructions from the Imperator to issue this scroll to his faithful servant Gaius Visellius Varro, who in turn, had handed both the baton and the scroll to his son. As far as the decision that culminated from this confrontation, however, it was actually a sound one, as much as I hated to admit it. Neither the Turoni or the Andecavi are large tribes, and most importantly, the number of warriors who had taken up arm numbered in the hundreds combined. According to the message, the Tribune Aviola was already marching on the Andecavi, leading a single Cohort of the 7th that had been sent north from Lugdunum as the first Roman force on the scene. Knowing this, Varro's decision was to dispatch the third line Cohorts of the 2nd to march against the Turoni, while the rest of the army was to continue on to Augusta Treverorum, because of these three tribes, the Treveri were the most dangerous. What I could not help noticing, and I was not alone, was that when the Cohorts detached themselves and began marching to the southwest in the general direction of Divodorum, although the Turoni lands were beyond that, further southwest, Varro did not go with them.

"I suppose that military glory isn't that important to him," Macer had commented as we watched the Cohorts march away.

The delay had taken more than a third of a watch, but soon enough, we resumed, making camp about ten miles east of Augusta Treverorum, making our first fortified marching camp, both as a precaution and as a message. We arrived the next day just before noon, but the only people who seemed happy to see us were the Romans who lived there, whereas most of the inhabitants just watched us march down the street in a sullen silence.

"I don't see many men," I commented to nobody in particular, and it was my *Cornicen* Macrinus who commented in reply, "And the ones you do see are all old."

This was also true, and as we had learned in Germania, this was the most potent sign of trouble coming. There is an auxiliary camp in Augusta Treverorum, but it was not nearly large enough to hold us, so Silius marched us through the town, which was by design, to the western side, where we built another marching camp, during which Macer attended a meeting with his counterpart, the two *Praetors*, and the Prefect. He was not gone long, and the Legion *Cornicen* sounded the notes for all Centurions to attend to the Primus Pilus, which meant I only had to walk a few paces.

The rest of the Centurions came up at a trot, and once we were assembled, Macer informed us, "We're going to be here for at least a day, but probably longer to wait for the third line Cohorts to report back about the Turoni. While we wait, we're going to be sending out Cohort-sized patrols in the cardinal directions to see if we can't find where all those Treveri who were missing in town are skulking about."

It was a message that we all received and understood, the sign that our Primus Pilus was as aware as we were of what this meant, and it was a reminder to me of the little ways in which a leader can both inform and assure his men that they are speaking the same language, and that their concerns are aligned.

Macer dismissed us, but indicated I should stay, whereupon he told me, "The Prefect is still fuming about Varro. Gnaeus," his expression became worried, "I'm worried that he's going to try and fight Varro somehow."

"He'd be mad to try," I replied immediately and without hesitation. "The fact that Varro has enough influence with Sejanus to get the Prefect to give him this kind of cover should tell him it's a foolish idea."

"I know that!" Macer snapped, but immediately held up a hand. "I apologize. I know you're aware of it as well, but I don't know how I can broach the subject with him."

I thought for a moment, then I advised, "At the very least, he needs to wait for a bit, and let his temper cool."

"That's a good idea," Macer said immediately. Lifting an arm, he pointed. "He's right over there. Why don't you go tell him?"

"Me?" I protested before realizing what he was doing; it was not that he thought it was a bad idea, but that it was the wrong time to try and reason with the Prefect. Deciding to take a measure of revenge, I said, "I'll go with you if you tell him."

With a sigh, Macer said, "All right, let's go."

We approached cautiously to where Sacrovir had dismounted and was in the process of giving one of the slaves who cared for the riding stock of the officers instructions, but to our intense, mutual relief, he waved a hand in our direction.

"Don't worry," he said as we reached him, "I'm not going to do anything foolish, like challenge Varro right now." Neither of us tried to hide our relief, which earned us a sour smile from the Prefect, although he did admit, "Oh, I'm tempted, make no mistake of that. But no, I've been dealing with these *cunni* for more than ten years as Primus Pilus, and now as Prefect. I know how to play their game. But," his smile returned, but it was a cruel one, "I'm going to be watching that bastard and biding my time."

Before he could do anything like that, however, another

event took place that impacted our Camp Prefect even more than Varro's maneuvering.

We ended up in that camp for almost a week, the only action seen by any of the Cohorts, including my own, was the heels of fleeing Treveri as they dashed into the forests at our approach, who we were far too experienced to pursue into the thick underbrush.

I believe it was Macrinus, my *Cornicen,* who let out a string of frustrated curses then said, "It was easier hunting rabbits back when I was on my Tata's farm than running down these *mentulae*! Are we going to spend an entire season like this, Centurion?"

Despite secretly agreeing with him, at least as far as the frustration, I also knew better than to say this aloud; at moments such as this, Centurions and Optios are expected to behave as if they are not as frustrated as their men, and that any moment, they will achieve success at whatever they were doing. In this case, it was punishing the rebelling Treveri who, at least to this point, were rebels in name only. Mainly because of our relentless pursuit of them, aided of course by our cavalry that was constantly scouring the countryside, and the fact that most of these rebels were on foot, the insurgents had not had the opportunity to inflict much, if any, damage save for an occasional burned farm belonging to a Roman. Confined to camp as we were when we were not out on patrol searching, it was also natural that men with time on their hands spent it gossiping, and it was inevitable that some enterprising ranker would figure out a way to have some sort of congress with one of the locals, usually a woman, and it was from these women that the fodder for the gossip was obtained. What this meant in a practical sense was that every morning we would be confronted with news of another tribe rebelling and joining the Treveri; the fact that none of these phantom tribes were ever spotted, let alone captured during our pursuit of the rebels flitting about did not quell the gossip at all. Finally, I was forced to resort to my *vitus* out of frustration, laying into men when I caught them chattering about something they had heard, although they, quite wisely, learned very quickly to shut their mouths whenever I approached.

Then, two days short of a week after our arrival, the Second of the 2nd finally managed to surprise a group of rebels who foolishly decided to stand and fight. Numbering about two hundred Treveri warriors, they were quickly cut down, save for a handful of men that the Secundus Pilus Prior ordered spared for the purpose of bringing them back to crucify within sight of the walls, the standard message to rebelling tribes. The other result of this skirmish was that it gave the boys in the 2nd the ability to gloat about having gotten stuck in first; the fact that it was only one Cohort was meaningless, so a man of the Sixth Cohort would shout insults at the 1st with the same enthusiasm as if he had been in the Second. As maddening as this may be, we all knew that if the *caliga* had been on the other foot, we would have been doing the same thing, and if there was a positive, it was that it fired the enthusiasm of the 1st to have their own opportunity to get their *gladii* wet. It was a day short of a week that the third line Cohorts returned, led by the Tribune Aviola, who ordered the standards garlanded with ivy in the ancient sign of victory, something that caused a bit of a stir.

"That's a bold move for a Tribune to make," was how Clepsina put it during our meeting with Macer in his tent, which was greeted with agreement from the others.

"If he made it on his own, yes it is," Macer replied, but there was something in the manner in which he said it that told us he had more to say about it, which he did. "But I don't think he did," he continued. "I think that he was either given a hint to do it, or told outright to do it."

"By who?"

This came from the only Centurion present junior to me, the Primus Hastatus Posterior Marcus Glaxus, and I am afraid to say that Glaxus and I did not get along. First, he was significantly older than me, and was only a couple years from retirement, having risen as high as he ever would, but the second reason for his antipathy towards me had to do with my status as a paid man. To men like Glaxus, it did not matter what I did or how much I achieved on the battlefield; the fact that I had entered the Centurionate immediately was an insult to men of the old school like Glaxus. And, earlier in my career, his view of me would not have been unwarranted, but I am not that Gnaeus Volusenus, nor have I been for some time. Thankfully, men like Glaxus are in the minority, and I had come to view Glaxus in the same manner I view a part of my *caliga* that rubbed me raw to the point that a callous had formed. Do not mistake me; Marcus Glaxus is something of an idiot, and it is an open secret in the 1ˢᵗ that he owed most of his rise to Tiberius Sacrovir's predecessor as Primus Pilus, Prefect Crescens, whose retirement had enabled Sacrovir to follow in his footsteps into the post of Camp Prefect.

Macer, who has always had a diplomatic streak, answered the obvious question by saying, "If I had to guess, I'd say that it was at the behest of Varro the Younger, as a way to solidify his standing as co-commander of this campaign, such as it is."

"Ah," was Glaxus' only comment, looking a bit embarrassed, as he should have been.

We were dismissed to our Centuries with the order to warn the men that it was likely we would be marching soon, but I was barely done with my Century when Lucco, who was now the chief clerk of the entire Legion, hurried up.

"The Primus Pilus wants you," he said, slightly breathlessly because he had come at a brisk trot. I began to head for Macer's tent, but Lucco stopped me. "No, Centurion. He wants you to meet him in the forum. He said he'll explain there."

Intrigued, and a bit concerned, I gave Vinicius command of the Century, albeit only to sound the dismissal, then copying Lucco, I moved at a brisk trot, thankful that this was only a two Legion camp so it did not take long to get from the First Cohort area to the forum, where I found Macer. He did not look concerned as much as a bit bemused, but it was a shade compared to my own even after he explained.

"The Prefect wants to talk to me," Macer explained. "And he said to bring you along. That," he shrugged, "is all I know."

Since there was no question of not obeying, I followed Macer and we walked over to the tent of the Camp Prefect, which is currently the same size as the tent belonging to the Tribunes, but inside, it is configured differently. Whereas the tents of Centurions are exactly the same depending on the grade; first Cohort Centurions like me have a tent the size of a Pilus Prior because the part of the tent that serves as the Century office must be bigger because the size of the Century is twice as large. Some Prefects, while technically second in command of an army behind the Legate, which in this case was also the *Praetor*, preferred to have larger private quarters because, frankly, they do not have nearly as much paperwork to do, despite their position. For whatever reason, perhaps because it was what he was accustomed to, the portion that served as the outer office was essentially the same size as it had been when he was Primus Pilus, and as always, Melander was there to greet us, but he looked agitated, which was unusual.

"The Prefect is expecting you," he whispered, "but he's very upset about something. I just don't know what."

With that ominous warning, he walked to the partition, then rapped on the wooden block. In another sign that all was not as it normally was, Sacrovir, who was famous for letting men stew in their own juices as he kept them waiting, barked permission, and perhaps if I had been in a better frame of mind, I would have found the expression on Melander's face, one that practically screamed, "Better you than me," amusing. Even though I was behind Macer, because of our respective heights, I could see the Prefect, and my alarm only deepened, as did Macer's, which I learned later. In simplest terms, neither of us had ever seen Tiberius Sacrovir look this agitated, not during the revolt of the Legions nor during the campaigns against Arminius. He was pacing back and forth, head down and hands clasped behind his back, and after a bare acknowledgement of our presence, resumed muttering something under his breath that I could not catch.

"P-Prefect? Primus Pilus Macer and Hastatus Prior Pullus reporting as..."

"Yes, yes." He did stop pacing to look at us, and now I was confronted with yet another unfamiliar sight, Sacrovir appearing embarrassed. Gesturing to his table, he said, "You two take a seat. I...I need to stand."

Melander, either because Sacrovir had given him prior instructions, or more likely because he knew his master so well by this time, had already placed two cups on the table and poured wine into them, which he did not cut with water. When I signaled him that I wanted mine watered, he cut me off with a warning shake of the head, and Macer and I took a seat, watching the Prefect as he seemed to gather his thoughts.

Finally, he said, "I'm going to ask you to swear on the eagle that what I tell you remains with you..." I was expecting him to say something like, "until you die," but I was surprised when he said instead, "...until such time I release you from that oath."

The fact that I am now divulging what he said should be taken not as a sign that I am breaking my vow, but that Sacrovir gave his permission to speak of it.

"The boys of the 2nd were able to crush the Turoni, but not alone," he began. "They also had some help from some Gallic tribes who remained loyal, acting mostly as the cavalry." He stopped pacing long enough to snatch up the cup that was already sitting on his desk, taking a deep draught before he continued, "One of those tribes allied to us was the Aedui."

He stopped then, looking in our direction, but while I could tell this was supposed to mean something, I had no idea what it could be. Macer, however, clearly did because he suddenly stopped his cup a couple inches from his own lips, then set it down on the table.

I have never liked feeling as if I am the one who does not get the joke, or does not understand something that others do, which was why I snapped at him, "I'm glad you know why that matters!"

As soon as I said it, I winced, waiting for Macer, or Sacrovir, or both to chastise me for using that tone with someone who, while he was my closest friend, was also my superior. Therefore, I was deeply surprised when Sacrovir muttered a curse that was not aimed at me, but at himself, and I swear I heard him call himself an idiot.

"I apologize, Gnaeus," he said. "I told Marcus more about...my family, and that's why he understands." He went on to explain, "As I recall, I did tell you that Gaius Julius Sacrovir is my half-brother." I nodded, and he continued, "But I realize that I didn't explain the rest of it. My father divorced my mother because he supposedly had fallen in love with a noblewoman of the Aedui, and wanted to marry her." His face suddenly twisted into a mask of bitterness that was understandable when he said, "I was about five years old, and I was left behind. I never saw him after that since we lived in Massillia, and he didn't particularly want to be reminded of his old life. You see," he smiled then, but there was no humor that I could discern, "my father was blessed by Fortuna to fall in love with a woman who was not only of noble Aedui blood, but she was a widow...an extremely wealthy widow. With her money, he was able to be elevated into the Equestrian Order in Rome, so his son is both an Aeduan noble and a Roman Equestrian."

As I listened, something occurred to me, so I asked, "Your father named your half-brother after Divus Julius. Did your father march with Caesar?"

"No," Sacrovir replied, and sounding a bit ashamed, he added, "My father never served under the standard. But the reason my half-brother is named for Divus Julius is because he's half Aedui, and they name their children after Divus Julius quite often."

Which, I realized, made sense, given the fact that it was Caesar who came to the rescue of the Aedui, then forgave them after they threw their lot in with Vercingetorix, gaining the entire tribe as clients in the process.

What I did not understand was why the Prefect was agitated, and I was about to ask when, either because he read my mind, or it was just the logical thing to do, he went on to explain, "The reason I'm upset is because Tribune Aviola made sure to sing the praises of the tribes who remained loyal, but there was one man he mentioned by name as leading the barbarians and distinguishing himself..." his mouth twisted and he almost spat, "...my half-brother."

At first, I could only stare at him uncomprehendingly.

"I don't understand," I said after a heartbeat. "Isn't that a relief to you? To know that he's not actually involved?"

"*But he is!*" Sacrovir shouted this, not in his normal bellowing manner, but I heard a note of what I thought was hysteria in his voice. "I know he is! This was just a ruse! In fact," he suddenly sounded triumphant, as if what he was saying vindicated his belief, "he didn't wear his helmet so that he could make sure he was seen by enough of us that it fooled them into thinking he's on our side. But he's not! He didn't fool *me*!"

"Did you tell the *Praetor* about this?" I asked what I thought was a reasonable question, but Sacrovir laughed at this, though again, it was not with any humor.

"What do you think?" he countered. "Of course I did! But that's when that bastard Varro made his move."

"His move?"

Sacrovir had snatched his cup again, and he was in the process of draining it, so it took a moment before he answered.

"Somehow," he replied bitterly, "he found out my connection to my half-brother. Not only that," he added, holding up a hand to forestall both Macer and me, the both of us about to try and reassure him this did not necessarily mean that Varro knew the specifics, "but he also found out about...other things. Not everything," he emphasized, "but enough to make it look as if I had some sort of grudge against my half-brother that made me unreliable."

I let out a low whistle, mainly because it was the only thing I could think to do, but matters were about to get worse, and more complicated.

"What did Silius have to say about it?" Macer asked. "Because even if he's technically outranked because of that scroll from Sejanus, his word has to carry a fair amount of weight."

"It would," Sacrovir seemingly agreed, but when I glanced at Macer, I saw that he had noticed the odd wording the Prefect used, saying "would" instead of "did," and we learned why he said that, "but Varro has decreed that he will be the only source of reports and dispatches back to Rome, in order to," Sacrovir actually did a credible job of imitating Varro's voice, which is quite nasal and pinched, "'avoid confusing the Imperator with conflicting information.' So, if the *Praetor* wants to send a dispatch to Rome, he has to give it to Varro to review. At least, that's how he put it to Silius." Suddenly, his features darkened as blood suffused his face, another thing that those who served under him understood meant that Sacrovir was struggling to control his rage. We understood why when he hissed, "That's what he told Silius. But me? He flat out forbid me from writing up any kind of report!" Lapsing back into Varro's voice, he mimicked, "After all, Prefect, you didn't rise to your post because of your skills at rhetoric, did you?"

It was an astonishingly rude thing to say, yet in that moment, I actually felt a bit vindicated myself, because to my ear, especially with Sacrovir's attempt to sound like Varro, I felt like I could have been standing in front of the man back in Mogontiacum, and this was exactly the kind of insulting thing he had said to me more than once. The Prefect stalked to the table, snatched up the pitcher to refill his cup, and the silence stretched out as we silently watched him drain his cup, then fill it for a third time since we had been in his presence, and I had the strong suspicion that he had already downed at least a cup before our arrival.

Finally, Macer broke the silence, and I knew my former Pilus Prior well enough to see that he was truly struggling to find the right words.

"Prefect, is it...*possible* that your information about your half-brother was incorrect? That perhaps he's loyal to Rome? If he was there, and in the thick of the fight, and wasn't wearing his helmet, surely that means something, doesn't it?"

I braced myself, but instead of exploding, Sacrovir admitted, "I've been wondering the same thing, Marcus. But," he shook his head, "the source who gave me this information is someone I trust with my life, and she...*they* are not likely to exaggerate or give me bad information. No," he said flatly, "he's involved in this uprising. The fact that he was seen fighting the Turoni is actually the kind of thing that cunning bastard would do in order to alleviate suspicion. I'm sure of it!"

"Where is he now?" I asked, and this pleased Sacrovir.

"That's the right question to ask, Gnaeus." He nodded with approval, and I felt the kind of flush of pride that I felt whenever he complimented me as my Primus Pilus. His tone returned one of something resembling triumph. "Because while I don't know where he is, I can tell you where he's *not*. He's not here! He left with his men from the battlefield and told Aviola that he needed to return to his lands because there were rumors of Aedui who were talking about rebelling."

What was clear was that he thought his half-brother's absence was incriminating, but I risked glancing at Macer, and I sensed that our thoughts ran along the same lines; what the other Sacrovir told the Tribune made perfect sense given the current climate. One thing we *did* learn during our week here was that there was unrest rippling throughout Gaul, brought on by a number of factors, but I will cross the river with the belief that the catalyzing event was the lingering anxiety that was unleashed by the death of Germanicus, exacerbated by the resulting anger when Piso escaped justice in the eyes of most Romans, particularly in the lower classes, including my former order of the Equestrians. Yes, he committed suicide, but the fact that he was acquitted of Germanicus' murder did not sit well with most Romans, and with the entirety of the Legions, including myself. Along with that, for the people of Gaul, the tax burden they were under, although in fairness, it was felt most keenly by the nobility, contributed to the air of discontent. All of this added up to the fact that, on the surface, Sacrovir the Aedui had good reason to return to his own lands and Augustodunum (Autun), the tribal capital that Divus Augustus had constructed to replace Bibracte, mainly due to the fact that Bibracte was an almost impregnable position. Nevertheless, we both trusted the Prefect implicitly, so neither of us were willing to completely discount his suspicions. We were dismissed not long after that, and I realized that Sacrovir had not been looking for advice as much as wanting to vent his anger and frustration to someone he trusted, and it was not lost on me that I was included in that select group of men that he trusted.

"What do you think?" I asked Macer as we walked back to our area. "Do you think Sacrovir is right? That his brother is up to something?"

"I wish I knew," Macer sighed. "But I know that I've followed Tiberius Sacrovir for a long time, and he's not the type to exaggerate or worry about something for no reason."

We remained in our camp for the next three weeks, the word being that we were waiting for instructions from Tiberius now that both the Andecavi and the Turoni had been put down. Meanwhile, it was more of the same chasing of phantoms, with the same results, as the men, of all ranks, began to believe that the rebels were being given information by someone within our camp that enabled them to avoid being brought to battle. When the relay courier came cantering into camp, it being around the Ides of May, carrying a dispatch from Rome, there was a fair amount of anticipation that the Imperator would be issuing instructions that allowed the Legions to begin taking more punitive actions against the Treveri as a tribe and not confine our actions to just the rebels. However, when Silius summoned Carbo and Macer to the *praetorium* a watch after the courier's arrival, the two Primi Pili were informed that the instructions that we were expecting from Tiberius were not forthcoming.

It was not until Macer and I were alone that I learned more, and we were in his quarters where he had summoned me before the meeting with all Centurions when he said grimly, "Tiberius wants us to stay here for the time being. And he refused to make a decision about the Aedui Sacrovir in particular." Since I thought this was a foregone conclusion based on what the Prefect had said about Varro barring him from adding his own report to the dispatch to Rome, I said as much. Macer smiled, and replied with a nod, "Yes, Varro did. But while I don't know the details, what I do know is that somehow Silius got several accounts from some of the prisoners that Aviola took who are Aedui, and their story backed up what the Prefect insists is the case, that what his half-brother did was a ruse to lull our suspicions of him."

This was good news as far as it went, indicating that Silius was finding ways to get information, but Macer had indicated that it did not work, and he had already relayed that we were to remain here for at least another week in Augusta Treverorum, so while it was nice that the Prefect was not completely isolated in his view about his half-brother, it still did not change anything in a material sense.

Finally, the Treveri rebels did something that not only inflicted more damage than burning a homestead, but roused the anger of the men who, at least to this point, were more annoyed and frustrated than anything else. It was near the end of the day when a cavalry trooper came pounding up to the camp, and as it happened, my Century had the watch on the walls, which meant I was at the *Porta Praetoria.* Because the cavalry is so far-ranging, they rarely know the watchword of the day, which meant that we rely on recognizing troopers more than expecting them to know the watchword, and while I did not know the rider's name, he was familiar to several of my men.

"He's a horrible dice player, Centurion," Macrinus confided after the trooper was allowed into the camp and we stood on the rampart watching him heading for the *praetorium.* My *Cornicen* grinned. "Which is why he's always welcome at the Faun."

It was less than a third of a watch later that there were horns blaring in the camp as both Legion *Corniceni* sounded the notes that summoned all Centurions to attend to the forum. Leaving Vinicius in charge, I hurried to the center of the camp, running into Clepsina and Aulus Gratianus, the Princeps Posterior, and the three of us speculated on the cause for the summons.

"A messenger from the cavalry arrived not long ago," I was able to inform them, "but he wouldn't say anything about why."

By this time, we were on the edge of the forum, and we were surrounded by other Centurions, all of them involved in the same speculation as we were, but Gratianus wasted no time in informing the other men about the courier, making it sound as if he had been the one who had been standing watch. It is a small thing, and I knew it at the time, but it was difficult for me to swallow my irritation, although it was Clepsina's look of amusement, telling me he knew me too well that did more to stop me from making an issue of it than my own recognition of how trivial it was. As is customary, while we were not in any kind of formation, even a casual observer would have seen us standing in two distinctive groups composed of the 1st and 2nd, but a sharper-eyed individual would have noticed smaller groups among the two large ones as, like rankers, Centurions tend to stick with their own Cohort, with some exceptions. If

Macer had not been Primus Pilus, for example, I would probably have been standing with him with the Second, or the Cohort from which I got my start, the Fourth, but now he was standing with the five of us, although the Pili Priores of the front line Cohorts were with us as well.

"I sent Lucco to drop off the daily report as soon as I heard about the courier," Macer informed us, eliciting some chuckles since we all knew this had been by design, although I felt certain that I was the only one who knew that this trick had been taught to our Primus Pilus by his Optio, who had arrived from the 8th after an incident triggered by the death of his brother, my uncle Sextus, who I never met. "But," Macer made a face, "he couldn't find out anything, other than something bad has happened."

Fortunately, we did not have long to wait, as Silius and the Prefect emerged from the *praetorium*, but while I kept my eyes on the flap, Varro never appeared. I do not know why, but this was the first moment I realized something, and I took the opportunity as Silius and Sacrovir briefly conferred with each other at the base of the makeshift *rostrum*.

"Has anyone noticed that Varro has never once spoken to us?" I asked of no one in particular.

I could see by the reaction of Macer, Licinius, and a couple of others that it had, but they were in the minority, and the ripple of murmurs and muttered comments about the patrician earned me a glare from Macer for bringing it up. Fortunately, it was actually Silius who mounted the *rostrum,* and as was his habit, he did not waste any time with the kind of flowery oration that so many patricians seem to think that men under the standard need to hear but we universally loathe.

"We have learned that a convoy of Roman traders who have a regular route through Treveri lands was ambushed by men of our Treveri cavalry auxiliary," he began, pausing for the reaction, which was one of slightly muted anger, mainly because we had been waiting so long for news such as this. "They were led by Julius Florus," at this, he turned to indicate Sacrovir, who was standing there with his arms folded, "just as the Prefect anticipated. We have also learned that, since the ambush two days ago, other men have joined their standard,

35

and the Decurion in command says that the rebel force is now too large for him to engage with any hope of success. Therefore, they are following the rebel army, and it appears we know where they're headed. Primus Pilus Macer, Primus Pilus Carbo, attend to me in the *praetorium* for further orders."

He spun about and hopped down off the *rostrum*, and Macer followed, leaving us to return to what we had been doing, which meant I made my way back to the gate, and since Silius had given no orders to remain silent, I informed the men as much as I knew, and as soon as it was time, they would hear more. Macer did not return until after we had been relieved, so I was in my tent with Alex when Lucco popped his head into our tent to inform us that Macer was summoning us to his quarters.

Draining my cup, I pretended to grumble, "Let me go find out what this nonsense is all about. It will probably turn out to be a waste of time."

"Oh, where would you be if you didn't have someone to kill?" Alex teased in what had become a standard retort on his part.

As usual, I was determined to loose the last volley, so I waited until I was at the flap before I said over my shoulder, "And I think it's time you find something new, because that's gotten old."

Stepping out, I pretended I did not hear his retort that I only thought it had gotten old because it is true, and I saw the shadowy figure of Numerius Caudex, the Princeps Posterior, just a few paces ahead of me, and I hurried to catch up with him so that we entered Macer's tent together. I cannot say exactly where it comes from, but I have a fear of being tardy, so it had become a habit of mine to catch up to another person going to the same place for the same purpose in the event that I was late, thinking that at least I would not be alone if I was going to be chastised for my tardiness. To my relief, I saw that Glaxus and Clepsina were both absent, but I also saw that this was not a meeting just for the First Cohort, as Licinius was present, along with the Secundus and Tertius Pili Priores. Once everyone was present, it was slightly cramped in Macer's quarters, but there were stools for everyone, along with cups, but it was heavily watered wine, which was a sign in itself. Hanging on the back wall of the tent was a map, a smaller version of the one that the *Praetor* has, and which is copied by a scribe in the *praetorium*, with information added to it on a daily basis while on campaign.

"We're going after the rebels," Macer began, then turned and pointed to an area that was actually north of Augusta Treverorum and due south of Ubiorum. "The *Praetor* has sent a courier to Ubiorum with orders to mobilize the rest of the 1st, and they're going to march south, while we, along with the front line Cohorts of the 2nd are going to march north." He was using his stylus to point, and he moved it to a spot farther west of Augusta Treverorum, and I was close enough to make out a dot with the word Vungovicus (Vonq) next to it. "The ambush was a mile outside of this station, Vungovicus, and the information from the cavalry is that Florus tarried here for a full day after they slaughtered the merchants. Without knowing anything about the identities of these merchants, if I had to guess, given they were coming from the southwest, I'd say it's very likely they were transporting wine, and we know how much these Gauls like wine. Whatever the reason, the *Praetor* believes that this has given us an opportunity to cut them off from reaching," he moved the stylus back to the original spot, which I confess I had not looked at that closely, "here."

He paused to sip from his cup, and I took the moment to examine the area that was roughly oval in shape, although the western end of the oval bulged outward and slightly south, and it was easy to see why the rebels would be heading for this area, because that part of it was not far from Vungovicus.

"What's so special about that area, Primus Pilus?"

This came from Spurius Caecilius, the Tertius Pilus Prior, and Macer, while he did not hesitate to answer, still looked grim, the lines in his face that I barely noticed normally suddenly looking like crevices when he answered, "It's called the Arduenna Silvia (Ardennes Forest)...and it's the Gallic version of the Teutoberg."

This unleashed a ripple of cursing, and I was among those doing it; none of us would forget the Teutoberg, and even now, eleven years later, the mere mention of the Teutoberg is enough to send a chill up my spine, and I know that I am not alone.

"Yes," Macer nodded. "Now you can see why we want to cut these *cunni* off before they get there. And," he set the stylus down, "we march in the morning. I know," he held up his hand to forestall the inevitable protest, "that it's short notice, but now that you know where they're headed and what we're likely to face if we let them get there, I don't see where we have any choice. Do you?" he asked pointedly, and with a tone where anyone who knew him understood there was one and only one answer.

His reward was a chorus of assent, and we were dismissed to go get our men ready.

The eight Cohorts of our Legion and the 2nd departed camp, with the rest of the 2nd lined up along the *Via Praetoria* to see us off, men calling out to friends the kind of thing that I know civilians who have never served would find ghoulish.

"Opimius, remember that you promised to give me that phallus you took off that Cherusci *cunnus* at the Angrivarian Wall! Be sure and remind your *Tesserarius*!"

"Turpilius, you bastard, you better not die! Our dice game isn't finished and I need to win my money back!"

Since the rest of our Legion was in Ubiorum, or more likely already on the march south, the banter was exclusively aimed at the men of the 2nd, who were in the vanguard. Given the nature of our foray, all but two of the wagons were remaining behind, the pair coming with us designated to carry any casualties, while the number of mules was cut in half and were carrying rations for three days. If it had been earlier in the season, or later, I doubt that we would have been marching without our tents, but the weather had been quite pleasant for a couple of weeks, which meant that the men would be fine wrapping up in their *sagum*. Not lost on anyone was the fact that, while both Silius and Sacrovir were leading our column, the latter looking as unhappy as always whenever he was mounted, the younger Varro was nowhere to be seen. The official story was that he had been eager to lead this foray against the rebels, but had reluctantly yielded to Silius' request that he be the one to lead this effort, which nobody I knew believed.

The road heading west that was on the northern bank of the Mosella (Moselle) River and paralleled the river was not a Roman road, but since we were not encumbered by all of our wagons, and it had been dry, we made good progress. Our information was that the southern edge of the Arduenna was about ten miles directly north, but we were heading west with the intention of linking up with elements of our cavalry, which was still being reinforced, both by other tribes who were remaining loyal to Rome, but by men of the Treveri who had held fast. Macer had informed us that Silius had made it clear to both Carbo and himself that, in the event we could not get into position to block Florus and his rebels from entering the Arduenna, we would not be penetrating it without being guided by someone with knowledge of the area. This was reassuring, but at the same time, given the kind of treachery that we had been forced to deal with when it came to dealing with barbarian tribes, I know I was not alone in thinking that there was a possibility that our guide would secretly be working in concert with the rebels, and would try to copy Arminius by leading us into an ambush. Frankly, it was not a huge concern, because the circumstances were far different than they had been twelve years earlier. Nevertheless, it was certainly in the back of my mind, and I felt certain I was not alone, but first we had to reach the force that was still being led by Aviola, who was proving himself to be a competent leader of both infantry and cavalry.

By midday, we had made a bit more than ten miles, but there had been no sign of our cavalry, nor any indication that the rebels were anywhere about either. Naturally, we were in full armor, and we uncovered our shields at the midday stop, while the normal chattering became more desultory with every mile west we went. We had two *turmae* of cavalry, which was not enough for comfort, and when we resumed after the midday break, we were at the point where the Mosella turns south, which meant that we were soon scanning both flanks as we marched now that we did not have the protection of the river on our left. It was about a third of a watch after we resumed that Silius' *Cornicen* blatted out the notes for a halt, but being the penultimate Cohort, we were too far back along the column to see why, but without waiting to be summoned, Macer was already trotting forward to find out what was happening. Macer was not the only one who did not need to be given instructions, and I felt a stab of pride at the manner in which the men of the two outermost files on each side pivoted to face the nearest flank, dropping their packs and unslinging their shields, though they rested them on the ground and leaned them against their legs. No, I thought with real satisfaction, no barbarian rebel is going to get close to us without being seen. Macer was not gone long, returning to the Cohort, where his Centurions had hurried to stand next to the eagle, whereupon he held a quick meeting.

"The reason we stopped was a scout from Aviola's force arrived," he explained. "Aviola and our cavalry and the allies are waiting at a village called Orolaunum (Arlon, Belgium). There's a junction with a road that heads north into the Arduenna, and we're going to be taking that road north in the morning. This village is another ten miles, so we should be getting there with just enough time to make a marching camp. Once our forces are combined, then the *Praetor* and Prefect Sacrovir will decide what to do next."

The march resumed in a matter of heartbeats after that, but at a slightly increased pace, not much but enough that, even if the men had been so inclined, they would not have had the breath to talk, and I count myself among them. It is a funny thing how quickly a man will lose his fitness when sitting in camp; even with the other activities, and going out on patrol, the weeks we had spent outside Augusta Treverorum had sapped our marching legs, as we like to say. Fairly soon, I began watching the sun as it slid downward towards the trees, which were dauntingly thick to our right, or north, the direction we would be marching in the morning, and perhaps we would be doing battle tomorrow. It was possible that it would be today, I knew, but I did not think it would happen; by this time, I had developed a feeling about such matters, which is both impossible to describe, or for a man who has survived as long as I have, to ignore when it hits them. Tomorrow, I thought. It will be tomorrow. We saw the smoke trails from the village, which was screened from view by the trees, which had grown thicker with every mile, and I realized that the representation of the Arduenna and how it bulged out to the southwest had essentially been accurate.

"So, we're actually already in the Arduenna," I murmured, unaware that I said it loudly enough for Lentulus to hear.

"If this is as bad as it gets," my *Signifer* commented, "then I'm not worried." I sensed he looked over at me because I saw his headdress move. "Are you, Centurion?"

"Me? Of course not," I scoffed. "Even if it gets worse, I'm not worried." Knowing the game Lentulus was playing, I raised my voice so I could be heard more than just a couple ranks away. "Not with these misbegotten bastards with me! I'd go cut Cerberus' balls off with this lot!"

As I expected, and hoped, this was met by the Century's promise to follow me in the form of a guttural roar that was less than a cheer but more than just a ragged chorus of murmured assent. No matter what comes, I thought, I know I can count on these men. One of the advantages of being the Centurion of a First Cohort Century is that the men are all veterans, drawn from the other Cohorts, which makes sense since we do the brunt of the fighting. That was why I was unprepared for what was coming, because I would not be commanding the Fifth in battle for what would have been my first time.

Chapter 2

While the men created their marching camp, about a furlong from the walls of Orolaunum, Tribune Aviola and five noblemen from the tribes who remained loyal, Silius, Sacrovir, and the two Primi Pili met in the lone tent that came with us that was serving as both the *praetorium* and, if the gods were not kind, as the hospital tent. Alex, because he was also trained as a *medicus*, was one of the clerks who was accompanying us, as was Lucco, the pair riding together with the baggage train, Macer having purchased his clerk a horse as a gift, making him and Alex the only two in the 1st with mounts, which had created some problems with their peers, and for their two Centurions, although Alex was actually riding Latobius, having left Lightning behind, claiming at the time that he had noticed I had not ridden my horse very much recently, which was true. Now, the pair approached, though not on horseback, but I was completely unprepared for Macer's clerk to inform me that I was wanted in the *praetorium*. I followed him to the tent, which as custom and practice dictates, had already been erected. Lucco was ahead of me and entered the tent first, but the senior officers were actually standing in the outer area, which was slightly unusual, and they all turned to look at me with a variety of expressions. Not surprisingly, Macer and Sacrovir, while not smiling, were clearly friendly, while Silius did not look either pleased or displeased, which did not surprise me since this was how he normally appeared. The tribesmen, three of whom were clean-shaven in our manner, with the other two sporting long mustaches in the Gallic fashion, while each were attired in a mishmash of styles and colors that bespoke their tribal affiliation, seemed more curious about my appearance than anything else. Carbo, on the other hand, was the only one who viewed me with overt hostility, clearly unhappy with my presence, not even deigning to nod his head, although I made sure to render a salute, turning my body in such a way that he could not easily say that I was only rendering it to Macer, Sacrovir, and Silius.

"Primus Hastatus..." I began, but Silius held up a hand.

"There's no time for formalities, Centurion," he said, though not unkindly. Then, without warning, he inadvertently gave me a hint about my immediate future. "I understand that you've fought from horseback while serving as cavalry when the Alaudae helped put Catualda on the Marcomanni throne, and that you're an experienced horseman with his own mount. Is that correct?"

I was caught by surprise, though not for the seemingly obvious reason, that he was aware that one of the forty-eight Centurions present owned a horse. No, what startled me was his knowledge about my role with the Alaudae, which must have registered on my face.

"I read the report by Primus Pilus Nerva," Silius explained, although he had no need to do so. "He spoke very highly of you, as," he indicated Macer, "does your Primus Pilus, which is why you're here. This," he turned and indicated one of the Gauls, one of the three clean-shaven men a few years older than I was, "is Julius Indus. He's Treveri, but he's remained loyal to Rome. And," he added what was the most important part, "his clan's lands comprise a good part of the Arduenna."

Indus was of stocky build, a few inches shorter than me, but taller than the other Romans to varying degrees, with sandy-colored hair that, in the Gallic fashion, was long and pulled back and tied in a knot, not on the side like the Suebi, but at the nape of his neck, and he was wearing a torq, though not nearly of the size or quality of that of Dumnorix that my father had won in battle. He was wearing what appeared to be a Roman *spatha* at his waist; all in all, he presented an image that was part-Roman, part-Gaul, and when he spoke, while his Latin was very good, he still spoke with an accent that was quite noticeable.

"Not only do I know the land," Indus assured me, "but I am quite certain that I know where Florus and his rebels are going. And," he smiled, though it was a wolfish one, "if we move quickly, we will be waiting for him when he and those traitors get there."

Silius resumed speaking to explain, "What Indus has asked for is a hand-picked force that he will lead deeper into the Arduenna, which will be mounted." He turned to indicate me. "And I know that I don't have to tell any of the Romans present of Centurion Pullus' prowess on the battlefield. He upholds the standard set by Prefect Pullus, and then by his father, who fell during the rescue of Segestes." He turned to address Indus. "But as you may have gathered from what I said, Centurion Pullus is also an experienced horseman, which is one reason that I'm *strongly* recommending that you include him in your party. As you can see, he is clearly a formidable..."

Indus, who had been listening with what I thought was a polite indifference, held up a hand in a gesture that was both astonishingly rude yet completely in character for a member of the nobility of a barbarian tribe, who are every bit as haughty as our patricians.

However, I was completely unprepared to hear him say, "*Praetor*, there is no need for further explanation. In fact," at this, he looked at me with a smile that at least seemed genuine, "the moment I saw Centurion Pullus, I knew who he was just by his size, and I am well aware of both his lineage and his own exploits, but his great-grandfather is a legend as one of the original Equestrians who rode with Divus Julius when he confronted the German chieftain Ariovistus. I," he actually bowed, not to me but in my direction; a nobleman of any sort can only bend so much, I understood, "would be honored to have the Centurion under my command."

For his part, Silius looked startled, giving me the impression that he had been expecting some sort of resistance from Indus; as for myself, I cannot say I was particularly happy at the manner in which Indus put how he would be my commander, although in fairness, I knew that this was how it would be.

Still, I held out a faint hope that Silius might object on my behalf; it lasted only long enough for him to say, "Ah, yes. Well, it's settled then. And," he assured Indus, "the Centurion will obey your orders to the letter."

This seemed an odd thing to say, but before much more

time passed, I would learn more about why Silius seemed so eager to convince Indus I could be counted on. Silius and Indus spoke for a few more moments, and it was almost dark when a plan was formed that we would depart in two watches at midnight, with Indus leading a force of almost a thousand men, half infantry and half cavalry, including the Batavian *turmae*. I was not particularly surprised when Indus indicated that of the infantry, most of the men would be from the Cohort of the 7th that had been involved with this uprising from the beginning, while the Tribune was named second in command to Indus. The First Cohort would be represented, but with only a half-dozen men put forward by Macer, while Carbo insisted that the 2nd receive the lion's share of the rest of the empty spots, which at the time, I put down to the normal competitiveness between Legions.

I was walking back to camp with Macer when, taking a glance over his shoulder to ensure we were not being overheard, he said quietly, "Gnaeus, you need to be careful."

I laughed, thinking that he was being overly concerned.

"I'm always careful," I replied with a straight face, then after a pause, I added, "Most of the time anyway."

Rather than this amusing him, he shook his head, replying irritably, "I'm not talking about fighting, Gnaeus." Now I was completely mystified, and I said as much, to which he repeated his glance around us; we were now inside the dirt wall of the camp but just a few paces from the *Porta Praetoria*, and he lowered his voice. "I think there's a reason Silius made a point in choosing you to accompany this Treveri, Gnaeus. Something," he added pointedly, "that involves more than your ability to kill a man...in battle."

Slowly, his meaning started to dawn on me, or at least so I believed, but I refused to voice my suspicions, mainly because I was ashamed that, like my father, I had been maneuvered into performing tasks for the man who rules Rome. Besides that, I could not deny I felt a twinge of anger at Macer for his suggestion that there could be another reason for my inclusion, even as I knew deep inside that he was probably right.

"I'll...be careful."

It was all I could think to promise, then we parted and

headed to our Centuries, where I took Vinicius' report that the men were in the process of preparing their evening meal, which I could smell cooking, reminding me of my own hunger. Vinicius was clearly curious about what had transpired; although he could not have heard the discussion, he, and every other man of the Fifth Century, had eyes, and it is not often that a lowly Centurion of my grade is summoned to a meeting in the *praetorium* with the *Praetor*, but to his credit, he did not ask the obvious questions I knew he wanted to, and I dismissed him to enter my tent. Alex was there with Euphemios, who was busy placing the boxes containing the precious Century records against one wall of the tent, each one holding the wax tablets for two tent sections, so there were sixteen boxes, with each box marked with the marching section number, there being two tent sections for each marching section, just one of the differences that mark a First Cohort Century. I had heard from more than one old hand who had supposedly been around for what are now called the Augustan reforms that the original idea for a one-hundred-sixty-man Century was to create a tent for all sixteen men in a section, but this was quickly abandoned. The story that is commonly accepted as true is that, while the official reason given for the abandonment was the difficulty presented in carrying it, being too large for a section mule to carry, the real story was that the Centurions were unsettled by the idea that there would be too much opportunity for mischief when putting sixteen men under one roof. This approach of having two definitions of a section is an example of the kind of compromise that we Romans excel at, adapting things to work to our advantage. None of which was in my mind when I entered to this scene, gesturing to Alex to follow me into my quarters. By this time, I trusted Euphemios almost as much as I trusted Alex, but this was as much about protecting him as it was hiding anything from him, and accordingly, I lowered my voice to a whisper once we were in my quarters, explaining to Alex what was going on, and Macer's warning.

I suppose I should not have been surprised when, without hesitation, Alex said, "The Primus Pilus is right, Gnaeus. I think Silius is up to something beyond what it seems."

"What do you think it is?"

Just as he opened his mouth to answer, we both heard the sharp rapping on the wooden block hanging outside the tent, and he whispered, "I'll tell you later."

He was nearer to the flap than I was, so he led the way into the outer office just as Euphemios was pushing the outer flap aside.

Despite being able to see over Alex's head, Euphemios' body blocked my view, and I did not recognize the voice of the man who said, "I bring the Centurion a message from the *Praetor*."

Euphemios looked over his shoulder, and I beckoned him to step aside; when he did so, I did recognize the man, though I did not know his name, but more importantly, I knew what he was not. He was one of the men who traveled as part of the *Praetor*'s staff, but he was as much a clerk as I am, though he did not look like a torturer like Canus had been. Despite not knowing what he did, I was sufficiently on guard that I was not surprised when he requested to speak to me privately, yet while I was tempted to demur, I did not want to give him the impression that I was afraid of being alone with him.

"Follow me," I said curtly, then returned to my quarters.

He obeyed, naturally, but I could see by his expression that he did not care for the peremptory manner I had shown with him, confirmed by the way in which he thrust out the small scroll and said flatly, "You're to read this in my presence, acknowledge your obedience, then give the scroll back to me."

"What if I decide not to obey?" I asked, trying to sound innocent, suddenly overtaken by an urge for mischief.

For the first time, he smiled, but it was the way he did it that suddenly reminded me of Canus, and he sounded almost cheerful as he replied, "Why, then I suppose the *Praetor* will arrange for you and me to spend time together, Centurion!"

I had to suppress the almost overwhelming urge to grab him up and thrash him, and I was proud of myself for sounding as cool as I could manage given the sudden rush of anger.

"You might find that things wouldn't go the way you think."

My reward was how his smile vanished as if it had never been there, but I was also surprised when he replied, "I could say the same to you, Centurion. Besides, you're assuming that it would just be me."

He was holding the scroll out as he said this, and I took it, certain that I felt a slight tremor through it, which made me feel good. I was surprised to see that, while it was sealed with wax, it did not have the *Praetor*'s seal, which is a portrait of Tiberius in profile as a sign that this was an official government document, but neither was it Silius' private seal, which I had seen before. Paying no more attention to this, I broke the seal and unrolled the scroll, wondering if Silius had written it himself, not that I would be able to tell. The message was very short, but I almost immediately felt a sudden chill, along with a feeling that I had not experienced since I had been in Rome serving with the Praetorians, and the best way I can describe it is that I believe it is something akin to what an animal caught in a trap must feel as it sees the human approaching it with an ax in hand. The taste of bile was strong in my mouth, which I had to swallow down, the burning in my throat from the effort making me sound hoarse when I spoke.

"I acknowledge receiving this order, and I..." I had to swallow again, "...will obey if it becomes necessary."

For the first time, the messenger looked almost sympathetic, which made me feel bad enough, but he murmured, "That's a wise choice, Centurion...for both of us," which made me feel even worse, because I knew he was right.

Alex had already lit a lamp, and the messenger used the flame to burn the vellum after stripping it from the spools, and when it was done, he said, "I'll relay that you will obey the order as it was given, Centurion. Hopefully, it won't be necessary."

I did not see him out, choosing instead to drop onto my stool at my desk, and I would not have reached the count of ten before Alex appeared.

Before I could say a word, he said quietly, "Silius doesn't trust Indus, and he wants you to kill him if he tries anything treacherous."

I thought I had become accustomed to Alex's insights and his ability to see a situation for what it is, but he constantly surprises me, and this time was no exception. In fact, I was about to demand to know if he had been listening with his ear pressed against the canvas partition; fortunately, I managed to avoid making a fool of myself since I had never uttered a word aloud about the contents of the message.

"How did you know?" I managed to gasp, to which he just shrugged.

"Because it's obvious," he replied evenly. "And Silius is being prudent...and wise in his choice."

"Oh, go piss on your boots," I muttered, though I was flattered by Alex's words, especially because I know he would not offer them just to soothe my feelings.

"You know that you have no choice, don't you?"

There was a note of anxiety in Alex's voice that was touching, but it also irritated me that he thought I did not understand the reality. All things being equal, however, I would rather have him more concerned with my welfare than sparing my feelings about whether I am an idiot or not.

"Yes," I sighed, "I know." Then, I moved to what I saw as the practical problem. "But it's easy enough to say I'll do it, and another thing to kill Indus and live to tell Silius I obeyed his order." Shaking my head at the thought, I added, "I can't imagine that however many Treveri who will be with us will be very happy about it."

We sat there in a glum silence for a fair length of time, until Alex finally stood.

"I'm going to go prepare your meal. You don't have much time to rest."

"I need to borrow a *spatha*," I mused. "I'll go find Herminius now that we're all together."

"No you don't," Alex assured me, and when I asked why he said that, he shrugged. "Because I packed yours."

"Is there anything you *didn't* bring?" I asked with a laugh. "Are you a diviner now? You knew I'd need my horse, and now a *spatha*."

"Not anything you wouldn't need," he retorted as he got up, leaving me to ponder on yet another situation where I had no real choice in my actions.

As the plan went, my Century would be commanded by

Vinicius in my place, and the eight Cohorts in our camp would be departing camp at dawn, which would give us a two-watch head start. I trusted Vinicius as my second in command for normal duties, but we had never been in battle together, which meant that I was even more nervous than I would be with the prospect of a fight coming. Without knowing the exact numbers of Florus' force, whether it was growing in size, men were deserting, or was remaining static, it was impossible to know what we in Indus' force would be doing. While Indus had boasted that his thousand-strong command would take advantage of his intimate knowledge of the ground and launch an ambush so devastating that the Legions would not be needed, I was not so sanguine. Frankly, I believed that the best we could do was drive the rebels into the waiting Legions, who as I understood it, would be waiting farther east of where were headed, deeper in the Arduenna. What Silius had planned was what we call the hammer and anvil, although in this particular plan, there would be two anvils in the form of the rest of the 1st that was coming from Ubiorum, led by a guide who I had overheard Indus say was his cousin, who had been sent with the courier ordering the mobilization of the 1st, and the combined front line Cohorts of the 1st and 2nd who were following us to a point where there was another track that intersected with the northern road we were taking that branched farther east.

According to Indus, there were only two routes eastward that a force the size of Florus' could take, and the other Cohorts of the 1st would be waiting at the northernmost route, with our combined Cohorts the southernmost. Without knowing how large Florus' force was, I was uncomfortable with the prospect of being led by an ambitious barbarian seeking glory for himself and redemption for his tribe, although I cannot say that I blamed him. If I had been in his *caligae*, I would be thinking along the same lines, hoping that by my actions I erased the stain of Florus' actions, and most importantly, removed the need to punish my tribe, at least to the extent that the action by Rome would not be punitive in nature, but a stiff fine, or the execution of a handful of noblemen deemed ringleaders. Nevertheless, despite my understanding his motivation, that did not mean that I necessarily wanted to suffer the consequences if Indus' ambition overwhelmed his judgment. Since we were marching with infantry, we could not move as quickly, which was why we departed at midnight. We were aided by a clear sky and a moon not quite full, and even in the darkness, I quickly found Herminius, not surprised to see Arnfrid, Barvistus, and the other Batavians who had been the entire cavalry force for what had turned out to be the folly of installing Catualda on the throne.

Not surprisingly, this was almost immediately the topic of conversation among us, with Herminius commenting, "As much as I liked seeing Catualda thrown out on his ass by that bastard Vibilius and his Hermundusi, I do not like that he is sitting on that pampered ass in Forum Julii." I saw the glint of his helmet as he shook his head, and there was no mistaking the sadness in his voice. "But I believe we made a mistake in the first place, Centurion. Maroboduus was a good king, and he ruled the Marcomanni fairly." He turned to look at me and asked bluntly, "What do you think, Centurion? Did we make a mistake?"

My mouth was opening to agree with him wholeheartedly, as this was something I had thought about more than once in the intervening time since Varro had essentially forced me to participate in his machinations, or whoever was behind it, but just before I uttered the words, I heard Alex's voice in my head.

"You can trust Herminius, but it's still not a wise thing to say out loud."

Still, at the same time, I did not feel right in refusing to agree with Herminius aloud since I did silently, so I compromised by saying, "I think that neither of us are in any position to make a judgment, Herminius. But," I added quickly, seeing him stiffen at the implied rebuke, "I agree with you about Maroboduus. When it comes to the two of them, Catualda isn't the *cac* on the bottom of Marobduus' *caliga*. He wanted to be king for the wrong reason. And at least now," I shrugged, "he's been taken out of the position where he can cause mischief."

Herminius did not reply, though he did nod, but it was actually Wigmar, who was riding right behind us who spoke up.

"He is being supported by Rome now, Centurion! Just as Marobduus is in Ravenna," he said indignantly. "That is what upsets us, that he was a weak king who could not even defend Casurgis from the Hermundusi." I could not see him since he was behind me, but I heard the contempt in his voice, reminding me that, despite being part of Rome for decades now, the tribes of this part of the world have grudges with other tribes that run back for centuries. "And now he has received as his *punishment*," it was impossible to miss the lacerating scorn in that word, "living in Narbonensis Gaul and be supported by Rome! Maroboduus deserves being supported by Rome, but Catualda does not!"

It was rare for Wigmar to say this much at one time, but there was a ripple of murmured agreement from the others, and I felt it was safe enough to add my own. I changed the subject to something else, I do not remember what, and Catualda and his unearned good fortune in not having his head parted from his shoulders returned to the past where it belongs.

We rode through the night, but at a pace that, while not quite the same as if it had been daylight, was close to it, stopping only two times. Latobius was full of energy, though not excessively so, which I ascribe to the fact that Alex had been riding him on the march, while I felt the ache in muscles that are not used marching but get used riding, signaling that I would be sore the next day. However, I also knew that, if my instinct was correct and we saw battle in a matter of watches, I would not feel any soreness, and just the thought of what lay ahead got my right hand flexing. I was wearing my *gladius*, while the *spatha* that I had been given by Germanicus as a gift when I had left the Praetorians I had secured to my saddle, my feeling being that I would be more comfortable using my *gladius* if I was out of the saddle, while on horseback, the extra reach of the *spatha* is not just nice to have, it is vital. The sky was beginning to pinken when Indus sounded the halt, though it was done verbally; while we had a *Cornicen*, he had been ordered to not use his horn until the moment we began the attack, so the stop was a bit ragged, offending my Centurion sensibilities at hearing the muttered curses that accompanied the sound of bodies smacking together when men or horses collided. Uncertain what I was supposed to do, I dismounted and, leading Latobius by the reins, walked away from the column so that I had a better idea of what the ground around us looked like. Before I had a chance to perform any kind of examination, however, I heard my name called, and I turned in the direction of the voice to see the dim figure that I recognized as Indus waving to me, which I took as an order.

When I reached him, his manner was more like the host of a gathering, because he began by saying, "Centurion Pullus, I must ask your forgiveness. I have not asked if you have met Tribune Aviola."

I had not, and I saluted the Tribune, who was quite lean and a few inches shorter than I was, which he returned, and I was surprised that he did not seem to be haughty at all, returning my salute as I offered my congratulations on his successes to this point.

"It's not me, it's the men who should be thanked," he said, and with a modesty that was both quite shocking yet at the same time seemed completely sincere, but I was completely unprepared for him to add, "but it's truly an honor meeting you, Centurion. Your name is well known where I come from."

Despite his unassuming demeanor, I had to suppress a shiver that seemed to start at the base of my spine as I thought, I was only in Rome a few months! How could he know about me?

"Were you in Rome during my time in the Praetorians?"

It was all I could think to ask, but my confusion deepened when he laughed.

"I'm not from Rome, Centurion," he answered. "I'm from Arelate. Actually," he amended, "my father has an estate a few miles north on the river. *He* is from Rome, and of course, I've been there several times."

As he was speaking, I had to struggle to control my reaction, and to avoid making it clear that I was examining him more closely as I searched his face for any resemblance to Lucius Aviola, either the Elder, whose remains are now lying on the bottom of the ocean floor near Alexandria as fish *cac* after Alex and I hunted him down to retrieve as much of my family's fortune that he had gulled from Gaius Pullus, or his son also named Lucius, who as far as I knew was still a legitimate citizen of Arelate, and in fact had been instrumental in helping us locate his thieving *cunnus* of a father.

Deciding to keep my thoughts to myself, I said honestly enough, "I have visited Arelate to see my uncles and aunt, but it's been some time."

"Ah," he nodded, "so you knew Gaius Pullus then?"

"I met him briefly," I replied, in a tone that I hoped would indicate I had no intention of discussing my dead uncle, particularly the cause of his demise, sensing that this was a road that neither of us wanted to go down.

He was opening his mouth, but I would never learn what he was going to ask because Indus cleared his throat, indicating that it was time to move on, for which I was thankful; it also helped that the other officers and leaders of the various contingents had arrived, including the Batavian Decurion, Chlothar, and the other tribal leaders.

"I thought it would be wise to have the Centurion here to discuss our plan, Tribune," Indus began. "He deserves to know what I intend." This was an interesting comment, and I understood why in the time it took him to say, "I know that we are supposed to harry Florus' men and drive them to where your Legions are waiting." He paused, then, with the kind of dramatic flair that is inherent in all barbarians, he thumped his chest as he declared fiercely, "But *I*, Julius Indus of the Treveri, will be the one to end this rebellion by Julius Florus, *not* Rome. This is a matter of honor, and it should be settled within our people." Without any warning, Indus turned to face me directly, and with a challenging tone, asked, "Do you have an issue with this, Centurion Pullus?"

I was stunned, but I was also angry, and I desperately wished for a moment to think, or even better, have an opportunity to talk with Alex, since Macer was with the Cohorts and was just now departing the camp.

It felt like a long moment, but apparently, it was not too long because Indus did not seem to notice my hesitation before I answered, "I was told by the *Praetor* that you're in command,

and that the Tribune is your second in command. I'm here because of my experience, and because I know how to ride a horse and fight without falling off." There were some chuckles at my attempted humor, and suddenly, I felt inspired to say, "Frankly, sir, I'm a bit puzzled why you feel like my opinion matters."

As I hoped, this caught Indus by surprise, and even in the dim light, I could see by his expression that he understood what I had done, and that he had been outmaneuvered. He could hardly accuse me of being sent to spy on him by Silius, which was exactly what Silius had done, and it did make me wonder what Indus suspected I was really there for; hard on the heels of that was wondering if I needed to watch my own back around this Treveri nobleman.

"I...I...was thinking more of what *Praetor* Silius might think about my intentions," he fumbled, and I felt certain that he knew how weak this sounded. "Yes, well, you have answered my question, at least to the extent that I am satisfied. Now," finally, he turned his attention to his actual plan, "knowing Florus as well as I do, I am very confident that we are still several miles east of him. After all," he pointed out, "he lingered around Vungovicus to let his men drink themselves senseless after they ambushed the Roman traders, and Florus is more Treveri than Roman."

This was a curious thing to say, but Aviola beat me to it by asking, "What does that mean, Indus?"

"It means," Indus said scornfully, "that they were up drinking and telling stories last night, and his entire force has sore heads and sour stomachs this morning, which means that they will not rouse themselves from the camp they made until," he glanced up at the sky before finishing, "about a third of your watches from now."

I cannot say why, but I was suddenly struck by something that prompted me to ask, "Do you know exactly where they are right now, sir?"

Indus shot me an amused look.

"Of course I do," he boasted. "They are about three miles west of here. There is a spot that we use as a base for our hunting parties, and although Florus does not know this area as well as I do, this spot is well known." This was promising, but it still seemed to me to be a fairly large risk, yet when I opened my mouth to press him further, he added smugly, "And if you are about to ask if I am guessing, I assure you that I am not. I have men watching them, and I received word shortly before I called the halt from a messenger that they are exactly where I thought they would be."

Now I can admit that this stung me, which was why I began thinking, and in turn was why I was only partially listening as he talked about the spot he intended to use for an ambush of Florus and his men that was nearby. The more I considered my idea, the more impatient I became waiting for him to pause. This was why, when he did not, I suddenly interrupted.

"Why wait?"

Indus understandably looked startled, while the others all turned to look at me, more than one of them not bothering to disguise their hostility at my speaking out of turn, or so I believed.

"Er, what do you mean, Centurion?"

Realizing that just blurting that out was not helping, I explained, "We know where they are, and you believe that they're...lax in their discipline and are probably not even breaking camp yet. If we move now..."

"We can hit them when they are still unprepared." Indus immediately began nodding in a sign he understood what I was intending. "Even if they have broken camp, they will not be expecting anything so soon." Without hesitation, he raised his voice to announce, "We are mounting up and riding west to crush Florus and his scum while they are still lolling on their bedrolls and holding their sore heads!"

He was striding to his mount as he finished this, and I heard him snap at one of the other Gauls who spoke in their own tongue, clearly uninterested in what this other nobleman had to say. Since I do not speak any Gallic tongue, while it has some similarities to the Germanic languages, they are not numerous enough that I could pick anything out, so I had to go by what my eyes told me. Clearly, the other Gaul resisted Indus' sudden change in plan, which I could understand to a degree, especially if Indus had a reputation for being intemperate and flighty, but it seemed as if there was something else. Not that it mattered, because when the other Gaul—as I recall, he was a member of the Caerosi, a smaller tribe whose lands are north of the Treveri and who supply a Cohort of auxiliaries that are stationed at Bonna—tried to press his case, Indus snarled something and deliberately turned his back to vault into the saddle. I walked over to Latobius and did the same, and within a few heartbeats, all of the men were in their saddles or on their feet, but as I nudged my horse back to where I had been in the double column, Indus called my name and pointed to the spot next to Aviola, who was in the third rank.

"That was a good idea, Centurion," Aviola commented as we began moving.

"Thank you, Tribune," I replied, but my mind had returned to the place it had been as I realized that the man sitting next to me was connected to the family who had robbed mine.

We set out, moving at a fast walk that I knew from experience meant that the infantry with us would be hard-pressed to keep up, and I wondered if Indus intended to leave them behind at some point as we got closer.

"You *do* know who I am, don't you, Centurion?"

Aviola said this so quietly given the sound of clattering hooves as we trotted that I was not sure I had heard him, but then I saw him looking directly at me out of the corner of my vision.

"Well," I admitted, "I wasn't sure until just now. But, yes, I know who you are. Or," I thought to amend, "who your family is. Who was Lucius Aviola to you?"

"If you're referring to the Lucius who is still alive and living in Arelate, he's my cousin." He paused. "But if you're referring to Lucius the Elder, he *was* my uncle, and he was living in Alexandria when he vanished. But I'm guessing you know more about that part of it than I do, don't you?"

Within the span of perhaps a third part of a watch, I had been confronted first by Indus, who may or may not have suspected that I was spying for Silius, when the reality was even worse for him, and now I was riding next to a Tribune who was a member of a family who had stolen from mine, and had indirectly led to the death of my uncle Gaius, although even as I dictate this to Alex, I must be honest and acknowledge that Gaius' demise was probably foreordained because of his twisted nature and desire for Algaia, or Juno, as he called her to his dying breath. And, while I had not been the one to slit his throat, that being done by Demeter, the Rhodian master of the *Persephone*, the ship that Bronwen, Alex, and young Gaius Gallienus, my dead uncle Sextus' son and Alex's half-brother had sneaked aboard without our knowledge that took us to Alexandria, it was only because Demeter beat me to it. How, I wondered, did the Tribune view this?

Since I did not reply immediately, Aviola said, "Whatever you did to my uncle, Centurion, know that I bear you no ill will. That man," I saw his mouth twist into a sneer out of the corner of my vision, "was a stain on my family's name and honor, and I'm sure whatever happened to him was a result of his own foul deeds."

At the moment, I was surprised, although when I thought about it, I realized this was a natural place for his mind to go given the topic, but there was one thing that caught my attention, except that I was unsure how to proceed.

Hesitantly, I began, "Our information was that while Lucius Aviola came from Rome, he came from the..." I fumbled then, unsure how to characterize the Subura in a manner that was not offensive.

Thankfully, he understood, because he shot me an amused look. "The Subura? Is that what you were going to say? And," he went on before I could respond, "I suppose the natural question is how does a member of the Head Count become a Tribune like me?"

I tried to hide my relief, nodding as I replied, "Something like that."

"We're not from the Subura, Centurion," he assured me, "and we're not members of the Head Count. I come from the *gens* Acilia." This was said with the kind of pride that many of us possess, but as I learned when I was Gnaeus Volusenus, when one is highborn, being proud of the achievements of other men who just happen to share your name and lived long before you were born is as natural as if you performed the deed oneself. "Yes, we're plebeian, but we're an ancient family, and

58

we've had a Tribune of the Plebs and a *Quaestor* in our line."

"I apologize, Tribune," I began, but he waved me off.

"Oh, there's no need, Pullus, I assure you." He laughed, but there was a bitter edge to it, which I understood when he explained, "That nonsense about being from the Subura was an invention by my uncle Lucius, although there's some debate in my family about why. Most of us think that it was his way to convince the fools he was gulling that he was a self-made man who rose to his station and wealth because of his cleverness and business acumen, using it as a way to impress his targets. Although," he added, sounding grudging, "there are some members of my family who insist that he did this, along with using other names, in order to shield the rest of the family from the shame he brought onto himself." I was not surprised when Aviola sighed, "And my cousin Lucius is one of them, I'm afraid." He turned to look up at me directly. "I mean it when I say that I bear neither you nor any member of your family any malice, Centurion. What happened to my uncle, whatever it was," he emphasized, "he brought on himself, and the one thing I'm certain of is that he deserved however much pain he endured because of the things he did to the people from whom he stole." While he paused, somehow I sensed what was coming, though he did drop his voice to finish, "Including your uncle Gaius."

When I am uncertain what to say, this is usually the moment where I utter the first thing that pops into my head.

"So you know about what happened to my uncle?" I asked, then realized how vague this was given there were several answers to that, but before I could say anything, he countered with a question of his own. "Which part? How my uncle convinced yours to invest a huge sum in one of his schemes and lost it all? Or about how he died?"

Since he had essentially summarized the original crime and the details did not really matter, I replied, "The second."

"Not all that much," he answered with a shrug that did not convince me in the slightest. Whether that was conveyed to him, I do not know, but for whatever the reason, he continued, "Of course, you hear all sorts of things." He grinned. "You know how we members of the upper orders like to gossip." I gave a polite laugh, but the grin vanished. "And, as I said, your family is well known in Arelate...and it's highly respected, Centurion, although I suspect you know that." Aviola hesitated then; I suppose he was considering how much to share, because he admitted, "But I won't lie and tell you that there wasn't...talk about your uncle and some of his...habits. And, we all knew that he was smitten with one of his slaves, and I recall my cousin telling me that your uncle Gaius had become obsessed with her. I never saw her, but from everything I heard, she was a rare beauty. Besides," he laughed again, "I suppose that's one of the many downfalls of owning slaves. More than one of us has found themselves ensnared in the clutches of a barbarian beauty, the more exotic the better."

"This barbarian beauty has a name," I said coldly, feeling the stirring in my gut. "And it's Algaia Alexandros Pullus." Aviola looked over at me, an expression of uncertainty and, I was happy to see, a fair amount of concern on his face. "She's the wife of Alexandros Pullus, my clerk, whose family has been joined with mine since Pharsalus." I looked him directly in the eye, but I tried to sound pleasant enough when I asked, "Do I need to say anything more about the subject of Algaia, Tribune?"

"N-no, Centurion," he answered quickly. "And I apologize for any insult I might have given. It wasn't intended, I assure you."

I knew this was true, so I did not hesitate or belabor the point, simply saying, "There's no need, Tribune. I just wanted to make it clear."

Obviously relieved, he nodded, then said, "Er, yes, where was I? Ah, well," he cleared his throat, "as far as your uncle, there are so many different versions that it's impossible to know which one is near the truth. But," he said carefully, "the one that was repeated the most often was that there was a dispute over the...Algaia, although she had been manumitted by..."

"My father," I supplied for him, explaining in brief terms the circumstances.

"I see. So," he continued, "when she returned to Arelate for some reason, despite her being free, your uncle tried to stop..."

It was somewhat amusing watching the play of emotions cross his face as Aviola began to realize that not only had I been present for this event that clearly was the source of a great deal of gossip in Arelate, I could see that within a matter of heartbeats since this hit him, his mind had worked out something else, that I might have been the man wielding the *gladius*, because the one thing I was certain of was that Tribune Aviola had a much better idea of what had taken place than he represented.

Therefore, I was not surprised when he finished weakly, "Yes, well, you no doubt know the rest."

"Yes," I answered dryly, "I do."

He fell silent then, which was a good thing, because we were about to initiate an attack on what we hoped was at worst an unprepared force of rebels, and at best, still in the process of breaking camp.

We did not catch Florus and his men still lounging in their bedrolls as Indus had boasted, but it was close. In fact, Indus' gamble to throw caution to the winds and not pause to send scouts ahead, preferring to come bursting into what was actually a clearing in a thick forest that, as he had informed us, had obviously been used quite often, with several small but snug shelters present that he said had been constructed several years earlier, paid off handsomely. The biggest difficulty was the narrowness of the track leading to the clearing that precluded us from shaking out from the double column into a line, but over his shoulder, Indus shouted the order that once we entered the clearing, we would peel off in both directions to form a line, and since I was on the left side, I would be wheeling in that direction to spread out before advancing into the camp, yet as inexperienced as I was, and am, fighting from horseback, I knew this is a standard maneuver. I was also thankful that I was on horseback, because the infantry had been struggling to keep up from the beginning of our short march, and while Indus tried to restrain himself from sending us to the trot, a mile into our march, he could not restrain himself. We did not stop, but Indus dispatched Aviola to drop out and take command of the mixed force of Legionaries, auxiliaries, and tribal warriors that Indus had selected, giving him the order to follow as quickly as possible to act as both a reserve and as a second line to catch any of Florus' men who managed to evade us. This was a sound plan, yet I could not help feeling a bit sorry for Macer and my boys, who had just departed from camp at dawn to move into a position roughly at the spot where Indus had halted us, expecting to be the main effort in stopping and crushing Florus' army before they got too deeply into the Arduenna. Not, I cheerfully admitted later, badly enough to remove myself and go be with them, something that Macer and every other Centurion in the Cohort would be reminding me about in the near future. In the moment, however, we barely paused to make these changes, then broke into a canter at what I assumed was the half-mile mark, since this was where Indus had said we would increase our speed.

With Aviola absent, his spot was taken by one of Indus' Treveri moving up a spot, though there was no time to make introductions, but what mattered was that it would be Herminius who would be to my right, and Chlothar to my left, the Decurion being directly in front of me when we were in column, which helped soothe my nerves a bit, knowing that they at least spoke my tongue. It was a bit less than a third of a watch after dawn, so there was more than enough light, and I could see ahead the lighter background that indicated a clearing, prompting me to reach down and draw the *spatha*, cursing myself for not thinking to either draw or borrow one of the flat cavalry shields with the pair of leather loops, nor would I have my *vitus* since I was not willing to let go of the reins like most of the men around me. The wind had begun whistling between my helmet flaps and my cheeks, reminding me I had also forgotten to tie my chin thongs, but my hands were full, so I could only hope for the best and that it would remain in place. Truthfully, I was not all that worried about it because, just as it had with my father, and with the Prefect, since all Roman helmets are made the same size, my helmet already fit snugly, and with the felt liner on, it felt as secure as if I had tied it on; provided nobody struck me in the helmet, I thought I should be fine, and I quickly had other things to think about, tightening my thighs against Latobius' sides, his ears pricked forward in the sign that he was as eager for action as I was.

When we were about a hundred paces from the edge of the clearing, Indus bellowed the command and we went to the gallop, whereupon everything from that instant on occurred so quickly that I was left with bits of impressions and flashes of scenes in my memory. The first thing that became obvious instantly was that, while Florus' men were all standing on their feet, and most of their bedrolls were rolled up, they were gathered around a series of fires consuming their morning meal. Those nearest to the eastern edge of the clearing from which we appeared were naturally the first to die, but Indus either chose to ignore or forgot his own orders because, instead of breaking to the right, he plunged directly into the middle of the camp, followed by the Treveri, who I had deduced were members of his personal bodyguard. I witnessed this out of the corner of my eye because I was following Chlothar as we galloped along the edge of the clearing, and my attention was perhaps a bit too much on him, because it was only by Fortuna's blessing that the Treveri rebel who hurled a short throwing spear at the huge Roman wearing a black transverse crest missed, the missile slashing across my front less than a full hand's breadth from my chest just a few inches above Latobius' neck.

There was no time for me to even react, the spear gone and past before I could have dodged it, then Chlothar executed a sweeping turn to the right to face the camp, which I copied. Ideally, we should have been closer together, but by this point, some rebels were already running for their own mounts gathered on the opposite side of what passed for their camp, some rebels were dashing for the edge of the clearing nearest to them, while a handful of them appeared to want to stand and fight. Four of these men were now standing together, but in the brief instant we had, I saw that only two of them were wearing armor of any kind, while the pair of men clad in tunics were wielding spears and nothing else, the manner in which they handled them betraying their inexperience. I cannot say who made the decision, me or Latobius, but before I had any thought to do so, I felt him veer slightly, seemingly heading straight for them, which in turn forced me to use my reins to adjust his path so that his head was aligned to the immediate right of the Treveri standing on the right side of the line they had formed, another sign of their inexperience being that they did not spread out but stood close together. Given how rapidly everything was happening, how Latobius moves so quickly despite his size, and the fact that the Treveri I had selected as my first kill was one of those wearing the tunic, I suppose it was inevitable that his panic-stricken thrust was launched too soon, hitting nothing but air. Before he could recover his spear, Latobius' chest struck it, sending it flying from his grip, while the impact spun him partially about so that it was almost as if he presented his neck for my *spatha* as it swung down, and I only saw his head tumbling into the air in a spray of blood out of the corner of my eye. Then I was past and faced with a choice of turning Latobius about or plunging more deeply into the camp, which was now a boiling mass of activity, with panicked shouting and screams of men being cut down adding to the chaos.

Glancing over my shoulder, I saw Herminius who, naturally, was more experienced, expertly driving his horse into the surviving three Treveri, and this proved too much for the second tunic-clad rebel, who threw his spear down and began sprinting towards the southern, or nearest edge of the clearing. I did not see what happened, but I did not need to because Decurion Chlothar saw the same thing and headed for the fleeing rebel. Not satisfied with just one kill, I scanned the area, as by this moment, most of the mounted contingent under Indus were now well into the clearing, slashing, thrusting, and cutting down at the rebels, but seeing that it was getting crowded, I looked towards the far end of the clearing to see that about a dozen men were now mounted. I cannot say exactly why my eye was drawn to one Treveri in particular, although in hindsight, I believe it was because, to my Roman eye, the man bore a striking resemblance to Indus, and somehow I knew that this must be Florus. He was one of the men in the saddle; perhaps it was also the manner in which the other mounted men surrounded him, and as confident as I was, I was not about to attack this group alone.

Looking over my shoulder again, I saw Herminius, along

with Arnfrid and Ellanher, the pair having arrived in time to finish cutting down the remaining duo of the four who had foolishly chosen to stand and fight. Shouting Herminius' name, it took two attempts before he looked in my direction, and I pointed my *spatha* at the cluster of Treveri, although by this time, we were not the only men to have spied them. A group of about eight of our force were now moving at the canter from our right, so thinking that we would take advantage of their movement and how most of the Treveri were now looking in their direction, I beckoned to the three Batavians and they did not hesitate to follow me as I kicked Latobius, but instead of heading directly for our foes, I swung around from the side opposite of the larger group which, even as I was maneuvering around the shelters, I could see was growing in number as other troopers spotted the prospect of action. The truth was that I was too intent on the idea of closing with Florus, because I was almost killed when, without any warning, a Treveri rebel hiding in one of the shelters suddenly launched himself bodily at me from my left. My head was just turning in that direction as my eye sensed the movement when I was struck in the middle of my body, with enough force that I instantly knew I would be losing my saddle, although I had just enough time to twist my body slightly so that when I slammed into the ground, my right arm would not be pinned under me. What this did mean, unfortunately, was that I landed more on my back, the impact driving the wind from my lungs, and I learned what forgetting to tie my chin thongs cost me as the flange that protects my neck slammed into the ground with enough force that my helmet was knocked off, though I suppose it did keep my head from striking the ground full force. This was the instant when I saw my foe for the first time, his face just inches from mine as he tried to drive his dagger into my throat, although this was his mistake; I suppose that because of my size, he decided he needed to use two hands to drive the blade into my chest, thereby robbing him of the ability to use his left hand to at least try and stop me from defending myself. That did not mean that I was out of danger, and even in the moment, as I struggled to draw air into my lungs while using just my left forearm to block him, I cursed the longer length of the *spatha*, which made it next to impossible for me, even with my longer arms, to drive the point into his side. His bearded face, inches from mine, blazed with the kind of hatred and fear that had so unsettled me the first time I had encountered it, during the brief campaign under Germanicus when a pair of tribes, the Tencteri and Sugambri had crossed the Rhenus north of our current location.

Now, while I while will not say it did not faze me, I was more annoyed with being sprayed with the man's spittle as he put every bit of strength into driving the dagger into my chest, having shifted his weight to his upper body, hoping that between his own strength and his mass, it would be enough to overpower just my left arm. Leading with the pommel of my *spatha*, I aimed the iron knob atop the wooden pommel for his temple, confident that even with just my arm's strength, it would be enough, but in the instant I began to swing my arm, I saw his eyes dart in that direction, and he threw himself forward so that, instead of striking him in the temple, it was a glancing blow that bounced off the back of his head. Frankly, his bellow right next to my ear was more painful than anything else during our struggle, but I also could feel my left arm weakening, so I swung again; this time, he moved his head violently to his right, and it was another glancing blow, then finally, the third time the iron knob struck him in the temple, and I felt the bone of his skull give way, although it was the manner in which his body went instantly limp, his eyes rolling into the back of his head so that only the whites were showing that told me the fight was over.

I threw him off me, though not before some of the blood that was now streaming from the side of his head spattered onto my face...and into my mouth as I gasped for breath. This is something that, while not all that common, does happen, yet in this case, my gagging and spitting out another man's blood as I scrambled to my feet distracted me just enough that my attention was diverted to the larger situation. Certainly it was not long, perhaps a full heartbeat, but it was just enough that I was a fraction of a heartbeat slow in reacting to the sudden rush of movement by a spear-wielding Treveri who, although he was wearing armor, bore the same kind of wild-eyed, panicked expression on his face that most of the rebels who were clad only in tunics were wearing, while in one of those odd moments I noticed he was actually completely clean-shaven. Still, he somehow managed to slide to a stop just out of reach of my *spatha* to launch a thrust of his own that was poorly aimed, and I barely had to lean a bit to my right to avoid it. He had managed to snatch up a shield, but I was confident that he also had never faced a man of my size who moved as quickly as I do, yet somehow, while it was close, he managed to raise his shield to deflect my *spatha* just enough that the blade skipped off the top of his shield, the point punching into his left shoulder with enough force to break the links of his mail, eliciting a bellow of pain from my foe, though the thrust was not particularly damaging. The look of panic on his face changed into one that I also recognized, one of the kind of iron determination when a man recognizes that the only way to see another sunrise is to kill the man across from him, and this time when he lunged, it was more what one would expect from a veteran warrior. Fortunately, both of our flanks were somewhat protected, because the shelter from which the first Treveri attacked me was on one side, while Latobius was standing there on the other, although he was tossing his head and blowing loudly enough I could hear him over the other noise.

With our flanks secure, we only concentrated on each other, and my foe's thrust was well-aimed and clearly meant for a man without a shield, because he held his arm out from his body a bit more than normal so that the point was slightly angled and, if it had landed, would have struck me in the left ribcage. Thanks to Fortuna, I had actually noticed him push his elbow out, and I correctly anticipated his intent so that when I moved my left hand outward in a wide swipe, it was actually not to knock his spear further outward so that the point would pass just behind my back, which would have been more likely. My reason for doing so was that I was going to do something that, if anyone had known about it, they would have called me mad, not only because it was dangerous, but I had never attempted it before, at least not exactly like this. I had learned it from my father, though not because he had demonstrated it but because I had read about it, so that when the palm of my hand struck the spear shaft several inches below the head, I wrapped my fingers around it and got it in my grasp, albeit with a backhand grip that was far from ideal. He understood what I was about, but his recognition was perhaps an eyeblink too late, so that when he yanked the spear with all of his strength, it did not budge in my hand, then when I returned the favor by doing the same thing, he was experienced enough to know he should just let go of the spear and at least try to draw the long Gallic *gladius* at his waist, yet for the second time, he was just a fraction late in doing so. Therefore, his lurch towards me was not much, his body only moving perhaps a foot in my direction, but the motion did cause his shield to move slightly, offering me a gap not much wider than my *spatha*, and if he had still held his spear, he could have used the shaft to parry my thrust, or at least deflect it towards his shield so that he could absorb the blow with it. He did not have his spear, however, having relinquished it rather than being pulled onto my blade, but while this was the reasonable thing to do, it only earned him another fraction of a heartbeat as, this time, I managed to put my hips into a first position thrust that swept up and caught him just under his breastbone. As normally happens, his eyes went wide and his mouth dropped open, but more to save time than any sense of mercy, I did not twist my upper body while locking my arm against my side as we are trained, actually kicking him straight off my blade, whereupon he took a single staggering backward step then collapsed, his eyes never leaving my face as he tried to say something, though his mouth filled with blood too rapidly for him to do anything but spew his lifeblood in a fine spray. I felt his eyes on me as I stepped over his body, though I did think to toss the spear out of his reach then leapt into the saddle, and it is difficult to describe how disappointed I was to see that the battle was essentially over. However, I learned very quickly from Herminius that this was not entirely the case, after he came trotting up wearing a broad grin and with three severed heads attached to his saddle, a habit that, as much as Rome has tried, we have been unable to break the Batavians from completely whenever it is with a tribe with whom they have had some sort of grudge, even if that grudge happened long before any of us were alive. Seeing those heads told me more about their tribal history than anything else, that at some point in the last hundreds of years, some Treveri had insulted a Batavian.

"Pullus!" he shouted, then pointed down at the heads with a broad grin. "One of these is yours, but I did not think you wanted it!"

He was right, of course, but I had other things on my mind, and I moved Latobius at the trot in his direction, shouting as I did, "Where's Florus?"

"He got away," Herminius replied, though he did not seem all that upset about it. He pointed back in the direction from which we had come. "He got past Indus and his minions here in the clearing and are trying to get deeper into the Arduenna."

"Maybe the men we left back there have caught him," I suggested, but the Batavian scoffed, "Florus and his lot are still mounted. How are men on foot going to catch them?"

I was about to offer an angry retort, but then I caught his grin, understanding that this was part of the normal barbed banter between cavalry and infantry, who heartily detest each other.

"Go piss on your boots, cavalry boy," I shot back. "Florus is as good as caught."

Fortunately for my pride, I was only partially wrong.

As Herminius had predicted, Aviola and the men under his command, while they managed to harry the remnants of what turned out to be more of an armed rabble than an army, and cut down dozens of horsemen, Florus and a handful of his bodyguards got past them. Aviola and his men did whittle down the men of Florus' bodyguard, and the Tribune reported to Indus that only Florus and three other warriors were with him as he vanished into the thick forest to the west. Indus was naturally and understandably impatient to hunt Florus down, but he was also adamant about something else.

"We are going to be advancing on line, but none of you are to harm Florus if you find him," he commanded. I was close enough to see the malice in the smile he offered. "Killing that rebel and traitor to Rome *must* fall to me! Is that understood?"

Speaking personally, I bridled at the tone that Indus was

using, along with the idea that he did not even glance over at Aviola, who was the ranking Roman officer present. He did, however, look in my direction, but to my eye, it was more of a speculative look, which made me think that perhaps he was viewing me as the one most likely to disobey his order, and he was absolutely right. I would not begin with the intention of not heeding his directive, but I knew myself well enough to know that if I saw Florus, who I had learned from the description of him had been the man I thought when I spotted him at the far end of the clearing, my instinct to kill an enemy would likely overwhelm any order given by a barbarian nobleman. Thankfully, I was saved from myself because, while I heard shouting off to my left about a third of a watch after we began sweeping west, I never laid eyes on any Treveri rebel. However, countering my disappointment from not having the opportunity to send Florus to the afterlife was the knowledge that, despite having been left behind, the rebel leader was not struck down by Indus either. Instead, it fell to the men of the Cohorts of the 1st and 2nd, who had arrived at the prearranged meeting spot to be greeted by a lone messenger given the unenviable task by Indus of informing the two Primi Pili that, if Indus was successful in his changed plan, they would have nothing to do.

I do not want to give the impression that it was a Roman who struck Florus down, even if the Legions were the cause of his demise. Macer was understandably bitter that it was not in the 1st's area that Florus and the last three men of his bodyguard blundered into an ambush, but once more while his men fell, Florus initially escaped the volley of javelins from men of the Second Century of the Third Cohort of the 2nd, but his flight to freedom was short-lived. With the area swarming with Legionaries, and the *Corniceni* of each Century signaling the others, as the net tightened, Florus dismounted, sat down at the base of a tree, and cut his own throat. He was found slumped over, his horse nearby, which meant that it was Carbo and his men who had the glory of returning to the camp outside Orolaunum where Silius, Sacrovir and Varro were waiting for the news, but it was the former Praetorian who also stole a march on my Primus Pilus and Legion.

"The bastard didn't let us know a fucking thing about what was going on," Macer raged, albeit in his tent that night. "We heard the horns off to the north, but Carbo never sent a runner to tell us what was happening. Then," he slapped his desk in frustration, "they marched away back here without informing us! The only way we knew anything at all, let alone that Florus was dead, was when Decurion Chlothar sent one of his troopers," he thought for a moment, then identified him, "Wigmar, I think his name is, to let us know it was essentially all over." He glared at me, though I was not the real target. "Can you believe that *cunnus*?"

I was certainly not as angry as my Primus Pilus, but I was not unaffected, and I felt a flash of my own anger, and even in the moment, I was not blinded to the fact that Carbo's status as a former Praetorian played a role in my own ire. What he had done smacked of the kind of thing Praetorian Centurions do to each other every chance they get, even when it is within their own Cohort, in an attempt to grab glory for themselves while belittling others they consider rivals.

It was this thought that prompted me to say, "Well, I suppose it's a compliment of a sort, isn't it?"

I believe that Macer was too worked up to understand my meaning, and he demanded challengingly, "Compliment? How by Pluto's cock is that a compliment?"

"Because he clearly views you as a rival for favor from Silius," I began, but then another thought occurred to me as I remembered something else. "Or, more likely, he thought this would be something that Varro would want, to embarrass Silius since he commands us, and he commands the 2nd."

He considered this, then seemed to accept it when he expelled a harsh breath, then muttered, "Fucking patricians and their fucking games."

We chatted a bit longer, then I left to go to my own tent and inform Alex of what had transpired.

I was not surprised when, as he handed me a cup of wine, he replied simply, "We heard." Taking the cup, I downed it in a couple swallows then thrust it out to him, and he frowned, clearly not wanting to indulge me, but when he saw I was serious, he sighed and refilled it, explaining as he did, "Carbo made quite the entrance into the camp. He had Florus' body across the saddle of his horse, and from somewhere, he found some ivy garlands to wrap around his eagle, while the men sang their ridiculous song they love so much."

My first thought was to wonder if Macer knew this, and if he did not and inevitably found out, what his reaction would be, but my irritation that had been somewhat muted flared up when he mentioned that song. It is some ditty that a wag of the 2nd composed long before, around the time my father was transferred from the 8th, and it is responsible for the majority of the brawls that erupt between men of the 2nd and other Legions because of the words. It is natural for men of a Legion, any of them, to be proud of their accomplishments, but the 2nd's song went to great lengths, in several verses to belittle the other Legions in the Army of the Rhenus, the 1st in particular. I will not soil the vellum that Alex is scribbling on with the specifics, but the essence is simple, and rests in the numbers of our Legions; despite being second, the 2nd's song insists that they are actually the first, of all the Legions, and are always called on to fix the mess created by the others, particularly the 1st. Once Alex explained this, I realized something else; in all likelihood, this was the reason Carbo had not sent a runner to his counterpart that they were returning to the camp, because if they had, and the 1st had been marching with them, there is no doubt that there would be violence, particularly since the men were already frustrated from not participating in what we would quickly learn was the ending of the uprising of the Treveri. However, as we would also discover, not only would the 1st get the last laugh, and more glory than the 2nd, Camp Prefect Sacrovir's insistence that his half-brother's participation in the crushing of the Turoni had been a ploy was vindicated, which in turn created some difficulties for Varro, a happy development as far as we were concerned, at least at first. Only now is it turning out that Varro's embarrassment is what is likely fueling the events that are only beginning to become fully formed, as once again, the son of the nominal *Praetor* of Lower Germania proves to be not only vindictive, but with a growing power; that is for later, however. In my life, things were about to once again become more complicated because of the return of Marcus Sempronius, Tiberius' agent, into my world.

"Sacrovir has marched on Augustodunum and taken it!" We were still in the camp outside Orolaunum, and almost a week had passed since the Treveri's rebellion had been put down, culminating with Indus returning to Augusta Treverorum with the head of Florus on a spear, accompanied by Varro, his personal bodyguard, or rather, his father's bodyguard, including the six lictors...and the First Cohort of the 2nd, where they entered the town in much the same fashion as they had the camp, sending the signal to the Treveri that their rebellion was over. Varro reportedly put on a great show of holding court and dispensing justice to men who were accused by loyal Treveri of having aided or abetted Florus in some way, but in the end, no executions were carried out, with Varro declaring to the packed forum that by order of the Imperator himself, those found guilty would be granted clemency, in exchange for a huge monetary fine. It probably will come as no surprise that there was a great deal of speculation about whether this was actually by order of Tiberius, who has never been known for his forgiveness when there is some sort of transgression, or if this was something concocted by Varro himself in order to enrich himself. Macer, who was normally the pragmatic one, was certain this was the case, and in fact I had to talk him out of seeking an audience with Sacrovir as the first step of initiating a formal request to investigate whether Varro the Younger was actually acting on his father's orders back in Vetera, and if he was not, that he be brought up on charges of corruption.

"To what end, Marcus?" I asked him in the privacy of his quarters where we were alone, of course; I would have never used his *praenomen* otherwise. "What do you think you'll accomplish, aside from your own destruction? At the very least, this will destroy your career, and it may get you killed."

Frankly, I was in a mild state of shock at the vehemence, and the seeming determination of my Primus Pilus to go through with this, although I also felt confident that, even if I could not talk him out of it, that the Prefect would make sure that the man he had personally championed to be made his replacement as Primus Pilus did not do anything rash.

"Something needs to happen to stop that *cunnus*," Macer insisted. "If not me, then who?"

"He's backed by Sejanus, Marcus," I replied quietly. "Nobody like us, no matter how high up in the ranks, can afford to draw the wrath of the Praetorian Prefect. And," I leaned forward, and to emphasize my point, I stabbed the table with my pointing finger, "you need to trust me when I say this. Remember, I know Sejanus, and I know Varro. One reason they're on the same side is because they see the world the same way, and they're both ambitious. Neither of them will rest in eradicating anyone who tries to stop them from attaining their own goals."

I stopped then, sensing that it needed to be Macer to be the next to open his mouth, and my heart sank when he shook his head, but that lasted less than a heartbeat before he finally muttered, "You're right. I know it. I just..." He made a helpless gesture, and of all the things he could have said or done, that one sign of surrender to the realities of our world was one that I understood and shared completely.

Everything changed when, two days after Varro and the others returned from Augusta Treverorum, a courier galloped into the camp, carrying the message that Alex came bursting into my quarters to announce, that Prefect Sacrovir had been right about the Aedui Sacrovir. Very quickly, the camp began buzzing, while Centurions who did not like to wait for orders to be issued began swatting their men with the *vitus* to get them moving in preparation for marching, Centurions like me, although I was not alone since this had been taught to me by my first Pilus Prior, who was now the Primus Pilus, but as I knew, Marcus Macer had learned this from my father, back when my father had been his Optio. Consequently, it was the First Cohort of the 1st that would be ready to march the soonest, and as the men worked, Macer sent Lucco while I sent Alex to the *praetorium* to learn as much as they could glean about the circumstances.

Augustodunum is in the heart of the lands of the Aedui, and while it is not as formidable as their original capital of

Bibracte, the hillfort that my great-grandfather had seen while a *Gregarius* marching with Caesar, it is still a fortified town, which meant that the wagering among the men was strongly in favor of some form of siege.

"Sacrovir would be an idiot trying to face us in open battle," Clepsina commented on the night we learned the news. "His best chance is to hide behind his walls." He thought of something, and asked the rest of us, "Have any of you been to Augustodunum before?"

"I passed through a few years ago," Glaxus spoke up, but when we all turned to look at him expectantly, he reddened slightly. "But," he mumbled, "I didn't look at it very carefully, so there's not much I can say."

Then why did you bring it up? I thought sourly, while Clepsina and I exchanged a glance, and I was heartened to see him roll his eyes; unfortunately, Macer caught it, earning me a silent warning in the form of a glare. Like my real father, I have never been able to completely hide my true feelings, and even those times I do manage to maintain an expression that does not divulge my actual sentiments to most people, Macer is one of those who can still tell, as can Alex and, of course, my wife. Fortunately for me, my antipathy for Glaxus was shared, and not just by Clepsina, but Glaxus also had a powerful patron in Prefect Sacrovir, although the real connection was between Sacrovir's son, who had been an Optio in the Eighth Cohort but was now the Hastatus Posterior of the Sixth Cohort, not in the 1st but in the 8th Legion, which is still in Siscia, the younger Sacrovir making the transfer because of his father's elevation to Camp Prefect, neither of them wanting the son's career to be tainted by the appearance of nepotism. Glaxus had saved the younger Sacrovir at the Angrivarian Wall, and the whispers were that his elevation to the First Cohort was the repayment of that debt, but if that was true, it was extremely unusual for our former Primus Pilus, and my personal feelings for Glaxus aside, I cannot say that he was a bad Centurion. He was competent enough, but there was just a timidity in his character that I found off-putting, and as he did at this moment, he had a tendency to speak up when he did not really have anything to contribute.

"Anyone else?" Macer asked, in another signal that this was not the time to have some fun at Glaxus' expense, and it was actually Caudex, who was something of a wit, who looked the most disappointed. When we shook our heads, he said dismissively, "Then we'll have to wait to get there to find out with our own eyes." He consulted his wax tablet before he continued, "Now that we're two full Legions, our supply situation has changed. Also, when the *Praetor* sent the orders for the rest of our boys to march down from Ubiorum, he didn't want to wait for a full baggage train, which means that we have no siege equipment or any of the other heavy baggage items, nor does the 2nd. Rather than wait for the 2nd's heavy baggage to come all the way down from Vetera, the *Praetor* has informed Varro that he is authorizing the 20th's complement of artillery to be used by the 2nd." He looked up then, and offered us a smile, but it was not warm, nor was it friendly, and there was no mistaking the satisfaction in his voice when he added, "Let young Varro try to make an issue of that!"

The rest of us offered up our approval of the idea, each of us understanding what he meant, because the Imperator, whatever his faults may be, is an experienced general, and he would have never made the mistake of putting a Legion in the field without having at least the capability of calling for his artillery in a timely manner, and Ubiorum was much closer to our current position. One benefit of the reunion of the entire 1st, who had arrived late on the night of Florus' death from their position a couple miles north of our blocking position, was that we were no longer outnumbered by the 2nd, which in turn meant that we no longer had to worry about trouble from them, and as it happened, the artillery, for both Legions, arrived three days after we were informed of Sacrovir's treachery. Naturally, we did not see the cavalry much, as they were now kept busy ranging all over the region, but when they did return, they brought troubling news.

On the night before we departed, as Macer gave all of the Centurions their final orders, he informed us, "There are a lot of rumors floating around right now, and since I just came back from a meeting with the *Praetor* and Prefect, I wanted to share with you the absolute latest information that we have."

I glanced over at Clepsina to see if he gave a sign that he had caught Macer's singular use of *Praetor*, and that he had not mentioned Varro, but it was impossible to say; besides, Macer was continuing, "There are a number of tribes," he held up his free hand to extend a finger, "starting with the Remi," another finger went up, "along with the Cataluni," a third finger, "the Tricasses," a fourth finger, "the Leuci..."

"Is he going to run out of fingers?" Clepsina whispered, and I had to suppress my urge to chuckle.

"It seems that way," I whispered back, or thought I had.

"Pullus, maybe if you spent more time listening and less time trying to be clever, you might learn something," Macer snapped.

"Er, yes, Primus Pilus," I mumbled. "Sorry. Won't happen again."

Thankfully, he did not belabor the chastisement, continuing with, "the Lingones, and the Sequani, where there seems to be a strong sentiment towards joining with the Aedui." He paused for the murmurs of dismay, concern, or the combination of the two that were inevitable, then he plunged on with the news that he knew would give us the hardest time with our men. "Since this isn't our normal area of responsibility, let me just inform you also that the territory of the tribes I mentioned are along our line of march to Augustodunum, and because of that, the *Praetor* has ordered that we march in armor, shields uncovered..." there were inevitably some groans at this, but the worst was coming, which he delivered now, "...and in *agmentum quadratum*."

Macer ignored the instant uproar, snapping his tablet shut in a sign that, at least the officers of his Cohort knew, meant that he was not willing to entertain any kind of discussion about the orders, relying on his Centurions to relay them, and to quell the grumbling that would inevitably be coming. Marching in the *quadratum*, as we call it, is a cumbersome process, one where, depending on where you are in the square, means that you might find yourself turned outward and sidestepping if you are under strong pressure from an enemy, or even worse, walking backward and begging the gods not to put something on the ground for you to trip over as you walk backwards.

Although it is the most secure method of moving a large group of men while at the same time protecting the all-important baggage train, it is also the easiest in which to make a mistake, and depending on what is happening, it can be a fatal one. To a man, the *quadratum* is loathed throughout the ranks, including by most Centurions, yet at the same time, if we were forced to choose the formation that provided the most security and the chance to see another sunrise...it would be the *quadratum*. On the day of our departure, Fortuna chose to smile at us, or most likely *Praetor* Silius and the Prefect took it upon themselves to set the marching order, knowing that Varro was too ignorant of Legion business to notice that his pet Legion would be given the hardest task of being the halves of both sides, and the rear line of the box. The 1st, on the other hand, particularly the First Cohort, occupied the middle of the front rank of the formation, with the Second and Third on either side, the Fifth on the far left, and the Fourth on the far right. Not surprisingly either, the *quadratum* requires a great deal of space, but for most of the first day, this was not an issue, because this area of Gaul has long since been settled, and the road we were on took us to Durocoturum (Reims) after turning south at a ford of the Mosa (Meuse) located at Mosomagus (Mouzon), where there is a trading outpost.

From Durocoturum, which is a four-day march from Orolaunum, we would turn directly south for Augustodunum, located more than a hundred fifty miles from Durocoturum. Normally, we would have covered that distance from Orolaunum to Durocoturum in three days, but another issue with the *quadratum* is that it is much slower than a normal marching column, and this was even more the case after we turned south and the terrain began undulating. Durocoturum is in Remi country, yet even before we reached the town, which is the Remi capital, there were signs that, while the Remi were not quite willing to break out into open rebellion, it was easy to see where their sentiments lay, and they were not with Rome. The grumbling about being in *quadratum* had steadily increased with every day we were on the march, until we arrived in Remi lands, when, upon seeing the open hostility on the parts of the odd tribesman as we marched past, the complaining, while not vanishing completely, did die down. It was when we marched within sight of the walls of Durocoturum, however, when tensions were at their highest, and in my case at least it had as much to do with the fact that it was our turn to be at the bottom of the *quadratum*, and there is actually a thick expanse of forest immediately northeast of the town, which is situated on a tributary of the Axona, (Aisne). There is a bridge, but since it is directly underneath the walls, Silius ordered that we use the ford, which is about five hundred paces south of the town, and while it was not a difficult crossing, as the current is not very strong and the river bottom is sound, we were effectively the rearguard, charged with watching the treeline of that forest.

While everything went smoothly enough, it was just when it was finally our turn to begin crossing that Vinicius, standing at the rear of the formation as he was supposed to, shouted my name. When I spun about, he did not need to point out what it was that had caught his attention, as I was in time to see a mounted man, clearly not one of our cavalry, emerge from the underbrush. His presence was one thing; the fact that he was wearing armor, and most importantly, he was joined by what I initially counted to be a dozen men also clad in armor, although most of them were wearing boiled leather, was alarming enough, but then the numbers grew until there were a couple hundred men that I assumed were Remi warriors standing motionless, watching us. For a brief instant, I considered ordering Macrinus to play the notes that alerted the other Cohorts who were sharing the bottom of the *quadratum*, but they had already crossed in a method we call collapsing, where the center Cohort remains on the original side of the ford as one of its Centuries after another crosses until there is just one left, which in this case was my Century, but after watching for about a dozen heartbeats, once I saw that the Remi numbers did not swell any more, nor did they make any move in our direction, I decided against it. Nevertheless, I only breathed easier once we were across the river, while the talking among the men did not resume until the walls of the Remi capital were no longer in view.

We built a fortified camp, and in a sign that our officers

had noticed the attitude of the Remi, we were put on one-quarter alert, which the First Cohort escaped by virtue of our day at the bottom of the *quadratum*. That did not mean it was a quiet night; twice, one of the guard Cohorts sounded the alarm, which did not endear them to the rest of us. Fortunately, at least from the Centurions' perspective, one alarm came from the 2nd, and one from the 1st, which balanced out the complaining at the interrupted sleep, but what was becoming clear was that the need for constant vigilance was wearing on all of us.

Our next challenge came just a day later, after we entered the lands of the Catalauni tribe, and one thing became immediately clear, that the closer we approached the Aedui, the more the sentiment against us grew with their neighboring tribes. Whereas the Remi had contented themselves with angry glares, and a lone demonstration of defiance as we forded the river, it was as we approached Durocatalaunum (Chalogne-Sur-Marne), on the banks of the Matrona River (Marne) that we ran into our first sign of overt resistance. On this day we were on the left flank of the box, but when our progress suddenly stopped because of a horn call, it was at the leading edge of the *quadratum*, which was screened from our view because of a low rise, the terrain having become hillier as we marched south.

"Drop packs! Face outward!"

I bellowed this, as did the other Centurions of the First, and overall, I was happy with the speed, although I did use my *vitus* on a couple of men who usually needed it, but I for one certainly did not expect that we would be standing there for a third of a watch. In fact, it was not until later that we learned the cause of the delay.

"There were felled trees across the track, and they went to the trouble of felling trees for about twenty paces outward on either side of the track so that the wagons couldn't get past them," Alex informed me after I had sent him on a trip to the *praetorium* that night. "It took the pioneers a lot of time because of the way the trees were interlocked together."

"They did that in Britannia," I commented, recalling my

great-grandfather's account of what the tribes there had done to delay the Roman invaders. "They felled them in different directions so they overlapped." Thinking of something else, I asked, "Were they lashed together? And were there any other traps, like sharpened stakes?"

Alex said he did not know, but by the next morning, we had heard that neither of these conventions that Prefect Pullus had spoken of had happened, which I chose to take as a good sign, thinking that if these Catalauni had actively attempted to hurt us, we would have been required to stop to deal with them. Even with their activities being confined to this harassment and an incident during the night, when an occasional missile was launched over the wall at odd intervals, although the only casualty was a mule who was lamed and had to be put down, I know that none of us relished the idea of having a potential Aedui ally in our rear. Yes, Gaul belongs to Rome, and yes, there were many of the sixty-four tribes who are friendly to Rome, but it was growing harder to see these tribes as such as we marched the almost two hundred miles to Augustodunum.

What should have taken a day and a half to cover took two full days for us to leave Catalauni territory, entering the lands of the Tricasses tribe, one of the few tribes in the region that were not rumored to be at least sympathetic to the Aedui. At the time, I believed this was the reason that, instead of bypassing the town that serves as the tribal capital, Augostobona Tricassium (Troyes), we marched through it, but in fact we were there for an entirely different reason, while I was in for a deep, and quite unsettling shock. On the day of our arrival, a halt was called a half-mile from the town to break down from the *quadratum* into a single column, with the 1st leading the way since we were once again at the top of the *quadratum*, while the First Cohort was given the vanguard, over the apparent objections of Varro, if I am any judge by the manner in which he was pointing emphatically in the direction of the 2nd's eagle, where Carbo was standing, as Varro said something to Silius. The Prefect was sitting on his horse, but while he looked uncomfortable, I did not put much thought into it since it was the expression he normally wore when he was sitting astride a horse. Silius was obviously unconvinced by whatever the other man said, and this was confirmed by the manner in which Varro yanked his horse's head viciously around and kicked his mount into a trot away, but it was the sight of Sacrovir smiling at his retreating back that was good to see, as there had been precious little of that for weeks now. Soon after this, the *cornu* sounded and we resumed our march into Augustobona Tricassium.

Since we were in Century order, I was a bit far back to pick a familiar face out of the crowd of spectators who were lining the central street that was a continuation of the main road that we had been following, which paralleled the left bank of the Sequana (Seine) River. Unlike Durocoturum and Durocatalaunum, while it would not be right to say that the people were overjoyed to see us, there was certainly not the hostility from the people in the other towns we had passed by, but I also noticed that there seemed to be more people, both men and women, dressed in Roman garb, making me wonder if this was any different than the places that we had actually bypassed. Most of them appeared to be tradesmen, but I saw a couple garbed in the Equestrian tunic, and what smiles there were came from these people, but it was one man in particular who almost brought me to a sudden stop, which would have been hard on Macrinus, who was marching just behind me.

"*Marcus Sempronius?*" I gasped, but it was under my breath, so I called out, "Marcus! Marcus Sempronius!"

Naturally, he was looking in my direction, but there was not a flicker of recognition from him, yet I was absolutely sure that it was him. Yes, his hair was a bit grayer, and I could see a scar at the edge of his hairline that disappeared into it that he had not had before. So surprised was I that I stepped away from the formation and stopped to stand in front of Sempronius, who eyed me nervously, and in fact, it reminded me of our early time together when I had almost thrashed him on learning who he was, and most importantly, for whom he worked, but I had believed that we at least had developed a working relationship where we were not trying to kill each other.

"Y-yes, Centurion? Is there something you needed, perhaps?" He gave a nervous laugh. "I'm a simple trader of grain and olive oil, but I'm not very big, so I don't know that I could supply your Century."

"Why are you pretending you don't know me, Sempronius?" I demanded, although some instinct told me to keep my voice low, not that it would have mattered since I was acutely aware that all eyes were on us....and my Century was marching past, watching this transpire.

"Because I don't have any idea who that is, Centurion," he replied in clear surprise, and in that instant, I remembered how thoroughly Sempronius had fooled me when we first met on our arrival in Rome, pretending to be an admirer of the Pullus family and merely eager to help. As this occurred to me, he thrust his arm out, and said, "My name is Aulus Cordus Macula, originally from Arelate and now living here in Gaul. Although," he laughed, and it did sound genuine, "I'm afraid I'm never in one place long enough to claim it."

It was an automatic reaction on my part to accept his arm, and only later did I recognize the shrewdness of his reply, because I heard myself say, "Oh? My family is from Arelate."

"Then that explains it!" he exclaimed, giving me a broad smile that did not reach his eyes, which were blazing a warning to me if I was any judge. "That's why you thought I was this Marcus Sempronius person! I obviously resemble him. Actually," he brought his hand to his chin and stroked it in the manner of a man thinking about something, "I think I know the man you're talking about! Before I moved away, I was confused with him more than once." He laughed. "In fact, I remember now! I was once chased by a gang of one of the local *collegia* because they thought I was this Marcus Sempronius person!"

"That must be it," I said, trying not wince at how lame I sounded while forcing myself not to glance at the other onlookers around us who were clearly curious and entertained by this exchange. Completely flummoxed about what I should say next, and seeing the standard of the Sixth Century just passing me by, I stammered, "Er, yes, well...*Salve*, I suppose."

I did not wait for a reply, turning to trot back up the column to step back into my spot, and Lentulus wasted no time.

"What was that about? Did you know that man?"

"I thought I did," I replied, and I am afraid I gritted my

teeth a bit as I added, "but clearly I was wrong."

Although we could have continued on for at least another watch, the horn sounded the first of the several calls to halt, followed by the command summoning the senior officers, and we watched as Macer went moving towards the command group.

He was not gone long, returning with a bemused expression to inform us, "We're making camp here, and we'll be here for at least two days." His demeanor changed slightly to a more recognizable mien, a kind of wry resignation that signaled that he knew how what he was about to say would be received. "And it's our turn to dig."

The chorus of curses that arose was not surprising, since digging is the most loathed of the duties in making a marching camp, but as always, within a count of a hundred, the men of the First Cohort were spread out, waiting with their spades for the men of the *Praefectus Fabrorum*, which in this case was another Tribune, Gaius Censorinus Paullus, to use the colored wooden stakes to mark the layout of the camp. This was somewhat unusual; normally, this party of men range ahead so that the site of the camp has already been selected when we were marching west of the Rhenus, but this was a sign of just how unsettled matters were.

Nevertheless, soon enough dirt was flying, while the pieces of the *praetorium* were hauled to the center of the camp, and in this relatively short period of time where there was no dirt wall to impede my view, I watched the three senior officers as they stood, dismounted, waiting for the tent to be erected, with each of their wagons drawn up to transfer their belongings into it. The Prefect's tent would go up next, and I noticed immediately that he was standing with Silius, engaged in what appeared to be an intense conversation, while Varro was standing with Aviola, Paullus and the gaggle of Tribunes who the younger Varro had dragged along with him from Vetera, comparing it to the two that Silius had detached from Ubiorum. What amused me was both the pointed manner in which Varro stood with his back turned to Silius and Sacrovir, and how Aviola seemed to alternate between nodding his head to whatever Varro was saying, then glancing over at the other two men, and while I was quite far away, I convinced myself that I could read his expression of longing for being with them instead of Varro.

"So I heard you saw him."

I almost jumped out of my skin, whirling about to glare at Alex, who looked anything but repentant for startling me.

"You could get hurt doing that," I growled, but he brushed it off in his usual manner.

"Then who would be left to tell you that you aren't losing your mind?"

"So it *was* him," I exclaimed, feeling quite triumphant that I had not been wrong.

"I'm positive that it was," Alex assured me, and this caused me to wilt a bit as I realized that, for some reason I could not have articulated, I assumed that Alex and Sempronius had had some sort of interchange where the agent working for Tiberius admitted that he was who I thought he was. I did feel better when he explained, "We locked eyes for a heartbeat, then he turned and vanished into the crowd before I got there. It," he said with a quiet but unmistakable emphasis, "was him."

"Not according to him." I leaned away from him and spat, then went on to give him the full account of our brief encounter.

"I wonder what he's doing here?" Alex wondered.

"If I had to guess, I'd say it has something to do with the Aedui," I ventured, earning me a scornful look.

"Yes, I gathered that much," he scoffed. "Because I seriously doubt that someone goes from being a...working for the most powerful man in the world to, what was it? Selling grain and olive oil here in the middle of Gaul?"

"I suppose we'll never know," I sighed.

Chapter 3

By the time camp was finished, I had at least learned a couple of things, namely that the reason for our prolonged stop had nothing to do with Varro wanting to avail himself of the charms of Augustobona Tricassium and sleep under a roof, which was the prevailing belief among most of the men, of all ranks.

"Decurion Chlothar and his men have been busy, and they've gathered new information," Macer told me in confidence in his quarters since he did not want to share this with either the rest of the First Cohort Centurions or the Pili Priores, knowing that they would demand to know what this information was. "It concerns Sacrovir, of course, but namely how he's built up a formidable army, and how he's gone about doing it." He paused for a moment to take a sip of watered wine while gathering his thoughts, then continued, "Apparently, when he took Augustodunum, he sent out a call to the tribal nobility of several tribes offering to educate their sons for free, in the Aedui capital. He claimed that he wanted to put all of Gallic nobility on an equal footing with us, and that the only way to do that was through education." He shook his head as he continued, "The thing we don't know are the exact numbers, but the truth is that there was a large number of young Gallic nobles sent to Augustodunum by their families for this...academy."

"That," I breathed, "is bad."

"It gets worse," my Primus Pilus assured me. "Because when a handful of these youngsters either got bored, or perhaps they sensed all was not as it seemed, when they tried to return to their homes, Sacrovir took them as hostages, in exchange for pledges from their fathers to supply warriors for his army. An army," Macer finished grimly, "that is growing in size every day."

Sacrovir's Revolt

I was too stunned to say anything in that moment, although I do recall there was a part of me that mentally saluted the Prefect's half-brother for this cunning turn of mind. It is an article of faith that, as assimilated as most Gauls have become in an astonishingly short time, there are still lingering feelings on the part of both parties, with many Romans, particularly members of the upper orders, who still view Gauls as barely educated savages, while many Gauls, not surprisingly of their nobility, are determined to prove that they are every bit as Roman as those born inside the *pomerium*. Sacrovir the Aedui, who was uniquely positioned to straddle both of these worlds by virtue of having a Roman father, took advantage of their desire, and now he was using the love fathers have for their sons as leverage to swell his numbers. Macer, however, was not through, and he said as much.

"There's more," he went on grimly. "He also liberated several *ludi* in the region, and he supposedly has more than a thousand gladiators trained as *crupellarii*."

"*Gerrae!*" I was so startled that I had to set my cup down. "I thought those were a myth!"

Since I cannot foretell the future, I have no idea at this point whether or not the *crupellarii* have become more widely adopted, so I will provide a brief description of this style of gladiator. Naturally, the traditional styles; the *Retiarii*, the *Murmillo*, which was what Divus Augustus decreed the *Gallus* be called in order to avoid offending our newest class of Roman citizen, and the *Thraex* are undoubtedly well known to you, my future reader and descendant. However, not long after the death of Divus Augustus, those who are ardent followers of the gladiatorial sport began talking about this new type of gladiator. Like the majority of the Legions by this time, they were armored with the *lorica segmentata*, but instead of using the segmented armor plates just for their torso and shoulders as we did, they use it to cover almost every inch of exposed skin, which was one reason that most of us did not believe it existed, for the simple reason that only someone of my size and strength could possibly bear the weight of that much armor and still be able to move with enough speed to be effective in the arena. What Macer was saying was that they did exist, and they were

87

waiting for us.

"Apparently, they're not," Macer replied. "But, Gnaeus, that's not all. According to the *Praetor*, Sacrovir has been busy manufacturing armor and weapons so that about a fifth of his men will be armed exactly like we are, and they've been trained as Legionaries to a reasonable degree."

My natural instinct was to deny the idea that it would have been possible for someone to manufacture so many weapons and armor, but before I said this, something else occurred to me, and I asked, "You said that about a fifth of the men under his command will be armed and trained like us. How many men is that, exactly?"

I instantly knew that I had asked both the right, and the wrong, question by the manner in which Macer grimaced, but he lowered his voice to barely above a whisper to reply, "Before I tell you, swear on the eagle that you'll keep it to yourself. Although," he held up a hand, "now that I think on it, if you want to tell Alex, go ahead. The gods know he can be trusted, and he's got sources that even I don't have in the *praetorium*, so maybe he can find out how accurate this is. But," he actually took a breath, "to answer your question, the number that Silius gave us is...forty thousand men."

My initial reaction was to burst out into a roar of laughter, thinking that Macer was making a jest because the number was so absurd, but he stared at me as if I had gone mad, and snapped, "I'm glad you think it's funny, Gnaeus!"

The laugh died in my throat as I stared at him in disbelief. "You...you're serious."

"Yes, I'm serious, Gnaeus," Macer assured me. "And," he grinned, "I won't lie and say that wasn't my first instinct as well, because that sounds so absurd, but believe me, Silius wasn't laughing. And," he added what was to me the most important part, "neither was the Prefect."

"What about Varro?" I asked, and now Macer actually chuckled.

"I think he was close to fainting," he answered, then added offhandedly, "although I think that's because he was more concerned that Sacrovir would rub it in his face."

"He has every right to," I heard the indignation in my voice, but I believed it then and I believe it even more now, "because if that pampered ass had listened to the Prefect about his half-brother, he'd be in chains at the very least." Macer nodded his agreement, but my mind was also moving on to something else. "Do you have any idea where this information is coming from?"

"No," Macer replied. "And Varro is being *very* tight-lipped about it. So is Silius, for that matter, but that's not unusual for him. He's been around for a long time and he knows better."

Promising that I would only tell Alex, I left for my tent, where I found him sitting with Euphemios, and he immediately rose, telling me he would start preparing my meal, but I stopped him, beckoning to him to follow me into my private quarters.

"Euphemios, I need to speak with Alex about something, so I want you to go start my meal. He'll be along shortly."

"Yes, Centurion," he answered, but I chose to ignore the face he made; preparing my meal was usually done by Alex, who knows how I like my food, and in the past when Euphemios had been given the task, things had not gone well, so I did not blame him all that much.

Mainly, I wanted him gone, but I listened for the outer flap to drop before I told Alex what I had learned. He did not laugh as I had, although he did go a little pale.

"I'll find out what I can," he said immediately after I was finished. "But if those numbers are right..."

"It means that even if most of them are worthless, it almost doesn't matter," I finished for him, to which he nodded. I was about to tell him about the *crupellarii*, then decided it could wait, so he left to rescue Euphemios from my possible wrath for not making enough to eat.

This was his intention, but I had just unbuckled my *baltea* and shrugged out of my armor when I heard a rapping on the wood, then an exchange of words between Alex and the visitor, but I could not make anything out. I had been about to sit down behind my camp desk, where a wax tablet lay awaiting my examination, but I remained standing as I waited to see what was transpiring in the outer office. When Alex pushed through the flap, although I could not readily pinpoint what his expression meant, it instantly put me on alert.

"Centurion, there's someone who wants to speak with you," Alex spoke formally, which did warn me in one way, but his expression was unreadable. Then, he added, "He *said* his name is Aulus Cordus Macula."

"I have to admit that when I saw you coming, I thought I might *cac* myself," Sempronius said genially. "Then I offered up a prayer to every deity I could think of that you didn't recognize me. That," he chuckled, without any visible rancor, "didn't work either."

We were in my quarters, but I had deliberately chosen to take a seat behind my desk and not at the small table, although I did offer Sempronius refreshment in the form of water with a dollop of wine.

Deciding not to waste time, I asked bluntly, "What are you doing here? And why are you using a different name?"

"How do you know it's different?" Sempronius asked, not in a necessarily challenging manner, but it shook me nonetheless as I realized, with some chagrin, that he was right; I had simply assumed that Sempronius was his real name. "Although," he added after a heartbeat, "Marcus Sempronius *is* my real name. As far as why I'm Aulus Cordus Macula?" He shrugged. "It suited my needs."

"And those needs are?" I asked pointedly.

I was not expecting a direct answer, but Sempronius was, and is a man of surprises.

"Why, to act as a spy for Gaius Julius Sacrovir, of course!" he replied with an obscene cheerfulness. Perhaps it was the manner in which I shifted my weight in my chair, because he hurried on, "That's my role, anyway. I had to convince him that I'm valuable because of my ability to move about the province without arousing suspicion. Once I did that, he began using me for carrying messages around Gaul." He paused and took a sip from his cup. "And since I'm still alive, I know he trusts me."

"So you're the source of information about his numbers and the fact that a fifth of his men are armed as Legionaries," I said this as a statement, and when he nodded, I continued, "and that there are twenty thousand men under his command."

I had timed it perfectly, so that my lie was uttered just as he was lifting his cup to take another sip, and while it was barely perceptible, I saw the hitch in the movement before the cup touched his lips. After he took another swallow, he set the cup down, but kept his eyes on it as he asked, "Is that what you heard, Pullus? That Sacrovir has twenty thousand men?"

"Yes," I lied again.

"That," he shook his head, "is wrong. It's twice that."

While I was heartened that he did not choose to perpetuate a lie even though he did not know from where it originated, I still was troubled, and I brought up my next concern.

"Given that, and that he's been manufacturing weapons," I said carefully, "it's hard to understand how he could manage to do all that so quickly."

"What do you mean?" he asked coolly, but now he was not looking down at his cup but directly at me.

"I think you know," I countered quietly. "What we were told in Ubiorum was that this was some sort of spontaneous uprising. And," I acknowledged, "when we ran Florus down, it didn't take much to crush the Treveri, or the Turoni and Andecavi for that matter. By the way," I decided to add, "in case you weren't aware, the Prefect warned Varro that Sacrovir's participation in the attack on the Turoni and Andecavi was a sham designed to lull us into believing that he was still loyal."

This clearly startled Sempronius, who admitted, "Now, that I did *not* know. And," he frowned, "I had an extensive conversation with the *Praetor*'s representative, and he made no mention of that." He paused then, and I had the impression that he was considering something, while I also noticed that he had not called what could only have been Varro the *Praetor* but his representative, which was accurate; I learned why he paused when he said carelessly, "I noticed that you didn't mention that the Prefect and the Aedui Sacrovir have a…connection. As in," he looked at me again, "they're half-brothers."

"I didn't see the point," I countered, "since I was sure you already knew that." However, I was not going to be thrown off my line of inquiry, deciding on the fly to press a bit myself.

"But if I was a suspicious sort, I'd think that you're trying to throw me off by bringing that up so that I'll forget about how unlikely it is that the Prefect's half-brother would be able to do all this in the space of just a couple of months."

For the first time, Sempronius betrayed a hint of impatience, setting his cup down with an audible sound.

"What are you trying to say, Pullus?" He did smile, but it was not particularly friendly. "It *has* been a while since we were in Rome together, but as I recall, you were always very direct, yet now you seem to be dancing about."

Careful, Gnaeus; he's trying to get you to lose your temper, I told myself, but hard on that was another thought: he's seen what I can do when I'm truly angry, so why would he be trying to make me do that?

Nevertheless, I was still irritated, though I managed to quell it enough to reply lightly, "I suppose my experience with the Praetorians has made me cautious. However," I hardened my voice, not much but enough he could not miss it, "I *will* stop dancing about. There's no way that Sacrovir organized this in a matter of weeks. Just to manufacture enough weapons to outfit almost two Legions' worth of arms and armor, especially if they're *segmentata* would take several months. So, it stands to reason that you've been involved with him for some time as he prepares for this since it's not likely that, just a matter of weeks before he enacts whatever he has planned, that he'll start trusting a man who's just shown up to take messages about the provinces about this uprising."

I made sure I was looking him directly in the eye as I said this, but to his credit he did not flinch, which made sense given how coolly he handled my confronting him in the street.

The silence stretched out, with neither of us willing to break our gaze, and he finally broke it by asking quietly, "Do you really want the answer, Pullus? Do you *really* want to know?" When I did not answer immediately, he changed his approach, and his words sent a chill up my spine. "Do you remember what I told you once in Rome? That the man we answer to is *not* forgiving, in any sense of the word? And," now it was his turn to harden his voice, "that he isn't likely to be content just with punishing you? You've had another child, yes?" In proof that he knew me very well, he immediately added, "This isn't me threatening you, Pullus, please believe that. I've seen firsthand what you're capable of, and only a fool would threaten you...or someone far more powerful than either one of us. I'm just stating a simple truth, and I suspect that you know that. Now," he repeated, this time sounding almost gentle, "I will ask again. Do you really want to know?"

"No."

It is impossible to describe how much it took for me to say that, and I will also acknowledge that, if this had been a few years earlier, I undoubtedly would have given him a different answer, but I now have so much more to lose.

With this settled, I decided that a change of subject was in order, and I asked the next question that had been nagging at me, "What about these *crupellarii*? I always thought they were a myth."

"They're no myth," Sempronius assured me seriously. "I've seen them fight at a game that Sacrovir hosted. They're...something to watch."

"Are they really armored from head to toe?"

"They are," Sempronius confirmed, "but while I don't have any experience in these matters, the one thing I noticed is their helmets."

"What about them?" I asked, curious to know since I realized that I had assumed that it would be like a *Murmillo* helmet.

"It looks like a big upside-down metal bucket, but with a couple dozen small holes drilled in the lower half so that they can breathe easily, and the helmet is attached to the gladiator's armor with two leather straps."

"How big are the eye holes?" I asked, thinking again that they were like the *Murmillo*'s. "And do they have a mesh covering to protect them?"

He surprised me when he shook his head. "They're not holes; they're slits, about," he held up his hand and held his pointing finger and thumb about four inches apart, "this wide and," he reduced the space to perhaps an inch, "this high." I was completely unprepared for him to say, "Oh, and they have this...ridge, I suppose, that runs down the middle of the helmet where the nose is, from the top of the helmet to the bottom."

I had never heard of anything like this, nor did I see what the possible utility could be, but after a few more moments of him trying to explain it, I grabbed a wax tablet and handed that and my stylus to him.

"Draw it," I commanded, and he did as I bade, looking slightly ridiculous as he stuck his tongue out while he worked.

Finally, he handed it to me, yet even after seeing it, I still could not really see the purpose.

"Unless," I guessed, "it's there for reinforcement and to protect the nose."

"They can't move very well, but since they only fought each other, it didn't really matter," Sempronius commented.

"And does he really have a thousand men like this?"

"He's got a thousand sets of that armor," Sempronius confirmed, then shrugged, "but does he have the men to fill them who know what they're about? That's another question."

"What about the men he's outfitted like us?"

"They've been training for more than a month, Pullus," Sempronius answered quietly. "How long is the training for the Legions? Four months?" I nodded. "Then I suppose it's safe to say that they'll be about a quarter as effective, although that also depends on how rapidly *Praetor* Silius marches you to Augustodunum."

This, I thought, is something that a man with no experience with not just the Legions, but any fighting force would say.

"Yes," I replied, "and no. If Sacrovir has found enough experienced warriors who are veterans of a few battles, then it won't be nearly as long to teach them our tactics. Still," a thought occurred to me, "I'm not sure how much fighting any Gauls have been doing for the last twenty years." Even as I was speaking, something else he had said stuck in my mind, and I asked him, "You just said something about how quickly we march to Augustodunum. What we were told was that we're only here for two days, and we assumed it was because Silius and the Prefect were being informed of the latest developments by someone. Which," I pointed at him and grinned, "turned out to be you." As irritated as I was with Sempronius, at the same time, as we spoke, I recalled how, for the most part, I enjoyed his company, and he seemed to feel the same way. "But now that you've told them the latest, I assumed we're going to be marching, probably day after tomorrow since we usually receive orders by this time of day if we were moving in the morning. So," I finished with a shrug, "I don't think the Aedui are going to have much more time to train these men."

Sempronius was clearly listening, his face betraying nothing, but when I finished, he offered a small shake of his head.

"That's not the only reason you're stopped here." He took a sip, and I sensed that he was trying to decide how much to divulge, because he gave a shrug of his own, then explained, "Silius dispatched orders to summon several Cohorts of auxiliaries, apparently when you were still in Orolaunum. You're waiting on the first of them to arrive here."

I considered this, aware of the crawling feeling in my stomach that comes from having missed something, because by rights, this was something that Alex would have sniffed out while we were encamped there. This is not meant to disparage Alex, who is glaring at me even as I dictate this, because he is unparalleled in his ability to ferret out information, but as I was about to learn, my dismay was based in a misunderstanding of the facts.

"So they knew there are forty thousand men waiting for us." I heard the bitterness in my voice, though even in the moment, I could not have said why I felt betrayed in some sense, and my anger was aimed more at Prefect Sacrovir, who I was certain would have warned us beforehand.

Fortunately, my misapprehension lasted only long enough for Sempronius to shake his head, and say flatly, "I just told them about the numbers today, and I could tell by their reaction they had no idea. No, the orders for the auxiliaries are for another reason. Silius intends on sending them against the Sequani, as they've been mobilizing as well, almost as long as the Aedui."

I briefly considered asking Sempronius how the Sequani had managed to escape the attention of the scores of faceless men like him whose only job is to keep Rome informed, then thought better of it. Hard on the heels of that thought, however, came another one, and it was completely on impulse that I stood up, gestured to my small table where I take my meals, then refilled Sempronius' cup, but this time with just wine, then did the same for myself.

"I don't know whether to be flattered or worried," Sempronius joked, but I saw the alert interest in his eyes.

"Probably a bit of both," I answered honestly. Then, as is my habit, I plunged ahead. "Tell me what you know about Varro."

I should have known better, because with a straight face, Sempronius replied, "Well, he was appointed as *Praetor* by the Imperator…"

"You know who I mean," I snapped, but Sempronius was not so easily cowed.

"Even if I do, why would I stick my neck out just to be chopped off?" he shot back, and while his tone was bantering, that sense I had that he was as concerned as he was piqued by my interest was reinforced.

Deciding to be as forthright as I could be, despite knowing it was a risk, I was also counting on our past relationship; after all, I reasoned to myself, the man had risked his life for me once before when we were in Rome and he had tried to take the blame for the death of Marcus Livinius Appius.

"Because you know you can trust me," I replied, then added, "just like I know I can trust you. Besides, Varro and I have a…history."

"Yes, I heard about that." Sempronius nodded. He paused to take a sip, then signaled his acceptance of my argument by saying, "He did try to stitch you up in a sack with that business with…what was his name?"

"Catualda," I answered, hearing the bitterness in my voice, not that I cared all that much. "That bastard who couldn't manage to stay on the throne we handed him for more than a year."

"Yes, that's right. But, Pullus, if he was dangerous then, he's even more dangerous now."

"But how?" I could not hide my skepticism. "He had to flee Mogontiacum because of what a disaster the Catualda affair turned out to be. He just…vanished one day. Honestly, I was shocked to see him back here, but then when I found out that his Tata was made *Praetor*, I just assumed that was why."

"Assumptions are a dangerous thing, Pullus," Sempronius warned. "Yes, there was some talk about how he had overstepped with the Catualda business. But," he lowered his voice, "he has a powerful patron, so whatever…setback he suffered was temporary."

"Who?" I asked, though I felt certain I knew the answer, yet for some reason, it was important for me to hear him confirm my belief. "Who's his patron?"

Sempronius shifted on his stool, clearly uncomfortable.

"I think you know," he answered evasively, but I would not be put off the scent.

"I want to make sure I'm right, or at least know if I'm not."

His shoulders actually slumped slightly, and he suddenly sounded tired as he admitted, "Praetorian Prefect Sejanus, who else? And, Gnaeus," he leaned forward, while I was startled, trying to remember if he had ever used my *praenomen* before, but I could not remember, "just like Varro has become more dangerous, so has Sejanus, but Varro's rise is a shade compared to Sejanus. There's…*something* going on with the Imperator." He shook his head, the frustration boiling out of him. "I've served him for many years, long before he became Princeps, and he's changed in ways that I can't describe. He's begun to spend less time in Rome, which means that he leaves Sejanus in charge, but even when he's there, it's as if he can barely be bothered with the details of running the Empire, and he leans on Sejanus when he's there almost as much as when he's gone."

"When he's not in Rome, where is he?"

"Oh, he has several estates." Sempronius waved a hand, as if this were the most natural thing in the world. "They're all close to Rome, but he doesn't stay more than a night or two in the same one, and the only man who knows which one he's going to be staying in is Sejanus."

"Why? Have there been attempts on his life?"

Sempronius looked at me with sardonic amusement, but I found his reply a bit cryptic.

"The real question is how many attempts have there been

in Tiberius' imagination, and how many have there been in reality?" He held his hands out, palms upward. "I only know of one, by some madman who was convinced he was the living incarnation of Tarquinius Superbus, and he wanted his throne back. That poor bastard didn't get within a dozen paces before he was cut down by the Imperator's bodyguard. But in Tiberius' mind, everyone around him is plotting. In fact," suddenly, Sempronius looked sad, "I used to have a face-to-face meeting with him at least once a month whenever I was in Rome. Then, it became once every three months, then every six, and now," he shook his head, "I haven't laid eyes on him for almost a year." He paused to take a sip before he finished with a sigh, "And if what I've heard about his plans for building that villa on Capri are true, if I had to guess, once it's finished, he'll move there and never set foot in Rome again."

I considered this, but while all this about the Imperator was interesting, I believe I can be excused that my concern was more about Sejanus, and as he had been talking about Tiberius, my mind had been chewing on something, which I blurted out now.

"Do you think Sejanus knew about what Sacrovir and the Aedui were up to before a few weeks ago?"

In answer, Sempronius actually winced and despite the flap to the outer office being down, and there not being any sounds indicating that Alex and Euphemios had returned, he glanced over his shoulder. When he answered, it was not a whisper, but it was close.

"Hopefully, I don't have to warn you to never utter anything like that again," he warned.

I was a bit nettled, but when I saw that he had no intention of saying anything until I responded, I promised, "This is the last I'll speak of it."

This clearly reassured him, because he did not hesitate to answer, "Yes, I'm sure that he's known for some time. And," for the first time in our association, I could see that Marcus Sempronius, or Aulus Cordus Macula, which was how I referred to him from that moment on in public, was not just nervous, he was terrified, "I know that because I ran into one of the men he employs to do the…same kind of things I do for

Tiberius, and he told me that not only did Sejanus know about it, but he's been one of the sources of funds for Sacrovir."

I felt as if I had been punched in the gut, actually having to draw in a breath to replace the one that had escaped as a gasp, but there was something that did not make sense to me; if I had had the time to think about it, I would not have asked.

"Wait, he just volunteered this to you?"

I know how skeptical I sounded, but it was because I was, and suddenly, Sempronius' attention went back to his wine cup. When he lifted it to his lips, even in the lamplight, I could see his hand trembling slightly, and later, I realized why; he was essentially putting his life in my hands.

"No, he didn't just volunteer it. I had my suspicions because of other information that I had learned, and I...persuaded him to tell me."

It took a heartbeat for the real meaning of his words to hit me, and while I regretted broaching the subject, I was sufficiently curious to hear myself ask, with a casual tone that even I could hear was forced, "And once he was...persuaded, is there any chance that he might feel guilty about it and run to tell Sejanus?"

"No," Sempronius replied quietly, and he made it a point to look me in the eye. "I swear on Jupiter's black stone that he'll never, ever be in a position to tell Sejanus anything...or anyone else for that matter." Without warning, he reached across the small table to grasp my forearm, and it was impossible to miss the pleading tone. "Gnaeus, I'm trusting you with my life by telling you this. I know you're an honorable man, but..."

"I understand," I assured him immediately, "and I swear on my Legion standard that I won't betray you."

"Thank you," he blew out a long breath, his relief impossible to mistake.

He was about to say something else, but there was a commotion at the outer flap, then we heard Alex call out, "Centurion, we're here with your meal!"

I was not surprised when Sempronius used this as his excuse to leave, but before he left, he whispered, "If I can, I'll get some sort of word to you if it's something that might save you and your boys some grief, Pullus. I don't want to see any Romans die because of the Prefect and his plots."

Nodding to Alex on his way out, Sempronius disappeared into the night, and as I watched him leave the tent, I was surprised at the feeling of worry I had for his well-being. After all, he had chosen this life for himself, I told myself, but immediately on the heels of that thought was another one; did he, though? Did he really choose it, or was he like me? I had come to realize that, while I may not have been bred to the profession of arms as the supposed son of Quintus Claudius Volusenus, I was certainly born to it as the real son of Titus Porcinianus Pullus, and I am now convinced that, no matter what path I took, I would have ended up standing here in a tent in a Legion camp, the only possible difference being which Legion I was in. Perhaps Marcus Sempronius was similar in that way, that he was serving Rome in not only the best way, but the only way he was born to, as a man of the shadows. Pushing this from my mind, I sat down to my meal, ignoring Alex's pointed stare as he expected me to divulge what I had learned, and while I did, it was certainly not the whole of what Sempronius had told me, especially about Sejanus, which I have only now divulged in the last few moments all this time later.

Our reason for stopping, that we were waiting for Cohorts of auxiliaries, was common knowledge by midday the first full day in camp. While I told Macer of Sempronius' visit, I made no mention of my questions about Sejanus or what I had learned, keeping it from him as I had from Alex. I sensed that he did not fully believe me, but he thankfully did not press; besides, fairly quickly, there was another rumor that occupied our minds.

"It's not just that we're waiting for the auxiliaries to march up from Lugdunum," Alex informed me at the evening meal of that second day. "Silius and Varro are at *gladius* points about what to do with them."

"What about?"

Alex could only offer a shrug to my question, saying, "That was something I couldn't find out, just that Varro wants them for one purpose, and Silius for another."

Shortly before the call to retire, Lucco appeared with a summons from Macer, and I followed him to the Primus Pilus' tent, where I at least learned the specific issue.

"Varro has been frightened by the numbers of Aedui waiting for us, and he thinks that Silius is mad to send the auxiliaries east to subdue the Sequani, while Silius' argument is that as we advance the rest of the way south, it will put the Sequani in the position to sever our supply line if we don't do anything about them." To me, this was simple logic and was so obvious that it did not seem worthy of argument, but when I expressed this, Macer actually was not quick to dismiss Varro's position. "Gnaeus, as much as I know you despise Varro, with," he added quickly, "good reason, and you have certainly had more dealings with him than I have, I think he has a point."

"Which is?" I asked coolly.

"That the auxiliaries are actually marching north from Lugdunum, and if they're able to do so unimpeded, then why shouldn't we expect to be supplied from that direction if the Sequani actually do as Silius fears?"

It was, I thought unhappily, not a ridiculous question, and I bring this up because it actually would serve to remind me that, while Varro was inexperienced as a military commander, he was still clever. More importantly, sometimes a novice can bring up a point that experienced men might miss.

Fortunately, it did not take me long to think it through, although I did allow, grudgingly, "That's a fair point. But," I went on, "there's a big difference between the Aedui stopping, or trying to stop, an armed column of however many Cohorts of auxiliaries there are coming, which would require them to divert men and send them east from Augustodunum in enough numbers to stop them, and to stop a supply train, which could be accomplished with just a few hundred men, even less if they're mounted."

"That," Macer replied with a wry smile, "is the argument the Prefect made. Which," the smile vanished, and I could see he was worried, "Varro didn't take well, so he enlisted Carbo to take his side, which he did. Although," he added, probably upon seeing my expression, "he was clearly unhappy about it, and I take it to mean that while he's a Praetorian, he may not be a totally political creature."

He paused then to take a bite of bread from his late meal, but I know him too well; also, I had continued thinking about it, which was why I said, "So that would make it a tie between Varro and Carbo, and the *Praetor* and the Prefect. How did that get resolved?" Even before he opened his mouth I had my answer in the form of his unhappy expression, so I put him out of his misery by saying it for him. "You broke the tie by siding with the *Praetor* and the Prefect."

"No," Macer responded immediately, "I didn't. At least, not yet."

"Why not?" I asked, torn between the relief that my friend had not put himself into a bad position, yet at the same time wondering if he secretly agreed with Varro's caution.

Macer hesitated for a moment, turning the cup in his hands as he stared at it with a frown, before admitting, "Because the Prefect predicted this moment was coming, and he didn't think the time was right for me to do anything like that. Not yet, anyway. He said he would tell me when."

I felt the sudden ball in my stomach start rising up into my throat as I recalled everything I knew about Varro. "And whenever that happens, as far as that *cunnus* Varro is concerned, you will have declared yourself his enemy."

"Yes, he was clearly upset that I wouldn't make any kind of declaration," Macer allowed, then insisted, "but I think you're being a bit dramatic that he'll think I'm his enemy when I side with the Prefect and Silius."

"Remember what you said just a few heartbeats ago?" I challenged. "That I'm the only one between us who has had any dealings with him? No, Marcus," I sighed, "you're going to have to trust me that Varro now views you as someone who is likely to thwart him in whatever he has planned, because he's a clever bastard. He knows that your refusal to make a decision and openly declare yourself for the Prefect's side isn't a matter of if, it's a matter of when."

"Well," now it was Macer who sighed, "he did manage to drop a turd in the honey, because he refuses to move until he receives further instructions from his Tata in Vetera, and in this Carbo not only backed him, but said that since the 2nd is part of the Army of the Lower Rhenus, he's bound to obey the orders of his *Praetor*, and until he hears from him, we're not going anywhere."

I listened in a growing state of anger and disbelief.

"So, you mean that we're going to be sitting here on our asses, giving this traitorous bastard more time to train those *eight thousand men* outfitted like us to *fight* like us?"

"Well, when you put it like *that*," Macer joked weakly, "I can see why you're upset. But," his faint smile vanished, "yes, that's about the size of it. And," he added to forestall the question he knew was coming, "yes, both Silius and Sacrovir argued that very point. Not only about that, but that it's giving him time to fortify Augustodunum. The gods know that he's got more than enough men to do both."

"So we're going to be conducting a siege," I said bitterly. "And he's going to outnumber us." Something occurred to me then, which I voiced. "Although feeding that many men, along with the civilians, will be a tough task if it's a protracted siege."

"We have to get there first," Macer said glumly. "There's no telling how long that will take."

It took almost two weeks, of which ten days was spent in camp, despite the fact that the last auxiliary Cohort had arrived exactly a week after our arrival, although they created their own camp instead of enlarging ours. The next three days were spent with the men growing increasingly restless, partly from the inactivity, but mostly because of the inevitable gossip that is as impossible to quell as it is to tie a knot in a column of smoke. Whether it was conducted openly around the fires, albeit with men keeping an eye out for a prowling officer, or in whispers once Macer gave us permission to start using more vigorous methods, the speculation was as varied as it was rampant, but there was one version that we would only learn later at least had the distinction of being repeated in the streets of Rome, and that was that every tribe in Gaul, all sixty-four of them as designated by the Senate, had thrown in with the Aedui.

"No matter how many times I try to tell the stupid bastards that if that was true, those Cohorts in the camp next to us would be attacking us right now since they're all from one of the tribes, it doesn't make any difference with Publius," Clepsina complained one night, using the term we use for the average ranker, though I have no idea why since there are not more rankers named Publius than any other *praenomen*.

This was met by a couple chuckles, but mostly agreement from the rest of the Cohort Centurions, and I include myself, because I had run into the same issue. No matter how obvious the answer about how this belief that every single tribe in Gaul had thrown in with the Aedui was not based in any kind of reality, there were men who stubbornly clung to it. I do not believe it was lost on any of us that these men were also the ones who could always be counted on for the gloomiest predictions, who saw dire omens all around, and in general seemed convinced that at any instant, some catastrophe would befall them. Understanding this did not make it any easier to deal with, at least for me, but I did take some solace in knowing that these idiots seemed to be evenly distributed through the First Cohort, the most experienced in the Legion. It was not until we were back in Ubiorum that we learned that, at least in the case of the Legion, the uproar was only verbal in nature, whereas in Rome there were supposedly a handful of incidents in the Forum where passions, and panic, became inflamed to the point where there were riots, and despite my overall feelings about the Praetorians, I did worry about my former comrades, like my former Pilus Prior Creticus or my *Tesseraurius* Dido, and Valerius, the former ranker from the Third Cohort of the 8th, wondering if it was true, and if it was, if they were safe.

I had never seen what the mob of Rome could do, but I had heard enough stories, and it was not until my time there when I saw just how many people of the Head Count could cram into the Forum that I began to appreciate just how dangerous the mob can be. It was a passing thought, the men of my Century and their chattering being my major concern, and I found myself prowling up and down our street, but despite being liberal in my application of the *vitus*, it did not seem to help until, struck by an inspiration, I began promising men that on our return to Ubiorum, their punishment would be to face me in the sparring square. Only then did the boys of the Fifth settle down, but when Macer called me in to his quarters to inquire as to why my Century seemed to have moved on from this fixation about a massive uprising by all the tribes of Gaul and I told him, he actually threw his stylus down in disgust.

"Well, the rest of us can't do that," he complained. "Especially since I'm fairly certain that there are a couple of their boys who could beat Glaxus and Caudex quite easily." Suddenly, a look of alarm flashed across his face. "And don't you dare tell them I said that!"

"Tell them what?" I asked innocently, but as soon as his expression relaxed, I added, "You mean that their Primus Pilus doesn't think they know which end of the *gladius* to hold, and that every one of their boys could thrash them?"

"That's not what I said!" he protested, and I was just pleased he seemed fooled.

Rubbing my chin, I mused, "That would seem to be a secret that a Primus Pilus would be willing to pay a pretty price to keep."

This was when he realized what I was doing, and he gave me a glare.

"Go piss on your boots, you big oaf," he grumbled.

It was a lighthearted moment during a period of growing tension, because along with the rumors, the tensions between what Macer reported had become two distinct factions within the command group down to the Tribunes had only increased as the elder Varro did not seem to be in any hurry about sending an answer to his son's query. Finally, a rider came in from the north when it was our turn to stand duty on the wall, and it did not take long before Alex came trotting up to whisper that it was indeed the courier from Vetera that had arrived, which engendered a long wait that lasted through our relief and return to our Cohort area. Finally, one of the slaves from the *praetorium* came to the Primus Pilus' tent, where I happened to be with Macer, although the other Centurions were on their way there. Of my fellow Centurions, while we all knew that prior to this point during this dispute between Silius and

Sacrovir on one side, and Varro and Carbo on the other, Macer had to this point still refused to declare his allegiance, I was the only one who knew that this was by the express instructions of Sacrovir.

"He wants me to let Varro think that I'm more aligned with his viewpoint that we need the auxiliaries with us rather than marching against the Sequani," he had explained one night before the courier's arrival when it was just the two of us, but when I expressed my skepticism that Varro would believe him, he surprised me considerably. "Actually, Gnaeus," he admitted, "this is one time where I think Varro might be right. Yes, having the Sequani in our rear and not pinned down is a concern, but your spy friend seemed very sure that Sacrovir has forty thousand men. And," he hurried on, seeing me open my mouth, reminding me, "you were the one who said that with that many men, it might not matter how well-trained and veteran they are."

The truth was that I had in fact said that very thing, so I did not try to deny it, nor could I argue that, whether it was sincere, or he had just accidentally stumbled onto it, Varro's concern was a valid one. Nevertheless, there was another thing that concerned me, and I asked about it now.

"If you agree with Varro, and he refuses to budge, or his father backs him, what are you going to do since we both know why Sacrovir wants you to cozy up to Varro and lull his suspicions?"

This irritated Macer, who snapped, "He didn't tell me to cozy up to him, Gnaeus! The Prefect just wants Varro to…" His voice trailed off, and he suddenly gave me what I suppose was a rueful grin. "I suppose I *am* cozying up to him now that you mention it." The grin faded, and he shook his head. "As far as what I'm going to do? I hope that Varro the Elder tells his son to defer to the men who are actually experienced in warfare."

This was an awfully thin reed to cling to in my opinion, but I did my best not to betray how I really felt about it; I doubt I was successful, though I did not bring it up again, and the arrival of the others would have precluded it.

Now, after a brief explanation to the others, Macer rose,

adjusted his tunic then grabbed his *vitus* before he exited his quarters, stopping at the flap to the outer office to address us.

"You may as well wait here," he told us. "I can't imagine this will take all that long, and I'll be back..." Because he was standing nearest to where I was seated, I think I was the only one who heard him mutter, "...I hope."

Once he was gone, we were left to our own devices, and almost immediately, we broke into what I suppose one might call our factions, which meant that it was Clepsina and me, while Gratianus, Caudex, and Glaxus formed a little circle with their backs to us, but rather than offend the two of us, we shared a grin. It was something that Clepsina and I had spoken about at length, and the conclusion that we reached was that, whereas both Clepsina and I had been Pili Priores, the other three had not, giving us a completely different perspective on things. Naturally, since we were in such close confines, none of us said anything that we did not want the people in the other group to hear, but I was not particularly surprised that the topic the other three were most interested in was the fresh shipment of whores that one of the brothels in Ubiorum had gotten in just before we departed. As profitable as the Dancing Faun was, and is, there has been a long-running debate between Alex and me about whether or not we branch out into the very lucrative business of prostitution, either by converting part of the Faun into a brothel, or more likely, purchasing one of the buildings on either side. To be precise, when I say that the debate is between Alex and me, that is not accurate; the debate *is* between Alex and me...and our spouses, with both Bronwen and Algaia firmly against it, although for slightly different reasons. In Algaia's case, and to me for the most understandable reason, it reminds her of her own past; while she was not a whore, she was a slave, and the property of my uncle Gaius, who did things to her that none of our family ever speaks about. For Bronwen, however, the reason is much more straightforward.

"I can barely stand the idea of you being around those women who serve drinks," she has declared on more occasions than I can count. "Being surrounded by women whose business is pleasuring men?" She always shakes her head in a manner that makes her magnificent head of hair, still the color of burnished copper, whip about her face in a manner that I am sure she knows inflames me, but it is always accompanied by something that has the opposite effect, and I believe the manner in which she says it so sweetly actually compounds rather than diminishes the threat, "I would cut your cock off if I ever found out about it, my love."

While the other three talked about whores, Clepsina and I were focused on more immediate concerns.

"Who do you think is going to win this argument?"

I considered Clepsina's question carefully, both because it was important and I was as curious to know what he thought as he was about me, and after a moment, I answered, "I think that this is one of those questions where there is no right answer. If Silius prevails and sends the auxiliaries to suppress the Sequani, and then we're unable to crush the Aedui, heads will roll, from bottom to top." Before he could respond, I continued, "If Varro prevails, and the auxiliaries are with us and we subdue the Aedui easily enough, but then the Sequani cut us off, heads will roll from bottom to top." I did pause then, but it was to gauge Clepsina's reaction, because I was not through. When I saw him nod, this was when I introduced what I thought was the deciding factor. "But from everything we've heard so far, Sacrovir intends on staying behind his walls and force us to besiege Augustodunum. If he does that, we *must* have a stable supply line because only the gods know how long we'll be here. So," I concluded simply, "given what we know, I think that's why Silius is right. We need to send the auxiliaries against the Sequani."

It was only then that I noticed it had gotten quiet, and I glanced over my shoulder, surprised to see that the other three were listening intently.

Glaxus was the one who broke the silence, saying dismally, "*Cac*. I didn't think of it that way."

"Neither did I," Caudex put in, then added sourly, "Leave it to Pullus to find the turd in the porridge."

"Don't blame him because he's thought it through and you haven't," Clepsina snapped, and I began feeling a bit uncomfortable.

Yes, it had been a couple of years since I had moved up into the First Cohort, and yes, I would put my reputation up against any of these men, but this was the first time we faced the prospect of battle, and I still imagined that there were men wearing the transverse crest who remembered the paid man, Gnaeus Volusenus, the haughty young Equestrian who thought that there was nothing any of these men could teach him anything that was valuable, until the only man in the Legion who matched him in size and strength, and overmatched him in experience had taught him that he had so much to learn.

"I agree with Pullus," Gratianus put in. "And I hope that the Primus Pilus sees it the same way."

It was the manner in which, suddenly, they were all looking at me expectantly that told me that, even if it had not been planned, they had trapped me into divulging Macer's thoughts, since it was no secret that we were close friends.

"I think he does," I answered, knowing how evasive it sounded, but I refused to be pinned down, not that they did not try for the next few moments.

It did serve to pass the time, and when Macer reappeared, I was initially relieved, but I did not need to be his close friend to notice his pallor.

Still, he sounded steady enough when he announced, "I was wrong. There has been no decision yet, but it should be settled in the morning."

He dismissed everyone, but signaled me silently to stay behind, which was not unusual, nor were the glares and muttered comments, which I ignored as I always did. Only when Lucco assured Macer that he had stood at the flap to make sure the others actually returned to their tent and were not lingering about did he inform me of what had taken place.

"Varro's Tata backed his son," he said grimly. "He said that it would be 'imprudent'," he stressed the word with a grimace of disgust, "to worry about a possible threat with the Sequani when we know there was a host of that size waiting for us."

I cannot say I was all that surprised, but I still felt a twinge in my gut at what I was about to ask.

"Did you have anything to say?"

Since I was unsure exactly how forthcoming our Primus Pilus had been with the others, save Clepsina, who I knew Macer had told everything to because he had said as much, it was the only way I knew to put it.

Macer gave me a look that expressed I had made the correct decision, replying, "Yes, Pullus. I was asked my opinion by Varro, and I gave it. I...agreed with the Prefect and *Praetor* Silius."

"Was this before or after Varro said that his Tata was backing him?"

"After," Macer replied to Glaxus' question, and even he was unable to hide his irritation as he asked pointedly, "Why on Gaia's earth would I declare myself before he told us what his father decided?"

"Ah, yes," Glaxus fumbled, "I see. Yes, that's a good point, Primus Pilus."

He did at least have the grace to look embarrassed.

"Yes, I thought so myself." Macer rarely spoke with this kind of acid courtesy, but privately I knew that he was as frustrated by Glaxus' seeming obtuse nature as I was. He did moderate his tone, saying disgustedly, "Not that it made any difference. Varro said that this wasn't a vote in the Senate, and that as far as he was concerned, since he was acting as his father's representative, *and* his father had given him the baton of *imperium*, what he had done in consulting his father had been more of a formality. He actually picked the fucking thing up and waved it around!"

I do not believe he meant to be humorous, but we nevertheless all burst out laughing; in my case, it was the expression of indignation on his face as he said it that struck me, but it did help dispel the tension a bit. However, the issue was still there, which Clepsina brought us back to addressing.

"You said that there will be a decision in the morning, Primus Pilus?"

"Yes," Macer nodded. "At least, that's what the *Praetor* told me. When I was dismissed, he and Varro were still...talking."

We were dismissed shortly after that, and I returned to my tent, Alex staying only long enough for me to inform him of the details before he left for the *praetorium*.

"Let me see what I can find out," he said as he left, "but I doubt it will be much."

This was one of the rare times he was wrong, because he was not gone long, and when he returned, he was clearly bursting with excitement, which I understood as soon as he spoke.

"Gnaeus, go tell the Primus Pilus that it would be wise of him to let the Centurions know that we're going to be receiving orders soon to prepare to break camp."

"When are we leaving?"

"In the morning," he replied, to which I could only stare at him, openmouthed; at least this is what he claims.

"But that's not what Macer was told," I protested, and it was not that I did not believe Alex, as by this time, I had long since learned that he was almost always right, but Macer had been told by Silius.

"I know," Alex agreed, then allowed, "and I don't exactly know why, but I overheard Silius' chief clerk telling Melander that the *Praetor* had decided to do what the Prefect suggested. So," he grinned, "I cornered Melander and he's the one who told me that we're leaving. The orders should be coming soon."

"We, as in the whole army? Or we, as in just the 1st?"

"Orders are being written for us…and for the auxiliaries," Alex explained. "And the auxiliaries are being sent to Sequani territory."

"What is he about?" I wondered aloud.

"I think that he's forcing Varro's hand," Alex guessed. "He's going to have to make a choice between letting us march alone to Augustodunum, and then if we're defeated, he's going to not only share in the shame, he's going to be blamed for letting us march against forty thousand men. And," he offered a grim smile, "if we win, then Silius will probably earn a triumph, and he'll be in disgrace for holding back. It will probably ruin his career."

"That's what I thought would happen with Catualda," I grumbled. "But here he is, still meddling in things he's not qualified to be involved in. This is the second time I've found myself in the *cac* because of him!"

"Yes, Gnaeus," Alex replied dryly, "you've figured Varro out. His only reason for being here is to drop you in the *cac* at every opportunity."

"Go..." I caught myself, recalling Alex teasing me recently about an expression that I had never used until I was an adult under the standard, but, according to him, I overuse, so I finished lamely, "...make yourself useful while I go tell Macer."

Thanks to Alex's warning, the 1st was already well underway in their preparations to leave the first thing in the morning when the orders arrived, while Macer sent Acco, who was the second of the three clerks assigned to the First Century of the First Cohort, over to the other side of the camp, and he reported back that, at least to that point in the first night watch, the 2nd was not making any overt preparations that would be expected of a Legion marching in the morning.

"There's no way that Varro won't hear all the clatter of one half of the camp making preparations to leave," I commented, not aiming at anyone in particular.

We were back in Macer's tent, ostensibly to report the status of our Centuries, but the truth was that we were all too aware of the tension and were all anxious about what I know I believed was an inevitable confrontation the next morning.

"Yes," Macer spoke up, with an enigmatic smile that was not aimed at anyone in particular, "I received a message from the *Praetor* that complimented us for our initiative in making ready. Reading between the lines, I think he was a bit embarrassed that he didn't think of it himself. Now, Varro isn't likely to sleep very well."

"That would be a shame if Varro didn't get a good night's sleep," Clepsina intoned, and I suppose it was the way he said it that made us all roar with laughter, or perhaps it was just a sum total of the nerves, which I would not compare to those we experienced the night before we went into battle, but there was an edge there that was impossible to ignore.

We were dismissed to return to our own quarters, but Clepsina and I took the long way around the edge of the forum to walk down the *Via Praetoria* towards the *Porta Praetoria*, the border line between two Legions in a camp, and we saw that the streets belonging to the 2nd were all deserted save for the pairs of men on walking posts.

"They're in for a rude surprise," Clepsina commented, and I agreed, though I wondered if they were the only ones.

We parted, and I entered my quarters to find my cot ready, and aside from taking off my *baltea* and *caligae*, I dropped onto it without any other preparations, falling asleep almost immediately, although I remember my last thought being essentially a continuation of what had been running through my mind for the previous watch, whether or not we might find ourselves fighting more than rebelling Gauls.

What transpired the next morning seemed to be quite anticlimactic; it would only be a few years later that we realized just how deep the enmity Varro held for Silius ran after this incident, and the lengths to which he would go to exact revenge. At the time, however, while the auxiliary Cohorts broke camp without incident, and under the command of one of the Tribunes from Ubiorum, Sextus Papinius Allenius, who, while he did not impress me or my fellow Centurions as much as Aviola, who was remaining with us, was still regarded as competent, although I feel quite certain that it was his reputation for loyalty to Silius that was his recommending quality. Most importantly, it was the direction in which they marched, towards Sequani lands, that informed Varro that the auxiliaries were following Silius' orders and not his. To his credit, Varro did not attempt to do anything silly like gallop out of our camp to try and block the auxiliaries from marching away, but one did not have to know him to see he was absolutely outraged. Compounding his anger was the humiliation that stemmed from his being forced to request that our departure be delayed in order to allow the 2nd to finish breaking their part of the camp down; we learned from the guard Cohort that Carbo had finally roused his men at the beginning of the last night watch, but they were still not ready to depart at dawn. Varro's slaves were working frantically to carry the various pieces of furniture and odds and ends that he had moved into the part of the *praetorium* tent that served as his private quarters; despite his seniority, and the fact that he actually *was* not just the *Praetor* but the Legate, Silius had ceded the part of the large tent that was reserved for the commanding officer to Varro. I offer this as an example of how, when he chose to, Gaius Silius knew how to play the game that our upper orders seem to be born playing, because it was common knowledge throughout the ranks that he had yielded that traditional space to a more junior Varro. However, in reality, the partitioned area that is used as the officer's mess is actually larger, which most men in any given Legion do not know since the chances of them finding themselves inside the officer's mess are very slim.

Being as veteran as he is, the other advantage Silius possessed was that he had long since learned that the higher the standard for luxury he rewarded himself with, there was a commensurate drop in the amount of respect the men he led held for him, officers included, which meant that his furnishings would not be sneered at by a Spartan. Perhaps the best part, at least as far as the men were concerned, was that they were standing in formation in the forum, with one half of the camp now completely bare of tents, watching as the 2nd scrambled about, and Varro's slaves carried out a number of busts, rolled carpets, and wooden floor squares. And, perhaps, some of the Centurions were a bit lax in enforcing silence in the ranks as they sniggered and muttered comments about Varro the Younger, some of which were quite witty. Finally, about the end of the first daylight watch, the command group swung into their saddles, whereupon Varro immediately kicked his mount and separated himself from Silius and Sacrovir, who looked even grimmer than he normally did whenever he was astride a horse, the reminder that we were now on the final march to face his half-brother. Some of our days waiting had been spent by the artillery *immunes* breaking out their pieces, checking the torsion bars and frames for cracks, the ropes for fraying or signs of stretching, and the stone ammunition for chips that knocked them out of their perfectly round shape necessary for accuracy, by order of our Primus Pilus, and I took a secret pride in why he had done so.

"It's something I learned from your father," he told me the night before he gave the order. "Rather than let the men's imaginations run wild, I want to remind them that if we do have to besiege Augustodunum, we have more than enough artillery to accomplish the job. And, it reminds them that this is our business."

Not lost on any of the officers of the 1st was that the 2nd had done nothing of the kind, their Primus Pilus preferring instead to hold a series of inspections that betrayed his origins as a Praetorian, where varnish jobs must be spotless, and chipped paint on a shield must be fixed, neither of which amount to a rotten fig when it is time to fight. What I noticed, and I was not alone, was that seeing the artillery shaken out seemed to light a fire under the men, and they showed their eagerness in their demeanor as we began the march. It is as impossible to describe as it is impossible to miss when one sees it, as if they are all hunting dogs straining at the leash, and, in fact, Silius called a halt earlier than normal, not to chide the Centurions for their men lagging, but to admonish them for setting too fast a pace.

"He said he's tired of us running up his horse's ass," was the way Macer put it to us, and while I doubted that Silius was quite that colorful, at the same time, I had heard the *Praetor* speaking around us rankers enough to know that it might be accurate.

Whatever he said, somewhat to my surprise, this fervor of the men did not wear off as we settled into the march, which would take another three days, even less if the men exhibited this kind of spirit into the next two days. As far as we knew, there had been no change in the situation, although we were in a position near the front of the column where we could see any riders approaching from the south, the direction in which we were heading, but it was not until shortly before the noon break that we saw the first of a pair of riders, making for the command group who were now riding behind the vanguard after leading the column as was customary at the beginning of a march. Then, at the noon break, the Prefect immediately detached himself from the command group to come jouncing up to where Macer and the rest of the First Cohort Centurions were gathered under a tree, most of us sucking down water from the flask our clerks carry for us since it is unseemly for a

Centurion to show any kind of weakness on the march, like thirst or fatigue.

I was not; I was consuming a couple of hard cheeses, and as Sacrovir slid from the saddle, he saw it, shook his head and said, "I suppose I should feel good that some things never change, Pullus. Every chance you get, you're stuffing your mouth."

"I'm still a growing boy, Prefect." I grinned, making sure he saw the cheese when I did.

"Marcus, I know you saw the messengers," he addressed Macer. "Decurion Chlothar sent them to report that they reached Agedincum (Sens) and they found a message from Macula waiting for them." It took me a moment to make the connection that he was speaking of Sempronius, so I missed the first part of the spy's message. "...and that there doesn't seem to be any real sign of what Sacrovir intends as far as whether he's going to defend Augustodunum or withdraw. But," he took a breath, "the message also said that he stands by the figure of forty thousand men." He cocked his head then, which was unusual, but then he looked over at me, and said, "It was something else that he mentioned that I think must be meant for you, Pullus." He squinted slightly as he tried to recall, something that he seemed to do more now that he was in his late fifties. "Let me see if I remember it right. Ah, yes...'Tell the big man that Sacrovir found enough men his size to fill those tin suits we talked about and they'll be hard to miss because of where they're going to be.'" Since I was watching him, I noticed the flicker of some emotion when the Prefect used his own *cognomen*, though it did not last long. "I'm assuming he means those *crupellarii*?"

"I believe so," I nodded, "but I'm not sure what he means with that last part."

"Probably that Sacrovir is going to put them on the walls," Macer ventured, but while this made sense, and my counterparts all nodded their acceptance of this, there was something that nagged at me, and I glanced up at the Prefect, who was watching me steadily, but I was not prepared for him to say, "Pullus, you look like you don't agree with your Primus Pilus."

Startled, I replied without thinking, "No, it's not that..." Then my mind caught up so I had to amend slightly, "...at least, not exactly."

"What is it, then, Pullus?" Macer asked evenly; if he was upset that I seemed to be disagreeing it did not show, nor was it in his character.

At the same time, I knew that he expected me to be able to articulate why I might feel differently, and despite the shade and the relatively cool breeze, I became aware of the sweat trickling down my back, acutely aware of all the eyes on me.

"I can't say, exactly, Primus Pilus," I replied, and while I was being honest, I knew this was not enough. "I agree that the most obvious answer to that riddle by Sem...Macula is that they'll be lining the wall whenever we go up the ladders. But," I took a breath, "have we been wrong in assuming that Sacrovir is going to stay behind those walls?"

Any further discussion was cut off by the sound of the *cornu* signaling the end of the break, and I could see that I had not persuaded anyone that there might be some other meaning in what we at least all agreed was a reference to the *crupellarii*, and I included myself. As we dispersed to rouse our men, Sacrovir nudged his horse to walk beside me as I headed for the Fifth.

"Keep thinking about it, Pullus," he urged. "I don't know my half-brother well, but what little I do know, he's likely to do something unexpected, and Sempronius clearly trusts you to figure it out."

He turned and trotted his horse back to the command group before my mind could register that he had used Marcus Sempronius' real name, and there would not be an opportunity to speak to him about it for the next few days. Not that it mattered; trying to decipher what Sempronius was trying to tell me occupied my entire attention, which at least helped pass the time on the march.

When we made camp that first night, we Centurions learned that not only was the enthusiasm and impatience of the men of the 1st not dampened by the day's march, it had spread to the men of the 2nd as well, so there was this air of anticipation

117

and excitement that none of us could recall seeing in the recent past.

"Maybe at the Wall," was Clepsina's comment, using the short version for what was the final battle against Arminius. "That's the last time I remember seeing the boys this ready to get stuck in. I have to admit," he sighed, "it's a nice thing to see."

There was a chorus of agreement from the rest of us, both Centurions and Optios on this occasion, making it a bit more crowded than usual in Macer's tent, but the reason they were there was to discuss this development.

"It is," Macer agreed, "but it also means we need to be vigilant, because it looks like the 2nd has finally joined the party as well, and you all know as well as I do that when the boys are spoiling for a fight, they're not all that particular about who it's with."

This, we all knew, was true, although we did have an advantage in that we were not back in Ubiorum, or any other town with enough *tavernae* to lubricate the men's fighting spirit even further. The Legion's wine supply was now under guard, by order of the *Praetor*, ostensibly to preserve it for the victory celebration that we were all certain would be coming, but what I found interesting was that, while the number of rebels had initially been met with, not fear perhaps, but with a fair level of trepidation, now it did not seem to matter to our men. To this point, much to our collective surprise, the news about the *crupellarii* had managed to remain a secret, but I was of the opinion that, if the fact that we were apparently outnumbered by a ratio of about four to one did not make any difference to them, the idea of a thousand men clad head to toe in segmented iron plate armor would not either. However, when I broached the idea to Macer in private of letting the men know after the larger meeting broke up, my Primus Pilus was clearly skeptical, but he also sensed that there was a reason behind my request.

"What is it, Gnaeus? I can tell there's something about these *crupellarii* that is bothering you, but whenever I ask you, you can't give me a reason."

"I know." I actually raised my voice enough that Macer

winced, because I was so frustrated. "I know that, I do! But I can't put my finger on why I think that the message Sempronius left means more than meets the eye." I snatched up my cup to take a long swallow, temporarily forgetting that it was not wine but water, my reaction making Macer laugh. "I'm glad you think it's funny," I muttered, but I returned to the topic. "The problem is that you're probably right that these *crupellarii cunni* are going to be on the wall because it makes the most sense. Sempronius actually has seen them in action," I recalled, "and the one thing that he said that's stuck with me is how clumsy and slow they are. Which," I admitted, "is all the more reason it makes sense to put them on a rampart where they don't have any need to move about."

"Then why are you still bothered by it?"

"Because I don't think Sempronius would have gone to the lengths to send a message just to me if Sacrovir is going to use those gladiators to defend a wall," I explained. Before I could think about it, I blurted out, "In fact, I don't think he's going to allow himself to be penned up in Augustodunum at all. I think that he's going to want to face us in open battle."

This clearly surprised Macer, which was understandable since the prevailing belief, at all levels of the army at this point, was that we were going to be attacking Augustodunum. The only question was whether we would settle in for a protracted siege or, after a brief period of preparation, we stormed the walls, with the opinion being equally divided, which of course meant the wagering was spirited.

"Why would he do that?"

I did not blame Macer for his obvious skepticism, but I realized that, while I had consciously tried to avoid dwelling on this, in the back of my mind, I must have been thinking about it, because the words came easily.

"Nothing we've seen or heard about this *cunnus* suggests that he's a dullard," I began. "Look how he fooled everyone but the Prefect with his ruse of joining with Aviola against the Turoni. And," I pointed out, "you and I both know that this rebellion has been *months* in the making. There is no way that he managed to not only recruit that many men, even if most of them are low quality, then manage to create enough arms and armor for eight thousand of them to be outfitted like us. He's been working on this for far too long to put himself in a position where he is risking not just this rebellion, but his life on one throw of the dice."

I had been encouraged by Macer's head, which had begun nodding as I spoke, but it stopped abruptly, although it was the frown that was most disturbing because I thought I had lost him. That was not why, however.

"I don't follow you," he said. "Yes, he's risking it all, but this is what he's been building towards. I completely agree that he's been planning and organizing this uprising for months. Which," he said suddenly, "I've been thinking about myself. How did he manage to do all this without drawing our attention?" My heart felt as if it had skipped a beat, and I braced myself for him to begin examining this more thoroughly, which might force me to make a choice about lying to him about what I had been told by Sempronius. Fortunately, he gave a curt shake of his head. "No matter. Anyway, I suppose I'm having trouble following you. Why wouldn't he want to give his army the best chance for success, which is to use the walls of Augustodunum?"

"Because," I replied quietly, "there's no escape for him if he does that. He can't live to fight another die if he traps himself inside the walls."

I could tell that I had at least planted a seed, but I also saw that he was not convinced, and he said as much.

"Let me think about it," he had said, and I left it at that.

We reached Agedincum before noon the next day, with the next settlement some twenty-five miles south, called Bandritum (Bassau), an otherwise unremarkable village except for one thing; it marked the northernmost completion point of the Via Agrippa, and once we reached that, our progress would undoubtedly become more rapid. It was entirely possible that we could cover the final seventy miles in two days of hard marching, but this was where the eagerness of the men to close with Sacrovir and his host was not necessarily a positive thing, because it would do no good to be exhausted upon our arrival. Unless, of course, the Aedui were content to be waiting for us behind the walls of Augustodunum; then it would not make any difference, because we would be there for a siege. Macer told me later this was in his mind when, at the noon stop, he came to where I was sitting with Vinicius and Macrinus, telling me peremptorily to come with him. I leapt to my feet and we walked to where the command group was gathered, all dismounted and seated on stools provided by their slaves, but as had become the habit, in two distinct groups separated by a few paces.

Most telling was the manner in which they sat so their backs were mostly to each other, and I listened with a growing dread as Macer explained, "I've thought about it, and I think that at the very least we need to tell the *Praetor* and the Prefect that you think it might be a possibility that Sacrovir has something special in mind for the *crupellarii* that doesn't include them being used to defend the rampart."

By the time he was through speaking, even if I had wanted to balk, it would have been too late, as both Silius and Sacrovir were sitting facing in our direction and were now looking directly at us as we approached.

We came to *intente*, rendering our salutes in unison, and it was Silius who returned it as the ranking officer, though he did so seated, something that rankles me a bit, but Macer was already speaking, saying crisply, "*Praetor*, Prefect, there's something that Hastatus Prior Pullus brought to my attention that I've been thinking about." Turning slightly, he addressed Sacrovir, "It concerns that message from Macula that was waiting for us in Agedincum."

"I've been thinking about that quite a bit myself," the Prefect agreed, which surprised me. Now, he addressed me, "So, Pullus? Clearly there's something about it that's bothering us both. What is it with you?"

During the time Macer had been ruminating on what to do, I had been doing the same thing, so it was slightly easier for me to expand on my misgivings; I also remembered to avoid referring to the Prefect's half-brother by his familial connection.

"I believe that Macula discovered that Sacrovir has something specific in mind for those *crupellarii*," I began, but suddenly, Varro, who had still been sitting with his back to us, spun about on his stool and cut me off by saying impatiently, "Yes, yes. We know all about that, Pullus. He's going to be using them to pack the rampart of their sad little wall protecting their collection of huts. This is nothing new," he gave what I can only describe as a smirk aimed at me, "to your officers, even if it *is* new to you."

I knew that he was baiting me; it had been a favorite game of his when he was the *Quaestor* with enough power to send me marching across hundreds of miles of hostile territory, but knowing it and being able to bite my tongue and not retort were two different things. Thanks to Fortuna, I was saved by an unlikely ally.

"Actually, Varro," Silius spoke up, and because he was facing me, it meant that Varro was behind him when Varro had turned around to confront me, yet the *Praetor* did not even deign to glance over his shoulder, "I feel quite certain that the Centurion here is well aware that this is the belief about how the Aedui intend to deploy these gladiators. Is that correct, Pullus?"

"Yes, sir," I was more than happy to answer, and while I could have been content with that, I could not stop myself. "You're exactly right. We all know that this is what we're expecting, sir. But," I shook my head to emphasize my point, "I don't believe that's his intention at all. I don't think that he's going to wait for us at Augustodunum."

"Why?" Silius frowned. "Give me your reasons."

So, I did, although I was able to explain a bit better than I had to Macer, ignoring Varro's snorts and muttered comments to his pair of pet Tribunes who tittered dutifully, because I only cared about what Silius, and only slightly less than him, Sacrovir, thought.

I concluded by saying, "I don't think that he wants to sacrifice himself for the cause, sir. I think he's also not in a position to withstand a prolonged siege with that many mouths to feed, but if he has to fight, he's going to do it in a manner that gives him an option to escape to try another day."

Silius did not reply to me; instead, he turned to look at the Prefect, who had been listening with an expressionless face that did not give me the slightest hint of how he felt.

Apparently, Silius felt the same way about this, because he asked, "Well, Prefect? You look like one of your ancestors' death masks. I can't tell what your thoughts are."

Sacrovir shifted on his stool, but his eyes stayed on me as he answered, "As we've discussed before, Prefect, I don't know my half-brother very well at all, so it's difficult for me to know exactly." He hesitated, and in that brief instant, I realized how deathly quiet it had become around us. "But," he resumed, "I must say that what Pullus says strikes some sort of chord in me. What little I do know about him indicates that Pullus is likely right, that he's not going to put himself in a place where there's no escape, which is what staying in Augustodunum would mean." I thought he was through, but then he added something that I had not considered, "And it wouldn't just be him that had the chance to escape. His army would be just as trapped inside the walls as he was, and the slaughter would be immense. By facing us out in the open, if things *do* go badly for him, his men will have more of a chance to escape than if they were inside the town. Which," he concluded, "would also give him a chance to rally and reorganize then come up with a new strategy."

Silius considered, then said, "Very well, let's say that this is true, and that he plans on either trying to ambush us at a place of his choosing, or meet us on open ground. What do those *crupellarii* have to do with it?"

"I believe that what Macula was trying to tell me was that Sacrovir intends to use them in one mass formation, probably in the center of their line, to punch through ours. And," I took a breath before I finished, "try to get to the command group, either to kill you, or to take you all as hostages."

Since I had no idea how this would be received, I cannot say that the stir it caused surprised me, but neither was I expecting it; however, Varro's laugh was not a shock. When he saw Silius rub his chin, I guessed that must have been a habit of the *Praetor* that indicated that he was taking my words to heart, because Varro could not contain himself.

"Surely you're not taking this seriously, Silius!" he exclaimed incredulously. Then, he gestured in the direction of

Sacrovir, and in an astonishing act of rudeness, scoffed, "I expect the Prefect here to fall for his kind of nonsense! He's a ranker at heart! But I expected better from you, I must say!"

This proved to be enough to get Silius to come to his feet before he turned to face Varro, which meant that his voice was slightly muffled, though I clearly heard what he said.

"Once you accrue as much as experience as I have, Varro," Silius replied, a coldness to his tone I had never experienced firsthand that I found quite impactful, and not in a good way, for Varro, anyway, "you learn that these men," he indicated us with one hand, "possess knowledge that can only be gained through hard-won experience on the *battlefield*. Not from a treatise written by another man reclining on a couch based on what they think a battle is like." This would have been devastating enough, but Silius clearly had been needled and prodded beyond his capacity to endure it without complaint, because he continued, "Perhaps if you had ever led men in battle, I would be more inclined to take your chastisement and your constant snide comments more seriously, but this is the closest you've actually ever come to being in battle, isn't it?"

Judging by the manner in which Varro sat there, openmouthed and with a face drained of all color, it seemed likely that nobody had ever spoken to him in this manner; that it was a man who, despite Varro's pretensions and proclivity to wave his Tata's ivory baton about, was more powerful in his own right meant that I will cross the river believing that, along with the things I have already mentioned, this was the true cause for all that was to come between these two. In that moment, however, it was Varro who signaled defeat by breaking eye contact with Silius first, which apparently satisfied the *Praetor*, because he then turned to address Macer and me.

"You've given me something to think about, Centurions, but I can't say that I'm completely convinced. But, for the sake of this discussion, let's say that I am. What do you propose we should do about it, the *crupellarii* in particular?"

Honestly, this had been my primary concern, and I realized in the moment that I had assumed that both Sacrovir and Silius would immediately agree with my reasoning, so I had moved on to the next problem, how to counter the effects of a heavily armored mass of men who might act as a giant battering ram, using their collective weight and the protection afforded by being armored head to foot, because the one thing I felt fairly certain about if I was correct in Sacrovir not using the walls of Augustodunum, that his goal for an open battle was to use those *crupellarii* to their maximum effect as a method to achieve victory. The question was, what did victory look like? Did he really believe he could overwhelm two battle-hardened Legions, even if one of them was led by a Primus Pilus who had never been tested in battle, which I suspected Sacrovir knew? Yes, he had overwhelming numbers, but of the forty thousand men supposedly under his command, I was concerned with perhaps ten thousand of them: the *crupellarii* and the approximately eight thousand men who would be equipped like the Legions. This was why I believed that Sacrovir's goal was not to overwhelm us, but to make a concerted effort to cut off the head of the proverbial snake by either killing or capturing the members of the command group, although from the Aedui's perspective, taking Silius in particular hostage would be preferable to killing him outright. I was also aware that in some ways, Varro would be more important given Sejanus' power, but I did not think that the Aedui rebel would have known that, while Sacrovir as Camp Prefect would be the most expendable to a Gallic nobleman, despite the reality being that, to the Romans doing the fighting, the order of importance would be exactly opposite, especially with the men of the 1st, the vast majority of them having served under Sacrovir as our Primus Pilus. Not lost on me as I had been thinking about the possibilities was how dangerous it was to think that you knew your enemy well enough to predict his movements and tactics, yet at the same time, I could not think of any other alternative actions the Aedui rebel could take if my supposition that he would not trap himself inside Augustodunum was correct. Consequently, I was ready with my suggestions, and I received a minor reward at the sight of Varro blanching at my mention of using the command group as bait by placing them closer to the line of battle than normal, whereas neither Silius nor Sacrovir reacted at all, though they did exchange a glance that did not tell me anything.

"How many men would that take?"

It was all Silius asked at the end of my comment, and at this, I heeded Macer's warning about asking for too much.

"Two Centuries' worth of men from the 1st, and two from the 2nd, but since I don't know any men from the 2nd, I'll need some assistance from Primus Pilus Carbo, sir," I answered immediately, proud of myself that I did not ask for a full Cohort, which was my initial estimate, and even then we would still be heavily outnumbered. "I need the best individual fighters each Legion can provide, preferably from the front line Cohorts if possible. We're going to be moving fast, and not in any kind of formation that we normally use, because we're going to use the *crupellarii*'s lack of mobility against them."

I should have been paying attention to Varro, but fortunately, Macer had his eyes on the man while I was watching Silius closely, who sat there, silent for a long moment before he leaned over towards the Prefect, beckoning to him to do the same, and the pair held a whispered conversation that seemed to last for a third of a watch but was only a handful of heartbeats before the *Praetor* sat back up and began staring down at the ground at his feet.

Finally, he said, "While I won't make the final decision right now, what I will say is this. When we make camp tonight, I want you to go ahead and select the men from the 1st that you want in the event that I decide to give my permission for this." He stood again, glanced up at the sun, and decided, "It's time to resume the march. Centurions, return to your spots."

We saluted, and as we hurried away, I heard Silius say Varro's name, but I did not want to glance over my shoulder, thinking that it might curse things.

"It sounds like Silius is telling Varro to have Carbo do the same thing," I offered, but Macer did not reply immediately, and when he did, it was in the form of a noncommittal "Maybe."

It was the tone as much as the words that caused me to look over at him, and I saw his expression matched his tone.

"What is it? Why are you looking like that?"

I knew I sounded nettled, but I could not help it; I thought it had gone quite well, considering, and seeing my Primus Pilus not sharing in my optimism stung me.

"Because I don't think Varro is going to let Carbo participate," he answered dourly. "I was watching him while you and Silius were talking, and I don't think he wants any part of this."

"He doesn't have any choice!"

I realize now that I was so indignant then because Macer had spoken truly, and on some level, I knew it, not because I had been paying attention to Varro's demeanor, but just because I knew the man.

"What do we do?" I asked.

"The only thing we can," Macer said grimly. "If Silius decides to do this, it will be completely up to the 1st to do it." He looked at me then. "Which means you're going to have a long night tonight, Gnaeus. I can't afford to weaken just the front line Cohorts, so you're going to have to choose men from the second and third line as well in case we're right that the 2nd doesn't contribute any men."

Chapter 4

Macer was correct; I did not get much sleep that night in camp, which was south of Autessiodurum, (Auxerre) and still in Senones territory, although it did not take all that long to select the men from the front line Cohorts, whose Centurions had been warned by Macer that they would be surrendering some of their men. It should not come as any surprise that, along with men of the First Cohort, I went immediately to the Fourth, making sure to stop at Licinius' tent first, although I knew he had been alerted by Macer to expect me. Thankfully, the period of tension between us that stemmed from him being named Quartus Pilus Prior after I had been presumed lost at sea, then it being made permanent on my secondment to the Praetorians, as brief as it turned out to be, was long in the past. Still, I could see he was not all that happy at the idea of losing men for something that was still not fully fleshed out, but I did not blame him for that, knowing I would feel the same way.

However, when I informed him of something else, I was a bit surprised at the vehemence of his reaction, which was to snap, "*Gerrae*! You're not stealing my Pilus Posterior!" He began shaking his head, "No, Pullus. That I won't stand for!"

"He *was* my Optio," I replied mildly. "And I put him up for promotion, so I know his qualities, Vibius. That's why I want him as my second in command for this."

This got Licinius to subside a bit, though he was still clearly unhappy about it, but by the time I was through running down the list of men I wanted, he was even unhappier.

"You're gutting my Cohort!" he fumed. "Those are the best I've got! You said yourself that Fulvius is the best ranker with a *gladius* in the Cohort!"

Determined to keep my composure and not just snap at him that this was done with Macer's blessing, I pointed out, "Four of them were with me in Britannia, Vibius. Surely you can understand why I'd choose them. And I know I don't have to tell you why I chose Clustuminus; you're the one who brought him with you into the First Century." Deciding a little flattery was in order, I confessed, "I wasn't sure about him at first, but you were right, and I trust him for what we might be doing. Still," I held my hands out in a gesture of surrender, "if you feel that strongly about it, I'll take him off the list. And Fulvius too, if you insist."

I was taking a gamble that Licinius would not want it to get back to Macer that he had balked, and it paid off, albeit with a grumbled, "No need for that. I suppose we'll get by without these men for what's coming."

"And Saloninus?" I pressed. "What about him?"

For a heartbeat, I thought he would refuse, but then he waved a hand in a gesture of defeat, and I left a few moments later to find my former Optio. As reluctant as Licinius had been, Saloninus' lone eye lit up at the prospect of the kind of action that I knew he preferred, one where he had a *gladius* in his hand and was getting stuck in himself instead of performing the more traditional role of the Centurion in supervising his Century, bone whistle in mouth and sounding the relief while listening for the *Cornicen* of the Cohort or Legion for orders.

When I told him the names of the men from the Cohort, he agreed for the most part, but there was one in particular where his reaction was decidedly different from Licinius', and in fact, he said flatly, "You're making a huge mistake with him, Pullus."

"Why?" I asked, completely mystified. "Cotta was one of the men I counted on in Britannia, and he's one of the best with the *gladius* in not just the Century but the Cohort, not to mention he's been the Cohort wrestling champion!"

"He *was* a good man," Saloninus agreed. "But that was before he settled down with that shrew Delphinia."

"Pluto's *cock*," I groaned. "I thought that was over!"

"No." Saloninus shook his head. While I knew it was not his intent, he actually made me feel worse by trying to make me feel better. "I know that you've got other things to worry about than what happens at the Faun, Pullus. And," he added, "believe me, both the Pilus Prior and I tried to keep him away from her, but now she's pregnant, and he's been shirking, malingering, and just being generally worthless. And," he took a breath before he finished flatly, "I don't trust him anymore. Not for a fight. He's lost it."

This was bad news, but once Saloninus informed me that Numerius Cotta had become entangled with one of the women who served drinks in The Dancing Faun, and who that woman was, I cannot say I was surprised. Delphinia was from Thrace, and she had been a mixed blessing from the beginning; she was extremely popular, and had a knack for getting customers to buy "one more cup," but she also brought a fair amount of trouble and drama because of her popularity. Of the eight women who worked at the Faun, Delphinia was the one Bronwen was the most suspicious of, something that I was reminded about as I talked with Saloninus.

"She is a sly one, husband," she had said in response to my comment about how pleasant in manner the Thracian girl was early on in her tenure. "She does this," my wife had batted her eyelashes, then gave a trilling laugh as she squeezed my bicep, and I recall being impressed by how uncannily Bronwen had captured Delphinia's manner, "but I watch her eyes. They are *never* smiling! They," she warned, "are always watching, and waiting. You should dismiss her immediately!"

Obviously, I had done no such thing then, and I had also ignored Turbo, who was no longer the owner but was still managing it, when he had brought up the problems that seemed to center on the Thracian girl.

"I'm not saying that she's the cause of most of the trouble," was how Turbo had put it, "but I'm not saying she's *not*. She," he had sighed, "is just really good at not getting caught at it."

And now, I thought, she had clearly gotten her claws into Cotta to the point that his Centurion did not trust him. Aside from the case of Cotta, who I substituted with the Sergeant of the Fifth Section of the Fourth Century, Gnaeus Pictor, I left the Fourth with the complement I had expected, making my way to the Second Cohort next. By rights, I should have selected men from the Third Cohort, but I am afraid that, at the risk of seeming petty, I had never forgiven the Third for their unforgivable behavior during the rescue of Segestes, which had directly resulted in my father's death. The old Pilus Prior Maluginensis had been replaced by Tiberius Pompilius, and their performance since then had been credible, but I could not bring myself to rely on men of the Third. That meant the Second, but once again, I already had a list, this one from Macer, who had been the Secundus Pilus Prior up until Sacrovir's retirement two years earlier, so that by the time I was through speaking to everyone, it was the beginning of the first night watch, and I had one Century's worth of men. This was when Lucco found me with orders to go meet with Macer, and when I entered his quarters, I knew just by the expression on his face that the news was not good.

"Carbo has refused to provide any men," he said without any preamble.

Despite not being surprised since Macer had predicted as much, it was still a bitter blow, and I unleased a string of invective that, had Varro been listening, might have gotten me scourged. This was all the time I spent on feeling sorry for myself, turning about and heading for the second and third line Cohorts, the former having been warned I would be coming.

"Wait," Macer called out. "I'll go with you," he said wearily. "This way, it will save time when Gallus, Camerinus, and Regulus come running to complain."

These were the third line Pili Priores, and while I appreciated the gesture, it was as much for the company as anything. By the time I was through, I had almost five Centuries' worth of men, most of whom I at least knew by reputation, men that I believed were best suited for what was coming, where they would be fighting more as individuals than is normal in the Legion, although I did intend to pair men up the next day after we stopped to make camp, which would be our penultimate day on the march before we were close enough to Augustodunum that contact was possible.

Not surprisingly, the closer we came to Augustodunum, the higher the tension, but in a continuation of what had begun on the first day, the men seemed every bit as eager to get there on this day, urging their Centurions to let the command group know that they were perfectly willing to march at an even faster pace. Being on the Via Agrippa, which is still relatively new and well-repaired, it meant that our progress was such that we could do more than thirty miles with relative ease, and my hope was that this would persuade Silius to call an early halt, because now it was also a matter of timing. Thanks to the series of milestones that are an integral part of all good Roman roads, we knew exactly how far Augustodunum was, but what threw some of us off, and I include myself, was the difficulty in calculating exactly when we would arrive the next day, which depended on our speed of march.

"If the boys keep pushing us to keep this pace tomorrow," Macer had mused at our first rest stop, "we're likely to get there with enough daylight for Sacrovir to do…whatever it is he has planned, but we'll be tired."

He was not the only one with this concern, and I was one who shared it, but try as we might, none of us felt confident in our calculations about our possible arrival time because there were a number of possible answers depending on whether Silius continued to let the men have their heads, as we say, in setting our pace, or if he chose a more prudent course. Ideally, we would arrive at a time when it would be too late for Sacrovir to sally out, if that was what he chose to do, which I confess I had begun to doubt as we got closer.

Just before the call to resume the march sounded, I said, "There's one person I know who can figure out all the possibilities based on how fast we march."

I did not need to name who it was, Macer instantly nodding his agreement.

"Yes, go have Alex chew on this. Tell him we need to know by the noon stop what we might expect."

I found Alex with Euphemios, Lucco, Acco, and some of the other clerks of the First Cohort, and not wanting to put him on the spot in front of the others, I drew him aside to tell him what we needed.

"Why me?" he grumbled, but he did not fool me then, nor does he fool me now; as proud as I am of my prowess with a *gladius*, Alexandros Pullus is no less proud of his powerful mind, and I have always been of the belief that, as long as one can back up one's words with deeds, then it is not boasting, and he is every bit as formidable in his own way as I am in mine. Nor was I surprised when he said simply, "I'll be able to figure this out well before the stop. I'll ride Latobius up the column to let you know."

I was still walking back up the column to our spot just behind the 2nd when the march resumed, which forced me to begin trotting, reminding me of the one drawback of marching on a paved road, that it is much harder on the legs of the men who are doing the marching and not riding. It may seem a small thing, and it is when it is only a matter of moving from one place to another, but with the prospect of battle ahead, it was just one more thing that worried me because of the plan I had formulated to defeat the *crupellarii*. This was about the point where I began hoping that I was wrong, that Sacrovir would in fact remain on the defensive and keep those gladiators on the rampart, something that I did not divulge to anyone, not even Alex. I firmly believed that the key to defeating the heavily armored *crupellarii* was by exploiting their lack of mobility, and men with legs already sapped from the pounding they took on the paving stones coupled with the fatigue from the increased pace, which would be exacerbated if we did not time our approach correctly, would have that mobility advantage at least partially negated. It felt as if all the enthusiasm and conviction that had spurred me to broach the idea in the first place was slowly leaking out of me, and it was not only an unusual feeling, it will probably be no surprise that it was quite unwelcome. The same could not be said for our men, and the only reason they were not singing was because Silius had set the pace that the men demanded, which in turn meant they simply did not have the breath to sing, or even to engage in any banter, making the predominant sound the sharp, crunching sound of thousands of hobnailed soles slapping the paving stones in a rhythmic cadence that, if one could manage to empty their mind of extraneous thoughts, like what awaited us, is quite hypnotic and actually can help pass the time of a hard march.

Unfortunately, my mind was anything but empty, so I actually welcomed the call from Vinicius at the rear of the Century warning me that Alex was approaching on Latobius.

My happiness was short-lived as I realized just before it happened that Alex would be unable to stop Latobius from rushing up to me and thrusting his nose into my midsection, and I was thankful for my mail, although the impact still sent me staggering back a couple of feet, the Century erupting into a roar of laughter despite not having much breath to spare.

Keeping his voice down, Alex warned, "If Silius sets this same pace tomorrow, we're going to reach Augustodunum around beginning of third watch."

"Which will be more than enough time for Sacrovir to shake out to face us," I said glumly.

"If we march at our normal quick time," he went on, "then we'd arrive a watch later, and while it still would be light, there will only be the time it takes for both sides to deploy, and I doubt Sacrovir wants to fight at night," Alex ventured.

However, I was not so certain, because as I thought about it, I realized that, if his goal to have a fight out on open ground was to give him the ability to escape should the day turn against him, then the coming of night would be welcome to him.

"All right, I'm going to inform the Primus Pilus. He can decide whether or not to bring it up with the *Praetor*, and," I shrugged, "then it's in his hands and the hands of the gods, I suppose." Alex nodded, but before he turned about, I told him, "And give this spoiled beast an apple when you get back to the baggage train."

I could see by the manner in which his ears pricked at the word "apple" that my horse thought this was a wonderful idea, while I girded myself to run up the column to consult with Macer. He was not surprised, having guessed as much, but I knew that he wanted it confirmed by someone he trusted; however, he refused to commit himself about whether or not he would speak to Silius, and I stood there catching my breath as I waited for my Century to arrive. No matter what the next day held, I was not looking forward to once we made camp, when I would assemble the men I had chosen, first to pair them up then inform them of my plans for the next day. The very thought of it made me offer up a prayer that, in fact, the next day would not be the day when we finally ended this rebellion once and for all. Not only were the gods not listening, they had one more surprise in store for us, which will serve me as a reminder about how trying to predict what the enemy will do is usually folly.

As I had anticipated, the men were already fatigued from the hard march of that day, yet they conveniently forgot when I pointed out to them that it had been at their behest and because of their agitation that they were complaining. My first task would be selecting them as pairs, with the help of Saloninus and the two Optios I had selected, the first being Publius Closus of the Fourth of the Fourth, and to everyone's surprise but Alex's, Publius Sabinus, my former Optio from the Praetorians who was now back to his old post, but in the First of the Seventh Cohort. My initial misgivings about him had proven to be erroneous for the most part, and what hesitation there might have been because of our time together in Rome had been erased by the reports of his performance back where he rightfully belonged with a line Legion. I was acutely aware, if only because Macer mentioned it more than once that, with a bit more than four Centuries' worth of men, I was light on officers with only these three, and a handful of Sergeants sprinkled throughout the ranks. However, as I stressed to Macer, we would not be operating in the traditional manner, and in fact, I was depending on the individual qualities of the men I had chosen to be more important than their instant obedience to orders. Because of the circumstances, and the time limits, I had not availed myself of the records of any of these men, even in the abbreviated form of the single wax tablet for each man that we take into the field, but I would not have been a bit surprised to learn that a healthy number of them, probably the majority, had run afoul of the regulations at some point in the past. This is very common with men who possess an independent streak, but for what we hoped to accomplish, this was absolutely essential; I needed men who required less supervision, who could think on their feet, and could take initiative. That said, there was still structure, as I designated a Sergeant to command not eight but sixteen men, and several of these were Sergeants in name only just for this task, then more or less evenly divided the sections between the four of us.

"The problem," I informed the men, though only after taking them outside the walls where we would be able to perform some maneuvers, and at least be away from prying ears, although it was impossible to miss the line of men on the packed earthen rampart who were watching with understandable interest, "is that until we see exactly what the Aedui Sacrovir intends, I don't even know whether we'll be needed. If he shakes them out like I think, that's when we're going to be used, and that's what we're going to train for now."

This was when we had the men pair up, and while for the most part it went swiftly, it was inevitable that there were odd men out from one Cohort or Century who had to pair themselves up with a man in the same situation in another. Sabinus proved useful with the men of the third line Cohorts, being more familiar with them than we were, and it served as a reminder of how, in many ways, the men of the third line Cohorts are almost as foreign to us as those from another Legion. Whereas it is true that the third lines are most often held in reserve, and at least since our last battles against Arminius we had not been pressed hard enough for the Legate to call them forward, they are also the Cohorts who are most often used for independent duties such as manning a satellite outpost, or used to guard supply lines. I mention it now because this was the first occasion I can recall where I actually began to think what I might do differently if I were to ever be in the post of Primus Pilus, and as time passed, I found myself doing it more often, to the point that, just a few months ago, Alex approached me with an idea.

"You need to start writing these things down," he said, though my initial reaction was to scoff.

"*Gerrae!*" I exclaimed. "And what happens if Marcus finds out about it? He'll think I'm after his job!"

"First," he countered matter-of-factly, "you are, and we both know it. But secondly, so does Macer. Gnaeus," he actually grasped my arm and squeezed it to emphasize his point, "of all the possible candidates, Macer wants you more than anyone else, even Clepsina. Why do you think you're in the First Cohort already?"

It was something that I had often wondered, but never allowed myself to think about, thinking it was quite presumptuous of me to do so, but I suppose that it is something like a new pair of *caligae* that take some time to break in and get accustomed to, and when I finally did as Alex suggested, at the top of the list is this thought I had that late afternoon a day's march from Augustodunum. Fortunately, by the time I had tucked this away, the final pairings were complete, and now that we were divided into four groups, I began showing the men what I had in mind. Almost immediately, I was forced to call a halt as men began balking at what I was trying to get them to do, not because they were daunted at the idea, but they saw areas for improvement.

"We need siege spears instead of javelins, Centurion. If those bastards are as heavily armored as we hear, our javelins will just bend," was one of the first shouted suggestions, and I immediately realized this was a good idea.

"Working in pairs is fine, but if we both have siege spears, then neither of us can get up close when we see an opening," one of my men from Britannia, Quintus Gallus, put in.

By the time I raised my *vitus* in a signal that I had heard as much as I was willing to, I was feeling better; more importantly, I could see the men felt the same way, and I realized that this plan, as hastily thrown together as it was, had been a bit too nebulous. Now that we had a better idea, and with the light beginning to fail, I broke the men down so that half of them acted as the *crupellarii*, ordering them specifically to behave as if they were encumbered, moving more slowly than they normally would have, and since we do not march with training weapons, we used our sheathed *gladii* and reversed the javelins to use the blunt end. Among the many things we did not know was whether or not the *crupellarii* we would be facing would be carrying shields; Sempronius had told me that, while he had been told they did use shields in the sand, for whatever reason Sacrovir had forbidden them from using them for his games. Whether or not that meant they would be going into battle without them was anyone's guess, just another thing that I had to worry about, but I made the gamble that there had been a reason Sacrovir had made the *crupellarii* face each other without shields, so the men who portrayed them discarded theirs. All in all, it was a slapdash effort, and I suspect the men knew it, yet to a man, they all behaved as if what we were doing was valuable and might serve to save their lives if it came to that, for which I was, and always will be grateful. It was past dark and getting next to impossible to see when I finally called an end to the training, but just when I was about to dismiss them, Saloninus cleared his throat in a manner I had learned when he was my Optio was meaningful.

When I glanced over at him, he whispered, "Perhaps you'd like to say a few words, Centurion?"

"Ah, yes. I suppose I should," I mumbled. Despite the darkness, although it was now Junius, the time of year when even after the sun goes down, it is not completely dark, I could see the sheen of the sweat on the faces of the men who, I was pleased to see, were not in any semblance of a formation but were still in their four groups. Taking a breath, I commenced, "I want to begin by apologizing that...whatever this was," I made a waving motion with one hand, but I was heartened that the men understood, signaled by the ripple of chuckles, "isn't nearly as thorough as I'd like it to be. And," I reminded them, "there's no guarantee that we're going to be facing these *crupellarii cunni* tomorrow, but we all know that we're a day away from Augustodunum. Depending on when we get there, we might have another watch to practice..."

"We don't need any more practice, Centurion! Just lead the way at those Gallic bastards, and we'll chop them into bloody bits! Right, boys?"

The roar of agreement was not only instantaneous, but I could also hear it was heartfelt, so that despite recognizing that the voice belonged to Sabinus, I would not have chastised him for it. I held up a hand, and they fell silent readily enough so that I could continue.

"That's good to hear," I resumed, "and I'm proud that you feel that way, and I know that each of you will do the 1st and your Cohort and Century proud by your deeds." Even as I was speaking, I could tell that I was losing them, so it was as much from desperation as inspiration that I added, "And we'll show those *fellatori* of the 2nd that we didn't need their help in the first place!"

Just that quickly, I had them on my side again, and their roar was even louder this time. It also took me bellowing at them to quiet down before I could finish, dismissing them to return to camp, and admonishing them to get some sleep.

I walked back with Saloninus and the two Optios, trailing behind the men who were trotting for the *Porta Principalis Dextra*, and once the slowest were fifty paces away, Saloninus asked, "Did you mean to shout that bit about the 2nd when you were facing in the direction of the camp?"

"No!" I answered, startled, but then I thought about it and realized I had done that very thing. "We were on our side of the camp, though," I offered, "so it's not likely that any of the men on the wall were theirs."

"So you didn't pay attention to who had the first guard shift," Saloninus replied, then laughed at my expression.

"No," I admitted. "I didn't. Pluto's cock," I groaned. "This is all I need, to have that fucking Praetorian knowing my name."

"Oh, he already does."

I looked over at Sabinus, who was on the opposite side of me and had been the one to say this.

"How do you know?" I demanded, and while I was disturbed, I was not angry...yet, and Sabinus suddenly looked nervous.

"I-I'm sorry, Centurion! I thought you knew," he replied. "But when Carbo came to the 2nd, he didn't come alone. He had about a half-dozen of his bunch with him. I ran into one of them right after he showed up."

His voice trailed off, and I had the impression that he was hoping that I would just deduce the rest, but I was not in the mood.

"Well?" I demanded. "What happened?"

"You...your name came up," he said, sounding miserable. "And...I won't repeat what he said, but what matters is that Primus Pilus Carbo knows who you are, and he's warned his men to steer clear of you."

This was not actually bad news, and I said as much, then

we were inside the camp and we parted to our respective areas, while I headed to my tent looking forward to a meal and a chance to rest.

Instead, I was greeted by Alex, who, without any preamble, said, "The Primus Pilus wants to see you in his quarters immediately, Centurion."

Just by the tone, I knew this was not for the purpose of a social visit, and I stifled a curse before executing an about-turn and walking up the Cohort street. My second warning was, on entrance into the Primus Pilus' tent, Lucco jumped to his feet and hurried to the partition, stuck his head in, and within a handful of heartbeats, I was entering Macer's private quarters, forcing myself not to come to a dead stop when I saw that he was not alone.

I did remember to salute the Prefect first, then Macer, deciding to play it safe by being formal. "Primus Hastatus Prior Pullus, reporting as…"

"No need for that, Pullus," Sacrovir said, and while he was technically within his rights as Prefect, he immediately reddened slightly, turning to Macer to say apologetically, "I'm sorry, Marcus. Some habits die hard, I'm afraid."

"There's no need, Prefect," Macer assured him, and I knew him well enough to see that he meant it; Marcus Macer is not known for his jealousy like some men are, but I also saw that Sacrovir was truly embarrassed. However, he was not smiling when he addressed me. "Now, would you care to explain why I got a visit from a very angry Primus Pilus Carbo who claims that you uttered a number of slurs against the men of the 2nd?"

"Juno's *cunnus*." I somehow managed to mutter this softly enough that neither of them heard me, or more likely, they both chose to ignore it. Loudly enough for them to hear, I replied, "That's not true, Primus Pilus! It wasn't a number of slurs; it was just one."

I honestly had not said it to be humorous, but Sacrovir suddenly coughed in a manner that sounded suspiciously like he was trying to stifle a laugh, while Macer snatched up his cup and brought it to his lips, though not quickly enough I did not see the beginning of the smile.

Only after he took a swallow and set the cup down, did he

ask, "And what slur was it that you uttered?"

"I…it's hard to recall, but I believe I might have called them…*fellatori*, Primus Pilus."

"Well, that was *one* of them he said you used," Macer agreed. "But there were a few others."

"He's lying," I said flatly, which caused Sacrovir to stir a bit.

"Gnaeus, it's not wise to call a senior Centurion a liar…even if he is," he admonished, and I knew that he was right, but he was not through. "But it's downright dangerous when it's a man like Carbo."

Naturally, my first instinct was to bluster, but these were two men who knew me well and neither of them were willing to indulge my fit of temper, though it was Macer who snapped, "Enough with this nonsense, Gnaeus!" He took a breath, and in a calmer tone, said, "Nobody doubts your ability to handle yourself. Least of all," he indicated Sacrovir then himself, "the two of us who have seen you in action. But you're one man, and you don't have eyes in the back of your head! And Carbo is threatening to make a stink about this with Silius. Not," he held up a hand to forestall me, "that you have to worry about that, because even if he does, it won't go anywhere."

"I made sure to let Carbo know that if he does, as Camp Prefect and his superior, I'd be inclined to start asking some questions myself," Sacrovir put in.

So, if it's not going anywhere, why are you telling me all this?

This was what I wanted to ask, but aloud, I heard myself say as humbly as I could, "I understand, Primus Pilus. And," this was at least heartfelt on my part, "thank you for warning me. I will be more…circumspect in the future."

"See that you are," Macer said, then changed the subject to more pressing matters. "Now that you've had a chance to see the men you chose, what do you think?"

"It's hard to say," I began, then saw Sacrovir's frown deepen, and while I was very briefly tempted to say something that might have gotten them both to rescind their endorsement of my plan, my pride came to the fore, and I do not believe they noticed my hesitation. "But I know the boys are eager and ready to get stuck in, and I feel that I've chosen the best type of men for what we need to do. Still," I finished, "it's in the hands of the gods."

This clearly satisfied them, because I was dismissed immediately after that, while Sacrovir seemed comfortable and in no hurry to go anywhere, which made me both curious…and nervous.

My legs ached the next morning, and judging from the manner in which the men were moving, they felt the same way, but I also had had trouble sleeping the night before, though not because of any concern about a Praetorian Primus Pilus whose feelings I had hurt. No, my sleepless night was caused by my very first taste of what it is like for a commander who is responsible for his men on the eve of a likely battle. This may sound strange coming from a seasoned Centurion, but this was the first time I was going to be leading an independent command where, once we were engaged, if events transpired as I thought they would, I would be essentially on my own in the middle of an enemy formation. Superficially, it was similar to what I had done at Idistaviso in ordering the Fourth Cohort to change its orientation on my own, without any orders to do so, but that had been done spontaneously. This time, I was going to be responsible for just less than a Cohort's worth of men and would be leading them directly for the strongest part of the Aedui formation, and depending on circumstances, we might find ourselves beset on all sides. In the darkness of night, lying on my cot, the predominant thought running through my mind was a sort of incredulity that I had ever suggested this in the first place, and I could not seem to banish the idea that my Hubris had finally met its Nemesis with this endeavor.

It was Alex who actually helped settle my nerves when, in the predawn darkness after the call to begin the day, he brought me not just the leftovers from the night before, the usual way we break our fast, but a freshly baked loaf, along with a bowl of soldier's porridge, saying quietly as he set the items on the table, "You're doing the right thing, Gnaeus. I think you're right about what Sacrovir is going to try, and this is the best way to stop those *crupellarii* if they're going to be used the way you think."

Frankly, in that moment, I was skeptical, thinking that he was just saying this to make me feel better, but his gaze did not waver when I looked him in the eye and asked bluntly, "Really? Or are you saying what you think I want to hear?"

As he usually does, he not only won the argument, he convinced me by retorting, "When have I ever done that before?"

This helped soothe my nerves, but I could not stifle the groan as I stood up to walk to the table, feeling the stiffness in my legs. The march would help loosen my muscles up, but we were still marching on the paving stones of the Via Appia, which I tried to put out of my mind by assuring myself that if the moment was to be today, I would not notice nor, hopefully, would the men. Donning my armor, as the men struck the tents and loaded them up, I went to the horse enclosure to give Latobius a hunk of bread, apologizing once again for not riding him, although he was getting more than enough exercise with Alex riding him every day. Spending time with Latobius, who had been my father's horse, I actually find comforting, but more importantly, it is when I feel closest to my father, and sometimes I find myself having a conversation with Latobius that is actually with Titus Porcinianus Pullus and not my horse, which was what I did then. I bring this up because it was the reason I was not paying close enough attention to my surroundings, and as a result, I took the most direct route back across the camp to my Cohort area instead of retracing my original path around the perimeter of the camp along the wall, which Silius had decided to leave intact, the sign that he intended on returning the same way we came. The consequence was that I almost literally ran into a similarly preoccupied Primus Pilus Carbo who was exiting from the latrine area, surprising and discomfiting both of us equally, judging from his expression, which at first was to look up at me with widened eyes. Most gratifying was his initial look of naked fear, though it was gone quickly, no doubt helped by the fact that, while we may not been paying attention, there were men from both Legions who were standing in one of the lines waiting to relieve themselves, the latrines being the one area where, by long custom and common consent, the natural antipathy Legions have for each other are held in temporary abeyance.

Unfortunately, Carbo recovered more quickly, his thin lips twisting into a sneer that I felt certain was overdone and meant more for his watching men, which also meant he said more loudly than necessary, "Oh, it's you, Pullus. The man who found the discipline of the Praetorians too harsh for him and he had to come running back to the kind of place where men are slovenly and feel free to utter slurs against their brothers! Isn't that right, Centurion?"

Don't do it, Gnaeus. He's baiting you and trying to get you to say something he can use against you.

"Actually, Primus Pilus, I got tired of playing toy Legionaries and decided to come back to where the *real* Legions are defending Rome, where how we fight is more important than how we look." I cocked my head and feigned puzzlement. "But why did *you* leave the Praetorians to come here if you feel that way about the men you're leading, Primus Pilus?"

Oh, how he wanted to strike me, or perhaps even draw his *gladius*; I could see it in his eyes, and in the manner in which his entire body seemed to vibrate. If looks alone could have killed me, I would have been dead on the spot.

"How *dare* you speak to me that way?" he hissed. "You *insolent*, puffed-up piece of *cac!*" With every word, his rage seemed to grow, and while my attention was on him, there were men standing on either side of us who were within my range of vision, some of whom I recognized, and some I did not, meaning they were from the 2nd, but what I noticed was the uniformity of their expressions, all of them indicating that they did not appreciate Carbo's obvious contempt for his own men. He was clearly unmindful of this as he continued to rage, "You think that I should bow to you because of your name? Because of who your Tata is?" He smiled then, a feral grin that displayed a mouth full of teeth that were black with decay, common in men who have a fondness for wine, but it gave me a hint of what was coming. "Of course, there's a question, eh? *Which* Tata are we talking about?" He laughed, but it was so obviously feigned that it actually did not anger me, much. "Mayhap we should ask your mother about where you got your mouth from, eh? Or," he widened his eyes, again overdoing it, but this time, it was to turn and look at the men around us, "maybe *she's* the one who was the bad influence on you. She clearly loves the company of men under the standard, eh, boys?"

This was the moment when Carbo realized something, that none of his men who were present for this appreciated his wit; it was not until later that it was pointed out to me that it was not just that Carbo had unintentionally let his true feelings about his own men show.

"You're a Pullus," Macer said, a bit impatiently to my ear. "You're the great-grandson of one of the first Prefects, the grandson of a Pilus Prior, and the son of...well," he had shrugged, "your father is a legend in his own right to men under the standard in the Army of the Rhenus."

In this moment, while I could see that the men he had expected to support him were watching in silence, I was still struggling with my temper, but then Carbo made his mistake.

When I still did not react, he suddenly lifted his *vitus* to brandish it at me in a manner that could have easily been construed that he intended to strike me, arousing a ragged but clearly audible gasp of shock from the onlookers, though it did not drown out Carbo screeching, "You miserable cur! I should thrash you where you stand for your disrespect!"

The *vitus* swung down on his last word, the sound of it striking flesh making what, to my ears, was the loudest, sharpest sound so far; however, the flesh it struck was the palm of my hand caused by my blocking the twisted vine cane from striking my body. I suppose to those watching, it looked as if it happened in one motion, with the *vitus* striking my palm, my fingers closing around it then yanking it from his grasp with an ease that the men would be talking about for some time, then tossing it behind me, where I heard it clatter on the beaten ground. The buzzing of the men whispering to each other that had begun with Carbo's dramatic and violent act ceased as abruptly as if I had barked at them for silence, which only amplified the noises around us as the rest of the army, oblivious to this drama, continued in breaking camp. For his part, Carbo looked frightened, suddenly deprived of his *vitus*, while I stared down at him, not bothering to hide my look of contempt, but when I took a step in his direction, it elicited a sharp yelp of fear as the Primus Pilus of the 2nd Legion leapt a step backward in response to my own move. This was his intent, at least, but his feet got tangled with each other, and he lost his balance, staggering back while windmilling his arms in a vain attempt to keep his feet, instead landing, hard, on his ass, in a manner completely unbecoming of the dignity of the Primus Pilus of a Legion of Rome. I did not offer a hand to help him up, nor did I say a word; instead, I stepped over him and resumed heading to the First Cohort's area, not even giving him a glance as I did so.

The men scrambled to get out of my way, but then I heard a voice say, "It wasn't right what the Primus Pilus did, Centurion, but we heard what you called us last night. That weren't right neither."

I probably should have ignored him, but I did not, though I continued walking as I said, "You're right. I shouldn't have said it, and I offer an apology. But," I did turn my head a bit since I was past them, "your Primus Pilus didn't want any of you to stand with the 1st against these gladiators. Maybe you should talk to him about it."

I waited to hear Carbo shout at me to stop, but he did not, though I did hear him snarl at one of his men to help him up, while I told myself that I would undoubtedly be standing in front of Macer again; provided, I thought, that I survived whatever was coming, whenever it was coming. However, I am still waiting to hear, which is another way of saying that Carbo never made a complaint, officially anyway. Undoubtedly what the Aedui had planned for us later in the day played a role, as once again, I was reminded of something that my father said more times than I could count. When it comes to warfare and the plans we make for success, the enemy also has a say in how those plans go.

It was before the noon stop when, from the front of the column, the *Cornicen* in the vanguard sounded the warning call that told us that a mounted party was approaching, which is distinctly different than the call they use for a single or pair of riders. Despite being closer to the rear than to the front, we could all see the cloud of dust hovering above the helmeted heads of the rest of the army in front of us.

"That's too much dust for just a couple of scouts," Macrinus commented from behind me, and I heard the worry in his voice. "I wonder if that's some Aedui cavalry coming to make some mischief."

While the thought had crossed my mind as well, I had also only been partially paying attention to my *Cornicen*, so I could answer with some confidence, "The vanguard would have sounded the call if that was the case. No," I shook my head, raising my voice since I knew everyone within earshot was paying attention, "this isn't the Aedui."

"Then what is it?" Lentulus asked, earning my *Signifer* a glare from his Centurion for asking a question to which I did not know the answer.

"We'll find out soon enough," I replied confidently, though I had no reason for being so.

However, while we did, I cannot say that the news was all that welcome, and it began when Macer's *Cornicen* blasted the signal for us to attend to him, and when I arrived, Macer was still puffing from dashing up the column to the command group then back.

"The cavalry's returning to us," he began, his features set in a grim expression that served to deepen the crevices in his face that reminded me that he was now more than forty years old. We quickly learned why he was looking this way, but first, he turned to address me. "Pullus, you were right. Sacrovir isn't going to use the walls. He's going to meet us in open battle...much sooner than we expected."

"What does that mean?" Clepsina demanded, but while I thought I had an idea, I was as unprepared as my comrades for what was coming.

"It means that he's already formed up and waiting for us...about three miles ahead."

It took a moment for one of us to work it out, but somewhat to my annoyance, it was Glaxus who gasped, "But we just passed the twenty-mile marker to Augustodunum! He's picked a spot *seventeen miles from there*?"

"That's what I'm saying," Macer agreed.

"There must be something special about that spot," Gratianus mused. "Like the ground must be to his liking."

"We're going to find out," Macer said, then looked at me. "The *Praetor* told Carbo and me to draw spare mounts so that we can ride ahead with Chlothar and the cavalry that's here, and he told me to have you come along, Pullus."

"At least Latobius will get some exercise."

It was all I could think to say; frankly, I was in as much a state of shock as the others. Yes, I felt somewhat vindicated that the Aedui leader had chosen to behave as I had predicted, but it had never even occurred to me that he would move so far away from Augustodunum. And, as Gratianus had said, it had to mean that there was something especially advantageous to him than just being closer to us. Macer put Clepsina in command, then we trotted back to the baggage train, and in my case, it was just a matter of Alex dismounting and I taking his place, which my horse took as the appropriate time to arch his back and give a couple of hops, though not a full buck; those he reserved for the occasions when nobody had exercised him for several days and he wanted to express his displeasure.

"Not today, you," I said sharply, using the tone that I do not use very often with Latobius; frankly, I have been told quite often that I do not use it enough, but my response to this is that there are not many horses of a man like me who are known by name by the likes of Germanicus Julius Caesar.

Fortunately for both of us, Latobius signaled his understanding by blowing a huge gust of air, which I had learned was his way of agreeing, albeit under protest. Macer was not quite as…grim…a horseman as Prefect Sacrovir, but he still looked anything but comfortable as he bounced alongside me on a bay gelding that was one of Tribune Aviola's spares. While I should not have been surprised, I cannot say that I was very happy when I saw Carbo, riding a roan stallion that I recognized as one of Varro's mounts, handle it with an ease that spoke of a great deal of practice, consoling myself with the thought that he was probably not the horseman

I was. The column had been halted, the men given leave to ground their packs, but the outer files were required to remain standing, facing outward, while all shields were now uncovered, the men not nearly as boisterous as they had been when the prospect of battle was still a day away. This is not saying that they looked downcast, nor were they mute, talking quietly amongst themselves as we trotted past, with some of our men calling out to us as we rode past.

"Centurion Pullus, if it looks like you can handle those Aedui on your own; go ahead and do it without us!"

"If you're not careful, Percennius, I'll sling you across my saddle and take you with me!" I shouted back, pleased at the laughter of all but one man.

"He thought I wouldn't recognize his voice," I commented to Macer, who was grinning broadly.

"I don't know why they think that." He shook his head. "We've been listening to them chatter like women at the fountain for years. You'd think they would figure out that if they can recognize our voice, we can recognize theirs."

Our conversation was cut short by our arrival at the head of the column, and I spotted Herminius and the rest of the Batavians, save one, so I asked him, "Where's Wigmar?"

"He is with the rest of the *ala*," the Batavian explained. "Tribune Aviola is in command there while the Decurion came back here. There is a forest between us and where the rebels are formed up. They are watching them from there."

"What does the Aedui position look like?" Macer asked, but we were disappointed when Herminius shook his head and replied, "I was patrolling to the east when we were recalled here, so I have not seen it. But," he finished grimly, "if what I am hearing is correct, it is easy to see why this Sacrovir chose it."

By this time, everyone who would be part of the scouting party was gathered, and Silius was opening his mouth when Varro, looking quite ludicrous in a muscled cuirass decorated with gold filigree and embossed with a snarling lion's head with gold-capped teeth that was completely at odds with his soft, pale body, beat him to it.

"We are going to observe where these rebel scum have

finally decided to face us," he shouted, a bit unnecessarily since the officers who mattered were sitting their horses a couple paces away all around him, "so I expect complete silence from this moment forward! We don't want to alert them that we're anywhere nearby and looking them over. Is that understood?"

"*Quaestor*," Sacrovir managed to sound both respectful and amused, but it was the use of Varro's actual official title that we could see had the most profound impact on him, "how are we going to give the command to begin the march if nobody is allowed to give the command? After all," he reminded Varro, "they're more than three miles away, so I think it's safe at the moment."

Somehow, I managed not to laugh, but others were not so successful, and for a moment, Varro's face was almost a perfect match to another of his affectations, the scarlet sash he insisted on wearing around his waist that is only worn by men of Legate rank. The fact that Silius had put up a half-hearted fight about this had been a topic of conversation very early in this campaign, but he had clearly given up, probably when Varro pulled out that ivory baton that even now he was clutching in one hand in much the way a Centurion carries a *vitus*. Somehow, Varro managed to refrain from lashing out at the Prefect, and in fact tried to play off the barb as if he shared in the joke, offering Sacrovir what could only charitably be called a smile.

"That is an excellent point, Prefect. We're blessed by Fortuna to have someone of your...experience to remind their commanders when they make an error, however minor it may be!" Turning to the mounted trooper carrying the *bucina*, which is used by the cavalry because it is smaller than the *cornu*, he ordered him to sound the advance, which was met by a nervous glance by the trooper over to Silius, which not surprisingly enraged Varro. Nudging his horse closer, he pointed a finger in the man's face, and while he did not shout, I was close enough to hear him hiss, "By the *gods*, I gave you an order, you *oaf*! Now..."

"B-but, sir," the trooper stammered, and his Batavian accent was accentuated by his distress, "until you give the order for column, or close order, I c-cannot play the correct notes!"

"Oh." When Varro had moved to chastise the trooper, he had turned his back to me, so I could not see if his expression showed the embarrassment we heard in his voice. "Yes, very well. Sound the advance for a column of two's."

This time, it was Silius who cleared his throat, and when Varro looked at him, the *Praetor* said expressionlessly, "At some point, we may have to change formation from column to close order if we run into Aedui cavalry, but you've ordered total silence. So," he held his free hand out, palm up in a gesture that needed no translation, "perhaps you might think of modifying them?"

"Fine!" Varro shouted this, clearly agitated now, and I realized I was thoroughly enjoying myself, at least until he savagely jerked his horse's head about so he could face most of the men. "I rescind the order of total silence! Just…just keep the talking to a minimum! Now, may we begin?"

Naturally, nobody offered anything more, and within a dozen heartbeats, we were formed into a column of pairs, although there was some whispered commentary about how a column of four's would have been better since it makes the column shorter, and if we needed to form into some sort of battle order, it would not take as long. Macer was next to me, while Carbo was called up to ride next to Varro at the head of the column, prompting me to glance over at Macer, who rolled his eyes. Silius was next to Sacrovir just behind them, while Decurion Chlothar and the horn player were immediately ahead of us, which meant that we could not talk as freely as I would have liked. Varro set the pace at a brisk trot, which was the first correct decision he made, and the rest of the army was left behind as we approached the northern edge of the forest that Herminius had informed us lay between our army and where the Aedui were located. We were soon joined by more of the cavalry who had been ranging about the countryside, usually in groups of four or six men, so that by the time we reached the spot where Tribune Aviola was waiting, my guess was that most of the cavalry was back with us, the first time since we had set out from Ubiorum we were all together.

"From here, only the senior officers, including the Primi Pili, and a bodyguard of three sections are coming," Silius announced, beating Varro to it, which I saw he did not like in the slightest. I suppose that my uncertainty about whether I was included showed, because the *Praetor* added, "That means you as well, Centurion. You and your chosen men need to have an idea of what you're going to be facing."

With this settled, we set out, with the Tribune leading the way, guiding us to where, just ahead of us, we could see the lighter background that signaled the southern edge of the forest, whereupon he veered off the road, leading us a few hundred paces into the forest on the western side of the Via Agrippa before he dismounted.

"We should walk from here," he explained, pointing ahead to what appeared to be a natural barrier created by an uprooted tree where the dirt clung to the roots, which was surrounded by a thick bramblebush. "The men created a bit of a hideout there where you'll have an unobstructed view of the hill. Although," he turned to address both Macer and Carbo, "I would suggest that you take off your helmets. Those white crests might be spotted by the advance guard they have down at the bottom of the hill."

None of us were wearing red crests of the Pili Priores, which would have been even more likely to be spotted, but while they both doffed their helmets, Carbo muttered something under his breath as he did so, which I believe was due to his thinning hair that he grew long then combed over in the manner supposedly originated by Divus Julius, and I remember wondering in the moment if that was why Carbo did it. We walked more slowly than normal, not wanting the movement of a party of seven men to draw the attention of one of the sentries that Aviola had mentioned, and I saw that the Tribune had described our observation post accurately. There was a hollow space surrounded on one side by the roots of the fallen tree, while in between us and the hill was a thicket of thorny bushes, with the berries on them fully formed but still green, it being too early in the year, while our left flank was obscured by three trees growing closely together and with more of the thicket clustered around the trunks. This was where

I found Wigmar, who was lounging on his cloak, at least until he saw who was approaching, but I saw with approval that he did not leap to his feet, since that kind of sudden movement is what attracts the eye, choosing instead to slowly rise to a crouch. He stepped aside to give us room, and naturally, Varro pushed his way forward, with Carbo right next to him, in exactly the kind of movement that Wigmar had known to avoid, and a part of me wished they would raise the alarm by the Aedui.

"I wonder if either of them knows what they're looking at?" Macer whispered, and I stifled my laugh, mindful of Varro's warning and not wanting to incur his wrath when he actually had a legitimate cause for complaint.

Yes, we were too far away to be heard, and it was a good thing, because once we all saw what was waiting for us, I do not believe there was one man who managed to keep from at least groaning aloud.

"Pluto's thorny *cock*," Macer contributed, though he did it in a whisper, and not lost on me was how everyone turned to look directly at me, but it was the Prefect who spoke first.

"Pullus, judging by the way that they're formed up, it looks like you're right. But I also don't think it would be a good idea if you..."

"Nonsense," Varro interrupted. "As you said, it appears that the Centurion is correct in how these rebels intend to use those *crupellarii,* and if so, we will need him and his men that he chose to stop them." He did look at me and smirked. "I suspect that those men won't thank you for the honor you did them once they lay eyes on that bunch, Centurion. Rankers," he chuckled, "do love their skin, don't they?"

"No more or less than the men of our order, *Quaestor.*"

I have never had the urge to kiss a man before, but I could have kissed the *Praetor* at that moment, saving me as he did from my own mouth, because the gods know that I was opening it to say something that Varro would have found even more offensive. For his part, Varro gave Silius a glare that was as impotent as it was furious, while I took the opportunity to squeeze past them to get a bit better look through the foliage at where what could only be described as a teeming mass of men were arrayed on the open slope of a hill that appeared to be a natural clearing and not manmade. The grade was not all that great; the Via Agrippa, like all Roman roads, was running straight north and south directly up the middle of the clearing, which was off to our right from our hidden position, and not switching back and forth as it would if the grade was too steep for wagons to traverse it. Men were milling about, but Sacrovir, who obviously had his own scouts who knew our whereabouts, had somehow managed to convince them to remain in their groupings, of which the largest by far was the kind of disorganized mass of native tribesmen, although they were organized to the extent that they were identifiable by the color schemes of their garb. The largest group, which I judged to be about ten thousand men, were wearing the normal motley collection of armor, but there were enough men just wearing tunics that I could see the muted reddish color that reminds one of rust being predominant, along with a hint of green, which I had been told were the Aedui colors.

They occupied roughly the center of the slope, directly behind the neater rows of men that, to a civilian perhaps, looked identical to the two Legions waiting for us three miles to the north. However, it did not take long for me to notice the differences, mainly in the lack of discipline, and the absence of men carrying horns, which told me they would be unable to communicate with the same level of efficiency. As informative as this may have been, my eye naturally traveled down the slope to a spot right in the middle of the host and straddling the road, to the mass of heavily armored men, whereupon I learned something; hearing about these *crupellarii* and seeing them were two vastly different things, but my first impression was how it hurt my eyes to look at them, and it took a heartbeat for me to understand that, between the amount of iron it takes to clad a man from head to toe in plated armor, the relative newness of the armor, and that there were at least a thousand of them, the light from the bright sunshine, which was almost directly overhead, was almost as if I was staring at the sun itself when it was behind clouds.

"I wonder if that's going to be a problem."

I had murmured this to myself, unaware that both Macer

and Sacrovir had come to stand on either side, and it was my Primus Pilus who gave a chuckle that held no humor.

"Which part?" he asked. "The fact that there's more than a thousand of them like we were told? Or trying to figure out a way to poke holes in them?"

"No," I answered, barely hearing him. "I'm talking about how I have to squint to look at them."

"*Cac*," Sacrovir muttered. "You're right. I didn't think of that. I just thought I had to squint at them because I'm so fucking old."

"That doesn't help," Macer put in, and despite the tension, this made the Prefect chuckle. "But," Macer turned serious, "I don't think it will be a problem once we're closer, and on level ground. It doesn't help right now because they are higher than we are, and farther away."

Although I was still slightly skeptical, it did make me feel better; what did not was the presence of shields, not as large as ours and round instead of rectangular, though I was too far away to see if they were curved or flat, which is the Gallic style. They were all armed with spears, which most of them had thrust into the ground, the vertical shafts looking like a strange forest of denuded, small branchless trunks, each of them next to a man in glittering iron, although, to a man, they had their helmets off as they waited.

"Those helmets must be hot and uncomfortable," I commented. "Once they have them on, it probably doesn't take long for them to start sweating. I just wish we were close enough to see if they're as they were described to me, because their vision is going to be limited, and if they're strapped on, then it must mean they can't turn their heads much."

"Attack them from the sides then," Macer suggested. "A man on each side, coming at them from the flanks, with the man with the siege spear on their strong side, and the man on the weak side with the *gladius*."

"Trying to parry with a spear is harder," I agreed, but I was not quite convinced. "But remember, these are supposedly gladiators, and they'll have been specifically trained to counter a different kind of weapon from the one they're using."

"True," Macer allowed, but he is one to always look on the

bright side, which was why he reminded me, "but we also don't know just how well trained they are, or how many of them are trained at all. Although," he did add, "while it's hard to tell from here, they do look bigger than those missile troops on either side."

"They would have to be to wear that much armor," Sacrovir commented, but when I glanced over at him, I saw that his eyes were not on the *crupellarii*, who were down nearer to the bottom of the slope, but on a party of mounted men who at that moment were moving at a trot across the hill near the top from our left to right.

Macer obviously noticed as well, because he pointed at the cluster of horsemen just as they came to a stop.

"That's probably…"

"Yes," Sacrovir cut him off, "I'm sure it is. That's my…the Aedui commander," he amended. "But I don't see any cavalry."

"He probably has them on the other side of the hill where we can't see them," Macer guessed.

"It doesn't matter where they are! We're going to crush these vermin and end this once and for all!" Varro declared, making me realize that I had forgotten he was even there. "I think we've seen enough." He was turning to leave when he stopped, and looking slightly embarrassed, asked Silius, "If you're satisfied, *Praetor*? Or is there something else you need to see?"

"No, I think we know what we're facing," Silius replied. Then, in a surprise, he turned to one of the Centurions, except that it was not Macer, nor Carbo, but me to ask, "What about you, Centurion? I confess I was a bit skeptical, but given how this Aedui has positioned his *crupellarii* in the front line, and not in a position to exploit some breakthrough by the men equipped like us, I believe that you've been right all along. They're going to try to punch through our front line and get to us, and it will be up to you to at least whittle them down, so it's actually a question for you. Have *you* seen enough?"

Even if I had not, I was not about to say so, and I assured him that I had seen everything that I could from this distance, whereupon we turned to go, allowing Wigmar and the other trooper who I did not know to return to their spot to continue watching. Walking back to the horses, I was only partially paying attention to the talk between the others, my mind struggling to cope with the stark difference that comes from an abstract idea like men being clad in *segmentatae* from head to foot and the concrete reality of seeing them arrayed on a sunny slope in Gaul. I thought Macer was right, that if it was possible to do so, we would attack from the flanks; naturally, this all depended on how the *crupellarii* themselves were deployed, which we would not know until the moment it happened. I barely noticed the ride back, and Macer quickly gave up trying to engage me in conversation, while I was only vaguely aware that, for the moment, Varro and Silius seemed to set aside their feelings for each other, and were talking animatedly about what was coming. Since they saw us approaching, the men were all on their feet, and I saw that there were even more horsemen present in the sign that our full cavalry complement was present, which was comforting, although we still had no idea how strong the rebel cavalry was, or exactly where they were for that matter. There was a flurry of activity as both Primi Pili rearranged their Cohorts from their marching order into the order in which they would be deployed, and this was when Macer came to me.

"Hand command over to your Optio," he said. "The *Praetor* has decided that he wants you and your chosen men separated out now, and you're going to be in between ours and the 2nd's first line Cohorts. We're going to be on the right side of the road, and the 2nd on the left. You're going to be right behind us, in between the main lines."

While this made sense, it was also at this moment I realized that, as little time as we had spent in training for the fighting, we had not prepared at all for something as mundane as how we would be arranged for a march.

"But we don't even have any standards!" I exclaimed. "I didn't choose any *Signiferi*, and we didn't actually divide up in Century order! We're just evenly divided into four groups, and Saloninus and Closus command two, and Sabinus and I command the other two. We," I tried not to let the dismay show, "are going to stick out like a Vestal in a whorehouse!

Sacrovir will see us coming out of those woods, and he'll know something is afoot!"

"Gnaeus," Macer said gently, "I think that he's going to have his hands full with that bunch. I seriously doubt that he'll notice that there's a group of Romans marching without standards and in a different-sized formation. But," he held up a hand, "if it will make you feel better, I'll have a couple of *Signiferi* from the Tenth march with you."

After a brief discussion, what we settled on was to arrange ourselves as if we were two First Cohort Centuries, the ruse being aided by the presence of two *Signiferi*, then at the last moment, we would further subdivide into four groups. All I could think to do was offer up a brief prayer that the Aedui did not notice that we were actually about twenty men more for each of our counterfeit Centuries. There was one blessing, and that was that while I had been gone, Saloninus had been using his head.

"I took some men to the baggage train, and we broke out the siege spears, Centurion," he informed me. Before I could ask, he added, "And I made sure they deposited their javelins in the wagon. It wouldn't do for the fucking army to charge the boys for them."

It may seem a small thing, and in some ways, it is, yet it is impossible to understate how important it is to rankers to know that the hated entity known as "the army" is prevented from conspiring to cheat men in the myriad ways that have sprung up over only the gods know how long, although it was certainly an issue when my great-grandfather was marching for Divus Julius. I thanked him for his foresight, then once Closus and Sabinus were there, explained what was happening.

"We're going to have to give the boys a moment when they lay eyes on those *crupellarii*," I told them. "because I know I felt like I was kicked in the balls. For one thing, there's more than a thousand."

"How many more?" Closus asked in dismay.

"Close to a couple hundred, I think," I answered, though I very briefly considered giving a smaller number, but instantly understood that they could count as well as I could. "But," I felt it necessary to add, "it's not just the numbers. I've never seen anything like them in my life. The only thing I can compare them to is the description of those Parthian cataphracts I read about…somewhere," I finished vaguely, not wanting to get into a discussion about where I had actually read about them. However, this was also when the seed of another idea was planted, one that threatened to take over my mind, yet this was not the time for it. Shoving it to the back of my mind, I gave the necessary orders to get the men into their proper spot behind the eight front line Cohorts, and finally the column began marching to face the Aedui. The chatter was now at a minimum, which I actually welcomed because it allowed me to think more about what had come to me when I mentioned the Parthians, specifically the manner in which the Equestrians, when my great-grandfather was Primus Pilus and under the command of Publius Ventidius Bassus, or as he was more commonly known, Ventidius the Muleteer, had defeated the cataphracts at Mount Gindarus.

The tactics that had been developed by Ventidius were two-pronged; the first was the use of sling bullets made of lead, where the rough edges had not been filed off as is customary, and which had proven to be devastatingly effective in punching through the lamellar armor of both horses and riders. This was not what I was thinking about; not only did we not have any kind of ammunition for that, nor had we practiced with the sling for a few seasons, I was not sanguine that the missiles would be effective against the *segmentatae*, having seen how the smooth, curved plates tended to deflect sling bullets on those occasions where the barbarians we were facing used them. Nor was I considering how the Equestrian and Parthian positions were essentially the reverse of what we would be facing, since the Equestrians had been upslope, and had used the slope of the mountain to help build up speed as they went plunging downhill to dart in among the Parthians.

What I remembered was the Prefect describing what happened when the cataphracts were unhorsed, and how if the Parthians were knocked off their feet, it was next to impossible for them to get back up. What we need, I thought, is a way to get these gladiators off their feet, because with that heavy armor, they won't be able to get back up before one of the boys does for them. The question was, how to do it? Judging by what I had seen, I thought the comments about the relative size of these *crupellarii* were correct, that these men were larger than average, and that was for Gauls, who are larger than Romans. While size was also a criteria for the men I had selected, more than that was their fighting ability on their own merits and not as part of a team, and now that this idea was blooming in my mind, I cursed myself roundly for not thinking about pairing men so that one of them was larger than their partner. This, what I could only think of as an oversight on my part, did serve to occupy my mind so that I was barely aware of the two-mile march to the spot where Tribune Aviola was still waiting to report that there had been no movement on the part of the Aedui, who were clearly determined to fight this day. Packs were dumped, the Centurions and Optios performing the last-moment checks of their men, while the Pili Priores relied on their Optios to do that for their Centuries so they could inspect their entire Cohort. I took the limited amount of time available to inform Saloninus and the two Optios of my thoughts about trying to knock the *crupellarii* off their feet, but we could not arrive at a consensus until it was Closus' turn.

"Take out their legs," he suggested. "Use the siege spears, aim for their legs and try to hamstring the *cunni*."

"They have plate armor covering their legs," Sabinus pointed out.

"The front of their legs, yes," Closus countered. "But I was thinking about it, and I don't see how they could make sure the backs of their legs are armored as well, because how would they attach the plates? Did you get a chance to see if it's on both front and back, Centurion?"

Fortunately, I had seen several of them turned about, and I shook my head.

"It wraps around from," I pointed to the side of my leg in front of the tendon that is just below the kneecap on the outside, "here to here." I moved my hand around to the same spot on the inside. "The back is where it's laced on, and there's a decent sized gap between the segment protecting the lower thigh to the plate covering the lower leg, which is more or less a set of greaves."

"So if we target the back of the leg or the side of the knee, that should do it," Closus said, and while I knew this was an oversimplification about the ease of doing so, it was also the best idea; in fact, it was the only one.

With this decided, I was about to address the men, but the *cornu* sounded, forcing me to improvise, doing so by standing on the side of the road, which we were going to use the rest of the way since they knew we were coming.

"All right, boys," I bellowed repeatedly as the men under my command marched past, "you lot with the spears, I want you to look to take their legs out! That's the weak point, and if you can get them off their feet, those *cunni* won't be getting back up again! Your partner can finish him for you, but do *not* waste your time chopping them up into bits or looting their corpses! We're outnumbered as it is, so no fucking about!"

"You can count on us, Centurion Pullus!"

"We're going to gut these Gauls, Centurion! Mark our words!"

"With a Pullus leading us, how can we lose?"

This last comment was shouted by Vibius Perperna of the First of the Fourth, who I had used as a runner at the Angrivarian Wall, giving me a smile that was notable for the lack of teeth as he marched past, and I felt a surge of emotion at this show of loyalty and confidence. Once I shouted my instructions to the last of the handpicked men, I moved at a brisk trot back to where one of the borrowed *Signiferi*, this man of the Sixth of the Tenth, was marching as if this was his normal spot.

"What's your name?"

"*Signifer* Aulus Donatius, Centurion," he answered.

"Well, I have good news for you, Donatius." I grinned. "You don't have to stay with us once things get hot."

To my surprise, he actually looked disappointed, but we were still within the screening confines of the forest through which the Via Agrippa passes, but shortly after our exchange, I saw the open area a hundred paces ahead. As usual for an experienced Primus Pilus, Macer had thought things through, because rather than the standard practice of the First Cohort anchoring the right, with the other three Cohorts aligned to its left, since the road was roughly going to be the center of the battle line, he had arranged it so that the Fourth Cohort was leading the way, and once they were a couple hundred paces into the clear area, they executed a right turn. Carbo, on the other hand, had not done that, so that their First Cohort was immediately behind the First of the 1st. It could have been a mess, but thankfully, the Secundus Pilus Prior of the 2nd had kept his wits about him, meaning that he ordered them to execute a left turn even before the First Cohort did, enabling his Cohort to march behind the First to their spot to the left of the First Cohort, with the other two Cohorts following the lead of the Second. It is unusual to have two First Cohorts next to each other, but this was obviously what Silius wanted, although I had not been present for the instructions, but while it was definitely an accident, the confusion actually seemed to aid our own cause, because following the Fourth of the 2nd as we were, it meant that when I led my group of men to our spot just to the left of the road, we were immediately behind but about fifty paces away from the front line Cohorts, roughly halfway between the first and second line. To the Aedui, who were still arrayed in front of us but had stopped their fidgeting, with men dashing back to their spots from whatever they had been doing as they waited, it would appear as if we were just a part of the formation. In reality, we were essentially in the space between the front and second lines, which would become obvious when each of the 2nd's Cohorts executed their flanking march to move up to align with the First, who was already in position.

Stepping away from my men, I watched as Saloninus marched his men into position next to me on the opposite side of the road, and as planned, they were aligned in the normal spacing we use between Centuries and Cohorts, which is wide enough to allow mounted couriers to move in between carrying orders, part of the fiction we were trying to present that we were simply two Centuries from the First Cohort. Once the battle started, we would separate ourselves even more in order to flank the *crupellarii* from either side, who at least were now all wearing their helmets, which they had begun strapping on when we appeared out of the forest. Macer had seemed confident that the Aedui Sacrovir would not notice what would seem to be spare double-sized Centuries who were not in a spot that anyone with any experience facing Rome would expect, but I felt quite conspicuous, not seeing how Sacrovir, who I could not pick out but was certain was part of the mounted group sitting just behind the rearmost of the center formation, would not at least divine we had some special purpose.

"C-centurion."

I turned to look at Donatius, and despite our short association, I could see how pale he had gotten, perhaps because of the contrast with the wolf headdress.

"What is it, *Signifer?*"

As I expected, especially now that I saw his eyes seemed fastened on the gleaming mass of ironclad gladiators who were hoisting their shields and pulling their spears from the ground as they made themselves ready, the *Signifer* was obviously having second thoughts.

"Y-you said something about returning to my Century," he began, but I reached out and squeezed his shoulder, cutting him off.

"It's all right, Donatius," I assured him, and I meant it. "If I had a choice, I wouldn't want to face these bastards either. So," I gave a gentle but firm push, "get back to your Centurion, and give him my thanks."

Despite all that was happening, and my own tension, I could not suppress my grin at the manner in which he dashed away, although he was forced to dodge out of the way when the command group came trotting up, yet another change, since they would have normally either been with the third line, or perhaps just ahead of it and behind the second line.

"They're baiting him," I murmured, then felt a bit foolish since I had neither *Signifer* nor *Cornicen* standing with me.

Despite not having anyone to listen to my muttering, I knew without a doubt that this had to have been either the *Praetor* or the Prefect's idea, because Varro was not only lagging behind the others as they came and drew up immediately behind my men and between my force and Saloninus' on the road, but I caught a glimpse of his expression, and if anything, he was even paler than the departed Donatius. Later, I would learn that he had argued vociferously against placing themselves closer to the *crupellarii*, arguing that it would tip the Aedui off that there was some sort of trap in the offing. Which, I knew, was true enough, but I also was certain that this was not the real reason, nor was I alone. None of which mattered now, and I found myself switching my *vitus* back and forth so that I could continue wiping my hands on my tunic, although it was not all that warm. The sun was now about midway between noon and sunset, giving us more than enough time to slaughter each other, but we also knew that the next move was the rebel general's to make. We were not about to advance to contact; despite the slope being as gentle as it was, even a foot uphill makes it harder on the attacker, and if I had guessed correctly, they would make the first move. Additionally, because of the placement of the gladiators, with the Aeduan version of the Legions immediately behind them, to my eye there was no other option for them but to begin to move. Naturally, this was when they proved me wrong, because it was not the *crupellarii* who moved first, it was the missile troops on either flank who, immediately after a high-pitched horn call sounded, began moving downhill.

Lightly armored with boiled leather, if they were wearing any armor at all, these men, numbering what appeared to be about two thousand men apiece on either flank, moved rapidly, flowing downhill to where the ground leveled out a bit more than a quarter-mile away before spreading out in front of the center to present a line that roughly matched our eight Cohort wide front. As they assembled, we saw that they were in three groups composed of men carrying sheaves of light javelins, with these men naturally in the front since they had to be closer to fling their missiles, while behind them were slingers. The last group was the largest, roughly half of the total, archers dressed in what I discerned were four similar but subtly different colored tunics, the sign that there was at least three other tribes involved in this rebellion besides the Aedui, although I did not know enough about Gallic tribal colors to know which they were.

Because of our position, we were essentially spectators,

although I did bellow out a warning order for the men to lift
their shields up off the ground in the event that the archers
arced their missiles over the front line Cohorts, which I would
take as the sign that the enemy had an idea we had some sort
of special role. Happily for the men, their shields were not
needed, but very quickly the racket of missiles striking the
protection of our comrades ahead of us in their double Century
lines was so overwhelming that I could not have been heard by
Saloninus on the far side of his bunch. And, as inevitable as it
was unfortunate, the thudding of iron points striking wood was
soon joined by sharp cries of alarm, and even worse, of pain as
a man was either careless or unlucky and struck by either a
javelin or arrow. To this moment, the slingers had seemed
content to stand there, making me wonder what the plan was,
and I assumed that since their missiles travel on a flat
trajectory, once the javelineers expended their supply; I
counted that each man had about ten missiles in their quivers,
they would retreat, their day essentially done.

To this point, the front-line Centuries who were absorbing
the brunt of the punishment had managed to block most of the
missiles, although there was a trickle of men either limping or
dragging themselves out of the formation, with the men behind
them stepping forward as we are trained. The easiest way to
judge the casualties a Century and Cohort is suffering is by
looking at the rearmost ranks; the more ragged and uneven, the
heavier the losses, and to this point, at least the losses were
light. This was about to change, because I was wrong in my
assumption, and it was a mark of cunning on the part of
whoever made the decision, because instead of trotting
backward to a spot behind the slingers on some clearly
prearranged signal, the javelineers simply dropped flat to the
ground., while in the heartbeats before this, the slingers had
actually begun swinging their arms about so that, just as the
javelineers hit the ground, their missiles were already streaking
into the ranks. Compounding the damage, the slingers had
clearly been instructed to aim low, forcing the Legionaries in
the front rank to make an impossible choice between keeping
their shields elevated in order to block the arrows plunging
down from overhead or protecting their lower extremities. The

moans and screams that had been coming sporadically before increased in both quantity and volume, and from where we stood, it appeared as if some invisible force swept across the lines of both First Cohorts, which also informed us that the rebels were focusing their attention on them.

"Pluto's cock! They're getting slaughtered!"

"Shut your mouth, Fulvius!" I snarled.

Titus Fulvius had been in the First Section of the First of the Fourth since my father was the Pilus Prior, and more specifically, in the first file. He was considered, first by Marcus Macer, then by my father, and finally by me, to be the best of the rankers with a *gladius*, and the only reason he had not been snatched up as part of a plumping by the First was that he loved fighting too much to stay out of trouble. His back was a crisscross of old and newer scars, and the only thing that had saved him from scourging was that his Centurions valued his fighting ability too much to see it ruined, and I include myself in that. Now, in this moment, he had not said anything that I, or any of the other men watching was not thinking, but this is the sort of talk that, if it gets out of hand, can infect an entire Century.

"We haven't done our bit yet," I lowered my voice so that only he, and perhaps the men immediately around him, could hear, "so keep your nerve, Fulvius."

As I knew it would, this stung him, and he replied angrily, "You don't have to worry about my nerve, Centurion! When we get stuck in, I'll…"

He did not finish, because this was the moment that, on another horn signal, those archers, slingers, and javelineers positioned immediately in front of the *crupellarii* suddenly turned to their left or right, and dashed out of the way just as the gladiators began to move. The attack had begun in earnest, and on a day that was already full of surprises, there was yet another in store for us.

With the missile troops out of the way, my expectation that the *crupellarii* would use the momentum created by being higher to come at us at a rush proved to be ill-founded, and in the moment, I wondered if it was because Silius had not arrayed us closer to the base of the slope. Whatever the reason, the other thing I realized was that I had not seen these *crupellarii* in motion; they had been standing there waiting for us for almost two watches, the only change being that they had put on their helmets, and as we watched them descend the hill, something else became apparent.

"They can't move very easily at all, can they, Centurion?"

Even in the moment, I knew what Fulvius was doing, but he was right, and I said as much, then added, "That may be another reason they didn't come running down the hill. They may not be able to control themselves with all that weight."

The archers had continued their assault, albeit from a slightly different angle, but it was still focused on the first line of Centuries of both First Cohorts, and I began to wonder if Macer would order a relief in place with the second line of Centuries just fifty paces ahead of us, which included my Fifth. Since we had not been subjected to any punishment, I had been able to split my attention between what was going on to our immediate front and to the Fifth, although they were partially obscured by Caudex's Century. With Vinicius in my spot, it put my *Tesseraurius* Hybrida in Vinicius', and I noticed that he kept glancing over in our direction, which told me he was aware that I was watching, and the thought that, even with all that was going on, my officers were concerned that I was keeping an eye on them made me happy.

To this point, there were only two files that were short, and only by a man, but it was impossible to know who had been hit, or how badly, as the *medici*, of which Alex was now considered fully trained, and the clerks like Euphemios acting as stretcher bearers, had been steadily at work removing men to the rear. This was not the case for the Centuries in the front line, as the slingers and archers made it impossible for unprotected men to reach them, with the less injured men expected to remove themselves, or with the aid of one of their comrades provided they could do so while keeping their own protection up and in place since it does not just protect them but the man behind them from plunging arrows. The most severely wounded were identifiable by virtue of the fact that they curled themselves up in a ball under their shields, with as

R.W. Peake

little of their body sticking out as possible; the easiest were those who had collapsed where they fell and no longer needed help or protection. Because the second line was in between us, I could not see just how bad it was in Macer's Century, but there was a moment when the eagle of the 2nd suddenly vanished from view, although it was the sudden roar of alarm and anger that was most telling.

"They lost their *Aquilifer*! By the gods, they lost their *Aquilifer*!" someone shouted, from what sounded like about the third or fourth rank, but since these were not all men who had been under my command, I did not recognize the voice, and I confess, I was sufficiently rattled myself that I probably would not have reprimanded him even if I had known who it was.

It is impossible to overstate just what a bad omen an *Aquilifer* falling is among rankers, and officers, with only the loss of the eagle or the death of a Primus Pilus considered worse, but I certainly did not associate what befell the 2nd as any kind of hint of what was in our future, and their *Aquilifer* was quickly replaced as the eagle reappeared within a matter of a few heartbeats. The racket was still incredibly loud, and I did wonder if this was also part of the rebel strategy, to weaken the shields of the men they thought they were about to face, but frankly, since we had not taken any kind of punishment save for a handful of arrows that had overshot the mark, it was only an abstract worry. With the *crupellarii* moving towards us, our moment was approaching, yet they seemed in no hurry, moving with a ponderous slowness that indicated just how difficult it might be wearing this much armor, although I was not yet altogether convinced that it was not a ruse. Up on the hill, the men equipped like us had begun moving as well, but instead of following directly behind the *crupellarii* to move into their vacated spot, they instead shook out in a line that spread across the slope to roughly match the width of our formation. In doing so, they demonstrated that just because they wore our armor and helmets, it did not mean they were trained to our standard, because instead of marching in unison in distinct units, they looked like a mob of *tirones* rushing from one spot to another. Regardless, by doing so, they made it

168

essentially impossible for our Cohorts on the wings to collapse down onto the *crupellarii*, who were now about fifty paces away from our first line, which forced the slingers to suspend their onslaught of the center of our line. Shifting their attention to the Cohorts on the wings did help quiet things down, but it was not much of a blessing because now that the sharp cracking sounds of stone bullets striking shields had subsided, the moans of pain, and calls for a *medici*, were impossible to ignore. The archers loosed one last volley on the First Cohorts before following the lead of the slingers, whereupon Paterculus, the 1st's *Cornicen* sounded the notes that signaled the Centurions of our Legion to begin bellowing their own orders.

"Ready javelins!"

The *Cornicen* of the 2nd followed a heartbeat later, which seemed to be how things were going, with Carbo essentially waiting for Macer to give a command, which in turn made me nervous because, in a similar manner to what the Aedui missile troops had just done, our counterattack hinged on the men in front of us getting out of the way quickly.

"*Release!*"

This was my signal, and I bellowed, "All right, boys! Shields up and out! Wait for my command!"

By the time I was finished, the javelins of the first volley had landed, but I was too busy looking at the men under my command, both my groups and those commanded by Saloninus to see the effects.

"Ready javelins!"

This time, I turned just in time to watch as the second volley was launched and able to witness for the first time what I learned later had already been noticed by our comrades during the first onslaught.

"They're not raising their shields!" I heard someone gasp, and since nobody ever spoke up later, I assume that it was me, since that was the first thing I noticed, but it was the second thing that made my blood freeze, although this time, it was not me who shouted the most important part.

"Our javelins didn't do a fucking thing to those bastards!"

This time, I did not utter a word of reprimand to Fulvius,

because I was every bit as dismayed to see that, for the most part, the rightly famed and feared Roman javelin, designed by the great Gaius Marius, had very little effect. One reason our javelins are so devastating is that, even if the enemy blocks it with their shield, the hardened triangular point punches through wood, even when it is several layers thick, while the combination of the soft iron shaft and the wooden pin that is designed to shear off by the weight of the shaft as it falls towards the ground, thereby causing the soft shaft that is still affixed to the wooden part of the shaft with a second pin of iron, to bend immediately, rendering the shield useless because of the effort it takes to yank the triangular point out and how awkward it is to wield their protection with a shaft hanging from it. However, the Aedui had negated this by simply refusing to raise their shields, but while this should have meant devastating punishment to the men wielding them, we learned something else this day, that our *lorica segmentata* and its smooth, curved surfaces are uniquely suited to deflect our javelins. It would not be until after the fight, and the *crupellarii* armor was examined and the gouge marks and deep grooves where the point of our javelins had struck then slid off were found that it was determined why this had happened. In the moment, it was as if we all suffered a collective punch to the gut when we saw, with no more than a dozen exceptions where a particular Gaul's gods had turned their gaze away so the unfortunate was stricken in the one vulnerable spot, the eye slits, that the *crupellarii* formation was still standing amid a few hundred bent and ruined javelins, seemingly impervious to one of our most potent weapons. It was probably no more than four or five heartbeats, during which it was as silent as it could have been on a battlefield where men had already been struck down, that the same high-pitched horn sounded from the Aedui side, whereupon the *crupellarii* began moving, still not running, or even moving that quickly, directly for our center. This elicited an immediate response from behind us, when Silius' *Cornicen* blew the one, long single note that had been agreed on beforehand that was our signal.

"Right, boys! Ready!"

It was a needless order; I could see that every one of my

men had their shields up off the ground but held out to the side, which is the only manner in which we can move at full speed, while our First and Fourth Centuries, the pair immediately in front of Saloninus and Closus, immediately pivoted to their right and went running in the same direction in the manner of a curtain being drawn aside, nor was I surprised to see that Saloninus was ready, and with a huge collective roar from not just the men given the assignment of stopping these heavily armored gladiators, but every comrade in the entire 1st Legion, they went rushing at the *crupellarii*...leaving us behind. As I sit here, dictating this to Alex, I realize that when I say that the 2nd was only perhaps two full heartbeats behind Macer and the 1st, it does not seem like much, but when you are standing there, already soaked in sweat despite doing nothing more than standing there for perhaps a sixth part of a watch, and you see the coordinated attack that is absolutely crucial to success being destroyed because of what, especially in the light of later events, was proven to be due to the incompetence of one Primus Pilus, perhaps it explains why, if Carbo had been anywhere near me as, at last, I led my men in an even faster rush at the *crupellarii*, I would have cut him down where he stood; thankfully for both of us, he was standing with the Legionary who was now acting as his *Aquilifer* just a pace or two out of my reach, his eyes wide with the kind of fear that is understandable with a *Tirone* in his first battle, or even a paid man like I was at one time, but not the man leading one entire Legion.

Even so, despite the fact that I launched into an all-out sprint that was much faster than I had planned, I still managed to bellow, or snarl, "Go back to the fucking Praetorians, you useless *cunnus!*"

He shouted something at me, but not only was I already past him, I was looking ahead at our foes, seeing that even in the less than a heartbeat I had had my attention on Carbo, they had *finally* broken into a run at us, the first understandable thing they had done to this moment. I call it a run, but that is being charitable, yet even with what was coming, I can recall sensing in that moment why they had not done so until the last possible instant given that it was more of a lurching, rapid stumble forward that was barely the speed of a trot. Even so, it meant I had even less time to give the next order, the one that we hoped would give us the advantage.

"Follow me, boys! Time to flank these bastards!"

I was already veering to my left as I shouted, and I could see Fulvius out of the corner of my eye, but he was already a step ahead of the others in the front rank, yet just when I was about to cut my stride to restore our cohesion, I saw that there was actually an advantage to be had, as Saloninus and his men had been just a couple heartbeats ahead of us in their sudden turn to the *crupellarii*'s left. With their peripheral vision so restricted, and in the sign that, while they may have been trained to a certain point they did not possess the same level of discipline expected of the Legions, I saw that several enemies on our side who should have been completely focused on us had actually turned their bodies slightly in Saloninus' direction, another sign that their head movement was restricted by the straps that secured their helmets.

Consequently, I made the decision to take advantage of this momentary distraction rather than leading my men a bit closer to the base of the hill before assaulting them from the flank, and I pointed with my *gladius*, roaring, "At 'em now, boys! *Kill these mentulae!*", or words to that effect, even as I selected the gladiator closest to me who had his body turned towards Saloninus' side the most.

The noise was overwhelming, yet it only seemed to be us doing it, though there was another noise I had never heard before in a battle; only a few heartbeats later did I realize that, contrary to my initial impression, the *crupellarii* were not silent, and were answering our shouts and bellowed challenges with their own, but their helmets muffled their voices to the point that it sounded as if one was shouting into a bucket. As I hoped, my first adversary was unable to pivot about quickly enough to bring his shield around, yet I had the impression that he was not all that alarmed, something that others would confirm later, counting instead on the combination of their size and their *segmentata* to protect them, and as most of the men would learn very shortly, they had good cause to feel this way. However, such was not the case with my foe, who only made what could be called a half-hearted attempt to knock my blade aside with his spear, seemingly content to allow me to execute my thrust, confident that his segmented armor would protect him.

If it had been Fulvius, or any of the other men, it might have been justified, as we were about to discover, but despite it being more than sixty years old, the *gladius* that had once cost a huge Gregarius more than a year's pay, with its darker metal with the barely visible whirling patterns, punched right through the iron plate, yet even in that instant, I felt the extra resistance, and I suspect that if it had been anyone but me wielding that blade, while it might have penetrated, it would have not likely been a killing blow. The shriek of pain that issued from the *crupellarius* was one of the oddest I had heard, with both a muffled yet echoing quality to it, while he immediately dropped both weapon and shield to grab at my blade in what I assumed was an attempt to keep me from ripping it across his midsection, but I did not do that on this occasion, choosing instead to try and use my *gladius* as a method to steer my dying enemy into the man standing next to him, who was even then just beginning to turn clumsily about and bring his shield up. I was only partially successful because the second *crupellarius* managed to get his protection up just in time to catch his dying comrade on it as I was forced to compensate for the greater weight of my initial foe, between his size just a couple inches shorter than me, large through the chest, and the extra pounds from being clad in iron from head to toe, my legs churning as I felt the blade sink deeper into his body.

For the first time, my face was close enough to see my enemy's eyes through the large slits, wide with the pain and fear to the point that I saw more white than the colored part, while he continued shrieking something that, even if it had been in Latin, would have been unintelligible because of the helmet. My progress was stopped suddenly as the second man dug his own heels in, and for a moment, there were three of us pressed together, then with one last audible moan, the first *crupellarius'* helmet slumped forward, though not much because of the securing straps, but it gave his comrade an opportunity to make an offensive move of his own. Fortunately, I saw him let his spear slide down a bit, putting his hand closer to the point, making it more of a close quarters weapon, so I was ready with my own *vitus* to knock the point aside when he thrust it at my face, just over his dying or dead comrade's helmet. He tried it again, then again, but before he could execute a fourth thrust, he gave a scream that sounded almost identical to the noise my initial foe made, then vanished from sight behind the slumped corpse of the first rebel who I was still holding up through the hilt of my *gladius*; most crucially, his dropping to the ground freed my victim from the pressure from behind that was holding him more or less erect, and he slid surprisingly smoothly from my blade.

This was when I saw Fulvius, who was armed with one of the spears just as he made a well-aimed thrust with it down into the eye slit of the second *crupellarius*. Something that I have noticed that both my great-grandfather and father have mentioned in their own accounts, which makes sense given how we expect those who will be reading this to follow in our footsteps, is how that all that I have just described takes much longer to dictate to Alex than it took when it happened. As difficult as it is to gauge time at moments like this, my best estimate is that from the instant I initiated my attack on the first *crupellarius* to the moment where Fulvius finished the second gladiator off after almost amputating his left leg at the knee with the siege spear, no more than three or perhaps four heartbeats had elapsed. It was long enough, however, for most of the men with me to slam into the *crupellarii* from their front rank to several ranks deep, while Sabinus and his group, just behind us, actually did what I had originally intended, rushing past us to press the attack farther towards the base of the slope from the left flank. I paused just long enough to determine that we were now fully engaged with the *crupellarii*, and had for the moment stopped them. This was the last moment where things went as expected, for the entire battle.

Chapter 5

The Gauls are renowned for their abilities at working metals of all kinds, but while the quality of their weapons is well known, and which the Prefect's Gallic blade is a testament to, what we learned on this day facing the Aedui and the *crupellarii* was that this extended to their armor, at least as far as the *crupellarii* were concerned. Despite the fact that our approach in pairing men up and attacking from each side was proving successful, it became apparent very quickly that at least one more pair had to devote themselves to protecting the attacking pair, and just as rapidly it became a completely disorganized mess of a fight. While I was wearing my bone whistle around my neck, I never used it for the simple reason it was not needed, the fighting looking instead more like the kind of brawl one would see in a *taverna* between men of different Cohorts or Legions, and since there was no reason to supervise and call a relief, I got stuck in myself. It was immediately after Fulvius and I dispatched our first two *crupellarii* that, over the clashing of metal and deeper thudding when a shield blocked a blow, one of my men, Manius Caninus of the Fourth Cohort, shouted in frustration.

"Our fucking blades are useless, Centurion! We can't stick these *cunni* with them!"

This was the first such statement, but it was far from the last as it became apparent that only the siege spears proved effective in penetrating the *segmentata*, which in turn meant that, as long as an individual gladiator kept his feet, he only had to worry about one of his attackers, treating the second as more of a nuisance. Before I could respond to Caninus, I saw an example of what he had shouted, when one of my men in the first rank, Lucius Curio, executed a first position thrust that I would have been proud to claim for my own, aiming for the *crupellarius'* right side underneath his arm, which was extended because he had just executed a thrust of his own on Curio's partner, Numerius Spinther, who blocked the thrust with his shield. It should have been a killing blow, but instead, to my utter shock and dismay, while his blade pierced the plate, I could plainly see that it did not penetrate more than an inch or perhaps two at most. Certainly, it was painful, as I just barely heard the muffled shout of agony from the *crupellarius*, who yanked his spear cleanly from Spinther's shield to make a wild, sweeping blow that Curio dodged, though it did serve to send him a step backward, momentarily taking him out of range, and most importantly to his foe, remove the blade from his side. Only because Spinther did not hesitate, and remembered to aim for the *crupellarius'* legs, although the gladiator did manage to drop his shield and partially deflect the point downward, did my man score at all. While it did not drop him, the *crupellarius* did stagger slightly, but when Curio drew his arm back in preparation to step forward to make another thrust, I am afraid that I none too gently shoved him aside, certain that it would be as futile the second time.

The *crupellarius* was making noise, yet it did not sound like a shout of pain, and while he had staggered a bit to his left, Spinther having managed to slice into the back of his calf in the area where the greaves were laced, he was clearly able to see me coming because he aimed a thrust of his own that caught me by surprise, his cause aided by my closing with him. This was just another occasion where I have no memory of what I did or how I did it, just that in one instant there was a spearpoint less than an eyeblink away from plunging into my chest, then it was caroming off the double layer of mail of my shoulder, enough to slow me slightly but not stop me, and once the point was past me, he was a dead man, and I suspect he knew it.

Now that I had experienced what it took for a killing blow, this time, there was no question of not using enough force, putting my weight behind the thrust that I aimed for the center of one of the plates, not wanting my blade to be trapped where they overlapped. Despite being prepared for it, there was no denying the extra amount of force that it took to penetrate the plate and drive my blade deeply into his body, while my reward this time was a sudden spew of blood that sprayed through the holes in the helmet in front of his mouth, and I was close enough to feel the spatter on my chin and throat, yet I no longer cared, feeling fully in my element now that the battle was joined. As satisfying as this victory may have been personally, it only took a glance around me to see that the problems Curio and Spinther encountered were shared by all of my men. It was not so much that we were not inflicting any damage; it was just not nearly enough to keep the *crupellarii* at bay, and I watched with a growing horror as they absorbed what punishment we could inflict, yet despite this, they had resumed their movement towards the command group. The only positive was that they were not moving quickly enough to stop Silius and the others, which included Sacrovir, from simply removing themselves, but it was at that very moment when I began thinking that the situation was not as dire as it appeared that the high-pitched horn used by the Aedui sounded again, followed instantly by another roar of thousands of men, this time from the throats of the rebels equipped like us, and since they were not as heavily encumbered and used the slope to build up their speed, they came hurtling towards our front line with a terrific speed.

I only had enough time to register what was happening in the larger sense before a shout in Latin drew my attention away, which I instantly regretted because while I was in time to see one of my men, a ranker from the Seventh Cohort recommended by Sabinus, knocked down by his foe, I was unable to do anything but watch helplessly as the *crupellarius* slew the man, his shield having been knocked from his hand. What took a heartbeat to register was that when the *crupellarius* swung his arm down, it was not the kind of motion one performs if using a spear or a *gladius*, and I barely caught the sight of the ax that slashed down into my ranker's face, which instantly vanished in a welter of blood, bone, and brains. For the span of about a heartbeat, the *crupellarius* was vulnerable as he tugged at the ax, which he had swung with such vicious strength that the blade must have gotten trapped in the dead Roman's helmet and skull, and the slain man's partner did not hesitate attacking with his siege spear while unleashing the kind of thrust that would have normally transfixed his foe at the precise instant he freed his own weapon, yet while it was a killing blow, once again, the segmented armor proved especially tough to penetrate. Regardless, the *crupellarius* dropped to his knees, the ax dropping from his hand before he toppled over onto his victim, although my attention was on the ax, though as I admitted immediately afterward and repeat now, it was more out of desperation than any idea what I had in mind would work.

"You there!" I bellowed at the man with the spear, having forgotten his name. "Drop your spear and grab that ax and come with me!"

He was clearly startled, and when he looked at me, I saw that, even in this moment as men were trying to kill each other all around us, he was as anguished by the death of a comrade as he was infused with the kind of rage that it takes to survive, but what mattered was that he gave a curt nod, then snatched the ax lying next to the corpse of both his friend and the foe he had just dispatched.

"You're with me," I told him, although I still did not have a real idea of what I was doing. Catching sight of Sabinus, who was directing four men who had formed a line that was effectively preventing a handful of *crupellarii* from getting to one of their comrades who had become isolated and was fending off a pair of men who were employing the original tactic we had developed, I grabbed the man by the shoulder to turn him in that direction. Using my *vitus* to point one of them out, I ordered, "I want you to go bury your ax in that *cunnus'* back!"

"Do you think that will work, Centurion?"

I could not blame the ranker for his skepticism given how this battle was progressing, but I had begun to sense that, along with the frustration that the men were experiencing, there was a growing apprehension that these *crupellarii* might prove to be too much for us to handle, and while none of us would like asking for aid, albeit from the second line Cohorts now that we could see that the counterfeit Legionaries of the Aedui were now all around us and engaged with our front line, I felt certain that I was not alone amongst my men when I did not see how the rest of our army would have any success with these heavily armored bastards, given that they did not even have the siege spears.

Nevertheless, I snapped, "There's only one way to find out," then gave him a shove. "So go do your fucking job, eh?"

Normally, the glare he gave me would have earned him a swipe with the *vitus*, but what mattered was that he was moving. The *crupellarius*, occupied as he was knocking aside the spear thrust by one of the pair who had singled him out, did not even bother trying to avoid the slashing blow from the second man's *gladius*, which inadvertently put him in the perfect posture for the Legionary to bury the ax between his shoulder blades. Whether it was because of the extra power created by the kind of overhead, downward slashing movement used with a weapon such as the ax, or the weight distribution where most of the mass is concentrated in the head of the ax, what mattered was that, despite the segmented armor plates protecting his back, the blade sliced through them and severed the man's spine. I heard the blow even over the din, the *crupellarius* not surprisingly collapsing immediately, as both his spear and shield slipped from hands he could no longer feel as he toppled over to land facedown.

This was all I needed, because in that short span of time as I waited for my man to attack the gladiator with his appropriated ax, I had seen that it appeared as if one out of every four of the *crupellarii* wore an ax on their *baltea*, and I spotted a couple who had either lost or discarded their spear and were wielding them, causing me to bellow over and over, "Take every ax that you find, boys! Take every ax from these *cunni*! That's the only thing that will kill them!"

I have no idea how many times I shouted this, but gradually, men began paying attention, naturally searching among the dead or disabled *crupellarii* first, but when it became obvious there were not enough to arm more than about four sections' worth of men, I had to decide how to address it. By this point, perhaps a count of five hundred into the battle, the situation was as confused as I had ever seen it, with the front line Cohorts too heavily engaged to divert any men to help my group, who at least had not suffered all that many casualties, only because as impervious as they were to every *gladius* but mine and perhaps a dozen other men, including Saloninus and Closus, both of whom had invested a substantial amount in a Gallic-forged blade of their own, they were too slow in their movements to pose much of a threat against men who were paying attention or did not make an error.

Our main problem was that it was clear that we were essentially a nuisance and not much more to the heavily armored *crupellarii*, and while the siege spears were proving to be effective, we did not have enough, nor were we killing or disabling enough of the gladiators with axes to completely stop them. Their progress had been slowed, yet they were still moving, so that I now had to worry about the rear ranks of the Aedui who had flowed downhill around us to attack Macer and our comrades in the First, and Carbo's Cohort, who were now about fifty paces away from the rearmost rank of my men, who were no more than two men deep, with those men bracing a comrade with a siege spear as he thrust at one of the gladiators. We were not losing, by any stretch, but this was far from the easy victory that even Silius expected, especially given the remarks I later heard he made to the Cohorts near his position shortly before the battle was joined, which I saw with a growing concern, he had not moved from his spot immediately behind the first line, and of course none of the others would budge as well. I briefly considered trying to send a runner back to the baggage train to retrieve as many axes as he could gather and convince some volunteers to bring them back, but I could not see a way to do it with any hope for success.

Deciding that our only hope was to seize more axes from the *crupellarii*, I was beginning to think through how to go about that when, from our left flank, the mystery surrounding the location of the Aeduan cavalry was solved. Using the bulk of the hill for cover, they had taken the long way around to come slamming into the left flank of the 2nd, the Fourth and Seventh Cohorts taking the brunt of what was later calculated to be about five thousand horsemen, many of them from our own cavalry auxiliary units throughout this part of Gaul. Because Silius had positioned our cavalry in the customary spot on the right wing, and because of the mass of men trying to kill each other in between, they had to turn about, then gallop across the rear of our line before swinging around the third line Cohorts of the 2nd to engage with the Aedui cavalry. Which, we quickly learned, was exactly what that bastard rebel Sacrovir wanted, although even in the moment, I had to give the man a bitter salute for waiting until Decurion Chlothar led his force until the inevitable laggards were about even with the Eighth Cohort of my Legion, dead in the middle of the third line before, for yet another time, that fucking thin wail of the Aedui horn sounded again, this time to unleash the twenty thousand men who we had dismissed as nothing but a mob that would pose no threat on their own, which was true enough if we were not already hard pressed. Also, for yet another time, we witnessed the one advantage the lack of order that is a feature of barbarian tribes possess over Rome, and that was in how rapidly they came bounding down the gentle slope, flowing like a raging tide of rusty brownish water, except that this flood was armed with spears, swords and axes.

I cannot lie; when I saw how they immediately changed their direction to go streaming past us off to our right, clearly intending to slam into our comrades in the same manner as their cavalry was doing to the 2nd, I was more relieved than concerned, and all I can say in my defense was that I had my own problems. More quickly than I could have imagined possible, we went from being confident of victory to being enmeshed in a fight for our very survival, and in that moment, I did not see a way to win. Then, matters became even worse when, from behind us to our left, another horn sounded, but while this was a Roman *cornu*, it was the notes being played that almost created a disaster.

"The 2nd is withdrawing? *What the fuck are they doing?*"

Despite myself, and all that was happening with my command, I could not stop myself from spinning about, just in time to see the 2nd's eagle, which was all that I could see between the counterfeit Aedui Legionaries slashing and thrusting against the front ranks of the First Cohort, begin moving backward, hearing the shrill sound of the bone whistles as the Centurions performed the count we use when we withdraw. As confused as it was, as little as I could see, I did know that, depending on how far the 2nd retreated, we might be in imminent danger of being surrounded on three sides. Then, the gods intervened, but as I had read from my great-grandfather's and father's accounts, and learned firsthand, the gift given to the Pullus men is one that carries with it a great price, and in this case, it was that, during my instant of inattention, Sabinus found himself cut off and surrounded by himself, with his men unable to reach him.

"*Centurion! Sabinus is in trouble!*"

I do not believe that I could have turned about any more rapidly than I did, and I will say I was already moving, albeit for the spot I had last seen Sabinus, but all it meant was that I was just in time to see him slain with a thrust from behind by a *crupellarius* who had managed to take advantage of the confused fighting to thrust his own spear, similar to our siege weapons, into my former Optio's back with enough force that he was transfixed, the point bursting out of his chest, his head dropping, and I was in the unfortunate position of seeing his expression, more of surprise than pain. In that instant, I was assailed; not physically, but by a rush of memories and images of my short time in the Praetorians, where I had an Optio I did not fully trust but who turned out to be a capable, and most importantly, loyal man, a proven veteran of the very Legion who was in that moment deserting us, one who I felt strongly enough to prevail upon Primus Pilus, now Camp Prefect, Sacrovir, who at that moment was sitting his horse not more than fifty paces away, to offer this man a spot, not at his rank, but as a Gregarius. While it was a different kind of combat in the streets of Rome, and was waged mostly against fellow Praetorians, Publius Canidius Sabinus had proven steadfast, and had regained his rank within a year of his return to the Legions. Now, he was dead, and I was barely conscious of the fact that I was moving, my great-grandfather's *gladius* in my hand as the beast that resides in me, that scares me as much as it terrifies those who have seen it aroused, came roaring up from deep inside my gut, and I only recall one, overwhelming desire...to kill.

(*Alex: Even now, almost four years later, Gnaeus does not have much memory of what took place, or he claims not to, but*

Sacrovir's Revolt

I spent the next several days doing nothing but listening to the men who had been present, including attending the questioning of a handful of the crupellarii *who survived immediately after the battle. In fact, it is still a fairly common topic of conversation in the* tavernae *in Ubiorum even now, particularly since there has been relatively little action of that sort otherwise. On that day, I was working as a* medicus, *with Euphemios and Lucco acting as stretcher bearers, so I only had an occasional moment to glance over to where Gnaeus was leading his chosen men against the* crupellarii, *and I definitely noticed that while he and his men had managed to slow the gladiators, who had clearly taken the bait provided by Silius, they were still moving, albeit slowly. I was too far away and too involved in my own tasks to understand what the problem was, that the standard issue* gladius *carried by virtually all of the men was unable to pierce the iron plates that comprised the armor of the rebel gladiators. What I was aware of was that this fight was much tougher than anyone, from* Praetor *down to the lowest* Gregarius Ordinarius, *had expected, and that was even before* Primus Pilus Carbo's *nerve failed, for that is exactly what happened, no matter what the official record may reflect.*

When the Aeduan cavalry suddenly appeared from the clump of trees that screened the view of the shoulder of the low hill to our left, I was in the process of tying a tourniquet around the lower arm of a ranker, lying to him that the surgeon would be able to save his arm, something that a medicus *learns to do with a conviction that is important to the wounded man, and to the bearers who have to carry him back to the rear. The sudden roar, quickly accompanied by the vibration up from the ground created by thousands of pounding hooves, caused me to tighten the tourniquet too tightly, in turn causing the ranker from the Fifth of the First to groan and writhe, making me feel terrible, and I apologized profusely. Euphemios and Lucco were loading him onto the board, and I saw my fellow clerk staring over in the direction of the 2nd, reminding me that while he has some experience in these situations, he had never been in a truly hard-fought battle, not being in the Legion for either Idistaviso or the Angrivarian Wall, and I am afraid I had to*

183

speak to him rather sharply to get his mind back on his job, while I tried to forget the ordeal at the Long Bridges, my first real taste of a hard fight where I became a combatant.

In the momentary lull before I heard another call for a medicus, I took the time to more carefully examine the scene, and even with the bulk of the 2nd in between where I was standing and their left flank, I felt my stomach lurch at the sight of how quickly the enemy cavalry had already penetrated, their longer blades slashing down onto the upraised shields of the surprised men of the Fourth Cohort while, as I watched, more horsemen arrived, flowing around their comrades to slam into the Seventh Cohort, with similar effect. I suspect that within the span of twenty normal heartbeats, the Aeduan cavalry had already rolled back the outermost two Centuries of the Fourth in their double line, shoving them into the Centuries to the left. I waited for Carbo to sound the signal for the third line, which for some reason the Aeduan horsemen had not engaged, to move into position to support their beleaguered comrades, but while I was expecting the cornu to sound, the notes that were played were so utterly unexpected and shocking, that if a stray Aeduan had managed to get close to me, I would not be here today.

"What is that cunnus doing?" I heard from behind me, turning to see Primus Princeps Posterior Caudex.

The answer was obvious, but I was close enough to see the collective look of shock and dismay on the part of not just the nearest men of the 2nd, but their Centurions, yet I was not altogether surprised to see them clench their bone whistles in their mouths, then begin blowing the count. As Romans under the standard, the habit of obedience is so ingrained that by the time a man is wearing the transverse crest, there was no hesitation on their part to obey an order that it was plain to see with which they did not agree. My attention was diverted by the shout for a medicus, and I turned away, a bit nervously I will admit, not liking the idea of having enemy cavalry behind me, especially when the Romans in between us were being withdrawn. That, however, was before what came next, perhaps ten heartbeats after I had turned about and spotted the ranker waving to me as he stood over a fallen comrade who *was writhing on the ground as he clutched his thigh. I was still a couple paces from reaching him when, from up the slope another blast from the higher-pitched Aedui horn that sounded to my ears more like the* bucina *sounded, but it was the unleashing of the relatively colorful mass of rebels attired more like what we had become accustomed to facing the German tribes to come sprinting downslope that stopped me in my tracks.*

"Pluto's thorny cock! *Those bastards are heading for our flank!"*

I had no idea who shouted this, but that was exactly what they were doing, yet I somehow managed to shake off my fear to kneel down to check the ranker, the hardest thing next to ignoring the idea that some twenty thousand barbarians were now streaming down the shallow hill to attack my Legion actually prying the ranker's hands from his wound. When I finally managed, I did not know whether to laugh, or curse, or cry for that matter, but for the first time, I looked into his eyes and saw that he was very young, with the wide, frightened eyes that are the normal look of a Tiro *experiencing his first battle.*

For the first time, it occurred to me to look up at the nearest standard and realize that I was not in the First but the Fifth Cohort, and when I looked up at the man's comrade, he explained disgustedly, "He got nicked by an arrow when their missile troops were pasting us. I told him it was just a scratch, but Afranius here kept picking at it, and now he says the bleeding won't stop. He," he shook his head, "is a useless bastard, our Afranius."

"I'm not lying, Sergeant!" Afranius began, but frankly, I was already done ministering to him, and I told him as much.

"I've already dressed it, Gregarius,*" I told him. "And the only way you're going to bleed to death from that is if you keep trying to widen it."*

It was the look of guilt that flashed through his eyes that told me the truth of it, but I was already standing, and I mention this only as an illustration of just how quickly the situation was changing, because I naturally looked in the direction of our right flank in time to see that the most eager of the lightly armed rebels had arrived to throw themselves at the Fourth, the Seventh, and unlike their cavalry, they had the numbers to assault our Tenth Cohort as well. In fact, it also became obvious that Sacrovir the Aedui, or perhaps whoever he had put in charge of these men who I know that we had discounted as a serious threat except for their numbers, had ordered the swiftest men to run the longer distance to engage with the Tenth first. Another difference, however, and one that would ultimately spell the difference was that the Pili Priores had not bothered trying to change the orientation of their outermost Centuries. Instead, they simply ordered every rank to face to the right. This served to make for a narrower rank but a deeper file for relief, and it also had the disadvantage of men fighting in our manner doing so with men on either side they do not train with regularly. The sight of the reinforcements clearly invigorated those Aedui who were equipped like their Roman foes, but it did not take an expert, or even someone like me who has witnessed several battles, to notice that, while they were similar in appearance to us, they were not organized in Centuries, nor were they commanded by professional Centurions who sounded the relief to rotate men. Instead, they fought in their normal style, as individual warriors who just happened to be equipped like their foes, which meant that their only options were either to withdraw from the fight on their own volition, only after vanquishing their foe of the moment, or to die after being overcome by exhaustion as our Centurions went about their business of blowing their bone whistles for the relief.

Not surprisingly, the 2nd's withdrawal had given the entire rebel force renewed energy, while the cavalry and the native warriors were still fresh, the horsemen now moving into the spot vacated by the front four Cohorts of the 2nd, the ground already littered with shattered shields, discarded helmets, and while there were not that many Roman corpses, given our practice of pulling men we can reach out of the fight, that did not necessarily mean our losses were light. I had just returned my attention back to where I had last seen Gnaeus, thankful that he at least is easy to spot, both because of his crested helmet and towering over other Romans as he does, but it took me an extra heartbeat to spot him; when I did, I almost wished

I had not, because what I saw was that he was now in the midst of what I guessed to be a half-dozen crupellarii, *without any of his men anywhere near him. Without thought, I felt my legs moving in that direction, when from the middle of the front line, I heard someone bellow for a* medicus. *Still, I did not move immediately, watching and hoping that another man would heed the call, despite recognizing I was closest, but I finally answered on the third shout for help, pushing up the file to where the fallen man had been pulled a couple ranks back. I do not recall anything about the wounded man I tended to, nor the next few after that, as the battle raged and my thoughts were completely on the fate of my friend and the Pullus it has been my fate and my choice to serve after his father, and I found myself offering up prayers to both Mars and Bellona that they had seen fit to bless him with the divine madness that makes him a threat to anyone within reach, which was exactly what happened.*

As of now, the official version of the final battle of what is now known as the Revolt of Sacrovir is that the battle was over quickly, the casualties suffered by Rome were relatively light, that the only slight difficulty was presented by what was later counted to be one thousand, two-hundred thirty-nine crupellarii, *whereas the bulk of the rebel army was dispatched with ease, including the eight thousand men attired in our armor. While Gnaeus has counseled me to be discreet, since this part of his account is mine and mine alone, he still has no real memory of his exploits other than the flashes of images that he says is usually all that he can recall, and considering for whom this is intended, I want to make it clear that the official account is a load of* cac, *an account that has been heavily influenced by the son of the official* Praetor *of the Lower Rhenus who, after his and his Tata's return to Rome, with the elder Varro dying shortly after this, has become even more powerful and is no longer disguising the fact that he is a patron of the Praetorian Prefect Sejanus. This is not to say that this is not understandable, given the conduct of not just the Legion representing the Lower Rhenus, but Varro himself, whose cowardice only escaped more notice and censure*

R.W. Peake

because of the actions of Primus Pilus Carbo.

While the battle would have been harder than any of us expected even if the 2nd had not withdrawn, their exposing the left flank of the 1st turned it into a desperate fight with half the men expected to battle a force of some forty thousand. Yes, twenty thousand of the Aedui rebels were lightly armed, poorly trained men, but there is a saying under the standard: "When the quantity is enough, the quality doesn't matter." That was certainly the case when we were shorthanded and tactically exposed. As much as I do not like to, in the spirit of the kind of honesty that we have both vowed to our household gods to uphold, as begun by the first Titus Pullus, the 2nd's withdrawal was temporary. Immediately after the battle, that night and the following day, the story around the camp was that it was due to Prefect Sacrovir, who galloped away from the command group to confront Carbo, berating the former Praetorian in front of his men and essentially shaming him into marching his Legion back into the fight. Unfortunately, the Prefect was not available to confirm or clarify this, but that is for later, and is Gnaeus' story to tell.

Nevertheless, the timing could not have been more propitious, that must be said, because with their withdrawal, the Aeduan cavalry had begun pressing the 1st, so that for a short period of time, our Legion was hard-pressed on three sides. However, even more than the tardy return of the 2nd, the consensus among the men of all ranks around the fires was that there were two other factors. One was when Decurion Chlothar, upon seeing the warriors on foot launch their attack shortly after he began leading his troopers around from the right to the left flank to confront the rebel cavalry, reversed his men on his own authority, a huge risk but one that paid off, both for him personally and, more importantly, for the 1st. The speculation among the men of the 1st was that his decision to come to our aid was based in how the Batavians have been attached to the 1st and 20th far more often than with the 2nd and 14th up in Vetera. According to my sources in the praetorium, *both Varro and Carbo tried to make an issue of it, but the Decurion stuck to his story, insisting that, in his view, twenty thousand infantry posed more of a threat than the five thousand*

188

cavalry, and nothing ever came of it, at least officially.

The second factor was the stopping of the crupellarii, *and to a man from Saloninus on down, they insisted that it was Gnaeus unleashing his rage, although I did not learn any of the particulars until after the* Corniceni *of the Cohorts began sounding the recall to their standards, which is the sign that the battle is over, and the process of attending to those wounded who had not yet been treated and recovering our dead can really begin in earnest. I am afraid that I disobeyed Primus Pilus Macer, although I pretended not to hear him calling my name, choosing instead to walk towards the slope, intent on one thing and one thing only, and that was to find Gnaeus. The fact that he was not immediately visible was disturbing enough, but I did spot Saloninus, who was in the process of getting a butcher's bill, but without the normal organization, with this* ad hoc *formation, it was a bit of a confused mess.*

I confess that by the time I reached his side, I was almost beside myself with worry, because I had naturally been scanning the faces and the shapes of the men lying strewn across the ground and had not seen a large Roman. Once one has witnessed the aftermath of several battles, one learns how to "read" the field, judging the ebb and flow, and the climax, of a fight, and the ground here told a tale of a hard-fought battle, where a disturbingly high number of the enemy dead appeared to have succumbed only after being hacked into bits. At the time, I was not aware of the ineffectiveness of our gladii, *but when I reached Saloninus, it was one of the first things I learned from him, though honestly, I was not as interested in this as I normally would have been given my state of anxiety about the whereabouts of Gnaeus.*

He saw me coming just after he pointed to a heap of entangled bodies where he wanted one of the men acting as a Sergeant to check for our wounded and dead, and without any preamble, he said grimly, "I thought we might lose this one, Alex. I truly did." His face was spattered with blood, though I could see it was not his, but when I pointed to the bloody bandage around his left forearm, he waved me away. "That's fine. It might not even need to be stitched up. We," he shook his head, *"couldn't penetrate their* segmentatae *with anything but the siege spears, and we didn't have enough of those."* I *suppose he realized how this sounded, that he might be blaming Gnaeus, because he added hastily, "Not that it's anyone's fault. I mean," he shrugged, but with just one shoulder, which indicated that he had another injury he was not telling me about, "how could we have known? The fucking Germans never had that much problem piercing our* segmentatae, *so why would we think we couldn't do it to these cocksucking Gauls?" He gave a laugh that was both humorless and bitter, saying something that would stick with me, "The gods know the Gauls know how to work metal, but it had to take a lot of time to fabricate armor of this quality...and a lot of money."*

I realized that Saloninus was rambling now, which is quite common with men after a battle; besides, my patience was already thin, so I asked bluntly, "Have you sent anyone to look for Centurion Pullus?"

It was the look that flashed across his features, the concern and guilt easy to see even in just his one good eye that made my stomach lurch, and he lowered his voice so only I could hear him admit, "I've been scared to, Alex." Turning, he pointed at a spot, and it was the one part of the battlefield that I had guessed might be the place where we would find him, where it looked like someone had directed the bodies to be piled, although it was far too early after the battle for this to happen. With a visible reluctance, he began walking towards that spot, some twenty paces away, and as I went with him, he said, "I didn't see what caused it, but one of the boys who saw it told me what started it. But," his voice took on a quality that, as grim as it was, I could clearly hear something like awe...and dread, "I saw what he did. It was like the other times everyone talks about with him and his father, but this time was...different."

This made me stop in my tracks, despite my desire to find him.

"What do you mean 'different'?" I demanded as I tried to recall if Saloninus had ever borne witness to the divine fit experienced by the men bearing the same name and the same

dark gift.

"*Remember, I was there for Segestes,*" *he reminded me, and I remember you telling me what he did to that big Parisii bastard Berdic. But before, we were facing Germans wearing their usual collection of armor and never men who were wearing this.*" *He kicked contemptuously at the helmeted head of a dead* crupellarius, *his chest plates split open and exposing his interior organs seemingly floating in a gleaming, gelatinous pool of congealing blood and gore. Suddenly, without any warning, he reached out to grab my arm, staring into my eyes with his one good one with an intensity that was unsettling.* "*But, Alex, I will tell you this now, before the gods, and I am going to tell the Primus Pilus, the* Praetor, *the Prefect, and the fucking Imperator if I have to, but Gnaeus singlehandedly broke this attack. They got so fixated on trying to kill him after he laid into them that the boys he armed with axes were able to cut dozens of them down. Then,*" *he shrugged,* "*they turned into typical barbarians, and were more concerned with running off than sticking together and acting like soldiers instead of a fucking mob. And,*" *he laughed then, but it was a mocking, cruel one,* "*I've seen tortoises that can move faster than these* cunni *could.*"

It was then I realized something else; Saloninus was as reluctant to confront the horrible possibility that Gnaeus had followed his father across the river as I was, so I forced myself to resume heading towards the heap of bodies. As we got there, Saloninus shouted for some men nearby who were absorbed in trying to determine the best way to strip the dead crupellarii *to loot their corpses, and while they joined us readily enough, it was easy to read in their expressions and the looks of sympathy they were giving me that they knew for whom we were looking.*

It took me a heartbeat to recognize one of the men as Quintus Gallus, who had been with us in Britannia, and he was the one who said simply, "*He saw Optio Sabinus fall.*"

This brought me up short again, and Saloninus apologized, "*Pluto's cock, I'm sorry! I forgot to tell you that. One of those* cunni *got behind him, and Gna...Centurion Pullus,*" *he corrected himself since it was no longer just us,* "*saw it happen.*"

I instantly understood then; as leery as Gnaeus had been about Sabinus on our arrival in Rome, he had proven himself beyond doubt, showing a kind of courage that was even more notable because it was actually not *on the battlefield against barbarians like this, but fellow Romans in the streets of Rome, and I knew that Gnaeus held him in high regard. In fact, I was struck, almost literally, by a random memory that Sabinus had been a guest at one of our meals in our apartment in Ubiorum about a month before we left on this campaign, where he had introduced his woman, a lovely young lady named Claudia Petronius, the daughter of one of the most prosperous bakers in Ubiorum, where he had proudly announced that she was carrying his child, their first, and even as I felt as if I had been punched in the stomach, I was reminded that it is this kind of loss that unleashes that thing inside these men bearing the Pullus name.*

Offering up a silent prayer for Sabinus and his widow as I worked, we began dragging the first corpses off a heap that was between my knees and my waist, quickly learning that not all of these men were dead, and I saw firsthand the difficulty involved when one of the men tried to finish them off. Because their helmets are strapped onto their armor, it was not a matter of just yanking it off and slitting their throats, and the men did not even try to end them with a thrust with their gladius, *a potent sign of their recognition of how ineffective they were. Fairly quickly, the preferred method became using their* pugio *to thrust it deep into one of the eyeholes, ignoring the muffled, echoing pleas for mercy, some of them even in Latin, but there was no mercy to be had by us, and I freely admit that I would have been incensed if any of our men had shown them any.*

Finally, I spotted a bare and very muscular arm, and I began shouting for help in dragging a corpse out of the way so that, for the first time, we could see his face, although it was completely covered in blood and gobbets of flesh, making him look like a general celebrating a triumph. His helmet was on but his eyes were closed, nor did he respond when I shouted his name, hearing the frantic edge to my voice and not caring; only later did I become aware that I tore a fingernail loose as I grabbed for any kind of purchase on the blood-slick armor of

Sacrovir's Revolt

the final corpse lying across his lower body.

"Is he...?"

Saloninus' voice was almost unrecognizable from just a few heartbeats earlier, but my own mouth had gone so dry so quickly that I couldn't get anything out. Then, I saw a flutter of eyelids, followed by Gnaeus opening his eyes, the whites standing out in such stark contrast to the blood caking his face that, as unreligious as I am, I still found myself making the sign against evil. He began blinking rapidly, which is not uncommon, but I also knew that it could be a sign of brain injury, yet there were no dents, or worse, punctures in the part of his helmet that was visible, as he was lying on his back, almost as if he had simply reclined on the ground for a quick nap. After what felt like a watch but was probably a half-dozen heartbeats, his eyes finally began moving about, and I could tell that he was looking at the faces peering down at him, going from one to the next, but then he frowned, and I almost fainted from the relief when he spoke, demanding, "Why are you all just standing there looking like oafs?"

While I had been praying for a miracle, that the blood that literally coated Gnaeus from his crest, which was so sodden that it had to be burned, to the soles of his caligae, belonged to the men he slew, in fact, Gnaeus suffered six different wounds. However, what was close to a miracle was that none of them were life-threatening, all but one of them involving his extremities, with the last one being the most visible, running equidistant from the edge of his helmet and the top of his left ear, moving diagonally down across his cheekbone, which was laid open to the bone, exposing his back teeth and ending just below the left corner of his mouth, not straight as one might expect from a bladed weapon, but in a jagged line that looked a bit like a lightning bolt, which I suspected would be noticed and commented on by the more religious men; even so, I have to admit that I have been quite surprised just how what might seem to be a battle scar has become a much more powerful symbol to not just his men, but the entire First Cohort.

He wanted me to stitch it up as I did with the other five, but I refused, something that he still reminds me about to this day, but as I said then, "As vain as you are, if you don't like the way it looks, I'd never hear the end of it."

While this was certainly part of it, the main reason was that, because of the jagged nature of the cut, I did not feel I was skilled enough to stitch it in a manner that minimized the scarring, thinking of Bronwen and how she was going to react upon seeing him. Otherwise, all in all, it was an astonishing thing that, once we had him back in camp, by which I mean that those slaves not involved as stretcher bearers or orderlies had performed the task of erecting our tents, their normal duty while the Legions dig the ditch and build the wall enclosing it, which was now missing, and in his quarters, where I washed away all the blood, which required four fresh basins of water, that he was in as good condition as he was. Despite his protest he could do so unaccompanied, I went with him to the quaestorium tent, which was already crowded, with the wounded still streaming in through the opened flaps, and I did feel a twinge of guilt that I was not there helping, but it was not strong enough to change my mind. Being a Centurion, he was given first priority, although he flatly refused to enter into the area sectioned off for officers, growling that he would not go lie down for a "couple of scratches" at one of the senior medici, Praxides, for trying to usher him in and sounding so much like his father when he did so that I felt the welling of tears threatening to unman me.

Fortunately, for all of us, Praxides is accustomed to dealing with Centurions, and he was not intimidated, retorting in his heavy Thracian accent, "Well, Centurion Pullus, unless you want your children to run screaming from you every time you enter the room, you better let Philippos attend to this. I am a fair hand, as," he nodded at me, "is Alexandros here, but if it was my face, and I wanted to fuck a woman again, there is nobody I would trust for this but Philippos. Not," he added meaningfully, "even Asclepios Solon himself. Now," he pointed to one of the benches placed next to the leather partition separating the officers, "sit down and I will fetch him immediately." He turned away in such a manner that only I could catch his wink, while I mouthed a silent thank you, both for his deft handling of Gnaeus and for the subtle manner in *which he handled another matter, one that I felt certain Gnaeus was unaware of, and that was the low regard in which the self-styled Asclepios Solon was held, not by his patron, Gaius Silius, but by the men who did the brunt of the work keeping Legionaries alive. In the judgment of Praxides, and essentially every other man who I had heard voice an opinion, Solon, who was in his fifties, and I will say did look the part of the Greek physician, was a fraudster who spoke knowingly of the great healers and the humors of the body, but had actually suffered the indignity of vomiting at the sight of one of the wounded men he was supposed to attend to soon after his arrival, but his greatest sin in the eyes of men with centuries of combined experience and the wisdom that comes from the battlefield is that he was in favor of things such as dung poultices for wounds that would not heal cleanly. More to the point, I knew that Gnaeus implicitly trusted Philippos, who had handled what was in essence a demotion from his post as the chief* medicus *for the Legion when Solon arrived, and perhaps most importantly at this moment, Philippos had at least been present for the aftermath of another of Gnaeus' fits, and would know what to expect with his mental state, and the lethargy that always sets in after one of them.*

This was what was running through my mind when Praxides called out over his shoulder, "After all, the Centurion is the hero of the day! The men coming in are talking about him and not about their wounds, which makes our job easier!"

I decided that it was best to determine what he did recall sooner rather than later, hating myself for doing so nonetheless.

"Do you remember what happened?" Thinking I was being unclear, I added, "I mean, to…"

"I know what you mean," he interrupted. He was sitting on the edge of the bench and staring at the ground, not looking at me, which was not unusual for his current state, saying dully, "Sabinus. I saw him…" He could not finish, heaving a sigh that was laden with so much emotion, and I saw the gleam of a tear rolling down his cheek, causing me to glance nervously about, which was somewhat silly given that there were men all around crying tears of pain; whether it was from physical

agony, or the kind of torment caused by the death of a comrade did not really matter.

Just as he was about to continue, Praxides reappeared with Philippos in tow, with the former carrying the necessary items, but I was watching Philippos, who was studying Gnaeus' face as he approached. He looked up at me with a raised eyebrow, and I felt certain I knew what he was asking, and I gave a slight nod, which he confirmed with one of his own.

Usually, Philippos could be counted on to give Gnaeus a few verbal jabs, usually about how frequently he found himself under the physician's care, though not this time, saying instead, "I know that you must be exhausted, Centurion, so let us get this taken care of. No," he held out a hand, "you do not need to go anywhere. I can do it well enough right here, provided," he turned to Praxides, "good Praxides here brings the tall stool so we can both be comfortable."

While Praxides was gone, Philippos carefully grasped Gnaeus' chin to tilt his head slightly as he squinted at the gash.

"Who cleaned this?" he asked, and when I said I did, he grunted, "Not bad. When it is jagged like it is…" Suddenly, he drew his head back a bit, cocked it and said, "I just realized that it looks like one of Zeus' lightning bolts! That is a good omen, Centurion! You have been marked by the great Zeus!"

He smiled broadly at Gnaeus, but Gnaeus did not seem ready to look for anything positive out of what he had just undergone, muttering, "It's not Zeus; it's Jupiter Optimus Maximus…" then, I saw the slightest hint of what might charitably be called a grin, "…you Greek pederast."

"It is Zeus, you Roman thief," Philippos retorted. "You Romans steal everything! You are a race of bandits, that is all! Stealing our wisdom, our women, even our gods!"

"Maybe," Gnaeus' grin started to widen, but it obviously hurt because he gave a sudden wince, though he still finished, "but at least we're good at it."

"Yes, yes, I know, I hear all about it all the time! How great is Rome! How mighty is Rome!" Philippos grumped just as Praxides returned with a stool with longer legs, onto which Philippos dropped down. "Now, shut your mouth, or," he waved a large needle that I knew he would not be using for this kind of work, and I hid my own grin at the sight of Gnaeus' eyes going wide, "I will use this needle instead of a small one, and I might just get carried away and sew that other big hole shut!"

"Oh, go piss on your boots," Gnaeus muttered, but this was the last thing he said for the duration of his ordeal.

Fortunately, Philippos is quite skilled, and I moved to a spot behind him to watch him work, noticing how much more closely he executed each stitch, while I was secretly proud of how the only sign of Gnaeus' distress was in how heavily he was breathing, otherwise not moving a muscle, or even blinking that much as he stared off into space. As he worked, Philippos explained why he was doing what he was doing.

"With the stitches this close together, and if you leave them in two days longer than normal, it will make the scar less noticeable," he explained, but I was not certain this was something Gnaeus cared about.

"Well?" I asked. "Who do you want to impress? Your wife? Or your men?"

Gnaeus did wait until Philippos signaled he was not about to stick him, and replied, "My enemies."

Both of us laughed, but then I saw Gnaeus was deadly serious; for his part, he must have seen my expression of surprise, and concern, because he explained, "Bronwen will love me no matter how I look. The boys?" He shrugged just his right shoulder. "They know me by now. No," he finished flatly, "I want to give anyone who thinks they might want to have a go at me to see this," he pointed to the side of his face, which was only partially stitched back up, "and have second thoughts."

"I don't think it's your face that gives someone a pause," I countered, then pointed at his arms. "I think it's those."

"Scars help," he said, and I knew by his tone he was serious...and that he was, and is, correct.

"Well, I am not going to undo what I have already done," Philippos grumbled, "but I will throw in just enough so that nobody can see your cheekbone and your teeth. And," he added, "you will have to drink and chew with the right side of your mouth."

He was working as he talked, and true to his word, he spread the remaining stitches out wider apart, but when he tried to bind Gnaeus' head with a linen bandage so that it wrapped under his chin and around the top of his head, he did not even make it around once before he was stopped just by Gnaeus' glare.

Only because I nudged him did Gnaeus deign to say, half-apologetically, "It's just that I won't be able to open my mouth very wide, or wear my helmet, Philippos."

"Then you are in danger of the wound corrupting the first two or three days before the stitches set and the scab hardens, so, Alex," he addressed me, "you must be vigilant and watch for the signs of corruption." I nodded, then Gnaeus was stitched up, which was good because the casualties were now flooding in, and I extracted a denarius *from my coin purse, which Philippos tried to wave off.*

Gnaeus reached out and grasped the medicus *by the shoulder, giving it a gentle squeeze, and I heard him whisper a thanks, but when Philippos tried to wave the coin off, which I had handed to Gnaeus, again, this time, Gnaeus said sternly, "No, this isn't for me. This is for my boys. See to them, eh? Both the boys in the Fifth and the men who were with me today. They deserve it."*

I could see that this both surprised and moved the medicus, *who could only nod, then we left the tent, just in time to see the return of a Legion, it taking us only a moment to see that it was ours, and that instead of marching into the forum before being dismissed, Macer led them directly to our area, which is an unofficial way to signal that it has been a hard fight. Despite my best attempts to convince Gnaeus that our Primus Pilus would not take it amiss if he returned directly to our quarters, he insisted on seeking Macer out, and within a matter of moments, I was feeling quite smug, at first anyway, though it turned quite rapidly into worry. That, however, is for Gnaeus to tell.*

I will be the first to admit that I did not really want to seek Macer out, desiring nothing more than to go to my quarters and drop onto my cot for some sweet oblivion, especially now that

I was in the time where the bits and flashes of images were coming back to me, almost always involving sprays of blood, or a severed limb tumbling into the air, or eyes widened in terror beseeching me for a mercy that would not come as I was ending their lives. Nevertheless, I was still sufficiently worried about my Century and how they had fared under Vinicius in particular, and the Cohort as a whole that I knew that I would lie on my cot, unable to rest. As Alex mentioned, the slaves not involved in shuttling the wounded had erected the tents as they normally did, with the only thing missing the ditch and walls that we would have constructed but instead had been involved in fighting for our survival. That made it easy to see the area surrounding the place chosen for our camp, which was just south of the strip of woods from which we had emerged, meaning that the hill was visible, its lower slope littered with bodies, amongst which were our field *medici*, and those clerks like Euphemios who doubled as stretcher bearers, searching through the piles of bodies for our men who were still on this side of the river, and when they found a man who had already taken Charon's Boat, they were separated and laid gently out in a line, from where they would be claimed by the survivors of the section to whom the dead man belonged. I did wonder about the men who had been part of my group and how their comrades from their regular Centuries would find them.

"Well, Centurion, you've looked better."

I had become so absorbed in my own thoughts that I did not see Macer approach me from up the Cohort street. Spinning about so quickly made me lightheaded, while bringing my arm up to render my salute tightened the muscles of my forearm, which had five stitches in it, and I felt the sharp stab of pain that briefly overshadowed the dull ache that I was now experiencing from my wounds. For his part, our Primus Pilus had his left hand wrapped, although he was holding his *vitus* well enough, but while he had clearly wiped his face, the lines in it that show his age were still embedded with grime, accentuating them to the point that it reminded me of the kind of makeup used in mime shows when one of the actors is supposed to portray someone much older. However, it was the expression on that face that concerned me, a grim one that, if one knew what they were looking for, was almost as good as reading the actual butcher's bill.

Once salutes were exchanged, I asked, "How about the Fifth? How many boys did I lose?"

I got a warning by his grimace as he extracted a tablet from the leather bag slung across one shoulder, opening it and squinting at its contents.

After a heartbeat, he confirmed my suspicions, replying grimly, "The entire Cohort took a beating, and your boys are no exception, I'm sorry to say. You've got eleven dead, two headed for Charon's Boat if they're not already in it, three men who lost an extremity and will be cashiered, two men who, if they survive the night, have a chance. And," he finished with a huge expulsion of breath, "you have twenty-seven wounded who are expected to recover to full duty, but almost half of them are too seriously injured to assume full duties for at least the next week, probably more."

At that moment, I was regretting my decision, if only because I would have preferred to at least be sitting down for this news, as it made me literally stagger, and it took a heartbeat for me to make the calculations.

"That's *forty-five* men!" I gasped. "I had one hundred seventy-two effectives when we left Ubiorum. That's," it took me another moment, "twenty-five percent of my Century!"

"Clepsina has fifty-eight men out of action," Macer replied, I suppose to console me, or perhaps not, since he allowed, "although he only has nine dead."

"What about the First?" I asked, bracing myself since it is inevitable that the First Century of the First Cohort is always the recipient of the most attention by the enemy because of the eagle, and because killing a Primus Pilus of Rome is a good way to achieving legendary status among your fellow warriors.

He was opening his mouth to answer when there was a shout of alarm from the general direction of where the *Porta Praetoria* would have been, facing south, which meant that Macer had to lean over to look past me, and by the time I was looking in the same direction, we saw the cause, a horseman, identifiable as a Tribune by the black-crested helmet that was all we could see over the top of the rankers' tents at first, but it was not until he turned onto our Cohort street that we got a clear view of his features and saw that it was Aviola.

"He was with the cavalry," Macer reminded me, and I was curious as to their whereabouts, but there was no time to ask because he slowed from a brisk trot a few paces away to draw up in front of us, which meant that I had to suppress a groan as I pivoted and rendered another salute.

To my utter shock, Aviola did not address Macer but me, though that was just the beginning of the surprises.

"Primus Hastatus Prior Pullus," Aviola spoke formally, and as if we had not had any kind of interaction at all, let alone a detailed discussion about the entangled nature of our families' history, "I bring a request from Camp Prefect Sacrovir. Although," he hesitated, then nodded his head to indicate my newly stitched face; or, perhaps it was the four bandages wrapped around my leg and arms, "he didn't give any kind of instructions in the event that you're too severely injured." He hesitated, then seemed to make a decision. "However, given who you are, I'm going to go ahead and state his request, which is that you saddle your horse, which he knows accompanied us, and come with me to meet with him."

"Tribune, he can't ride!" Macer broke in. "Just look! And," he added before the Tribune could respond at all, "I know that you were with the Decurion doing your bit killing these bastards, but you're going to be hearing what Centurion Pullus did on his own to beat those *crupellarii* back!" The more he spoke, the angrier he seemed to be getting. "The men are talking about nothing else, Tribune, so the Centurion has done his part and then some! It's not right for the Prefect to…"

"Primus Pilus," Aviola cut Macer off, and while it might have been within his rights to do so because Tribunes do outrank even a Primus Pilus, only very foolish Tribunes would dare to do so, and nothing Aviola had done or said to this point made him seem a fool, but it was also his quiet tone that helped soften the discourtesy, "that's why the Prefect took great pains to remind me to make sure that the Centurion understands this is a *request*. And," he turned away from Macer to look me directly in the eye, "he also wanted me to tell you that this involves Aulus Cordus Macula. He's in need of help. And,"

Aviola added the most important bit, "he supposedly knows where the Aedui Sacrovir is located."

I confess it took a moment, my head seeming a bit foggy, first for me to recall that he was actually referring to Sempronius, then for the second part to register, yet rather than respond to the Tribune, I looked over at Macer.

"What?" I gasped. "Sacrovir got away?"

Macer looked a bit embarrassed, which to my mind was totally understandable, and justified, though he did not hesitate to admit, "Yes, he and a handful of the barbarians who serve as staff officers got away somehow."

"And Macula managed to get a message out from wherever he is that he's trapped and needs our help," Aviola put in.

While I cannot say that the emotion I felt was the same as if he had said that it was Macer, Alex, or even one of my men, I was sufficiently concerned that Sempronius might be in trouble that I did turn in the direction of where the horses should have been.

"I'm fine, Primus Pilus," I told Macer, who, thank the gods, did not truly believe me, but it was the ranker who was just unfortunate enough not to have entered his tent who caught his Primus Pilus' eye who was sent to where the livestock was kept with an order to have one of the livestock slaves, who Latobius at least knew, to saddle my horse, and I made a mental note to find out who the man was and to reward him later.

Given the inevitable delay, I did have time to hurry back to my tent, where I had another battle on my hands with a clerk who was absolutely determined to stop me from going anywhere, not caring in the slightest that Prefect Sacrovir was making the request. So set on it was he that I ended up having to enlist Euphemios, who, as accustomed to our bickering as he may have been, clearly wanted no part of our quarrel, but he nevertheless helped me into my *hamata*, which Alex was only too happy to point out was still caked with congealed blood, gore, and only the gods know what bits of the human body embedded in the links. Only now will I acknowledge that my stomach almost joined the Aedui in a rebellion at the sight, the smell, and just the idea of donning it without it being thoroughly cleaned and oiled.

Nevertheless, I was back in the proper attire for a fight, and despite his resistance to the entire idea, Alex did take the time to affix a new crest to my helmet, although somewhat oddly, when I asked him why the crest needed to be replaced, his answer was a tart, "You don't want to know."

Impulsively, I did think to grab the *spatha* that Germanicus had given me, although I had absolutely no idea what was ahead; I think it was more that I just wanted to be prepared for anything. Because my wounds were to my extremities, I was thankful that it was not that painful to don my *hamata*, greaves, and helmet, but I was finding it increasingly difficult and painful whenever my face made any expression whatsoever, nor could I seem to discipline my tongue from moving to my left cheek to run along the sutures, which at least did serve to distract my mind a bit from the pain in other spots. In terms of wounds, I cannot say that this was the most painful I had experienced; however, I had never suffered gashes in so many different spots, and when I allowed myself to think about it, I could not seem to banish the idea that the sum total of my wounds on this occasion were more painful in the aggregate than any single wound I had incurred. This was certainly a factor in the overall sense of malaise I was experiencing, and I realized that it was also at least partially due to the fact that, in the past whenever I had experienced one of these moments, while I had been almost overcome with fatigue, I had always had the opportunity to rest immediately afterward. This was not going to happen, but I nevertheless managed not to spend any extra time in my quarters, emerging from my tent to walk down the Cohort street at least trying to appear as if I was unaffected. It was during this short trip down what was already becoming a heavily trodden path, when men began calling out to me that I got my first indication of what has now become accepted as fact by the men of the 1st Legion.

"We saw what you did to those fucking gladiators, Centurion!" someone from the Fourth Century shouted. "You turned the tide, right enough!"

If this had been the only thing of this nature said, I would have attributed it to simply the kind of thing rankers who like to draw the attention of a Centurion do by using flattery, but by the time I was passing the tents belonging to the Second Century, it was obvious that this was a widely shared sentiment. Only later, the next day, actually, would I have heard enough to know that, once again, this...thing that resides in me, and in my father, and my great-grandfather that had been unleashed ultimately had had a positive impact on the outcome of a fiercely fought battle. In the moment, it was more confusing than anything else, but what mattered was seeing Latobius, saddled and ready, with Tribune Aviola sitting his horse next to mine, giving me something to focus on; what that was, however, was the sudden horror at the thought that, as men were now congregating in the Cohort street, not knowing exactly what it was that was taking place but that it was something interesting, I was going to be expected to vault into Latobius' saddle. Normally, this would not have been worth mentioning, but while the wound to my outer left thigh, a shallow slash that only took a half-dozen stitches to close bothered me, it was the one wound that had not required being stitched shut, a puncture wound right in the middle of my left calf that sufficiently convinced me that the idea of leaping into the saddle was not guaranteed.

Thank the gods, Macer somehow sensed this, because as I approached Latobius, he pointed to one of the rankers who had been drawn by the small spectacle, snapping, "Figulus! Get over there and down on your hands and knees. You were just shouting about how Centurion Pullus pulled our fat from the fire. Show your appreciation, man! He's a hero of Rome and deserves to be treated as such!"

As thankful as I was, I was not willing to say so publicly, hoping that the look I gave him was sufficient; since he never brought it up, I assume that it was. I had expected that having my thighs wider apart would be painful, but I immediately discovered that holding the reins caused me more discomfort, making me worry slightly about what Alex had described as a stab wound with a wide-bladed weapon when he stitched it up, and of course what I did was continually flex my left hand, simply because it was so uncomfortable. Regardless of my discomfort, what mattered was that I was in the saddle, and without any forewarning, Aviola went immediately to the trot, then the moment we were beyond the last row of tents that would have put us either just within the wall or just outside it, he began cantering his mount, though Latobius immediately matched his counterpart's pace without me having to kick him. I had deliberately waited until we would be away from any prying ears, but I quickly saw that there was a *turma* of cavalry waiting to serve as our escort, so as soon as it was possible to do so but before we reached them, I wasted no time.

"All right, Tribune, what's going on?" I demanded.

To my surprise, Aviola did not prevaricate, nor did he seem put out by my peremptory tone, replying, "What I told you is true. Macula is in Augustodunum, which as you can imagine, is in a panic. Sacrovir managed to escape our cavalry and got there first, but he didn't stay there long, just switching out horses. He's gone to ground somewhere nearby, and Macula insists that he knows the location."

This was useful information, if it could be trusted, but it did not answer the main question as far as I was concerned.

"But why does he want me?"

"That," Aviola admitted, "I don't know. At least," he added hastily, "not with any certainty." He paused for a moment, and I saw him give me a sidelong glance. "Would you like to know what I think, Centurion?"

"Of course," I snapped, then modified my tone a bit. "It will just help me understand what's really happening."

This obviously mollified the Tribune, because he did not hesitate to explain, "I don't think the Prefect feels safe right now, Centurion, and I think he wants someone he can trust with him, as well as someone that Macula trusts. And," he added with a frown that suggested he was deep in thought, "I would want someone who was not only experienced as a fighter, but someone who's an experienced horseman himself. I mean, if you need to ride hard without any warning. And," he grinned over at me, "you're not just experienced, you're…you."

I certainly did not want to hear this part about the possibility of galloping about, yet at the same time, I had a deep and abiding loyalty to my former Primus Pilus, and I confess it was nice that this Tribune was clearly aware of my abilities, but I was about to learn that he was very familiar with the things I had done about which I had no memory.

When moving at a canter, it is difficult to hold a conversation under the best of circumstances; when you're being reminded of the wounds you received less than a full watch earlier by your horse's impact with the ground, it also makes it difficult to recall anything but the pain, but what I do remember was Aviola talking about the battle from the perspective of our cavalry.

"It was all due to the Decurion," he told me. "If he hadn't made the decision to turn about and hit the Aeduan infantry, I don't know what would have happened. But," he finished with the kind of confidence that is the purview of young Tribunes, "I think both the 1st and 2nd should be making sacrifices to the cavalry."

At this point, I had not heard much besides the shouting of some rankers, while at the same time, between my own experience whenever I suffered one of these divine fits and how they usually occurred at crucial moments, and what the men had shouted at me when I was about to mount Latobius, I knew that what we had done against the *crupellarii* had played some role, and it was with this in mind that I challenged, "But what about my men? They had to stop those *crupellarii*. And," I pointed out, "I can tell you now that we didn't have enough siege spears to go around, and that unless one of the men had something like this," I tapped the hilt of my *gladius*, "they weren't doing a fucking thing to that armor."

Aviola surprised me then, because his mind immediately went to more practical matters, which he showed by musing, "How do you suppose they managed to fabricate so many sets of *segmentatae* to that level of quality that your men weren't able to penetrate them with their *gladii*?"

While it was certainly the case that I was distracted for the reasons I mentioned, I retained enough of my senses to immediately become alert, because this had the potential of being dangerous, given what had been said about this very topic earlier.

"That," I admitted, "is a good question, Tribune." I thought for a moment about how far I was willing to go, and I supposed that this hesitation prompted Aviola to offer, "Sacrovir had to have had some sort of help, surely. And," he did glance over his shoulder since we were riding at the head of our column, with a pair of advance riders about a hundred paces ahead, "it had to be someone with not just a great deal of money to purchase the raw materials, but," he did lower his voice even more, "someone with enough influence to keep whoever it is in Rome whose business it is to keep track of resources that are important to the Empire from noticing a province that is suddenly consuming more ore than normal...like iron ore. So, I suppose the question is, who would this person be?"

"I think you would know that better than I would," I replied, knowing that he would recognize I was being deliberately evasive, even as I tried to make a joke of it. "I'm not a fine young man of Rome on the *cursus honorum.*"

"I may be a 'fine young man of Rome'," he retorted, though it was with a genial smile I took as acknowledgment of my attempt at humor, "but I've never actually been there. You have. And," he shrugged and did a creditable job of sounding casual, "I just thought that during your time there, you would have learned a bit more how things work in that regard than a provincial like me."

I have a habit: when I am trying to avoid making some sort of outburst or remark that would indicate that I have been caught out by whomever I am engaged with in an exchange where I do not want them to know they have elicited a reaction, I tend to bite down on the inside of my cheek. My bellow of agony was enough to make Latobius slightly stumble, the men behind us shout in alarm, and at least one of them drew their *spatha* judging by the rasping sound, while Aviola's eyes went wide and I did not need to know him very well to read the expression of a man who is trying to decide whether he should be ready to fight or cut his losses and flee.

"I apologize," I mumbled, then spat a gobbet of fresh blood onto the ground even as we continued moving, then pointed to my face in explanation since he was on my right side and was not subjected to my newly stitched wound. "Latobius stepped into a hole and I bit down on the inside of my cheek, and it hurt."

"I can imagine," he commiserated, and for the span of a couple of normal heartbeats, neither of us said anything, giving me the hope that perhaps I had inadvertently managed to thwart this line of questioning, because Aviola was right, I did have a very good idea of who it was in Rome who would be aware of every lump of ore and every ingot of finished iron, and to where it was going. That hope lasted just long enough for him to gently remind me, "So we were talking about who in Rome might at least be aware of that much iron being consumed by a province that has been at peace since Divus Julius pacified them." At least this time, I did not bite my cheek, if only because it was throbbing so painfully that I thought I might go lightheaded and lose the saddle, but I managed to remain silent. Even over the hoofbeats and creaking of leather and wood, I heard the Tribune's exasperated sigh, though he mostly managed to keep it from his voice as he said, "I understand, Centurion. I truly do. So, perhaps this might be a good way to proceed. I'll tell you what *I* think. If you hear something that makes sense, or you agree with, perhaps you'll just…nod?" I did so then, and it would have been hard not to grin if I had not been injured when I heard him snort. Nevertheless, he went on, "I know that, in the days of Divus Augustus, every aspect of Imperial administration was run from his villa on the Palatine." He stopped then, and I was unsure if he expected something, so I started to nod, but he was already continuing, "But our current Imperator isn't that…interested in the minutiae of how many chickpeas Publius is eating, or the cost of a wooden peg for our javelins the way Divus Augustus was, and he's delegated a great deal of the responsibility to others."

This was all generally true, though not entirely accurate in a specific sense, and before I could stop myself, I heard my voice reply, "That's true, but only the first part. He hasn't delegated responsibility for most of the administration to *others*, just to one man."

"Ah," I saw Aviola nod out of the corner of my eye. "And that would be…?"

This was as far as I would go doing this dance, and I turned to look at him directly, while nudging Latobius closer to the Tribune, ostensibly so that I would not have to raise my voice, although this was not the real reason, and I saw by the look of alarm that he understood this.

"I'm done playing at this, Tribune," I said coldly. "You're trying to get me to say his fucking name, but I won't do that. You clearly know as well as I do who we're talking about, so if you feel the need to hear the name spoken aloud for some fucking reason, you can say it yourself."

"Very well," Aviola answered without any hesitation and with an even tone, "I will. We're talking about the Praetorian Prefect, Lucius Aelius Sejanus."

I almost said, "No, *you're* talking about Sejanus, not me." Fortunately, I managed to keep that unworthy and cowardly retort to myself. Still, I was not altogether convinced that Aviola was not playing some game.

"So it's Sejanus we're both thinking about," I said. "But what does that mean? The gods probably aren't even able to keep track of all the things said about him, and most of them are untrue. After all," I suddenly recalled one of the more bizarre rumors that I had heard while I was in Rome, "I don't really think that his mother and sister are the same person, do you?"

"No," Aviola acknowledged with a laugh, "not even I believe that. But," the grin vanished, "that aside, the fact is that *someone* very, very powerful is likely behind what the Prefect's half-brother tried to do, although thanks be to the gods, he didn't succeed. Not," he added something I thought both curious, and grossly inaccurate, "that he even came close."

"*Gerrae!*" I exclaimed, deeply shocked. "Aviola, you were there. That *cunnus* came very close to succeeding. Although," I added bitterly, "you're right that it shouldn't have been that close, and it wouldn't have been if Carbo hadn't run like a fucking rabbit."

Now, it was the Tribune's turn to look nervous and a bit apprehensive, glancing once more over his shoulder. Then, he said something that, in the moment, I found odd and disquieting in equal measure.

"Centurion, I admire you a great deal." He made sure to look directly at me. "I truly do, and I believe that, based on what little I saw, and just what I heard from your men when I came to fetch you, that you had a great deal to do with helping to defeat the Aedui, and I fervently hope that you're suitably rewarded for your deeds today. But," his voice sharpened, "if you repeat what you just said to me, I'm afraid that not only will you not reap that reward you deserve, it will do irreparable harm to your career. So, I beg you to let this be the last time you say such a thing, at least when you're not alone or only with someone you trust with your life."

Although it made me wonder what he knew, I also was aware that it was good advice, but before I could make any kind of reply, there was a shout from the advance guard, who had just crested a low hill similar to the one that was now a few miles behind us. Through a series of hand signals, we were warned that there was an armed force ahead of us, but when we reached the crest of the hill, it was this moment that I learned of the whereabouts of the 2nd.

"*Praetor* Silius sent them on a hard march to Augustodunum," Aviola explained. "I passed them on the way back to camp. And," he chuckled, "Primus Pilus Carbo is certainly pushing them hard. I had expected to catch up with them two or three miles ago."

I had briefly wondered where they were, not seeing them anywhere around the opposite side of the forum in our unfortified camp, but I was sufficiently distracted that I did not really spend much energy thinking about their whereabouts. They were marching in Cohort order, in column, which I thought was somewhat reckless; yes, we had shattered the Aedui host, and yes, most of the time when a barbarian army is defeated so decisively, especially when it is composed of more than one tribe, the remnants scurry back in the direction of their own tribal lands, moving as rapidly as they could manage. However, the Aedui Sacrovir had managed to surprise us, both by his location so far from Augustodunum and with the tactics he employed, and it was because of this, and the memory of that shock still being quite fresh that, if I had been in Carbo's position, I would have been marching in open formation. They were not marching with their baggage, or I saw almost immediately, even with their packs, so it did not need to be in the *agmentum quadratum*, but even one or two thousand men led by a competent commander could have posed a problem for a Legion marching in column. None of which was my concern, but as we trotted up the line and got nearer to the head of the Legion where I could see the afternoon sun was catching the golden wings of the Legion eagle, I was growing increasingly tense. I had, after all, cursed at the Primus Pilus of a Legion, and while I never asked, nor did Aviola ever mention why, I did not then, nor do I believe now that the fact that the Tribune had chosen to veer his mount to the left just before we reached the last Century of the Tenth Cohort was an accident, given that it put us on the side opposite the eagle. Of course, a mortal can propose to do whatever he pleases; if the gods do not endorse that man's plan, then we are left floundering, as we were when, to my horror, I saw the white crest of the Primus Pilus seemingly materialize on the left side of the 2nd's formation. It was certainly not planned by Carbo; he was simply doing what all Centurions do on a long march, moving around the formation so that he could be seen by all of the men in his command…and so that he can keep an eye on them. The fact that he had chosen to stop marching for a moment so that his Century could march past him, thereby enabling him to consult with his Optio before cutting across the back of his formation to the other side meant that he was essentially standing there watching us approaching. Or, I suddenly realized, he had either seen us coming, or had heard the shout from farther down the column and was waiting to speak with us, and of course we would be expected to do so.

While we were too far away for me to read Carbo's expression, there was no missing the manner in which his entire body went stiff, the clear sign that he had recognized me, not that it is difficult, especially when I am on horseback. He did not stop, instead turning back about to resume marching at the tail end of his Century, while I tried to be discreet in my examination of his Legion as we rode past. I was not surprised to see that there were not any men sporting bandages, nor were there any uneven ranks in the third, or even the second line Cohorts, and I felt the tightening in my gut at this testament to how little of the fighting the 2nd had done. Whenever I had undergone this transformation when the beast that dwells so deep inside me is roused, afterward, when it returns to its lair down in my gut, I am so exhausted that the idea it could be roused again within a watch had always been so unfathomable that I had not considered it possible. However, when we reached the Sixth of the First, and I saw the disturbingly uniform ranks and the paucity of bandaged men, it was impossible for me to deny that I felt the shifting sensation inside me.

My temper was not helped when Aviola murmured, "Centurion, you have as many wounds as one of Carbo's First Cohort Centuries does altogether."

It was an exaggeration, of course, though not by much, and even Latobius must have sensed my tension as we drew up alongside Carbo given the manner in which my horse began blowing, and almost prancing, the sign that he wanted to break out into a full gallop, forcing me to curb him more firmly than I normally did, offering up a silent prayer to the gods that Carbo did not say or do anything to poke and prod the beast inside me.

The gods were not listening, or more likely, they thought it might be amusing to have Carbo give me a smile that bore no relationship to the glittering malice I saw in his eyes as he said loudly enough for the men in not just his Century, but the Second to hear while trying to sound jovial and as if he was engaging in the kind of banter between comrades who actually like each other, "I see you've been playing the hero again, eh, Pullus?" He turned his head to his Optio, who he was marching next to at that moment, and nudged him with his elbow. "What do you think, Plautus? Eh? You think that if we unwrapped those bandages there'd be anything there? A scratch maybe? Although," he allowed, pointing to my face, "that one *is* a right nasty gash, I'll tell that to anyone. But," to my ears, his laugh sounded like the braying of a mule, "his wife should thank the barbarian who did that, because it improved his looks! Isn't that right, boys?"

What saved Carbo, and me, was the reaction of his men, who looked more embarrassed, his jibe earning a ripple of chuckles that anyone with a set of ears knew was half-hearted, and that was putting it kindly.

It was clear to me that the men knew that their performance had been shameful, even if it was through no fault of their own, and this did more to settle the beast back down than anything I could have done, yet I could not stop myself from commenting, at least as loudly as Carbo had, "I suppose that's what a Centurion who leads from the front can expect, Primus Pilus Carbo." Before he could say anything, I pointed to my face, and I would have smiled, but it was far too painful, so I tried to express that I was simply matching Carbo's bantering, "Thank Fortuna, she's already my wife so she doesn't have any choice." I made a show of shuddering. "I hate to think what it would be like if I was in your position and had to pay for it every night!"

I had not anticipated the roar of laughter from Carbo's men, and clearly neither had the Primus Pilus, judging from how his mouth dropped open, his face going deadly pale for a heartbeat, then flushing a deep red as he glared up at me. It was how his hand dropped to the hilt of his *gladius* that prompted me to nudge Latobius so that, before Carbo could react, I had moved my horse immediately next to him, but on his right side, meaning that he could draw but not wield the *gladius*, while I leaned down in a manner that made it appear as if I simply wanted to speak to him without being overheard, which was not my intent but suited my purposes.

"I don't want any trouble, Primus Pilus Carbo," I said to him, using the laughter as cover, though it was quickly dying down as the men watched us. "Besides, I think you have your hands full already."

"What do you mean?" Carbo demanded. "I haven't done anything that would warrant it!"

He was lying, and I knew it, yet this was also to my advantage, because I feigned surprise.

"I didn't mean to suggest that you had. I," I nodded my head in the direction we were marching, "am talking about what's ahead in Augustodunum. There's no telling what kind of reception you and your boys are going to get, especially after a hard march, and it will be dark when you get there." I knew I should not do so, but I could not stop myself from adding,

"Be sure you thank your household gods that your boys haven't already been badly chewed up." His color had been returning to normal, but the flush came rushing back, and his mouth was opening when, seemingly of his own mind, Latobius suddenly sidestepped and brushed against Carbo, not hard enough to knock him off his feet, but enough to cause him to stagger a bit, while I raised my voice to shout, "May Fortuna bless you, boys! Root the rest of these rebel *cunni* out so we can all go home!"

As I hoped, this earned a rousing shout, which precluded Carbo from being able to say anything, and I wasted no time, kicking Latobius from his walk to the trot, doing so without saluting Carbo, who could only glare at me in impotent fury as I left him behind. Aviola hurried to join me, while the rest of the escort followed us, the Tribune pulling alongside me though not saying anything at first, which was good because I had just learned something; opening my mouth wide to do something like shout was extraordinarily painful, but it was Aviola who noticed something else.

"Centurion, did you know your face is bleeding?" I had thought it was sweat, but when I gingerly touched my cheek and examined my fingers, they were red. Aviola nudged his horse closer, and with the ease of an experienced horseman, leaned over to look more closely. "I think you may have ripped a stitch out, Centurion," he said helpfully.

I would learn later that was exactly what had happened, but there was no way that I would trust anyone other than Alex or Philippos to put it back in, and it stopped bleeding soon enough.

"By the way," Aviola commented, sounding casual. "That was a neat trick." Not taking his meaning, I looked over at him with a raised eyebrow, and it seemed as if he was considering not explaining, then shrugged and said, "Remember I was on your left side. I saw you kick your horse into the Primus Pilus. That was a good way to get out of that situation." He chuckled. "I'll have to remember that."

I only grunted; my mind was already on other things, especially the practical issues of what was coming next, and I had resigned myself to the idea that I would not know why the

Prefect wanted me with him until I saw him. Once we were past the 2nd, we started seeing people from a distance on the road ahead of us, yet without exception, the instant they spotted us, they went dashing for the nearest cover of the trees on either side of the road, which told us they were rebels who had been among the earliest to flee the battle.

There was no discussion about trying to run them down; not only was it not our job, we did not have the time or the numbers, and I am ashamed to say that this was the first time it occurred to me to ask Aviola, "You said that the Prefect received information from Macula about the whereabouts of Sacrovir?" The Tribune nodded. "But you also said that Macula is in some sort of trouble." Aviola nodded again, which was the part that did not make sense to me. "How did Macula get word to the Prefect if he's hiding somewhere in Augustodunum?"

I did not know what answer I was expecting, but it was not him simply pointing to a cluster of buildings about a mile away.

"You can ask him yourself, Centurion. That's where we were told to meet. That's an inn and Augustodunum is only two miles farther on, which is where Decurion Chlothar and the cavalry are."

"They went into the town?" I asked, and Aviola must have heard the alarm in my voice, because he assured me, "No. The Prefect gave strict orders for them to do nothing but guard all the gates and wait for the 2nd to arrive."

We had traveled another five miles since leaving the 2nd behind, and there was less than a watch of daylight left, which meant that Carbo and his Legion would be arriving after sundown at Augustodunum, and they would be near exhaustion when they did. They had been traveling light, leaving their packs behind and I assumed that the 2nd's complement of wagons and mules would be used to carry that gear to them, but even if they had left shortly after I did, the baggage train would not arrive until close to midnight. Whether or not they entered the town, and most importantly, what they did when they entered, I had no idea, but I felt certain that Prefect Sacrovir, who was the ranking officer, would have thought it through and would not risk the 2nd any more than necessary. It did not occur to me, at least in those moments before we arrived at what I could now see was a rather large inn with several outbuildings, while there were a dozen horses outside the largest building, that Sacrovir might have other things on his mind.

"You look terrible," the Prefect commented, even before I took the offered seat at the table in the dining area of the inn, which had been commandeered by him and the men with him acting as bodyguards. "And that," he indicated my face, "is a right nasty gash."

"So I've been told." I tried to hide my irritation at his stating the obvious. "By Primus Pilus Carbo of all people."

"First," Sacrovir went on, ignoring my reference to the other man, "before we talk about anything else, I wanted to tell you that, no matter what happens, I've already dictated my official report about the battle, and a separate account of your actions against the *crupellarii*. And," he raised his voice slightly, I supposed so the others could hear; although most of them were Batavian, I did spot Tribune Paullus, who had been joined by Aviola at another table, "in that account, I make what I believe is a strong case that your actions, and your actions alone, stopped those fucking gladiators from putting the *Praetor* and myself and everyone in the command group in dire peril. Now," he added with a slight shrug, "whether that's enough that you're officially recognized, I don't know, but I also wanted to take this moment to thank you personally." Suddenly raising his cup, he stood, and as custom dictated, this brought the others to their feet, but in a manner that told me they had received forewarning, because they all had cups in their hands, leaving me the only one seated, knowing that I was supposed to remain this way now that I understood what was happening. "To Primus Hastatus Prior Gnaeus Volusenianus Pullus of the 1st Legion, slayer of the *crupellarii*, and a hero of Rome, whose heroic actions saved his commanding officers, and probably his Legion from disaster!" He paused a fraction of a heartbeat, then barked, "To Pullus!"

"*To Pullus!*" the others roared, and because of the close confines, it made me jump, whereupon the only noise was the sound of more than a dozen men slurping down whatever they had in the cups, then in a ragged unison, slamming their cups onto the table.

I sat there then, trying not to squirm in embarrassment as the other men in the room came to offer their congratulations, and I noticed several things; most of them were sincere in their thanks, though if I was any judge, Paullus seemed ambivalent about it as he offered his arm, temporarily forgetting our different ranks, yet Aviola seemed almost as pleased as I was, even though I dearly wished that at the very least Alex could have been there with me to see this. The Batavians were the most enthusiastic, though none as much as Herminius, who I had not seen when I first entered the inn, and frankly, his thanks meant more to me than just about anyone else present, save of course for the Prefect, who was watching the proceedings, yet despite the fact he was smiling, he seemed somewhat distracted, but I dismissed it as understandable since he had unfinished business of his own.

"It seems a long way from our time together in Mogontiacum, Centurion," Herminius said with a grin, and without thinking, I laughed, knowing that he was referring to how we had met, when we were both in the holding cells in the *Praetorium* basement, immediately regretting the show of humor because of the sharp stab of pain to the side of my face.

"Ah, you *bastard*," I gasped, clutching my cheek only partially for show, "don't make me laugh! It hurts too much."

As I expected, and hoped, Herminius was cheerfully unmoved.

"It is repayment for you putting me in danger all those times," he retorted, and in the same bantering tone, I reminded him, "And you're still attached to the 1st, you Batavian savage. Be careful or I'll bribe a clerk to send you to go check on our friend Catualda."

He gave an exaggerated shudder, holding up his hands in mock surrender. "I take it back, Centurion! Please, do not do anything like that! If I never see that *mentula* again, I will die happy!"

He actually did not use the Latin word, but one in Batavian that I knew means the same thing, though I could not spell or pronounce it if there was a knife to my throat. Once the men were done, they drifted back to their table, by common consent leaving the Prefect and me alone, and I fumbled for the right words to express my gratitude, which he dismissed with a wave.

"There's no need, Gnaeus. I just wrote what I saw." He leaned forward to put his forearms on the table and lowered his voice. "And I saw *why* it happened. You were…stricken, weren't you? By that…whatever it is?" Even if I had been disposed to do so, I could not lie to Tiberius Sacrovir, although I only nodded. "That's what I thought," he sighed. "And," his tone turned careful, "I also heard about Sabinus. I know that you took a chance on him when you asked me for a spot for him when we were in Rome, but you were right about him. He had a bright future in the 1st, and based on what very little I know about these…fits you and your father…"

"And great-grandfather," I interjected, though I do not know why this was so important to me.

"Yes," he nodded, "and the Prefect, of course, but what I do know is that there seems to be a moment or an event that causes these fits." He paused, though I knew what was coming. "Was it losing Sabinus? Was that what did it?"

"Yes," I answered honestly, though I did not really want to discuss it, but Sacrovir was not quite through.

"And was it the same as before? You don't remember everything that took place?" I nodded again, and he looked at me thoughtfully, giving me the impression that there was something specific he wanted to say, or to ask.

More to forestall this, I asked, "What's the plan, Prefect? Aviola told me that Sempronius is in trouble, but that he knows where Sacrovir is heading."

An expression that I had learned was irritation flashed across his face, but rather than continue with his own questioning, or chastise me for attempting to change the subject, he nodded and explained, "Yes, that's the bare bones. He sent a man, I think it's his slave who helps with his pretense of being a traveling merchant, to tell me that his master has information that will help us locate Sacrovir." He pointed at the ceiling, "He's upstairs in one of the rooms. One of the

Batavians is guarding him."

"He doesn't know himself?" I asked, and Sacrovir grimaced, giving me the answer.

"No, and that's no accident," he said bitterly. "Sempronius is hiding out somewhere in Augustodunum, and he instructed his man that he won't tell me until we're face to face…and outside the walls."

"Someone must have discovered that he was spying for us," I guessed, and Sacrovir nodded.

"And he's being careful to make sure that he's safe before he tells us. Not," he admitted, "that I blame him. I'd probably do something similar, but it's still fucking inconvenient."

"Do we have enough men? Or will we have to wait for the 2nd? What's the situation inside the town?"

"The last report I received from the Decurion is that they've been kept busy keeping people from leaving, which is strictly forbidden by order of the *Praetor*. He doesn't want anyone leaving, or going in, who isn't Roman, although I don't think there's much chance of that. As far as whether we have enough men or not," he finished grimly, "it doesn't matter, because we're entering the town to find Macula, then once we get Sacrovir's location from him, we're going to go hunt him down and kill him. This ends tonight."

He was standing up as he said this, and though he did not indicate I should follow him, I did so more out of habit, and I followed him up the stairs to the room nearest the stairway where the door was closed. Sacrovir rapped on it, and I was in for another surprise when the door was opened by Barvistus, while sitting behind him on the single bed was a thin, terrified-looking man who appeared to be about thirty, attired in a filthy tunic and sandals. In fact, probably the most valuable item on his body was the bronze placard around his neck, and he scrambled to his feet when Barvistus beckoned to him.

"Are you ready to take us to your master?" Sacrovir asked, though it was not really a question.

"Y-yes, Master," the man stammered, his accent marking him as a member of a barbarian tribe, but while I could not place it immediately, it struck me as something I had heard before, just not recently. "As you command."

R.W. Peake

"Remember," the Prefect warned, "if you and your master are playing tricks, you're both going to pay, but you're going to be the first to die. Barvistus here," Sacrovir nodded at the Batavian, "has orders to gut you the instant anything goes wrong. Understood?"

"I…I understand, Master," the slave said, which only made me more certain I had heard the accent before, but I still could not place it.

Descending the stairs, I saw the room was empty, and we went outside to find the party already mounted, including Aviola and Paullus, while there was a spare mount for the slave. This time, there was nobody to help me into the saddle, and I gritted my teeth, expecting the pain, but it was still difficult not groaning aloud, and within a few heartbeats, I sensed the bandage around my calf getting wet. We moved quickly away from the inn, the northern wall of Augustodunum coming into view with perhaps a third of a watch of daylight left, and we saw that the cavalrymen who had been assigned by the Decurion to guard the northern gate were dismounted, but holding their horses' reins in the sign they were ready for trouble. I had been informed by Sacrovir that while there were four gates, the northern and southern were directly aligned across the town, which looked to be smaller than Ubiorum, but the eastern and western were misaligned, with the western gate closer to the southern one.

"The slave told me that where Macula is hiding is closest to the western wall, so we're going to head straight for it," Sacrovir announced to those of us who would be going with him into Augustodunum, which were the men who had been his bodyguards at the inn, and me, while Aviola and Paullus would remain outside the walls. "Since I don't know where we're going, I want Tribune Aviola to stay here, and Tribune Paullus to go to the eastern gate since the Decurion is at the southern gate." He took a visible breath. "Now, everyone make sure that you can draw your blade, but wait for me to give the command. I don't think the people in the town are going to be eager to try and stop us, but in case they are, you have my permission to do whatever you need to do in order to protect yourself."

I was wearing my *gladius*, which I had been told by Alex I was still holding in my hand when they found me underneath all the *crupellarii*, but I had grabbed up the *spatha*, which was attached to my saddle, and I reminded myself to check to make sure that it slid easily from the scabbard since if I had to use a blade from horseback, I would prefer the *spatha* because of its longer reach. We were moving then, riding west along the northern wall before turning the corner, and I immediately saw why the western gate was closer to the southern wall. Augustodunum is located on the Icauna (Yonne) River, and the bridge was located at a spot where it crossed the river directly into the town, which is closer to the southern wall. While I was not overly concerned, I was certainly alert, and I could see that the other men with us were as well, although we entered the town to an almost deserted scene, although deeper into the town, I could see figures darting into one of the buildings lining both sides. By this time, I had been in enough towns in Gaul not to be surprised that, for the most part, it looked Roman, with tile roofs and whitewashed walls, although there was an occasional building whose owner I supposed clung stubbornly to his Gallic roots, and I was quite surprised when the slave, who was riding next to Sacrovir, suddenly pointed to one such structure, though it was two stories.

"Pullus, you come with me." Sacrovir surprised me, swinging off his mount, and it must have shown on my face, because he explained in a reasonable tone, "You know him better than I do. I've only met him once."

This was true enough, though he hardly needed to take the time, since I would have followed him without being told, but I dismounted my horse without thinking, doing so normally, and my leg almost buckled under me.

"Are you sure that you're all right?" the Prefect asked, but with the kind of impatient tone I recalled when he was my Primus Pilus that I knew meant he did not want to hear anything that might displease him, and I assured him that I was, though I could not disguise my limp.

Sacrovir was second, behind one of the bodyguards while I was behind the slave, who was behind the Prefect, and we all had to pause inside because the shutters were closed and there was no fire or lamps lit. While I was not overly concerned, I still put my hand on my *gladius*, just in case this was a trap.

"Master?" the slave called out nervously, and inadvertently, he solved one mystery for me. "It is Lugotorix, Master! I have come with the Prefect as you ordered."

That's it! I thought, with more excitement than the revelation warranted. The slave was from Britannia, that was why I had recognized his accent but could not immediately place it.

Any thought about this was put away for the moment when I heard the Imperator's spy reply from up above, "I'm up here, Lugotorix. I'm coming down!"

I expected to hear his footsteps clattering down the stairs, but he moved with obvious caution; that, at least was my initial thought, though I would learn differently when the Briton moved over to the table I could just barely make out, and after a few strikes of his flint, lit the wick of a tiny lamp. Sempronius, for that was how I thought of him despite everyone else referring to him as Macula, descended the stairs, and because of where I was standing, I actually saw why he was moving so slowly even before I caught a glimpse of his face, seeing a bloody bandage wrapped around his right thigh before he appeared fully. Not surprisingly, he was looking at Sacrovir, but he glanced over in my direction, coming to a sudden stop just before he descended the last step.

My first thought was that he was startled to see me there, which I thought odd since the Prefect said that he had specifically asked for my presence; I learned differently when he exclaimed, "Pluto's thorny cock! And here I was feeling sorry for myself because some *cunnus* stuck me in the leg, but look at your face!" He gave me what could have been a grin or a grimace; the light was not sufficient to tell. "I can't imagine Bronwen will be very pleased when she sees you've gone and ruined your looks!"

I cannot say that I cared for Sempronius speaking so familiarly about my wife, yet at the same time, I reminded myself that he had put himself at risk to help both of us when I was in Rome, so I replied genially, "It's not my looks she's in love with, and as long as," I looked down at my groin, "that remains intact, I'm sure she'll be happy." I was pleased that this earned some chuckles from the other men present, but I also wanted to know about his own wound, which I pointed to and asked, "And what about you? Who stuck you in the leg? And," I asked the more important question, "why?"

"I got careless," Sempronius admitted simply. "I thought I could trust a man who turned out to be a piece of *cac*. But," his expression changed, the flickering of the lamp accentuating the cruel smile, "he might have struck the first blow, but I struck the last." He surprised us by jerking his thumb upward. "He's up there."

"You have a dead man in your home?" Sacrovir gasped. "What are you thinking?"

"It's not my home, Prefect," Sempronius replied calmly. "And what I'm thinking is that he was the man who knows, or knew," he corrected, "where your half-brother fled to. I assume that's of interest to you?"

"Of course it is," the Prefect snapped, and I suspected that his irritation was exacerbated by Sempronius' emphasizing their familial connection. Then, what had already occurred to me clearly struck him, because I saw the sudden expression of worry on his face. "As long as you got the information we need before you killed him."

"I did," Sempronius assured him, and Sacrovir's shoulders sagged with relief, but it was destined to be short-lived, because the spy was not through. "But while he…volunteered where Sacrovir is most likely to be," Sacrovir's more relaxed demeanor evaporated and he went rigid again, "what he didn't know was how many men are going to be with him." Sempronius looked over at me, and asked, "How many men are with you, Pullus?"

"What do you mean 'most likely to be'?" Sacrovir interrupted. "I asked if you knew where he was, and you said yes! Now you're changing your tune!"

Despite the dim lighting, there was enough illumination to see Sempronius' face darken, but he replied calmly enough, "No, Prefect, you asked me if I had the information you needed, and I said that I did, but in my business, there's always a possibility that the information is incorrect. Diviciacus was a treacherous bastard in his own right, but he was a tough man, and he was loyal to Sacrovir, so he might have lied to me…but I don't believe he did. Not," he shook his head, and there was an expression that was there for only an instant that indicated, to me at least, that Sempronius would be having his own nightmares, "after what I did to him."

There was a silence that stretched out for a couple of heartbeats, then Sacrovir grunted, "Fair enough. But you seem to be more worried about our numbers. What did this Diviciacus tell you?"

"That Sacrovir's surviving councilmen are still with him," Sempronius answered readily enough, but I sensed there was more, which we learned with his next words. "He had ten advisors, and Diviciacus was one of them, and they all have at least five bodyguards, although I can think of two of them who have ten men. Diviciacus had five men, but he sent them with Sacrovir while he stayed behind."

"So there's a minimum of fifty men," Sacrovir said flatly, though I knew him well enough to hear the tension in his voice. "I know that each of our Batavians can handle more than one of these rebels, but can you guarantee that there won't be more than fifty?" He addressed this to Sempronius, and I was not surprised when the spy shook his head. "Then I'm going to need to speak to Chlothar and arrange for at least ten more of his men." With this settled, he asked, "And where is the place that he *might* be?"

Sempronius flushed again, but he was ready, answering, "He has a hunting lodge four miles from here, in the hills to the southwest. He said that it's easy to find. There's a stream that feeds into the river, the first one from the south wall, and you just follow it up into the hills. The lodge is on the bank."

Sacrovir considered this for a moment, then said thoughtfully, "We'll be approaching in the dark, but since we can follow the stream, we shouldn't have a problem finding it. But, will the darkness negate their numbers?" He turned to me. "What do you think, Pullus?"

I did not care for being put on the spot, although I knew it was a sign of his respect for me, and I thought for a moment before I replied, "I'm not sure that it will, Prefect. Yes, it will help us get close, but they have to be expecting us." Something occurred to me, and I turned to Sempronius. "Did this Diviciacus say anything about what Sacrovir intends to do once the sun comes up?"

"Actually, he did." Sempronius nodded. "He plans on escaping to Britannia, but he didn't know if he was going to try immediately, or wait for the search to move beyond this area."

"A large party is going to draw too much attention," I pointed out. "And right now, even fifty men would be too large for him to move west." This more than anything made my mind up, and I tried to sound as confident as I could, telling Sacrovir, "If he did allow his council to bring every bodyguard with them, it would draw too much attention. Prefect, I don't think there's that many men at this lodge."

I was surprised when Sacrovir actually nodded, saying immediately, "That's my thought. So," he decided, "we leave immediately, and we're riding with the men we have." He smiled then, pointed at me, and said, "With your face in the condition that it's in, you're good to scare at least two of these bastards to death." The others present chuckled, and I might have joined in just to show that I was not offended, except that I had learned my lesson about making any kind of overt facial expression, but Sacrovir was not done, and his words only became meaningful in retrospect. "Besides, I can think of no man I'd rather have with me for this final battle than one bearing the Pullus name." Before I could respond one way or another, Sacrovir addressed Sempronius, "And what about you? Can you at least ride with that?"

He pointed to the leg wound, but I was not surprised when the spy offered the Prefect a grim smile.

"Considering the alternative if you leave me behind, even if this leg was gone, I could ride," he assured the Prefect.

"What does that mean, 'considering the alternative'?" I asked, though I thought I knew.

"Someone figured out that I'm not who I have been saying I am," he explained. "They broke into my home before dawn this morning, and I only got away after I got this," he pointed down to his leg, "and jumped out of the window."

"How did they find out?" Sacrovir asked, but Sempronius

could only shrug.

"I don't know, but I do know they planned on holding me for Sacrovir to deal with after he and his army beat us. Which," Sempronius smiled, "they clearly didn't do since you're standing here."

"You mean you don't know what happened?"

I was the one who asked this, quite surprised, and he shook his head.

"I've been holed up here since I had to leave my home," Sempronius explained, then pointed up again. "Dealing with getting answers from Diviciacus. Oh," he added, "I could tell by all the shouting in the streets that started about a watch ago that whatever had happened was bad, but nothing more than that. So," he asked eagerly, "how did it go?"

Sacrovir held up a hand, cutting off the conversation.

"You can hear all about it later," he said. "We need to leave, now."

Sempronius obviously did not like it, but he nodded his understanding, and we headed for the door. Outside, there was a slight delay because of Sempronius' slave, who Sacrovir ordered give up the mount he had been on for his master, which Sempronius did not allow, and on this, he refused to budge.

"Prefect, Lugotorix is the only reason that you have the information about Sacrovir's whereabouts, because I'd be dead if it wasn't for him," Sempronius argued. "I won't leave him stranded here inside the walls without a horse."

Thankfully, the Prefect did not argue or try to impose his authority, though he was clearly unhappy, snapping, "Very well. But you can see as well as I do that we don't have a spare horse, so you're going to have to ride double until we get outside the walls. Then, you can leave your slave with Decurion Chlothar and his boys. Is that acceptable?"

This last Sacrovir asked with a lacerating sarcasm, but Sempronius ignored this, behaving as if it was a sincere question.

"Yes, and thank you very much, Prefect. I'll never forget it. And," he nudged his slave, who had just hopped onto the horse behind the spy, "neither will Lugotorix. Will you?"

"N-no, Master," the slave assured him, then offered the

Prefect a smile, the kind that a slave uses when he is not certain that he will not be hit for being impertinent. "Thank you, Prefect."

Sacrovir's response was a grunt, and he clumsily turned his horse about, heading not for the eastern gate, but the southern. The eastern was closest, but Sacrovir clearly believed that using the southern exit was the quickest, and it would have been except for the fact that one of the townspeople saw us; more crucially, they saw Sempronius.

"Macula!" I heard the name shouted from behind us, and was just turning my head when the spy was struck in the chest by what was probably a paving stone, and while it did not knock him from the saddle it was only because of Lugotorix sitting behind him, and with his free hand he clutched his chest.

Because the instigator was shouting in the Aedui tongue, I could not determine the cause of the attack, but what mattered was that, seemingly from nowhere, the street was suddenly filled with angry civilians, except that their ire was not directed at us but at Sempronius. That was just the first object thrown at him, and this time, I saw a woman snatch up something from the street, hurling it at Sempronius, but this at least turned out to be a turd. While her aim was not perfect, it still struck him on the upper leg, spattering all over Lugotorix, who shouted what sounded like a curse, while Sempronius was now focused on controlling his mount, which was growing increasingly agitated as more people seemed to materialize from inside the buildings, it becoming immediately obvious that they had been lurking inside, watching us.

Finally, someone shouted something that we understood, when another man, this one bearded and missing an eye, shouted, "Macula the spy! Macula the spy for the Romans! We know what you did!"

"*Pullus!*" I recognized the Prefect's voice, but since I did not want to take my attention from Sempronius, who was now surrounded by a half-dozen clearly angry people, I raised a hand to let him know I heard him. "Go to Sempronius! Protect him!" Then, he bellowed an order that, while I understood, also chilled my blood. "Draw *gladii!*" Meanwhile, I kicked Latobius, who responded immediately, forcing a pair of Aedui men, one of whom was shaking a stave at Sempronius in a threatening manner, to leap out of the way, while Sacrovir addressed the townspeople in Latin. "Anyone who throws another rock or threatens Citizen Macula, or any of my men, will be cut down like dogs!"

This was enough, thank the gods, and I grabbed the bridle of Sempronius' horse, the spy clearly still dazed and, somewhat worryingly, wheezing from the blow from the rock.

"If we ever see you again, we will cut your balls off, you Roman pig!" one of the men shouted, though not the one missing the eye, and I guessed that this was the man who hurled the rock.

It was his misfortune to decide to utter this threat just as I was passing him, with Sempronius' horse's reins in my right hand and trailing behind me, and since my left hand was holding my reins, I used my foot, wincing at the pain in my thigh from raising my leg, but it was worth it, my hobnailed sole striking him in roughly the same spot he had hit Sempronius with the stone. Unlike Sempronius, who had stayed in the saddle, this man left his feet and slammed into the wall of the building, the air rushing from his lungs loudly enough I could hear it over the dull uproar as the townspeople muttered under their breath, while the Batavians cursed them in a mishmash of camp Latin and words that I guessed were similar enough that the Aedui understood them judging from their reaction, which fortunately was restricted to shaking of fists and grabbing of crotches. We reached the southern gate without any other incident, and Sacrovir called a brief halt to speak to Decurion Chlothar; later, I would learn that the Prefect lied to the Decurion, telling him that we still did not know of Sacrovir's whereabouts, while I took the moment to check on Sempronius, who had just helped his slave off the back of his mount.

"Are you all right? You're wheezing a bit."

"I think so," he answered, still rubbing his chest, "but it hurts like Dis."

"But you're not going to die."

"No," he replied, looking at me warily. "I don't think so."

"Good. Now," I grabbed him by the arm, squeezing it, hard,

"tell me what that was about, Sempronius."

At first, I was certain he was going to insist he had no idea, but then his shoulders slumped, and he closed his eyes.

"I told you that someone must have figured it out," he admitted. "And they clearly talked."

"When?"

"My guess is earlier today." He shook his head. "Not long after Sacrovir led the army north. If it had been before that, there's no way that he would have left without taking care of me first."

"That's what that's from?" I pointed down at his bandaged thigh, to which he nodded, but I was suddenly certain I knew even more of the story. "And that Diviciacus that you were...questioning," I continued, "he did that." He nodded again. "So you weren't there to question him, were you?"

"No." Sempronius shook his head.

This was when I was struck by a horrible suspicion, but I saw Sacrovir bouncing back in our direction on his horse, and knowing my time was down to a few heartbeats, I tightened my grip on his arm until he actually groaned slightly.

"Do *not* tell me that you made this *cac* up about where that *cunnus* is hiding so that you didn't have to admit that you've been exposed as a spy!"

"No! I would never do something like that!" Sempronius looked surprised, but I reminded myself that given what he did, lying had to be second nature to a man like him. "Pullus, I swear to you that I told the truth!" He must have seen I was not convinced, and I saw his eyes look past me to where Sacrovir was almost up to us, and he lowered his voice, though there was no mistaking the urgent tone to his voice. "I admit that wasn't why I was there, but once I got the best of him, I began questioning him because he was one of the men who was supposed to flee with Sacrovir, but the *cunnus* stayed behind here in Augustodunum to hunt me down." His features twisted into a mask of both hatred and triumph, and he continued, "He was an ambitious bastard, and he had suspected me for some time, but Sacrovir refused to believe him. So, he stayed behind to try and catch me, and he thought he had, but I was too clever for him. And now, he's dead. But, Pullus," he whispered, "I swear to you that I'm not lying about where Sacrovir is. You believe me, don't you?"

I did not answer immediately, but I finally nodded.

"Yes, I believe you."

"Sempronius," Sacrovir called out, "are you all right? Are you fit to come with us? Or do you want to stay behind?"

"No, Prefect," Sempronius replied without any hesitation, but his eyes were on my face. "I'm fine. I wouldn't miss this even for a chance at a Vestal."

"Good," the Prefect said. "Now, let's go finish this."

With that, we moved at a trot, following the stream in the last few moments of daylight.

Chapter 6

Our cause was aided by the almost full moon and few clouds, although even if it had been pitch black, we could have used the sound of the stream flowing past as we headed upstream. Nobody was speaking, which was not unexpected, but I did not welcome it that much because it was giving me time to think, and the more I thought, the more worried I was about Sempronius and his role in this entire affair. He was riding next to me, but I noticed how he looked everywhere but in my direction, as if he was no more eager to talk to me than I was to him. My face hurt abominably, while the aches from all the other injuries that I would not know anything about even after I finally stripped out of my armor and tunic and saw all the bruises had begun to throb. Frankly, I did not know how I was still upright in the saddle, because I was exhausted; I had been counting on whatever it is in a man that supplies him energy after something like a battle to keep me going, but it had run out even before the sun went down, and now I wanted nothing more than to sleep. If the rebel Sacrovir and however many men were with him put up a fight, I had no idea how I would perform, but what kept me going was the knowledge that my former Primus Pilus, a man I respected a great deal, had asked for my help in whatever lay ahead. At the same time, I could not keep my thoughts from going to my boys in the Fifth, wondering about who it was on the butcher's bill. Oh, I knew the numbers that Macer had given me, but he had not put any names to the numbers, which meant that until I was reunited, I would not know which of my boys was still in the land of the living, which were not, and how many of them I would see standing in the ranks again.

The surrounding countryside was completely dark, which was not that surprising; I could guess fairly easily how those Aedui who were not fighting men, or had chosen not to participate, were probably huddled in their darkened farmhouses, waiting for word about the rebellion and whether it had succeeded or failed. Not, I will say, that I could really see how anyone with a modicum of sense or knowledge of Rome could entertain any idea that Sacrovir would have been successful. Hard on the heels of that thought was another, one that shook me to my core then, and I still find troubling now, and that was when I remembered just how close he actually came to defeating us earlier that day, although his rebellion had no chance for success beyond winning a battle. Even if he had defeated us, the 1st and 2nd, the Imperator would have devoted every single man at his command, the entire might of Rome, to crushing Gaius Julius Sacrovir and every one of his followers. None of this would have mattered to Bronwen, or to any of the women who love a man under the standards of the 1st and 2nd, but it would have mattered to us, their husbands. Knowing that you will be avenged does provide a sense of security that is as hard to deny as it is impossible to explain to someone who is not under the standard, but that did not matter, because we had not been defeated, and in fact we were now on our way to slay Gaius Julius Sacrovir. It is funny, but only later did I realize that the Prefect never once mentioned the idea of taking him alive, nor did any of us who were with him, in my hearing, anyway.

The terrain was relatively flat and open for the first two miles, then the stream entered a forest, and although it was not dense, it was sufficient to slow us down, while Sacrovir ordered a rider out on either flank of the track that ran along the northern bank.

"I'll wager that this is the track to that lodge," Sacrovir commented, then addressed Sempronius, "Have you ever been to this place?"

"No, Prefect. But I've heard them talking about it. There's the main lodge, which is about the size of a modest country villa, and the area around it has been cleared of trees and underbrush."

"Any other buildings?"

Sempronius actually looked annoyed at my question, and I

learned why when he pointedly replied, "Yes, I was about to say that there is a stable, and slave quarters, along with a cookhouse that is attached to the rear of the lodge."

"Is it Roman?" Sacrovir asked.

"No." Sempronius shook his head. "It's built in the Gallic style, of wood and with a peaked roof made of thatch. What I was told was that it has been in the Sacrovir family's possession since before the Aedui allied with Rome. Divus Julius is involved somehow, but I don't know the details. What I do know was that he made sure that they were allowed to keep it in their family."

"So they betrayed their own people at some point, and Rome allowed them to keep their lands and holdings," I guessed, not that it mattered.

"The fact that it's made of wood is something we can use," Sacrovir's expression was impossible to read in the darkness, but I could hear the thoughtful tone there, though I did not think anything of it. Setting that aside, he ordered, "Right, Wigmar estimates we've gone almost three miles, so we're going to slow down. If he's got as many men as Sempronius says they might, they're going to put some sentries out farther than we might expect. So, be alert. If we're spotted, then we're going to move as quickly as we can before they have a chance to prepare."

One of the difficulties in offering this particular part of my account is that I am attempting not to color my narrative by the events that were about to transpire, and in that moment, I did not think anything of the Prefect asking about what kind of materials the lodge was constructed with, and the truth is that I was a bit more surprised by his order to increase our pace if we were spotted. Not, I will say, because I disagreed with it, but it was a bit more aggressive than I would have expected from him. Regardless, we resumed moving, and I rode with my hand, not on the *spatha* but on my *gladius*, mainly because it was hanging in the normal spot at my waist and not lashed to my saddle. The only sound now was the rushing water, the creak of leather, and an occasional clicking sound as one of the iron-shod hooves struck an embedded rock in the track, which was just barely wide enough for a single wagon. We no longer rode side by side, but staggered, following the lead of the Batavians with us, counting on their greater experience, although I knew why they did this because I had learned it when I was with Herminius and we acted as the cavalry for Varro's scheme to put Catualda on the Marcomanni throne.

"If you are attacked from either flank in a forest," he had explained, "and are riding side by side, then you are at a disadvantage no matter what kind of attack it is. If it is a missile attack, an arrow or javelin, or even a sling, if your enemy misses the man nearest him, he still can hit the man on the opposite side. If it is an attack with spear or *spatha*, then the man being attacked cannot be supported by his comrade on the other side, but by staggering the column, you reduce those risks."

They only did this in forested terrain, counting on the ability to spot a threat from enough of a distance over open ground, but at this moment, I just welcomed not having Sempronius right next to me, as the very sight of him ignited in me a number of questions that had no bearing on what we were about to do, and I was already having enough difficulty with distracting thoughts. None of us expected to see any kind of light ahead, yet that was exactly what happened, a pair of them actually, separated from each other, though it was impossible to gauge the distance between them. It was enough to get the Prefect to whisper the order to halt, passed down the column, followed by the order to dismount, and gather around, holding a quick discussion.

"If I had to guess," Sacrovir whispered, "I'd say that there are torches at either end of the lodge." When he stopped, I was about to open my mouth, but then he added the very thing I was going to bring up as an alternative. "Or it's by the stable entrance. The question is, which is it? And which torch is the one next to the lodge?" I assumed the Prefect was not expecting an answer, and was more thinking aloud, which seemed confirmed when he went on, "Right, here's what we're going to do."

Over the span of perhaps a hundred heartbeats, Camp Prefect Tiberius Sacrovir used the decades of experience to come up with a plan that accounted for as many of the unknowns as I believe it was possible to do. "First, we're going to get closer, but still dismounted, while Wigmar and..." He looked over at the Batavian, who supplied, "Tiwaz," "...yes, Tiwaz are going to move forward on the sneak to look for sentries posted farther out from the lodge. The rest of us are going to be divided into mounted and those of us on foot." He turned to me. "Pullus, because of all that you've already been through today, I'm going to leave it up to you about whether you're mounted on Latobius or with me on foot."

While I suspected I knew the answer, I asked him, "What are the mounted men doing, and what are you on foot doing?"

"We're rushing the lodge," the Prefect confirmed my guess. "You men on horseback are going to keep anyone from escaping, and stopping anyone outside from getting organized. So, now that you know, what do you want to do?"

There was only one answer, I knew; I just was too tired and battered to be on foot, and I was a good enough horseman that I could acquit myself even as sore as I was.

"I'm going with you, Prefect."

Even in the darkness, I saw the gleam of his teeth as he smiled, though it was the smug tone that was more instructive that I had done exactly as he expected, even as, in my mind, I was roundly cursing myself.

"As I hoped," he confirmed.

Standing erect, he gave Wigmar and Tiwaz the order to begin moving up the track, with those of us going on foot handing the reins of our mounts to the cavalryman the Prefect had designated to hold the horses of the men who would be on foot, of whom there were four others besides the Prefect and myself. Because of his leg, Sempronius would be with the mounted contingent, and it was with some reluctance that I drew the *spatha*, bringing it and handing it to him hilt first.

"That was a gift from Germanicus, so if you lose it, or break it...just keep riding," I warned him.

The spy reacted by chuckling, then leaned over a bit to peer at my face, and I saw the smile vanish when he saw that I at least looked deadly serious.

"I...I will guard it with my life, Pullus."

This was when I smiled, replying, "That's what I wanted

to hear."

The Prefect had been keeping a count, and when he reached a hundred, he whispered that it was time for us to move, slowly, staying on the track. This was a calculated risk on our part; while it was more likely that Sacrovir would place any sentries on or near the track, we did not want to go blundering through the woods in the dark and leave them alive behind us. Essentially, we were gambling that our smaller numbers would be able to move more stealthily and achieve surprise, reaching the lodge and the Aeduan who was responsible for everything that had transpired before their larger numbers could be brought to bear on us. I was just happy that we were not moving very rapidly, and I hoped that walking would loosen up the muscles that had tightened up while I was on horseback. I heard the hiss before I spotted the shadowy figure standing to one side of the track, but the Prefect did not hesitate, moving to what turned out to be Wigmar, who was standing over a body.

"Here is one of them," the Batavian whispered, then pointed in the direction of the lodge. "Tiwaz is still moving forward."

The corpse was lying face down, with the blood pooled around the area of his throat gleaming black in the moonlight, and I confess I felt a surge of pride for Wigmar, who, like Herminius and the other Batavians who I had first met in the cell next to mine in Mogontiacum, had proven himself during our time together in the campaign to put Catualda on the Marcomanni throne, and while I did not know Tiwaz, I felt cautiously confident that he was at least as skilled as Wigmar, since he had been the man to recommend Tiwaz. This seemed to be borne out because, no more than twenty paces up the track, we found him in an almost identical posture, but he had a surprise in store for us. Unlike Wigmar, Tiwaz did not speak Latin, at least not well enough that he felt confident in conversing with the Prefect, therefore using Wigmar to interpret.

"There is another man," Wigmar whispered, "over there." He pointed in the direction of the stream, which was about fifteen paces from the track. "Tiwaz found him first, took care of him, then," he nudged the second corpse with his toe, "this one."

This was impressive, even more so because we had not heard a sound of any kind, though, to be fair, the stream was swiftly flowing over the rocky bed, making the kind of noise that creates a constant backdrop of noise that many people find soothing. Nevertheless, this was welcome news, and we were now at the edge of the clearing, with the lodge, stables, and slave quarters roughly in the middle of it, which meant that we had disposed of the men guarding the track. We could also see that, as suspected, there was a single torch attached to a bracket next to the main entrance of the lodge, though we could not tell if it was one single, wide door, or a double doorway. What we could see was the pair of men lounging outside on either side of the entrance, one of them sitting on a barrel that I felt certain had been rolled to this spot to serve as a seat. The second torch was a few paces away from the wide opening of the second largest building, although the entrance was not guarded, another sign that it was the stables. That left the third building of any size, the quarters reserved for the slaves, though I felt certain there were none present, which meant that this building was probably empty. Thank the gods I did not whisper this, because just as I was opening my mouth to do that very thing, we saw a figure suddenly materialize from around the corner where the door was located on the lodge side. Because of the clearing, there was nothing to obstruct the silvery moonlight that reflected off the long mail vest the warrior was wearing, and we watched as he pulled his trousers down and began to piss.

"That must be where at least some of those bodyguards are," the Prefect whispered. "The question is, how many?"

"And," I thought aloud, though I was also whispering after expelling my breath as the Prefect had, "is it because the lodge is already too full of men to hold any more?"

When I said it, I had assumed this had already occurred to the Prefect, but the soft gasp that caused me to look away from the slave quarters to where he squatted, and seeing his mouth hanging open in shock, told me that it had not. For a moment, just one, I thought that the Prefect was about to cancel our attack, and I confess that a large part of me would have been relieved. As badly as I wanted this rebellion to be over so that I could return to Ubiorum and my family, at the same time, I realized that I had consciously ignored the nagging worry about how outnumbered we might be, and while I wanted this to be the last fight of this rebellion, I did not want it to be the last fight of my life.

Then, his mouth snapped shut with an audible click that actually made me wince, thinking that it was louder than it was, but he said only, "Wait here."

He rose from his squat, though he remained bent over at the waist, and moved quickly back up the track, heading to where I could see the large shadow of darker shapes were gathered that I knew were our horses and the rest of the men. Since they were too far away to be heard, I strained my eyes, watching as the Prefect presumably explained the situation to Sempronius and the others, although a trooper named Gerbald was in nominal command of the cavalry, if ten men including Sempronius could be counted as such. Resigning myself to finding out only after the Prefect returned, I decided to keep an eye on the lodge and slave quarters, Wigmar whispering that the man who had come out to relieve himself had returned to the quarters, but most importantly, he pointed towards the stable, where I just caught a moving figure turn the corner of the lodge.

"It is a walking post," Wigmar whispered. "He showed up there," he pointed to the opposite end of the lodge, "and walked around the lodge."

"Did he stop to talk to those two?"

"Just a word," Wigmar replied.

"All right, let's see if he just walks around the lodge and that's all," I decided. "Keep watch for him."

When I turned back to look up the track, I was surprised to see the Prefect moving quickly back to us, but there was no sign of most of the horses and their riders, only the trooper holding the reins of Latobius and the rest of the mounts of my party in sight.

As soon as the Prefect reached us, he explained, "I've sent them through the woods in the direction of the stables to the other side of the slave quarters. When however many men are in there hear us going into the lodge, they're going to come out and their attention will be on us." He did not explain further, but there was no need, although he did say, "I told them I'm giving them to a count of three hundred before we begin." He looked over at me, and asked, "Pullus, now that you've seen how far it is, do you think you can run that far with your legs like that?" He pointed to the bandages.

This was not the time to let my pride get in the way, so I answered honestly, "My calf is bothering me more than my thigh, and I won't be able to move as quickly as I normally would...but I'll keep up, I swear it."

"I have no doubt," the Prefect assured me. Then, seemingly out of nowhere, he whispered, "Fifty-seven...fifty-eight."

It took me a heartbeat to realize that he had been counting in his head, and giving the count aloud gave me an idea how much time was left, which in turn gave me time to make my own preparations. I had not been exaggerating or minimizing the fact that my calf was bothering me more than my thigh, and when I glanced down at both bandages, while there was just a dark spot on the bandage covering the slash wound on my thigh, the one on my calf was soaked through to the point that only the very edges of the bandage were white. It was when I flexed it, as I would be doing when I ran, that I had to bite my lip from groaning aloud, yet all I could think to do about it was bind it tighter.

I was just bending down to do that when I heard the Prefect whisper, "...two hundred...two hundred one..."

There would be no way to untie the knot securing the bandage, especially knowing that it was Alex who had bound it up—his knots are notorious for the difficulty in untying them—then rewrap the bandage more tightly, and be ready to break out into a run to cover the roughly one hundred paces to the lodge, so all I could think to do was to offer up a prayer to Mars, Bellona, Fortuna, and even Virtus, asking for whatever it was that each god, or goddess, could offer to me to help me support the Prefect in his quest to salvage his name. Even without knowing what was just moments from transpiring, I was under no illusions that the Prefect's half-brother was going to be returning back to the army with us, and if necessary, I was more than happy to be the one who cut the Aedui's string in the event that the Prefect suddenly had qualms about killing his own blood, not that I was overly concerned this would be the case.

I had just finished when I heard the Prefect, slightly more loudly, intone, "two hundred ninety-nine…three hundred."

I had just enough time to take a deep breath, then with my great-grandfather's *gladius* in hand, I followed the man I had been following since I first arrived as a paid man as he broke into a run.

It is commonly accepted as fact, one that I have seen firsthand, that we Romans take sentry duty more seriously than any other of the nations with which we have come into contact. That certainly seemed to be borne out at this moment, because while we did not shout or make any kind of noise, just the fact that there were five armed and armored men running directly for the entrance to the lodge should have elicited an alarm by either the pair of men standing there, or the man who was roving about, the instant we entered into the cleared area since, thanks to the moonlight, we would have been clearly visible. Instead, the pair of sentries appeared to be engaged in some sort of quarrel which had them looking at each other and not the area around them, while the gods arranged for the number three hundred to coincide with the roving sentry turning the far corner of our end of the lodge and putting it in between us and him. Consequently, we had covered almost half the distance when the Aedui bodyguard facing in our general direction but who was focused on his comrade, either looked over the other man's shoulder, or perhaps his eye was drawn to the movement.

I am ashamed to say that, for the first time in my life, I was not leading the way in our headlong dash, and in fact, was lagging a couple paces behind Wigmar and Tiwaz, who were a pace behind the other two Batavians, all four of them burdened with their shields, the flat cavalry type that they had strapped to their back until this moment. Naturally, the Prefect was leading the way, moving at an impressively rapid speed for a man of his age, yet despite my laggardly pace compared to normal, I was moving quickly enough that the wind whistling through the tiny space between my jaw and the iron ear flap of my helmet made it difficult to hear, but I thought I detected a shout of alarm from one of the sentries by the lodge. If I was right, now it was a race between how quickly the men inside both the lodge and the slave quarters reacted and how much of a fight the pair of sentries guarding the entrance put up. When a man reaches the rank that Tiberius Sacrovir had, it is easy to forget that one reason they have reached that grade is because of their ability, not only to stay alive but to kill, and because of my being slow to reach the lodge, I was in the perfect spot to watch as the Prefect, not even armed with a *vitus*, executed a thrust that only he knew was a feint, as it completely fooled me as well as his opponent, provoking a lunged counterthrust from one of the bodyguards clad in the counterfeit *segmentata*, his spear punching nothing but the empty space that had been occupied less than an eyeblink earlier by the Prefect, who had somehow managed to take a leaping sidestep that placed the second bodyguard between him and his first opponent.

Naturally, and understandably, the second Aedui pivoted to address the nearest threat, putting his back to his comrade, but with a speed and precision that was impressive, even more so given the man's age, the Prefect was already moving his right arm, held low and with the blade parallel to the ground. If his opponent had his shield, he could have blocked the Prefect's thrust, but because of their haste and excitement, it was still leaning against the side of the lodge next to the door, as was his comrade's immediately adjacent to it. Unprotected as he was, and armed with a longer, Gallic-style *gladius*, he was too late in bringing his blade sweeping across his body to deflect the point of the Prefect's *gladius* and keep it from punching through his armor, which, unlike his comrade, was the traditional Gallic long mail vest with sleeves. I took all of this in as I was closing the last dozen paces, while Wigmar attacked the first bodyguard who had missed the Prefect, but this Aedui had catlike reflexes, recovering his spear from his miss so quickly that he had time to knock Wigmar's *spatha* aside just enough that the slimmer blade struck the smooth

R.W. Peake

shoulder plate instead of the center of his chest and slid off in a small shower of sparks, but because the block placed his spear out of position for an offensive move with it, he threw himself bodily at Wigmar, who did manage to get his shield up in front of him, though it did not keep him from staggering backward, opening up space so that the Aedui, who recoiled in the opposite direction from the collision, had the space to use his spear.

Wigmar's cavalry shield provided protection, but it is useless as an offensive weapon, the boss being almost nonexistent because it is not held by the hand grasping a handle like ours, but by running the forearm through a pair of leather loops, which frees the hand up to grasp the reins. This also means that it is impossible to hold the shield so that it can become an extension of the hand, where the plane of the shield is perpendicular to the plane of the forearm and hand. Now, with barely a half-dozen paces between us, I chopped my stride, ignoring the stab of a deeper agony from the strain on my calf while I reached out with my left hand to grab the back of Wigmar's mail and yank backward with as much strength as I could muster with my left arm. Wigmar would insist immediately afterward, and still does to this day, that he did not need my help, and that may be true, but what it accomplished was that, when his enemy made a second thrust with his spear, there was nothing there, and since he had put all of his weight into his attack, no matter how experienced he was, he could not avoid taking a step forward, right into my blade and the high second position thrust that caught him at the base of his throat. A twist of my wrist sliced through the big vessels of his neck, sending a spray of blood that I felt spatter on my arm, which did not bother me; however, the Prefect had just kicked his own foe off of his blade and was stepping into position to aid Wigmar and received a face full of the second Aedui's blood.

"Pluto's cock!" he managed to gasp, then started gagging. "I got a mouth full of that *cac*!"

"Why did you pull me like that?" Wigmar shouted. "I did not need your help!"

As odd as it may seem, I actually welcomed the fact that,

242

at that very instant, one of what we now saw were double doors was thrown open by a bearded warrior, a *gladius* in one hand, but while he had obviously been drawn by the disturbance outside, it was also apparent that he was completely unprepared for what greeted him, a giant Roman with a stitched-together face and a *gladius* dripping blood, so that within less than a heartbeat, he was staggering backward, vainly trying to keep his intestines inside his stomach. I did not withdraw my blade this time, using it to push him into the lodge, ignoring his shrill screams as I took in the immediate area. This was an entry vestibule, with a short unattached wall set about three paces from the double door, commonly used to keep cold winds from blowing directly into the main room, but it did block my view of the larger chamber, forcing me to steer my victim to the right to get around the edge of the wooden wall so that I could see into the lodge. I immediately regretted this, because what I saw were what seemed like a hundred men, all armed, most of them with a *gladius*, rushing towards me, bellowing things that I did not need a translator to know were promises to gut me in the same manner that I had gutted their comrade, who chose that moment to finally give up his attempt to remain in the land of the living, his legs collapsing from beneath him as his arms dropped to his sides, his head slumping forward. Just before he slid off my blade, I shifted my weight to one leg, hearing someone cry out in pain and only dimly aware that it was me, lifted my other leg and placed that foot against the now-dead man's chest, and kicked, hard.

It worked better than I could have dreamed, the corpse flying back, with his arms flailing in a grotesque parody of a man trying to wave a swarm of gnats away, to slam into the Aedui who had either been the closest to the door or the quickest to react, the dead weight taking this man at the knees and sweeping him off his feet before landing on top of the dead man. The Aedui behind him, who, I noticed by the light of the roaring fire in the center of the room, was clean-shaven and looking more Roman than Gallic, was unable to either stop himself or leap over the two bodies cleanly, though he did try, but he did not clear his comrade trying to disentangle himself, one foot striking this man in the side with enough force to make him cry out in pain, while the leaping Aedui pitched forward in such a way that he had to choose between using his hands to break his fall before he landed on his face, or use his *gladius* in a desperate attempt to stop me from killing him. It is one of those instantaneous decisions that, if a man has time, is easy to make; a foe trying to kill you is more of a threat than landing awkwardly on the floor, but it is also one of those where a man's body is likely to make a different decision, in the same manner as when someone is suddenly knocked off balance, it being extremely difficult not to thrust your arms away from the body in an attempt to restore balance. In this case, the Aedui's body betrayed him, both hands reaching out to break his fall, and I saw the despair on his face as his eyes helplessly followed the track of my blade as it thrust down into his body at the junction of his neck and shoulders, and I felt the jarring grating from my blade cutting through his spine that at least meant his agony only lasted an eyeblink.

Just that quickly, there was a pile blocking the other men in the room from getting to me, yet they did not hesitate nor did they bother trying to drag their comrades out of the way, while the lone warrior still living was vainly trying to extricate himself from under the dead weight of the man I had just slain, his comrades offering no assistance as they instantly pivoted to try and flank me from the opposite end of the screening wall, where, thank the gods, the Prefect was already there, waiting for the Aedui to come. I felt a hand grab my harness, though I did not spare a glance, instead watching and waiting for the moment when the second Aedui finally managed to throw off the corpse of the last man I had slain. Taking advantage of his comrades' lack of attention, or concern for him in their eagerness to kill the Romans who had entered their domain, he had just come to his feet when I darted forward a step, though I confess I was not paying attention to him as I should have, equally concerned that one of his comrades who was barely more than a pace from me but facing slightly away was not alerted by my movement. Also, not wanting to step farther away from the protection of the screening wall, my target was at the outer edge of my reach, forcing me to rely on the strength of my arm, so that between my partial attention and not having my body behind it, I missed the mark. Given the orientation of his body at the time I launched my thrust, I had aimed for his throat since that was the closest vital spot to me, not accounting for and anticipating his own movement, but while it was only a matter of inches, it was as good as a miss as the point shattered his front teeth and sliced open his cheek. His bellow of pain had a sibilant, gurgling quality to it as his mouth filled with blood and teeth, but his shout also had another effect, drawing the attention of the very warrior I had been concerned about, and he did not hesitate, swinging his *gladius* in a downward blow that forced me to dodge back behind the screening wall, where I saw that we had been joined by Wigmar and one of the other troopers with us, and I was about to ask where the other two men were, but Wigmar beat me to it.

"The bastards in the slave quarters have started coming out! Tiwaz and Hunfrid are going to stay outside to…"

His words were cut off by a chorus of shouts, too numerous to be just a pair of men, though it was the answering cry from one of the Aedui inside that confirmed that the bodyguards who had been in the slave quarters were now in the battle. The Prefect had been joined by the other man with us, Thancmar, effectively blocking both ends of the entry area, but by this time, we had had enough time to get at least a good idea of how many men we were facing inside the lodge, but before we would confer, the Aedui I had maimed decided to get vengeance, leaping and this time clearing the pair of corpses on the floor, blood streaming from his ruined face, the lower part of his left cheek hanging outward like a flap, exposing the shattered stumps of his teeth, snarling unintelligibly as he swung his *gladius* in the kind of wide, sweeping blow that is a hallmark of the Gallic tribes that is designed to decapitate their foe, but because of the screening wall, he had to perform it backhanded. Even caught slightly by surprise, my blade was on the right side to use it to block the blow, and my reflexes, even without the help from the gods, are quick enough that I could have defended myself rather easily. Instead, I chose to duck, feeling the disturbed air as the blade swept above me, and just as I hoped, buried itself in the edge of the screening wall, but I was already moving, except this time, I took an extra step forward to ensure that I was in range to deliver my low thrust with enough power while watching my *gladius* in, as we say, using my eyes to pick the spot, just above the Aedui's *baltea*, for my point to plunge through his mail vest, feeling the fraction of an eyeblink's of resistance from the iron links. Unlike other such moments, on this occasion when I was blasted in the face with the last breath of my foe, it was literally a mixture of air and liquid, the blood that had still been pouring into his mouth spraying me fully in the face, and I could see by the hate-filled glare he gave me even as he sank to his knees that this had been his last act of defiance. Or, given what was about to take place, perhaps he hoped to distract me long enough for his comrade whose back had been slightly turned to me to sense the movement, but it was a forlorn hope on his part, because when the Aedui lunged at me, I had already oriented myself so that I was protected by the screening wall to my left, my blade in the first position with my arm pulled back, ready for whatever came.

What came was nothing, at least from my prospective foe, because from the opposite side of the screening wall, the Prefect appeared after driving his own foe back a step, putting my opponent in an untenable position. Suddenly, for the first time, there was a shout that was clearly not the kind of bellowed challenge or promise to slay an enemy but an order, because of the manner in which these Aedui instantly obeyed, withdrawing into the center of the room. I did try and take advantage of my opponent's move to withdraw since he now had to worry about both the Prefect and me, so that when I saw his eyes dart in the Prefect's direction, I moved a step closer before I executed a high second position thrust, hoping to catch him by surprise and take advantage of the fact he did not have a shield. It was unsuccessful, the Aedui managing to dodge the point of my *gladius* before he backed away to join the bulk of the men who were now arrayed from one wall to the other in a double line just behind the firepit. As disappointed as I was that I had not managed to inflict another loss on what I now counted as more than twenty men, I realized that this respite was necessary, for both sides, if only to determine what was happening outside the lodge. It was clear that there was a fight going on, the ringing sound of metal on metal penetrating the log walls of the lodge, but I had not heard the pounding hooves of our mounted men arriving, and I could not imagine that just Tiwaz and Hunfrid could hold off however many men had been in the slave quarters. Just as I was about to call to the Prefect, who was staring fixedly at the double line of Aedui, and suggest that one or two of us go to aid the pair outside, as if in answer, I heard the neighing of a horse, followed by another.

"Wigmar, go to the door and see if Gerbald has everything under control," the Prefect shouted, though his eyes never left our foes across from us. "If he does, bring Tiwaz and Hunfrid back with you. This bunch looks like they've still got some fight in them."

As Wigmar darted for the door, like the Prefect I watched the men across from us, trying to discern from their collective demeanor how much their hearts were in what they had to know was their last stand. Then, my eye was caught by movement at the far end of the lodge, but it was the kind of furtive, darting motion that I somehow felt certain was by one man who had no intention of standing and fighting. It was this moment when I remembered something else, and I felt a stab of what was not exactly panic but was close to it.

"Prefect, there at the far end! That's the door that leads to the cookhouse! I just saw someone head for it! Sacrovir is escaping!"

The Prefect instantly understood and accepted that I had identified the likely identity of the figure who, rather than stopping at the sound of his name, dashed the last couple of paces to what only later we identified as a low door that, as I suspected, led the half-dozen paces to where the meals were prepared, and I could only watch helplessly as I saw the door open and the man I knew was the cause of all the pain and suffering escape into the night.

I should have had more faith in our spy, who was the only one of not just Gerbald's group, but of all of us, who remembered the cookhouse and that it would mean that there was a passage of some sort between the two, so that instead of going with the other nine mounted men led by Gerbald, who timed their attack perfectly, although Tiwaz and Hunfrid argued the point, slamming into the men from the slave quarters only after he was sure they had all vacated the building and were near the entrance to the lodge; instead, Sempronius rode directly to the opposite end of the lodge. Consequently, when the Aedui Sacrovir tried to make his escape, he was met by the man he thought was Aulus Cordus Macula, still unaware that Sempronius had been identified as a spy earlier that day. That led to a mistake, understandable given Sacrovir's ignorance, that the Roman spy was actually there to rescue him, a misjudgment that he quickly learned when, instead of thanking Sempronius, he barked at him to give up his horse, which prompted Sempronius to swing Germanicus' *spatha*, though he retained the presence of mind to use the flat to strike Sacrovir, and when the Aedui leader persisted in trying to grab the bridle of Sempronius' mount, the spy kicked the horse and it leapt forward, sending Sacrovir reeling. When Sempronius pressed his advantage, Sacrovir's only real choice was to dash back into the lodge through the door that was far too small for a mounted man to enter, stunned and confused, and when the Prefect saw his half-brother reappear inside the lodge, he did not bother trying to determine why.

"Gaius! Gaius Julius Sacrovir!" While he had not had the need for some time, it was clear that the Prefect's ability to speak with the kind of power and volume honed over decades on the forum and the battlefield had not diminished, and I saw very clearly that the attention of even the Aedui bodyguards was arrested. Even more telling was how every head turned, at least partially, in the direction of the doorway on the opposite end of the lodge, and I got my first good look at Sacrovir, the Aedui rebel, who was now standing just inside the doorway. For a moment, it seemed as if he was considering trying his hand at escape one more time, but then a figure appeared in the far doorway, though just outside the lodge, my *spatha* in hand. The Prefect began moving, with deliberate slowness, towards the firepit, his *gladius* in his hand, the firelight causing the fresh blood coating his blade to gleam. To me, who knew him fairly well, he sounded almost genial as he said, more softly but still audible for everyone present, "*Salve...*brother."

Their similarity was undeniable, and I was struck by the thought that it was as if I was looking at not an Aedui rebel, but the man who introduced himself as my new Primus Pilus a decade earlier. The Aedui version was taller, and his hair was not black but a lustrous brown and long enough to brush the back of his muscled cuirass, but there was no mistaking that these men shared their blood; it was also clear that his men had no idea that their leader had a brother, one wearing the muscled cuirass and helmet with a longitudinal white crest of the Legions of Rome, and one of the rebels, forgetting our presence, turned his back to us to address the younger Sacrovir, in a tone that made it clear that he was unhappy. It was completely understandable that the attention of everyone present was on the Prefect or his half-brother, which I took advantage of by sidestepping to my right, with the intent of giving myself some space and the ability to attack from a different direction than the Prefect, Wigmar, and Thancmar, who were standing a pace apart just in front of the screening wall, while Tiwaz was on the door side of the screening wall, guarding the entrance.

At first, the Aedui leader did not move from where he was standing just behind the second line of his men, but nor was he bolting for the far door, and he whispered something, prompting a pair of warriors from the second line to turn and face where Sempronius still stood, not trying to enter but sending the clear message he would try and stop anyone from leaving. Initially, I did wonder why the Aedui Sacrovir did not order some of his men to rush Sempronius in order to make their escape, although we could all clearly hear noise outside, not just of fighting, but the thrumming of horses' hooves as their riders galloped back and forth, and after listening for a couple heartbeats, I understood why; either the fighting had shifted, which I did not think based on what I heard, or enough of the Aedui from the slave quarters had been dispatched that Gerbald had sent a couple of his troopers to the far end of the lodge to join Sempronius, which I thought likely. Since the Aedui Sacrovir had no real idea of exactly how many men were with us, I could see why he was hesitant to subtract from the men facing those of us inside if there were enough of us outside to cut them down. What became apparent was that we were in a standoff, because as of this moment, we did not have enough men to overwhelm almost two dozen seasoned warriors, while the Aedui Sacrovir was faced with the opposite dilemma; he had enough men to keep us at bay, but he did not know what was waiting for him outside, though we could all tell from inside the lodge that the fighting was dying down, and there was nothing to indicate that it was in the Aedui favor since there was no attempt by any Aedui to force their way inside. Finally, the Aedui Sacrovir moved towards his half-brother, pushing his way through his men to stand with the stone firepit to his immediate left, a clever move on his part, given, like everyone else among his party, he did not have his shield, a sign that they had not expected to have any trouble here.

For a long interval, the only sounds were of some of us inside the lodge panting from the exertions of a moment earlier, and the sounds of the fighting outside that, even in that period of relative silence, we could hear a shrill scream of mortal agony, followed by a diminishment of the noise, and I guessed this was what prompted the younger Sacrovir to say bluntly, "What do you want, Tiberius?"

This was the moment when I realized something, and I felt a bit foolish for not actually asking what was an obvious question beforehand, and I could not stop myself from blurting out, "Have you two actually met before?"

For the first, and only time, the pair of Sacrovirs seemed to be equally amused, but it was the Aeduan who asked the Prefect, "What, you did not tell him, Tiberius? That you came for Tata's funeral rites? And how we spent a month together?"

"No," the Prefect answered coldly. "In fact, I forgot about it. I suppose," he offered his half-brother a shrug, "you didn't make enough of an impression on me that I thought it worth mentioning…to anyone."

"There it is," the Aeduan sneered. "The Roman arrogance!"

"For someone who adopted a Roman *nomen*, who likes to dress like a Roman, and who tried to equip his traitors to Rome like men of the Legions, for you to speak of 'Roman arrogance' is hypocrisy at its finest," the Prefect responded with an eerily identical sneer of his own. "But it's not surprising."

The younger Sacrovir pointed a finger at his half-brother; I saw that it was shaking, and I wondered if it was anger or fear.

"Your Imperator is to blame for this!" he shouted. "He has bled us dry, and for what? For his banquets, where he serves oysters and larks' tongues to hundreds of patricians, for no other reason than because he can! He is building that villa on Capri! Oh," he nodded emphatically, "yes, we know all about it. Even here," he snarled, "here in this backwater! Is that not what you call it? But we have said no more!" Poking his thumb into his chest, his voice grew shriller. "*I,* Gaius Julius Sacrovir, whose great-grandfather was awarded lands by Divus Julius himself, whose family has served Rome for…"

"Shut your fucking mouth," the Prefect cut him off, and while he did not shout, there was something in his tone that seemed to reach his half-brother, who did indeed snap his mouth shut. "Don't you talk to *me* about *my* family serving Rome!" To my shock, he suddenly pointed at me, and demanded, "Do you know who that is standing there, *brother*? You who *dares* to speak of his family serving Rome?" The younger Sacrovir did not answer, clearly thinking, as I did, that it was a rhetorical question; we were both wrong, as the Prefect suddenly bellowed, "*Well, do you*?" Again, his brother did not reply, though he did turn to examine me more closely, and I saw the expression change, a dawning recognition that the Prefect clearly interpreted the same way. "That's right, *this* is the great-grandson of someone who served Rome, faithfully and well, for more than forty years, not as a grasping, scheming barbarian who betrayed his own people to gain favor with Rome. But," he smiled then, the kind that a man offers another when he is certain that what he is about to say will be a staggering blow, "beyond that, it was this man who almost singlehandedly stopped those *crupellarii* you thought would give you victory today." He pointed again, and I was torn between embarrassment, a touch of anger, but mostly pride when he added, "You can see the scar he will bear to his dying day that will always serve as another reminder of all that his line has sacrificed for Rome. And, brother, our family hasn't sacrificed anything near what theirs has. Our father never served under the standard, but…" He stopped suddenly; I had been watching the younger brother and his men as the Prefect spoke, and when I glanced over at him, I saw that his expression had changed, one of grief that I did not comprehend until he gathered himself and resumed, "…I saw the Centurion's father fall trying to save his son, and *brother*, trust me when I tell you that our father would have never lifted a finger to save you. Or," he finished bitterly, "me, for that matter. He was a coward who abandoned his legal wife to fuck a Gallic whore and whelp a bastard who tried to overthrow Rome…and failed."

If the Prefect had walked over and slapped his brother, I do not believe the effect would have been as dramatic, his mouth dropping open to give an audible gasp, his face going pale, and when he looked over at me, I saw the shock of recognition on his face, though it only lasted less than a heartbeat before his lips twisted into a hate-filled grimace, yet when he actually moved, it was not in my direction but towards the Prefect, raising his weapon as he did so, which was not a long Gallic *gladius* but a *spatha*. This was when I realized that this was what the Prefect wanted, and I for one was certainly prepared to do whatever was necessary to ensure that they faced each other, but then one of the Aedui bodyguards said something in their tongue, pointing his own blade at the Prefect. While I did not understand the words, I believed that this man was offering to be the younger Sacrovir's champion in facing the Prefect, which got me moving a couple of paces back towards the middle of the lodge, though I took care not to advance any closer to them.

"If that man," I spoke up and pointed at him with my *gladius*, "is offering to fight the Prefect for you, Sacrovir, you need to let him know that he'll have to face me first."

The younger brother proved that he had correctly understood the Prefect's reference to my great-grandfather by replying with my name, "I understand, Centurion Pullus, but that will not be necessary." He looked at the Prefect, his lip curling up in contempt. "I want the pleasure of sending my arrogant half-brother into the afterlife myself. However," he returned his attention to me, smiling coldly, "if Dumnorix here requests the pleasure of gutting you like a pig, I am only too happy to give my permission. Not only is he the commander of my personal bodyguard, but the man who commanded the *crupellarii* was his cousin, so it is understandable that he wants the pleasure of killing you for himself, after all. Or," he shrugged, "perhaps after I dispatch my brother here, I will kill you the same way I personally slew a half-dozen of your fellow Roman Legionaries today."

While it was true that I did not remember a significant portion of our fight with the *crupellarii*, I was confident that I was speaking truly when, with a mocking laugh, I answered, "You're a liar, Sacrovir. I saw you sitting on your horse at the top of the hill, well away from any fighting." Turning my attention to the other Aedui, I said, "But I probably am the one who killed your cousin. There was one man in particular who begged me to spare him. He even offered sexual favors if I let him live. But," I gave him a grin, "he squealed like a pig as I used his own ax to gut him like one."

I was unsure how much this Dumnorix understood, but it was clearly enough for him to bellow in rage, and completely ignoring his commander's shouted command, come rushing at me, which was exactly what I wanted. Frankly, I expected more from the commander of the leader of the rebellion's bodyguard, although it is possible that the younger Sacrovir had lied about this Dumnorix's role, or perhaps the man was just out of his mind with rage at the death of his cousin. Whatever the reason, he charged at me with his long *gladius* raised above his head in preparation for the downward blow favored by barbarians on both sides of the Rhenus, and it is a devastating blow…if it lands. However, it is also easy to defend against such a blow; if you are in a tightly packed formation and have a shield as we do, simply lift it above your head. I had neither a shield or even my *vitus*, but I had room to move, which I used, though I waited until he had fully committed to his attack before I did so, admittedly something that not many men can do, even if they are smaller than me. Hopping to his left in the fraction of an eyeblink after his blade swung down, the blow was delivered with enough force that the tip and several inches of his *gladius* buried itself in the wooden floor, and I saw a look of resignation in his eyes as I plunged my *gladius* deeply into his side, just under the ribcage but with the blade angling upward to pierce his heart so that there was no need for me to rip the blade out, the Aedui dead even before he finished collapsing at my feet.

"This is the best you can do?" I pointed down at Dumnorix's corpse, making no attempt to disguise my contempt. "If you're not better than this, you're not long for this world, Sacrovir."

It was as I was saying this that we learned in a way that left no doubt that Gerbald and his mounted force were victorious, when he appeared with four of his men, along with Tiwaz and Hunfrid from behind the screening wall, while Sempronius finally entered a heartbeat later with the rest of the mounted party through the cookhouse exit. The atmosphere in the lodge palpably changed then, the expressions of despair, and fear, impossible to misinterpret...with one exception.

"Tiberius," the younger Sacrovir stepped away from his men after giving them a whispered order that seemed to be a warning to keep their weapons lowered, "I have a proposition for you."

"Unless it's your unconditional surrender, there's nothing you have to offer that I'd be interested in," the Prefect replied.

"Be that as it may, it can do no harm for you to hear it, surely." I had to admit, grudgingly, that the younger Sacrovir did not react to the Prefect's dismissive tone, sounding as if he was trying to convince a friend to go for the next round of wine. The Prefect did not reply, surprising me by looking in my direction with a raised eyebrow, to which I responded with a shrug that indicated my indifference. He interpreted this as agreement, which he signaled with a gesture of his own, and his half-brother did not hesitate. "It is clear that you and I have...unfinished business between us, Tiberius. My proposition is that we settle our business, right now and right here, just you and I. We send our men outside, and if I am the man who emerges..."

"No," the Prefect cut him off. "I know what you're going to say. If you defeat me, Centurion Pullus as the ranking officer is supposed to let you and your men go free. And that…"

"You do not know me as well as you think, Tiberius." His brother returned the favor of stopping the Prefect in midsentence. "That is not what I was going to say. I know it will be too much to expect to allow me to go free. But," he turned to indicate the men behind him, and for the first time, I saw what I believed was a real, genuine emotion from Gaius Julius Sacrovir, the kind of sorrow and regret that a leader has when he feels he has failed the men under his command, the kind that only another leader recognizes, and understands, "I *do* ask that these men be allowed to return to their homes. Their only crime was loyalty to me, and to the cause that we all believe in, and I do not believe they should be punished for that. And, all that I ask for myself is that I be allowed to stand trial so that I can state our grievances before your Imperator has my head parted from my shoulders."

Not surprisingly, all eyes in the now almost full lodge went to the Prefect, the tension so thick, and understandably so, that anyone making any kind of move, such as grabbing for or raising a drawn *gladius*, would have been responsible for initiating a bloodbath in the close confines of this lodge, even with the furniture having been shoved against one wall by the Aedui, and I only realized that I was holding my breath when I started getting a bit dizzy.

Despite the fact they had only been in each other's presence for a month at some unspecified point in the past, the younger Sacrovir had clearly learned something about the Prefect, or perhaps he just knew what type of man the Prefect was, because he broke the silence by replying, "Very well. I agree to the terms." He paused, I supposed to let his brother to translate, though just watching the Aedui, there was no need, or perhaps it was because he knew what was coming. "As part of this agreement," he resumed, "you will order your men to lay down their weapons." This was met by howls of outraged protest, with more than one of the bodyguards shaking his head, but I noticed that, while they did not drop their *gladii*, neither did they lift their points above their waists, while the Prefect raised his voice, his tone harsh and unyielding. "If you want your men to see another dawn, *brother*, you're going to convince them to surrender their weapons. If you defeat me, they will be allowed to return to their homes. But if they refuse to do so," he pointed at me, "Centurion Pullus will finish the job he started with your *crupellarii*. With," he added, thank the gods, "the rest of these men to help, of course. And that means that you'll die with them, without any chance of airing your grievances."

Since there was never the opportunity to ask him, I have no idea whether it was the chance to save his men's lives or the idea of being able to have his voice heard in Rome that convinced him, but what mattered was that he turned to address his men. There was some back and forth in their tongue, though not as much as I expected, but I believe it was when their leader pointed to the corpse of Dumnorix, lying in a pool of his own blood, that clinched his argument, because within the span of a couple heartbeats, the first bodyguard dropped his *gladius* to the floor with a clattering that was the loudest noise since my short fight with Dumnorix, but he was quickly joined by the others, until there was a pile of weapons.

"My men do have a request," the younger brother said, and I knew what it would be, since I would have made the same request.

"Yes, your men will be allowed to take their weapons with them," the Prefect proved that he was thinking the same way I was, but he added, "but only if you best me. If not, then they will be bound and the *Praetor* will decide their fate."

That was when his brother said something that caused the Prefect and me to exchange yet another glance, both of us wondering if the other took it the same way.

"Oh, I trust Varro will be just," the younger Sacrovir said, but with an assurance that indicated, to me anyway, that he might have a good reason for his optimism, but the Prefect regarded him with a raised eyebrow, and his version of a smile that was nothing more than a slight lifting of one corner of his mouth.

"Varro?" he echoed, as if he were confused. "If you mean Varro the Elder, he's not here, and the son isn't *Praetor*. In fact," he cocked his head to one side, acting as if this had not been a subject of a couple watches of speculation by this point in the campaign, "I'm not even sure what posting he holds." Looking at me, he ventured, "Tribune, maybe? Pullus, what do you think?"

"He was a *Quaestor* when he was here for that nonsense he cooked up with Catualda," I pretended to muse, "but he had to flee back to Rome in disgrace. Honestly," I shook my head, "I don't know what post he holds, but I know it's not *Praetor*."

I cannot really describe how unsettled this clearly made the Aedui, nor can I describe how happy it made me, knowing what was coming next.

"No," the Prefect put in just as I expected, "I'm talking about Gaius Silius. He's the ranking officer here. He will decide what's to become of your men. And he's just, but," he shook his head, "he's not known for his merciful nature."

It was decidedly odd to hear these two discussing what everyone present knew would be a fight to the death of one of them, behaving almost amicably, with none of the overt hostility that had been present a short time earlier. Wigmar had taken it upon himself to supervise gathering up the *gladii*, and the Aedui were understandably nervous, but when the younger Sacrovir called out to them, pointing to the main door, they followed as Tiwaz led the way out. However, the Aedui Sacrovir had something else on his mind, because he turned to face the other end of the lodge, where Sempronius and four of the formerly mounted men were standing.

"So, Macula," he began, his voice cold. "Or is that even your real name?" Before Sempronius could reply, the younger Sacrovir made the kind of dismissive gesture that seems to be favored by the upper classes. "No matter what your name is, not really. No, what I want to know is, are you the man who betrayed me? Who gave my *loving* brother here information about my whereabouts?"

Honestly, I did not expect Sempronius to answer, but he did, not flinching as he looked directly at the Aedui.

"No, Gaius, I didn't betray you," he said evenly. "I'm a loyal Roman, and you can't betray a traitor to Rome. I," his chin lifted slightly, but there was no mistaking the pride in his tone, "did my duty to my Imperator, nothing more."

I happened to be looking at the spy, so I was completely

unprepared for Sacrovir to shout, almost screech in fact, "*You lied to me, Aulus! You told me that you cared about the Aedui and our plight. That you cared about* me!*"*

Truly, it was not what he said, but the way that he said it that made me look over to the Prefect once again, looking for some sort of reaction that he was thinking along the same lines that I was, that there was…something else going on here, and what I saw in his expression told me that he was, though neither of us said anything.

"I did my duty to Rome," Sempronius replied, except that this time, he sounded uncomfortable, causing me to turn my attention away from the Prefect, but when I looked back at Sempronius, he averted his gaze to stare at a spot somewhere above our heads.

"Well," the younger brother agreed bitterly, "you did it well." Then, in a clear signal, he pointedly turned his back on the spy to look at the Prefect.

"Go make your preparations," his older brother said. "I need to speak to the Centurion."

He beckoned me to follow him towards the main doors, but I also noticed the surreptitious gesture he made to Sempronius and the Batavians with him to remain where they were, effectively blocking the exit leading to the cookhouse, just in case his younger brother's nerve failed him.

Leading me to the screening wall, he turned to face it so his back was to his half-brother, who seemed to be engaged in some sort of prayer or meditation, hands out from his sides at his waist, with palms up.

"Gnaeus, there's something I want you to do for me, but before I tell you what it is, I want you to swear on the eagle that you'll do it."

I bridled at this, pointing out, "You can't really expect me to swear on the eagle when I don't even know what I'm swearing to. That's not fair!"

"No," he agreed, "it's *not* fair. But I'm still asking you to do it."

Ultimately, I consented, though it was just as much because I wanted to know what it was he wanted, but I was not even close in my guess about what he would ask, although I immediately understood why he had asked for my oath beforehand. As I listened, it felt as if my heart had turned to stone, sinking down from its position in my chest down, down, down into my gut, cursing myself for agreeing to something like this too readily.

Nevertheless, when he was finished, all I could bring myself to ask was, "Are you sure about this, Prefect?"

"I've never been more certain about anything in my life," he replied without hesitation.

It took me two tries, but finally, I managed, "I'll do as you ask, Prefect. Not," I felt compelled to add, "that I'm happy about it."

"I understand, Gnaeus," he said quietly. Then, he offered me his arm, and I came remarkably close to grabbing it and dragging him out of the lodge with me, but I could not bring myself to shame him in that way.

"Mars and Bellona."

It was all I could manage to say, and he repeated, "Mars and Bellona. And Gnaeus…thank you."

It was the one time I did not want to be thanked for something. Signaling to Sempronius, I pointed to the main door, and he and the other men walked the length of the lodge, disappearing around the screening wall. I stopped there, looking over my shoulder to see the Prefect and his brother, both of them holding their *gladii*, facing each other…then I left, and closed both doors, certain that I would not see Tiberius Sacrovir, my first Primus Pilus, alive again.

Chapter 7

It is only now, these years later, that I offer the full story of what actually transpired, but first, I will relate the version that became the official description of the end of what is now known as Sacrovir's Revolt, although this was not the case in the days immediately after the final battle. Initially, we called it the Aeduan Uprising, or the Revolt of the Aedui, but within a month, a couple weeks after our return to Ubiorum, Macer returned from the *Praetorium* and called a meeting of all the officers, including Optios.

"From now on, whenever the boys are out in town and talking about where we've been, they're to refer to our bit with the Aedui as Sacrovir's Revolt," he announced, squinting as he read from his tablet. "Or the Revolt of Sacrovir. Same with the Treveri and Florus. Call it Florus' Revolt. Actually," he snapped it shut, "I think all the Imperator cares about is that the tribes aren't referred to in any way. The way the *Praetor* put it, Rome wants people to know that this wasn't an uprising by the tribes but by a few disgruntled members of the nobility who managed to attract a gang of debtors and assorted malcontents to join their cause."

Honestly, this was close enough to the truth as we saw it that it was not difficult to get the men to go along, although it took a few swipes of the *vitus* for the more forgetful among them. Accordingly, we heard there was much rejoicing in Rome, mainly due to the fact that, as the mob is likely to do, they had convinced themselves that every tribe had risen up, and Tiberius was hailed for his swift and decisive action in suppressing the rebellions. Unknown to us, the downfall of Gaius Silius had already begun, the seeds of which were planted during the campaign. What I am about to relate is not the official version of the ending of Sacrovir's Revolt, which is that he was tracked down to his hunting lodge, which is true, with the lodge being surrounded and, when he refused to surrender, set afire, whereupon he burned to death, which is not. No, what happened was set in motion by the Prefect, after his half-brother made his offer, when he took me aside.

"Gnaeus, I'm going to kill this *cunnus*," he began, which I expected, and wholeheartedly agreed was the desired outcome, but he was not through. "But I'm not going to leave this lodge alive either."

I was so shocked that I could not find my voice at first, instead staring at him in disbelief before I finally managed, "*Gerrae*! Why are you talking this nonsense?"

"It's not nonsense," he replied sharply, as if he were offended. "I'm serious, Gnaeus. I know what the future will hold for me now that he," he jerked his head in the direction of his half-brother, who was now standing there, watching us, "has done what he's done. I'm a Camp Prefect, and I'm also seen as an ally of the *Praetor*. And, Gnaeus, believe me when I tell you this. Gaius Silius is in grave danger as it is, and I'm going to be a liability. Besides," I will never forget the smile he gave me then, "I'm tired, Gnaeus. This is a good way to end my career, and I'm…tired. Ever since Aurelia died, and with Sextus now in Pannonia and with a family of his own, I'm happy to see the end of my life, provided that I kill Gaius."

"You really hate him that much?" I asked, without thinking, but I was shocked when he looked surprised.

"I…I haven't actually thought about it much, but honestly, I don't hate him. My *father*," the laugh he gave was laced with a bitterness that was almost palpable, and I recall thinking in that moment of the other Prefect, my great-grandfather, and his father Lucius, "him, I hated. I hated him even before he left my mother. He was weak, he was a coward, and I despise him now as much as I did when he was alive. Gaius?" He shrugged. "I actually enjoyed the month we spent together, if only because he hated our father as much as I did. But with this…" he waved a hand in an encompassing motion, "…thing that he's done? No, he has to die, but I think he'd rather be killed by his own flesh and blood than face what's waiting for him in Rome. You know as well as I do what Sejanus will do to him." He paused, then whispered, "Especially if everything we've heard is true.

He's going to kill him, but first, he'll want to make sure that he hasn't uttered a word to anyone about where the money to supply and equip that army came from, and if he has, the names of the people he told. Now," he drew his shoulders back, "leave me to it."

This was when he offered his arm, and I departed after that, jumping a bit when I heard the locking bar slam down, happy that the men were gathered too far away to see it happen in the darkness. The trooper holding the other horses had moved up the track, and I went directly to Latobius, needing the feeling that I got from his solid presence, finding his single-minded desire for obtaining something for him to munch on without any concern for me oddly comforting. However, to my surprise, on this occasion he did not thrust his nose into my midsection, instead lifting his head to my head, his huge nostrils almost touching me as he smelled the left side of my face, his exhalations blasting me as he performed what I can only describe as an examination of what is even now still a livid, jagged scar. Once he was done, he nickered softly, then lowered his head slightly in a manner I recognized, and despite the waves of emotions that were battering me as my mind grappled with what was coming, I had to laugh.

"I have my helmet on, you big oaf. I can't do that now," I chided him, but when he persisted, nudging me insistently, I made a show of sighing as I untied the chin thongs and removed my helmet, then lowered my chin so that our foreheads were touching, aware of but not really caring that the other men were undoubtedly watching.

I do not know how long we stood there, as I stroked his neck with my free hand, listening to his breathing as my horse and I experienced this moment of togetherness, but it was long enough that I was startled when someone cleared their throat behind me. Oddly, I did not feel all that foolish when I turned around to see Sempronius standing there, wearing an expression that I recalled seeing on him when we were together in Rome.

"They've begun fighting, Pullus," he informed me. "Do you want us to find something to break down the doors? I checked the rear entrance and it's barred as well."

"Why?" I felt the anger flare, although I was thankful that I was as close to exhaustion as I was since it dulled the edge a bit. "You don't think the Prefect can handle that *cunnus*?"

"I've never seen the Prefect with a *gladius*," the spy countered, "but I have seen his brother, although it was only sparring. And, Pullus," he cautioned, "he's very good."

This was the last thing I wanted to hear, but I also knew what the Prefect was capable of, recalling how we had actually sparred once, in the bathhouse in Ubiorum, with nobody but Macer present as judge.

"It's a tradition that everyone who wants to can challenge a Pullus," he had explained at the time, then gave me one of his rare smiles, at least back when he was still Primus Pilus. "I faced your father, and I want to see if you can thrash me as badly as he did."

As I am certain he knew I would, I did not put in a full effort; despite his assurances that he would not hold it against me, the idea of thrashing one's Primus Pilus and then him not seeking retribution for said thrashing was far-fetched just enough that I could not bring myself to move as quickly, or put as much power behind my thrusts. Regardless of my effort, the outcome was exactly as he had predicted, yet I had come away impressed with Sacrovir's skill, and the ferocity that he was able to unleash even in a sparring session, which is a problem for most men, and I had just witnessed him less than a third of a watch before this moment easily handle himself as he dispatched his foe.

Now, facing Sempronius, I managed to quell my rising anger and assure him, "I've faced the Prefect myself, and I'm not worried. Besides," I pointed out, "there are only two ways out of that building, and we have men standing outside each of them. Even if that Aedui *cunnus* manages to be blessed by Fortuna because the Prefect slips or makes a mistake, he's not going anywhere."

"Pullus," Sempronius sighed, "I hope you're right. But don't be surprised if Sacrovir, the Aedui one, has some secret escape. This is his family's lodge, and he knows every inch of it." Something seemed to occur to him, and I learned what it was when he asked suddenly, "How thoroughly did you search that lodge?"

My stomach suddenly clenched, and I was forced to admit, "Not at all." Though I hated to do so, I asked, "Why?"

He did not reply immediately, turning instead to survey the area, and when he spoke, it was in the tone that one uses when talking to oneself. "The trees are too far away, and the cookhouse is too close. So," he turned and pointed to the slave quarters. "We need to search there, and," he moved his arm to point at it, "the stables."

"Search them for what?" I asked, not having caught up yet.

"A tunnel entrance," he answered immediately. "Or, exit, since it's not very likely that a man is going to want to sneak into the lodge."

Cursing bitterly, though it was aimed at myself for not thinking of it, I was about to call out to Wigmar when, from inside the lodge, there was a muffled shout, one that experience told me was of pain, but with a tinge of rage that was the sign it was not a mortal blow.

Sempronius confirmed his agreement, commenting, "Someone drew first blood."

I called to Wigmar and Gerbald, who were standing with their comrades, holding the reins of their mounts as they watched the lodge, as if they could see the fight inside, and it was impossible to miss their reluctance, leading their horses as they approached.

"You won't need your horses," I began, then quickly explained what I wanted them to do, sending Wigmar to the slave quarters, and Gerbald to the stables.

"It will be well-disguised," Sempronius warned them. "That means you're going to have to move things around in the slave quarters." Addressing Gerbald, he mimed the action he wanted the Batavian to do. "Use your *gladius*, and stab it into the dirt at least," he held his hand up, his thumb and pointing finger about three inches apart, "that deeply. Be especially careful where the hay is piled, and in the corners."

"I know how to search a barn, Roman," Gerbald grumbled, but he was moving as he did so.

Watching the pair for just a moment, I turned my attention back to the lodge, and I supposed I had been blocking out the sounds of the combat taking place inside, probably because of the impossibility of being able to determine who was winning. The windows were shuttered, of course, yet while there are always cracks or spaces between shutters, it was impossible to see anything unless I was willing to walk up and press my eye to one of them in the same manner as a child might who wants to spy on his parents, and while I was tempted, I suppressed it, choosing to go stand with the rest of the men, Sempronius joining me. The conversation was desultory, as we stood there, listening to the ringing clash as one of the combatants blocked or parried a blow, trying to determine what it might mean.

"It should be over by now," Sempronius said in just above a whisper, "shouldn't it?"

"Yes," I answered tersely. I did not want to say more, but I suppose I felt compelled to acknowledge, "You were clearly right about the Aedui's skill. Like I told you, I've faced the Prefect before, back when he was still my Primus Pilus, and he is good, very good."

It was not long after that when there was a shout from the direction of the stable, and our heads all turned as one in time to see Gerbald emerge, but he did not come to us immediately, instead shouting something in his own tongue, whereupon Tiwaz responded, then addressed me excitedly, "Gerbald says he found a hole in the ground! It is in the far corner of the stable, but he does not want to leave it in case the Aedui inside there," he pointed at the lodge, "tries to use it."

I was about to ask him to expand on what he meant by "hole," since that could mean something other than a "tunnel," but I remembered that Tiwaz's Latin was not very good; besides, this was not the time to quibble about his vocabulary, so instead, I said, "Go join him. Both of you stay there until I tell you."

He did not salute, just nodded, but what I cared about was that he was moving, at a run, to join his comrade.

"Thank you for thinking of that," I told Sempronius, but he waved it off.

"When you're in my line of work, you're always looking for ways to escape."

"Centurion."

I turned to look at Hunfrid, who had called to me, but he was pointing to the lodge.

"Is that smoke?"

It took a heartbeat for me to see it because of the darkness, but then I spotted a thin plume that had found a crack between the shutters.

"Pullus," Sempronius whispered, "it's gotten brighter in there too."

He was still speaking when there was another crash that could only come from iron striking iron, and he had just finished when there was another sound, one that every man who has been in battle recognizes and, no matter how many times I have heard it, still makes the hair on the back of my neck stand up.

"Someone just made the killing blow," Sempronius said quietly.

I did not respond, nor did I react, keeping my eyes on the lodge, watching as the light from the interior not only intensified, but began to spread, the crack between the windows to the left of where the firepit was located now glowing almost as brightly.

"Gnaeus? Gnaeus! Can you hear me?"

I could, though just barely, and I moved closer to the lodge; this was when the heat hit me, and I offered a prayer that the Prefect had changed his mind, but it was not destined to be answered, either by the gods, or by the Prefect.

"I can hear you!" I called out.

"Come to the door!"

I obeyed at a run, groaning from the stabbing pain the sudden exertion caused me, though I still quickly reached the doors, but while I expected to hear the locking bar being lifted from the bracket, nothing happened, while I could just glimpse part of the Prefect's face through the narrow crack between the two doors. Because of the growing light from the flames and his helmet, most of his face was in shadow, but I could easily see that it was streaked with blood, though it was impossible for me to tell if it was his or his half-brother's.

"Prefect? What is it? Why aren't you opening the door?" Suddenly, the thought occurred to me. "Is your brother still alive?"

"No," he replied, his voice hoarse, which is quite common after a fight, though I have no idea why that is. "He's not. Look down at your feet."

As baffled as I was by the command, I did so, and instantly saw the gleam of gold, which was also when I realized what it was, and why he had offered it. Bending down, I picked the ring up, recognizing it as the one I had seen on the Aedui Sacrovir's finger, while the Prefect, unwilling to lift the locking bar and open the door, had instead shoved it under, making me think that he did not trust me not to try and drag him out, the final example of how well Tiberius Sacrovir knew me, since that is exactly what I would have done.

"They're going to want proof that Gaius Julius Sacrovir is dead," he explained. "But once you show that to the *Praetor* and that treacherous bastard Varro, I have a favor to ask."

"Of course," I replied automatically, though I was only partially listening; the heat was growing more intense, my eyes were starting to sting from the smoke that was seeping out through every crack and opening, and I was still trying to think of a way to drag the Prefect out of there.

"I want you to make sure this gets to my son," he explained.

This surprised me considerably.

"Why would your son want his dead uncle the rebel's ring?"

"Because it's *not* his fucking ring!" the Prefect snarled, and whereas many times when, as Primus Pilus, he acted as if he was enraged when he was not, I could tell this was not the case, that this was genuine, though it was not aimed at me. Fortunately, I kept my mouth shut and learned why. "That," I saw his hand raise and he pointed through the crack at the ring in my palm, "was my father's ring, and as his oldest son, it should have been mine, but he gave it to Gaius instead. And," he laughed then, filled with a bitterness that bespoke of a lifetime of anger towards a feckless father who clearly favored his other son, "Gaius lied and told me that it had been lost. But then I saw it on his fucking hand. And," just that quickly, his voice changed to a tone of a savage satisfaction, "I fucking took it back before he died. I wanted him to *know* that I was taking it."

Thinking that he would appreciate it, I said, "And I'd wager he died, crying like a woman and begging you for mercy, eh?"

"Then you'd fucking lose," he snapped. "He died well, with his *gladius* in his hand. He died..." his voice broke then, "...like he had been under the standard his whole life. Like a Sacrovir of Rome should."

I was reminded then of something that I had seen, experienced, and read about in my father's account, something that my mother had always been quick to remind me about, that as a child without any siblings, there was an aspect of sibling relationships that I just did not understand, particularly when it came to brothers.

"Well," I finally managed, "that's something, I suppose." Holding up the ring, I promised, "I'll do as you ask, Prefect."

"Good." I saw his head nod, then he stepped back away from the door so that I could no longer see him clearly, then called out, "And, Gaius, remember your oath."

Before I could respond, I sensed as much as saw a sudden motion through the crack, then the Prefect gave a short but sharp cry, followed by a gurgling sound, and I felt the tears pushing against my eyes as I rushed up to the door, intent on breaking it down somehow, but when I was about to press my eye to look through the crack, I recoiled from the heat, and I only caught the barest glimpse of two pairs of legs, one set lying atop another before I had to retreat several paces. My attention was so focused on the scene in front of me that I did not realize that Sempronius, and a couple of the Batavians, had walked up behind me.

"What oath? Pullus? What did he mean?" Once more, before I could respond, the spy cried out, "We have to get him out of there!"

He began to move, clearly intending to run to the door himself, forcing me to lunge to grab him, the sudden movement making all of the aches and pains come back to life, and I just managed to catch the back collar of his tunic, almost yanking him off his feet in the process.

"What are you doing?" he shouted, and he was quickly joined in his protest by the other men. "He's going to burn to

268

death!"

"No, he's not," I assured him, but I could not bring myself to say the word itself. Instead, I settled for, "Trust me, Sempronius. He won't feel it."

The spy stared at me for a long moment, and I was afraid that he would force me to articulate it, then he looked away from me to stare at the lodge, the roof of which was now smoking furiously, while the Batavians muttered to each other.

It was Tiwaz, who I had not noticed return from the slave quarters, who asked hesitantly, "This was what the Prefect wanted, Centurion?"

"Yes," I nodded, certain of at least this much. "This was what he wanted."

We stood there, though we had to remove ourselves and the horses a few paces farther away, and watched as the lodge became fully involved, the embers catching the cookhouse on fire as well, and the sky was just beginning to lighten in the east when the support timbers collapsed, leaving a heaping pile of blazing timbers, the thatch quickly burning away, the embers rising high into the pinkening sky. Once that happened, Gerbald and Hunfrith returned from the stable, reporting that there had been no sounds coming from below ground that might indicate someone had escaped the flames, extinguishing my last hope that perhaps the Prefect had managed to crawl over to wherever the tunnel entrance inside the lodge was located. Even if we had waited for the fire to cool down, there would have been no way to find it, the charred remnants of tables, chairs, cots and beams lying in heaps that we knew from experience would take days to become cool enough to be cleared away, time that we did not have. It was the spy who foresaw that this would be a problem.

"They're going to want some sort of proof that Sacrovir is in there," he indicated the blazing fire. "I hope you have some ideas about what that might be." I held up the ring, not surprised that he recognized it immediately, so he moved on to the next question, which I had put off thinking about. Jerking his thumb where the bodyguards were sitting together with their hands bound, guarded by four of the Batavians, he asked, "And what about them?"

It was true that the beast that resides within me had gone into the kind of deep slumber it falls into after it is roused, which means that I do not even have that as an excuse for my actions, and what disturbed me even then, and over the intervening time, disturbs me even more was that I was not particularly angry, nor did I hate these men for choosing the side of a half-Aeduan, half-Roman traitor. No, my decision was made for perhaps the worst reason possible; they were an inconvenience, I was tired, sore, my face throbbed, and I wanted to get some sleep.

"They're going to slow us down, even mounted," I answered. "And I don't want to waste any more time than we already have."

I was striding towards the men as I said this, my great-grandfather's *gladius* already in my hand though I did not remember drawing it, and I moved so quickly that I think even the battle-hardened Batavians were frozen in shock and disbelief as I butchered helpless men who could only resist by trying to get to their feet and flee, none of them managing to get more than a couple steps before I was on them. I was not only not surprised, but I was content to be left alone on the ride back to Augustodunum where, as I hoped, the *Praetor* and the rest of the command group were not yet present, and it was easy enough to avoid Carbo, the only individual I was worried about currently in the town. We returned to the place that Sempronius, masquerading as Macula, had lived, and have little memory of anything other than collapsing onto the bed that the spy said I could sleep in, other than the fact that I barely managed to pull off my armor before I collapsed.

Thankfully, Sempronius allowed me to sleep through most of the day, only awakening me when he overheard a pair of Legionaries who were on a walking post in that part of the town talking about the arrival of the *Praetor* and the 1st. It took me three attempts to get my feet onto the floor; as I had feared, lying still had made my body stiffen up, and his slave Dumnorix finally had to help me up. I did take the opportunity to query the slave, who Sempronius graciously put at my disposal for an oiling and scraping.

"You're from Britannia, aren't you?"

He had just poured some oil into his hand to warm it up, and I did not miss the slight tremor in his voice at my question.

"Yes, Master," he answered cautiously.

"I'm married to a woman of the Parisii," I informed him casually, and the slave suddenly relaxed. "But I can tell by your accent that you're not Parisii."

"No," he confirmed. "I am not. I am Trinovantes," he said, with the same kind of pride that I had noticed with Bronwen's people, and I could not resist having a bit of fun.

"That is a relief," I replied with an exaggerated sigh. As I hoped, this puzzled Dumnorix, and he asked why. Without thinking, I grinned, or I started to until the stab of agony as the flesh of my cheek protested at being forced to move, actually bringing tears to my eyes, yet I managed to deliver my jest. "If you had been an Iceni and I didn't come home with your head as a trophy for my wife, I doubt she'd ever let me between her legs again."

When jesting with slaves, it is, or should be, always in the back of one's mind that their laughter is at least partially due to their status, yet his amusement did not seem feigned, as he roared with laughter to the point that Sempronius appeared.

"What are you telling my slave that made him laugh that hard?" he asked, wearing a puzzled smile. When I told him, all I got was a blank stare, and Dumnorix explained, "It is about one of the other tribes in Britannia, Master. Master Pullus here is married to a Parisii, who hate the Iceni almost as much as we Trinovantes hate the Iceni."

"Ah." Sempronius nodded, though it was clear that he did not understand, but he turned to address me. "Actually, I came to tell you that I heard some talk, and I went to the forum to see for myself. *Praetor* Silius and Varro are here, and I saw your Primus Pilus with Carbo."

"What about the Legion?" I asked, but he shook his head.

"I don't know, but if they're here, they're going to be outside the town in the camp the 2nd constructed while we were...busy."

Dumnorix had continued to work on me, and while he had skill, I was still extremely sore, and I realized just how talented

Alex is at this kind of ministration. I did not have a fresh tunic, nor had there been time to launder mine, and it was still clammy from all the sweat, but I was surprised, shocked actually, when I saw that my mail had been thoroughly cleaned and oiled. When I looked over at Sempronius' slave in astonishment, he blushed a deep red.

"I did it while you were sleeping, Master. I can only imagine how unpleasant it must be to wear your armor in that state. I also cleaned your *gladius*, and oiled it as well. It," he shuddered, "was as bad as your mail."

I automatically reached for my coin purse, only remembering that I did not have it when I fumbled around, meaning it was my turn to blush.

"As soon as I am reunited with Alexandros, I'm going to show my appreciation for this, Dumnorix."

"There is no need, Master." He tried to wave it off, but anyone with eyes could see it was halfhearted, which I did not begrudge in the slightest.

"Oh, I know," I agreed, deciding that playing along with his lie was the prudent course. "But I am still going to give you coin. What you do with it is up to you."

"As long as it's not enough to buy his freedom," Sempronius muttered, which was an odd thing to say, though I did not comment on it, and the expression on his slave's face did not indicate his thoughts one way or another.

Dumnorix helped me into my armor, while Sempronius held my helmet, then it was time to go to the *Praetorium*, although I had heard the Gauls referred to it as something else, but the Aedui had long before become Romanized, so Augustodunum was laid out in the Roman manner, with the forum in the middle of the town, with all the temples and administrative buildings that are now a part of the Empire arrayed along the borders.

"I don't know if I'll be coming back here, but if I don't, can you bring Latobius to the camp?" I asked Sempronius, who reacted with surprise.

"I'm coming with you," he replied. "I have to speak with the *Praetor* myself, but yes, I'll make sure Dumnorix gets your horse to camp."

We left his residence, and the streets were practically deserted, and in fact, the only people we encountered were exclusively male, and almost completely composed of men from the 2nd, wearing their armor and carrying their shields and javelins, marching in pairs, the sign that they were part of the guard Cohorts. As few Aeduan civilians that we saw, those we did all had essentially the same reaction as my fellow Legionaries when they got close enough to see more than my size, and that was to recoil as their eyes went from my frame to my face, where they took in the blood-crusted, bruised wound. If I had been in a better frame of mind, it might have been amusing, but my initial desire for something memorable that would inspire dread in any man who was considering facing me with a blade in hand had cooled considerably, as the practical implications of how my wife and children would react began to sink in.

I suppose that, finally, Sempronius felt moved to comment wryly, "Well, it *is* quite a scar, Pullus." Rather than reply verbally, I gave my answer in a warning glare, but he did me a service by pointing out, "If you think this bothers you now, what do you think it's going to be like when you're in front of Varro? And Carbo? They're likely to think of all manner of witty things to say, just to get under your skin."

As soon as he said it, I realized it was true, and thanks to his warning, I was as prepared as I think it was possible to be for what was coming. Anything else he might have said was cut off by our arrival at what, to my eyes, appeared to be the kind of building any Roman, especially one under the standard would recognize in the brick two-story building with a red tile roof, the only sign that it was not in a purely Roman town was the Aeduan tribal symbol affixed on a wooden post, although there was a curious looking patch of slightly darker brick directly above the entrance, which Sempronius explained.

"There was a banner in the Aeduan colors hanging there," he explained. "I suspect that the *Praetor* ordered it taken down as a reminder to the people that they're under Rome's control, because they clearly forgot."

The pair of Legionaries standing at the entrance were another sign that Rome was present and in command of this large town, and my gut tightened when the mouth of the man directly in front of me dropped open, his eyes fixed on my cheek.

When he waved us through, I was about to make an issue of it, since we should have been challenged, but it was the other Legionary who saved his comrade, saying crisply, "We were told to expect you, Centurion Pullus. *Praetor* Varro's representative gave us instructions to tell you to go to the main office. It's," he turned slightly to indicate the door directly to the left of main entrance, "right there."

This was a superfluous comment; the office of the *Praetor* is always in the same place, or it least has been in every *Praetorium* I've been in, but I was sufficiently embarrassed that I had been about to give these rankers a hard time simply because of the natural reaction of one of them when, in fact, they had been given specific instructions about me. I was also sufficiently distracted that the meaning of his words, specifically the reference not to the *Praetor* himself, which would have meant Silius, but to his "representative," escaped my attention, as there was only one man who would have met that description, and the fact that he had been the one issuing instructions about me should have alerted me. Somewhat unusually, the small desk that is usually occupied by a Tribune at most, or at least by a senior clerk, usually attached to the serving *Praetor* and not part of the permanent staff, was empty, so I took the lead, rapping on the door, prepared for the waiting game that seems to be a requirement for the man occupying that office. The fact that a muffled voice immediately barked at us to enter also should have alerted me that something at least unusual was taking place, but I suppose I was still somewhat distracted by the throbbing in my face, the ache in my calf, and the fact I had only gotten perhaps two full watches of fitful sleep because I have always had difficulty sleeping when the sun is up.

Nevertheless, I made sure my helmet was oriented properly under my arm, whispered to Sempronius to follow me a pace behind, then opened the door and marched into the office. My initial thought was that everyone I had anticipated was present, with Macer, seated next to Carbo, although there was a space between them in the center of the desk, twisting around to greet me with a smile, while Silius sat behind the desk, his face as usual looking like one of his ancestors' death masks, betraying not a flicker of human emotion, as Carbo, pointedly in my opinion, remained sitting looking straight ahead. Finally, there was Varro, the only man standing next to the desk on the right side, though perhaps a half-pace closer so that his left side was even with the midpoint of the desk, which I only realized too late was not accidental.

"Primus Hastatus Prior Gnaeus Pullus, reporting to the *Praetor* as ordered, sir!"

This was also the instant when I learned something else, which Sempronius later confirmed; because of the pain and the row of stitches along the inside of my cheek, I had unconsciously been mumbling, because crisply enunciating words like I had done just then was quite painful, to the point that my eyes began to water, causing me to blink rapidly.

"Why are you crying, Centurion? Are you so overcome with emotion on seeing the *Praetor* alive and well? Or did you have a chance to see yourself in a mirror and still haven't recovered from the shock?"

The words were outrageous, and infuriating, in themselves; the fact that Varro had spoken first before the *Praetor*, who I must reiterate was also the Legate, and would have been even if the younger Varro was a *Praetor* himself just by seniority, was an astonishing breach of not just custom but regulation, yet Silius did not reproach him. It took all of my self-control not to turn my head even the slight amount it would have taken to look at Varro directly, my eyes on Silius as I rendered my salute, who returned it.

"It's good to see you, Centurion," Silius spoke then, his eyes locked on me in the same way mine were on his, and I understood that the *Praetor* was doing the one thing that would infuriate Varro more than an overt insult—ignoring him—and in apparent confirmation, I saw him stiffen out of the corner of my eye. For the first time ever that I could recall, Gaius Silius actually adopted a sympathetic tone, pointing at my cheek. "That is a right nasty gash, Centurion. It must be quite painful, eh?"

Knowing what he was doing and why, I admitted, "Yes, sir. It is. Especially when I speak."

"I can only imagine." The *Praetor* actually winced, though it was somewhat clumsily done, as if it was something with which he was unfamiliar. Reverting back to his more formal tone, he continued, "Nevertheless, before we go onto other business, I want to commend you, and the men you personally chose to stop those *crupellarii*. Your men performed admirably, but you…" Silius suddenly stopped, and it was the first and only time in the admittedly sparse number of times I had been in his presence he seemed at a loss for words, finally shaking his head. "…truly, there are no words that adequately describe what I saw you do yesterday. And I want to be the first to tell you that your actions are mentioned in the report I'm writing, and I'm mentioning you by name to the Imperator."

Yesterday? That was yesterday? So stunning was this realization that I am afraid I missed the next few words, only realizing by the sudden silence that Silius had asked a question.

"I…I'm not sure I know how to answer that, sir. I apologize," I stammered.

Which, by complete accident, turned out to be not only acceptable to the *Praetor*, but understandable.

"No, I should apologize." He waved a hand. "That was a poorly worded question." He paused, clearly thinking about how to rephrase whatever it was he had asked me, then began, "It probably won't surprise you, Centurion, that I thought quite highly of your father, and while I never witnessed his exploits personally, I heard about them from men I trust." He inclined his head to Macer, which, being seated to my immediate right as he was, meant that I could not gauge his reaction. "After I witnessed what you did today in shattering the *crupellarii* attack, I asked the Primus Pilus if what I saw was the kind of thing that your father had done, and he said yes. What I asked you, quite clumsily, was, is this…gift…something that you can summon on command?"

I actually relaxed a bit, because this is one of the most common questions I get, second only to whether I can recall anything, and if so, how much.

"No, sir," I answered honestly. "Not only can I

not…summon it, I don't know when it will happen." I actually laughed then, and I have no idea why, especially since it made me immediately wince from the pain to my cheek. "There have been times where I wished I could make it happen, at times when I thought my boys or I were in the *cac*, I mean, in grave danger," I corrected hastily, but while it was not a real smile, Silius' lip did curve upward for a brief instant, "but I couldn't." Thinking I would forestall the next question, I added, "And I don't recall anything after it…happens."

The expression of disappointment that flashed across his features told me I had made the correct choice, but just when he opened his mouth, Varro chose that moment for a strategic cough, and when Silius looked over at him in obvious irritation, in my opinion, he purposely mistook what was a clear rebuke instead as an invitation to speak.

"As interesting and informative as it may be to hear about the Centurion's exploits, I believe there is a more important question to be answered. We've already heard from Primus Pilus Carbo," he looked at the 2nd's Primus Pilus, who was seated on my left in the same position as Macer, also putting him at the very edge of my vision, "whose Legion performed quite well yesterday, both in the first battle with his strategic choice to withdraw his men to lure the rebels in, then in their assault on Augustodunum…"

I cannot say if Varro expected the reaction he got from Macer, Sempronius, who I heard gasp behind me, the *Praetor*, or me, but if not, he should have.

To my surprise, it was Macer who exclaimed, "*Strategic choice*? *Gerrae*! And, what assault? Every man Sacrovir could muster was facing us!" Since I was standing in between them, Macer had to lean forward to look past me at Carbo, so I could see his glare at his fellow Primus Pilus, and I saw that he was genuinely angry, which was not only understandable, but which I shared. "What tales have you been telling, Carbo? You pulled your Legion back because you panicked! And there were no signs of a fight when we got here earlier today, and there's no way you had enough time to clean up!"

I expected Carbo to bluster and snarl, but to my ears, he sounded aggrieved, and a bit petulant.

"I haven't told any tales! All I said was…"

"It doesn't really matter, does it? These are questions that can be discussed later!" Varro interrupted, and I sensed that he was keenly interested in reasserting control of the conversation, which was confirmed when he plowed ahead, "What does matter is that we were informed by Primus Pilus Carbo that Prefect Sacrovir and less than a *turma* of Batavians had gone in pursuit of his brother, but now, we have neither the Prefect nor his traitor brother to inform us of what happened. So," he pointed at me and finished coldly, "you're all that we have to tell us."

My beast had clearly slumbered long enough to at least partially recover, and I did not trust myself to speak, so instead, I reached down to my *baltea* and withdrew the ring from where I had tucked it away. Varro did not hesitate to thrust his hand out in a clear silent command to hand the ring to him, which was the moment I realized that his positioning had been no accident since it enabled him to interpose himself between me and Silius, but I very slowly, and very deliberately, leaned slightly to my right so that I could reach around his arm and hand the ring to Silius instead, expecting Varro to try and snatch it; I was disappointed when he did not. For his part, Silius seemed startled at first, though he reacted quickly, reaching out to take it; when he did, our eyes met and I could see in them that he understood and approved of my insult to Varro, who clearly comprehended it as well, giving me a venomous look in return, but since I had seen this from him before and I was still standing, I replied with a smile, despite the fact it hurt.

Silius examined the ring, but Varro was not through, as he scoffed, "A ring? That's all you have to show us? That," he pointed at it in Silius' palm, "could belong to anyone!" In a slightly more respectful tone, he asked Silius, "Do you recognize that as either belonging to the rebel Sacrovir or his brother the Prefect?"

Silius shook his head, and Varro gave me a triumphant look, but then the *Praetor* asked me, "Can you tell us how you came to possess this, Centurion?"

So, I did, shoving down the welling emotions as I described

the ride through the night, reaching the Aedui leader's hideout, and the series of events that culminated with the fiery destruction of the lodge. Since this was essentially a report, I did as I had been trained, speaking in a flat tone with a minimum of verbal flourishes while staring at a spot just above Silius' head, but one of the first things one learns is how to use the edges of your vision without moving your eyes, and I saw the expression of the kind of sadness that I was feeling as I related what took place between the two half-brothers. I finished, and there was a long silence, during which I actually turned my head to look at Macer, and I saw the sheen in his eyes, threatening my own composure, which I had managed to retain as I spoke, if just barely.

"So, you have no proof that Gaius Julius Sacrovir is dead except for a ring that you *say* belonged to the Sacrovir family," Varro said, and if he was trying to sound matter of fact, to my ears, he sounded anything but, instead seeming more like a man who is certain he has gotten away with something. "I'm afraid that with just a ring that we have no proof…"

"Actually, you do have proof."

I confess I had forgotten about Marcus Sempronius, which I suppose is a testament to his ability to blend in and not be noticed.

"Oh?" Varro asked, and I heard the concern there. "And what proof is that?"

"As you know," Sempronius began, and I was forced to use only his spoken words as a guide since I had been standing at *intente* and not given leave to go to *otiose*, which would have allowed me to pivot to face him, "I have been here in Augustodunum for several months, and during that time, I gained Gaius Julius' confidence. Because of the role I was playing as a roving oil and grain merchant, he found me useful to relay messages to other conspirators in this uprising, which meant that I was in his company quite a bit. And that," I assumed he pointed at the ring, which I had noticed Silius was still holding in his left hand, as if he was worried that Varro might snatch it off the desk, "is his ring. He wore it all the time. In fact, I asked him about it, and he told me that it was the ring his father had given him. Since he did not know my true identity, or the job I was sent here to do, he had no reason to lie about it, and that is definitely the same ring."

Varro was clearly aware that he had been defeated about the ring, so he shifted his line of attack to Sempronius himself.

"You say that you'd been with this Aedui for several months," he began, using the same tone and cadence that he would have been using if Sempronius was on trial. "Yet we were caught by surprise, not only in general, but yesterday in particular when he decided to not wait for us to reach here and use the walls to defend his army. How do you explain that?"

"The reason that I was unable to get to the army personally to warn you about yesterday was that someone worked out that I was not who I said I was. I was about to go to the meeting where Sacrovir was informing everyone who needed to know that he had decided to take the fight to us when my slave came to warn me. I had only enough time to send my slave in my place before that individual arrived to take me prisoner." Given what he said next, I had to assume he pointed down to his bandaged leg, which he had changed while I was sleeping. "As you can see, he wounded me, and I was forced to hide for a bit while I waited for the army to leave…"

"Yes, yes," Varro cut him off. "That's all very plausible, and it might even be true. But," now he pointed past me at Sempronius in a dramatic manner that confirmed, for me at least, that he was rehearsing for a court appearance, "that doesn't explain how you've been in Sacrovir's confidence for *months*, yet you didn't pass any information to Rome about his plans!"

"How would you know that?" Sempronius countered, though he did not raise his voice, but there was an element in his tone that was impossible to miss that Varro should have recognized as a warning, but he was not through. "How could you possibly know what I do, and don't, report to Rome? In fact," I desperately wanted to be in a spot where I could watch both men's expressions, "what's *your* role here, Varro? I know that he," he must have pointed to Silius, "is the *Praetor* of the Upper Rhenus. I know that he's the Primus Pilus of the 1st, and he," his tone altered slightly, just enough to imply contempt but not obviously so, "is the Primus Pilus of the 2nd, newly arrived from the Praetorians. But…what are you?"

Varro's face turned a satisfying shade of purple, and he shouted, "I am the duly designated representative of the *Praetor* of the Lower Rhenus, as appointed by the Senate of Rome!" Since I had not spotted it, I was surprised, but I realized I should not have been when he suddenly brandished that fucking ivory baton, which he must have had tucked in the back of his *baltea*. "And this is all the proof that I need that I belong here! Now, answer the question!"

"I don't report to you, Varro," Sempronius replied, sounding tired. "I take orders from one man and one man only, and he has ordered me to answer questions from only those of the rank of *Praetor*. If your father was here, he would qualify…but he's not." He must have pointed again. "That means that only *Praetor* Silius has the right to ask me questions." Sempronius fell silent for perhaps a heartbeat, then asked, "But why are you so interested in me and who I answer to? If I was a suspicious man, I'd think that you're working for someone else, because the Imperator is a *very* thorough man. I have served him for a long time, and I am as certain as it's possible to be that, had he desired it to be so, he would have alerted me to share what I know with anyone who might be serving someone else in Rome other than him…like the Praetorian Prefect, perhaps?"

To be fair, Sempronius never said Sejanus' name, but there was no need, nor was there any need for him to expand further. The battle lines had been drawn, and the message given to Varro that, just as we believed he served Sejanus, I, for one, *knew* that Marcus Sempronius worked for the one man more powerful than the Praetorian Prefect, and that Sempronius was not cowed by Varro's bluster, nor was he scared of Sejanus.

"So, how did the Prefect die, Centurion?" Silius asked quietly, and just that quickly, Varro's attempt to cast suspicion on Marcus Sempronius was cast aside, nor did I hesitate to explain the events of the night before, the death of both Sacrovirs, and the end, the real end, of the Sacrovir Revolt.

Stepping out of the *Praetorium* with Macer, I took a moment to draw in a breath of fresh air, feeling very much as if the air inside the *Praetor*'s office had been fouled, but that was not the real reason I did it. In simple terms, I knew the moment had come where I had to hear just how badly hurt the Fifth Century had been, and I was not eager to hear.

Macer clearly understood, which was not a surprise, because he asked gently, "Do you want to talk about it later?"

As tempted as I was, I also knew that it would be worse to enter the camp, walking down our Cohort street, and go from tent to tent to see for myself without any kind of warning.

"No," I sighed, "tell me now."

"The good news is that your Optio performed very well, very well indeed," he began. "I was quite impressed, and I think that in about a year, you're going to have to be looking for a new Optio, because based on what I saw yesterday, he's headed for the Centurionate, so start thinking about your list of possible replacements."

Naturally, I was pleased, though it was not just for Vinicius' sake; I do not know if I am unique, but the fact that I had taken something of a risk with Vinicius, given that he had been seen as one of the troublemakers when he had been *Tesseraurius*, and he had performed to a degree that the Primus Pilus of the Legion spoke so highly of him was as much a vindication of my judgment as it was an endorsement of his abilities.

Regardless of this piece of good news, I believe I could be excused for recognizing that whenever someone starts a conversation speaking of good news, it means there is bad news coming, which was why I asked bluntly, "So, what's the bad news? Or," I asked without much hope, "is there more good news coming?"

Macer sighed, then replied, "Not really, unfortunately. No, the bad news is that you're going to need a new *Cornicen*."

"Macrinus is dead?" I gasped, but thankfully, he shook his head.

"No, not dead. He's in the hospital tent here in this camp. He lost his right hand."

It was my turn to sigh, because while this could hardly be called good news, at least for Macrinus, it could have been worse, although I felt certain he probably did not see it that way in the moment. However, there was something else that caught my attention.

"You said he's here in the hospital tent in *this* camp," I said, then asked, "But where else would he be?"

"Before we broke camp to come here, Philippos came to me and said that we'd lose close to a hundred men if we put them in the wagons to transport them here, even on a road as smooth as the Via Agrippa, and that it would take two trips, even using the 2nd's wagons as well," Macer explained. "And there's another fifty where he said they would probably survive, but he couldn't guarantee it. So, we left them behind. With," he added quickly, probably because he saw my mouth open, "the Tenth to guard them."

I should have known better than to think Macer would leave our wounded unguarded, I realized immediately, so I moved to the next difficult question. "Do you have any idea how many of the men left behind are in the Fifth?"

"There were three of your boys when we left," he replied, but there was something in the way he said it that alerted me, so I was not completely unprepared when he added, "but there's one of them, I think he's from your Third Section, that Philippos said was more likely to die before sundown today whether we moved him or not."

Automatically, I looked up at the sun, seeing that it was about two fingers' width above the western wall, meaning that it was late afternoon.

"So he has maybe a watch," I mused. For a heartbeat, I tried to think of who it might be, but we were within sight of the northern gate, which meant we would be entering the camp soon enough, and I knew that it would not take long to learn the identity of this man, or any of the others once I spoke with Vinicius, and in all honesty, I was not in that much of a hurry to be told.

Deciding a change of topic was in order, I asked Macer, "It seemed as if this version about Carbo's…" I had to think to recall the word Varro had used, "…*strategic* decision to run that Varro tried to peddle was the first time you heard it."

"It was," Macer confirmed. "But that *cunnus* is in for a surprise. Actually," he amended, "both of the *cunni* are." He took a quick glance about, but also slowed because we were almost within earshot of the section of Legionaries from the 2nd standing at the gate, which was open, and he lowered his voice. "I was with the *Praetor* late last night as he was writing his report that he sent to Rome. And," there was no mistaking the satisfaction in his tone, "both Varro and Carbo are going to *cac* themselves when they find out."

"What did Silius say?"

"The truth," Macer answered simply. "Nothing more than that. He described the battle quite accurately, at least from where I was and given all that was happening. And," I saw his head turn in my direction and I looked over to see him watching me with a piercing gaze that was a bit unsettling, "he talked about you and the role you played, a great deal."

I was surprised, certainly, yet I was also concerned.

"What does 'a great deal' mean?" I demanded. "And what did he say?"

"He didn't read it to me," he said. "At least not all of it, but what he did read was impressive, Gnaeus. I don't think anyone not named Pullus has ever actually tried to describe the kind of things you do before. Until now anyway." On the surface, it seemed an odd comment to make, until I recalled that he was aware of the accounts that my great-grandfather and father had given; as far as I knew then, and know now, he is not aware I am doing the same, but Marcus Macer is a very clever man, so it will not surprise me at all if I learn that he has deduced I am following in their footsteps. "It took up one side of the wax tablet, I'll say that. And I don't see how you won't wind up earning some sort of decoration from the Imperator."

This was beginning to make me uncomfortable, not because of the praise, which as Bronwen is quick to remind me, I never tire of hearing when it's about me or my command, but because my mind was taking me places, like how such effusive praise would likely be read not just by the Imperator, but by Sejanus. Would that make me important enough to Tiberius to be seen as a threat in the eyes of the Prefect? I wondered. Given all that I had seen during my time in Rome, I believed it was certainly a possibility, and I reminded myself to speak with Sempronius about this.

Fortunately, Macer was moving on, both literally in resuming his walk to the camp, and to the larger subject of the battle, though he did pause as we walked past the Legionaries, Macer returning the salute of their ranking officer, while I pointedly ignored the stares at my face, reminding myself that once the stitches were removed and the bruising faded, it would not draw as much attention as it did now a day after I suffered the wound.

Once we were outside the town wall and far enough away, he resumed, "He accused Carbo of acting on his own without orders when he began withdrawing the 2nd, and while he didn't use the word, he plainly implied it was because of Carbo's cowardice that he did it."

This was so stunning that I suddenly stopped, believing that for some reason Macer was having some fun at my expense, but he returned my gaze without flinching, or any sign that he was jesting for that matter.

"That," I spoke slowly, "is going to stir up the *cac*, and not just here but back in Rome."

"It will." Macer nodded. "And I actually tried to change his mind, though not overtly. I just asked him a couple of questions about the phrasing, but he didn't change a word."

"Do you think he knows the risk he's taking?"

Macer did not hesitate in his reply, telling me that he had thought about it.

"Yes, but I also think he doesn't care about the risk to himself. Maybe," he shrugged, "he's counting on his record and his relationship with the Imperator to protect him from any kind of repercussions from Sejanus." We were nearing the *Porta Praetoria* of the camp, and I recognized the Optio in command of the guard Century covering the gate and wall as belonging to the Ninth Cohort, though I could not recall what Century. Macer did not stop walking, but he did slow, because he was not through talking. "But he didn't just talk about Carbo, Gnaeus. He talked about Varro, and how he tried to interfere with the campaign, specifically how he delayed our progress after we dealt with Florus by refusing to allow the 2nd to march with us here to take care of Sacrovir, and how that time we spent at Treverorum gave the Aedui extra time to prepare."

Out of habit, I puckered up my lips to give a low whistle, which was a mistake, the stab of pain to my cheek forcing me to abandon that attempt to just mutter something that expressed my shock, then added, "I can see why you tried to talk him out of it. It's one thing to go after Carbo. He's clearly subordinate to any *Praetor*, especially one who's the Legate as well, but Varro?" I shook my head. "Yes, he's not a *Praetor*, but that baton he likes to wave around means something, and I highly doubt that his Tata won't stand up for his son and insist that he was following his orders as *Praetor*. But while we think that Carbo is probably Sejanus' creature, I *know* that Varro is a client of Sejanus."

"Which is why I tried to talk him out of it," Macer replied with a fair amount of heat.

"I know, and I'm not implying that you didn't," I assured him. "It's just…dangerous."

"It is," Macer agreed, then grinned and gave me a light punch on the shoulder. "But at least we're going to be sitting with the rabble watching the play unfold. Now," he took a breath, "let's get back to our business and the things we have more control over."

With that, we entered the camp, and as I learned very quickly, it was going to take weeks before the First Cohort would be anywhere near normal; we had been badly hurt.

When I entered my tent, Euphemios was sitting at his portable desk, with dark circles under his eyes and a haggard look that told me that he had been hard at work, the stack of tablets separated into three piles a grim testament to the amount of work he had to do as the clerk responsible for recording everything that the army considers important after a battle. Alex was not visible, but then I heard a stirring on the other side of the partition, and he quickly appeared, with the same fatigued look and demeanor, perhaps even more pronounced, which was understandable given his dual work as a *medicus*.

He did not offer a greeting as such, instead walking up to me, his eyes narrowed almost in suspicion as he examined my face, then sniffed, "I see you pulled a stitch out, but I'm surprised it's only one. I suppose I should be thankful."

"Yes, you should be," I agreed. "Especially considering what I went through last night."

His expression softened, nodding as he replied, "We heard about the Prefect. I'm sorry, Gnaeus. He was a good man."

I heard the genuine sadness in Alex's voice, and I was reminded that his association with Sacrovir ran back longer than my own; I was struck by a thought that, if my father had still been alive, this would have hit him harder than either of us.

"Yes, he was," I agreed, but I was only partially engaged, thinking of my father. "What exactly have you heard? About how he died?"

"Nothing specific," Alex answered, and he searched my face, looking for some clue, I suspected, knowing me well enough to know there was a reason I asked. "Why?"

"I'll explain later," I promised, then turned to Euphemios. "All right, the Primus Pilus gave me numbers, but not any names except about Macrinus losing his hand." I actually had to think for a moment as I tried to recall the name. "Has anyone spoken to Siculus yet and let him know he's no longer the apprentice *Cornicen*?"

"I haven't," Alex answered, and a glance at Euphemios was met with a shake of his head. "If Vinicius has, he didn't tell me."

"Where is Vinicius?"

"If he's not in his quarters, he's in the hospital tent," Alex replied, then without me bringing it up, he added, "Gnaeus, next to what you did with the *crupellarii*, the thing the boys are talking about the most is Vinicius and how he handled everything."

"That's what Macer told me," I nodded. "In fact, he told me that we need to start polishing up our list of possible replacements for him."

Turning to the flap, I announced that I was heading for the hospital, but Alex had other ideas.

"We need to see to that stitch." He pointed towards my quarters. "It won't take long."

"It can wait." Seeing his eyes narrow, the sign that there

was an argument coming, I said, "I should have been there first thing to see the boys, Alex, but I wasn't. And this," I pointed to my face, "isn't going to look any different once it heals if I don't have that stitch put in for another watch."

One could have knocked me over with a strong breath when Alex actually nodded and said, very grudgingly to my ear, "You're right. But wait," he added, then pushed through the flap into my quarters. I was about to protest, but he returned with my *vitus*; or I should say, the replacement to the one that I assumed was still on that battlefield.

With it in my hand, I felt relatively normal again, and I left the tent, telling the pair that I would return from the hospital to get the detailed casualty report before I visited Vinicius and the other officers and the section tents. The Cohort street was not empty, but as was customary the day after a battle, the men had no duties, unless one considers resting and recovering from the exertions of the day before a duty, which most of us do, so the only men who were out and about were the men who had to go relieve themselves, or were on the prowl for a skin of wine or a loaf. A couple of the men were mine, but when they stopped and came to *intente*, I waved them off and told them that I was going to visit their comrades in the hospital. Without exception, each of them named a comrade and asked me to let them know these men were asking about them, or that they would be by to visit as soon as they could.

Perhaps the most memorable comment came from a ranker in the Second Section, an older veteran named Aulus Longus, who gave me a gap-toothed grin as he cheerfully admitted, "Personally, I hate Nobilior's guts, Centurion. But," he held his hands out in a helpless gesture, "he's a Second Section man, isn't he? So tell him that old Aulus will be along soon, will you?"

I assured him that I would, and for the rest of my walk to the hospital, my thoughts were about the nature of life under the standard, where one man can detest another, yet still show concern when he's struck down in battle, or risk his life to save that man in a fight. The gods know I had learned very quickly about Longus and Nobilior's antipathy for each other, which as far as anyone who had been around long enough could remember, was centered around a woman, which is undoubtedly the most common cause, yet here was Longus promising to visit the man, something that I believe is impossible for those who have never served to understand.

My thoughts were interrupted by the realization that I was close enough to hear, and to smell, the hospital, with the moans of the men inside, though I knew that it was not nearly as noisy as it would have been in the watch after the battle, but it was the smell, of *cac* because men could not go to the latrine and the waste was in buckets, waiting for the orderlies to take them to be emptied, and worst of all, wounds that were beginning to corrupt that was the hardest on me, and judging by the comments I have heard before and since this moment, on other men. I paused for a moment to gather myself, adopting the expression I had learned by observing my father when he made this kind of visit, then entered. My first thought was that it was a good thing that not all of the wounded were here in this tent, because it was already overcrowded as it was, which the *medici* had compensated for by narrowing the space between cots, which meant that they were required to turn sideways to navigate between ranks and files.

It was only by accident that it was Philippos I spotted first, where he was bent over sniffing the leg wound of a ranker, making my stomach flip, though not as much as the wounded man when Philippos straightened up and looked at the *medicus* standing next to him and gave a shake of his head. Immediately, the wounded man, who might not have been a *Tirone* but was at the very least no more than two years under the standard, began to moan in terror at what was coming, shaking his head vigorously as if by denying it he could change the reality. I caught the eye of and signaled the chief *medicus*, and he nodded, whispering instructions to the other *medicus* before he sidestepped up the row to the end of the aisle, and I hurried to meet him there.

I was not surprised at all when the first thing he mentioned was my face, saying severely, "I sewed that up just yesterday, and you have already torn a stitch out? Bah! I do not even know why I bothered to do my best work if you were just going to pull them all out!"

"It's one stitch!" I protested. "Stop being so dramatic. This isn't some Greek tragedy, you old pederast." Changing the subject, I asked, "Where are the men from the Fifth of the First?"

He did not know, though I did not expect him to as the chief *medicus*, but there is a tablet filled out by one of the junior *medici* that details where men are placed, and they are always placed together, by Cohort and, in this case with the casualties so heavy, by Century, a very Roman thing to do. Finding the tablet, he consulted it, then pointed to an area at the far end that, thankfully, was next to the partitioned area for the officers, and not Charon's Boat.

"When you get done, come back here and I will put that stitch back in," Philippos called out to me.

"Alex said he'd do it."

I thought he would be relieved that he would not have to worry about such a trifling manner, but instead, he said, almost angrily, "That is my work, and I should be the one to fix it!"

Startled, and a bit concerned, I assured him that I would seek him out, then walked over to the spot he had pointed out, where the first man I saw was the Sergeant of my Sixth Section, Vibius Porcina, whose shoulder was heavily bandaged.

"Sergeant," I greeted Porcina, who had been staring up at the tent ceiling, black with soot from the lamps, visibly starting in surprise, which wrenched a groan from his lips, and made me feel terrible for doing it, but I did stop him from swinging his legs off his cot to come to *intente*, even as I thought that there were Centurions who would require it. "*Pax*, Porcina! *Pax*! I didn't mean to make you jump! Please, lie back. I just came to check on you, nothing more than that."

He did so, then while he was clearly still in pain, he grinned up at me and pointed to his bandage, which I had noticed when he leaned forward had blood on both front and back, which told me that it had been a piercing wound.

"This is the golden wound, Centurion! The butchers said that it's clean, with nothing in the wound, and it went straight in and out without tearing the muscles, so it will heal up fine. It just means that I'm going to be on the no-duty list for a whole month!" He smacked his lips, making a show of stretching out.

"If I had to get wounded, this is the way to do it!"

I knew I should have been stern with him, but Porcina had a unique ability to make his officers laugh. Besides, he was as high as he would rise in the ranks, the third rung of the ladder, above *Gregarius Immunes*, and the lowest, *Gregarius Ordinarius*, so he had no need to try and impress me.

"I'm happy to see you so happy," I tried to growl, albeit unsuccessfully, but the moment of levity was not destined to last, because then I asked, "What about the rest of the section?"

The smile vanished as if it had never been there, and his eyes started to shine, which I understood when he could only get out in a whisper, "Orestes is dead, Centurion. He took a thrust right through the eye." He shook his head, and said bitterly, "I suspect I don't have to tell you how."

He did not; Gaius Orestes was Porcina's close comrade, and he was a solid veteran, like every man in a First Cohort Century, but this did not mean they do not have flaws, and in Orestes' case, it was an inveterate habit of letting his shield drop too low when he got fatigued. I had tried everything I could think of to correct this, even doing something that ran against my nature by asking other men, not just my fellow Centurions, but every man with a reputation for being exceptionally skilled with the *gladius* if they had any trick to offer, to no avail, and the memory of this got me cursing bitterly, using my *vitus* to smack myself in the leg to punish myself for my own failure. I was startled, and stopped, by Porcina reaching out and gently but firmly grasping my forearm.

"Don't blame yourself, Centurion," he said in just above a whisper. "You did everything you could; everyone in the section knows that." He laughed then, a jarring sound given the topic, "I remember the time you thrashed him so badly that he should have been on the sick, lame, and lazy list, but he was too terrified of you to put himself on it."

I recalled that as well, and I chuckled at the memory of Orestes trying to pretend that he was fine, which meant that he at least learned how to limp very rapidly.

"He was a good man, nonetheless," I told Porcina, and I meant it. "Were you able to be there to send him on his way?"

He nodded, and there was no mistaking the pride there when he said, "I'm the one who put the coin in his mouth, just as I should be."

I left Porcina, moving to the next man, and I bring my conversation up with him because it was typical of what transpired over the next third of a watch, as men alternately informed me of how they received their wound, with varying emotions, some of them with a sort of wry embarrassment because of a mistake they had made, others with a kind of fatalistic resignation, and thankfully, there were very few of these men who displayed angry bitterness because they did not see the failure as their own but by one of their comrades, for failing to protect them with their own shield. More than once, I had to suppress the surge of raw emotion as I listened to my boys recounting their worst moments during this fight, yet invariably, it was never about their own wounding, even from the three men who had lost all or part of an extremity that signaled their days under the standard were over, but upon either seeing firsthand or learning of the death of one of their comrades. Macer had been right, or I suppose Philippos had been, because along with the eleven who died outright, two of the men in Charon's Boat died before the 1st marched away to Augustodunum, while Macer had already mentioned the man in the Third Section, who I had learned was Spurius Cinna, who remained back at the camp near the battlefield, along with five other Fifth men. These were the moments that tormented the men more than their own wounds, and by the time I had spoken to the last one, I was exhausted and feeling battered. This was also the moment when I realized I was not done, when I saw a lone hand raise from roughly in the middle of the ranks of cots. When I saw who it was, it was as if my blood froze, because I recognized Gnaeus Pictor, one of my chosen men, making me realize that if I left the hospital after only seeing the men of the Fifth and not those men I had personally chosen to stop the *crupellarii*, I would never forgive myself. I reached his cot with some difficulty, banging my shins on a cot several times, although judging from the groans, it was more painful for the occupants than it was for me, yet somehow I reached Pictor, whose right thigh was heavily bandaged and raised on blocks.

"*Salve*, Pictor." I greeted him with a heartiness that I could only hope did not sound feigned, because I was certainly forcing myself to appear cheerful. "It looks like you're in for an easy time for a few weeks, eh?"

The veteran, who I had known from the time I had arrived in the Fourth Cohort, gave me a smile that I thought was as counterfeit as my greeting had been, though he sounded cheerful enough.

"Usually, I can count on Fortuna to squat right over me, and the only difference is whether she chooses to piss or *cac*," he joked. "But this time, she looked at old Gnaeus and felt sorry for me." His grin vanished as he continued, "And she sent you, Centurion. I will cross the river knowing that, I swear it. I had gotten knocked down by one of those tin bastards, and I swear on the black stone, he had me, because when I went down, I lost my shield, and it was just out of my reach. He had his spear pulled all the way back," he actually shuddered, "and I knew right then this was it. But then, we both heard this...sound," he shook his head, "one that I know I'd never heard before. And," Pictor pointed up at me, "it was you. I only found out later that Optio Sabinus was killed right before that." His expression changed then, and I learned why when he added awkwardly, "I didn't know Sabinus that well, but I had heard good things about him from his boys, and what little I saw with my own eyes told me they were right."

"Yes," I managed to get out, "they were."

"All I know is that, if it was his dying that caused you to do what you did, then his sacrifice saved a lot of lives, Centurion."

Perhaps if his tone had not been so fervent and full of conviction, I would have been able to retain my composure, but his face started shimmering in my vision, because while there was no way for him to know it, Pictor had articulated my own silent prayer, that Sabinus' death had been necessary and part of the gods' plan for that day and that moment.

I could barely manage to get out, "I...I hope you're right, Pictor."

"I am," he said flatly. "Some of the boys that were with us

yesterday were in the same wagon as me when we came here, and we talked about it. Centurion," he sat up and grabbed my forearm in much the same way Porcina had, "*you* saved us yesterday, nobody else. Not the rest of the Legion, and," his mouth twisted into a scornful grimace that accentuated his words, "certainly not those gutless, faithless *cunni* in the 2nd and their Praetorian Primus Pilus!"

Despite my wholehearted agreement, I did feel it necessary to admonish him, "Careful what you say, Pictor." Suddenly, I was struck by an inspiration and pointed out, "As you say, Primus Pilus Carbo comes from the Praetorians, and he's likely to have ears all around us. That's how things work in the Praetorian Guard. Men spy on their brothers all the time."

"How?" he scoffed, then indicated the tent around us. "There aren't any 2nd men here, Centurion! They didn't suffer a scratch. There's only us here, and trust me when I tell you that every man in the 1st knows the truth, and feels the same way." He turned to address the man in the cot next to him who was pretending not to be listening, demanding, "Right, Falco?"

While Falco, whose abdomen was wrapped in a bandage that had one large spot low on his right side, did not appear to be happy about it, he did not hesitate to reply, "You are, Sergeant." Tilting his head to address me, Falco added, "About everything, Centurion. We all know that what you did broke those fucking gladiators. And if you hadn't done that?" He shrugged, which caused him to wince. "Only the gods know how things would have turned out."

Leaving Pictor, I realized that I could not leave without seeing the men of my force, but they had been placed with their original Centuries, which meant they were scattered all about. Nevertheless, I was determined that I would thank these men, although it was from Philippos that I learned that, as badly hurt as the 1st was overall, the losses among the more than four Centuries' worth of men were savage.

"I have not added it up yet, but my estimate so far is that the casualty rate with your force of handpicked men is easily fifty percent." I could not stop myself from gasping, which sent a shock of pain coursing through my head, yet this time, I did not fight it, accepting it as the least I should suffer for losing half of my men; however, there was another question to ask, but I was spared from asking it, because Philippos added gravely, "And as of now, I think almost half of those men are dead, and I expect four or five more men of your group will die. They're most of the occupants of Charon's Boat back at the other camp."

It is impossible to know, since it only happened the way that it did there in the hospital, but I wondered then, and still wonder now, if hearing Pictor echoed in more or less the same tone if not the exact words about how these men credited me for turning the tide made it easier to bear the knowledge that so many of the men I had chosen perished, or if it made things harder. However, I did my duty to the best of my ability, spending a few moments with each man, and listened to essentially a different version of the same story, one where my name was always mentioned. Since then, even Bronwen has commented that my burning desire for accolades has cooled considerably, and she is not wrong.

As I sat there, trying to listen without shouting at them in guilt and frustration, there was a part of me that would not stop silently chiding, "This is what you want, Gnaeus. You want men to say your name, to laud you and thank you for saving their lives."

By the time I staggered out of the hospital tent, it was almost dark, I was exhausted, yet I still had to visit every section tent, but I decided instead that I would put that off until after the morning formation, which would be the first one since the battle that marked the official end of the period of recuperation, although we all knew that the formation would be short, and when the men were dismissed, it would be back to their area for more rest. Instead, I decided to visit the Optio's tent, and I was not surprised to find Vinicius, stretched out on his cot, though he was alone, his body slave that is assigned to every Optio nowhere to be found.

When he leapt to his feet, after he bade me enter and saw that it was his Centurion, I waved him back down as I apologized for not giving any warning, to which he replied, "Not necessary, Centurion. I sent Fusco out into the town to see if he can scrounge up a couple of *amphorae* of wine. Or," he grinned, "if he can find enough, some mead."

"*Gerrae!*" I was shocked. "A couple of *amphorae* just for you?"

"No." He laughed. "For the boys, of course!" His smile faded, "They could use something to take their mind off of yesterday, don't you think, Centurion? Pluto's cock!" he exclaimed before I could reply, shaking his head in a manner like a man waking from a dream that seems impossible in the cold light of day. "It *was* yesterday…wasn't it?"

I knew exactly what he meant, and how he felt, because I had caught myself asking the same thing.

"It was," I nodded, "and no, it doesn't seem like that. Especially after the night I had."

This was when I told him about the events that signaled the end of the rebellion, though I was also deliberately vague about the details surrounding the death of the Prefect, and if what he took away from what I said was that he and his half-brother fought to the death, and that the fire was an accident, that was perfectly acceptable to me.

When I finished, Vinicius sat there on the edge of his cot in silence, staring at the dirt floor for several heartbeats, then said hoarsely, "I wish I had a cup right now, to toast the Prefect. He was the Primus Pilus when I enlisted, and he was the only one I knew until Primus Pilus Macer. Next to your father, he was the man I most wanted to emulate under the standard, Centurion. He," Vinicius heaved a sigh that was more eloquent than his words, "will be missed."

Deciding that a change in subject was in order, I cleared my throat, immediately regretting it because of the bloody mucus that I had been hawking up for several watches by this time, the sign that the wound was still leaking blood and mixing with my saliva, forcing me to hurry to the tent entrance and spit it out. My Optio looked a bit alarmed, but I pointed to my cheek.

"It's still bleeding on the inside of my mouth," I explained. "But the Primus Pilus told me of your own performance yesterday."

"I was just doing what you trained me to do," he said, but his modesty actually irritated me.

"Stop it," I snapped. "You don't need to pour honey in my ear, Optio. I..."

"I'm not!" Vinicius cut me off, and I saw that he was actually angry. "I'm telling the truth, Centurion! Remember how you found the Fifth when you took command and what a mess we were! And," he pointed out, truthfully, "remember that you thought I was one of the problems in the Century because I wasn't willing to tell you what you wanted to hear. Yet you were still willing to give me a chance to prove myself, and that's something that I've been doing, or," he amended, sounding rueful, "at least trying to do with the boys."

He was exactly right, and while I did not want to, I acknowledged that, then I had to offer my current version of a smile.

"The reason I chewed on you was because I want to impress upon you that you need to learn to take a compliment without trying to diminish what you did. And," before I could stop myself, I chuckled, which at least did not hurt as much as laughing outright, "here I am doing the very thing I was telling you not to do. But there's more, and that's another thing I want you to know, Vinicius. I just was in the hospital tent, and it's not just the Primus Pilus who told me that you kept our boys together and in the fight." I pointed in the direction of the *quaestorium*. "They told me as well. And, I wanted you to know that after what I heard today, I'm going to press the Primus Pilus to see that you're decorated." He did not say anything, but he did not need to; the flush that crept up from the neck of his tunic bore testimony. On an impulse, I also decided to add, "And when Primus Pilus Macer brings this up, you need to act surprised. If you don't," I warned, "you and I are going to be in the sparring ring...once I heal up."

He laughed, then swore he would pretend he had no idea, and I told him that he would be on the list for the Centurionate sooner rather than later, his broad smile all the thanks I needed.

"What about you?" he asked. "Our boys might be talking about me, Centurion, but the entire fucking Legion is talking about you and what you did."

On this matter, I decided to remain silent about what Macer told me about the *Praetor* and his report, saying vaguely,

"We'll see."

I could tell, just by the way that the atmosphere in the tent altered, what was coming.

"It's the same kind of thing that happened to your father, isn't it?" I only nodded. "And you don't recall anything?" The truth was that, as usually happens, by this time, some fragments of memory had returned, flashes of images, and some of them actually coincided with what I had been told just a short time earlier when I was in the hospital, but to Vinicius, I simply shook my head. He seemed to consider something, then clearly decided to share it. "I didn't see that much since I had my hands full at the time." I chuckled again, which he clearly appreciated, but then he did so himself. "But I don't think there was any way to miss that fucking head."

He stopped, and I guessed that he was waiting for me to query him on what he meant, but I did not, and I did feel a bit badly for him because he was clearly disappointed, yet I had already heard about the head of one of the *crupellarii* and how I had separated it from the rest of the gladiator's body, sending it alternately ten, fifteen, or even twenty feet in the air depending on which version one believed, despite the pair of straps securing the helmet to the *segmentata*.

I felt badly enough that I threw him the proverbial bone by admitting, "I heard something about it from some of the boys from my command in the hospital, but they didn't seem to agree on how high it went."

"At least fifteen feet," he answered instantly. "But it's not just how high it went. That fucking head landed nearer to our eagle than to where you were standing."

This I had not heard, and while I did not think Vinicius was lying, I also knew how these things tend to grow over time, because from what I recalled, just before Sabinus' death, I had glimpsed Macer's white crest and the eagle next to it almost a hundred paces away. The gods know that when I am in that state, I am even stronger than I normally am, which, thanks to my real father, and to my great-grandfather who, as far as he knew, was the first of his line to be born so large and naturally strong, means that I possess far more power even without the help of the gods.

Shrugging, all I could think to say was to repeat, "I don't remember doing it."

"Those *crupellarii*," Vinicius thankfully changed the subject. "What made them so hard to beat?"

Normally, I would have bridled at what could have been perceived to be a criticism, but it was the simple truth, and I had certainly given it a great deal of thought even over the short period of time since the fight.

"Their armor," I answered.

I was surprised that my Optio seemed skeptical.

"I can see how wearing *segmentata* from head to toe would be more difficult," he spoke slowly, thinking as he went, "but I already heard from some of the boys who were with you that their *gladii* couldn't penetrate."

"That's exactly what happened," I agreed, growing uncomfortable now because of where this would naturally lead. "For whatever reason, those plates were tougher to penetrate."

"I looked at a couple of them, and their plates were a little bit thicker, but it didn't seem to be that much that would make it impossible to penetrate," he mused. I said nothing, offering a prayer that he would drop it, but he did not. In fact, he frowned suddenly, sitting up straight from where he had been leaning with elbows on knees, exclaiming, "Wait, there was something else. Did you notice something else about their *segmentatae*?" I decided that I would delay by drawing it out, because I felt certain that I knew what he meant, but unfortunately he did not wait for me to answer him. "It was darker than ours. It was like…" He stood then and pointed to my left hip. "…your *gladius*. That *is* Noricum iron, isn't it?" Although there is nothing in my great-grandfather's account where he mentions the origin of the iron that makes this blade, my father had figured it out, and told me about it, so I nodded. "That's what that the *crupellarii* armor was made with, I'm certain of it." My heart sank as he let out a low whistle. "That's the most valuable iron in the known world! How much money would it have taken this Aedui to buy that much Noricum iron? Centurion…"

I stopped whatever he was going to say with a chopping

motion of my hand, accompanied by a sharp command.

"Stop. Stop now. Do not say another word, Optio. That's an order."

Not surprisingly, this clearly startled him, but I still said nothing, watching the range of emotions as Vinicius went through the progression as his mind worked; the startlement was quickly replaced by puzzlement, then his eyes narrowed in anger as, I assumed, he realized that there was no practical way that Gaius Julius Sacrovir would have been able to acquire what is, understandably, one of the most closely guarded resources in Rome's possession, in sufficient quantities to equip more than a thousand men in Noricum iron, not on his own. Later investigation would reveal that, contrary to what we believed just a few watches after the battle, the *crupellarii* were not clad in the Noricum iron from head to toe; instead, only the plates of the torso portion and the helmets were made of this superior metal, but this was also when the Gallic ability at metalworking showed itself to advantage, because even the plates protecting the extremities were tougher to penetrate. I did not try to hide my relief when, after a span of several heartbeats, I saw the expression I was looking for on my Optio's face, one of resignation.

"I…understand," he murmured. "Nothing is going to come of this, is there?"

"Only if someone who's clever enough to figure it out isn't clever enough to keep their mouths shut," I said, and despite feeling somewhat confident that Vinicius truly understood, I wanted to make sure, and I pointed at him. "But all that matters to me is that it doesn't come from you, is that clear?"

He did not like it, but I would have been unsettled if he had not been upset, but apparently sensing I required more than just a nod, he replied formally, "I understand…and will obey, Centurion."

I left not long after that, almost staggering from the exhaustion, thinking how, in some ways, this day had been almost as trying and fatiguing as the fight, though it was my emotions that were taxed more heavily than my body. Entering my tent, I was greeted by the aromas of baking bread and a haunch of roasted pork still sizzling from the fire, the timing indicating that either Alex or Euphemios had been watching Vinicius' tent, seen me enter, and started preparing the meal, not that I was complaining.

"Once you eat," Alex did wait until I had a mouthful of food, then pointed at my face, "we're taking care of that. And," he had to lean over to look under the table, "that bandage on your calf is soaked through. We'll have to change it."

I only grunted, unwilling to take even the time to utter a word from devouring the food that, as I am constantly reminded, would easily feed three men, finishing quickly while remembering to chew on the right side of my mouth, then as promised, Alex tortured me. That, at least, is my story. It also turned out that, while there had only been three stitches closing the puncture wound on my calf, I had torn all three, which explained all the blood on the bandage, and that actually hurt more than the single stitch to my face. Indeed, now that everything is fully healed and some time has passed, my calf wound has turned out to be the one that left me with a slight limp whenever I am fatigued, but I was aided in this by recalling my father's account and how, as he grew older, the aches and pains lingered longer. With the ministrations to my wounds finished, Alex gave me an oiling, scraping, and most importantly, and pleasurably, a good massage. I doubt if I had counted I would have reached five after I fell onto my cot before I fell into a deep sleep, blessedly free of the kinds of dreams that have plagued me after one of these divine fits. They returned the next night.

Chapter 8

We stayed at Augustodunum for another eleven days before the *Praetor* deemed publicly that our wounded had either recovered to the point they could march, albeit without packs, or if they were still unable to march, could survive the wagon ride back to Ubiorum; as some of us wearing the transverse crest suspected, we would learn that the real reason was that it had taken that long for word to be sent to Rome, and instructions from the Imperator to return. Matters between the two Legions were tense, although the *Praetor* acted quickly in issuing orders that forbade any man from crossing the forum to the other side, which is the standard action when there is the kind of hostility that was present. Every man below the rank of Centurion was forbidden from going into the town, but in a decision that proved unpopular by all of us in both Legions, Silius also gave strict instructions that the Aedui were not to be punished any further than they already had been in the loss of so many of their tribesmen.

"The *Praetor* is choosing to believe the headmen, that the Aedui were led astray by Sacrovir, and have been punished enough by the loss of so many men," Macer told us, but although his heart was clearly with the rest of us, he did make a point that resonated. "If he sends word to Rome that he doesn't think the Aedui have learned their lesson, where do you think we're going to be wintering?"

There was something else that was a topic of much debate, though it was of the kind that, whenever an officer approached a fire, the men immediately stopped, but it did not take long to learn what was of such interest.

"It concerns the *crupellarii*," Vinicius informed me on our third night. He had spent the previous day prowling around, talking to other Optios, and some of his friends in other Cohorts, one of the advantages a man who starts out as a

Gregarius Ordinarius has over a paid man like me. "Specifically, the fact that Varro forced some of the townspeople to strip the dead, and every scrap of armor was collected and loaded into wagons."

"Is that what those wagons next to the *Praetorium* are?"

Vinicius answered my question with a nod. "But I don't know if you've noticed something."

"That only men from the First of the First of the 2nd are guarding it," I answered, though I was honest enough to admit, "Actually, I learned that from Alex."

"Since we're not allowed to mix, it's hard to know why," Vinicius commented, but he was wearing what I thought was a sly expression, then added, "but it's not impossible."

"Do I want to know how you found out?"

"Probably not," he laughed, then assured me quickly, "but nobody got roughed up, Centurion. I swear it." Deciding this was good enough, I indicated for him to continue. "All of that iron is going back to Rome. Nobody seems to know why, but the rumor is that it's not going back on the Imperator's authority."

"Sejanus." I breathed the name. "He's the only one who would have the power to order that. The gods know the Senate might have the authority, but every man, woman, and child in Rome would know about it before the day was out." Curious, I asked, "What do you think he wants to do with it?"

"Melt it down, of course," Vinicius answered without hesitation. "Can you imagine how much that Noricum iron is worth?"

This made sense to me, but when I mentioned this to Alex later, I knew just by the manner in which he started paying attention to the scroll he was reading that he had other ideas.

"All right," I sighed. "I can tell you've thought about this and don't believe that's why he's snatching it."

"I'm not saying I don't believe it," he protested, swinging his feet over to sit up and regard me with the kind of look that he uses when he is trying to get me to reach the conclusion he wants me to on my own.

I sat at my desk, trying to think of what else he could have in mind, but I finally threw my hands up in frustration. "What's another way that all that iron could have even more value than if would be melted down into ingots?"

"What happened the other day when you took on the *crupellarii*?"

"We…we couldn't kill them," I answered, my mind just beginning to catch up as I thought it through as I spoke. "Vinicius said that he actually examined the plates that they used to protect the torso, and they were only slightly thicker than our *segmentatae*, which shouldn't have been enough to stop us from penetrating them with our *gladii*." I had already figured out that the reason my great-grandfather's *gladius* was the only one that could pierce that iron on that day was because it was the same, although later, I was distressed to see a slight nick in the blade, the first and so far only one it has sustained over the previous seventy years and only the gods know how many battles. I signaled the moment when I finally reached the point where Alex wanted me to be when I gasped aloud, "He wants to equip his Praetorians with that *crupellarii* armor!" I looked at him, and I saw the same troubled expression on his face. "He would have a force wearing armor that the issue weapons couldn't penetrate."

This was bad enough, but Alex made it worse.

"And given what we know about the bastard and how cunning he is, he'll tell Tiberius about it, but convince him that it's for the Imperator's own protection. He'd be surrounded by men who can't be struck down by anything other than axes, or siege spears, not the normal kind of weapons."

We had all heard by this time how the Imperator seemed to grow more paranoid with every passing year, suspecting the relative handful of men whose social standing and lineage was roughly equivalent to his own of coveting his position as Princeps, the First Among Equals, the fiction started by Divus Augustus that only the most gullible Romans believed was actually true. Consequently, I could easily see how someone as slippery as Sejanus could convince him that having Praetorians, undoubtedly those in the First Cohort, who were wearing armor that made them virtually invulnerable to the standard weapons of *gladius* and the Marian javelins, would make Tiberius safer. I just had to wonder if, as rumors suggested, Tiberius trusted Sejanus more than anyone else in his circle, whether the Imperator had the ability to recognize that this was a double-edged *gladius*, where the thing that gave him the most security also provided the greatest threat. None of which was our concern in a practical sense, but as my great-grandfather observed, trying to keep Romans from talking incessantly about politics is a fruitless endeavor, and I would put it second only to talking incessantly about the sexual antics of the upper orders, along with chariot racing and gladiatorial games.

While I was not as senior as most of my fellow Centurions in terms of longevity alone, I had come to the 1st after the Varus disaster but before the death of Divus Augustus and the revolt of the Legions, so I had endured a hard course during the turmoil and upheaval of that period, which was second only to the periods of civil war that dominated the career of the Prefect, but I knew that it was my brief period in the Praetorians that was the cause for men more senior and experienced in a general sense than I was coming to me and asking my thoughts on the larger implications of the Sacrovir Revolt. The most common question in the days immediately after the fight was the likelihood that the reason we were staying was that Silius was waiting for orders from the Imperator about how punitive to be with the Aedui, despite the fact that Macer had already announced this would not be happening.

"Yes, but there's no way that Silius has heard back from Rome yet," Clepsina had argued that evening after Macer made his announcement. "And the *Praetor* has to be guessing that the Imperator won't want to take any more action, not because he's been in contact with Rome yet."

He was correct, at least in the sense that there was no way Silius had issued these orders to not punish the Aedui further based on instructions from Rome, but I sensed that this was not the real reason Clepsina had come to my tent, where we were now seated in my quarters. We had certainly talked since the battle, but this was our first private conversation, which began with us commiserating on the losses each of our Centuries had suffered.

However, Clepsina was the first man besides Macer who,

without any warning, reached across the table to give me an awkward pat on the arm as he said quietly, "But you lost a lot more than the rest of us, Gnaeus. I was sorry to hear about Sabinus, and I know that some of those boys with you taking care of those gladiators were from your old Cohort."

I think I was so overcome with emotion at this simple but clearly heartfelt gesture because it was unexpected; that it was Clepsina, with whom I had, and have, a relationship that I think can best be described as wary on both of our parts, though I have no idea why, made it even more impactful. In fact, all I could muster was a nod and a whispered thanks. I do not believe that his sudden switch of subject was meant maliciously, but it was obviously intentional since it was essentially a return to the larger question.

"How long do you think it will take for Silius to hear from Rome?"

I considered for a moment, before thinking aloud, "He's undoubtedly using the *cursus publicus* and the Imperial courier system, so it should take them about five days to get there, give or take a day. So," I shrugged, "the courier should be arriving in Rome tomorrow, but then it will depend on how long it takes Tiberius to make his decision."

"If he consults with the Senate, we're going to be here all fucking winter," Clepsina commented, with such a glum expression that I wanted to laugh, but it was still far too painful.

I also agreed with him, yet while I could not give a reason for my feeling, I still said, "I don't think he will. Our absence from the Rhenus is going to worry him since Arminius is still lurking out there somewhere, and as long as that bastard is drawing breath, I don't think the Imperator is going to be willing to run the risk of a prolonged absence."

This all turned out to be true, at least in effect, as we marched away from Augustodunum eleven days after the battle, but what we certainly did not know at that time, and I have no way of knowing if Tiberius knew, was that our rushing back to the Rhenus was unnecessary because, at long last, Rome's greatest enemy since Vercingetorix, known to us as Arminius and to his fellow Germans as Herman, saw his string snipped short as Fortuna finally turned her face away from him, being murdered by his own peers in the nobility of tribes other than the Cherusci, having grown tired of his arrogant ways and insistence that he was the only man who could lead such a fractious confederation. Frankly, what consumed my thoughts for most of the next week were two things; the first was those wagons full of Noricum iron armor, but I confess this was not the most pressing issue that concerned me. Alex had removed most of the stitches from my face the day before we departed, but the spot where he had had to replace the stitch was proving troublesome, and I had sought out Philippos to provide some insight as to why I was now on the third replacement stitch.

After a brief examination, he declared, "You talk too much, Centurion." This earned him both a glare and a growled prophecy of a beating in his future, but he had dealt with my father and me for too long to be intimidated. "That spot," he indicated the area right under my cheekbone, "is the one where the muscle that you use to open your mouth is located. So," he shrugged, "the more you use that muscle, the longer it will take for it to heal, and the more strain is put on the thread of the stitch."

While I had suspected it was something like this, it was still dismaying.

"I can't command my Century using hand gestures and angry looks!" I protested. Something else occurred to me, and the very thought was so troubling that it made me nauseous. "Is it because I'm raising my voice so I can be heard by my boys? Remember, I'm a First Cohort Centurion, which means I've got twice the men." As soon as I said it, the reality that this was no longer the case, something that I tried to avoid thinking about, came rushing back, and I could not stop myself from adding bitterly, "Or, at least I used to have twice the men."

To his credit, Philippos wisely ignored my self-pity, adopting a thoughtful tone and musing, "That actually might have something to do with it, Centurion. I had not thought about it, but you have to open your mouth more widely to shout loudly enough to be heard. Do you remember Lysippos?" I did not until he reminded me, "He was Germanicus' personal physician. He served as the physician in charge when he was here." This brought it back to me, although I did not mention that my father had a relatively close relationship with the Greek, just nodding and mumbling something. "Well, he showed me a technique that might solve your problem. However," he warned, "I only watched him do it, though it is simple enough. And, it is…uncomfortable for the man who is being treated."

I was tired of hearing Alex complain about me "ruining his work," and my cheek constantly throbbing from having a needle poked through it multiple times, which was why I did not ask any questions, saying only, "If you think it will help, go ahead."

It did not take me all that long to regret my haste, but my pride kept me from calling a halt to what Philippos was doing, which was essentially to have another *medicus* have me open my mouth as widely as I could, then shoving a block of wood between my upper and lower teeth on my right side that pried my jaws open even further, bringing tears to my eyes, then have Philippos put most of his hand in my mouth to apply not one but two stitches, although they were very close together, on the inside of my cheek. I am not ashamed to say that tears were streaming down my cheeks, and I kept gagging on the combination of saliva and the thin trickle of blood caused by the needle piercing the tender flesh of my mouth, unable to swallow for some reason. For two or three agonizing heartbeats, the *medicus* was unable to remove the wooden block, finally forced to yank it out with enough force that I thought it broke a tooth. Completely by instinct, I lashed out with a fist, but thankfully for both of us, the *medicus* anticipated my likely reaction, leaping backward so that my fist only grazed his chin. It was enough to knock him on his ass, but I did not have to face the *Praetor* to explain why I had killed or incapacitated a *medicus.*

"You agreed to this, Centurion," Philippos reminded me as I came to my feet, and I was gratified to see that his gaze flickered between my clenched fists and the *medicus* who was trying to get to his feet, for the first time appearing noticeably nervous. "Please keep that in mind."

"I know," I mumbled, having to make an effort to keep my

tongue from automatically going to the two fresh stitches, and it brought a real problem to my attention. "But those stitches sticking out are going to be a problem. I can feel them and my tongue…"

"Yes." He nodded. "Lysippos told me that the chief complaint the men who had this cure made was that they could not stop their tongue from touching the stitches." He paused, trying to think, "Ah, yes. That is it. Lysippos said that one man told him something that made sense, that it was the same as if he had some piece of gristle stuck between his teeth, and his tongue kept worrying at it." This was exactly how it felt, and I nodded, but I wanted to know what I could do about it. Philippos did not answer immediately, instead telling me to wait where I was, then disappearing. He was gone for what seemed to be a long time, returning with something in his hand, and when he reached me I saw that it was a scrap of leather. When he held it out for me to examine, I saw that it was not a piece of the stiff kind that we use for *caligae* or *balteae*, but an extremely soft and pliable scrap that had come from a kid goat. Using one of his brass knives, he cut a smaller piece in a roughly oval shape, then handed it to me. "Place that in your mouth, between your cheek and teeth."

I felt a bit foolish, and I grunted in pain when I pressed the thin leather against the wall of my cheek where the two stitches were located, though not for long, shaking my head and removing it.

"It needs to be trimmed," I told him, pointing to the top where it would be lodged between my upper teeth and cheek. "It's poking me and that will drive me mad."

He took it without comment, shaving off a bare sliver before handing it back to me. It took two more tries before I was satisfied, and I endured the pain of pressing the thin leather hard against the stitches long enough for the blood still seeping from the small holes created by the needle to create a bond.

"How often will I have to change this out?"

"You should not have to," Philippos replied. "Yes, it is kid leather, and it is not very thick, but as long as you make sure that you only chew on the right side of your mouth, and when you drink, tilt your head a bit to your right to keep it from coming into contact with it, the patch should last long enough for the stitches to do their work."

He, or more accurately Lysippos, was right. It took me a day to become accustomed to it, and Alex did ask if I was feeling feverish or if I had a toothache because it made my cheek look a bit swollen, but it did prevent my tongue from bothering the interior stitches. Peeling the piece of leather away from the inside of my cheek when we arrived in Cambete turned out to be the most painful part of the ordeal, while I barely noticed the removal of the two stitches. However, what mattered was that the wound was now fully healed, although it was a vivid red that has only now begun to fade these years later. The scar tissue is not just on the outside; there is a corresponding line along the inside of my cheek, along with a slight lump where the two interior stitches were that I was constantly biting for weeks afterward, but it has now toughened up, or perhaps I have just learned how to cope without chewing on the inside of my cheek.

Meanwhile, men who had begun the march riding in the wagons, of which we had appropriated an even dozen from the Aedui to accommodate the higher number of casualties, recovered sufficiently to rejoin their comrades, though without their packs, while sadly, and as inevitably as men recovering, there were those who suffered relapses and returned to the wagons to get over the relapse…if Fortuna was kind. Wounds that had managed to escape becoming corrupt initially, during the most dangerous period of time, somehow fell prey, perhaps to some foul humors, or as many men believed, because the *numeni* who inhabited the area through which we were marching became offended. No matter the cause, the result was the same as it always is after a tough fight; men who believe they have escaped a brush with death find themselves with chattering teeth, smelling the rot that is consuming their body, wondering what they did to displease the gods. That was the case with Macrinus, who actually began marching with us, joking that since it would be his last, he wanted to participate in all the banter, recounting of tales that are rarely about battles, unless it is something humorous, and singing the songs that help the miles pass. I noticed that he was pale at the end of the first day, but when I suggested that he might skip the next day and ride in one of the wagons, he became a bit indignant.

"There's nothing wrong with my legs, Centurion!" I am certain it was without thinking that he began to point down at his lower body with his right hand, but it was still in a sling. He flushed deeply, muttering a curse under his breath as he switched to his left hand, giving a self-conscious laugh. "I'm going to have to learn to do a lot of things with my left hand, Centurion." He made a motion down below his waist that every man recognizes, and if his goal was to make me laugh, he succeeded. "Especially the most important one, eh?"

It is only with hindsight that I realized this was a strategy by my former *Cornicen*, who, despite being unable to perform his duties, I insisted march in his normal spot just behind me, although Siculus was next to him. The next morning, he was not only pale, but his face shone with sweat, despite it being a cool morning, but once again, he managed to dissuade me from sending him to the wagons, this time with a jest about how he had not heard the end to the story that Vibius Merula of the Fourth Section had been telling when we stopped for the day. This is actually another common occurrence on the march, where long, drawn-out stories are a favorite of the rankers, depending of course on the man's ability as a storyteller, and in the Fifth Century, Merula is something of a legend for his ability to weave a tale that I confess has had me listening as avidly as the men. It was at the noon stop on the second day when Vinicius came to me, clearly concerned.

"It's Macrinus, Centurion. He doesn't look good, but he refused to let me look at his arm."

"He refused?"

That got me to my feet, yet honestly, I was more irritated than concerned because this was happening in front of Macer and the other Centurions, where we had settled under a tree to have a drink and chat. Reaching Macrinus, my anger dissolved, because he was clearly very ill, but it was only after I raised my *vitus*, though my heart was not in a thrashing, before he very reluctantly took his arm out of the sling. The bandage protecting his stump extended up to mid-forearm, but not only was the end of the bandage still stained, which it should not have been almost two weeks after he lost his hand, I immediately smelled the odor that sends a stab of fear into every man's heart. However, it was the livid red streaks running up the length of his arm that made me gasp in shock.

"How long has it been like this, Macrinus?"

It was the manner in which he suddenly looked everywhere but up at me that warned me, so I was not altogether surprised when he shrugged and offered weakly, "I...I'm not sure, Centurion. Maybe a day or two."

"Don't give me that *cac*," I snapped. "Come on, we're going to see Philippos. At the very least, you've marched your last mile."

I could see he wanted to protest, but I also sensed that, because of how miserable he felt, his heart was not in it, and he meekly obeyed, following me as we walked down the column to the wagons, where I found the chief *medicus* taking a rare break, sitting on a stool next to one of the wagons. When I briefly explained the situation, then gave Macrinus a shove towards the *medicus*, I made sure to watch Philippos, and when Macrinus extended his arm to be examined, the tale was told by the expression on the *medicus*' face.

When Philippos finished his examination, he did not say anything to Macrinus, or to me, calling instead for one of the orderlies, and when he arrived, he said, "Take the *Cornicen* here to Wagon Number Two," enunciating it in such a way that told me this was not just a method of identifying the wagons in their order in the column. To Macrinus, he said gently, "Go with Demeter here, *Cornicen*. He'll get you settled in, and I'm going to prepare an elixir for you that will help you."

To my surprise, given how resistant Macrinus had been with Vinicius and me, the Legionary meekly walked away, and my guess about the wagon was confirmed when Wagon Number Two actually turned out to be the fifth one.

Seeing my gaze, Philippos said quietly, "That's Charon's Boat, Centurion."

"*What?*" While I knew Macrinus was in danger, I thought that it would be at the expense of the rest of his arm. "How can you say he's that far gone?"

"Two things," he replied calmly, and without any

hesitation. "When you looked at his arm, how far up did you look? Did you have him pull up the sleeve of his tunic?" I had not, and I shook my head. "What about having him pull the neck aside so you could see his shoulder?" I had not done that either, and I realized that Philippos had done both those things, so I was at least prepared for him to say, "I did, and those streaks have moved all the way to his chest. He is a dead man, Centurion," he concluded.

I felt as if I had been kicked in the groin, and I immediately blamed myself for not paying closer attention, but my mind grabbed on to something else.

"You said there were two things," I reminded him. "What was the other thing?"

"That your *Cornicen* wants to die," he answered quietly, and with a tone that suggested that he was about as certain as he could be. "I looked at that bandage, Pullus. It has not been changed in days, which means that he has not been reporting to the hospital tent, because along with changing the bandage, the *medici* are instructed to inspect the wound for that kind of sign that you saw for yourself. He clearly did not."

"I should have been paying closer attention." I felt absolutely miserable, but Philippos surprised me considerably, replying with a rough-edged empathy, "That is a load of *cac*, Centurion. An absolute bunch of nonsense. When a man decides he no longer wants to live, there is nothing that anyone can do about it, other than perhaps prolong the inevitable. You would have had to watch over him for every watch of every day, and to do that, you would have to neglect those men under your command who still want to remain alive. No," he shook his head, "I have seen this many times. Macrinus saw what his future held, cashiered from the Legion without a full pension, and he decided he wanted no part of that future."

The *cornu* sounded, interrupting our conversation, and I returned to my Century, informing Vinicius about Macrinus and what Philippos said, then we resumed the march. Macrinus died two days later, but Philippos, honoring my wishes, sent an orderly to alert me, and I was with my *Cornicen* when he crossed the river; it was the least I could do for him.

We reached Cambete at midday of the fourth day, and Silius had sent word ahead that we would be using the river route, so the docks were lined with barges, but there was not enough room, meaning that the river was packed with so many vessels that men scraped together a pot for any comrade bold, or desperate, enough to try and cross the river by leaping from one ship to the next. The Rhenus is not nearly as wide this far up its length as it is in Ubiorum, yet it was still a daunting challenge, and when there were no takers, the amount in the pot increased, despite the best attempts of the Centurions from both Legions to identify the culprits behind it. Once it got to more than a year's pay, it was inevitable that someone tried it, and speaking for myself and every other Centurion in the 1st who I spoke to about it, we were just happy that it was an idiot in the 2nd who made the attempt. At the last moment, the rules for the endeavor were changed, requiring that the man making the attempt wear his *segmentata*, helmet, and greave, while the attempt itself was naturally held after dark to avoid the prying eyes of anyone wearing a transverse crest. Consequently, it should come as no surprise that when the sun rose the next morning, we were greeted by the news that the 2nd had suffered a loss during the night.

It was Vinicius who provided me the details. "The poor bastard actually was almost to the other side when he lost his footing and went in. A couple of his comrades went in after him. Tied off," he added hastily, "but with his armor on, he sank like a stone."

Ignoring how suspiciously well-informed he was, since Macer had given strict instructions that we remain aloof from this endeavor, I did muse aloud, "I wonder what happens to the pot?"

"It's going to his family," Vinicius answered, and this was when he seemed to realize this was something that betrayed a level of knowledge he should not have had, so he added lamely, "That's what I heard, at least."

I did not press any further, mainly because I was about to leave for a meeting of the Centurions with the Primus Pilus, the topic being the order in which we would be leaving, because as many ships as there were on the river, there were not enough to transport both Legions, especially when one of them was still transporting so many wounded. Our complement of commandeered wagons had been reduced to ten as men recovered, or as in the case of Macrinus, they did not, but there were still too many wagons. The question was which Legion would be spending another two weeks in Cambete, and not surprisingly, the overwhelming consensus was that it was the 1st who deserved the chance to return home first. I certainly agreed with the sentiment, and the logic behind it that said that since we had suffered the brunt of the casualties, we had earned that consideration, yet while I did not voice it to anyone, not even Alex, I was not quite as eager to return to Ubiorum, not because of how Bronwen might react to the wound to my face, but because of my children. Titus and Giulia were still very young, and while I would certainly not blame them, or punish them for their reaction to their Tata's face, the idea that they would be frightened of me was such that the idea of a two-week delay was not all that unappealing. I also was acutely aware that I was in the vast minority, and I was not about to express my feelings at this meeting, especially once we were informed of the decision of the *Praetor*.

"I've just come from the *Praetor* and Varro," Macer began, his lips in a thin, bloodless line that we knew meant he was trying to contain his own fury. "He informed me that since the 2nd has the farthest to travel, they will be returning to Vetera first." This unleashed a small uproar, but while I opened my mouth like everyone else around me, nothing came out of my mouth, even as I felt a twinge of guilt. Macer held up a hand, and when it quieted down, he went on, "It's not all bad news, because the *Praetor* has sent out a call for more shipping to come here. He doubts that it will be enough for the entire Legion, but he's given us a choice. We put the wounded in their wagons on the barges that show up, and however many men of the walking wounded will fit, while the rest of the Legion marches."

"That's a week's march!" Caecilius protested, though he was simply the first to articulate it.

"It will take those barges six days to take the 2nd to Vetera, and then another eight days for them to get back upstream,"

315

Macer explained patiently. "Then it's four days by barge to Ubiorum."

"Did Silius tell you how long he thinks it will take for more barges to get here?" Clepsina, who was standing next to me, asked.

"No," Macer replied, and while it was not unexpected, it was still disappointing.

"So we don't know how many days we're going to be here waiting for more barges," Clepsina muttered.

"That's right. It's possible we're going to wait a week, spend a day loading the wounded and however many men we can cram onto however many barges show up, then go on a march of a full week and only save about three or four days time," Macer explained.

This created a discussion that at times came perilously close to a heated argument as our Primus Pilus allowed us to debate the merits of waiting or staying, the opinion almost equally divided.

Finally, it was the Septimus Pilus Prior, Marcus Isauricus, who made a point that resonated with everyone present, by asking, "If we return to Ubiorum piecemeal, who's the one willing to tell all the widows and children of the men whose Cohorts haven't returned yet?" Addressing Macer, he said simply, "Primus Pilus, I think the only thing that matters is that the 1st returns all together, however long it takes."

It was not long after that the decision was made that the 1st would remain in Cambete, only leaving for Ubiorum together, with Macer allotting four days for shipping to arrive before we departed overland, either with our wounded safely on barges, or still in the wagons with us. The 2nd was leaving the next day, which meant there was one more surprise in store for me.

"Gnaeus, a messenger has arrived from the *Praetorium*," Alex informed me as I lounged on my cot that evening. "Your presence is required immediately."

"The *Praetor*?" I asked, a bit alarmed, but that was about to increase, because he shook his head.

"Not Silius," he replied, his expression grim and worried. "Varro. Varro wants you."

My initial instinct was to don my armor since it is the only acceptable way to justify wearing your *gladius*, and given that the first time I met that bastard I ended up in a cell, I did not think I was being unreasonable in thinking that I might have to fight my way out of trouble.

Knowing me as he did, Alex warned me, "That's not a good idea, Gnaeus. But I'll go alert the Primus Pilus immediately that you're heading to the *Praetorium* to see Varro. I'm sure he'll be there quicker than Pan."

It was a good suggestion, and I knew it, but I still felt naked with just my *vitus* and my *pugio*. I also did not want to give Varro any excuse to make my life miserable, so I left the tent with Alex, who headed immediately for Macer's quarters. Being strategically important as the beginning of the river route on the Rhenus that goes all the way to the sea, the town is walled, and has its own *Praetorium*, which was where I knew Varro would be, while Silius occupied the tent in our camp. We had heard that matters between the two men had deteriorated to the point where they avoided each other unless absolutely necessary, and I recalled as I made my way out of our camp into town that I had barely glimpsed Varro on our march from Augustodunum. When I entered the building, Tribune Paullus was seated at the small desk guarding the office that Varro occupied and where, to my surprise, the Tribune did not play the little game of pretending that he was too busy to return my salute. Coming to his feet, he did give a curt command to stay put while he went and knocked on the door, and I was struck by a sense that I had done this before, the only difference being that I knew nothing about Quintus Licinius Varro back then.

My musing was interrupted when Paullus returned and said with what almost sounded like sympathy, "The *Praetor*'s representative will see you now, Centurion Pullus."

Without thinking, I asked, "Did he make you say it that way, Tribune?"

He clearly knew what I meant, because he actually smiled sheepishly and nodded. The door was ajar, and before I pushed it open, I took a breath and squared my shoulders to prepare myself, then entered his office. The desk was directly across from the door, which is customary, and Varro was seated behind it, reinforcing the sense of time repeating itself, but it was as I was marching up to his desk that I sensed the presence of someone else out of the corner of my eye, seated at the small desk that is normally occupied by a scribe, though I did not look over at him, assuming that it would be the man I had seen most often hovering around Varro with a wax tablet.

"Primus Hastatus…" I began, but Varro held up a hand.

"I believe we can skip these formalities, Centurion," he said in what, for him, was almost a genial tone, and he actually bared his teeth in what I supposed was his version of a smile. "After all, we have had an…adventure together already, neh?"

"Yes, sir." I did my best to match his tone, yet I could not help myself, though I did try to sound as if I was asking innocently, "Speaking of those days, how is Catualda? Do you still keep in contact with him back in…where did the Imperator send him after he was deposed?"

Despite knowing it was a foolish thing to do, I cannot deny how pleasing it was to watch the blood drain from his face, and I could see he was struggling to maintain his composure, though he did try to sound jocular as he forced a chuckle. "No, I can't say that I do, Pullus."

There was an awkward silence then, as his head dropped to seemingly look at a scroll on his desk, which gave me the opportunity to glance over at the man I assumed was a clerk and expecting to see the face I had associated with Varro, hearing someone gasp while feeling like an invisible hand was squeezing my heart at the sight of what I would have sworn on the black stone was Gaius Fonteius, whose name I had not known until just before his death at my hand and who I had only known prior to that as Canus. It was not Canus; in fact, after a heartbeat, I was chiding myself for my reaction, because this man did not resemble Canus in any way, not physically. However, in a way that was as indefinable as it was unmistakable, he could have been a twin to Varro's former agent, with an air of quiet menace, and cruelty, that marked him as indelibly as Canus' replacement as if he had been wearing a bronze placard around his neck proclaiming that fact. For his part, Varro clearly did not miss my reaction even as quickly as I tried to cover it up.

"Forgive my ill manners, Centurion, and allow me to introduce you to my…associate, Marcus Curio Libo. No," Varro waved at Libo, who was coming to his feet, "no need for that much formality."

Libo had a sleeker appearance than Canus had, wearing a ring that marked him as an Equestrian, with regular, even features and very curly black hair, but when he had begun to stand, he had put both hands on the desk, and I noticed the scarred knuckles. More than anything, it was the flat, emotionless look he gave me that most reminded me of Canus, but what surprised me was the sudden flare of anger that I felt as I recalled something.

This was why I pointedly turned away from Libo to ask Varro bluntly, "Is this Canus' replacement?"

I was disappointed that Varro did not look upset; if anything, he seemed happy that I had asked, because he did not hesitate to answer.

"I suppose you could put it like that, Pullus. And," he looked over at Libo, and adopted a tone that I would liken to a man who is proud of the horse had just purchased, "I must say that in many ways, Libo here is an improvement over Canus. He's more…efficient."

The anger came rushing up with enough force that I asked coldly, "What did you do with his children?"

A look of what I felt certain was alarm flashed across his features, though his voice was even enough when he asked, "What do you know about his children?"

"Just that Maroboduus tried to buy their freedom from you, and he was unsuccessful," which was the truth.

I had been quite surprised when I learned through roundabout means that the deposed chieftain of the Marcomanni had followed through on his promise to try and rescue Canus' children, but while we never learned the details, we had heard that he had failed.

"Yes," Varro said vaguely, apparently trying to look regretful. "He did make an offer, if you can call it that. It was such a paltry sum that it was quite insulting, frankly."

I waited for him to finish, but when he did not, I demanded,

"Well? What happened to them?"

"Why do you care, Centurion?" He laughed, but it was obviously forced, and I shot back, "Why don't you?" I pointed at him, bringing Libo to his feet, which I ignored as I jabbed my finger at Varro to emphasize my words. "He died for you, Varro. He was loyal to his last breath…"

"And he failed," Varro cut me off coldly. "He was well paid, and I…cared for his children, but he failed."

"And you were foolish to send him to kill a man when I was anywhere nearby. You sent him to his death."

There is no way to describe the satisfaction I felt in that moment, with Varro looking the way I imagine he would have if I had leaned over and slapped him, but that satisfaction did not last long.

Pretending he had not heard what I said, Varro addressed my first query, echoing, "Yes, what *did* I do with those spawn of his? Oh yes," he snapped his fingers, "the boy I sold to a *collegia* in Rome, where I was told he would be working in a brothel for men with that sort of appetite until he's old enough to be turned out onto the streets and earn his keep in other ways. The girl," he looked directly at me and smiled a smile that was impossible to misinterpret, for both his intentions and the menace of a coward protected by one of the most powerful and dangerous men in Rome who knows he is safe, "I kept for myself. She…amuses me. For now, anyway."

I did not reply to Varro, instead choosing to look over at Libo, who had remained standing, his eyes never leaving me.

"Do you know the kind of man whose coin you're taking, Libo?"

For a moment, I did not think he would answer, but when he did, I was surprised by how high-pitched his voice was, though he only shrugged and said indifferently, "It's not my business, Centurion. Besides," he offered what might have almost been a smile, "if I got picky about whose coin I take, I'd starve."

"I wonder if Canus felt the same way," I scoffed, but Varro was ready to move on.

"As touching as it is to reminisce about a man who once served me, that's not why I summoned you." When it became clear I had no intention of asking, he explained, "It's about Aulus Macula." I did not react, because I honestly did not immediately recall the name, which irritated him and he snapped, "Very well, you want to play Stupid Legionary, which I've learned all about here." He slowed down, and enunciated his words in the same manner one does to someone who is simple. "I want to know where Marcus Sempronius is."

The truth was that he was not the only one, although I did feel a bit foolish for not recalling the name Macula had been using while spying on the Aedui for us, but I answered honestly, "I haven't seen him since the last day in Augustodunum."

He stared at me for a long moment, then looked over at Libo with a raised eyebrow, and while I refused to behave as if I cared about his opinion nearly as much as Varro clearly did, I did see him shrug out of the corner of my vision.

He looked back at me, saying neutrally, "I see." He paused, seeming interested in something on the scroll on his desk, but I could not read the writing, and he asked suddenly, "What did you and he talk about the last time you did see him?"

I pretended to think about it for a moment, then shook my head and said as sincerely as I could and still be believable, "I honestly don't remember." Somewhat inspired, I pointed to my face, and could not resist a jab of my own. "In case you were looking elsewhere, I was in a bit of a fight trying to keep those *crupellarii* from chopping you and the *Praetor* into tiny, bloody pieces...no thanks to the 2nd."

"Yes, the *Praetor* made sure to mention your name," Varro waved a hand as if he was trying repel a pesky gnat, "several times, and he made it clear that he was going to mention you in his report. If I'm being honest," he sniffed, "I think our dear *Praetor* may be a bit enamored with you, Pullus. It's not as if you're Hercules defeating the Nemean Lion, after all. But, to be clear, you're saying that you have no recollection of what you and Marcus Sempronius may have spoken about? Such as, oh," he tapped his chin with a finger, "where he planned on going from Augustodunum?"

This was something that I could answer easily, and honestly.

"No, he made no mention of where he intended to go. The only thing I do know was that his true identity became known just before the battle, and it wasn't safe for him to remain there."

He was clearly disappointed, choosing to stare up at me for several heartbeats before his body ever so slightly relaxed.

"Very well," he said at last. He turned to Libo, but he continued to address me, "Libo is going to return with you to Ubiorum. He is going to wait there in the event that Marcus Sempronius chooses to come to see you. If he does," now he turned to look back at me, "it would be in your best interest to alert Libo."

"And then what?" I demanded.

"Then nothing," Varro replied. "That's where your part ends, Centurion."

"I won't be your spy."

Varro did not seem surprised, and he leaned back in his chair, regarding me for a long moment before he spoke.

"Do you think that you're safe from Praetorian Prefect Sejanus, Centurion?"

I was surprised; no, I was shocked that he would threaten me so nakedly, and for a moment, an admittedly brief one, I considered countering his threat with one of my own, about my association with Tiberius. Thankfully, not as much for myself but for my family, both by blood and by oath, who I would have undoubtedly endangered by my choice, I did not.

Instead, I tried to sound cool as I replied, "No more safer than you are, I imagine."

"Oh, that's not true," Varro countered. "I've never angered him as you have. Don't think that he's forgotten your time in Rome. In fact, he spent a great deal of time on the last occasion I was in his presence talking about not just you, but about your father. He hasn't forgotten that insult either, I regret to say."

While none of this was a surprise, although I did not know if Varro had any idea that I knew a great deal about my father's clash with Sejanus back when Sejanus was still sharing the post of Praetorian Prefect with his father and he had accompanied Tiberius' son Drusus to Pannonia during the revolt, it was still chilling to hear this man talk about it.

"What do you want from me?"

"Nothing more than your word that you'll do as I expect, that if Marcus Sempronius...under any guise," he added meaningfully, "contacts you, that you alert Libo so that he can ask Sempronius some questions that I did not get the opportunity to ask him before he...left."

This was a moment where I realized that it was better to make a tactical retreat, and lying to Lucius Varro would not make me lose any sleep, so with as much sincerity as I could muster, I swore that I would do it.

"Libo will show you out," Varro said. "He has some questions about where he might lodge in Ubiorum."

"I'll make an offering that your barge doesn't sink," I could not resist on my way out.

"That wasn't very nice," Libo commented, though without any kind of heat. "Or very wise."

I did not say anything until we were outside the building, then came to an abrupt stop, giving me an opportunity to get a better idea of Libo's size. Naturally, he was several inches shorter than I was, but I realized that one other similarity he held with Canus was in the wiry, muscular build on a frame that had no fat.

"Turn around," I said impulsively, but when he demurred, I assured him patiently, "I'm not going to stab you in the back, Libo. I don't need to." He flushed, but he did as I asked, and I made a grunting noise once I was satisfied.

"What?" he asked suspiciously.

"I was just checking to see if you used some sort of trick like Canus did," then described the long dagger he wore horizontally against his back.

"I don't need anything like that," he replied, evenly enough, but I noticed something, that his nostrils flared slightly in the same manner my mother's do when she is controlling her temper.

"Canus was a brave man," I said, "and in his own way, he was a good man."

"I wouldn't know," Libo replied indifferently. "I just know that he displeased Varro."

"So will you," I said suddenly, "if you think you can ever

hope to defeat me."

"Is that what Canus thought?" Libo asked, and he seemed more amused than angry.

"No," I answered honestly. "By the time he was in a position where he had to try and kill King Maroboduus, he knew that he couldn't hope to beat me." I leaned closer to put my height and bulk at its best advantage, and I was pleased to see him lean backward instinctively. "Just hope you die as well as he did, Libo, because if you try me, you're going to die."

Then, I patted him on the shoulder and began walking away.

"Centurion," he called out, and I turned to see him smiling. "Two things, actually. The first is, why would you think that I'd come for you? And if I did, that I'd come alone?"

"Bring as many men as you want. It won't matter." I was about to turn back around and resume walking away, but I recalled something. "You said there were two things. What was the other?"

"Just that I believe there is a...clarification that I believe is important for you to know in order for you to make the best decision possible."

Without hearing what it was, I felt the beginning of a fluttering in the pit of my stomach because, while I had no idea what this "clarification" was, I was certain I would not like it.

"Oh?" I was secretly proud of myself for my cool tone. "And what might that be?"

"Varro was...imprecise in his description of my role," he explained. "While it's true that I report to him, that's a temporary measure for a specific purpose. I normally don't serve him; I serve *his* patron. And," he held his hands out as if the matter was out of his hands, "once this particular task is done, there's no way to tell what my master is going to have me working on next."

"That's good to know," I said, and I was not being completely disingenuous. "But it doesn't change anything, Libo. If you come for me, whether it's on orders from Varro, or for Sejanus, the one thing I can promise is that you'll die."

He did not try and stop me this time when I turned about and walked towards camp.

"Gnaeus," Alex sighed. "Sometimes I wonder about you."

I was back in my tent, and had just recounted everything to Alex, and I had been prepared for his chastisement. We were sipping wine as I related everything, but I was quite disappointed when my wise friend could not provide any insight into Varro's purpose, for which I naturally gave him a fair amount of grief, while I had decided in that moment not to reveal for whom Libo was really working.

"What did *you* make of it?" Alex asked me challengingly, and when I could not offer any alternative, he hooted, "Then why are you talking *cac* about me?"

"Because I expected more from you," then did my best impersonation of my wife's Parisii accent. "Oh, why can't you be more like Alex and use your head for more than a place to wear your helmet?"

I thought I was doing a creditable job, but Alex disabused me of that, warning, "You better not let her catch you mangling her beautiful accent like that, or you're going to have to sleep with one eye open." Turning serious, he spoke in the kind of musing tone that meant he was thinking it through. "Clearly, Varro is worried about Sempronius, but the question is whether it's what he knows…or that he's going to tell Tiberius what he knows."

"You mean the Noricum armor," I said, rewarded with a nod, which made me feel quite clever, but I also continued thinking it through, and I realized something. "You don't think that Varro had that armor diverted to Rome for the purpose of protecting Tiberius and not to help Sejanus, do you?"

"No, I don't," Alex did not hesitate to reply. "Oh, I believe that's how it's going to be presented to the Imperator *if* he finds out about it, but I think the prospect of Sejanus having at least a full Cohort outfitted in *segmentatae* that can't be pierced by a standard *gladius* to use for his purposes and not Tiberius', that would be too much for him to resist."

I had been thinking the same thing, but there was another aspect that I pointed out then, "Those are just the sets that are intact. If they can find enough smiths in Rome with the skills to repair those sets that we chopped through with axes or pierced with siege spears, they'll have enough for almost two full Cohorts."

"That's true." He nodded. We paused from our rumination to sip, then he asked the next question that bothered me. "But why would Sempronius show up in Ubiorum? And why would Varro think that he'd come and seek you out, either back in Augustodunum or in Ubiorum?"

"Well, he *did* seek me out when he was trapped in Augustodunum," I pointed out. "But why he'd come to Ubiorum, I have no idea."

We finally decided that the likelihood of seeing Marcus Sempronius in Ubiorum was so remote that it did not merit consideration. As far as the armor was concerned, it was also something that was so far above our heads that, as troubling as it may have been, there was no reason to waste any time or attention to it. Or, so we believed, at least.

After two days and only a handful of barges appeared from downstream who answered the call put out by Silius after they had unloaded whatever cargo they were carrying when they were alerted to the opportunity for a fat purse of silver from the Roman army, Macer announced that we would not be waiting any longer, which, as one might imagine, did not make the masters of those barges who had hurried to Cambete very happy.

I felt quite smug because I had been with the Primus Pilus the night before and he had told me, "The more I think about it, the more I keep thinking about what Isauricus said about arriving in Ubiorum together, for the sake of our families. I think that it's probably more important than I would have thought initially."

Therefore, I tried not to let it show as he articulated to the other Centurions that we would be taking the overland route, with our wounded riding in the wagons, although I did believe that, if this had been perhaps five years earlier, he would have chosen to wait for the shipping because of the condition of the road. While it was not a fully Romanized road like the Via Agrippa, it was a far cry from the rutted, bumpy track it had been during my early years with the Legion, and it would have been a practical guarantee that a handful of the most seriously injured would have a wound open because of the jolting, thereby prolonging their recovery if they were blessed by Fortuna, or actually succumbing to their wounds if they were not. Consequently, I was not all that surprised that, once Macer explained his reasoning, most of the Centurions were in agreement, or if they were not, did not feel sufficiently moved to argue the point.

We departed Cambete with our longer than normal tail of wagons the next day, moving at what was not necessarily a leisurely pace, but was certainly slower than if we had been marching whole. I devoted part of the day either riding alongside one of the wagons carrying Fifth Century boys, or in one of the wagons with Latobius tied to it, though I confess I did not stay long. It was certainly better as far as the smell; those whose wounds had corrupted had either had the corruption cut away, albeit usually at the cost of a limb, or it had gone away on its own, or they had died, but there was still a faint odor trapped within the confines of the wagon that I did my best to ignore while I rode with them since they clearly did not notice it. I did not confine myself to just my Century; after what we had shared facing the *crupellarii*, I would not have felt right if I did not spend time with the men who had been with me, although it became clear on the first day that at least part of the time, instead of talking about what awaited them in Ubiorum, either in the form of their women and children, or the prospect of new faces, and bodies, in the brothels, the men seemed to feel the need to talk about what had transpired that day now almost two weeks ago. More specifically, I had to hear them talking about me and what I had done, yet, while at first I found it actually valuable, if embarrassing, because some of the fragmented memories in my mind now matched with what one of the men had told me they had witnessed, I soon enough realized something.

It was during our evening meal in my quarters the second night of the march that I complained to Alex, "If I were to believe what every one of those bastards in the wagons who were with us that day says, it's no wonder we almost got beaten. They were all watching me instead of doing their fucking jobs!" I do not know if it was my words, or the indignant tone, but whatever it was, I was not prepared for Alex to burst out laughing, quickly coming to the point he had tears streaming from his eyes. "It's not funny!" I protested, but that only made him laugh harder, grabbing his stomach until I finally cried out, "All right, fine! Explain it to me."

Wiping his eyes, Alex took a sip to compose himself before he said, smiling, "You sounded so much like your father then, so...offended, I suppose is the best word. And hurt." He kept smiling, though his expression changed, becoming a bit melancholy as he continued, "You're just like him in that way. You can't grasp exactly how remarkable what you did really is..."

"Because I can't remember it!" I knew I should not be raising my voice, but I could not help it, the frustration that I had managed to keep stuffed down inside me as I listened to my wounded comrades avidly describing my actions suddenly welling back up. "I don't know how I'm supposed to behave when I hear about lopping some poor *cunnus*' head off, or picking one of them up and throwing him a dozen paces away; at least," I added, "I *think* that's what he was saying, but it didn't make any sense because he talked about me doing something with a siege spear I didn't understand, or taking an ax and almost slicing a man in two from the top of his head to his balls!"

I knew that I was not only becoming angry, but that I was taking it out on Alex when he had done nothing wrong, yet I could not help myself.

"You're not supposed to behave in one way or another," he replied, but as agitated as I was, I still maintained enough of my faculties to know that Alex was choosing to be deliberately calm and unruffled by my outburst. He reached out to grasp my forearm, saying emphatically, "Gnaeus, believe it or not, what you're hearing from those men isn't about you, it's about them. They're letting you know that they were there, with you, that they witnessed what you did, and this is their way of expressing their thanks."

I cannot say why, but I had never thought about it in that light, so the next day, I was able to spend time with them without that feeling of discomfort and frustration, although I still could not shake the thought that, perhaps if they had been paying closer attention to their own jobs there would not have been a need for me to behave the way I did, something I never articulated until now. There was another thing I had been avoiding, and finally at Alex's quiet but stubborn insistence, on the third night, two days from Mogontiacum, I invited Saloninus and Closus to dine with me. Immediately after our cups were filled, I launched into the apology I had been rehearsing for avoiding them in the days after the battle.

"Part of it was I didn't want to talk about what happened with the Prefect since I was there with him at the end," I explained, which was certainly true. "Not until we had a chance for the *Praetor* to write up his report."

"What did Varro say?" Closus asked, reminding me that, despite his appearance as being a man of the ranks who barely knew how to write his name, he had a keen mind and a shrewd insight into human nature, and I understood that he had seen the problem. "Did he put up a fight of some sort?"

"Oh," I gave a dismissive wave that I hoped would convince them, "he made some noise, but we put it to bed quickly enough." Deciding that these two men deserved full honesty, it was still difficult for me to continue, "And then there was Sabinus…" I could not finish, but to my relief, there was no need for me to, their expressions of shared sorrow saying it all. Clearing my throat, I raised my cup. "To Optio of the First Century of the Seventh Cohort of the 1st Legion Publius Canidius Sabinus. His actions will never be forgotten, nor will his name as long as there is a 1st Legion of Rome, which is as eternal as Rome. May we meet again in Elysium."

"To Sabinus!" they both echoed, followed by a brief silence, if you could call the sound of three throats trying to gulp the contents of their cups so they could be the first to slam their cups onto the table a silence. As usual, there was no agreement on whose cup touched the table first, the argument continuing through another cup before, finally, Saloninus broached the other subject that I knew the mention of Sabinus would evoke.

"I know you've heard all you care to about what happened,

Gnaeus," he began, "so I'm not going to go on and on, but I never got the chance to thank you."

"Nor I," Closus put in, adding with an emphatic pointing of his finger at me, "but every man who was there knows the truth. Those *cunni* were fucking impossible to kill with just our *gladii*, and it wasn't until you did…what it is that you Pullus men do," even I had to laugh, even though it was a bit uncomfortable in both the physical and emotional sense, "that we had a beggar's chance to see another sunrise, because we were well and truly fucked."

"Whose idea was it to use axes?" Saloninus asked, and I answered honestly, "I don't really know."

Only in hindsight did I realize this was not really a question but an invitation, because I saw them exchange a glance, though I could not interpret it until Saloninus said quietly, "It was you, Gnaeus."

He went on to relate how I had ordered a ranker, who was destined by the Fates to only be alive a few hundred more heartbeats, to grab up one of the axes that what we later counted as a full quarter of the *crupellarii* carried as their secondary weapon, which I only recalled when he mentioned it. What I did not remember was sending men out to gather more axes or putting them into a semblance of a formation, because it was not long after that I saw Sabinus fall. As they talked, it became clear to me that they had probably agreed beforehand which of them would talk about which part of that day, because it was Closus who took up the story, staring into his cup as he continued talking.

"You didn't run, you walked, but I think those helmets they wore restricted their vision so much, and they had been so intent on Sabinus that they didn't see you coming. I was," he paused, squinting as he tried to remember, "oh, about fifty paces away, but on the opposite side with the boys of my group, and I saw you reach that bunch and you'd killed three of them before they even knew what was coming. Then I got busy," both Saloninus and I chuckled at the way he said it, "because I copied you and had some of my boys grab an ax, but then there wasn't many of those *crupellarii* left to fight, because they were all heading for you."

"You were completely surrounded," Saloninus said, "and they were about four deep all around you, but the last row turned around to hold us off. It was…" he took a heartbeat to remember the name, "that Sergeant of the Fourth Section from the First of the Fifth. Squatty bastard with that huge mole on his chin…"

"Appianus," I recalled his name, recommended by Clepsina, who had remembered him from his days as the Quintus Pilus Prior. "Sextus Appianus."

"Right, Appianus." Saloninus nodded. "He gathered some of men left from Sabinus' group and formed them up in a boar's head," he went on, describing what is essentially the infantry version of the cavalry wedge. "Then he led them at full speed, right at the outer rank, trying to break through to get to you."

Appianus had died in Charon's Boat the night of the battle, and I felt a wave of regret, and shame, that I had not at least had the opportunity to visit him and thank him for his heroism, or held his hand as he crossed the river, though I knew it was not Saloninus' intention to shame me by mentioning him.

"He had his shield tight against his shoulder and threw himself at one of those *cunni*, and it did knock him back a step, just not off his feet, but it was just enough of a crack in their line for the men on either side of Appianus to get stuck in," Saloninus said, then stopped to sip from his cup while giving Closus a nod.

"I had gathered about twenty of us, and nine of them had gotten axes, and when I saw what Appianus was doing, I copied him," the Optio explained. He was now hunched over the table, and using a combination of our cups, and picking out some chickpeas from the unfinished bowl of soldier's porridge we had consumed, created a map of the battle, the first time I had an opportunity to get a sense of what it looked like from an overhead perspective and on a scale larger than a couple dozen paces around me. Grabbing his cup, which he said was his group, he moved it across the table towards my cup, which he said represented me and the surrounding *crupellarii*. "We were coming from this direction, see? So we would have hit those bastards almost directly opposite where Appianus and his men were…" He moved a chickpea to the side of my cup opposite his, "…here. But," he suddenly sounded angry as he took another chickpea and moved it slowly across the table until it was interposed between my cup and his, but from his side, "their fucking commander and what I suppose was his personal bodyguard, they intercepted us before we got there."

"How did you know he was their commander?" I asked, which caused the other two to look at each other again.

"You don't remember one of those *mentulae* with the horsetail crest attached to the top of his helmet?" Saloninus asked in surprise.

I shook my head, yet even as I did so, I experienced a sudden image, a flash of memory, while my one-eyed friend laughed. "You should, considering you sent that fucking helmet so high in the air."

"Too bad for him his head was still in it," Closus put in, then the pair roared with laughter.

"So Appianus managed to cut his way to me," I said, but they both shook their head.

"No, and neither could my boys and I," Closus replied, and even if I had not known him so well, I would have heard the bitter disappointment.

I turned to Saloninus.

"What did you do?"

"I had to worry about those counterfeit Legionaries," he explained. "I don't know if it was the Aedui Sacrovir or one of his subcommanders in charge of them, but he sent about three Centuries' worth at us." When he saw I did not understand, he copied Closus, using a handful of chickpeas that represented his group, and another handful for the men who had been equipped like us to attack what was essentially our right flank. "As you know, we were attacking from the north, so I had to get enough men oriented facing to the west, or our right, but keep enough men facing the *crupellarii* to our east in between us and your men that they couldn't essentially cut us off. It was," he finished with a shrug, "an *orbis*, more or less, other than the fact we were protected somewhat by Macer's Cohort to the north."

For a second time, I was assaulted by a wave of guilt; that

was my responsibility, and it should have been me making that decision, yet I was also thankful that I had chosen Saloninus, who may not ever become a Primus Pilus because of his lost eye, thanks to the superstitious nature of his fellow Romans who believe that is a sign of the gods' disfavor, but if he does not, it will not be because of his lack of ability.

"So," I asked, still puzzled, "how did I manage to avoid being chopped to bits? I mean," I added quickly, "besides the obvious reason, because of my…" I waved a hand, but I could see they knew to what I was referring. "I was surrounded, Appianus couldn't get through to me, and neither could you because of this other bunch of *crupellarii*. So…what happened?"

"I think it was because you clearly spotted their commander," Saloninus said simply. "And it wasn't just because of that crest." He hesitated, and I heard the caution in his voice. "You *really* don't remember any of this?"

"No!" I answered, more sharply than I intended, but the gods know how tired I had become of being asked whether I remembered, as understandable as their confusion that I did not may have been. More softly, I repeated, "No, I don't remember, Aulus, I truly don't."

"He was at least your size," Saloninus explained, then amended, "although it was hard to tell with all that armor on." He turned to Closus. "What do you say, Publius?"

"He was at least as tall as you," Closus replied without hesitation. "Maybe taller."

"Naturally, we couldn't see his arms or legs, but just judging by his breadth compared to the other *crupellarii* around him, he was about your size as well. And," Saloninus shrugged, "you clearly saw him."

"You must have picked up a siege spear from somewhere," Closus put in, "and you used that to skewer the poor bastard standing directly between you and the *crupellarius* with the crest." This seemed somewhat odd to mention, but he was not through, although in the process, he did clear up one lingering mystery. "Then you lifted him up off the ground by the spear shaft, and you…" he was clearly struggling to describe it because it took a couple heartbeats for him to finally settle on,

"…swung him back and forth and knocked the gladiators on either side of him off their feet." I must have given him a look that relayed my confusion, because he got to his feet, and extending his arm out as if he was holding a spear at waist level, began swinging his arm horizontally back and forth in a sweeping motion. "Like that," he explained. "And you didn't just knock the pair on either side of the bastard you skewered; you started moving towards that big *mentula* just swinging this dead man back and forth like he weighed no more than a feather." He was clearly warming to the tale, continuing, "I swear on the black stone that you looked like you were a woman sweeping the floor of her house, back and forth, back and forth," he was moving his entire body as he talked, and even I was laughing harder than I had in some time, despite the pain, but he was not through. "The dead man was," he began waving his arms wildly in a parody of what I suppose a limp body being jerked back and forth looked like, but he put all but his lower body into the performance, including his head, which he jerked about, tongue hanging out, "flopping all over like that, and I think his comrades were just as terrified of the sight as they were being hit because of the way they tried to get out of the way! I," he dropped back down in his chair, panting from the exertion as he managed to finish, "have never seen anything like it."

While I had heard some allusion to using the corpse of a dead enemy in some manner, this was the most explicit description I have heard before or since. After his performance, Closus understandably felt the need to take a long draught from his third, or perhaps fourth cup, leaving it to Saloninus to finish.

"You cleared a path to reach their commander, but he saw what you were doing," Saloninus said. "And he recognized that you were trying to get to him, so he apparently ordered his men to move aside so that you and he could face each other. And," he pointed to my face, "he's the one who did that."

Without thinking, I reached up and touched the gash, wincing from the sudden flash of pain, not just because it was still quite tender, but because it seemed to trigger another fragment of memory, remembering that, since I did not have either a shield or even my *vitus,* I had been unable to completely dodge the high, overhead slashing attack from my foe's *gladius,* which I suddenly recalled was not the long Gallic style with a rounded tip but was more like our cavalry *spatha*, yet ultimately, what I felt more than anything was a cold satisfaction, knowing the outcome.

"I'm glad he's dead," I murmured.

"Oh, he's dead all right." Closus laughed. "You put paid to him and did it in a way that got those scum to start taking that first step backward."

"Some of the boys say they will swear on the black stone that his head still hasn't come back down yet," Saloninus added, shaking his head and joining Closus in laughing.

That's right, I thought. *That* was the image, one of the few I had recalled almost immediately, of a *crupellarius* helmet tumbling in the air with what seemed to me to be black blood but was instead the black horsetail crest, but immediately following that was another memory.

"Wait." I held up a hand. "They didn't break and run then, did they?"

"No." Saloninus shook his head. "Not right that moment. Instead, they all converged on you, and before we could do anything, you were surrounded all over again, except this time, it was more than just four ranks deep. But they seemed so intent on getting to you that, this time, they didn't bother turning even one rank around to protect their backs."

"And we took a moment to put the men with axes in the front and alternated them with the siege spears," Closus explained. His lips suddenly twisted into a cruel smile as he relived the moment. "We cut through those *cunni* like they were stalks of wheat, and that fucking armor didn't save them."

"It started a panic within a hundred heartbeats," Saloninus put in. "And while you may not remember everything, I know you remember how fucking slow they were." He laughed at the memory. "And they were trying to run uphill."

I did indeed recall that, when they began their charge downhill, it was at what could only charitably be called a trot, so it was not hard to imagine how ridiculous these same men who inspired the level of dread they had not long before when the first of our men shouted their *gladius* could not penetrate would look when trying to flee uphill in the opposite direction. We lapsed into a silence, and I assumed that each of us were lost in our own thoughts; I know that I certainly was, staring into my cup, oblivious to the fact I was being studied.

"Do you think that what we've heard about that *crupellarii* armor is true?"

I confess that my first reaction to Saloninus' question was disappointment, wondering if this had been the goal of the evening all along, before I reminded myself that I had invited them, and that Alex had informed me that we had not been the only ones to notice how closely guarded the wagons were and who was guarding them exclusively. Nevertheless, I wanted to be cautious, if only for Saloninus' and Closus' sakes.

"It depends on what you've heard," I said carefully.

"I've heard all sorts of things, but I can tell you what I think, that they're heading to Rome, and that it's not Tiberius who's in control of them but Sejanus," Saloninus answered me, his eye never wavering from my face, not in a challenging manner as much as letting me know that he felt confident that our thoughts were aligned, and that he trusted me.

"That's what Alex and I believe as well," I admitted.

I was trying to think of a way to sound Closus out, but there was no need, because he spoke next.

"And I think that it's that piece of *cac* Sejanus who wants that armor for his purposes, and his purposes have nothing to do with protecting the Imperator. I think," he poked the table with one finger to emphasize each word, "*he* wants to be Imperator."

He sat back in his chair to drain his cup, and I was concerned and touched in equal measure, as in this day and time, saying such a thing could be quite dangerous, especially when we were in a tent where the only thing between us and prying ears was a layer of canvas, but it was a show of his complete trust in his two companions and I was determined to reward it, thinking it was the least I could do.

"I think you're right," I replied.

"So do I," Saloninus nodded, then we fell silent for a period.

I was about to say something else when the *bucina* sounded the call to retire, and I honestly felt relieved, but not wanting to end it like that, I said simply, "We should make an offering to Fortuna that we're going to be far, far away from Rome, and it has nothing to do with us."

The march into Mogontiacum was something of a rehearsal for our entrance into our home camp, except for me, knowing that I would never hear the end of it if I did not go to see my mother, which of course meant there would be no hiding the fact that I had been scarred for the rest of my days. As much as I knew this would upset my mother, it would be a shade compared to my wife and children, but the truth was that it was my calf that was proving more troublesome, to the point where, while I pretended that it was so that I could spend time with the wounded men in the wagons, I spent part of my day on Latobius simply to let my calf rest. I would learn later that I did not fool anyone who knew me well, but at the time, I felt quite clever. Naturally, the people of Mogontiacum were expecting our arrival thanks to the 2nd passing through on the way to Vetera, but what we did not know, and was the topic of much discussion, was whether or not Silius would be there waiting for us, there being a fairly large segment among us who believed that he would already be on his way to Rome. Although not every ranker, or officer below Centurion for that matter, knew the details of the dispute between Varro and Silius and the role the 2nd had played, it was common knowledge that the two men, who had been wary allies at the beginning of this, now heartily despised each other, and that there was some sort of power struggle going on. Therefore, it made sense if he was absent from Mogontiacum, yet when we marched into the four Legion camp that housed the 5th and 21st to occupy the vacant huts and halted in the forum, the traditional spot for dismissal, the red pennant was flying over the brick *Praetorium* building, declaring the presence of the *Praetor*.

The wagons went directly to the hospital, and Macer dismissed the rest of us in the forum, allowing the Centurions to march their Centuries to their assigned housing, which we knew the location of because we always stayed in the same quadrant of the camp whenever we were there. It is a very practical, very Roman thing to do, but personally, I find it quite remarkable, and even soothing knowing that I could enter any permanent camp in the Empire and know exactly where the First Cohort of a Legion was located in relation to the forum and *Praetorium*. As we marched the short distance to our huts, a runner sent by the Primus Pilus came trotting up, informing me to attend to Macer as soon as the men were settled, which I acknowledged, fairly certain I knew why. Alex and Euphemios had already hurried to our designated hut, so that by the time I gave the Century their final instructions and dismissed them, when I entered my quarters, Euphemios was finishing up sweeping away the last of the dust and cobwebs that are inevitable, while Alex was pulling out a spare tunic, the last clean one, knowing where I was heading.

"You know you're coming as well," I told him, ignoring his protests that he did not want to impose on my mother.

"You just want me along so she won't be angry about that." He pointed at my face. "She'll feel badly about scolding you for being careless if I'm there."

"That," I admitted cheerfully, "is exactly right."

Deciding I would change after I spoke to Macer, I left and went to his hut, where Lucco was standing in the outer office, snapping at one of the other clerks about something, forcing me to hide my amusement as I recalled one of Alex's complaints.

"Being made the chief clerk of the Legion has gone to Lucco's head," he grumbled, more times than I can easily count. "He thinks his *cac* doesn't stink, and that he's never wrong, but he *still* has to come to me to check his sums."

Blissfully unaware that I knew this, Lucco pointed to the door leading to the Primus Pilus' private quarters, and I walked to it. Within a couple heartbeats, I was standing in front of Macer, who grunted a greeting, but in his hand was a scroll, which he extended to me.

"A pass so that you can see your mother," he explained.

"You're not giving the men the freedom of the town?" I asked in surprise.

He shook his head, but not for the reason I thought.

"I don't know yet. I need to speak with the *Praetor* first, because I just talked to Philippos, and he told me that if we spend two days here, we'll be able to clear all but the amputees and the last of the chest wounds out of the wagons."

"That seems like it would be a good thing," I said cautiously, because there was something in Macer's tone that suggested he had some doubt, "but you don't seem to think so. What am I missing?"

"It's not that I don't think it is, because I do. Yes, it means two more days before the men can be with their families, but I'm about as certain as I can be that once we explain it to the men, they'll agree. But I don't know if Silius will allow it."

"Why not?"

He had been looking everywhere but at me until my question, and he gave me a level look as he said, "Because I'm not sure that Silius is going to want us out in town saying the kinds of things about the 2nd that our boys will be saying to the boys in the 5th and 21st."

"It's the same thing we'll be saying to the 20th when we get home," I countered, but by the time I said it, my mind had continued working, "but yes, I can see that. It's the difference between one other Legion hearing what we have to say, and three other Legions hearing about it." I was struck by an idea, though not one that seemed to have much of a chance of success. "I'm going to delay leaving camp until you speak to the *Praetor*. If he says that he isn't willing for us to spend a night here because he wants us gone, let me know. I'll go talk to Primus Pilus Nerva…"

"Nerva!" Macer exclaimed, then gave a disbelieving laugh. "He hates you for what you did to Petronius!"

"He did." I nodded. "But that was before we served together when Varro sent us on that fool's errand to depose Maroboduus and replace him with that idiot Catualda. No," I said with more confidence than I actually felt, "if Silius wants us gone, I'll be able to work it out with Nerva. He owes me."

Macer eyed me, clearly skeptical, not that I blamed him considering that the last time he had been in Nerva's company when I was present had been in Rome, and the Alaudae Primus

Pilus had not hidden his feelings about me then, but finally, he agreed.

"Go back to your tent and wait for me there. I'll come and tell you what the *Praetor* says."

I did so, telling Alex what was happening, and I decided to take the chance that there was enough time for an oiling and scraping, though the rubdown was briefer than normal, which is the best part, especially if one is sore and tired. Once he was finished, I had just donned my fresh tunic when we heard the quick rap on the wooden block, so that Macer and I entered my outer office at the same time, if from two different directions.

He wore a bemused expression, which I misinterpreted, turning about to grab my *vitus* as I thought of what I was going to say to Nerva.

"He said that we can spend as long as we want, and that of course the men have the liberty of the town," he said. With a shake of his head, he admitted, "I'm surprised. In fact," he looked up at me, a frown creasing his face, "I got the sense that even if we were only stopping a night, he'd tell us to stay longer."

"What does that mean?" I asked, glancing at Alex, but all he could do was shake his head, as mystified as I was.

"He didn't say as much, certainly, but I got the strong sense that he wants our boys to tell the Alaudae and 21st about the 2nd."

I was about to chide Macer for letting his imagination getting away from him, but I glanced over at Alex, and recognized the expression on his face, so I kept my mouth shut.

"I'm beginning to think that our *Praetor* actually wants some sort of confrontation with Varro the Younger about this entire business," Alex said thoughtfully. Then, he added, "Or maybe his target is Tata and not his whelp."

Macer considered this, then shrugged.

"This is far above our heads, and I for one am tired of thinking about it. So," he turned to me, "go see your mother. Have Vinicius deal with your misbegotten bastards and sending them out into town."

I did not want to grin, but I could not stop myself, and I gave him an excessively elaborate salute that hearkened back to my time as a Praetorian, and after issuing instructions to Euphemios to go tell Vinicius he was in command, the three of us left my tent, with Alex and I heading for the *Porta Praetoria*. Now it was time to see my mother and let her fuss over me.

Crossing the bridge and navigating the now-familiar path to my mother's villa, I experienced my first taste of the kind of reaction that I could expect from civilians, who, for the first time in my life, did not react to my size first but the livid pink scar running down the left side of my face.

However, when I saw Alex's head turn to say something, I beat him to it, saying lightly, "At least they're not gawking at my size anymore, eh?"

He laughed, and if there was a forced quality to it, I chose to ignore it, but then we turned the corner and saw my mother's villa. The gate was closed, but that was to be expected, and we crossed the street to stand in front of it, and I noticed that the iron knocker had been replaced by a bell, which I rang. After a few heartbeats, we heard the footfall of someone approaching, and as they got closer, I could tell that it was a man approaching, then the small door that kept anyone from looking through the iron grill of the postern door opened, and I saw an eye, a blinking eye that went suddenly wide, accompanied by a gasp.

"Master Gnaeus? What happened to you?"

"I got careless shaving, Mandalonius," I joked, momentarily forgetting something about the former gladiator who was now in my mother's service, reminded when he replied seriously, "You should be more careful, Master."

The sound of the latching bar being raised muffled his words slightly, but when I stepped through the open door, I saw a gleam in Mandalonius' eye that told me he had not been completely serious, and I rewarded him with a grin and clap on the shoulder, but he suddenly looked uncomfortable.

"The Mistress is not alone, Master Gnaeus," he said, explaining his discomfort since I knew to whom he was referring, but I had already resolved to take the presence of Censorinus in stride.

"That's fine, Mandalonius," I assured him. "In fact, I'm looking forward to seeing Lucius Censorinus as well." He had already started walking towards the villa, so I tugged on his sleeve to slow him down. "How are they, Mandalonius? Are they happy together?"

I was relieved to see how quickly his battered features transformed and he smiled, unusual for him, nodding vigorously.

"Oh yes, Master Gnaeus! They are very happy together, I swear it! And Master Lucius treats her very well."

This was indeed good news, and we resumed walking as I asked, "And how is Carissa?"

"She," he sighed, but with a kind of moonstruck expression, "is wonderful, Master Gnaeus." Alex and I exchanged an amused glance, which he must have caught, because he went a deep red. "Oh, you mean how is she doing as far as her health, yes?"

"Yes, that's what I meant."

"She is very healthy," Mandalonius confirmed.

"And how are she and Grimhilt getting along?" I asked mischievously, and I was not surprised at the grimace he made.

"I am surprised they are both alive," he said frankly. "But as long as Mistress Giulia wants them both under her roof, neither of them are willing to slit the other's throat. I," he finished as he pulled open the door, "keep my mouth shut and stay out of the way, then at night when we are alone, I just listen and nod to whatever Carissa says about Grimhilt."

"That's a wise strategy, Mandalonius," I agreed, and I meant it wholeheartedly.

Even if I had wanted to say anything more, I would not have had the chance, because a figure darted into the hallway between the entry vestibule and the *triclinium*, a small, lithe figure attired in a rich green *stola* who moved with such impressive speed that, before I could even get my hands up and out, my mother was clinging to my neck.

"My *boy*," she whispered the words into my ear as, out of a long habit that had developed when I was all of eleven years old and already almost six feet, I straightened up so that her feet were dangling off the floor, "you're home!" I realized that she had not had the opportunity to get a good look at me during her headlong rush at me when she said, "And you're in one piece! You don't know how many offerings I've made to…"

"Mama," I interrupted, gently prying her arms from around her neck, "I don't think you got a good enough look at me."

Still gently, I held her out at arm's length, remembering to lower her so her feet were back on the floor, and as I watched her eyes take in my face, then suddenly well with tears, it felt as if I was being stabbed in my heart. I can only imagine the willpower it took for my mother to hold back those tears, though her eyes shone with them, and she tilted her chin slightly upward, the picture of the strong Roman matron.

"Well," she said, "you've always wanted a scar on your face since you were twelve years old, so I suppose congratulations are in order for finally achieving your goal. And," she smiled then, "I think that once Bronwen gets over the shock, she's going to find it very…appealing."

With that, she peered around me and saw Alex, and they exchanged a hug and kiss, then taking my hand, she led me towards the *triclinium*, but when she turned towards me, I recognized the expression, and I whispered, "Don't worry, Mama. I know Censorinus is here, and I'll be on my best behavior."

The expression of relief was impossible to miss, and we entered to see Censorinus coming to his feet from his spot on the couch my mother normally reclined on.

"Gnaeus," he began, then stopped abruptly, gasping, "By the gods! That is a right nasty…"

"Lucius, my love," my mother cut him off sweetly, but while Censorinus may have known my mother in a different way, I had known her longer, and I was curious to see if he heard the same warning there, "I think Gnaeus is well aware that it is a serious gash to his face."

He clearly did, saying meekly, "Yes, Giulia, of course. I didn't mean to state the obvious." I suspect to appease both of us, he said, "I actually met with the *Praetor* two days ago. Not just me," he added hastily, "I mean the various magistrates and former and present *Duumviri*, and he told us all about the campaign."

We settled down, with Alex and me taking up the spots that more or less had become ours by virtue of that was where we sat the first time we visited, and Carissa appeared with a tray bearing cups and a pitcher. She, unfortunately, was not as disciplined as my mother, letting out a shout of despair at the sight of my face; even worse, she dropped the tray, shattering the cups and pitcher, the contents of which spraying across the floor and soaking one of the carpets. Whether she was mortified by her mistake or too disturbed by my visage to remain, she turned and fled into another part of the house, leaving it to Grimhilt to come in to clean up. In a stark, and at least to me, humorous contrast, she barely seemed to notice our presence, let alone my wound, offering a bare grunt that had my mother groaning in frustration.

"Try as I might, I haven't been able to teach Grimhilt any manners," she complained once the two women left the room, whereupon there was an almost immediate eruption of voices that, while audible, were too muffled to hear what was being said but was clearly a quarrel, and even my mother gave a soft chuckle.

"That's another thing I've been unable to change," she said ruefully. "I'm afraid they are too much alike to ever become friends."

Carissa returned, her eyes averted from my face this time, at least until she set the tray down without mishap. Only then did she come to stand in front of me, offering me a curtsy of sorts.

"Master Gnaeus, please forgive my reaction," she apologized. "I was just…surprised." I assured her that no offense had been given, and she asked with a shyness that made her seem much younger, "Does it hurt?"

"Only when I laugh," I replied, then added, "or smile."

I was being serious, but Carissa, my mother, and Censorinus all laughed, and rather than make them feel badly, I forced myself to grin.

"It does make you look very fearsome," Carissa offered.

"So I've been told," I acknowledged, but my mother chose that moment to divulge, "Yes, Gnaeus has always wanted to be disfigured ever since he was a boy. One time I caught him with

Quintus' *pugio* in front of my mirror, trying to work up the nerve to cut himself."

"That's not true," I lied. "I just happened to be standing there when you came in, and you drew the wrong conclusion!"

Despite the subject matter, I felt more at ease since this was, and is the pattern of our interactions, one of teasing back and forth that is probably more akin to that of siblings than parent and child, yet even in the moment, I was aware of the manner in which she had referred to Quintus Volusenus, using his *praenomen* and not as my father. This was a change that had happened gradually ever since the revelation about who my father really was, and I took note that she had done this in front of Censorinus, who sat there with a grin on his face, clearly enjoying our back and forth. Carissa left, though only after my mother gave her instructions to start preparing a meal that made my mouth water, but once she was gone, I turned to Censorinus.

"So, tell me what the *Praetor* had to say about the uprisings."

By the time he was through, it seemed clear that Gaius Silius, the *Praetor* of the Upper Rhenus, was determined to tell the truth of what had taken place.

Chapter 9

We stayed for three full days in Mogontiacum, a period during which Macer had more than one opportunity to confirm what Censorinus had intimated during my visit with my mother.

"He seems determined to tell the truth as he sees it," was how the Primus Pilus put it, on our last night back at my mother's villa, at her insistence.

Given his association with our family, my mother had essentially adopted him, which I frankly found odd since they are about the same age, but most crucially, she trusted him as much as I did, and the feeling was reciprocated, which was why he was speaking so freely. Although, I thought with some amusement, it could have been due to the Chian wine, which is his favorite vintage, which had been flowing freely throughout the dinner. I was sated, not from the wine but because of the pork, with the skin crackling, along with chicken, and best of all, a nice haunch of beef, roasted in a manner that Grimhilt excels at, bringing it from her Suebi homeland. Censorinus was present, but seated on the *lectus summus* as a guest and not the *lectus imus*, which I shared with my mother, and I was a bit nervous that Macer was speaking so freely, but when I cleared my throat in an attempt to signal him, it earned me a nudge from my mother, who communicated her warning that she knew what I was doing and did not appreciate it, so I subsided, unhappily, but I did not do it again.

"I can tell you this," Censorinus put in. "There's been a fair amount of talk that Varro the Elder is close to the end of his string, and has actually been incapacitated for weeks…if not longer."

This got our attention, and a glance across the low table told me that Macer's mind was working in the same direction, that it had been longer, which meant that Varro the Younger had been making decisions in his father's name instead of carrying out his instructions as he had claimed. As I thought about it, I had to admit that it was cunning, but it was Alex who thought ahead.

"The only way the son can get away with it is if the father dies," he said flatly. "Because if there's any chance that Varro the Elder might contradict his son's account that he was getting instructions from the *Praetor*, whether intentionally or by accident, Tiberius will have his balls..." He immediately flushed a deep red, turning to my mother. "I'm sorry, Giulia." He grinned and looked over at me. "I'm afraid I've been in your son's company too long."

"You are forgiven, Alexandros," my mother said loftily, making sure to make a languid gesture that made us laugh. "My son is a bit of a barbarian, I admit. It must be his soldier's blood. But," my mother leaned forward a bit and adopted a conspiratorial tone, "I agree. The Imperator would absolutely have that young monster's balls."

We all laughed, except for Censorinus, who looked a bit discomfited, reminding me that he had never served, though he was not a bad sort. He also was thinking about what was being said.

"I did hear something that, at the time, I didn't think anything about it," he said slowly. Addressing Macer, he asked, "Do you recall what the son said about why his father wasn't present when the 2nd joined you?"

Macer thought for a moment, then shook his head. "Not anything that jumps out. He just said that his father was too ill to travel...and then he pulled that fuck...that ivory baton out."

As much to cover up Macer's blunder as anything, I groaned, "By the gods, him and that baton."

Between us, Macer and I briefly described Varro's propensity to produce the ivory baton carried by the *Praetor* as the symbol of his authority at seemingly every opportunity, but once we were finished, Macer asked Censorinus, "Why did you ask?"

"Because of something I heard." He suddenly turned to mother, saying a single name. "Casca. He's the one who told me." This clearly meant something to my mother, though she said nothing as her lover explained, "He runs a freight business, and he owns the contract to take supplies to Vetera, and as you can imagine, he was quite busy in the days before the 2nd left Vetera to join you. I just happened to be at the baths when we heard about the *Praetor* being too ill to accompany the Legion, and Casca was there. 'That's odd,' he said, and when I asked him why, he told me, 'I saw Varro the Elder just a couple days ago, and he was fit and eager to march. He said he hadn't felt this young in years.' Honestly," Censorinus admitted, "I didn't think anything of it then. But now?"

A silence settled on our small party, ostensibly as we either sipped some of our beverage, or in my case stuffed more beef into my mouth, though I am certain that it was to give us all time to grasp the possible meaning, yet when nobody wanted to say it, I swallowed my mouthful of beef, and said flatly, "That cowardly *fellator* tried to kill his father."

"*Gnaeus!*" my mother gasped, pushing herself up off her elbows to glare at me, but this was one time I was not cowed.

"He tried to have me killed, Mother." I heard the cold wrath in my voice, but I was sufficiently angered not to care. "He threw me in a fucking cell."

For a long moment, my mother and I locked eyes, then she settled back down and said, "That's true. So, you're right. He's a *fellator!*"

We laughed for a very, very long time, and it is a good memory of that evening. That ebullient mood did not last all that long, as we became immersed in the discussion about the various possibilities that could result in Silius' actions, one that lasted longer than it should have considering we were marching the next morning. Fortunately, as Centurions, we have the ability to make others share our misery, which in this case was a combination of a lack of sleep, a hangover, and a fair amount of concern about our *Praetor*. That night, when we were about to return to the camp, Mandalonius suddenly appeared in the *triclinium*, and he beckoned to me. I was a bit drunk, but I managed to weave my way to him, yet despite the wine, the expression on his face sobered me up a great deal.

"What is it?" I asked, slightly alarmed.

"Master Gnaeus, will you come with me? There is something I want to show you."

Gesturing to him to lead the way, I followed him out of the villa, but instead of walking to the gate, he headed for a spot several paces down the wall.

"If you lift yourself up and look directly in front of you, you will see a man," he explained solemnly, but I think the wine was still affecting me a bit, because I did not understand why he wanted me to do this.

"So? There's some drunk sleeping it off across the street?"

What he said next did more to sober me up than anything else, because he replied, "He has been there in the same spot watching ever since you came to visit the first time."

I did not hesitate then, hopping up to catch the edge of the wall and chinning myself, though I did think to be careful not to lift my head too high above the wall.

"He is sitting on that barrel, just to the right of the torch," he said, and I saw him immediately.

And, because of where he was seated, within the pool of torchlight thrown by one of the torches that are lit by the night watch, I not only spotted him, I recognized him.

"Libo," I breathed the name of Canus' replacement.

I dropped back to the ground, thanking Mandalonius, and I returned to the villa, but when the others asked me, I made an excuse that I do not recall. Somewhat hampered by the effects of the wine as I was, it took a bit longer than it should have for me to realize that his placement within the circle of light from the torch was no accident; it was a message from Libo that he was watching me. The question was, would this continue when we were back in Ubiorum?

The march from Mogontiacum to Ubiorum normally takes a bit less than four days, but such was the men's eagerness that by the midday break on the first day, Macer essentially gave up trying to rein in the Legion. He also ordered that we march a third of a watch longer since there was no need for a camp, which meant that the final day of the march only lasted the first daylight watch so that we arrived back home in midmorning. Once he knew our exact time of arrival, he sent Lucco ahead on his horse to alert the duty auxiliary Cohort who had remained behind, along with the families, making our entrance into a small scale triumphant procession. The Tribune in "command," Lucius Vitellius, was haughty even for a patrician, coming from a well-connected family, but he had been sufficiently cowed by Macer during our march, with a bit of help from me because I just "happened" to be standing with Macer whenever the Primus Pilus had some sort of "suggestion" for him to cede the decisions to the professionals. However, to the Tribune's credit, he independently came up with the idea to wrap our eagle and Cohort standards in ivy, so there was a delay as we stopped and went into the nearby forest to collect enough, which meant that the crowd had reached its full size by the time we came marching into the town, which is not the most direct route to our camp from the south, there being a smaller road that branches off that leads directly to camp.

"Smarten up, boys!" I shouted, "You don't want to embarrass your families now!"

I was far from alone in this admonishment, nor was it just my Century where some wit—in our case, it was Publius Geta of my First Section—who said loudly enough that the target of his jibe in the Tenth Section could hear, "I'm afraid that's not going to be possible for Mancia, Centurion! He's a walking embarrassment! He's the only man I know who can look worse coming out of the baths than he did walking in…and smell worse too!"

This was received by a roar of laughter, and it included me as well; it was funny because it was essentially true. Gaius Mancia was in the Tenth Section, and it was a mystery how, no matter how hard he scrubbed, he somehow managed to look dirty, with a yellowish cast to his skin that none of us could place. When I was in Alexandria, then later in Rome, I had seen men with almond-shaped eyes and skin that was similar in shade to Mancia's, but when I was told that they came from a land far beyond the Parthian Empire, I refused to believe that Mancia's roots extended that far east.

Mancia, long accustomed to this line of mockery, shouted back, "That's not what your Fulvia said the night before we left, Geta! While you were at the Faun, we were playing slap and tickle!"

Geta's bellow of rage was drowned out by the even louder roar of laughter, but this time, I was not laughing, and I took a quick step so that I could get just ahead of the first rank and look down to where Geta was located.

"Don't even think about it, Geta!" I bellowed, knowing by his guilty look that he had been about to drop his pack. "You know how it works in the Fifth! Don't run your mouth if you can't take it as well as you give it!"

"But he's talking about my woman, Centurion! My Fulvia!"

I was also reminded of something about Geta, and that was that he tended to whine when he felt he was being wronged, which was what he was doing then, and I was unmoved.

"I don't care if he was talking about your mother, Geta. If you break ranks...I'll break you. Now shut your mouth!"

He did so, with the kind of sulky expression that I was beginning to see from Titus, who would be five on his next birthday, and just like I did with my son, I ignored it. I do not want to give the impression that this was happening in just my Century, or Cohort; when spirits are high, as they were that day, these kinds of exchanges are happening up and down the column. In my case, my nerves were vibrating with tension as we approached the crowd lining both sides of the street, with children of varying ages darting out in front of us as we marched as they searched the ranks for their fathers, or just for the sport of it, while the hobnailed soles were cracking on the paving stones as the men marched in a rhythm that is music to a Centurion's ears. It is a truism shared among men who wear the transverse crest, that their Centuries, Cohorts, and Legions march better whenever there is an audience, and when it is their own families, they march their absolute best.

Aside from the ivy, Macer had not required the men to varnish their leathers, nor were we wearing our *sagum* over one shoulder like we do when we are on parade, but the gods know that it was still an impressive, stirring sight that never fails to make my heart quicken with pride, and one glance at the Fifth told me they all felt the same way. I could have quibbled and barked at them to wipe the broad smiles from their faces, but that would have been excessively harsh; we *were* coming home, after all. My own eyes were scanning the faces of the crowd, knowing that Bronwen and the children would make sure to place themselves on the right side of the street, using her status as not just the woman, but the legal wife of her Centurion husband, thanks to the dispensation given by Germanicus himself, now dead almost two years. It was something that Bronwen was never shy to bring up with any other woman attached to the Legion in some manner, despite my counseling her more than once that between that and her exotic background, coming from Britannia as she did, it would behoove her to be more diplomatic. Inevitably, she would scoff at this and toss her glorious mane of coppery hair, reverting back to being the imperious daughter of a rich merchant.

"It would do them well to remember who my *husband* is!" she would reply sweetly, or words to that effect since this was something that came up often.

Now, as I scanned the faces, I actually spotted her by that magnificent head of hair that I adore so much, which she was wearing swept up and held with pins, a style that she had adopted from my mother, knowing how I felt about it. She was holding Giulia, and I saw Bronwen say something to her that made her giggle, just as Macer marched past with the First Century with Gnaeus Calpurnius, our *Aquilifer* who was going to be retiring at the end of this campaign season next to him. Macer had turned his head in their direction, and I could tell that he had said something, technically a violation of regulations, but one that is largely ignored, especially by lofty personages such as the Primus Pilus. However, it was the figure that suddenly appeared from the other side of my wife to go darting out into the street, where he began capering beside the man he called Uncle Marcus that made my heart leap into my throat. Titus followed Macer a few paces before his mother called to him, and he came trotting back to her, and I saw his face turn in my direction. It did not take him long to spot the largest Centurion, and one of the largest men in the Legion, and the Army of the Upper Rhenus, lifting his arm to point at me and I assumed to call to his mother, as she turned in our direction, shading her eyes with her free hand, while Titus began jumping up and down from one foot to another, something he always did when he was excited, only recently growing out of it, much to the sadness of his parents. I knew that I was still too far away for them to see my face, and my stomach began churning as we approached, although I largely ignored the growing shift in the nature of the sounds from the crowd as women like Bronwen, and children like Titus eagerly scanned the ranks, all of them knowing the spot where their men were marching, a shift that, as much as we all prepared for it, was still difficult to hear.

"Where's Publius? I don't see my Publius!" This would be how it started, followed by, "You there! Gaius Manius! Where's your close comrade, eh? Why isn't he next to you?"

I had noticed that this was the one time where men suddenly took their orders for quiet in the ranks seriously, many of them choosing to look straight ahead, though some of them would respond in some way, usually with a shake of the head, which would be met with a shriek of agony, or even worse in some ways, an utter silence as the new widow stood there, mouth open, suddenly surrounded by women who, despite their own fears and concern for their men, would rally around her, offering support. Other times, it was not quite as bad, because the comrade would either point back in the direction of the wagons, or would tell the woman her man was alive and with the wounded. This was now taking place all around us, and it would only get worse as the rest of the Legion marched into town and more women and children missed their familiar face, but all I was paying attention to at this moment was my wife, now close enough that I could see her smiling, knowing that it was not going to last once I was close enough for her to see me. I saw her point to me, clearly telling Giulia that her Tata was coming, because I saw her head, full of black curls, turn to look, while my son, still hopping from one foot to another, stood next to Bronwen.

Despite knowing that Macer had not slowed the pace, my eyes were telling me a much different story, it seeming to take a full watch for the Fifth to reach a point where I saw it happen; Bronwen's smile fading away, close enough now that I could see her eyes go wide, then her mouth drop open, even as Giulia, despite her age, had the same reaction as her mother before she turned her face away and dropped her head to bury her face in her mother's neck. Ignoring the pain, which was still present but had diminished somewhat, I gave them a broad smile, which Bronwen, through the tears streaming down her face, returned, whispering something to my daughter, who clearly reluctant, did lift her head to look at me again, except it just made her cry even harder. I looked down at Titus then, noticing that while his eyes were bright and wide like his mother's had been, they showed no sign of tears, and I will never forget the long span of the heartbeat our eyes met, noticing how expressionless he seemed, making me feel as if I was looking at a slightly curious boy seeing a stranger and not his father, igniting a feeling of unease in me. Crying I would have understood, just like his mother and sister were doing, but instead, without a word, he turned and dashed into the crowd, disappearing into the crush of bodies…just as I was reaching them.

"I will go to him!" Bronwen shouted over the crowd. "We will be waiting for you at home!"

I could only nod, unable to get anything past the sudden lump in my throat at my son's reaction to seeing the monster his father had become, and she did not hesitate, turning away from us. The rest of the people immediately around her scrambled out of her way, allowing me to get just a glimpse of the heels of my son as he ran as fast as he could down the intersecting street, and I realized that my family had positioned themselves directly down the street from our apartment. Then we were past, continuing to march, but I sensed that I was being watched, seeing the orientation of my *Signifer*'s headdress turned in my direction.

"He'll get over it, Centurion," Lentulus said, and I did not know what was worse; the sympathy I heard in my *Signifer*'s voice, or the possibility that he was wrong, that my son would never look at me the same way.

Such was my return home.

"Does it hurt?"

Given who it was that was asking, I did not think it wise to offer the same response I had given to Carissa in Mogontiacum, yet at the same time, I did not want to scare my son by being honest. It had taken all afternoon to just before our evening meal before he would even look at me when I was not seemingly looking in his direction, and this was the first time he was gazing directly at me, though I was having trouble reading his expression, it being one I had never seen before.

Consequently, I admitted, "A bit. But," I stressed, "it's feeling a little better every day, and soon?" I grinned, a bit encouraged that he did not flinch, "I won't even notice it. And," I thought to add, "neither will you." I waited then, aware that Bronwen was watching intently from where she was preparing our meal, both of us watching our son as he considered my words, and I tried not to show my relief when he nodded, though he still wore a solemn expression. "Now, I have a question for you."

"You do?" he asked warily, and I noticed that while his eyes were trying to fix themselves on mine, they kept flickering over to my scar. I nodded, and he asked, "What is it?"

"Why did you run when you saw this?" I asked gently as I pointed to my face.

"I…I…don't know," he stammered, yet I sensed that he did know, and again I waited for him to work up whatever it is that takes someone almost five years old to be honest. I was rewarded, if one could call it such, with Titus lowering his voice to a whisper, forcing me to lean forward to hear him admit, "I was scared."

"Of what?"

"I just…I have never seen you hurt before."

I understood then, deciding in this moment to spare him from trying to articulate something that is complex for an adult to comprehend.

"I think I understand. You didn't think I could be hurt, did you?"

I saw the relief on his face, and I confess that there was, and still is a part of me that regrets that I had chosen a profession where a young boy must learn at such an early age how to cope with the fear that their father might die. Yes, it is a dangerous world that we live in, and death in one form or another is all around us, though most commonly, it comes because of illness, or by some mishap and not because another man is trying to part your head from your shoulders. This is true for rankers, but even more so for those of us in the Centurionate, and it is something both the Prefect and my father commented on in their accounts, about how we desire a job that is likely to kill us.

"Titus, what I do is very dangerous," I began, but he stopped me with a shake of his head, saying fiercely, "But not for you, Tata! You're the greatest Legionary ever born! I hear men say it all the time, that you're even greater than your Avus!"

Believing that he had our lineage a bit confused, I corrected him, "You're talking about *your* Avus, my son. He was my *father*, which makes you his grandson."

"Oh," he looked crestfallen, but it was about to be my turn, because he said more to himself than to me, "I'll tell Marcus that the Prefect was your father, and not your Avus."

"Ah," I was a bit embarrassed now that I understood. "You know what? You don't have to tell Marcus anything, because Marcus was right. He was talking about my *great*-grandfather, but yes, the Prefect is a legend that men still mention today. Although," I added, feeling my throat tighten, "*your* Avus, my father, is a legend as well. Did I ever tell you that he saved my life?"

"No!" Titus shook his head, his eyes suddenly shining. "What happened?"

"*Meum mel.*"

I lifted a hand to indicate I heard Bronwen, but I made the decision that it was time, especially given his reaction to what was, when all is said and done, a minor wound, to tell my son the truth. I spoke for the next few moments, though I spared the details of what that battle was like, but I did try to convey to him in a way that he would understand what the chaos, the confusion, and the fear was like, and how his father, being responsible for so many other men, had to maintain his presence of mind and give orders that accomplished his objective and kept as many of his men alive as he could. He listened intently, though I could tell that he was disappointed, eager to hear me talk of blood and gore, the kind of thing that fascinates little boys. In fact, when I reached the part where I described my father's last moments as he bought the time it took to drag me to safety with his life, I was the one who was struggling to contain my emotions.

When I was finished, he seemed to accept my words and consider them, the solemn expression never leaving his face, then without any warning, he asked, "So, why do you do it, Tata?"

Such was my surprise that I actually looked over to Bronwen, who had been standing there, a knife that she had been using to chop the root vegetables in her hand, her task forgotten as she looked at me with shimmering eyes.

"Because," I answered honestly, "it's something that I believe that I was born to do, and the gods gave me the same gifts they gave your Avus, and my Pro Avus to do them. And, I do it because I believe there is nobody who can protect my men better than me."

He considered this, then asked gravely, "Do you think the gods gave me those gifts, Tata? Do you think I can be like you?"

I heard Bronwen's sudden, sharp intake of breath, while I stifled the groan; this had already become a contentious subject between us, before he had even turned five years old.

Consequently, I chose to prevaricate and put this battle off to another day, telling him, "It's still far too early to tell that, Titus." He looked so crestfallen, I heard myself add quickly, "But you're certainly off to a good start. Your Mama tells me all the time how you're the tallest of all your friends, and you're very strong."

"I'm the fastest runner," he said proudly. "At the Vulcanalia, I beat everyone in my age group except for Marcus Potinus, and he's almost ten!"

Since the Vulcanalia is held eight days after the Ides of August, I had not been there, and while I believed my son, I still glanced over at Bronwen, who gave me a nod.

"It is true, Gnaeus."

"That," I swept him up and hugged him, the emotion

threatening to overwhelm me, "is so good, Titus! I am *so* proud of you! And," I had to pause for a heartbeat, "I'm sorry that I wasn't there to see it."

"That's all right, Tata," he replied, with a *gravitas* that was simultaneously quite amusing and heartbreaking. "You were serving Rome and the Imperator keeping us safe. That," he turned to look at Bronwen, "is what Mama said."

"Well," I winked at him, "Mama is always right."

This made him laugh, then he looked back at Bronwen again, and he must have had an inquiring expression on his face, because she answered seriously, "So is your Tata, so if he tells you that I'm right, what does that mean?"

I do not know whether it was the tone of resignation or the great sigh he heaved that was more amusing, but he answered, "That you are too."

"Which means," I tousled his hair, "that whenever you have the urge to try and hide something from us, you need to remember that."

Bronwen had resumed her work and announced that our meal would be ready soon, and I should have known better than thinking that I had escaped because, without warning, Titus asked eagerly, "Did you cut anyone's head off, Tata?"

I know that it was not his intention by bringing it up without any kind of warning, nor was it something unusual for a young Roman boy, the son of a Centurion at that, to ask, but without any kind of warning, I was assailed by the image of a helmeted head spinning up into the air.

In that moment, I took the easy path, one that would cause me some trouble in the near future, which I should have anticipated, patting Titus on his shoulder and lying, "No, I didn't."

His crestfallen expression was such that when he asked hopefully, "Did you at least kill any of those barbarians, Tata?" I answered, "Why, of course I did!"

More quickly than I could have imagined, his downcast demeanor vanished, and he asked eagerly, "You did? How many?"

"Oh, I lost count," I answered, happy I could tell the truth. "But it was a lot."

I offered a silent prayer to the gods when Bronwen gently but firmly took Titus by the hand, leading him to the basin where he washed his face and hands, with his mother's supervision, the signal that we were about to eat, and I used that time to sweep Giulia up, holding her aloft above my head so that she was almost touching the ceiling while she spread her arms out as if she was flying, squealing in delight as I rotated about.

When I lowered her back down, she surprised me by reaching out to run one tiny finger along my scar, examining it with an intense expression that I found unsettling, then she stated, "Tata was hurt."

"Yes," I nodded. "Tata was hurt, but he's all better now."

And, I was surprised to find that I meant it. I was home, with my family, and the campaign was over.

That night, as we lay in bed after our reunion as man and wife, I told Bronwen everything, at least everything that I remembered, and that I had been told, leaving nothing out. More than once, I felt her body stiffen as it lay next to mine, but she did not pull away as I described something that I regretted telling her, yet for some reason that I cannot really explain, I have always been honest with Bronwen, about everything, and to a degree that I feel confident would make Marcus Macer uncomfortable. I told her of the Prefect's suicide, and because it was dark, I could not see, but I could hear her weeping, her face pressed against my shoulder. I told her of the tension between Silius and Varro, and our suspicions that Sejanus had something in mind with the almost incalculably valuable Noricum armor that had nothing to do with protecting the Imperator.

When I was finished, her mind immediately went to the practical matters, and she asked, "What comes next for you?"

The truth was that I had not really given it much thought, so I was silent as I considered for a moment before I answered, "The one thing I do know is that the 1st is done for the season. We were too badly hurt to go out again, so it will have to be the 20th from here, and the 5th and 21st from Mogontiacum, and the 14th from Vetera if there's any mischief across the Rhenus."

"That is good," she declared, and I heard the satisfaction in her voice that made me instinctively bridle, and I opened my mouth to demand why she thought this was such a good thing. Thank the gods I kept my mouth shut, because she had some news of her own, and I had a moment's forewarning by the subtle change in her voice, becoming a bit huskier, and the manner in which she began that it was important, "Husband, I have something to tell you as well."

"Oh?" I asked warily, wondering if this was going to be something I wanted to hear.

"I am with child again," she said, almost shyly, another example of how well she knows me, hearing that caution in my voice.

Yes, it hurt, but the smile I gave her, and the kiss, were genuine, and it did serve to instigate another session of lovemaking, and after we were finished, before long, I heard her slow, regular breathing as she fell asleep, but sleep did not come so easily for me. I briefly wondered if Alex was in the same state that I was, unable to fall asleep, but decided against getting up to go check, choosing instead to lie there, staring up into the darkness as my mind jumped from one thing to another, some of them mundane, like remembering that I had several men who needed to be marched to the *quaestorium* in order to draw replacement equipment, including shields, and leave their damaged items that could be repaired, like their *segmentatae*, then thinking about this news that I was going to be a father again, and whether it would be a boy or a girl, accompanied as always by the lurking fear that is the purview of Pullus men, while following hard on that was wondering about that Noricum armor, and what was going to happen with it, unaware that I would be learning its fate much sooner than I expected; that was the last memory I had of that night before I fell asleep.

The 1st spent the next week almost as busily as we spent the week before we departed on campaign, although some of this was due to the fact that there were not as many hands to do the work. My final butcher's bill left me with one hundred forty-eight effectives in the Fifth Century, with fifteen dead, including Macrinus, and of the other thirteen, six of them had lost an upper extremity, five of them losing a lower extremity, although in two cases, it was because a wound had become corrupt and the only way to save his life was to take it, with one of them suffering so much damage to his thigh that there was not enough muscle left to support his weight, and the final man having been blinded by a slash across his eyes. Of the four men that had been left behind who had all been stricken with a fever that the *medicus* deemed serious enough they were not fit to march, three had fully recovered, while the fourth man succumbed a week after our departure. Even in the battles against Arminius, we had not suffered such heavy losses, and while they are always heaviest in the front-line Cohorts, because of the losses to my *ad hoc* force that had been drawn from every Cohort to face the *crupellarii*, it created a situation that was quite serious, as the Pili Priores of the Fifth through Tenth Cohorts banded together to resist Macer's call for their most experienced men to plump up the First.

I would not call it a rebellion, but it was certainly a serious situation, and while I supported Macer, both as Primus Pilus and as my friend, when he pressed me on the matter, I reluctantly said, "Naturally, you're within your rights as Primus Pilus, and the fact is that the First Cohort has been plumped this way since Augustus doubled the size." I took a breath before I added, "But I do see their point. I know how I'd feel if I was still the Quartus Pilus Prior after losing almost a fifth of my men already, and I then had to give up my most experienced men to the First."

I expected him to be angry and lash out, but in some ways, his reaction was much worse, because he heaved a sigh as he stared down into his cup as if there was some answer to be found there before he replied, "I know. They're not wrong. Every Cohort lost men this time because of your force and you picking men from every Cohort."

I felt my body stiffen, but I tried to keep my tone light as I asked, half-jokingly, "Do I hear a rebuke there?"

He looked up with a frown, clearly startled.

"Pluto's cock! No, not at all, Gnaeus. Although," he added, "I can see how you'd take it that way now that I think about what I just said. But, no. If you had taken from just the First we wouldn't have a Cohort left, and if you had taken from the front-lines, we'd be in even worse shape. All things considered, that was the best course of action, and none of us expected the problems that we experienced killing those *cunni*." His mouth twisted into a grimace. "I just wish Silius would have insisted that those bastards in the 2nd had been included to spread the grief a bit."

This was not the first, nor would it be the last time I heard this sentiment expressed, from more men than just Macer, yet while I agreed wholeheartedly, this was not relevant at the moment.

"So, what are we going to do?"

Macer laughed, though it held no humor.

"I was hoping that you'd have some ideas. Or," now he grinned, and this time, it was genuine, "maybe I should just skip this part and ask Alex directly."

"He doesn't give me the answer all the time," I protested, though not with much spirit, then I returned his grin. "But yes, you probably should have saved some time and just asked him directly."

We shared a chuckle, though the levity faded quickly. It was at the end of the duty day, and I needed to return to the apartment, which I signaled by draining my cup, and it was as I was finishing that Macer said soberly, "I think I don't have any choice but to inform the *Praetor* that we need to call an emergency *dilectus*. And," he closed his eyes, I suppose to envision the reaction from his First Cohort Centurions, "we're going to have to take on some *Tirones* ourselves and not plump up from the other Cohorts to the degree we normally do."

I had suspected this was where things were headed, yet hearing him confirm it aloud was impactful, but I had no idea how much it would mean to me, because while I had no way of knowing, I was a matter of weeks away from meeting…my brother.

It was on my return home from that meeting with Macer that I was confronted with another problem, one that was not quite as impactful on me professionally, but certainly was a

362

pressing matter within the Pullus household. In fact, if my wife was to be believed, the occasion of my son's first black eye was far more important than the readiness of the 1ˢᵗ Legion, and the instant I opened the door, I could sense the tension in the air. This heightened sensitivity to minute changes around me has proven extremely valuable in my professional life, but in my personal one, it has been a different story. Only relatively recently did I give any real thought to where this comes from, and the only conclusion I have been able to draw is that it is something I learned in my childhood, from the tension and shifting emotions that arose from the latent hostility that Quintus Volusenus held for both my mother and me. Consequently, I learned how to figuratively sniff the air whenever I entered the *triclinium* in the morning, trying to determine if it would be a good day or a bad day because of the quarreling between my mother and the man I thought was my father the night before. As I said, this has served me well professionally, but as I learned from my wife, when combined with my natural impatience, it means that quite often, when I entered my apartment and sensed something was amiss, I tended to follow my natural instinct to confront the "enemy" immediately. It took barely dodging a plate hurled at me before I learned that this was not a sound tactic to employ with my Parisii wife, although as I learned from my mother when I sought her support in the matter, this is not confined to tribes in Britannia.

"No woman wants to be confronted immediately about something that might be bothering her even before she's had a chance to think about how she wants to bring it up to her husband," my mother informed me. This was bad enough, but she shook her head and actually sounded sad as she added, "I thought I had raised you better than that."

However, on this occasion, I did not have any opportunity to exercise discretion, as I was met by an extremely angry Bronwen, but she was not alone, holding Titus, whose head was down so I could not see his face, and the arm by which my wife held him blocked my view.

"Do you see this?" she demanded, pointing at Titus, but I could only see his tousled hair, which prompted me to answer in bewilderment, "See what? I can only see the top of his head!"

She did look embarrassed, though it did not last long, but when she told Titus to raise his head, he did not reply, yet neither did he raise his head. Uttering something in her native tongue that I knew was one of her favorite things to say to me when she was exasperated, she took him by the chin, lifting his head and giving me the first look at the prominent black eye.

"Pluto's cock!"

It came out before I could think, earning me a hissed warning from my wife, then she snapped, "Well? See what has happened to our son? Are you proud of yourself, *husband*?"

I realized then that my confusion of a moment earlier was only a shade compared to now.

"What are you talking about?" I asked, then I gasped as what I thought she meant hit me. "Are you suggesting that *I* did this? That I hit our son so hard, it gave him a black eye?"

Fortunately for both of us, this did cause her to subside a bit as I suppose she realized this was a logical conclusion for me to draw.

"No, that is not what I am saying," she admitted. "But I *am* saying that this is because of you!"

Deciding that I would be better served, I looked at Titus, and I felt a stab of both anger and the kind of pain a parent feels when their child has been injured, which in that moment I realized is very close to what a Centurion feels when one of his men is injured, but even more intense.

Squatting down, I asked in a gentle tone, "Titus, what happened? Who hit you?"

For a long heartbeat, it seemed as if he was not going to answer, but he finally said slowly, "Manius Closus and I got in a fight."

It took me a moment before I realized to whom he was referring.

"Wait! You don't mean Optio Closus' son, do you?" Titus nodded, and now I felt a stirring of anger as I glanced up at Bronwen, explaining, "Manius Closus is Publius' son, but he has to be ten years old."

Before I could say anything else, Titus said fiercely, "He

is, but I don't care! He called you a liar, Tata! He said that you cut a barbarian's head off, but you said you didn't, so I told him he needed to stop lying! He said his Tata told him, and his Tata wouldn't lie, but he did! You said you..." His chin began quivering, then the tears came, and before he could say any more, I had swept him into my arms, hugging him close and hard as I looked up at my wife, her face wearing an expression I had never seen before.

It took a moment for him to subside, but then I picked him up and carried him to the lone couch, sitting down with him perched on my knee.

"Titus," I began, "I want to..."

"Tata only lied to you about what he did because I told him to," Bronwen cut me off, dropping down to kneel next to us.

"But why?" Titus asked, sounding as confused as I was at that moment.

"Because I thought you were too young to hear such things," his mother explained, but when he opened his mouth to offer what I was sure would be a protest, she held up her hand and added, "but I know now that I was wrong. You are the son of a Centurion of Rome, and you are a Roman. Not," I saw her eyes start to shine with tears, "a Parisii like your mother. With my people, we try to protect our children, particularly our boys, from the kinds of things that happen in war. But I see now," she shook her head sadly, "that especially here, in a place like Ubiorum, it is impossible."

"That's why Rome is victorious," Titus said proudly, and while I shared that pride, I also saw Bronwen flinch as if he had struck her, making me feel a sense of conflict that I had never experienced before, but when I reached out to her, she pulled away from my touch. Titus did not notice, instead suddenly looking troubled. "But that means Manius wasn't lying?"

"Yes." I nodded. "That's what it means."

"Then," I saw him swallow, "that means I need to apologize to him, doesn't it?"

"Was he hurt?" I asked, and he suddenly went from disconsolate back to answering proudly, "I gave him a bloody nose!"

"Well, I think it evens out, then," I said, earning me a glare from Bronwen, which in turn got me to add hastily, "But yes, we both owe Manius and his Tata an apology. What do you say we do it together?" I was not surprised that he thought this was a splendid idea, and I told him, "While we go to their apartment, I'll tell you the truth about what I did that day."

When I kissed Bronwen, I murmured my thanks, which she accepted, but with a distracted air, then Titus and I left the apartment, but while I told him the truth as I promised, we never went to the Closus' apartment, although I had a conversation with the Optio the next day, something that Bronwen will learn if and when she reads this.

Only in hindsight did we realize that we should not have been surprised when Macer's formal request to Gaius Silius to call an emergency *dilectus* was met by a terse refusal, nor was I surprised when Macer suggested that an invitation to my apartment the night it came was in order.

"Tell Bronwen that I miss her cooking," he suggested. "Which is true enough, but I need to talk to you two about what to do about this." He waved the wax tablet.

I also knew that when he was referring to the two of us, it was not Bronwen as the second person, but Alex, who left the camp early to warn Bronwen and Algaia so that they could begin cooking for our guest. While he was a frequent visitor, it was always an occasion, especially for Alex and Algaia, the former's history with Macer extending back in time farther than my own, while Algaia's affection for him was based in Macer being the man who informed her of her manumission when reading my father's will, so I was not worried about their reaction. The only awkwardness came when, after the meal, the children were led away to Alex's apartment, with Iras and Titus, who were no longer competing over baby Diocles now that he was toddling about and had developed a mind of his own, uniting to put up the biggest fuss about being excluded, it falling on Iras, as the oldest, to side with the parents. Once this small rebellion was quelled, with Bronwen and Algaia trooping them out, the three of us settled down to discuss the meaning of Silius' refusal.

After reading the message himself, Alex considered for a couple of heartbeats, then said flatly, "It's about the way you worded it." I glanced over at Macer to see if he understood any better than I did, but he did not, prompting Alex to explain, "If an emergency *dilectus* is called, what happens? What would cause it to happen?"

"A defeat, or a victory that incurred heavy losses," Macer answered, still frowning, but Alex shook his head.

"I apologize, I should have made myself clearer. Who has the authority to call an emergency *dilectus*?"

This was when both Macer and I understood, although what Alex was pointing out was not as straightforward as it would seem, because as it is inscribed on some bronze tablet moldering in the Tabularium somewhere, a *Praetor* has the sole authority to call for a *dilectus*, emergency or otherwise. That is how it has worked since the early days of the Republic, but that was before Augustus, who, in his wisdom, essentially took over the administration of the Legions, so that now, *any* decision made concerning the army, whether it is about the Legions, auxiliaries, cavalry, or navy for that matter, now comes from Rome. In practice, there was no way that Gaius Silius could take it on himself to declare a *dilectus* of any sort without Rome being involved, and by Rome, during this period of time, that means not one but two men, Tiberius and Sejanus. However, Alex was not through making his argument.

"Also, from what we've heard so far, the story that Tiberius told the mob isn't what happened, although I suppose it might have changed. But as of now, the official story is that we crushed both Florus and Sacrovir easily, with very few casualties. So," he held both hands up with palms up, "why would Silius need to call an emergency *dilectus*?"

"Pluto's *cock*," Macer muttered, slumping over to lean on the table, shaking his head. "You're right. I should have seen that immediately. Tribune Vitellius actually told me he had gotten a letter from his father, who lives in Rome, just two days ago. Tiberius addressed the Senate by letter, and the way he made it sound, the entire campaign was a trifling matter that was barely worth mentioning. He said that since it was never in doubt, and we did away with Florus and the Treveri so easily, there was no need for him to send Drusus, let alone go himself to face Sacrovir and his Aedui."

"Well, that's at least true for Florus," I commented. "They weren't much of a challenge."

"The best lies are those that have some truth in them," Alex replied. "Besides, by the time the elder Tiberius sent his letter, everyone in Rome would have heard from other sources about how easily the Treveri were put down. So," he shrugged, "there's no reason for them to suspect Tiberius isn't being truthful."

"Then what will that mean for us?" Macer wondered, clearly worried, which I shared, but only Alex seemed unconcerned.

"Gaius Silius has been out here a long time," Alex replied. "And he's got some of the most experienced clerks and scribes in the province. They'll know how to…finesse the reports they send back to Rome to explain why we're adding so many new men to the rolls." Macer considered this, then began nodding slowly in a signal that he accepted this, but Alex was still not through. "Also, if it was me, I'd spread it out over the entire winter…" the manner in which he paused caused me to look over at him in curiosity, but I understood why when he continued, "…and I'd invent a fever, or an outbreak of plague."

"*Gerrae!*" Macer exclaimed, then his eyes narrowed in suspicion. "Are you having a go, Alex?"

"No, I'm not, Marcus," Alex assured him, while I remembered in time that Macer had given Alex permission to use his *praenomen*, but not once have I heard Alex slip when others are around. Seeing that Macer was unconvinced, he went on, "Think about it. How else are we going to be able to plump back up to full strength?" Before Macer could reply, he pressed, "And if we're not at full strength, do you want to be the one to tell that to whoever Silius' replacement is going to be? And why we're not?"

"Maybe Silius will tell the truth," Macer offered, giving me a glare when I snorted in disbelief.

"He might," Alex, ever the diplomat, seemingly agreed, "but I think that ship has already sailed, Marcus. And now, it's almost as if he's got no choice. What do you think Varro and

Sejanus would do if it comes out that there's a *Praetor* out here on the frontier running around contradicting the Imperator, after he already wrote a letter to the Senate telling them that nothing much happened?"

I want to take this moment to point out that it is difficult for me, and for Alex, who is nodding his head, to try and avoid coloring this part of our account because of all that transpired just a few months ago now, but almost three years after that conversation. Regardless of what was to come, in that moment, we still believed that there was not an unavoidable catastrophe looming in the future of Gaius Silius.

Finally, Macer nodded again, saying slowly, "I understand...and I agree this will be the best solution. But, how do we go about it? Because there's no way we can do this without Silius at the very least turning a blind eye. Remember, he's not going to be relieved by the new *Praetor* until Februarius, and I'll be fucked if we're not at the very least through with the process of plumping up. Ideally, I'd like to have a full complement and training them by the end of Januarius."

This was the first moment I realized something else, and that was that we First Cohort Centurions were going to be involved in training to a much greater degree than ever before, or in my case, since I had been a Pilus Prior. Now that we had determined there was no way to simply grab up experienced men from the lower Cohorts, we would be putting raw *Tirones* into the First Cohort, men who would not know which end of the *gladius* to hold. I also determined very quickly that this was for later, and Alex already had a possible solution for the problem Macer had posed.

"Melander," he said with the kind of grin that he uses when he is proud of himself.

"Melander? What about him?" Macer asked.

"He's leaving for Pannonia very soon," Alex explained. "He's going to be taking the Prefect's effects...and his urn."

Now it was my turn to interject, not understanding.

"His urn? What urn? That entire fucking lodge burned to ash and there were a lot of bodies inside it," I reminded them. "Besides, it would have taken more than a day for it to cool down enough."

"He says he went back after it cooled, then found the Prefect's remains because they were by the door," Alex said quietly, yet there was still something that did not make sense to me.

"That may be true, but I remember seeing that his body was lying on top of his brother's."

"Gnaeus, does it really matter?" Alex asked. "As far as his son is concerned, those will be the remains of his father, the Camp Prefect Tiberius Sacrovir, and he'll be able to put that urn in the family tomb, just like we did with your father in Arelate."

I knew that he was right, yet at the same time, it just did not sit well with me, and I only dimly comprehended that it had to do with the idea that at least some of those remains in that urn would likely be his traitorous half-brother, yet neither was I willing to make a fuss about it.

"But what is Melander going to do regarding the *Praetor*?"

"Silius and the Prefect had become very good friends," Alex explained. "And when Melander passes through Mogontiacum, he's going to tell Silius that the Prefect had already begun to think about the problem of how to bring the 1st up to strength. He," he held his arms out, "is going to tell the *Praetor* that all of this was the Prefect's idea."

"So that if Tiberius is angry, he can blame a dead man for the idea," Macer mused. While he seemed receptive, he also pointed out, "But what if Tiberius is amenable to it, but Sejanus has other plans, and he sends one of his minions to find Melander? I know he was loyal to the Prefect, but how long could he take being tortured by whoever a bastard like Sejanus would send?"

"I understand," Alex replied, but there was something hesitant in his manner, until he finally explained, "but I don't think it's as much of a worry as you think. I actually asked him about that, and he said that he's returning to Thrace as soon as he's done his duty to the Prefect. The Prefect manumitted him in his will, so he's free to come and go as he pleases."

After more discussion, we were at least in agreement that it was unwise for us to expect and plan for an emergency *dilectus*, but aside from that, it was out of our control, and the best we could do was prepare for a winter season that would start earlier, and be unlike anything we had experienced before.

As the weeks turned into months, we marked the end of the campaign season with an official message from the *Praetor* that we would not be allowed an emergency *dilectus*; additionally, he informed us that there was no decision on the naming of a Camp Prefect yet to replace Sacrovir, and it would only be later that we deduced that this was not an accident, one designed to aid us in our cause of returning back to strength. Since the *Praetor* for Germania Superior is headquartered in Mogontiacum, the ranking officer in Ubiorum had been the Camp Prefect, so without Sacrovir's replacement, it meant that the senior Primus Pilus, Lucius Neratius of the 20th, was in effective command since Vitellius had accepted that his role as senior Tribune was to play the part, showing up for the morning and evening formations, in exchange for a generous gift of wine and free women at his favorite brothel in town. Fortunately, Neratius, who had one eye obscured by a patch that served all of us as a reminder of the one he had lost, not at the hands of an enemy, but by an unknown ranker who had flung a rock at him during the mutiny, was not a political creature, at least no more than any man who has achieved the post of Primus Pilus, and for his own reasons, he was as interested in seeing his sister Legion in the 1st returned to full strength as we were. It was a week after that official dispatch that another one arrived, in the dark of night, addressed to the Primus Pilus of the 1st Legion, from the outgoing *Praetor*.

"There's a report heading to Rome at this moment informing Tiberius that the 1st has been struck by a very serious fever, which has already claimed several lives," Macer announced, not in his quarters, or even in the camp. Instead, he had asked me to use The Dancing Faun, deeming it the one place where only 1st men could congregate without the risk of being spied on by unfriendly eyes and ears. He continued, "Additionally, there's a wagon arriving containing enough silver to pay bounties for new enlistees, but we will *not* be relying on *conquisitores* for this task. This," he moved his head to scan the faces of every Centurion and Optio, all one hundred nineteen of them, "is our job and our job alone."

Over the next third of a watch, we decided on the men who would be part of the recruiting party, and it was not restricted to just Centurions and Optios, but *Signiferi* and *Tesseraurii* would be included as well. To my relief, Macer told me immediately that I would not be venturing out into the province, though I would not be idle.

"You're going to have to devise a method for the First to train the men we take in," he told me. "You and Clepsina are the only two who were Pili Priores in the Cohort…"

"Are you forgetting something?" I laughed, pointing at him. "You were both the Quartus and Secundus Pilus Prior."

"And I'm too old for that *cac*," he growled. "Besides, you're the weapons instructor for the entire Legion as it is, so you're the best choice."

It might seem strange, but this was one of the few times when I was jolted by the realization that Marcus Macer *was* growing older and had reached a point now in his forty-fifth year where he had begun to slow down. Clepsina was about to turn forty, while I would be turning twenty-nine on my next birthday in a few months, and it was with this in mind that I approached my fellow Centurion with an idea, and I was not surprised when he readily agreed.

"Clepsina is going to conduct the part of training that includes drill, regulations, camp requirements and such, and I'm going to do everything that pertains to weapons training, including the javelin," I explained to Macer in his quarters, the day after our meeting at the Faun, with Clepsina seated next to me.

"You're not doing this all by yourselves," Macer responded skeptically. "Are you?"

"No," I assured him. "We'll need some help, which is what we want to discuss with you. I suppose the most straightforward way would be for me to use Vinicius, and for Clepsina to use Postumus," I named his Optio, "but that would mean…"

"You won't have anyone to run your Centuries." Macer nodded his understanding. He thought for a moment, then suggested, "How about Dolabella helping you, Clepsina?"

This actually made a great deal of sense; an Optio of the First Century of the First Cohort is generally considered to be a man most likely to be considered for the Centurionate, and when it came to the details of life under the standard, especially when it involved appearance and having one's gear in good order, the Optio of the Primus Pilus is probably the best choice.

For my part, I already had someone in mind, and either Macer sensed this, or more likely, just because he knew me so well, said, "I'd offer you a suggestion, but I suspect you've got someone in mind already, and it's not likely to be who I picked out."

Deciding to be somewhat politic, I replied, "Why don't you tell me who you're thinking of, Primus Pilus? We might be able to save time." He did so, and as he probably guessed, it was not the name I had in mind. "He's a good man," I said, and I meant it, "but I'm actually thinking of someone not in our Cohort."

"Closus," Macer supplied, then laughed at my surprised, and a bit peeved expression. "I clearly know you better than you think."

"Do you want me to speak to Licinius about taking one of his Optios?" I asked, but he said, "Let me talk to him. I'll present it as my idea. Let's see if he thinks it's a good one."

Of course he will, I thought with some amusement; when your Primus Pilus has it, it's always a good idea. At the same time, I acknowledged to myself that, despite it being a few years earlier, there had been some tension between Licinius and me, and while I felt cautiously confident that it had been resolved, one does not know for sure what is going on in another man's head. It would have been supremely embarrassing if I had been forced to come to Macer after discovering that he in fact did hold a grudge, so this way, the problem never materialized. With this settled, it was a matter of getting things organized, and I made a conscious effort to make myself scarce when the Primus Pilus worked on selecting the men who would be going out to do the actual recruiting lest I be accused by some of my fellow Centurions of being too involved in every aspect of this endeavor. Also, by this time we had learned something else, thanks to the informal but extremely reliable association of clerks and scribes, that helped our cause immensely.

"It turns out that the original butcher's bill that I gave to the *Praetor* was…lost," Macer informed us, back at the Faun, although this time, it was during the day before the normal opening time, completely understandable given the subject matter. "What that means is that the official report that he sent back to Rome for the Imperator's examination may have some discrepancies."

"And what does *that* mean?" the Secundus Pilus Prior demanded, and when I saw Macer's lips thin, I knew he was trying to control his irritation. Whereas in the past I have not named him because of his connections to a certain man in Rome, subsequent events have unfolded that enable me to identify that his name was Quintus Lucullus Felix, and I knew that Macer worried about how safe any of this was with this man involved, but there was no real way to exclude him. "Specifically what kind of *discrepancies* are we talking about, Primus Pilus?"

At first, it did not seem that Macer would reply, and later he told me that he was racking his mind trying to think of a way he could avoid answering, but after a long pause, he explained, "The list that will be going to Rome will be missing several names from those who fell against the Aedui. We're going to be receiving a list of those missing names for each Cohort." He paused to take a sip from his cup. "Over the course of the next few weeks, as we suffer the effects of this fever that we're going to be officially reporting, we're going to supply those names as the fallen."

I know that I had certainly never heard of anything like this before, nor had either the Prefect or my father mentioned using the names of men who fell in battle and listing them as victims of a plague instead, but it was an advantage of being on the frontier, because it was unlikely that anyone would be coming from Rome to investigate. That, at least, was our fervent hope.

While the recruiting parties were out scouring the province west of here, there was not much for those of us left behind to do, and I took advantage of the time by spending more time with Bronwen and my children. That was my intent anyway, but fairly quickly, a couple of things became apparent, and the first was that Bronwen was perfectly content with our normal camp routine, where I would leave just before dawn, and return in the afternoon. Having me underfoot and at loose ends even for a half-day, at least after the first two or three days, had her snappish and irritable, while it left me wondering what I was doing wrong. I partially solved the problem by resuming my rides on Latobius, with Titus accompanying me, which meant that a trip to the aqueduct was a requirement, and I was struck more than once how it had been less than a year since we had done this, yet how much had changed. Certainly I was happy that his issues with Iras were a thing of the past, but now all he could talk about was the new baby sibling coming, and I was amused at his certainty that it would be a brother.

Finally, one day I asked him, "How do you know you're having a brother?"

"Because," he said with the kind of confidence that comes from being young, "Mama had me first, then baby Giulia last, so that means it's time for another boy!"

For a brief moment, I considered trying to explain that this was not how things worked, but quickly realized that it would be a futile exercise; my son has inherited my size, and unfortunately my temper, but he has some of his mother's gifts as well, and between her stubborn streak and need to have the last word, I could easily imagine that we would be engaged in this argument all the way back to Ubiorum.

"What would you like your baby brother to be called?" I asked instead.

He thought for a moment, then shrugged. "I don't know. As long as it's not Gaius."

This surprised me, and I asked, "Why not Gaius?"

"Because I *hate* Gaius!" he said, with a fierce scowl that was equal parts amusing and unsettling, while I was reminded of the scarcity of *praenomen* among us, which forced me to ask, "Which Gaius are we talking about?"

"Why, Gaius Rebilius, of course!"

My son said this with a tone that made it clear he thought I should have known, and being truthful, once I heard his *nomen,* I did recall Bronwen talking about Titus' problems with Gaius Rebilius, the son of the Tertius Pilus Prior of the 20th Legion whose family lived at the end of our street. And, as I recalled the name and what my wife had told me, I felt a stirring, a slight one, of that beast, because Gaius was twice as old as Titus. That said, when Bronwen pointed out the boy, I saw two things that, in my mind, explained the issue. Despite being almost ten, Gaius Rebilius was small for his age, while Titus was…Titus, so that he was only perhaps two or three inches shorter, while the Rebilius boy had a narrow, skinny build. Gaius' advantage was his age, and that was all, but he apparently used it to the fullest, and it was clear that my son was intimidated by Gaius.

It was with this in mind that I said, "You need to be patient, Titus. I've seen that boy, and you're going to be his size in no time. Maybe," I remember noticing how the top of his head was now a couple of inches higher up my chest than it had been just a few months earlier, "by the time you're five, or maybe six."

"And?" Titus twisted to look up at me, eyes wide. "What does that mean, Tata?"

"It means," even as I spoke, I felt a twinge of guilt, knowing how Bronwen was likely to feel about it, "that soon you're going to be bigger, and stronger. And when that day happens, and if Gaius picks on you again, you're going to be ready. I'm going to teach you how to defend yourself, Titus. Besides," I added, "remember that you gave Manius Closus a bloody nose even if he did give you a black eye, and he's about that boy's age."

I will say that, even in the moment, I had reservations, but they were mostly about what his mother would say if she learned that I was teaching him how to fight. Never in my wildest imaginings did I think this would have the ramifications that it did.

I did not always take Titus with me, and it was on one of the days when I went out by myself that, on returning to the stables and after stripping Latobius, rubbing him down, then forking some hay into his stall, it was just dark, it now being in mid-autumn, but I did not feel the need to light a lamp simply to leave the barn.

Consequently, just as I reached the exit, a low voice called from one of the empty stalls in the darkest part of the barn, saying only, "Pullus."

Before any conscious thought, I had my *pugio* in my hand, had dropped into a crouch and pivoted to face the direction from where the voice had come, but when the shadowy figure materialized as it stepped away from the back of the stall, it was still light enough that I could see both hands out from his side, though I still could not make out his features.

"*Pax*, Pullus! It's me! No need for that!"

I immediately recognized the voice, yet I still hesitated to lower my *pugio*, confused as to why he would be here.

"Sempronius?" Remembering, I added acidly, "Or should I be calling you Macula still?"

"No." He chuckled, a reminder of how good he was at maintaining his composure. "Sempronius is fine."

Finally, I sheathed my *pugio*, but I asked bluntly, "What are you doing here?"

"That is a long story," he replied with a rueful tone.

"Well," I cannot say that I was gracious about it, "I'm going back to my apartment. You can tell me there over our evening meal."

I was torn between relief and concern when he shook his head, and said flatly, "That wouldn't be safe. For me, or for you and your family."

"Pluto's balls," I groaned. "What have you gotten yourself into now?"

"Doing my duty to *our* Imperator, Centurion," Sempronius replied coldly. "Do I need to remind you who we both serve?"

Oh, I did *not* like hearing that, yet at the same time, for some time I had had this nagging thought in the back of my mind how likely it was that, at some point, either this man, or one of the other faceless men, and I assumed women, who serve the Imperator in the shadows would step out of them to remind me, just as Sempronius was doing now, that I served at the Imperator's pleasure.

"No," I sighed. Taking a guess, I asked, "What do you need from me?"

"A safe place where we can talk, and I can stay out of sight for a couple of days," he answered immediately, but this confused me.

"Then why not my apartment?"

It was the manner in which he hesitated that prepared me, somewhat, for him to say, "Because it's being watched, Pullus."

"Why are they watching me?" I did not try to hide my alarm.

"They're not watching you," Sempronius assured me. "They're watching *for* me."

"Who?" I asked, then realizing I needed to be more precise, I added before he could reply, "I don't mean who gave the order. I know who that is, but who is it? Do you know?"

"Yes, I know him," he answered grimly. "He's been on my trail for the last two weeks after I lost him when I left Augustodunum. Somehow he found my trail."

"It's Libo, isn't it?" I asked, then realized that, just as Sempronius was known as Macula, Varro's replacement for Canus might go by many names, so I began to describe him, but the spy had heard enough.

"Yes, that's him."

"He was watching my mother's villa when we stopped in Mogontiacum."

"That's why we can't go anywhere he knows," Sempronius said, and I heard the edge to his voice that I would not describe as panic, but it was close.

That was when it came to me.

"He undoubtedly knows about The Dancing Faun," I thought aloud. "Just like he's got someone watching the camp in case I try and sneak you in there. But," I grinned, "there's one place he doesn't know about, because we kept the purchase of it a secret, and I mean from everyone, including our wives."

After my return from the campaign to depose Maroboduus, I learned that The Dancing Faun had become so profitable that we expanded the *taverna* by buying the building adjoining it. There was another business that Turbo, the retired Legionary who my father had bought the Faun from but kept him on to run it, had been pressing for, and that was a brothel. For a very,

very brief period of time, we considered converting the newly purchased building into that business, but both Alex and I were immediately faced with a rebellion at home that caused us both to agree to abandon those plans. About six months later, however, Turbo, who was quite persistent, had approached us again, this time with news that the woman who owned one of the brothels that catered to men of the 1st was eager to sell.

"Mistress Gaia's got grandchildren and she wants to spend the rest of her days with them," Turbo had said, giving us a smile that was missing more teeth than it had. "Best of all, she's best friends with my Pandora, and she's ready to take over and run it as is."

Pandora, whose real name was Antistia, had been Turbo's woman since the days when she was young and attractive and Turbo had all of his teeth, and it was no secret that it had been her ambition to own Venus' Passion because she had been employed there, and had been friends with the owner back when they both made their livings on their backs servicing the men of the Legions. Best of all, it was on the next street over from The Dancing Faun; that there was a secret passage between the building that we had just bought and the brothel was something that Turbo, Alex, and I agreed neither Algaia nor Bronwen needed to know about, nor did they need to know who the real owners were. Thinking a moment, I mapped the route to the brothel from the stables in my mind, then told Sempronius to follow me, but when I walked to the main entrance, he stopped me.

"Pullus, you obviously don't have any experience at this, because only a fool would walk out that way," he said. "Please tell me you know other ways out."

I did, and I pointed the way, then followed him as I directed him which way to turn. I learned a great deal during that short journey to Venus' Passion as I watched everything Sempronius did; crouching down at the corner of a building to peer around because he knew that anyone watching would be looking higher up; pressing his back to the walls of the buildings as we moved in the shadows between the torches, and when we crossed the street, he moved more slowly than I would have imagined, yet when he explained it I felt a bit foolish since I did the same thing he described as being a mistake.

"In the dark, the eye is attracted by movement, and the faster the movement, the easier it is to see."

Therefore, we arrived at the brothel safely, and I led him inside, only then realizing that I needed to find Pandora immediately to warn her to watch the entrance for anyone who was not a regular. Taking him to the room that was reserved for the upper class that had been dubbed *The Praetor's Triclinium* to make it sound special and which had couches, low tables, and most importantly given the purpose, a bed, we got settled, with one of the serving slaves bringing an amphora and cups.

"Why is Libo after you?" I asked, thinking a direct attack was the best.

"At first," Sempronius began, "it was trying to stop me from doing something, but he was too late. Now," he grinned tightly, "he's trying to kill me."

The way in which he said it was as casual as if he was describing a dice game where he won and his competitor was upset, nothing more than that, and I was struck by the thought that, in his world, this sort of thing was probably very much part of his everyday life.

"What was it he was trying to stop?"

"What do you know about the armor of those *crupellarii*?" he asked casually, which got me sitting up straight on the couch I had settled on, making him chuckle. "Clearly something."

I told him everything I knew, leaving nothing out, and I noticed that he seemed as if there were things he had not known, like how it had been the First of the First of the 2nd who had been assigned to escort the wagons.

"They weren't who was guarding them at Lugdunum," he commented. Seeing my confused expression, he went on, "I learned about that Noricum armor, and that Varro was trying to deliver it to Sejanus, and why."

"That's what we figured out," I told him, proud that we had done so, and Sempronius seemed suitably impressed. "It's been something that we've been worried about."

"When you say 'we'," Sempronius interjected. "Who are you talking about?"

When I told him, he relaxed, murmuring to himself, "They're trustworthy."

"Why, thank you," I said acidly, but he was unapologetic.

"You know who I work for, Pullus, and you know he's not a forgiving man." This caused me to subside a bit, and he continued, "I knew that I had two choices, either stopping that armor from reaching Rome, or somehow making sure that the Imperator received it first." I was about to open my mouth to express my misgivings, but thankfully, Sempronius had already worked it out. "The problem is that Tiberius trusts Sejanus too much right now, and I couldn't take the risk that he would simply hand over that armor to the Praetorians. So," he paused to take a sip, "the only two options were to gather together enough men to seize it, then melt it down so that it couldn't be used, or…"

He stopped then, and I realized he wanted me to work it out, and by doing so, gave me a hint about what he did, though it took a moment.

"Or, make it disappear somehow," I said tentatively, yet I was still uncertain about the method. "Bury it somewhere?"

"I thought about that," Sempronius admitted, "but the problem was that this wasn't a one-man job, and the type of men I hire sometimes get…ideas. And," he grinned as he lifted the cup, "I do like to be able to sleep with both eyes shut." After he took a sip, he said, "Actually, it was what I learned at Lugdunum that presented the solution. They loaded it up on a ship that was heading for Ostia, sailing down the Rhodanus, then coasting the rest of the way. I knew that if we sank it in the river, there was a chance that, knowing how valuable the cargo was, Sejanus would spare no expense in recovering it. So," he shrugged, "I rode south to Arelate, and hired a ship and crew that were more interested in silver than politics."

"That should have been easy." I chuckled, thinking back to my own experience on the docks in Arelate.

"It was," Sempronius agreed, but there was no way I could have been prepared for what was coming. "It took me less than a third of a watch to find a Rhodian who had just delivered a cargo from Alexandria, and was heading back empty and looking for a cargo. Well," he held his hands out, palms up, "I couldn't offer that, but I could offer enough silver that more than made up for it."

I had been about to take a drink, but my cup stopped halfway to my lips when what he said hit me, and I set it down.

"Wait," I stopped him, "you said this master was from Rhodes, and he had delivered a cargo from Alexandria?" Sempronius was clearly puzzled, but he nodded. "What was his name?"

"Demeter," he said, and I was happy that I had not taken that mouthful of wine. "I can see by your reaction that you know the name." Sempronius offered a smile that might have been nervous if he was the type. "How do you know him?"

I explained the story, and he reminded me that he was familiar with part of it, since I had told him about my trip to Alexandria in pursuit of what I now knew was a relative of the Tribune who had proven himself to be a valiant, capable leader and, from what we had heard, was now back in Rome enjoying the accolades that he deserved. What I had not ever mentioned was Demeter's name, nor the fact that, after my return to the Rhenus, my uncle Septimus had entered into an agreement with Demeter to supply him with the luxury goods, specifically the peppercorns, *kinnamon* and silk that had proven so popular. Most importantly, this new trade had transformed my family's fortunes, and Septimus had informed me some months before that they had more than enough money for my elevation to the Equestrian Order, should I desire it, something that I mistakenly mentioned to Bronwen.

"Well," Sempronius commented when I finished, "he's a capable man. And," he grinned, "he didn't ask any questions, even when I told him what we were going to do...once we were downriver."

"Which was?"

"I wanted to ram it, but Demeter refused." He laughed at the memory. "He said that the *Persephone* wasn't a barge or a..." he squinted as he tried to recall, "...bronze-beaked harpy bitch of a *quinquereme*." I laughed at that, knowing this was something that he would say about his beloved ship. "So instead, we laid to in an inlet in the bay that was angled in such a way that they couldn't have spotted us until they were past us even if they had been watching for us, which they weren't. Then," he used his hands to demonstrate, "we came up from behind at full speed, and sheared their oars before they even knew what we were about. Once they were crippled, Demeter moved *Persephone* into position to grapple their ship, and we threw jars of flaming pitch into it."

"How did you keep them from putting out the flames?"

"Four of the men I had with me were in the auxiliaries at one time," he said offhandedly, "and they used slings to keep their crew pinned down."

"I take it you were successful."

"That Noricum armor is at the bottom of the Arelate bay," he confirmed, but then he looked away from me, in a manner that indicated there was something else.

It occurred to me what it probably was, and I considered letting it lie, but I suppose I am enough of an honorable man that I felt he should acknowledge it.

"What about their crew?"

My guess was confirmed by the manner in which he did not respond immediately, choosing instead to drain his cup before he set it down.

Shrugging, he said flatly, "Dead." He must have read my expression, because he became defensive. "We couldn't let them live, Pullus. Surely you can see that."

He was right, yet I cannot deny that it did not sit well with me, given that these men were simply doing their jobs and had no part in any of the intrigue.

Putting this aside, I asked him, "How long ago was this?"

"A month ago," he replied. "Long enough that Sejanus knows by now that the armor isn't coming."

"Which is why Libo is after you?"

"I would imagine," he answered, not seeming very concerned about it.

"And," I asked politely, "how long do you think you're going to need to use this place to hide?"

His first reaction was to scowl at me at the last word, but he did pause to consider it.

"If he doesn't get my scent, then I think he'll move on in about three or four days," he concluded, causing me to wince.

This was going to require some delicate negotiations on my part; while I certainly trusted, and still trust, Turbo to keep his mouth shut as long as he was told to, Pandora was another matter entirely. An additional source of stress was the fact that, while I had as little to do with this business as possible, there was no way I could avoid hearing the gossip about the men who were regular users of *The Praetor's Triclinium*, and even worse, how frequently they were here.

Deciding to put this aside for the moment, I asked, "Do you know how many men Libo has with him?"

"At least a half-dozen, but if I had to wager my life on it, I'd say eight men," he answered.

"Do you have anyone here you can count on?" I asked hopefully.

I cannot say I was surprised when he laughed without humor before he answered, "Counting you? Just one."

This made me sit up straight, suddenly worried.

"Sempronius, I'm willing to help you to a point, but I won't get my men involved in this, do you understand?"

"I do," he said readily enough, but even in the dim lighting, it was easy to see he was disappointed.

Realizing the time, I stood up and as I walked towards the door, I told him, "You're going to be safe here tonight. I'll speak to Pandora, and I'll make sure that she's the only one who serves you. She'll bring you something to eat, and you can sleep here tonight." Tomorrow, I thought grimly, is another story.

Before I opened the door, he called out, "You're not going to make me sleep alone, are you?" I looked over my shoulder, and he grinned. "I mean, given where we are, and it *has* been a bit since I've gotten my prick wet."

I could not help laughing, though all I said was, "I'll see what I can do for you."

I found Pandora first, explaining what needed to be done, and she was amenable enough, until I mentioned the idea of him having company.

"Who's going to pay?" she demanded, scowling up at me.

I had not thought about it, so I made the mistake of saying, "Compliments of the house?"

One would have thought I stabbed Pandora in the heart, and very quickly, I found myself reaching into my purse and shoving coins in her hand, and I do recall thinking in the moment that this was something I needed to tell Bronwen, but I quickly dismissed it because of all the other questions it would inevitably raise. Promising that it would just be one night, despite knowing it was a lie, I left the brothel, taking care to use the private passageway so that when I emerged onto the street, it was from The Dancing Faun. Immediately outside, there were a handful of people, though this was not unusual; there were men who had stepped outside to have a private conversation, or relieve themselves in the narrow alley between the buildings across the street, while there were three or four women of the lowest class of prostitute, those who did not have the protection of a brothel and made their money one hump at a time, usually but not always in the alley. While I tried not to be obvious, I did a more thorough examination of the faces, relieved that I recognized almost all of them; almost, but not all. There was one man whose face I could not place, though it was not Libo, and in fact, he was quite young, with a fresh-faced, innocent air about him that, ironically, was what put me on my guard about him.

Nevertheless, I turned in the direction that would take me to our apartment, knowing that I was a bit late, and that Bronwen would have questions about it, which meant I would have to decide what to say. I was thinking about this when, from behind me, I heard a scraping sound, like a man who did not lift his foot enough when taking his next step, yet I did not react in a way that might indicate I had noticed, although I did turn the corner a block earlier than normal. Once I did, I quickened my pace to just short of a brisk trot so that I could reach an intersecting alleyway to the left, and I ducked down it, stopping just around the corner. My reward was hearing a muffled curse, followed by the sound of leather soles slapping on the paving stones at a run as my pursuer raced towards me, clearly worried that I had reached the next full intersection. He obviously spotted the opening to the alleyway because I heard him slow slightly before he appeared as only a dark shape, though I still saw the glint of metal, held low and away from

R.W. Peake

his waist on the right side, while my *vitus* was already moving as I swung the end of it towards the pit of his stomach. Essentially, he ran right into my *vitus*, his breath exploding in my face, the odor of wine and garum washing over me as he collapsed into a ball at my feet, whereupon I stepped on his right wrist with enough force that, if he had had any breath left in his lungs, he would have screamed in pain. More importantly, he relinquished the grip of what I could see was a *pugio*, though one that was a bit longer than we carry in the Legions, and I used the end of my *vitus* again, this time to send the dagger skittering across the paving stones safely out of his reach.

"Can you talk?" I asked, pleasantly enough given the circumstances I thought. "Or do you need to catch your breath?"

It took him two tries before he finally managed, "G-go fuck yourself." The next sound was a howl of pain when I stepped down harder on his wrist, and it made me wince, not from the pain I was causing but because I had no idea who heard it.

"You don't want to do this, boy," I still spoke conversationally, though I hardened my voice to add, "I can make you hurt in ways you've never imagined, but if you make too much noise, I'll cut your balls off and use them as a gag."

To emphasize this, I put a bit more weight on his wrist, quickly letting up when I heard him inhale to scream.

"Are you working for Libo?" I asked, deciding not to build up to it.

"W-who?" He shook his head. "I don't know anyone by that name!" I began pressing down again, and he writhed in agony, yet he did not scream, managing a low-pitched moan, telling me that he took my warning seriously. "I swear it! I don't know any Libo!"

This was when I remembered Macula, the name Sempronius went by, so I described him as closely as I could remember, and I was rewarded by seeing his head moving up and down.

"Yes, that's him. But he doesn't call himself Libo. He goes by Marcus Sura, and he says he's looking for his old business partner who stole from him."

"What did he say the man's name is?"

"He said that he calls himself Aulus Cordus Macula, but that his real name is Marcus Sempronius."

"So why are you following me? I'm not some fucking merchant; even an idiot like you can see that."

"Because," he panted, "Sura said that you and this Sempronius *cunnus* are friends and that you'd know where to find him."

I managed to avoid cursing, but I thought for a moment before I asked, "How many men has Sura hired?"

"I don't know," he began, except this time, I did not crush his wrist. I swung down with the *vitus*, striking him on the thigh with a meaty, smacking sound that made him gasp with the pain but I knew would not permanently damage him.

"Don't lie to me, boy," I snarled. "You need to assume that I already know the answers to most of the questions I ask. That way, I know you're not going to lie to the ones I don't know the answer to. Now," I repeated, "how many men does he have?"

"I...I don't know," he began, but I could see the whites of his eyes as he looked not at my face but at the *vitus* as I raised it. "No, that's not what I mean! I know how many men he's hired, but he was talking today about hiring more, and he said he was doing that today!"

This actually made sense, but I did not lower the *vitus*, holding it aloft as I said, "Go on."

"Right now, he has eight men, plus himself, but he said he was going to hire at least two more men, maybe three."

"Pluto's thorny cock," I muttered. Realizing that I had gotten all the information I was going to from this youngster, I lowered my *vitus*, then leaned it against the wall of the building and extended my left hand downward as I moved my foot off his wrist. "Here, get up, boy."

At first, I thought he was going to refuse, but then he reached up with his left hand, and I grabbed it and pulled him to his feet. He did not even see the punch coming, and I felt a deep satisfaction that, even in almost complete darkness, my aim was true, striking him on the point of his chin and I was certain that he was unconscious before he collapsed back to the ground just by the manner in which it seemed as if his bones evaporated. Grabbing one ankle, I dragged his limp body deeper into the alleyway so that he was not easily visible to another passerby, then found his *pugio*, which I scooped up and took with me. When I arrived at the apartment, I had to endure a tongue-lashing from my wife, which I survived with as much grace as I could manage, though I did not tell her why I was late. With the meal finished, I went to Alex's apartment, telling him about Sempronius, Libo, and the good news about the Noricum armor sitting at the bottom of the bay.

"You should have started with that," Alex grumbled. "All I'm thinking of now is this *cac* with Sempronius."

"I haven't told you everything," I said, and his expression made me laugh. "It's not that bad, it's just that someone is going to have to tell Pandora that she won't be able to use that special room in Venus' Passion for a few days until it's safe for Sempronius to get out of Ubiorum."

I cannot express the relief I felt when, after a heartbeat, Alex sighed, "All right, I'll talk to Turbo, and together we'll go to Pandora and explain it to her." He smiled then, but it was the kind of smile I knew did not bode well for me. "Besides, I've got some news of my own. Just before I left camp, I heard that we're going to be getting the first of the recruiting parties back, and you know that we get first pick."

I often wonder how I would have reacted if I had known what the next day was bringing.

As he usually is, Alex was right; there was a total of thirty-seven new *Probationes* who arrived in Ubiorum before midday. Since they were the first batch of the men who would become our comrades, it was no surprise that there was a large crowd at the forum, the word of their arrival at the *Porta Praetoria* flashing through our side of the camp. From my viewpoint, Alex was obscenely cheerful, although he swears he had no way of knowing what was coming. Matters began routinely enough, as I joined Macer on his stroll to the forum, although I eschewed donning my full armor and decorations like Macer did, but in his case, it was understandable since he would officially welcome the new men to the Legion. I was content with my *vitus*, although at Alex's suggestion, I chose one of my tunics that was on the smaller side, with shorter sleeves as well, that accentuated my bulk.

"You're going to be the man they have to face in the sparring square at some point," he had said. "They might as well see what they're going to be up against."

It was a good idea, and between that and the vivid pink scar on my face, even Macer's shudder seemed only partially feigned.

"If I was a *Probatio* just arriving to Ubiorum, and I saw you, I'd *cac* myself," he joked.

Clepsina came trotting up to join us just before we reached the forum, which was lined along our side about three and four men deep, buzzing with the excitement created by these new arrivals. We got there before the new batch arrived, escorted by the Tertius Hastatus Posterior Quintus Volcacius and his assistant, the *Tesseraurius* of the Second of the Sixth as I recall, but while I was content to stand near the back of the crowd who had arrived before us, Macer tugged on my tunic as he began moving through the crowd.

"You and Clepsina come with me," he ordered. "We're going to take the pick of the litter."

This surprised me, if only because Macer was always scrupulously fair.

"Before the other Centurions are here? They're not going to be happy about that."

He grinned at me over his shoulder as he replied, "If they were so concerned, they should have been here by now. Besides," the grin vanished, "if we're going to have to plump our Cohort up this way, I'm going to get the best available of the new meat."

I certainly was not going to argue this, but it helped that I agreed, and a glance at Clepsina, who offered his own grin, told me he was of a like mind. Macer marched out to the middle of the forum, standing in front of the *Praetorium*, roughly on the same spot where the Legate, Camp Prefect, or duty Tribune issued his orders of the day or made some sort of announcement. Despite it being out of the ordinary, both Clepsina and I knew to flank our Primus Pilus, one on either side, settling on our spot just in time to see Volcacius, who was marching alongside what could only be charitably called a formation, reach the edge of the forum. With the crowd growing so quickly; at that moment, I estimated at least half the Legion was present, with more men arriving with every heartbeat, though there was also a fair number of 20th men on their side of the forum, and since nobody had called men to *intente*, it was quite loud as men shouted to the new arrivals. More importantly in what was about to occur, it was also impossible to miss the largest of them, unusually in the last rank of the five man wide marching column, but before I could get a closer look, I heard someone call my name.

Recognizing the voice, I turned my head to see Vinicius, standing with Lentulus and Hybrida, the Optio having to cup his hands to shout, "I think I already know which of these boys you're going to be picking, Centurion!"

He was pointing in the direction of the approaching column, though they were still too far away for it to be clear he was pointing to the large *Probatio*, not that it took much effort to guess that was who he meant. Several things occurred next in rapid succession; I naturally turned my head back towards where my Optio was pointing, but before I could focus on the large *Probatio*, Macer's sudden gasp drew my attention to him instead, and while I was standing just behind him, I was offset enough to the side to see his face and that his weather-beaten features, darkened from years of exposure, had taken on a pallor that was quite alarming, his mouth hanging open in what could only have been a bad kind of shock.

Before I had a conscious thought, I was taking a step towards him, reaching out to grasp him by the shoulder because he was suddenly weaving, asking as I did so, "Primus Pilus? What is it?"

"He's seen a *numen*."

When I looked over at Clepsina, it was with the intention of snapping at him for making such a foolish comment, but when I saw that his demeanor and his shade matched Macer's, and that his eyes were fixed on the same spot as our Primus Pilus', I finally turned my head. I know that it did not take inordinately long, yet immediately afterward, it seemed as if a whole lifetime passed in the amount of time it took for my eyes to fasten on the largest *Probatio* and, for the first time, see more than just his size. Because of his height, towering over the other *Probationes* as he was, and given where I was standing, I suppose it was inevitable that our eyes met, so I saw the moment when he comprehended that he was essentially staring in the mirror, because, despite the age difference of about a decade and the scar on my face, he could have been looking at his twin. Such was his shock that he stopped marching, coming to a stop as we stared at each other, oblivious to the sudden change in the noise as, one by one, the onlookers surrounding us saw the same thing, the raucous shouting vanishing, and replaced by hushed whispering that rippled through the crowd.

The silence was not destined to last long, but the quiet was sufficient for me to hear Macer murmur, "Oh, Corbulo. What did you do?"

Chapter 10

Through no fault of his own, the *Probatio* Titus Corbulo was the cause for the postponement of the planned allocation and introduction of Clepsina and me as the Centurions who would haunt their waking moments as much as their dreams. Instead, we retired to the Primus Pilus' quarters, where, over Macer's objections, Alex was also present as we sat in his private quarters.

"You knew about this," I spoke flatly, but Macer shook his head, eliciting a snort of disbelief from me, while Alex sat there, seemingly still in shock.

"Gnaeus," Macer began, "it's…complicated. But what I can say is that, no, I didn't know with any certainty until after your father died."

"*That was six years ago!*" I bellowed, yet to his credit, while Macer certainly did not like a subordinate shouting at him, he kept his composure.

"I also didn't find out immediately after he died," he objected. "It was," he thought, "actually about four years ago when Manius Corbulo came to me."

"Corbulo!" Alex exclaimed, showing the first sign of animation. Turning to me, he explained, "Manius Corbulo was the *Signifer* of the Fourth Cohort when your father was transferred from the 8th." Turning back to Macer, he continued, "But he retired…" He had to think, "…right after we returned from serving with the *Legio Germanicus*." Something else seemed to hit him, and he murmured, "Pluto's balls, that was almost fifteen years ago." As soon as he said this, something occurred to me, but Alex beat me to it, pointing out, "Unless Titus Corbulo is the most overgrown fifteen-year-old since Hercules, that means that Corbulo didn't…"

"Raise him from an infant," Macer confirmed. With a touch of impatience, he said, "I'm going to tell you what he told me, but I want to be able to get it out without either of you constantly interrupting. Save your questions for after I've finished. Is that understood?"

Since he was using the tone that told us he was speaking as the Primus Pilus, we both hastily agreed, while I admonished myself to actually do it.

Addressing Alex, Macer asked, "Do you remember what Venus' Passion was called before Mistress Gaia bought it?"

"Of course," Alex answered immediately. "It was Juno's Grotto." There was something in the way he said it that got me looking over at him, and I could see how red he was. He did not turn his head, just giving me a sidelong glance as he shrugged. "I was young. Besides," he added quickly, "it was long before I met Algaia."

"Of course," I replied dryly, and I saw that Macer was grinning, though it did not last long.

"Yes, well, then you know that you weren't the only Pullus who was a regular customer." He hesitated, then asked, "Do you remember the one Mistress Gaia called Niobe, the Thracian girl?"

"Yes," Alex replied tersely, causing me to look over at him again, but this time, his eyes were fixed on Macer, and he said nothing more.

Now, Macer looked over at me as he continued apologetically, "At the time, I hadn't met your mother yet, Gnaeus, so I had no idea that this Niobe bore a...striking resemblance to your mother. And," he held up both hands in a helpless gesture, "she was the only woman your father would see."

"And, she got pregnant," I thought I understood, but I was wrong, because it was far more complicated.

"Yes, but she was terrified. Apparently, your father had been very forthcoming about the...problem you Pullus men pose to women bearing their sons. She also knew that Titus would never love her as much as he loved the Legions, and there happened to be another customer who was as much in love with her as she was with your father."

"Corbulo," I said, certain I was finally caught up, but I was wrong again.

"No, not Corbulo. In fact, not under the standard. He was a farmer, and was doing quite well, and before your father arrived, Niobe was his favorite girl. Apparently, Niobe was a farm girl herself, taken when she was very young during a Bastarnae raid and sold into slavery. She ended up as Mistress Gaia's property, and she could have had a worse fate. Gaia was a kind mistress, at least for someone in her line of business."

I was becoming exasperated, because I was certain that Macer was not being fully forthcoming, but when I glanced over at Alex, he was staring at the floor in seeming disinterest, and I finally could not hold it in.

"Would one of you tell me what by Dis is going on? You're both hiding something, I can tell!" I shouted this after coming to my feet.

"*Pax*, Gnaeus." Macer held out a placating hand, but his tone was firm. "And sit down. Now." I did so, albeit reluctantly. "This is hard to explain, for both of us, because it means breaking an oath we both made."

"Are you saying he *knew* he had a son?" I gasped, but both Alex and Macer answered immediately, and without any hesitation, saying, "No!" in unison.

Macer spoke then, explaining, "The oath I took was to never let you know that your father and Niobe were in a relationship of sorts, where he was her only customer."

I looked over at Alex, who nodded, though he would not meet my eyes.

"And this Mistress Gaia allowed that?"

"Given how much your father was willing to pay her, yes," Macer answered.

That, I understood, made sense, especially since this was before Gaius had lost most of the family fortune to Aviola, but there was still much that did not.

"So, what happened when she got pregnant?"

"She ran," Macer said. Seeing this was not enough, he went on, "Oh, there's no doubt that she had help, but we didn't know anything about it until a few years ago when Manius Corbulo showed back up."

The story Corbulo told was that Niobe, having heard the stories of the Pullus curse, had been certain that she would not survive the pregnancy, and she loved my father so deeply that she used that poor farmer, named Gaius Vatinius, who had a forty *iugera* holding near Juliacum (Julich), convincing him that his unrequited love for her, which had begun before Niobe became the exclusive lover of the huge Centurion with the famous name, was reciprocated.

"From what we could put together," Macer explained, "she told Vatinius some *cac* about how she was basically held prisoner by Mistress Gaia, who had sold her exclusive use to your father. And," he shrugged, "Vatinius believed her. So, while your father was in Pannonia with the *Legio Germanicus*, she and Vatinius just vanished."

"And my father didn't go after her?" I asked, finding this hard to believe.

"No," Alex spoke up, "because nobody knew anything about her connection to this Vatinius. She was apparently very good at keeping secrets."

"So how does this Corbulo enter into it?"

"That," Macer admitted, "is what I've kept from you, mainly because of when he showed up after your father died. By that time he had figured some things out on his own, namely that your brother, who he found abandoned when he was about three…"

"Abandoned?" I gasped. "What are you talking about?"

By the time Macer was finished, I was not sure I had been served well by insisting on hearing the story. In another example of the cruel humor of the gods, Niobe actually survived bearing my father's son, and from what Corbulo put together later, Vatinius had treated the boy well, as his own son, and she and the farmer apparently had a happy marriage, or at least sufficient to keep her with him. Yet, her fear of dying in childbirth was realized, though not because of bearing a Pullus. My brother was around three then, and by that time, Corbulo had retired more than a year before my arrival, and like so many men under the standard, had taken as his woman someone like Niobe, and in fact, his woman, Fulvia, had worked at Mistress Gaia's brothel as well, and was one of the only people Niobe took into her confidence; in fact, it was Fulvia who had helped Niobe flee with Vatinius. Perhaps the gods are not completely cruel and heartless, because they arranged for Corbulo and his new wife to come west to Juliacum, where he had purchased a holding from another retired ranker who, like so many retired Legionaries, had decided a farming life was not to his taste. From my perspective, this happens to about half of the Legionaries who opt for land instead of cash as their bonus if it is offered, or if it is not, purchase land.

From what Corbulo told Macer years later, they arrived at the Vatinius holding within a day or two of one of Vatinius' neighbors growing concerned and riding to their farm, only to find what had to be a grisly scene of a woman and dead baby strangled with its own umbilical cord, with her husband's corpse slumped over them after committing suicide, while a three-year-old boy sat on the floor next to the corpses of his parents and sibling, drawing pictures by using their congealed blood as paint. While the farmer who found my brother was sympathetic, he already had too many mouths to feed, while Fulvia, when she heard the names of the dead couple, knew who it was and made sure her new husband was aware as well that this was the son of Titus Porcinianus Pullus.

"Corbulo said his original intention was to bring the boy to Ubiorum to reunite him with your father," Macer explained. Then, he sighed before he continued, "But Fulvia was barren, and she threatened to leave Corbulo if he did that, so they raised him as their own son. He said that the youngster was too young to remember the real story, so that as far as he was concerned, Corbulo and Fulvia were his real parents."

"And he waited until four years ago, two years after my father died?" I asked acidly. "What changed?"

"Fulvia died," Macer answered flatly. "She had been sickly for some time, and she finally crossed the river. And, according to Corbulo, that's when the problems started between him and your brother."

"Problems? What kind of problems?" I asked.

"Oh, the usual between fathers and headstrong sons," Macer replied, but I did not care for the knowing look he gave me as he added, "especially when that son is already six feet tall, almost two hundred pounds, is very strong and has a bad temper."

Now, I was annoyed, but I was also feeling a bit sheepish since he could have been describing me, though it did explain the look he had been giving me.

"And he came to you for, what? Advice on being a father?"

I could have bitten my tongue off as soon as the words were out, knowing that this was also a sore spot with Macer. Our Primus Pilus had had several relationships with women, yet none of them had borne him children, which is why I believe the average length of each of these interludes was about three years at the most before he moved on to another woman, in search of an heir.

"No, Gnaeus," he answered in an even enough tone, but I knew that he was hurt. "He came to tell me that, at the earliest opportunity, he was going to have the boy enlist under the standard. The way he put it, it was about the only thing he showed any interest in." He chuckled then, adding, "He had already started training the boy, and he told me he just hoped that the boy didn't kill him sparring before he was old enough."

"That sounds familiar, but I can't really say why," Alex commented dryly.

The fact that he had not spoken a word during Macer's narrative had not escaped me, and I turned and asked bluntly, "Did you know about this? Did Corbulo come to see you too?"

He shook his head.

"No, he didn't." He hesitated, and I did not miss how he looked at Macer, who gave a slight shrug. "But Marcus told me about Corbulo's visit. And," to his credit, Alex turned his head to look directly into my eyes, "I'm the one who suggested that he not tell you about it."

I was too stunned to be angry…immediately.

"But, why?" I heard the bewilderment in my voice. "Why would you keep that from me?"

"Because we were about to leave for Rome and the Praetorians," Alex replied. "I didn't think that it was in your best interest to know about this, especially then."

This was when the anger started bubbling up from deep within me, yet I did manage to maintain my self-control, to a degree.

"Isn't that my decision?" I snapped. "I don't recall the moment I told you to make those kinds of decisions for me, Alex. Oh," I snapped my fingers, knowing that I was being dramatic but not caring, "that's why I don't remember. *I never told you*!"

"That's enough!" Macer snapped. "And keep your voice down, Hastatus Prior!"

I obeyed, recognizing an order when I heard it, but it did not mean I did not continue to give both of them an angry glare.

Macer responded by giving a weary sigh, then asked, "All right, Gnaeus. Let's say that we did tell you once we learned the specifics. What would you have done?"

To my utter annoyance, as soon as he asked the question, I realized that I did not have an answer; there was no way that I could have taken a strange teenager, blood relation or not, to Rome with me. Between the fraught nature of the assignment, acting as a *de facto* spy for Germanicus, though it was short-lived, and having a wife expecting our first child, it would have been not only irresponsible, given all that transpired, it would have been dangerous for a young teenage boy.

Nevertheless, it took quite an effort for me to admit, "Nothing. It would have been dangerous taking the boy with us. But," I could not resist, "I still should have been asked. Then," I addressed Alex, forcing a grin, "you would have had the satisfaction of talking me out of it." As I hoped, this relieved the tension, but it did not answer the larger question, which I asked now, "All right, now that we know who he is, and how he came to have the *nomen* of Corbulo, what's next?"

"That's up to you," Macer answered, surprising me. "I'm going to claim him for the First Cohort, that's obvious just by looking at him. As far as whether he's going to be in the Fifth with you, or the Fourth or the Sixth?" He shrugged. "That's up to you. Those are the only three Centuries I'd consider him for anyway."

Understanding why he would only consider Corbulo for the second rank Centuries, I turned to Alex, and I saw he was surprised when I asked, "What do you think?"

As is his habit when he is caught off guard, he did not answer immediately, thinking it through before he said, "As I recall, Uncle Titus considered Corbulo highly skilled with a *gladius*. Although," he added, "he didn't think much of the man's character."

This was when I recalled something I had read in my father's account, about an incident during his first campaign with the 1st, when the *Signifer* had been a secret witness against the Quartus Pilus Prior Vibius Fimbria, soon after my father came to the 1st, who had lost control of the Cohort during an attack on a Cherusci village, with the exception of the Third Century, which had been commanded by the man seated at the desk in front of me, and my father had been his Optio. Corbulo had been the Cohort *Signifer*, and while he had been a key witness that ultimately saw Fimbria relieved of command and Marcus Macer elevated to the post, there had been a sly quality to Corbulo's actions that had rubbed my father the wrong way.

"Well," I responded, "if he and *Probatio* Corbulo had been at odds to the point that he came to talk to the Primus Pilus about getting the lad off his hands, maybe that's a good sign." I could tell neither were surprised when I said, "I'd like him in my Century, Primus Pilus."

Macer nodded, then asked the next most obvious question. "What are you going to tell him?"

This was at least easier to answer, perhaps because I had had the time to think about it.

"The truth," I answered. "It's not like he won't be hearing all about it within a matter of watches. This is too tempting a secret for the rankers to keep quiet about it." This was when something occurred to me, and I felt a stab of alarm. "In fact, I don't want him spending the night in this camp before I talk to him. I'll speak to him immediately. Where are they at now, Primus Pilus?"

"I told Volcacius to take them to the *Quaestorium* to draw their gear," Macer said.

"Then with your permission, I'll talk to him as soon as his issue is done."

It was just a couple dozen heartbeats after that Alex and I exited Macer's quarters, and he asked me, "Do you want me there?"

I considered for a moment, then decided, "Not right away.

Just bring him into my quarters, then wait in the office for me
to call you. And," I warned, "don't give anything away when
you're escorting him."

"What if he has questions?"

I gave Alex an amused glance.

"He's under the standard now, Alex. His days of asking
questions are over."

It is hard for me to describe the range of emotions that were
swirling about inside of me, some in direct conflict with
another one, giving me a case of nerves unlike anything I had
ever experienced, but I was determined that none of this would
show.

"Primus Hastatus Prior Pullus," Alex's voice was muffled
by the closed door, which he had rapped on twice, "requesting
permission to enter with *Probatio* Corbulo?"

I had warned Alex what to expect, which was a silent count
to twenty before I barked, "Enter!"

Alex held the door open, and Corbulo marched in, and I
noticed that, while he had obviously been taught, or at least
told about keeping his eyes straight ahead, he was having
trouble doing so, his eyes going back and forth between the
wall behind me and my face. Frankly, I could not blame him
given the circumstances, but I did my best to keep my own face
expressionless, watching as he marched up to the spot a pace
away from my desk, then rendering what I had to admit was a
crisp, perfect salute.

"*Probatio* Corbulo, reporting as ordered to Primus
Hastatus Prior Pullus." He did his best to sound strong and
confident, but his youth and his nerves were readily apparent,
and I am certain I did not help when I did not return the salute
immediately, choosing to lean back in my chair and examine
him in silence while hoping that he did not discern that I was
every bit as nervous as he was.

Finally, I returned it, leaning over slightly to give Alex a
nod, his signal to close the door and sit out there and wait. I
could feel my heart beating against my chest with such vigor
that I almost looked down to see if my tunic was moving, but
Corbulo chose that moment to break his stare on the wall, his

eyes dropping down to my face, though he immediately looked back up, the only sign he had been caught his face turning a red that almost matched his fresh new soldier's tunic.

At last, I broke the silence, asking bluntly, "Do you know who I am?"

"Y-yes, sir. You're Primus Hastatus..."

"That's not what I meant," I cut him off, and in a gentler tone, I added, "and I think you know that."

"I...I...know that we must be related somehow," he ventured, and I relaxed slightly.

This was what I wanted to know, although it was possible that he was lying, but I did not think so.

"I'm your brother," I said, then corrected, "your half-brother, I mean. We have the same father."

He looked confused, which was explained when he asked hesitantly, "Do you mean my real father? Gaius Vatinius? Or do you mean Manius Corbulo? He's the one who raised me. He," his expression changed, subtly, "told me a few years ago that he's not my real father."

If he had punched me in the stomach, it would not have been much different than what I felt in that moment, and it was completely on impulse that I suddenly pointed to one of the stools that were next to my dining table.

"Pull up one of those and sit down. We have a lot to talk about."

He did so, and I saw his hand trembling as he picked up the chair, then when he sat in it, I saw the flash of concern on his face, recognizing it, and despite myself, I chuckled, earning a puzzled look.

"I see we share the same experience of having a chair collapse under our weight."

Corbulo's immediate reaction was a grin, but it was instantly replaced by a look of horror at the lapse, and I assured him that he was in no danger of being tripped up.

"It's just that my fat...Manius Corbulo warned me about some of the tricks some Centurions play on rankers."

"*Signifer* Corbulo was right to warn you," I told him frankly, "but this isn't one of those times. Now, shut up and listen."

He did shut up, and for the next sixth part of a watch, I told him everything, including what I had just learned, while he sat and listened, and I noticed with a mixture of approval and apprehension, how intently he watched me. I talked about the similarities between our stories, of how our father had been unaware of either of our existence, and how I felt drawn to the Legions even before I knew the real story, during which he nodded more than once. However, I also spoke of the differences, how my mother came from the Equestrian Order, the daughter of a merchant and a free Roman woman, how her mother had conspired to mislead my father by telling him that my mother had died, and her marriage of convenience to the man I thought of as my father. For the first and so far only time during my life under the standard, I stressed my status as a paid man, and how Quintus Volusenus had purchased my post as the Hastatus Posterior of the Fourth. It was not subtle, perhaps, but I felt it important that he know that we came from very different backgrounds.

"I worked my way up to Quartus Pilus Prior," I emphasized. "I also served in the Praetorian Guard, and I'm now a First Cohort Centurion. I might not have been in the ranks, but I've earned every promotion, something you'd do well to remember. Now, I'm sure you have some questions, but let me tell you now that this will be your last chance to ask me for the next few months. Starting tomorrow morning, after you take the oath as a *Tirone*, you're not going to be my brother, you're going to be a *Tiro*, and you're going to be treated accordingly. And," I pointed at his body to emphasize my words, "even if you don't carry the Pullus *nomen*, by this time tomorrow, every swinging cock in this camp is going to know you and I are brothers, and they will want to test you."

He had been obedient about keeping his mouth shut to that point, but this elicited him to declare, "Let them try! I'll do the same thing that I've done to every *cunnus* who's tried me! I'll break them," he actually demonstrated, acting as if he was snapping a branch, "just like that!"

"*Tacete!*" I roared, my eyes going to the door, and as I expected, it opened a crack, and I glared at Alex's lone eye, my reward being the door shutting immediately. Returning my attention to Corbulo, I said, "You're not on the farm, boy. You're in the Legions now, and whoever might be giving you *cac* and wanting to test you are men, men who have seen the wolf. There are brawlers in the Legion who lick their chops with every new *dilectus*, and they've forgotten more about fighting, and fighting dirty, than you might ever know. Besides, do you know the penalty for fighting?"

I was not all that surprised that he nodded, and he proved it was no boast by saying meekly, "It's a flogging, sir. The first time without the scourge, and every time after that with it."

"That's right," I nodded. "The *Signifer* taught you well."

"He said unless I control my temper, I'd be striped before I made *Gregarius*," he mumbled.

Despite myself, I felt my heart softening even more than it already had, understanding the challenge that comes with having this seemingly unquenchable rage that was so difficult to control.

"It sounds like we have even more in common than our size," I said, but he looked up at me with such expectation that I had the feeling he was waiting for me to teach him how to rein it in at that moment. "We'll have time to work on that once you're in my Century. But until then, consider this your first and final warning. You're not to lose your temper and retaliate. Is that understood?"

"Yes, sir."

"I'm sure you have a lot of questions," I said, in perhaps the biggest understatement of our conversation. "What are they?"

"How did you get that scar?"

It took a bit of effort to suppress my groan, but then I was struck by an idea, and I said impulsively, "You don't actually start your training until tomorrow. So, tonight, you're going to come to my apartment, meet my wife and your niece and nephew, and I'll answer your questions."

Looking back now, I am not certain this was wise, for a number of reasons; Alex clearly had reservations, but when I told him to go make the necessary arrangements with Volcacius, who at this moment was still responsible for the thirty-seven *Probationes* until the next morning, with my assurance that I would personally escort Corbulo back to the camp, when he hesitated, I thought it was going to be about the unconventional aspect, but it was about something entirely different.

"Do you really think it's wise to show up at home unannounced with your newly discovered brother with the wife that you have?"

I winced, because he was absolutely right, so in a quick switch, Euphemios was given Alex's task, while Alex hurried out of the camp to alert Bronwen and Algaia, and in what I cheerfully confess was a cowardly move, I told Corbulo to stay put, then trotted down to Macer's quarters.

"What are you doing for the evening meal?" I asked, trying to sound innocent, but Macer has known me too long.

He heaved a sigh, tossing his stylus down onto the desk.

"Why? Did you invite him back to your apartment to eat?"

"And? What if I did?" I tried not to sound defensive, but I was completely unprepared to hear him say, "Actually, I think it's a good idea. After tomorrow, he's not going to be leaving camp for four months, and he's going to be hearing all manner of things about you, and about your father. I think the more he knows, the better prepared he's going to be."

That had nothing to do with my reason for inviting him, but I pretended otherwise, and once he was done with signing a few reports, we both returned to my quarters, where to our amusement, we found Corbulo sitting in his chair apparently not having moved a muscle.

"The Primus Pilus is coming with us," I told him casually. "He was our father's best friend, and he can tell you even more about him than I could."

This is not strictly true, given my father's account, but there is more to a man than what he leaves behind in a couple dozen scrolls, and I could see that this excited and intrigued Corbulo. We walked down the *Via Praetoria* towards the gate, and the startled glances and stares that I barely noticed anymore were far more frequent, while it clearly upset Corbulo to the point that, without thinking of the impropriety, I put a hand on his shoulder.

"It's just because these ugly *cunni* have never seen two

such handsome men at the same time," I joked, earning me a wan smile.

"Is it always like this?" he murmured, and I did not lie. "We're two of the biggest Romans people have ever seen, and I suspect that our...resemblance is catching men by surprise. Don't worry, they'll get used to it soon enough."

"If you say so, sir," he said politely.

Leaving the camp, we made our way through the town, and I surreptitiously watched Corbulo taking it all in.

"Have you been to a town this big before?"

He shook his head as he replied, "No, sir. Just Juliacum, and it wasn't anywhere near this size. My fath..." I saw his eyes shift to me. "Manius Corbulo told me there wasn't anything worth seeing in towns or cities, except for Rome."

"You can call him your father, Corbulo," I told him. Then I explained, though I did not know why, "Even after I learned the truth about my real father, I still referred to Quintus Volusenus as my father for a long time. I understand."

He did not say anything, but he gave a grateful nod, and I could tell he appreciated it. Then, we were at the apartment, and I led the way, stopping outside our door.

It was that moment that I suddenly realized something, and I turned to him just as I was lifting the latch to ask, "By the way, what's your *praenomen*?"

He was clearly surprised, which I suppose was understandable, but he answered readily enough, "It's Titus. My *praenomen* is Titus. It's the only thing I remember about my mother, telling me that she named me for my father, but I always thought that meant Vatinius."

I looked over at Macer, and I saw my expression mirrored in his own, my throat tightening as I was struck by the horrifying thought that I would be crying in front of a *Tiro*. Before I did, I pushed open the door to find my family, both by blood and oath, standing there, waiting to greet my brother.

It would be another four months before I asked Titus Corbulo his thoughts about what had to be an extremely unusual evening, especially given what he was facing starting the next morning. That was not the case with me, however; I do not think I got a watch's worth of sleep because my wife was beside herself with excitement.

"You have a *brother*!" If she said this once, she said it a dozen times, seemingly happier every time she said it. "That is so wonderful for you, *meum mel*!"

Honestly, at that moment, I had not decided about how I felt, although even then, I did feel what I suppose was some excitement at the idea. Corbulo was understandably overwhelmed; I could not even imagine what it must have been like for him. He would have already been nervous when he was roused at dawn by Volcacius, knowing that he would be arriving in Ubiorum to begin his life under the standard, yet never in his wildest dreams could he have predicted that by that night, he would be sitting in an apartment meeting the family of the half-brother he had never known existed that morning. Those of my flesh reading this, however many years later, I suspect that you have many questions, and that one of them was why Manius Corbulo, who knew the truth, never told the youth he had essentially raised as his own the story, but despite my best attempts to find him, Manius Corbulo was never seen again after he signed the document attesting to his paternity of my brother, that he was a Roman citizen, and that he was of age, only one of which was true. Yes, dear reader, just like Titus Pomponius Pullus, thanks to his size and the willingness of someone to lie for him, Titus Corbulo entered the Legion at the age of sixteen, not seventeen. I could lie and say that neither Macer nor I learned this until he had already completed training, but that would not be true, because he blurted it out that night in my apartment.

This led to an understandably tense moment, as both Alex and I looked at Macer, studying his face for a hint of his feelings, but after a long pause, he took a deep draught of his wine, then shrugged, "I'm sorry, I must have drifted off thinking of something else. What were you saying?"

For a horrifying instant, I thought Corbulo would repeat it, but he either caught my warning glare or realized on his own this was something that was best left unsaid. Otherwise, it was a unforgettable evening, with young Titus absolutely fascinated, and taken, with his new uncle, who seemed to feel the same way about his nephew, while Giulia could not seem to decide which of us was her father, spending the time constantly looking back and forth from one of us to the other, with a confused expression on her tiny face. Corbulo was clearly smitten with Bronwen, but I had become accustomed to this, although it never made me very happy, yet to my surprise, he seemed most interested in listening to Alex, telling stories of his time with my father, starting when he escorted young Alex and his siblings and mother back to Arelate with Alex's father Diocles' ashes, to be interred with the ashes of the Prefect. In fact, we all listened in rapt attention as young Corbulo was given his first initiation into his real family by Alexandros Pullus, of his father's time as the Primus Pilus of the *Legio Germanicus*, and how highly Germanicus Julius Caesar thought of my father. Naturally, Alex did not speak much about the political intrigue, nor did he say much about the revolt of the Legions in the aftermath of the death of Divus Augustus, but about this, we learned that young Corbulo had his own source of information, the man who had raised him since he was three.

"He talked about your…*our* father during that," he said hesitantly, and I braced myself for it not to be flattering. Fortunately, there was no cause for concern, as he explained, "He talked about how he heard from old comrades about how our father rode to get Germanicus and bring him to the Rhenus, then was in Pannonia as well." He paused to gulp some wine, and I understood why when he said, "Whenever Manius Corbulo got drunk, he would talk about that, and he always blamed Divus Augustus for it."

Macer and I exchanged a glance, but I inclined my head in the signal that my more tactful friend handle this, and he began by saying carefully, "While he's not alone in that, it's still a complicated issue, and the fact is that the revolt happened *after* Augustus died, and Tiberius is the one who decided to keep those things that the men didn't like in place, like the length of enlistment."

Corbulo surprised both of us when my brother interjected, with a shake of his head.

"It wasn't that. I mean," he amended quickly, "that was part of it, but what my…Manius Corbulo said was the worst part was the *dilectus* he called in Rome that cleaned out the Subura of all the scum. At least," he finished shyly, "that's what Manius Corbulo said he heard from all of his friends who were still under the standard."

We both looked at each other, and I knew that our minds were running along the same lines, which Macer confirmed by mouthing a word, or more accurately, a name.

"Pusio."

I nodded, but since Macer had not said the name aloud, Corbulo did not hear it, and he continued, "He told me that if there hadn't been those men in the ranks, there would have never been a revolt."

There was certainly truth in this, and my father expressed much the same sentiment, although not to the same degree. He did think, and I agree, that in the Rhenus Legions, the addition of these men in the aftermath of the panic triggered by the Varus disaster created an atmosphere of discontent because of men like Pusio, who we learned was actually an Equestrian, and because of his education, was a persuasive force among the rankers. However, to say that it was only these malcontents who were responsible ignores the fact that the Pannonian Legions were every bit as involved in the uprising, and they had not been contaminated by rabble rousers like Pusio. Ultimately, I think the revolt was inevitable, but the effects were certainly exacerbated by these men among the Rhenus Legions. In addition to the revolt, Corbulo expressed a great deal of interest in the *Legio Germanicus*, which Alex knew the most about, and as he talked, I noticed that Corbulo seemed to be moving in a linear fashion, and I braced myself for what I felt certain was coming.

Nevertheless, it felt like a stab to my vitals when he turned and asked me bluntly, "How did our father die?"

Just as I opened my mouth to answer, I felt a gentle hand on my shoulder, and when I looked up to see my wife standing there, I reached up and gave Bronwen's hand a squeeze to let her know her silent support was appreciated. Then, I told him, becoming aware that the attention of everyone present in the room, meaning the adults since the children had been trundled to bed, against their wishes, were on me, and I realized that I had never really talked in any depth about this to Algaia, Alex, or Bronwen for that matter, although Alex has since written down my recollection of this event.

"We were sent to rescue Segestes," I began, then told my brother about the pursuit by Arminius, desperate to retrieve his pregnant wife, the failure of Maluginensis, the Tertius Pilus Prior, whom those who were there still under the standard place most of the blame for what happened, and I am one of them, and my own error when I led my Sixth Century to the aid of a Cohort that, had I been more experienced, I would have seen was already doomed. I spoke dispassionately; at least, that is what I believed, that I was delivering the equivalent of an after-action report in the manner in which a Centurion of Rome is trained, but when I got to the part about being surrounded, then struck a blow to the head that drove me to my knees, I paused to take a sip of wine. When I did, I glanced up to see Algaia and Bronwen, seated at their spots at the table, both of them with tears streaming down their cheeks, only then becoming aware of the wetness of my own, but I did not look over at Alex or Macer, knowing that if they were weeping, it would shatter my composure. Corbulo was dry-eyed, but I detected a barely noticeable tremor of his chin, while his eyes were wide and fixed on mine. I resumed, talking about how Arminius' Germans became so fixated on cutting down Titus Pullus that it gave our men the opportunity to drag me to safety, and by doing so, condemned me to watching our father die, succumbing not to a single thrust, but because of thrusts, slashes, and hacks coming from every direction, and in doing so, cemented his legend among the men of the Army of the Rhenus as a Roman that could not be slain by just one foe.

I erred then, because I finished by saying, "It was the last time he suffered one of our divine fits, but he not only saved my life, he thwarted Arminius because they shouldn't have been putting everything they had into killing a single man."

Two things happened simultaneously; I heard someone's sudden intake of breath, and Corbulo asked, "What do you mean 'divine fit'?"

Silently cursing myself, I said firmly, "That's something

we can talk about once you're done with training." Deciding this was a good time to end things, I stood up, signaling to Corbulo to do the same. "It's time that you return to camp." Something occurred to me, and I turned to Macer. "Where are they staying?"

"Those huts that normally are occupied by the Sixth Century," he reminded me, then laughed. "You don't remember?"

I had not, but once he mentioned it, it came back to me.

"I tried to put it out of my mind." I made a face. "Given how the boys behaved about it, can you blame me?"

He laughingly agreed. When Macer made the decision that we would be training *Tirones* in the First Cohort, he had ordered a consolidation, designating most of the Sixth Century huts as housing for the *Tirones* for the first part of their training. Once they were deemed capable of integrating with their Centuries, things would be rearranged, with the men of the Sixth returning to their original huts. This is not unprecedented; in fact, some Legions do this with their Tenth Cohort every season before dispersing them to the Cohorts that require plumping up, but to anyone's knowledge, this had never happened with a first line Cohort, let alone the First Cohort, yet another sign of just how badly hurt we had been. What surprised me, but should not have, was that the chorus of groans and complaints did not come from just the men of the Sixth, but from my Century as well.

"They don't like the idea of those thieving bastards from the Sixth fouling their living quarters with their presence," was how Vinicius explained it.

Once Corbulo said his goodbyes to Algaia, then Bronwen, blushing furiously as I looked on, then solemnly took Alex's offered arm, I picked up my *vitus*, but Macer stopped me.

"I'm going back to camp. There's no need for you to bring young Corbulo here back there, then turn around and come back to the apartment. Besides, I want to talk to Volcacius tonight." He grinned. "I'll make sure he's all tucked in."

I thanked him, but when I turned to Corbulo, I was not smiling, nor was I particularly friendly.

"As of now, you're just another *Tiro*, and I'm going to

haunt your fucking dreams. Do you understand?"

I was pleased to see how he caught on immediately, replying crisply, "Yes, Primus Hastatus Prior. I understand."

I closed the door behind them, and when I turned, I was faced by three people, two of whom wore broad smiles, while Bronwen actually clapped in delight.

"You have a brother!"

Yes, I did, and I do. I am still unsure how I feel about it.

Thankfully, there was no need for me to be involved in any of the training immediately, and I made it a point to avoid the forum and the Sixth Century area as Clepsina, along with Macer's Optio Dolabella, began introducing Corbulo and the newly sworn-in *Tirones* to their new lives. Macer did hold a brief meeting with the other Centurions of the First on their first real day of training, consulting from the pair of wax tablets Volcacius had given him.

"All in all, this seems to be a good group, above average in terms of fitness." He looked up from the tablet, and directly at me. As we had agreed, he added, "Of course, Pullus, your half-brother is at the top of that heap by a large margin."

Since we had discussed it beforehand, I was prepared for the eruption of exclamations from the other four Centurions, creating a babble of voices, although it was Gratianus who cut through the noise that I picked out first.

"Yes! What's that about, eh, Pullus? How did that happen?"

With a completely straight face, I feigned surprise and replied, "Why, Gratianus, when a man sticks his prick into a woman's *cunnus*, they…"

"You know what I mean," he snapped, his face turning a satisfying shade of red as our comrades hooted and jeered. His expression became sly, and I knew that he was going to try and repay me in kind. "But did your Tata have *another* family tucked away besides you and this one?" He looked around at the others, and he should have read in their expressions the clear signal that I saw in their faces, but I suppose he was either oblivious or decided he would plunge ahead anyway, because he finished, "Are there going to be any more huge Romans showing up and inundating this Legion?"

"If the gods are kind to this Legion," Macer beat me in being the first one to speak, probably a good thing, "and bless us with more men like Titus Pullus, are you saying that's a bad thing, Gratianus?" Before Gratianus could answer, he addressed the rest of us. "Do any of you agree with Gratianus here?"

The response was immediate, and unanimous, forcing Gratianus to raise his voice to protest, "I didn't say it was a bad thing, Primus Pilus! I…I was making a joke, that's all!"

"It wasn't funny," Macer replied coldly. "You're speaking of not only my best friend, but this Centurion's father," he pointed to me, "and a hero of this Legion. Or, are you forgetting that, Gratianus?"

To his credit, Gratianus knew what he needed to do.

"No, I'm not forgetting, Primus Pilus." He turned to address me, "Pullus, I humbly apologize. I didn't mean to give any offense, I truly didn't. I was just…surprised to hear about this. And," he finished weakly, "I was trying to be funny."

There were *so* many things I wanted to say, but while I was looking directly at him, I sensed as much as saw Macer glaring at me out of the corner of my eye, so what came out of my mouth was an equally weak, "Thank you, Gratianus. I accept your apology, and there's no need for any further discussion on the matter."

This last bit earned me a slight nod from Macer, which the others missed because they were all understandably watching Gratianus and me, but it provided the perfect opportunity for our Primus Pilus to continue, "That's all about Corbulo, and as I was saying, Volcacius said this isn't a bad group, although he did identify two men who began giving him some trouble on the march back here. I'm not going to tell you those names yet. Let's see how they shake out with you, Clepsina. If they turn out to be a problem for you as well, then we'll make a decision about whether to dump them on another Cohort, or throw them out."

With that, we were dismissed, and I made an excuse to Macer about going back to my apartment, relieved that he only gave a distracted wave and did not ask any questions. I had not told him about Sempronius and that he was hiding out in our brothel, deeming it something that, if possible, would remain secret from him until one or both of us crossed the river, telling myself that there was no real need to alarm him. When I reached Venus' Passion, it was early enough in the day that there were a handful of customers who had paid for a full night stumbling out of the place, making me feel a bit uncomfortable that I was entering. I cannot say I was particularly surprised when I saw Pandora, who, like all mistresses of such establishments, never seemed to sleep, standing there blocking my entrance, hands on her hips and glaring up at me, not intimidated in the slightest.

Indeed, she began by wagging a finger in my face as she scolded, "You need to do something about your guest, Gnaeus Pullus!"

"Why?" I sighed, already weary. "What now?"

"What now?" she echoed. "Why, he's completely dominated young Hecate's time, that's what! She's one of my newest girls if you'll remember! Barely sixteen, fresh, innocent, and while she's only been here a month, she's one of *our* best earners! But now?" She had begun wailing by now. "Now, she's not only not earning, but he's filled her head with all sorts of nonsense about how he's going to buy her from us and they'll run off together!"

Now, I was not as upset as Pandora, but I was certainly irritated; it was about to get worse, because I thought I could at least partially soothe Turbo's woman by pointing out, "Just because he's controlling her time, Pandora, he's still paying for it."

"Paying?" she scoffed. Suddenly, her expression changed, and she asked suspiciously, "Are you saying that you didn't tell him that all of this was compliments of the house?"

"For the first night, yes," I replied, then added with a sinking feeling, "At least, I *think* I did."

She said something else, but I was already moving to *The Praetor's Triclinium*, and if it had not been right down the hallway, I would have been running. I entered without knocking, and I am afraid I opened the door with a bit too much force, because it swung open and struck the wall with a loud bang that, understandably, elicited a shriek of fright from one of the two occupants of the bed who sat upright, one hand to her mouth, her eyes wide with fright, while I caught less than an eyeblink's glimpse of Sempronius' bare ass as he rolled out of the bed on the opposite side to drop out of sight behind it. He did not vanish for long, popping back up in less than a heartbeat, but with a *gladius* in hand and in a crouch that the part of my mind that notices such things approved of, though I thought his legs were a bit too wide apart. Hecate, or at least that was who I assumed it was, had not moved…nor had she made any attempt to pull the sheet up to cover her naked body, but while I cannot lie and say I did not notice and appreciate her gifts, my eyes were actually still mostly on Sempronius, noticing how, when he had come to his feet, he had positioned himself immediately behind the girl, and when our eyes met, his widened in recognition first, the hand holding his *gladius* dropping as his body relaxed, but immediately following that was what I believe was a look of shame, correctly interpreting by my expression that I had taken notice of what he had done, using this innocent girl, relatively speaking, as a shield.

"*Salve* Hecate," I said genially enough, and I was not lying when I said, "Pandora said you were a rare beauty, and she wasn't exaggerating, I see." She blushed prettily, but what I saw in her eyes did not make me think of an innocent girl in her teens. I was also not through, shifting my gaze to Sempronius, although I was still addressing her. "In fact, I can now understand why my friend here was so smitten with you that he promised to take you away with him. Isn't that right…" I realized with some dismay that in my attempt to be clever, I had in fact put both of us in a potentially dangerous position, which meant that I finished awkwardly, "…*friend*?"

Sempronius flushed, but he answered readily enough, "I intended to talk to you about that, Pullus." Addressing the girl, he said gently, "Hecate, *meum mel*, why don't you go and find something to break our fast?" He grinned at her. "You've worked up an appetite in me in more ways than one, eh?"

Since she had turned her face away from me, I could not see her expression, though I did hear her giggle, but it was what she said next that froze my blood, both for what she said and how she said it.

"Yes, Marcus my love."

She leaned over to pick up her shift, made of a gauzy material and brightly colored, designed to come off easily, and I was not fooled by her manner as she did so, moving languidly and much more slowly than necessary, my suspicions rewarded when I saw her glance up at me through her lashes to check to see if I was ogling her.

"She's a bit skinny for my taste," I said to Sempronius. "And a bit hairy. But," I gave an overly exaggerated shrug, "to each their own."

As I expected, the air of young innocence vanished, her face transforming and suddenly making her look much older as her lips twisted into a sneer, but it only lasted a heartbeat, and since her back was to Sempronius, all he heard was Hecate saying meekly in heavily accented but understandable Latin, "I am sorry that you are displeased by me, Master Pullus."

Then, she hurried past me, giving me a triumphant smile when Sempronius replied, "*Oy*! That's a bit harsh, Pullus! You admitted she's a rare beauty when you walked in, so what are you prattling about now?"

I did not answer, waiting for Hecate to close the door, which she did, but not before, using the door to screen her from Sempronius, she stuck her tongue out at me. Maybe she *is* a teenager, I thought with some amusement. Holding up a hand, I tiptoed to the door, but I heard her receding footsteps, though I did crack the door to check before I closed it.

Turning on him, I had to make an effort to keep my voice down as I demanded, "Are you *mad*?"

"About what?"

I could tell he was trying to sound surprised, but I heard the defensiveness there.

"You know about what," I snapped. I extended a finger. "First, why did you tell her that you were going to take her with you when you left?"

I was expecting a denial, or a lie, or a joke.

What I was *not* expecting was him to say quietly, "Because I'm in love with her, Pullus."

"You're *what*?" So dumbfounded was I that I actually

staggered over to one of the couches and dropped down onto it. "You've known her for two days!"

"I know that," he acknowledged coolly. "But I also know how I feel."

"Is that why you told her your real name?" I asked the second thing that was bothering me, determined that I would not let him have the upper hand.

It was a guess; as I have mentioned, and every Roman knows, we do not have all that many *praenomina* to go around, so it was possible that he had used his real *praenomen* but not his *nomen*.

However, it turned out to be a good guess, because he did reluctantly admit, "Yes. And," he held up a hand to forestall me, "I know why you think that was a mistake. And, it *might* be...but I don't believe it is."

I must confess that I was torn; it was not all that long ago that I created a multitude of problems for myself by falling in love with a young woman of the Parisii, while I was actually being held hostage by their tribe's chieftain, but I reminded myself that it was not over the course of two days.

There was the third thing that worried me, but instead of a frontal assault, I decided to act more subtly, asking suddenly, "If I recall correctly, you haven't worked in Germania much, have you?"

"No," he replied quickly enough, but his eyes were searching my face, and he asked cautiously, "Why do you ask?"

"Because it stands to reason that you don't recognize the various accents," I explained.

He was clearly reluctant to do so, but he did nod.

"That makes sense, I suppose."

"For example," I said, as if I was speaking in an abstract sense, "you wouldn't be able to tell the difference between an Ubii accent and a..." I pretended to think for an example, "...Cherusci, would you agree?"

Sempronius did not reply immediately, looking at me for a long period of time, then he finally asked quietly, "What are you trying to say, Pullus?"

"Did you ask Hecate her real name?" I asked, and I was

surprised when he nodded, but I should not have been surprised by her answer.

"She says she doesn't remember," he told me. "Apparently, she was taken when she was still an infant."

"Well, she may not remember her name, but she was old enough to have learned to speak Cherusci, because I recognize the accent. In fact, every man who's been part of the Legions the last twelve years would know a Cherusci accent if they heard it."

"So?" He shrugged. "That doesn't mean anything. Seriously, Pullus," he laughed, but I heard how forced it was, not fooling me in the slightest, "you're beginning to sound like someone in my line of work, seeing threats around every corner." He pointed in the general direction of where Hecate was. "Did you look at her? You really think that she could murder me?"

"No," I answered, clearly surprising him. "I don't get that impression from her. But she wouldn't need to. All she would need to do is let one of her tribesmen know she's sleeping with a Roman and let them know the best time to come for you."

"She'd never do that!" He almost shouted this, yet I felt certain that I heard the first hint of doubt, and I decided to drop this for the moment, thinking that it was best to let him think about this on his own and let the doubt build.

"How much are you planning on offering Pandora for her?" I asked, and I was rewarded by the sudden look of guilt that flashed across his features, and that was when the realization hit me. "Ah, you weren't planning on paying her a fucking *sestertius*, were you? But the question is, who are you lying to? Pandora? Or to…?"

Before I could say her name, the latch lifted, and Hecate entered, saying, "I brought bread, and some cheese and a jug, my love."

"Please," Sempronius whispered, "drop this for now, Pullus. I beg you!"

It actually was an easy request to grant, mainly because I still had a larger problem on my mind, and I signaled my acceptance by asking abruptly, "When do you plan on leaving here?"

He did not answer me immediately, choosing instead to walk to Hecate, thank her and kiss her as he took the food, then whispered something that sent her out of the room again.

Only then did he reply coolly, "As soon as it's safe."

"You've got one more day before you're going to need to be out of here," I said, using a tone that I hoped that he interpreted correctly for what it was, an order, and not a negotiation.

"Where else can I go?" he protested, while I took note of his use of the singular, thinking it odd that a man who had declared his love just a matter of a few heartbeats before was speaking in this manner. "I don't know Ubiorum, and I don't know who I can trust besides you. It's too dangerous to move!"

"It's too dangerous to stay here," I said flatly. "Sooner rather than later, one of the *Duumviri*, or a Tribune or whoever uses this room regularly is not going to take no for an answer."

He mouthed a curse, then gave a slight nod, but I was not prepared for what was coming next.

"Turn around and face the door, please, Pullus." When I just stared at him, he almost pleaded, "Please, Pullus. I need to retrieve something, and it's safer for both of us if you don't see where I have it hidden."

I cursed him, but I complied, turning about, though I did my best to try and identify what part of the room he moved to, and what he was doing, but I quickly gave up.

"All right," he said. "Ready."

I did not know what to expect to see when I turned around, but it was not a small scroll. When he turned it and I saw the red seal, and most importantly, the sphinx, my first instinct was to tell him to put it back where he had it hidden, because I wanted nothing to do with it.

As much to stall as for any other reason, I asked, "What is that?"

Sempronius was not fooled, saying impatiently, "You know what it is, Pullus. Don't act the fool. But," his voice hardened, "I'm telling you by the authority given to me by the Imperator personally to accept this scroll."

My mind screamed at me to refuse, yet it seemed as if I could only watch helplessly as my hand extended, then took the scroll from him.

"Now, you're to open it in my presence," he instructed.

"Why?" I demanded, expecting to hear him insist that I not ask why or declare it was not my business.

Consequently, I was surprised when he explained, "Those were my instructions from Tiberius' personal secretary, that if I had to use this, it was to be opened by you in my presence."

Such was my agitation that I missed something very important in what Sempronius said; more accurately, I made an assumption when he said that I was to open it, that he was making a general statement aimed at to whomever he handed it. It was a bad assumption, because when I cracked the seal, trying to keep my hand from shaking, then unrolled the scroll, when I saw that it was addressed to "Primus Hastatus Prior Gnaeus Volusenianus Pullus of the 1st Legion, stationed in Ara Ubiorum," I collapsed back onto the couch with enough force that it made a sharp, cracking sound. Numbly, I read the contents, though it was not long. In simple terms, it reminded me of my obligation to the Imperator, both by virtue of my status as a Centurion of Rome, but also by my oath, though I did not recall actually making one directly to Tiberius. Regardless of this formality, I also knew that it made no difference; in our world, if the most powerful man in the world decides you are sworn to him personally, it does not really matter if you intoned an oath to that effect. And, as such, this scroll ordered me to offer Marcus Sempronius; it even added, "or by whatever name he is known by at his moment of need," every assistance, up to and including sacrificing my life for his own safety. I had to read that passage twice before it registered, and when I looked up at him, dumbfounded, he did have the grace to look embarrassed, which told me something.

"You...you know what this says."

"I was there when it was written, Pullus," he replied quietly. He must have realized how this could be taken, because he added quickly, "I had *nothing* to do with what it says, Pullus, I swear it on Jupiter's black stone! And, if it makes you feel any better, it's not just you." Seeing my puzzlement, he explained, "That's why I had you turn your back. I have...more of these, each of them addressed to an individual who's like me and serves the Imperator in…different ways."

"I'm nothing like you!" I snapped, actually thankful that I was feeling an emotion other than this numbing dread, while reminding me at the same time to keep my anger in check, but Sempronius did not help matters.

"If you really believe that, you're a fool," he said scornfully. This brought me back to my feet, and I was grimly pleased to see the look of alarm flash across his features. "Even if you're not like me," he added hastily, "does it really matter right now?"

That stopped me in my tracks, realizing that this was nothing more than the truth, however unpalatable. It also got me thinking about the predicament we were both in, and the glimmering of an idea began taking shape.

"In that pile of scrolls you've got to force people to help you," he flushed at this, which was somewhat satisfying, "do you have anything that isn't addressed to an individual?"

He frowned, clearly not understanding.

"What do you mean?"

Once I explained, his face cleared, though he was still somewhat doubtful, or perhaps apprehensive is more appropriate.

"I do," he answered cautiously, "but I only have one of them, and the Imperator made it clear that it was only to be used as a last resort."

I shrugged at that, saying offhandedly, "Well, if you don't want to use it, I can't force you, but that's the only way I can think of to safely move you, and move you somewhere you're going to be safe even if Libo knows where you are."

"Turn around," he sighed.

"How do I know this is genuine?"

Of all the reactions I anticipated from Tribune Vitellius, this was not one of them, and I realized that I had made an assumption, which was that he had seen the seal of the Imperator before, which was the cause of my blunder.

"You've never seen the Imperator's seal before?" I asked, but that was not my error; laughing about it was.

"Of course I have!" he snapped, his face turning red. "But I've also seen forgeries, Centurion! And this," he sniffed, waving the scroll in the air, "is suspect, I can assure you!"

I was saved by an unlikely ally, in the form of Primus Pilus Neratius, who was standing behind the Tribune seated at the desk in the *Praetorium*, and who leaned to look over the Tribune's shoulder.

"That's genuine," he said flatly, then before Vitellius could react, Neratius turned to Macer, standing on the other side of the Tribune. "What do you think, Marcus? You've seen enough of these as well."

Even after Macer did the same as Neratius, or at least pretended to, Vitellius seemed inclined to argue, but when he looked over his shoulder at Neratius and was met by the cold one-eyed stare of the senior Primus Pilus, he clearly thought better of it.

"Fine," he muttered. "It's genuine. But," now he returned his attention to me, "what do you intend to do?"

"With Primus Pilus Macer's permission," I replied with what we had rehearsed beforehand, "I'm going to march two sections of my Century out into Ubiorum to this brothel, and escort Tiberius' agent back here to camp, where he'll be safe."

"Safe from what?" Vitellius cried out in exasperation. "You still haven't told me what this person is so scared about, and who's the threat!"

"He told me that it's better that we don't know, Tribune," I replied, also a lie. "Just that he needs protection. And that," I pointed to the scroll still in his hands, "is very clear, and it's genuine."

"So you've all said," Vitellius grumped, but I had the strong sense that he was more upset that he did not know any details than he was about being overruled. Finally, he tossed the scroll onto the desk, then gave a disgusted wave. "Very well, you have permission to muster your Century sections, enter Ubiorum, and retrieve whoever this important agent is and bring him back to camp. But," he added, trying to sound severe, "only two sections, is that understood? We don't need to create a panic."

Despite everyone present knowing the fiction that he was

actually giving permission, I still rendered a salute as if this was not all a farce, then departed with Macer.

"Go get your boys ready," he ordered. "Armor and shields, no javelins." I thought this was a bit excessive, but when I asked why he thought it necessary, he said, "It's just a precaution. Better to overawe Libo and whoever he's got working for him than give them any ideas that they can handle you and your boys if they're just in tunics and carrying cudgels."

This made sense, and as soon as I entered my hut, I had Euphemios run to fetch Vinicius and Siculus, deciding that I would leave Hybrida behind as the ranking officer while taking Lentulus with me, knowing it would not be hard to assemble the men since we were still in a recovery routine. When the Optio arrived, I gave him his orders, and while I could see he was surprised, like a good Optio, he did not hesitate or ask questions, hurrying out to rouse the men, which began with Siculus sounding the call, starting with the two notes denoting the First Cohort, followed by five quick blasts, except that he missed the fifth and final note, a sign that he was still practicing to replace Macrinus.

"I hope that the men don't use that as an excuse," I commented to Alex, and as I sat there listening to the shouts outside as men came running from wherever they were in the camp, I made a quick decision.

Getting up, I grabbed my *vitus*, but just as I reached my door, I heard the outer one opening, and I opened mine to find Vinicius already saluting, whereupon he announced formally, "The Century is assembled, Centurion."

"Good." I nodded my approval at the haste, although at the same time, I reminded myself there were significantly less men to be scattered about the camp.

It did not take long to give my orders, especially since I ordered the entire Century to don their armor before dismissing the men.

"I thought you were only taking two sections," Alex commented as he helped me into my own, although to save some time, I did not wear my padded tunic, nor did I strap on my greaves.

"I am," I replied, then grinned, "but they don't know that. This is good training."

"Oh, I'm sure they'll completely agree," Alex agreed, albeit sarcastically. "They'll love you for this, no doubt."

What mattered was that, despite my loud claim to the contrary to the Century, I was quite pleased with the speed with which they assembled, though I still did not make any mention of where we were going. Instead, I gave the commands to turn them in preparation for marching down the street, then turn the corner to the *Porta Praetoria* and out into town, taking my spot at the head of the column. The change I came up with was to have the entire Century in armor, but when we reached the main gate, I sounded the halt, then called Hybrida to attend to me.

"You're in command of the rest of the Century," I informed the *Tesseraurius*. "I'm taking the Optio and Lentulus with me to escort someone back to camp. I doubt there will be any trouble, but I want you and the men standing ready in case I have Siculus sound the call, or I send a runner to you for help."

"Yes, sir," Hybrida replied. He hesitated, then asked, "Should I know where you're headed?"

"Venus' Passion," I answered, kicking myself for not remembering that it might be important for him to know.

His eyes did widen a bit, but to his credit, the *Tesseraurius* saluted, and said, "I understand and will obey."

Leading the First and Second Sections, which in reality meant that I was marching the First, Second, and most of the Third in order to have two full sections, out of the camp, we passed through the city gate, and as always, I was struck by the thought that, even in the relatively short period of time I had been here, the position of the western wall, which was closest to the camp, had been moved twice, and how the inevitable cluster of buildings that always sprang up just outside the wall, usually within days after it has been completed, were now about three hundred paces from our camp. I had heard rumors that the Prefect had issued orders that forbade any construction closer to the camp, not wanting a situation where there were shacks hard up against the camp walls that might provide cover to attackers, but Prefect Sacrovir was dead, and there was no way to know if his order would be respected, either by his replacement, who had yet to be named, or by the incoming *Praetor* in Mogontiacum. Shoving that out of my mind, I led my men at a brisk march, just short of a trot, our presence creating a bit of an uproar among the citizens of the town who were going about their business, not expecting to be confronted by armed Legionaries and led by a huge, scarred Centurion.

Even in the moment, though it barely registered then, I saw the eyes go wide as a woman, or sometimes a man looked at my face, only after taking in my size, the latter something I am accustomed to, sometimes with a hand going to the mouth to cover the look of alarm. One thing I do recall crossing my mind was the amusing thought that perhaps some of these people thought that we were German warriors who had stolen uniforms, but aside from some gasps, and how quickly these citizens leapt out of our path, they did not impede us. When we reached the intersection where a left turn would put us on the same street as Venus' Passion, just before we reached the corner, I was forewarned by the sound of pounding footsteps coming at a run, but before I could react, a figure came careening around the corner, it taking me a fraction of a heartbeat to recognize that it was Turbo. So intent was he on reaching the camp that he had his head down, churning his arms and legs as he ran as quickly as he could, and I just barely got my *vitus* up and across my body in a blocking position before he came crashing headlong into me. I was not completely successful in catching him, because my hand was already full with my *vitus*, but I did manage to steer him around me, whereupon he came skidding to a stop, his arms windmilling wildly.

"P-Pullus," he gasped, his face actually ashen despite his exertion, and I understood why when he got out, "the brothel! There are men who broke into the brothel! They've trapped your friend in *The Praetor's Triclinium*!" I was already running before he finished, and I heard him shout, "He's barricaded himself inside, but I don't know how long he can hold out!"

I did not order my men to follow, or I do not remember doing so, but I heard the slapping sound of the hobnails of more than thirty men pounding after me, while I tried not to think of what might happen to me and my family if Sempronius did not survive.

I almost found out. Although we reached the brothel before Libo's men could finish the job, they had managed to break down the door to the room, and while Sempronius gave a good account of himself; there was a dead man on the floor in a pool of blood, while there was another man who was still alive but writhing about and, to Pandora's horror, bleeding all over what she swore was a very expensive carpet that had come from Egypt, and if she were to be believed, had once been in the palace of Cleopatra in Alexandria. She was incorrect; while there *is* such a carpet in Ubiorum, it is actually in the apartment of Alexandros Pullus, inherited from his father Diocles, who took several carpets when he was serving the Prefect during the period of time my great-grandfather was the *de facto* Primus Pilus of the 6th Legion with Caesar. Whatever its provenance, it was ruined, thanks to the spurting wound that Sempronius had inflicted to his attacker's arm on the inside of his elbow, severing the large vessel.

I barked an order to Aulus Taurus, one of my First Section rankers who had skills in such things, to fashion a tourniquet for the wounded man, then turned my attention to Sempronius, who was slumped against the far wall on the opposite side of the bed, clutching his side, his right hand covered in blood, though I did not see any spraying or spurting from between his fingers. He also had a wound to his right thigh, but it was not until I walked around the bed in which, just that morning, I had found him and Hecate lounging, that I learned there was another body in the room. Lying on her back, her eyes still open wide with the kind of shock that I had seen many times before, Hecate's shift was soaked in blood, making the material cling to her breasts in a manner that, under other circumstances and if the liquid had been something other than her blood, would have been quite arousing. Without warning, an image flashed through my mind, a recent one from that morning, of how Sempronius had leapt out of the bed and how he had positioned himself, and in that moment, I was certain that I knew what had happened. More importantly, I saw that Sempronius was aware that I knew by the way in which he refused to look up at me.

"That *cunnus*," he used his free hand to weakly point at the wounded man, "got me good, Pullus, when I was putting paid to that bastard there." He indicated the dead man. Still keeping his eyes away from the vicinity of my face, he asked dully, "What about the rest?"

"They scattered like chickens as soon as we got here," I assured him. "And now you're safe. We're going to take you to camp and get you fixed up." As much to force him to look at me as to examine the wound, I crouched down, pointing to it. "How bad is it?"

"It's not good," he said grimly. "It went in about," he held up his free hand with thumb and pointing finger about three inches apart, "that deep." He actually chuckled then, though it held no humor. "And I just stood there watching him bury that fucking blade into my body as if I was at the games watching a gladiator kill his opponent."

I had actually heard other men say something similar, how they had this moment of disembodiment where they seemed to be nothing more than an observer as their foe plunged a blade into their bodies, but I made no mention of that.

Instead, I moved my hand in a way so that, despite his refusal to look at me, he could not miss it as I pointed at Hecate's corpse, though I used a gentle tone as I asked, "And? What happened to Hecate?" He did not answer immediately, only shaking his head, but I was growing impatient, so I reached out and grabbed his chin firmly enough that he winced, forcing his head up so that he had nowhere to look but at me. "What. Happened. To. Her?"

The grimace that Sempronius made then had nothing to do with the physical pain he was experiencing, I was certain of that.

"She...she tried to help," he whispered. "When we heard them break down the door, she told me that they wouldn't hurt a woman, and to get behind her to give me time to draw my *gladius*."

"Well, she was wrong," I said, more harshly than I

intended, and despite my suspicions, when he visibly flinched as if I had struck him, I did feel badly.

Deciding there was nothing more to be gained from this, I stood up, saying as I did, "We can't let her sacrifice for you go to waste, Sempronius. We're going to get you back to camp, and I'll have Philippos look after you personally. I don't suppose you can walk?"

He surprised me then by struggling to his feet, or perhaps I should say trying to struggle to his feet, and he did make it halfway before his legs gave way, and he slid back down the wall to the floor. Signaling to a pair of other First Section men, when they reached me, I instructed them to carry Sempronius on one of their shields, which in turn meant that I had to threaten both of them for bickering over whose shield would get blood on it.

"If you two don't decide, I'll just make sure they're both bloody, but it won't be from him," I jerked a thumb at Sempronius, who seemed oblivious to this, his eyes now fixed on Hecate.

It was a bit of a struggle, but they got Sempronius lying in the concave side of the shield, which meant his legs dangled over the edge. This is an exceedingly awkward arrangement, which is why we only use it to remove men out of immediate danger, or in this case, out of the brothel so that I could find a better method of transporting him.

"Centurion, what about him?"

I turned to see Vinicius pointing at the wounded man, the bleeding stopped for the moment thanks to the tourniquet Taurus had fashioned from a couple of his *cingula*, for which I promised to pay.

"Take him with us," I said, then a bit more loudly, I added, "I think the torture detachment will be able to make short work of him with that wound."

"Torture detachment!" the wounded man exclaimed, making a sudden, darting movement for the door, but I was close enough to give him a good whack across the head with my *vitus*, which caused him to stagger backward, dazed and moaning but otherwise compliant.

"Are you really turning him over to the torturers?" Vinicius whispered.

"It depends." I shrugged. "I want to find out where that bastard Libo is."

This reminded me to ask Pandora, but she was too busy wailing over Hecate, yet while her tears were genuine enough, I did wonder how much of her grief was about the whore and how much was about the lost profit. There was also extensive damage to the outer door, which was hanging by one hinge, while the area around the latch was splintered, and I told Vinicius to detach a pair of men to stand guard until Turbo could sufficiently repair it. Outside, I was not surprised to see a crowd had gathered on either side, filling the street, but I was very pleased to see how Lentulus had taken command, dividing the men who had remained on the street into two groups, each facing the crowd while arrayed completely across the street, blocking anyone from getting too close. The crowd was mostly curious, but I sensed there was an undercurrent of anger as well, which made sense; the shopkeepers and residents who lived on this street did not want to see this kind of violence, but I was more interested in scanning for faces who I either recognized, such as the youngster who followed me, or whose type I recognized. It did not take me long, spying two men who reminded me of Vibius Cordus and Gnaeus Stator, two of Nasica's bully boys, who were trying to pretend that they were not watching intently as the pair of rankers dragged their wounded accomplice out into the street, though not before he tried to declare he was too weak from blood loss to walk; once I informed him that I would just cut his throat and leave him behind, he somehow found the strength to declare that he could move under his own power. Laying the shield carrying Sempronius onto the paving stones, there was a brief delay as a plank was found that was more suitable to carry him, and as this was happening, I watched as the pair conferred and in fact appeared to be arguing about something. Surely they're not going to do anything as stupid as trying to rescue their comrade, I thought; hard on the heels of this was another one that made me stiffen. No, they're going to try and murder Sempronius if they have the chance! With this in mind, I summoned Vinicius, and gave him my orders. He surprised me when he made a gesture with his head back over his shoulder to where the two men were standing.

"You talking about those *collegia* bully boy types over there, Centurion?"

"That's exactly who I was thinking about," I agreed, but when I glanced over, I saw that the original pair had been joined by two more men, one of them almost certainly having served under the standard.

"We'll form up in a square and put both your friend and the prisoner in the middle," Vinicius suggested, and I nodded approvingly.

No more than a count of a hundred elapsed before we were moving, but I gave the command to Vinicius.

"I've got something I need to do," I told him, and I saw by the way he eyed me that he was not fooled.

When we set out, I was in my normal spot, but Vinicius was next to me instead of at the rear of the formation on the opposite side, and since we were marching away from where Libo's men were, they were forced to make a choice; either follow us, or turn and dash down the street in the opposite direction to the next intersection, take the cross street in the direction of the camp and rush ahead of us to get into a position from which they could try and harm Sempronius. Gambling that this was what they would do, once we turned the corner, I dashed away myself, my original intention being to get ahead of them. However, before I had gone a dozen paces, I changed my mind, slowing down to a walk, though it was quite difficult to do so, then stopped at the next corner. Squatting down, just like I had seen Sempronius do, and is now something I do whenever I am in a situation that calls for it, I did remember to take my helmet off before I peeked around the corner, just in time to see the four men dash across the street, their cloaks streaming behind them, which gave me the opportunity to see they were all armed with *gladii*, the man in the lead shoving a woman aside who was too slow in getting out of the way and sending her sprawling. The last of them disappeared, without a glance in either direction, or at the woman, who was trying to get to her feet, and I turned the corner in pursuit, tying my helmet back on as I moved, then stopping long enough to pick the woman up, albeit a bit roughly, by grabbing her by the back of her stola and lifting her up and depositing her on the street.

"T-thank you, Centurion!" I heard her call out, but I was already moving to the next block.

I experienced a moment of concern because they had vanished, but I had forgotten about the narrow space between two buildings about midway between the two intersecting streets. Too narrow to be a street or a normal alley, I realized that it actually suited my purposes better because it negated their numerical advantage, it being only wide enough for two normal-sized men to pass by, although they would brush shoulders, giving me just enough room to use my blade without worrying about anyone getting on either flank. Taking a quick glance around, I looked for any sign that reinforcements were headed their way, and once I saw that it was clear, I entered the alley. With both buildings being two stories, it was a bit more dimly lit than out in the street, but it did not impede me, and I was careful to step over the pottery shards, pieces of old crates, and a couple piles of *cac* deposited by people who could not make it to the public latrine, of which there are now two in the town. While I did not recall drawing it, my *gladius* was in my hand, with my *vitus* in the other, and I approached cautiously, certain that one of the men, all of whom were now crowded together just inside the exit of the alley, would glance over his shoulder. They did not do so, all four of them intent on peering to their left, the direction from which my men would be coming, and I could tell they rounded the corner two blocks away by the manner in which they all suddenly leaned back and away from the edge of the building to avoid being seen. I was less than ten paces away when one of the pair closest to me finally glanced over his shoulder, not because he sensed danger, but just because it is something a person does occasionally, though I have no idea why. Our eyes met, his going wide in surprise, and his hand dropped to the hilt of his *gladius*, but I was already moving so that, before he could draw his own, or even say anything, the point of my blade was pressed against his throat.

"*Salve,* ladies," I said, which, not surprisingly, elicited an instant and dramatic response, the other three wheeling about, but when they did so, one of the men actually took a step backward, out into the street, and we all heard a chorus of shouts that I knew would be Vinicius and my men sounding the alarm that these men had been spotted. Consequently, I spoke calmly, "Let's not do anything that gets you boys chopped into bloody meat, eh?"

The largest of them, with the kind of flattened nose that is as distinctive a badge as a transverse crest that indicated his status as a *collegia* tough, with a rough, gravelly voice that matched his demeanor, declared with a bravado that was patently false, "We won't be the only ones that cross the river, will we, boys? We can take you with us!"

The nonresponse by the other three actually made me laugh, and it was not forced.

"It looks like you're on your own there, Publius," I said cheerfully. By this moment, we could hear the slapping din of several pairs of hobnailed soles heading for us, so I spoke quickly, "Nothing's going to happen to you as long as none of you do anything stupid." Turning to the man, standing next to the tough I had dubbed Publius, I stated flatly, "You were under the standard."

At first, I did not think he would answer, but I saw his eyes dart to his right, where Vinicius and the other men, about a half-dozen from the sound of it, were moving towards us, then he gave a nod.

"Yes, Centurion," he said flatly.

"Deserter?"

"No!" he answered, clearly angry. "Not a fucking deserter." With his right hand, which I knew was not an accident and sent a message of its own, he reached up and grasped the leather thong, pulling out the round iron disk. "*Gregarius Immunes* Spurius Ventidius, First Century, First Cohort of the 8th Legion."

Understanding that I had been given an opportunity, before I could address Ventidius, I bellowed, "Optio Vinicius! Halt!"

Thankfully, he recognized my voice, and I heard him shout the order to stop the advance, the men clattering to a stop, close enough that, even around the corner, I could hear them panting and coughing.

My blade was still at the throat of the closest man, but I did not move it as I called out, "Vinicius, put Lentulus in charge of Second Section with our prisoner back to camp, and you take the First Section with Marcus Sempronius to the *quaestorium*."

"I understand and will obey, sir!"

Vinicius began shouting, and since I did not want to raise my voice, I waited for him to make the necessary arrangements. I saw the eyes of the man I had dubbed Publius going back and forth from me, my *gladius*, and the men off to his right a few paces down the street, and I swore I could see the wheels of his mind turning, very slowly, so I decided it would be wise to preempt whatever he had in mind.

"You wouldn't make it more than a few steps," I said casually, looking directly at him as I did so, and his battered features flushed.

"I don't know what you're talking about, soldier boy," he said sullenly, but I glanced over at Ventidius, asking the veteran, "Is he always this disrespectful to his betters?"

Ventidius actually laughed, but it was humorless, and he replied sourly, "You have no idea, Centurion. This one," he jerked a thumb at the subject of our conversation, "boasts that there's not a man under the standard who's ever lived who could beat him."

The beast inside me stirred a bit at this, and I looked directly at the tough, locking eyes with him, and I saw exactly what I wanted, and expected, as he broke eye contact with me and looked away, signaling his surrender along with the abandonment of his fantasy that he would be able to cut his way through my men to escape. To, I will add, my slight disappointment, but I forced myself to keep my mind on the moment at hand.

To Ventidius, I commented, "So if you were in the 8th, you know Titus Domitius."

For the first time, the older veteran showed a flicker of emotion, though I would not call it a smile, but I learned why when he replied challengingly, "Is that a test, Centurion? Of course I know him! He retired the same year I did. Although," now he did smile slightly, "he was the Primus Hastatus Prior when he did, so he doesn't have to worry about money like I do." He regarded me for a heartbeat before asking curiously, "How do you know him?"

"I don't, really," I admitted, recalling a similar conversation with another former ranker who had fallen on hard times and rented out his *gladius*, this one working for Nasica in Mediolanum. "But he and my father were close comrades."

I was not altogether surprised when I saw the flicker of his own startlement, then recognition, in Ventidius' eyes.

"You're Pullus," he said flatly. "The son of Titus Pullus."

"I am," I confirmed. "Did you know him?"

He made a short, barking sound that sounded a bit like a dog, but now it was my turn to be surprised when he affirmed, "Yes, you could say that. I was in the First Section of the First of the First."

Ventidius did not say anything more, just giving me a shrewd look, and I confess it took longer than it should have for me to recall something.

"You served with my father," I exclaimed. "When he transferred into the First Cohort."

"I did," Ventidius confirmed, while I tried to recall what I had read in my father's account, but there was nothing much, just that they had served together. "Even then you knew he was going to be something special."

"You're a Pullus?" the tough asked, and it pleased me to see the sudden air of caution.

"Yes, which is why you need to listen to me now, you stupid *cunnus*." I did not raise my voice, nor did I speak in a hostile manner, trying instead to sound indifferent. "Go tell Libo that he failed, and that if he has any sense, he's going to go find the deepest hole he can find and climb in it." Suddenly, I was somewhat inspired to add, "Remind him that the master that Sempronius serves is far more powerful than the man Libo serves."

He flushed slightly, undoubtedly because of my characterization, but he seemed more puzzled than angry.

"Who's Libo?"

I was about to snarl something, but then I recalled what the young *collegia* member told me, and realized that this one likely did not know Libo's real name either, forcing me to rack my brain before coming up with the name the youngster had uttered.

"You know him as Marcus Sura," I replied, and seeing his expression, I added, "and I can see that you recognize his name, so trying to pretend you don't will only make me angry. And," I smiled, but there was nothing friendly about it, "now that you know who *I* am, that's not something you want to do."

I fixed him with a cold stare until, after the lump in his throat bobbed up and down, he gave a nod, but while I briefly thought about forcing a verbal response, I decided this would suffice, because I was not through.

"Brother Ventidius," I deliberately used the informal title that men will use for each other out in town, "I'm offering you this piece of advice, and it's offered by the son of your former comrade. I don't know the circumstances of your employment by this man you know as Marcus Sura, but if you can sever your ties with him immediately, I would do so now, and here's why."

Returning my attention to the first man, I reminded, "Remember what I said, but there's one other thing. You tell Libo that if I see him in Ubiorum after this, I'll kill him where he stands. I don't care who he serves. In fact," I suddenly remembered something, "tell him that he owes me. I'm the owner of that business you broke into, and I'm going to take my payment for the damage he's responsible for in blood. His attempt on Sempronius got one of my whores killed, and she was very valuable, one of my top earners, and he's going to pay for her if he stays here."

Satisfied, for the first time, I turned my attention to the man who I had pinned to the wall with the point of my blade, and to his credit, he had barely moved, but there was still a thin trail of blood trickling down his throat.

I smiled, and congratulated him, "You did very well not moving a muscle. It's a good thing my arm didn't get tired, eh?"

I had maintained my posture, with my arm straight out from my side as I engaged in this exchange by design, knowing that these men would at least know what it took to hold a *gladius* out and away from your body for that period of time, wanting to send a message of my own, but regardless of any outward sign that I was not fatigued, the relief when I dropped my arm was immense. Most importantly by this moment, my men had marched past and, judging by the sound of their movement, were almost to the town gate, which meant that it was time for me to join them.

"All right, boys," I pointed with my *vitus* around the corner, in the direction from which my men had come, "you head that way. I'm going to give you to a count of ten before I step out into the street, and if I see any of you," I made a show of looking from one face to the next as if memorizing them, "I'm going to think that you're looking for a fight, and I'm coming after you."

"You don't need to worry, Centurion Pullus," Ventidius spoke before anyone else could, which I saw infuriated the tough who clearly saw himself as the leader, whose name I learned when the veteran turned and gave him a flat, level look, "I'll make sure that old Tullus here doesn't do anything foolish. Right, Tullus?"

For perhaps a heartbeat, it appeared as if Tullus' temper would get the best of him, although it appeared that his ire was aimed at Ventidius, giving the veteran a hateful glare, and I took that time to glance at the other two, worried that I would be in a situation where I had to try and protect the veteran, but to my relief, they both were clearly more interested in getting out of the area.

Finally, Tullus spat on the paving stones before he addressed me, without taking his eyes off of Ventidius. "We're leaving, soldier boy. And," he tore his gaze from Ventidius to look at me, and smiled as he said, "you can be sure I'll tell Sura, or Libo, or whatever his fucking name is what you said, but you'll regret it."

I know he tried to make it sound menacing, but his bluster was completely unconvincing; what mattered was that, being closest to the corner of the building, he was the first to disappear around it, the other two men, one of them rubbing his throat, following without even glancing at me. With a nod, Ventidius made to follow, but I stopped him.

"Watch your back, brother," I warned him. "I suspect that Tullus might have some plans for you."

"Oh, I have no doubt." He chuckled. "But he's an empty jug. He makes a lot of noise, but there's no bottom to him."

That aligned with my judgment, but I was still not convinced it meant that he was harmless, "Still," I began, but he beat me to it.

"Oh, I'm not spending another night here," he assured me, then offered his arm. "Thank you, Pullus." I took it, though not after sheathing my *gladius*, and I was surprised to see a glint of tears in his eyes, which he explained, "Seeing you brought a lot of memories back of your father. He was a great Legionary, and I grieved when I heard of his death."

"Thank you, Ventidius." I had to get this out past the lump in my throat, and I hoped that the shade of my father would forgive me for telling a little lie. "He spoke highly of you as well."

I could see this pleased and moved him, but he only gave a curt nod before he followed the other three men. Realizing I had forgotten to count, I only went to five before I stepped out into the street, and while I expected as much, I was still a bit disappointed that neither Tullus nor the other two men were anywhere to be seen in the sparse crowd moving along the street. I never saw Spurius Ventidius again.

I caught up with my men just before they entered camp to find that the wounded prisoner had collapsed, lapsing into unconsciousness from the loss of blood that at least delayed a meeting with the torture detachment. Sempronius was semiconscious himself, and I confess I had mixed feelings about whether it would be a good thing or a bad thing if he did not recover. Regardless of my personal feelings, as I promised, I went to the *Quaestorium* to order the duty *medicus* to go get Philippos, then while we waited, I ordered Vinicius to take command and march the men back to our huts.

"An extra wine ration for the entire Century," I told my Optio, who was surprised.

"But it was only First and Second Sections that did anything," he said, which was true enough. "Do you really want to reward the rest of the men the same as them? All they did was stand there."

"They were ready quickly," I pointed out. "And it wasn't their fault that we only used the first two sections. Besides," I then gave the real reason, "are you willing to put up with the bellyaching and complaining if we only reward First and Second? Because," I was joking, but I did not act like it, "I'll be happy to tell the boys that it was their Optio who objected."

Watching the range of emotions flash across his face was amusing, but as I suspected, it did not take him long to say, "No, no. You're right, Centurion."

Only then did I grin.

"Of course I am! Now," I slapped him on the shoulder, making him wince, "get them out of here while I deal with this mess."

When I reentered the *Quaestorium*, I saw that Philippos had appeared, seated on a stool next to Sempronius, while the unconscious wounded man was on the cot next to him. By this time, the hospital was empty of the seriously wounded from our battle against Sacrovir, meaning that the few cots that were occupied were from fevers or the inevitable injuries that are part of life under the standard. Standing behind the chief *medicus*, I had a good vantage point, enabling me to see that Sempronius' wound was serious, but when Philippos sat up after sniffing the puckered hole in his side, I relaxed slightly, knowing by his demeanor that there was no puncture to Sempronius' bowel.

"That's good," Philippos murmured, which caused Sempronius' eyes to flutter a bit before opening. "Ah, I see that you have rejoined us..." His voice trailed off, and I realized why.

"This man's name is Aulus Macula," I lied. "He was a customer at Venus' Passion when it was attacked." By this point, Philippos had spun about on his stool at the sound of my voice, and he listened with a raised eyebrow, giving me a hint of what was coming.

"Was a Legionary involved in his wounding?" I shook my head at his question, having decided to say as little as possible. "Then why would you bring a wounded citizen here to the

Legion hospital, Centurion?"

As unsurprised as I was, I still had not managed to think up an answer to this obvious question, although I opened my mouth to answer, but when nothing came, I shut it.

"My name isn't Aulus Macula, it's Marcus Sempronius." Sempronius' voice was barely audible, just above a hoarse whisper. "And I serve the Imperator. That's why the Centurion brought me here."

"Is this true?" Philippos asked me, and I nodded, though I was looking down at Sempronius, and it was him I asked, "Are you certain you want to do this, Sempronius?"

"No," he made a rasping sound that could have been a chuckle, "but I don't think I have any choice."

It was hard to argue this even if I was inclined to do so, but what mattered was that this convinced Philippos, if only for the time being.

Turning back to his charge, I heard the *medicus* murmur, "Well, I suppose I better keep you alive then, Marcus Sempronius. It would not do to have the Imperator angry at me."

"Oh, he'd be a lot angrier with me for dying," Sempronius joked, and while it was a weak jest, it still made us laugh.

I decided to take advantage of the levity to switch subjects.

"Do you have any idea how they found you?"

He grimaced, though it might have been because Philippos had just begun his probing of the wound looking for any foreign object in it.

"We were betrayed," he said flatly, which I thought was the obvious possibility, and I forced myself to be patient.

"Yes, but do you have any idea by who?" I asked.

I was expecting two or perhaps three possibilities; one of the other whores was at the top of my mental list, followed by Pandora, or perhaps Turbo, and the latter two I was prepared to reject, but nothing could have prepared me for what was coming.

"You were right," he said bitterly.

He did not say anything more than that, even after several heartbeats' amount of time passed.

I was about to demand that he explain when it hit me, and

I gasped, "You mean it was Hecate?"

He nodded, but just when he began to explain it to me, Philippos, who had been working the entire time, pushed his probe deeper into Sempronius' side, so what came out was a shriek of pain before he fainted, his mouth dropping open and head lolling to the side, unconscious.

"What did you do that for?" I demanded. "He was about to tell me something important!"

"Yes, yes," Philippos replied testily, clearly unimpressed. "I know, whatever it was is more important than his life, yes? Nor could it wait a few watches until he is out of danger either?"

I knew this was one I could not win, so I did not try and argue, though I still salvaged some of my pride, snapping, "Send someone to me the moment he's able to talk." He waved a hand that could have been agreement or a dismissal, not bothering to look away from Sempronius' wound. "I need to go report to the Primus Pilus," I said grumpily.

Chapter 11

Marcus Sempronius survived, though he was in the hospital for more than a week, during which there was a guard on the hospital at all times. Once he was able to talk, Sempronius told me what had transpired, which I in turn related to Neratius and Macer, the 20th's Primus Pilus having arranged that we meet without the Tribune present, which meant that we were at The Dancing Faun before it opened to regular custom.

"The whore Hecate had been approached by someone hired by Libo," I explained. "If I had to guess, I'd say it was Tullus." It took a moment for them to recall the name of the man I had confronted in the alley, which I had put in my written report, but once they nodded, I continued, "She was supposed to…distract Sempronius at the right time so that his guard was down when they showed up." I could see that I did not have to describe the form of the distraction by the smirk on Neratius' face. "Sempronius said that she began, but then apparently had a change of heart at the last moment and warned him they were coming. So," I finished, "he was at least partially prepared for them to come."

"How did she die?" Neratius asked, but I could tell it was more idle curiosity than from any real interest.

"She tried to stop the men attacking Sempronius." I shrugged, repeating the lie Sempronius had told me. "She thought they wouldn't cut a woman down."

This elicited a derisive snort from Neratius.

"Foolish whore," he said. "I hope whatever they were offering her was worth it."

"She told Sempronius that they told her they would buy her from Pandora and give her her freedom," I informed him, aware now that Macer was looking at me, though I did not want to glance over to try and interpret it, worried that I would see that he was not fooled.

I was telling only a partial truth, which, as Sempronius had told me, made for the best and most believable lies. While Hecate had been approached, and what they offered was what Hecate had told Sempronius in what would be the last few dozen heartbeats of her life, Sempronius had been her killer, not Libo's men. This I had strongly suspected the moment our eyes met the morning of the attack, but I had been wrong about the cause.

"I lost my head," Sempronius said simply. "I was so angry that she had betrayed me that..." he had held his hands out from his sides lying in his hospital cot, palms up in the gesture one makes when they are helpless, "...before I knew it, I killed her." He had broken down then, sobbing in a way that indicated to me that this was the first time he had forced himself to relive the moment and truly grieve. In a voice choked with emotion, he continued, "I *did* love her, Pullus. Oh, I know," he said before I could interject, "it was foolish to think that she could feel that way about me, but I did. I believed her when she said she felt the same way."

I did not feel completely false when I pointed out, "She clearly cared about you, Sempronius. She did warn you."

"I know." He began sobbing again. "And I have to live with that for the rest of my days."

I had left him with my head full of thoughts about what kind of life it must be for men like Marcus Sempronius, or Tiberius Dolabella, my father's long-time Nemesis who, in the end found his soul, and lost his life because of it.

Now, in The Dancing Faun, once it became clear that this matter of the death of a Cherusci whore had been put to bed, at least with Neratius, it was time to move on to other topics, namely the larger implications of what it meant to essentially protect Sempronius.

"Vitellius isn't happy about it," Neratius informed us. "In fact, he sent a dispatch to Rome to Praetorian Prefect Sejanus..." He was clearly unsurprised by my alarm, which Macer shared, but Neratius held up a hand, "...which didn't make it to the first mile marker outside Ubiorum before it was...lost."

My initial reaction was to look over at Macer again, but he was clearly as shocked and unsettled as I was.

"That seems like a risky thing to do, Neratius," Macer commented mildly, but I knew him far too well not to hear the note of alarm in his tone.

"It is, a bit," Neratius admitted. "And I certainly won't do it again, but it bought a couple of months without Sejanus poking his nose into our Legions, Marcus. Besides, it's not all that uncommon for a dispatch rider to disappear out here on the frontier." He saw Macer stiffen, and added hurriedly, "No, nothing happened to a dispatch rider. We just threw the dispatch in the Rhenus instead of handing it off."

It could not be argued that, especially here on the Rhenus, the men who carried messages between places like Ubiorum and Rome, for example, sometimes vanished, or were robbed and their messages destroyed, and I was forced to silently salute the Primus Pilus for coming up with this solution, as temporary as it may have been.

"There haven't been any mentions of a man fitting Libo's description making its way into my morning report," Neratius commented, glancing at Macer, who shook his head. "So it sounds like he took your…suggestion, Pullus."

This was good news, but it led to the next question.

"And?" Neratius asked me. "When's this Sempronius bastard departing our camp so that we don't have to keep men outside the hospital with their thumbs up waiting for an attack that will never come? Our camp," he gave me a severe look, "isn't a brothel, Pullus."

Choosing to ignore the jibe, I was happy to answer, "Philippos said he's going to be ready to leave by market day, which is three days from now."

I thought Neratius would be happy with this news, but I was mistaken.

"I know when our market days are," he said acidly. "So that means we have to protect this scum for three more days, but after that?" He pointed a stubby finger at me, something I detest. "I don't want to see that bastard's face anywhere near our Legions."

For a brief moment, I thought about mentioning the small

trove of scrolls, which Sempronius had begged me to retrieve for him from the hiding place at the brothel, and how, if Tiberius' spy showed up waving one of them, Primus Pilus Neratius would be dancing to any tune that Sempronius chose. Fortunately, that stayed behind my teeth.

Instead, I said simply, "I will relay the message, Primus Pilus Neratius."

As expected, Sempronius left Ubiorum, using one of his precious scrolls I had retrieved for him to get a spot on one of the military barges that make the slow but safe upstream passage, yet when I asked if he was going to debark at Mogontiacum, or go further upstream, he was evasive.

"It's not that I don't trust you, Pullus," he assured me. "It's just that I don't know yet. Much will depend on what the situation is there."

This was understandable, and for perhaps the hundredth time, I wondered what the life of a man like Sempronius was like and whether he ever experienced any real joy that was not marred by the need to constantly look over his shoulder. He was pale, but I ascribed that to the wound, which thankfully, for his sake, had been clean and was healing well, but I also noticed that he had been quite subdued, which I had initially put down to the melancholy that sometimes afflicts seriously wounded men, but now I was not so certain that was the cause.

Consequently, I tried to sound as if I was joking when I said, "Don't take this poorly, but if I never see you again, I won't shed a tear."

He did chuckle, but it was not for very long, his demeanor turning grim.

"I understand and I wish I could make that promise, Pullus. But," he shook his head, "I'm afraid I can't. There's just too much happening, and it seems as if with every passing day, the Imperator withdraws a little more and trusts his advisors less, with the exception of that...*minion* Sejanus."

"Well, try your best," I believe I muttered, then after we clasped arms, I watched him descend the plank down into the barge, where he was the only passenger among stacks of bags of grain and crates, all part of the lifeblood that makes Rome the most powerful nation in the known world.

I did not wait to see them push off, walking back up the slope from the wharf that is now an extension of the camp and is adjacent to the commercial wharf but separated by a wall. By the time I was back to my quarters, I had already shifted my mind to what was coming next, and that was my turn at training the *Tirones*…and my brother.

I freely confess that I was quite nervous when the day arrived where Clepsina informed me that the *Tirones* had finished their third week of training, and were ready to begin learning how not to stab themselves, always the first obstacle in turning men from bumbling civilians into trained Legionaries. Even if I was not faced with the prospect of training my half-brother, I would have been a bit nervous, for the simple reason that, while I had taken my father's place as the weapons instructor for the entire Legion, my job had been to help each Century's instructors, spar with the men of the First Cohort, and finally, initiate every new *Tirone* into the 1st, a custom that had begun in every Legion with a Pullus in the ranks with the Prefect. However, I had never been responsible for introducing a raw civilian into our world and take him through the steps that have been part of the training for Rome's Legions for only the gods know how long. While I understood that much had changed with the Augustan reforms by reading the Prefect's account of his time as a *Tirone* with Divus Julius and the newly formed 10th Legion sixty years earlier, the basic form was the same. The training is broken down in increments of a week, and when men are introduced to the *rudis*, it will be two weeks before they begin sparring with each other, while the previous two weeks are spent on learning their forms, the first spent facing the wooden stakes that have to be replaced every year, which are just outside the camp walls. This would be where I met the thirty-six *Tirones*; it had been thirty-seven, but one of the men that Volcacius had brought back with him had vanished in the night, which still happens with some regularity. On the day Clepsina turned the *Tirones* over, I met with him in his quarters beforehand, and unsurprisingly, he was prepared with the information I would need.

Handing me a wax tablet, he began, "These are the names

of the men who I think are going to do very well with your part of the training."

I should have been listening more carefully, or at least paid attention to the expression on his face, but I realized I had made an assumption when I opened the tablet, expecting to see one name at the top of the list, and it was not. Then, after I scanned the two dozen names and did not see the name Titus Corbulo, I looked up at Clepsina, but he was holding out a second tablet.

"These are the men who will need some help," he said quietly. "They're weaker than they should be, and while Dolabella and I gave them strengthening exercises and they've gotten better, they still need work."

I would have been astounded if Corbulo's name had been on this second list, and he was not, but then I quickly added up the names on both tablets, my heart sinking when I saw that it only added up to thirty-five names.

"Why isn't Corbulo on either of these lists?"

"I've been dreading this," Clepsina confessed. "And I honestly don't know where to begin, Gnaeus."

"Start at the beginning," I snapped, then immediately apologized before amending, "Just tell me what I need to know."

"It's obviously not his strength," my fellow Centurion began. "And it's not that he's unwilling, or that he doesn't follow orders. He's just…wild, Gnaeus." He shrugged. "His temper is the worst I've ever seen, but most of the time when he gets angry, it's at himself. That's the only thing that's saved him from a flogging, because neither Postumus nor I can find anything in the regulations that says a man who hits himself should be punished, unless he does it to escape duty. And," he shrugged, "he's never put himself on the list, and is always standing in formation every morning."

By the time he was through, providing examples of what he was talking about, I was as nonplussed as Clepsina, yet at the same time, there was a familiarity to what I was hearing, because what very few people in my life knew was that, especially when I was younger and around Corbulo's age, a good deal of my rage was at myself, but because of my status as a wealthy Equestrian youth, I did not have to turn it on myself; as much as it shames me to say now, the way I viewed matters back then was that there were slaves for that, and they bore the brunt of that misdirected rage. This was when the beginning of a deeper understanding blossomed in my mind, and I resolved to myself that I would speak to Corbulo and ask him if my suspicion was correct.

Turning my mind to practical matters, I asked Clepsina bluntly, "Are you saying that he's not ready to move forward in training?"

"No," he replied immediately, and without hesitation. "He's more than ready in a physical sense and he knows as much as the others. But, you know how it is, Gnaeus. You give a *Tirone* a *rudis* and that's when he starts becoming dangerous. I just wanted you to be aware about Corbulo."

This was sobering, and concerning, but I was sincere when I thanked him, though I had no idea how I would approach the issue with Corbulo. As we were walking out of the camp, Clepsina did think to warn me about something.

"Corbulo has a bruise on his cheek," he informed me, though it took a moment for me to make the connection between this seemingly inconsequential fact, given how *Tirones* are always sporting bruises on some part of their bodies, and our conversation, but when it hit me, my stride faltered.

"*Gerrae*! Are you saying he hit himself in the face hard enough to leave a bruise?"

Clepsina nodded, and I resumed walking, trying to think of the power and resolve it would take to hit oneself hard enough in the face to leave a bruise, and I concluded that the only way he could have done it was that he had temporarily lost his head because of his anger at himself.

We exited the camp, making the right turn that took us to the stakes, where we saw the thirty-six *Tirones* who at least looked the part of Legionaries, although their bright red tunics betrayed their status as new recruits, standing in formation, their *rudii* held point down in their right hands as they stood at *intente*. Both Dolabella and Closus were standing there, turfcutter handles in hand, but it was Macer's Optio who acted as the senior officer, rendering us a salute, whereupon

Dolabella began the ritual of turning over command.

"Primus Pilus Posterior Clepsina, all *Tirones* are present and ready for training!"

Clepsina, his face set in the kind of mask that is expected of a Centurion, returned the salute.

"Very good, Optio Dolabella." Executing a half-turn to face me, Clepsina barked, "Primus Hastatus Prior Pullus, I transfer command of these *Tirones* to you for the next part of their training." Since he is senior, I rendered a salute, which he returned. Then, for the first time since our arrival, Clepsina acknowledged the presence of the *Tirones* by looking at them, and I was in the perfect spot to see the smile he gave them, and to learn something when he said, "I know that I told you to make a sacrifice to your household gods before today. For those of you who thought I was joking…" He shook his head as if he was sad, "…then pray to them for mercy now, because I've seen what Centurion Pullus can do, and he's not going to have any on you."

It was only after he pivoted in preparation to march away from us with Dolabella that he winked at me, but I did not acknowledge it, playing my own part. I did not do anything for a lengthy span of time, listening to their footsteps receding until I could not hear them before I reacted. I had made a point not to look at Corbulo, despite the fact that even without his bruised face, he was impossible to miss even being in the last rank, standing a head taller than his next tallest comrade. Without any warning, I was struck by the thought that this must have been what it was like for my father's first Centurion, Gnaeus Corvinus, the Quartus Pilus Prior of the 8th Legion, seeing a huge *Tirone* in my father, although it would have been especially difficult for Corvinus since he was my grandfather's best friend and fellow Centurion, replacing Gaius Porcinianus Pullus as Pilus Prior after he lost his leg because of the treachery of another Centurion, and had known my father since he was a child. Otherwise, aside from Corbulo, the *Tirones* in front of me were nondescript, appearing no better or worse than any randomly drawn group of thirty-five men from any Cohort in the Legion. This was when I was reminded of something, and whereas I had been struggling with how to begin, this served to be a perfect opening.

I broke the silence by beginning, "Normally, you bastards would be heading for one of the third line Cohorts first, but as I'm sure that Centurion Clepsina told you, there are…circumstances that mean that we don't have that luxury, and you men were chosen because it was felt that you might have what it takes to march with us in the First Cohort." I paused long enough for there to be a reaction, and there was one, though it was muted and consisted of a slight nod of the head, or a twitching of the corner of a lip that indicated they wanted to smile in agreement. I did not see Corbulo's reaction because I was pointedly avoiding his part of the formation. I resumed with a shake of my head, "I don't know who made that decision, but based on what I'm looking at right now, either they suffered from temporary blindness, or some *numen* cast a spell on him that made him see something that's not there, *because none of you* cunni *look fit to serve in the fucking city watch!*"

Naturally, I did not betray it, but I was quite pleased by the reaction to my bellowed last words, and while I did not look at him directly, choosing to look at the man in the rank ahead of him, I saw the expression of rage on Corbulo's face, clearly taking the insult more personally than the others.

Dropping back to my original tone and volume, I said, "But I'm willing to accept that I might be wrong. Maybe you *do* have what it takes to march with us, the *First* Cohort of the *1st* Legion!" I emphasized those words for a reason, telling them why with my next breath. "I want you to think about this and heed my words. We are the First Cohort, of the 1st Legion, Rome's first, and best, Legion. Why do you think we're stationed here on the Rhenus? Yes, Arminius is dead, but who knows if there's another Arminius out there?" I pointed east, across the Rhenus. "And that's just the Cherusci. There are more than twenty tribes who are less than a week's march from here, and believe me when I tell you this. They hate Rome." I paused again to scan the faces, and for the first time, I looked directly at Corbulo, pleased to see there was no sign of bravado there, nor with any of his comrades, not anymore. Satisfied, I walked over and grabbed a *rudis* from one of the men in the front rank before resuming my spot. Lifting it up above my head so that the wooden blade was parallel to the ground and across my body so that everyone in the formation had a good view, I turned my wrist so that they could see my fingers and thumb, and I began, "The first thing you're going to learn today is how every man in the 1ˢᵗ Legion holds their *gladius*. We call it the Vinician Grip. Does anyone know why?" My hope was fulfilled when, albeit with hesitation and after glancing around at his comrades, Titus Corbulo tentatively raised his hand. "Yes, Corbulo?"

I very briefly thought of pretending I did not know his name since I had not placed any of the names to faces for the rest of them, but immediately realized that the idea that the news of our connection was not common knowledge by now was next to impossible.

"It was taught to Prefect Pullus, your…grandfather?"

"Great-grandfather," I corrected, but said nothing else, specifically that it was his great-grandfather as well, noting how he grimaced in what I assumed was embarrassment, which indicated that he might have made the connection just then.

"Ah, yes, great-grandfather," he continued. "It was his Optio Vincius…" I did not correct his mispronunciation, deeming it close enough, "…who taught it to him when he was a *Tirone* in the 10ᵗʰ Legion."

"Yes," I nodded, then added, "very good, Corbulo. Who taught you about this?" I asked, without thinking.

"My fat…" he stopped suddenly, and I could have bitten my tongue off for putting him in this position, but then he finished, "…Manius Corbulo told me about it. He was under the standard, and he served with your father, Centurion."

"That's right, I forgot about that," I lied, lamely, but the others did not seem to mark it as unusual, and I reminded myself to send Alex out to learn what Corbulo's comrades knew about my half-brother. Deciding the history lesson was over, I moved to the practical advantages by demonstrating the grip. "As you can see, by wrapping my fingers over my thumb…"

Thus, my role in making these men worthy of marching in my Cohort began.

By the end of the first week, I had witnessed enough of Titus Corbulo to know that he posed as much of a danger to himself as he did to anyone who faced him.

"I've never seen anyone who's as hard on himself as he is," I told Bronwen one night as we lay in bed. Her belly was swelling nicely, and we were getting close to the time when the baby would begin moving, an event that Titus was awaiting with growing excitement since he had been too young to remember Giulia's birth. "He's very good," I acknowledged, trying, unsuccessfully as I would learn, to hide my pride, "but he *is* young and raw, so he's bound to make mistakes. But when he does, he beats himself up about it, sometimes literally."

In fact, just that day, I had been forced to admonish him about his habit of striking his thigh after I corrected him about his recovery on a thrust. I normally would not have bothered, but he had begun limping because of it, and since it was the time of year where we wore *bracae* every day, I had ordered him to drop them, gasping despite myself at the horrific bruises that provided the proof that this was not an isolated incident.

"How long have you been doing this?" I gasped, momentarily forgetting that I was his Centurion.

"For a while," he admitted. "Manius Corbulo taught me." I did not understand why he would do such a thing, but Corbulo explained, "He said that as strong as I am, when I lose my head because I'm angry, I'd end up killing someone. As long as it was a slave or a bandit or something like that," he shrugged, "then I wouldn't be executed. But he was worried that one day I'd lose my head with the wrong man, so he told me that if I needed to hit something, it was better that I hit me."

I was about to ask why Corbulo did not have him strike an inanimate object, but I stopped myself as I realized that I already knew why.

"And hitting something like a tree or a wall doesn't help," I murmured to myself, momentarily forgetting that Corbulo was standing there, "because it doesn't feel pain."

"How did you know that?" Corbulo gasped.

"Never mind that," I snapped, angry at myself that I had

slipped. Pointing down to his thigh, I ordered him to pull his *bracae* up, and as he did, I said, "You're going to be inspected every morning by Optio Closus or myself. And those bruises better be fading and not have any new ones added. Do you understand?"

"Y-yes sir," Corbulo answered. "I understand and will obey."

Without thinking, I said in just above a whisper, "We'll talk about this more later, once you're through your training."

I hoped that this would be enough, but as I was lying with Bronwen that night, I was not sure that it would be.

"I wonder what it is about us that we all seem to be cursed like this?" I mused aloud, though I felt certain that Bronwen had fallen asleep by this time, being in that stage of her pregnancy where she slept more than normal.

"It must have something to do with your size," she said drowsily. "Beyond that, I do not know, my love."

"There has to be something more to it," I insisted, staring up at the ceiling as I tried to think about it. "The Prefect? I understand; his father always blamed him for killing his mother in childbirth, and hated his son for that. Lucius was a drunken failure as a farmer. And," even as I formed the words, I thought of my daughter Giulia, and felt the wave of revulsion, "there was…what he did with the Prefect's sisters."

"I wept when I read about that," Bronwen said, but I was not fooled, knowing she was fishing for praise along with her agreement.

"Yes, your reading has improved a great deal," I replied, using a teasing tone that earned me a punch on the arm.

She was quite proud of her ability to read now, and Alex, her primary tutor, had been suitably impressed, although he had reservations about it.

"Thank the gods Algaia hasn't expressed the slightest interest in learning." He laughed. "That way, I don't have to worry about her learning something she can use against me. You, on the other hand," he had grinned broadly at me, "are a plucked and cooked goose."

Despite the levity, my wife had spoken truly; the circumstances of the Prefect's birth and childhood was an easily identified cause for the simmering rage inside him. However, my father had grown up under much different circumstances, yet had he not killed an adult male when he was only twelve, even if he was a dwarf? Naturally, I was acutely aware of my own issues with my temper, but my childhood was more like my father's in the sense of the kind of comfort that came from the fortune that had been amassed by the Prefect. In fact, I had long before determined that, despite my Equestrian status and the affectation that my father was quite wealthy, the fortune of my real family dwarfed that of Quintus Volusenus. Corbulo's childhood had clearly played a major role in his development into this huge youth with a temper issue, but none of the other Pullus men had ever directed that rage at themselves, at least to the extent that he did.

"It must have something to do with happened to his real mother and her husband," I mused, but this time, my comment was met by the sound of soft, gentle snoring, and I decided that I was doing all that I could for the moment. Soon, he would begin sparring with his comrades, and that would be the first real test.

The first day of sparring also marked the first day where we woke to a thin dusting of snow, the men's breath making little clouds as we marched out of the camp. Despite my pleas, Macer refused to honor my request that the only men witnessing these bouts be the *Tirones*, the four officers, and the small group of *medici* and slaves who were always present whenever men try to bash each other senseless, and, of course, the Primus Pilus. Dolabella and Closus had done a good job of keeping track of the various disputes and feuds among *Tirones* that are part of the first weeks of training so that we would pit these men against each other early on when they were not better trained and more able to inflict real damage on each other, yet another thing I had not experienced as a *Tirone* myself, although when I was in the Fourth, I had learned quickly enough the inevitability of such things when men are thrown together in close quarters. What made this a bit different was that everyone involved at this point was a fellow *Tirone*; we were still two more weeks away before these men would be assigned to a Century in the First Cohort, where a whole new process of establishing a hierarchy would begin. The new men would be judged all over again, this time by their comrades; the sharp operators in a section would be evaluating the possibility of gulling one of the new "chickens" as they are called, while other men would get offended by something a new man said or did, usually for no reason other than the veteran hated change. Part of the ritual was when the *Tirones* sparred with their veteran comrades for the first time, but since this time we had so many *Tirones*, and given the time of year, we had the luxury of letting the *Tiros* learn and make mistakes on each other. I had wanted to do this in private, but Macer was having none of it.

"The boys deserve some fun," he had said the night before when I made my final plea in his quarters. "This will be a good way for them to let loose, have some fun wagering, and your *Tiros* can get a taste of their new life." I knew by the tone of voice he was using that this was not an argument I could win, but Macer proved that he was nobody's fool when he asked quietly, "This isn't really about any other *Tirone* besides Corbulo, is it?"

There was no point in denying it, so I did not try.

"No," I admitted. "I just don't know how much control he's got himself under, and I'm worried that, depending on what happens, that he might lose his head, and if he does it in front of so many witnesses?"

I did not think I needed to expand, so I just shook my head, but again, Macer was aware there was more going on.

"Or are you worried that he's going to beat his fellow *Tirones* so easily that he's going to make himself a target of someone? Say," he pretended to think, "someone like Glabius?"

Once again, Macer had touched the needle to the boil. Quintus Glabius was Gratianus' Optio, and prior to my promotion to the First Cohort, he had been considered the best man with a *gladius* in the First Cohort, which in his mind meant the entire Legion. And, I will acknowledge, Glabius is *very* good. He is nowhere near my size, but he is extremely fast, perhaps the quickest man I have ever seen, yet he is also quite cerebral in his approach, watching his opponent and seemingly never forgetting a move that his foe makes, tucking something away for use later. Finally, he is patient, and I freely admit I underestimated him the first time we sparred, where Glabius put me in difficulty more than once. Perhaps the only thing we ever agreed on was when Macer stepped in and stopped our first bout, which Glabius was quick to claim was because the Primus Pilus did not want his friend and the newest Centurion in the First Cohort to be humiliated, especially given my own reputation, although he only said this after a few cups of wine and in the privacy of The Pride of Bacchus, the *taverna* that caters to the First Cohort. I said then, and say now, this was nothing but a load of *cac* hauled by a wagon requiring twenty oxen to pull; yes, he had me off-balance, but I was never really in any danger of being struck a killing blow, and I had taken his measure. In fact, I was in the process of planning out my final attack that would give me victory when Macer intervened, and as proof, I would simply point to the results of the second bout we had four days later, which I won in overwhelming fashion, and by common consent, it did not take to a count of one hundred before he was flat on his back, with me standing over him, a foot on either side of his body. This did not settle anything for Glabius, and he challenged me to a rematch, which by custom in the 1st Legion is a right as sacrosanct as if it has been inscribed on a bronze tablet; this match he did not make past a count of fifty, yet rather than gloat about it, I approached the Optio in private, complimenting his skills and offering to work with him. He rebuffed this so vehemently, I could have written him up on charges of insolence to a superior officer.

"The only reason you beat me is because of your size." He had almost shouted this. "If you didn't have that and your strength, I would have chopped you up!"

"But I *do* have my size and strength," I countered, mildly enough, although I felt a stirring of anger. "And," I pointed out, "you're likely to face a German who's closer to my size than he is to yours. Don't you want to know how to beat him?"

"I'd rather feed the crows than ask for your help!"

I gave up then, but it did not take much imagination to think that Glabius would be salivating at the idea of revenge; if he could not get it against me, then someone who everyone knew was my half-brother and my size and strength would do very well indeed.

"You worry too much," was how Macer had put it. "Besides," he added, "just because Glabius hates you, it doesn't necessarily mean he'll hate Corbulo."

This would be one of the few times I had something to hold over Marcus Macer's head in the near future.

By the time it became Corbulo's turn, the atmosphere among the watching men had gone from spirited to raucous, and I was sure that men had sneaked wine, but because of the chill, they were all wearing their *sagum*, making it next to impossible to catch them. For their part, after an initial spell of nerves, which included one of the *Tirones* dropping his *gladius* during his bout, earning him roars of mocking laughter from the veterans, the new men got into the spirit of things themselves. Very quickly, I decided to allow the onlookers to render the decision about the winner of each bout, realizing that what I was looking for was overall technique and not necessarily who landed the killing blow, and with the men in the mood they were in, it would have been an impossible task trying to explain it. One of the *Tirones*, slightly older at twenty-one, named Tiberius Appuleius, who I had observed had a fair amount of aptitude and I judged to be one of the top five *Tirones*, defeated his opponent, a strong boy from a farm down near Tolbiacum named Quintus Philus, in rather spectacular fashion that earned him a rousing cheer from the veterans, which he answered by acting as if he was a victorious gladiator, raising his arms with his wicker shield and *rudis*, his head tilted upward as if he was looking up into the seats of an arena as he made a slow rotation. Naturally, the spectators loved this, although there were a fair number of good-natured jeers and taunts thrown at him, but even with the wicker faceguard, I could see Appuleius grinning broadly. What mattered more was how he thrust the *rudis* into the hardpacked dirt to offer his hand to Philus, who took it and climbed to his feet, then as custom dictated, the pair clasped arms before walking back to the group of combatants, where they were met by their comrades, who alternately congratulated and commiserated with the two men, while I bellowed the names of the next pair, who had been prepared by Closus and Dolabella, helping them get on their padded sleeves and tying the wicker faceguard.

"Are you saving Corbulo for last for a reason?"

I had been so busy watching the next pair being checked over by the Optios I did not notice Alex approaching, although he had come with a cup of water, which I snatched and downed, only then realizing how thirsty I was.

Not until I finished draining the cup did I answer curtly, "Yes."

"Do you have something specific in mind, or are you just trying to delay it until the last possible moment?"

This earned a glare from me, but Alex was not cowed, and my irritation evaporated so that, with a grin, I asked, "What do you think?"

"I think you answered the question without answering the question." He laughed, and I joined him, because he was right.

I was spared from being forced to articulate why I had been holding Corbulo back by Closus raising his turfcutter handle, signaling the next two men had been checked and were ready. In answer to my nod, Closus gave them both a shove in the back, sending them into the center of the square, which unleashed a fresh spate of wagering by the spectating veterans.

"I'll take the one on the right, Galens! He at least is holding the right end of his *rudis*!"

"*Gerrae*! I've always known your wits were addled ever since you got bashed on the head at the Wall, Poplicola! Look at his opponent! He moves like a cat, light on his feet! Anyone can see it! But if you want to lose your money, that's your business!"

"Bah! Your boy will *run* like a cat; that's the only thing he'll do!"

As diverting as it was listening to this exchange between this pair of veterans standing with their comrades in the First Century, I had my own business to conduct, namely tugging on the padded sleeves from each man, who had proven they were paying attention because they both lifted their arms to enable me to do so, then grab the wicker faceguards, tugging on those as well. There was a slight delay because one of them needed to be tightened a bit more securely before my final act of checking that their chin thongs were securely tied. Satisfied, I pointed them to their respective sides of the square, then once they were in position, I put the bone whistle between my teeth, the onlookers now in full voice, while I let the tension build a bit before I filled my lungs, then gave a sharp blast of sound.

By this time, about ten pairs into the sparring, the *Tirones* still waiting to go had had the opportunity to see which strategy worked better than another, which meant in this case that neither of them went rushing at their opponent, both of them choosing to approach cautiously, circling each other as they searched for an opportunity.

Not surprisingly, this was not a popular approach for the veterans, and I heard Poplicola's voice, barely discernible over the noise, hooting, "He's a cat all right, Galens! Look at him! He's terrified…"

I never asked the *Tiro*, the son of a tanner named Sextus Diadematus, whether he heard this, but it certainly seemed as if he did because in the eyeblink after Poplicola shouted this, he charged his opponent, Decimus Caprarius, moving with a speed that he had never shown in training before, catching Caprarius by surprise. Caprarius was a heartbeat slow in bringing his shield into position, and if I was judging it strictly, the bout would have been over right then, but I refused to do that for the simple reason that this was about training these men and not giving their future comrades the opportunity for entertainment and making money off of each other. Therefore, I was not a bit surprised when I heard Galens howling a protest that Diadematus had scored a killing blow, which he had, but the bout was barely thirty heartbeats old when he had done it. Caprarius survived the initial onslaught, barely, then got his feet under him and began making offensive moves of his own, and by the time I finally blew the whistle, both contestants were exhausted, nor was there much protest from the spectators when I declared it a draw, with the exception of Galens, of course.

Finally, there were only two men left, and there was an air

of anticipation that had been building with every bout as the pair of combatants walked into the middle of the square and neither of them were Corbulo. I had thought long and hard about his opponent, finally settling on the *Tiro* who had impressed me the most outside of Corbulo, and who was the consensus choice of both Optios, and Clepsina, although my fellow Centurion did not participate in the weapons training all that much. This was how I knew it was not my bias showing when it came to Corbulo, but as far as who would have been ranked second best, there was no universal agreement. In fact, each of the officers favored different men; Dolabella, for example, felt strongly that Caprarius was the *Tiro* who was second only to Corbulo, whereas Closus was equally adamant that Appius Bestia was the only logical choice. The man I had chosen to face Corbulo, Lucius Scaurus, was nowhere near the second best man on the other three's list, and when they pressed me to explain why, I could not do so in a manner that made any sense. I just felt strongly that he was the one *Tirone* who could not only acquit himself well against Corbulo, but might prevail. The truth is that, if I had intervened when I should have, Scaurus would have, but since I did not, the men of the First Cohort who were watching were given a spectacle that they would be talking about for a couple weeks.

"What were you thinking, Gnaeus? That's what I want to know. No," Macer held up a hand, "that's what I *need* to know." Before I could reply, he muttered, "Thank the gods our new Camp Prefect is someone who has a soft spot for you. Still, he wants a report."

Our conversation, held the night of the sparring, took place in his quarters, and it was one I had not been looking forward to, even as I knew that it was inevitable.

"The good news is that Scaurus will be fine," I offered, knowing how lame it was to my own ears. "So, I *did* stop it before he was badly hurt."

"It should have been stopped the instant that Corbulo lost his head," Macer snapped. This was true, and I did not bother trying to deny it, but my Primus Pilus was not through. "And," he pointed directly at me, "you of all people know the signs better than anyone alive." Suddenly, he sat back, his expression changing, but it was his musing tone that made my stomach clench. "Now that I think about it, it's almost as if you wanted to see just how far he would go." The look he gave me then was cold, piercing, and without a hint of friendliness in it. "Was this your way of trying to determine if he was a true Pullus? You needed to see if he has that…beast as you call it, inside him?"

Given the audience for whom this is intended, there is nothing to be gained for me by lying, but the gods know that what I am saying now, and said then, is the truth.

"No," I replied, and I had to swallow twice before I could get the rest of it out, "at least not until you said it right now. But now that you've said it…" I could not finish, hoping my helpless gesture served as my admission.

"I thought as much," Macer said, then fell silent, and I did not feel comfortable speaking up. I realized that I was holding my breath when he broke it by saying, "That's all we'll say about it other than this." With the same, cold expression, he bit off the words, "That. Cannot. Happen. Again. Do you understand, Primus Hastatus Prior Pullus?"

As straightforward as it seemed, I was actually somewhat confused; was he saying that Corbulo could not lose his head again? Or was he saying that if he did, I had to act immediately? Or was he saying that, no matter how it happened, he would be holding me responsible, even if Corbulo did not end up in my Century?

That mystery was solved when Macer added, "But given that you're the only man in the Legion who could possibly handle him if he loses control like that, he's in your Century, and I know I don't have to worry about you treating him differently because he's your brother."

Certainly not, now that you brought it up, I thought sourly, but I think I was still reeling a bit so I did not say anything, just nodded dumbly.

It was not a case where I felt like I could blame Macer for how he felt, and it was certainly true that, whatever my subconscious mind was trying to do regarding Corbulo, his demonstration that day would leave an impression that lasted with the First Cohort. The bout had begun routinely, with Corbulo rushing straight at Scaurus while pulling his wicker shield up against his shoulder in the sign that he intended to knock his opponent flat, and judging by the manner in which Scaurus reacted, which is to say he did not, at all, just standing there not moving a muscle, it seemed as if Corbulo had caught Scaurus flat-footed and so surprised, he was unable to move. Perhaps I blinked, though I do not believe I did so, but even after talking about it with Closus, Dolabella, and Clepsina, none of us could really describe what took place other than to say that instead of having a massive collision, Corbulo went charging through the spot where Scaurus had been, while Scaurus seemed to magically appear on Corbulo's weak side, putting him at a massive advantage. To his credit, Scaurus did not hesitate, but there was a reason beside his size, strength, and his kinship to me that I considered Titus Corbulo to be the most advanced of the *Tirones*, because he reacted instinctively and instantly by swinging his *rudis* up behind his body in a sweeping move that, as awkward as it must have been to execute, struck the wooden blade of Scaurus' *rudis* with the kind of sharp cracking sound we had only heard a couple of times that morning, just as Scaurus executed his thrust that would have struck Corbulo on his unprotected side.

More than the sound was the manner in which Scaurus' entire body pivoted to his left from the force of his right arm being jerked across his body from the recoil of Corbulo's *rudis* striking his, though he recovered himself quickly and squared his feet, his shield in the proper orientation and elbow locked against his hip. He did so just in time, because despite his bigger size, Corbulo moved about as quickly as the smaller Scaurus, but what mattered was that his thrust was met by Scaurus' shield. The men of the First Cohort were in full voice, this being the last bout of the day, and it was shaping up to be better than expected given that the wagering was prohibitively in favor of Corbulo. Although it was difficult to read either man's expression because of their faceguards, I felt certain that Corbulo was growing frustrated, because starting with Scaurus' block of his first thrust, the smaller *Tiro* put absolutely no effort into trying to stand toe to toe with his larger foe. More than that, I noticed Scaurus doing something that I had never seen before, and that was actually using the force Corbulo was capable of putting into his thrusts to keep a separation between them.

"Is Scaurus hopping backwards whenever Corbulo attacks?"

I was surprised by this question, unaware that Closus had gotten close to me because I was watching so intently, but I shook my head.

"No, he's just using the force of Corbulo's thrusts to his advantage," I explained, though my eyes never left the pair. Seeing it was about to happen again, I hissed, "Watch!"

And, just as he had more than a half-dozen times before, rather than try and maintain his position by absorbing the thrust with his shield, Scaurus was relaxing his body and allowing himself to be knocked backward. It was not much, certainly, but Scaurus was saving energy by doing this, whereas we could hear Corbulo beginning to breathe more deeply, while shaking his head every couple of heartbeats, telling us that he was sweating heavily despite the cold. More informatively, I could hear Corbulo muttering under his breath as he relentlessly maneuvered Scaurus around the square, while the smaller *Tiro* relied on counterattacks, though not answering every time when Corbulo attacked, but it was clear that Corbulo was by far more aggressive. Under other circumstances, I would have warned Scaurus that this kind of strategy was not acceptable for a *Tirone,* but this was a time when I was essentially a prisoner of my own insecurities and concerns. It was common knowledge that Corbulo and I were related by blood, yet while I did not think that anyone would fault me for warning Scaurus and essentially require him to spar more like Corbulo, there was enough doubt in my mind that I did not open my mouth.

Matters were not helped when, after Scaurus once more absorbed a series of thrusts from Corbulo by seemingly floating backward before dancing nimbly out of danger, Corbulo turned to me and demanded, "Centurion, aren't you going to do anything about what that bastard is doing? He won't stand and fight!"

This was met by a chorus of jeers, which I could see

confused Corbulo, who was too inexperienced to understand that it was not that the watching veterans disagreed, because I had heard their calls to Scaurus to stand and fight just like Corbulo was protesting, but that a *Tirone* has no business complaining about anything.

"Do you think your enemy is going to always stand toe to toe with you and fight, Corbulo?" I snapped. "If what you're doing isn't working, then change what you're doing!"

I would have cause to regret my words, and I missed the first warning sign until it was too late. Honestly, when I heard the growling sound, I thought I was imagining it, but then Corbulo was moving again, shuffling into a position where, up to this point, Scaurus had always performed a dancing sidestep to get him more into the center of the square and away from the barrier formed by the watching men. Perhaps because of the exchange between Corbulo and me he decided to stand this time and go on his own offensive, although it was the same thing where he let Corbulo unleash his own attack first. Even in the moment, when Corbulo launched a first position thrust, it seemed as if his fatigue had finally caught up with him, because it was not with nearly the speed and power he had been exhibiting before, but that was not what was happening, and Scaurus was as fooled as I was. What followed took less than a full heartbeat to take place, as in the fraction of an eyeblink of time between Corbulo's thrust and Scaurus, believing that his opponent was finally fatigued, responding by putting everything into his own counterattack, Corbulo dropped his shield. By that, I do not mean he lowered it; I mean that he completely let go of it whereupon it dropped to the ground, leaving his left hand free to grab Scaurus' *rudis* while twisting his torso with enough force that the blunted point not only did not strike his *segmentata*, but the momentum of his upper body moving in the same direction as Scaurus' thrust, along with the viciously powerful jerk of his left hand yanked the *rudis* from Scaurus' grasp, which Corbulo discarded behind him in the same motion.

Corbulo could have conceivably picked his shield up, but instead, he kicked it aside and out of his path, while Scaurus, now armed with only his shield, instantly began shuffling backward, away from Corbulo, who was now with only his *rudis*. The noise that had been almost overwhelming had not vanished, but it had dissipated as men stopped shouting and began talking with each other, no doubt asking their comrades if they had seen anything like this before. To his credit, Scaurus did not panic, and in fact did what he had been trained to do, although I realized at this moment that we spent perhaps a third of a watch out of one day discussing what to do when a Legionary was reduced to just a shield, which was to use it as an offensive weapon. Unfortunately, that was exactly what Corbulo wanted Scaurus to do, but when he then tossed his *rudis* aside as he closed with Scaurus, I was convinced that he had lost his wits. When Scaurus dropped his hips just before he shot his left hand forward with a shield punch that Corbulo made no attempt to dodge, instead absorbing the entire force of the blow, this action informed all of the onlookers why he had discarded the *rudis,* because when Scaurus tried to recover his shield, he instead found the shield yanked out of his hand, which Corbulo tossed over his shoulder with seemingly no more effort than if he was discarding a plate.

So entranced was I that it was not until the last possible instant that I realized the wicker shield was spinning right for me with enough force that it would have likely injured me, and I threw myself out of its path with no time to spare, though I managed to keep my feet. Because of that distraction, when I returned my attention to Corbulo and Scaurus, my brother had already closed the space of perhaps the pace that had been between them, but I was in time to see Corbulo's left hand shoot into the space under Scaurus' wicker faceguard, his fingers wrapping around Scaurus' throat, and I heard someone gasp in horror. Thankfully, however, it was not to choke him, though I doubt that Scaurus appreciated this all that much, while what Corbulo intended to do became clear when I realized that, since I had been watching the hand heading for Scaurus' throat, I missed his other hand grabbing Scaurus by the *baltea,* then in one smooth motion that I was uncertain that even I could have done, he yanked Scaurus off of his feet and lifted him above his head, holding him aloft for a heartbeat before he then threw him bodily back into the middle of the square. Only by the grace of the gods did Scaurus have the presence of mind to try and tuck himself into a ball, so that he did not break anything, though I felt his impact with the ground vibrating up through my legs. The buzzing of the spectators, which had stopped as if cut by some imaginary knife, was suddenly replaced by a collective gasp, followed immediately by a cacophony of noise, with some men bellowing with the kind of savage exultation that comes during a gladiatorial contest when one contestant bests another in a manner that men would be talking about for days, or longer, while others shouted a protest about how what was supposed to be a sparring session had turned into something decidedly different. I think I can be excused because my first action was to look over at the Primus Pilus, but his mouth was hanging open in shock, seemingly as unable to speak as I was.

"*Centurion! Stop Corbulo!*"

I spun about at Closus' warning, which he had shouted to me as the one closest to the pair, seeing Corbulo standing over Scaurus, with his *rudis* that he had snatched up off the ground in his hand, and without thinking, I broke into a sprint. As often happens in moments like this, things slowed down, so I saw his arm drawing back, and while his features were obscured by the faceguard, in that moment, I held no doubt that he intended to plunge that *rudis* into Scaurus' face, knowing as well that the wicker faceguard would be useless, which was why I did not even attempt to shout at him to stop, instead launching my body from the full sprint with my feet leaving the ground, slamming into him with enough force to take him off his own feet, although he had the protection of his armor from the weight of my body driving him into the ground. The fact that he was protected by his armor was fine for him; I was wearing just my tunic, and the iron plates and edges of the *segmentata* left several bruises and a handful of small cuts all over my upper body, none of which I noticed in the moment. Straddling him, I rolled him over then reached down and yanked the faceguard free from his helmet, fully prepared and intending to snarl into his face that he was well and truly fucked and heading for a flogging, but what I saw stopped me cold. Staring up at me was a blinking, confused youth, and if I had been punched in the stomach, the effect could not have been more dramatic, seeing in this moment an image that could have been my own reflecting back at me from a polished bronze mirror.

"C-C-Centurion? W-what happened? What are you doing?" he stammered, but then, before I could answer, I saw the change, the look of dawning recognition flood his features, although it was the despair in his voice that I will take with me into the afterlife. "I did it again, didn't I?"

"Yes, Corbulo. You did."

It was all I could think to say.

"The first time I can remember I was about ten. My best friend Marcus had promised to give me a puppy from the litter his dog Lupa had just had, but then he said he changed his mind. He wanted a whole *sestertius* for it, and I didn't have it. When I went to Manius Corbulo, he said that he couldn't afford it right then because he needed to buy a cow since ours had just died. That," Corbulo shrugged, "was true, so I understood. But then I went back and I begged Marcus, and he just laughed at me." He stopped then, ostensibly to take a sip from the cup of watered wine, but I saw his hand shaking as he lifted it to his lips. Setting the cup back down, I noticed how he refused to look me in the eye, although I felt certain I knew what was coming, because what Corbulo was saying contained echoes of my own past. He resumed, "It was him laughing at me that did it. I just got...angry."

Since I knew exactly what he meant, I did not press for details, although I did ask, "And what happened to Marcus?"

"I broke both of his arms," Corbulo sighed. "But then Manius Corbulo was forced to pay Marcus' father some money, and it was enough that we couldn't buy a cow that year."

"I can't imagine he was very happy with you," I commented.

To my surprise, Corbulo shook his head as he replied, "He never said a word about it to me. If anything, he just seemed...sad."

"He was a good father to you?"

Corbulo considered, though not for long, then nodded.

"Yes, he was. Even after he told me that he wasn't my real father after…after something else happened when I was thirteen."

This was the incident I knew about, at least that something had happened, but while I was curious about it, I decided that it was not crucial to know the specifics.

Instead, I asked, "How many times has this kind of thing happened?"

"Not that many times," he replied, then thought for a moment. "Counting today, I think this is the fourth, or maybe the fifth time."

Despite my decision of a moment earlier, before I could stop, I heard myself asking, "Have you ever killed anyone, Corbulo?"

His eyes once again dropped to the floor of my private quarters to stare at the carpet that helps keep the floor warm, one of those that Alex's father purloined in Alexandria, but I knew he was not studying the pattern, however intricate it was, or even seeing it, and after a heartbeat, he nodded.

"And it was when you were in that…state? Like you were with Scaurus?" He nodded again, but this time, I was not going to be satisfied with just a nonverbal response. "Was it when you were thirteen? Don't just nod," I snapped, inwardly wincing knowing this was not the wisest way.

However, this did not upset him, reminding me of the almost overwhelming lethargy and disinterest in everything that seems to be one of the prices that men with Pullus blood must pay immediately after what those around us insist is some sort of divine fit, as if that explains why we have this volcanic rage simmering just underneath the surface.

"Yes, sir," he said dully, "it was when I was thirteen."

I will not divulge the details other than to say that the circumstances were unlike anything that my father faced when he was about the same age and he was secretly training at the *ludus* his family owned in Arelate. In Corbulo's case, his rage was triggered when he entered their barn and found one of the freedman laborers Manius Corbulo hired seasonally on top of one of Corbulo's daughters, the girl being eleven at the time and who, at that moment, Titus Corbulo believed was his sister.

Just as happened with Scaurus, he had no real memory of what took place, although the aftermath was undeniable; the freedman's face was crushed beyond recognition, and while his sister corroborated what had taken place, their relationship was destined to never be the same.

"She was always a little afraid of me after that," he said sadly. "Not that I could blame her."

This was the event that led Manius Corbulo to tell Corbulo the truth of who he was, and who his real father was, but it also marked the beginning of the trouble between the elder Corbulo and my brother, culminating with him sitting in front of my desk.

"Have you made things right with Scaurus?" I asked, and he grimaced, though I learned why soon enough.

"I'm doing his wash and varnishing his leathers for the rest of our training," he replied ruefully. "That was his price."

I hid my amusement, seeing this as a positive sign, and it turned out to be just that, although I was still quite surprised when I learned that the pair agreed that if they ended up in the same Century, they would be close comrades.

"The next time something like this happens, and it's not against an enemy, you're going to be flogged at the very least, and crucified at the worst. Do you understand that?" I asked harshly, not wanting him to get the impression that this was going to be a cozy get-together.

"I do, Centurion," he answered, but it was easy to see he was troubled, and he explained why. "I just don't know how. I never have any warning when it happens." He gave me a beseeching look then that made my stomach twist. "How do you do it? How do you stop from getting so…angry?"

The answer to that, at least for me, was and is easy to describe, yet it is difficult to do, and I also understood that it would do my brother absolutely no good whatsoever, so I did not bother telling him that what kept my temper in check was the knowledge of what it would mean to my wife and children.

Consequently, the best I could offer was to say vaguely, "I keep in mind what a flogging would do to my career." Slightly inspired, I did grin, "Remember, I've never been in the ranks, so I don't want to find out what it's like for you *Gregarii* now."

This did earn me a half-hearted chuckle, but I could tell this was not satisfactory; unfortunately, it was the best I could offer.

"You know that every eye is going to be on you, but there is one good thing about your situation," I offered. When he responded with a raised eyebrow, I pointed out, "Nobody is going to be willing to test you. If anything, they're going to go out of their way not to make you angry like you got with Scaurus."

He considered this, and I could almost see him turning it over in his mind before, after a long moment, he nodded.

"I can see that," he said thoughtfully.

"All right," I stood up, signaling the talk was over, "get back to your hut. And," I added, hardening my voice so he understood this was a Centurion speaking, "we're not going to have any more of these cozy chats for the rest of your training. Is that understood?"

To his credit, he did not hesitate, hopping up and coming to *intente*, and saying crisply, "I understand, and will obey, sir."

Fortunately for both of us, this turned out to be true.

When the day for integrating these *Tirones* into the First Cohort arrived, we were closeted in Macer's quarters for almost two full watches as the Centurions bargained, begged, and bickered about which *Tirones* would be going into their Century. There were thirty-five men left, with the second of the original thirty-seven suffering a freak injury that resulted in losing an eye when a training javelin caromed off a stake and struck him in the face as he was talking to Optio Dolabella. Although the regulations are clear on the matter, that Rome did not owe him a brass *obol*, a collection was taken up that meant that he was not utterly destitute when he left camp, but we now had two men less. Meanwhile, Volcacius and the other men acting as *conquisitores* had been busy, so that here on the Kalends of December, every other Cohort was busy training new men, while the original group including Corbulo were about to begin their last month of training, which would be conducted by the Centurions and Optios of the Cohort. This would still not bring us up to full strength, but after three months of submitting false reports that made it seem as if a plague had savaged the Legion, Macer had decided that it was impractical, and unwise, to have so many raw men in the First Cohort. None of us in the First Cohort were surprised at the vehement rejection of this change by the Pili Priores of the second and third line Cohorts, but finally, they were forced to accept the likelihood of the First sustaining higher casualties than would be expected if we were called to operate across the Rhenus in this upcoming season, and with the death of Arminius, there was such turmoil among the tribes that nobody was willing to wager that out of the void created by his murder by poison, another ambitious chieftain would not rise and try and solidify his power over the warriors of the various tribes by giving them what they wanted, a chance to kill Romans again.

Finally, a compromise was reached, whereby the First would still plump up with men from the second and third line Cohorts, but at a rate that would be more in line with what we did after the final campaign year against Arminius, while those Cohorts would be training more new *Tirones* than they had originally planned. Even so, we would still be slightly understrength, with a spare bunk in every section hut, but Macer felt that this could be hidden easily enough, especially now that the new Camp Prefect had arrived. That I was the one who my Primus Pilus sent to sound the new Prefect out about this little game we would be playing in our reports was because of who it was, although I was a bit worried when Quintus Nerva did not seem at all surprised to see me a few days after his arrival.

"I was wondering when you'd show your face here," he began, but I knew the former Alaudae Primus Pilus well enough by this time to detect the glint in his eye that signaled he was having some fun at my expense, and given what I was there for, I was, if not happy, then resigned to serve as the butt of whatever teasing he had in mind. "So, who have you offended this time enough that they want to kill you?"

"Nobody," I protested, then grinned as I added, "at least that I know of."

"Give it time," he grunted, then before I could respond, he said seriously, "It's good to see you, Gnaeus. I grieved when I heard about Tiberius down there with the Aedui."

Recalling that my former Primus Pilus and the man Nerva was replacing as Camp Prefect, who had never once referred to me by *praenomen* while he was my commanding officer, had almost always referred to me by that once he was Prefect, I did not read much into Nerva's familiarity.

"Thank you, sir. Yes, it was a bitter blow for all of us," I answered, bracing myself for the questions, but to my surprise, he did no such thing.

Instead, he sat back, lacing his fingers across his stomach as he regarded me under his bushy, iron-gray eyebrows that I suddenly remembered tended to move quite a bit whenever he spoke.

"Before you say anything about your visit," he broke the brief silence, "allow me to venture a guess." Even if he had not been Camp Prefect, I was not about to refuse, and I nodded my agreement. In a conversational tone, he said, "I'm guessing that Primus Pilus Macer sent you to talk about a potentially...sensitive subject, and he chose you because of our time together when we were aiding that useless heap of *cac* that just happened to be shaped like a man usurp Maroboduus."

I did not see any point in denying what was obvious, so I did not try, but I did say, "Just because we were together helping Catualda, that doesn't necessarily mean that I'd be the right choice. After all," I grinned, "as I recall, when we were in Rome and I was with the Praetorians, you didn't have much good to say about me to Primus Pilus Macer."

"That's true," he agreed. "But when we returned from that Marcomanni nonsense, I sent him a letter, telling him that I had misjudged you and that you're one of the best Centurions who has ever served under my command in any capacity."

"He never mentioned a word to me about it." I could not hide my surprise.

"Well," Nerva shrugged, "that was his decision because I never asked him to keep it to himself. Now," his tone became businesslike, "was I correct or not?"

"You were," I confirmed, but he was not through.

"Since I guessed correctly about that, would you allow me to guess as to what the specific topic actually is?" I nodded again, whereupon he proved he knew. "I saw the reports that were sent to Rome by Varro," he began. His tone became grim, which was understandable because he continued, "I also saw the reports sent by *Praetor* Silius, and I'm not going to put you in difficulty by asking which one is accurate, because I already know." This was a relief, which I tried not to show, and Nerva went on, "I also saw your reports since you've returned when I was still in Mogontiacum and making preparations to assume my new post." The glint of amusement returned to his eye. "How tragic, to whip those Aedui rebels with negligible losses, only to lose so many men to a fever. Not," he held up a hand, "from the plague, but fever."

It was certainly a valid concern, and it was something that was discussed quite a bit, but the problem facing Macer was there was no way to know how those reports were received in Rome, and we were just weeks away from the new *Praetor* arriving to replace Gaius Silius.

"That being said," Nerva continued, "I'm not happy at the idea of having an understrength Legion, or a Legion where the front line Cohorts, especially the First, has so much new meat. So," he made a tent out of his fingers, placing them under his chin as he gazed at me with an expression that gave nothing away, "to that end, here's what I'm willing to do."

By the time he was finished, I was the one struggling to contain my relief. Aside from this first draft of men, the First Cohort would be plumping up the rest of the way in the traditional method, and it would fall on the second line Cohorts to supply the rest, while the third line Cohorts would be supplying the Second through Fourth Cohorts. In terms of how we were reporting matters, it would not change; men would still be "dying" from a fever instead of how they really fell, months earlier by this point, but now we would have Nerva corroborating that we were being stricken by a fever. The urns that had gone into storage would be parceled out and sent to their families, yet despite the fact that none of us were happy that the families would be told that their loved ones had died a rather inglorious death lying on a cot in the hospital in

Ubiorum, even after weeks of discussion, nobody could come up with a method whereby the survivors were informed of the real circumstances of their Legionary's demise. When all was said and done, the changes made were minor, but I know that it was a relief to all of us, Macer in particular, to have a Camp Prefect firmly on our side.

None of those good feelings were present in Macer's quarters now, as Clepsina insisted that he was getting fucked, in our parlance, when it came to those names who were desired by more than just the Primus Pilus Posterior. Specifically, it was the fate of Diadematus, the tanner's son who, after his draw against Caprarius, had gone undefeated until his final bout, losing to the only *Tirone* who never lost, and I do not believe I need to name that *Tiro*. In fact, I was surprised and disturbed in equal measure that, contrary to my expectations, none of the others, including Macer, had put up any kind of a fight about Corbulo being in my Century. What was clear was that while, as I would learn, the reasons varied somewhat, there was a common thread.

"If he gets out of control like he did that first time, you're the only one who can put him down."

While somewhat flattering, it was more concerning seeing the conviction that each of my fellow Centurions had about the inevitability of Corbulo losing his head, but when I pointed out that I had never undergone one of these fits at any time other than during a moment where my life and the lives of others were at stake, Gratianus was simply the first but not the only man who pointed out that Corbulo had not been in any danger other than the humiliation of losing a sparring match.

"There's no doubt that he can fight, Gnaeus," Clepsina put in quietly, his calm demeanor a contrast to Glaxus' histrionics of a moment earlier when he evoked memories of the revolt and the horror of having a man like Titus Corbulo as one of the rebels. Thankfully, this was met by the others with a rolling of eyes or quiet snorts of disbelief before Clepsina began speaking, and he continued, "The question is how much time and effort are you or any of us going to have to put in watching him to make sure that he doesn't lose his head?"

While I could not argue this, I also thought it was both

unfair and excessive, and I pointed out, "How much time do any of us spend on an individual in our Century who might pose some sort of problem?" Deciding to pay Glaxus in kind, I pointed at him. "How much time have you spent on your man Quintus Cinna? He's spent more time on punishment than any other man in this Cohort."

"That's only because he loves Bacchus, not because he's beating…"

Glaxus stopped then, and I tried not to give him a triumphant smirk, because Cinna's last transgression, one that had gotten him flogged for a second time, was his attack on his close comrade after becoming convinced that the man had been filching Cinna's wine ration when, in fact, Cinna was so intoxicated that he had forgotten consuming it within heartbeats after getting it. Despite all this, the end result was that, along with Corbulo, I got five men, including Scaurus, though only after doing a bit of horse trading, taking advantage of Gratianus' ignorance that, despite their initial difficulty when my brother had bodily hurled him several feet, the two men had become close friends. While I never asked him, I feel confident in my belief that Gratianus gave up Scaurus in exchange for Decimus Philo, who was slightly older at twenty-one and had not distinguished himself during training, but neither had he brought attention to himself in a negative fashion because, in simple terms, Philo was one of those men who we Centurions would describe as dependable, the kind of man who forms the backbone of a Century. One way that I could tell that Macer had been fair was that when we left that meeting, none of us were wildly happy, but neither were we bitterly disappointed. However, I confess that I was probably more worried than the others, realizing during this meeting that there had been a part of me that hoped that one of the other Centurions, or best of all, our Primus Pilus, wanted Corbulo for their own Century, thereby relieving me of another headache. With these new assignments, all that remained was for the Pili Priores to offer up their lists of men who were transferring into our Cohort, but this would not be happening until just before the beginning of the new year, the traditional time for plumping up. Now, we had a month to finish the job of turning these semi-trained *Tirones* into men worthy, and most importantly, capable of marching in the First Cohort.

Despite Vinicius' impish suggestion that I not only put Corbulo in the First Section, but in the first file, which would put him right next to me, I decided not to place him in the last rank either, choosing instead to place him in the Fifth Section.

When I asked Vinicius why on Gaia's Earth he had come up with this idea, he tried at first to seem as if he was serious, explaining, "Can you imagine how those Germans would *cac* themselves to see *two* of you side by side? Between your size, and that," he pointed to the scar on my face, "I doubt we'd get our blades wet because they'd turn and run like rabbits!"

Fortunately for both of us, I had reached a point where I did not mind jokes about my disfigurement, and while I did not say so to my Optio, it *was* quite a clever idea. Still, my reason for putting Corbulo in the Fifth Section along with Scaurus, while promoting a Fifth man up into the First Section, was because of the senior Sergeant, Spurius Bibulus, who was on my list as a candidate for Optio, deeming his leadership style a better fit for Corbulo. While I am loath to compare any man to my Primus Pilus, Bibulus was cut more from Marcus Macer's cloth than my own when it came to his style of leadership. He did not yell, at least not often, preferring instead to set an example and encouraging his men to match or surpass it, and while he was no Glabius with the blade, I have him in the top five men with a *gladius* in my Century, and I do not believe I am boasting when I say that I would put up my Century against any in not just the 1st Legion, but the Army of the Upper Rhenus when it comes to overall skill. In short, I thought Corbulo would benefit from having Bibulus as his Sergeant, and I would benefit from easing one of the myriad headaches that are part of a Centurion's life.

One other unfortunate consequence of the changes to our training routine forced on us by the Sacrovir Revolt was that we had no choice but to conduct training in the dead of winter, which meant that the new meat, none of whom had been in long enough to receive their pay, were forced to endure the harsh conditions during our training marches with only their issue equipment, specifically the regulation, unlined *sagum* and without fur-lined socks, of which most men have at least two pairs, using the spare set for their hands. The normal process of marching out into the countryside then building a marching camp was out of the question because the ground was too frozen, and even if we had been allowed to do so, we would not have crossed the Rhenus with just a single Cohort. On the Ides of December, the men from the other Cohorts began shifting their gear from their section huts to their new homes in the First Cohort, although every section hut in the Fifth save four had an empty bunk, which may not seem crucial, but when a Century is missing about ten percent of their strength, it means that tasks take longer because there are less hands to do the work, although it should not be a surprise that no high-ranking officer ever gave us ten percent longer to accomplish a task.

Throughout it all, I had no more or less to do with Corbulo than I did with any of the new men, content to let Vinicius and Bibulus perform their duties, preferring instead to restrict my exposure to the sparring ring. By this point, every man new to the First Cohort, whether they be this special batch of *Tirones*, or those plumping us up, knew they had to face me in the square, so I resumed my third of a watch at the stakes, and sparring with those handful of men, of all ranks, who were willing to spar with me. This when I came to the realization that, because of the wound to my calf, my mobility would never be the same again, though it only began tightening up after I had been exerting myself for some time. Meanwhile, at home, Bronwen's belly was growing, as was both Titus and Giulia's excitement, especially when it became clear that the new baby might share Titus' birthday, or at least have one close to his, seemingly growing at the same rate. Algaia became pregnant again as well, but this announcement was more subdued, which was understandable given that her last pregnancy after baby Diocles had ended in a miscarriage, but I recall Alex's joke about our growing broods.

"Before long, we're going to have a whole *contubernium* for you to command."

The initial tension after the excitement between

Sempronius and Libo had gradually dissipated, while Hecate had been quickly replaced as the latest object of fascination and desire at Venus' Passion, and while I definitely took notice of how quickly Pandora's grief about the whore's death seemed to vanish, I made no comment about it to either her or Turbo, reasoning that this was just a normal part of that world. All in all, despite the eventful year, the subterfuge being undertaken with our reporting to Rome that would continue for the next few months until the men who had in reality perished months earlier were accounted for by the phantom illnesses, injuries, and handful of desertions that every Legion suffers over the course of the winter months, and the unusual training schedule that resulted from it, life was almost back to normal.

With the end of December came the Kalends of Januarius, which also meant that the thirty-five *Tirones* new to the Legion became *Gregarii,* and those veterans who were new to the First Cohort would undergo a ritual that, while I had nothing to do with creating it, I did not do much to fight, which Alex and Bronwen appear to enjoy reminding me. However, having learned my lesson during my time with the Praetorians, the sparring bouts were spread over an entire week instead of a single day, and thanks to Alex, who took the time to investigate the veterans who were transferred into the First Cohort, I would not be facing two of the more skilled men consecutively. Finally, after some discussion, I agreed that I would face the *Tirones* for their third and final bout with me at the end of the week, and the lustration ceremony was going to be the day after them, this having become the custom for the previous three or four years. One difference was that, in years previous, this initiation of sparring with me had been extended to all the new *Tirones* in the Legion, except this year, it was not possible because of our heavy losses against the Aedui, which, in the final tally, totaled over eight hundred men. Speaking of what had become referred to as Sacrovir's Revolt, there was what I can only describe as a pall that seemed to hang over the Legion, or perhaps it would be more accurate to describe it as the kind of lingering headache and sour stomach that plagues anyone who dances with Bacchus the night before. I know I was not alone in noticing, because it was the topic of more than one hushed discussion at The Dancing Faun, on those increasingly rare occasions when I appeared at the *taverna* to sit at the table reserved for the Centurions, and it was not confined to just us.

Over time, a consensus developed that what the Legion needed was a good, hard campaign across the Rhenus, over and above the punitive forays we make whenever a band of Germans forget themselves and slip across the river to steal a few cattle and burn a handful of farms. Unfortunately, we are still waiting for that opportunity, and in most ways, matters were and still are disgustingly peaceful. Speaking personally, in terms of the wound to my face, while I had become accustomed to the reaction from strangers, the comments and barbed jests from my comrades, I will only now acknowledge that the biggest adjustment, one with which I am still struggling, is the damage that was done to some of the nerves, or perhaps the muscles, that control that side of my mouth. Whenever I smile now, or laugh for that matter, the left side of my mouth remains more or less immobile, but strangely, only when my mouth curves upward in a smile; frowning is not an issue, both sides of my mouth turning downward the same as always, something that Bronwen insists I am doing more now than I ever have. My children have become accustomed to this change; I know this because I see their eyes fixed on the right side of my face as they are telling me something they hope will please me or make me laugh, since that is the only side that registers my pleasure or amusement. This bothers me more than it probably should, yet it does serve as a reminder of being careful what one wishes for, because the gods may use it as an opportunity for their own amusement.

Probably not surprisingly, the week of sparring passed quickly, and while to the observers that assembled every morning I might have appeared to be as fresh and ready as I had been the day before, none of them saw Alex's ministrations that, as the week progressed, lasted longer into the night, and he had to pay particular attention to my calf with every passing day. In only a small handful of bouts was I pressed, including against one of the veterans who had been Glabius' close comrade back when Glabius was a Sergeant in the Fifth

Cohort, and I immediately saw by his style that he had paid attention to the Optio's teachings. He managed to land two hard blows, but since neither of them were thrusts, they were not judged to be killing blows by Nerva, replacing Sacrovir as judge since this had become an unofficial duty of the Camp Prefect in order to avoid charges of favoritism by Macer. A slash may not be a killing blow, but when it is applied to the ribs, or to the unprotected thigh, it is extraordinarily painful, which I could not have hidden even if I had tried. While I never asked him, I suspect that this was suggested by Glabius, in a way of exacting his own petty vengeance, but all he ensured was that it did not come down to a decision by Nerva because, while I was not enraged, I was sufficiently irritated to make sure that there was no doubt about the outcome, finishing him with a thrust to the pit of the stomach that knocked the fight out of him with the same speed as the wind rushing from his body, and I confess I felt an enormous sense of satisfaction as I looked directly at Glabius, who was standing next to Gratianus trying to appear as if he was not bothered by his proxy's defeat. It was a few days later that I learned that Glabius and this veteran had been seen out on the training ground, working with each other as Gratianus' Optio tried to prepare his friend for our bout.

Otherwise, the biggest challenge I faced was fatigue, and what damage I did sustain invariably took place in the later bouts of the day, while I quickly lost count of the number of *viti* I went through since I still refused to use a shield, although this also marked the year where I decided that I was going to begin training with the shield more consistently. As brutally hard as it was, and is, for me to acknowledge, I knew the truth, that I was not as quick, nor did I recover as rapidly as I had just two or three years earlier. Fortunately, my strength and the power behind my thrusts have not suffered, but most importantly, I swore an oath to myself that I would not fall into the trap of self-pity that I have seen other men do when they grew older, choosing instead to view it in the same manner as my father, as something that happens to all men, and following his example of working harder. However, according to Alex, I have only been partially successful in this endeavor, at least the self-pitying part, and he is probably right. As the day approached for the *Tirones* to face me, the anticipation among the Cohort grew, although there was only one *Tirone* who drew the vast majority of the wagering, and as Alex informed me, the odds were overwhelmingly in his favor when it came to lasting longer than any other *Tirone*. As Alex described the various wagers, many of which were standard fare, such as whether or not it would be a decision or a killing blow, or if Corbulo would land a slash or thrust, I noticed that he seemed to be growing a bit more nervous.

Finally, on the day before the bout, we were discussing the matter when he came to an abrupt stop and suddenly seemed absorbed in staring at his fingernails, and I snapped, "All right, out with it! What is it that you're afraid to tell me?"

"I'm not afraid," he replied, though without much conviction. "It's just that it's…odd."

"Odd?" I could not see any reason why he would make that comment. "What does that mean?"

"I mean, I've never even heard of it happening before when you spar, with anyone, let alone a *Tirone*."

He stopped then, choosing instead to stare at me, clearly hoping that I would come to the answer on my own, and while it took several heartbeats, it did hit me.

"Are you trying to avoid telling me that someone has bet on me to lose to Corbulo?"

"No," Alex replied, but while I was relieved, I was also confused, though the relief was short-lived. "Not some*one*. Now," he held up a hand to add, "Turbo said there's not much activity, but there are some men betting that Corbulo will beat you."

To this point in time, I still have not experienced the mixture of emotions that I felt listening to Alex, which I suppose is understandable given that I had never faced this situation before, or at least this was what I told myself in the moment. What I was completely unprepared for was the sudden thought; would it be so terrible if Corbulo did best me when we sparred? This, thank the gods, was a thought that was destined to die within the span of a heartbeat of it forming in my mind, but the fact that it formed at all disturbed me quite a bit as I experienced the very first feeling of what it is like to have a sibling.

I slept poorly the night before the final day of sparring, though I pretended that was not the case with Bronwen, but I suspect she was not fooled. Alex left early to go into town to make sure that everything was ready for the celebration at The Dancing Faun when we welcomed the new *Gregarii* into the First Cohort. Licinius and his Centurions would be holding a similar celebration in a couple months, but since they were behind us in the training, I had made arrangements with him to make the Faun off limits for the Fourth that night in order to avoid trouble. Adding one Century from the First Cohort to the mix at the Faun had been successful and for the most part without a lot of tension, but adding the other five Centuries into the mix was asking for trouble. He was not particularly happy about it, but he wisely did not try to argue, knowing that, since I am the owner of the Faun, he and his boys were allowed to remain there on my sufferance. What he did not know, nor did I feel the need to tell him, was that one reason I was content to let matters stand and keep the Faun as the Fourth's *taverna* was that I did not want the trouble that would inevitably come if what was essentially two Cohorts in total numbers used my *taverna* as their drinking and carousing spot. After breaking my fast and visiting the public latrine around the corner from our apartment, I spent a few moments with my children, which consisted of tossing Giulia into the air to her peals of laughter, while simultaneously answering my son's endless stream of questions. It was a sign of his awareness that something momentous was happening with this sparring session that most of his questions were centered on what I would be doing shortly, whether I was scared about it, and if I felt badly about defeating my opponents, but interspersed among these were questions that at least seemed completely random.

One in particular stuck with me when, in the middle of me explaining there is a difference between nervousness and fear, Titus interrupted by pointing up at a bug crawling on the ceiling, demanding to know, "Does he know that he's upside down, Tata?"

I was so nonplussed that I completely lost track of what I had been saying, and my wife entered the room to see both her husband and son staring intently up at the ceiling, whereupon she turned about and returned to our bedroom, muttering something in her own tongue, of which I recognized the Parisii word for "mad." Finally deciding that, while the bug might be aware that it was upside down, it obviously was not concerned about it, I announced that it was time for me to go to camp, reaching for my *vitus* by the door.

"Tata, if Titus Corbulo beats you today, will you be sad or happy?"

How, I thought with a combination of alarm and a small amount of amusement, could he possibly know I was wondering that very thing?

"Your father will be happy either way because, at the end of the day, he will be coming back to us," Bronwen said after reentering the room at my announcement, and in the kind of tone that both son and husband knew meant the subject was closed. "Is that not true, my love?"

I was not fooled by my wife's sweet tone, hearing the warning there, and a glance at Titus, who was looking up at me with a broad grin, told me he was of a like mind.

"Absolutely, *meum mel*," I assured her, waiting to wink at my son until after I turned my back to her. "You're right as always."

After saying my goodbyes and accepting my wife's whispered promise of what awaited the victor on his return home, I closed the door just in time for Titus to resume his argument with his mother that he was a big enough boy to be present on the training ground to witness his father's demonstration of prowess, and I thought to myself that I was getting the better bargain between the possibility of some bumps and bruises or spending a watch arguing with my son.

Macer had issued orders that only the men of the First Cohort be present for this final day of sparring, but inevitably, there were townspeople who had taken advantage of the fact that the training ground is outside the camp walls, and while as Primus Pilus Macer could have dispersed them, it was too much trouble to send them back to town. We marched out in Cohort formation, accompanied by the normal complement of slaves, *medici*, and the cart carrying the equipment, and being at the rear meant we did not have to bother with scattering those civilians foolish enough to think that their early arrival guaranteed them a prime viewing spot. However, some enterprising souls had thought of this beforehand, because there were a half-dozen open-topped wagons, all empty, that once we had arrayed ourselves into a square, they maneuvered into spots just behind the rear ranks, whereupon they began charging people an *as* for a spot standing in the bed of the wagon. Even as distracted as I was, I could not help being impressed.

"I've never seen that before, have you?" I asked Macer, both of us standing in the center of the square while Alex was busy attaching the wicker faceguard to my helmet.

"No." He shook his head, then nudged me with an elbow, grinning as he said, "It looks like there's a lot of people in Ubiorum who like seeing you thrash poor, helpless *Tiros*."

"Or they're hoping to see a *Tiro* knock me on my ass," I commented sourly.

"Or that," Macer agreed, looking away from me.

He cleared his throat, which as all of his Centurions had learned, never boded well, and I groaned, "Pluto's cock, what?"

"Nothing!" he protested. "I just had something in my throat, that's all." I saw his eyes shift back to me without moving his head, and he must have seen I was not buying what he was selling, because he admitted, "All right, there is one thing. You know that we drew by lots." I nodded; Macer had informed me that he had decided that this was the best manner in which to handle this most unusual moment, and I confess that I had made a small sacrifice at my household shrine the day before that Corbulo's name would come either first, or in the top five, but clearly, the gods were not listening. He hesitated again, but before I could take issue with it, he said, "Somehow, I don't know how, Corbulo was chosen last."

"Of course he was," I muttered, which caused Macer to flush deeply, and I asked coldly, "Who drew the lots?"

"I did, Gnaeus," he replied evenly enough, but I knew him too well not to hear the anger there at what he thought I was implying.

I realized I had not worded it precisely enough.

"Who was responsible for making the lots? Who had you draw?"

It was the look, a combination of awareness, chagrin, and guilt that prepared me for the answer.

"Gratianus," he breathed, then closed his eyes as he groaned, "How could I have missed that?"

Deciding in that moment there was nothing to be gained by making an issue of it, I patted him on the shoulder. "Actually, it's better this way. I know there are men who have bet that Corbulo will beat me. Putting him last will get their hopes up."

I grinned down at him in a sign that I was sincere, yet I was somewhat surprised to realize I meant it, mainly because at the same time, an idea began forming.

"I need a few moments," I told Macer. "I'm going to go loosen up on one of the stakes."

Nodding his permission, while I did want to loosen up, that was not my main reason, and I signaled Alex to follow me, and as soon as I had pushed through the men who were beginning to get warmed up themselves, I told him, "I haven't seen him, but I'm sure that Turbo is here somewhere."

"He is," Alex answered. "I just talked to him."

"And?" I asked bluntly. "How's the action against me?"

"He said that it's...picked up," he admitted. "Apparently, the word got out that you're facing Corbulo last."

"Of course it did." Gratianus' face, and the smirk he liked to give when he thought he had outwitted someone, popped into my head. "Well, here's what I want you to do."

By the time I was through, Alex was having a hard time smothering a smirk of his own.

"I understand, and I will obey, Centurion," he assured me with a mock gravity, then practically skipped off to find Turbo, the first of the two tasks I had given him.

Chapter 12

By the time it was Corbulo's moment to step into the square, I was certainly tired, but not nearly as exhausted as I pretended to be, swaying on my feet and weaving about to the point where Alex gave a whispered warning that I was overdoing it. There is no doubt I was fatigued, and while I was not surprised at the identity of the *Tirones* who gave me the most trouble, the difficulty I had in putting them away did surprise me, particularly Diadematus, the tanner's son whose style proved problematic in single sparring. He would never be allowed to show that kind of individuality when standing in the ranks, but this final sparring session was not about teaching as much as it was a rite of passage and tradition that gave their veteran comrades fodder for the tales that would be told that night at The Dancing Faun.

All told, there were a half-dozen *Tirones* who forced me to extend myself, but it was at least partially due to the fact that I refused to overpower them by using my strength and battering their shield, forcing their arm down lower with every hammer blow so I could perform a second position thrust over the top of their shield to finish them, or rushed them and knocked them down. Instead, I relied strictly on technique, and the consequence was that some bouts took longer than they would have otherwise, and in fact, some of the townspeople who had been so eager to watch the huge Centurion face the huge *Tirone* that their eyes told them had to be related finally lost patience and went back into Ubiorum. My tunic was soaked, despite the temperature that was only slightly above freezing and the cloud cover that turned the sun into a silver disk in an otherwise leaden sky, and I had drained two skins of water. What none of the onlookers or the combatants realized was that, when Alex briefly disappeared, it was to retrieve two items. One of them appeared to be a normal *rudis*, the one I trained with on the stakes, though I was not surprised when Gratianus voiced an objection for no other reason than to complain. However, when I held it out, just out of the reach of Gratianus and indicated the handle, which I had shaved down and shaped so that it was identical to the handle of my Gallic blade, Macer stepped in and took it from my hand before I could stop him, and I watched with my heart in my mouth as he examined it for a moment, then made a show of hefting it.

"This is a perfectly acceptable *rudis*, Gratianus," he announced loudly as he handed it back, his face betraying no hint of his thoughts, despite the fact I knew that he had felt how much heavier it was.

This *rudis* has a double layer of lead lining the edges, while the handle is hollowed out a half-inch deeper than the standard *rudis* and filled with lead, making it significantly heavier, yet despite using it at the stakes, I had never used it for sparring before, and by the time I faced my thirty-fourth *Tirone*, Appius Bestia, who was now in the First Century, I felt confident that everyone, particularly Corbulo, had gauged my speed and would plan accordingly. It took longer than I would have liked before Bestia recovered his shield a bit too far away from the center of his body, and he did manage to get the wicker shield back in front of his torso in time to strike the edge of my *rudis* and slow the thrust down so that if it had been a real fight, it was unlikely to have been a killing blow. However, when the tip of the *rudis* strikes the torso of one of the contestants, the force behind the thrust it is not considered, and Prefect Nerva immediately blew his whistle, ending the bout not a heartbeat too soon as far as I was concerned. When I staggered back to where Alex was standing, I was only partially acting, and I noticed that when I tossed my *rudis* on the ground next to a pair of spares, none of the men standing there, all from my Fifth Century, gave any sign of noticing.

"Here, finish this skin," Alex ordered, extending a skin that was clearly almost empty. "There's no use in wasting water."

Our eyes met as I took it from him, which was when I understood and was therefore prepared not to gag at the bitter taste of the elixir, the second thing that Alex had retrieved from my quarters, though it took quite an effort to pretend to savor the contents as I tilted my head back. Smacking my lips, I dropped the skin, taking the other one Alex offered, happy that I did not have to act about the comparatively sweet taste of clean water washing away the foulness after what I had just consumed.

"Remember," he whispered as he took the second skin, "it takes a bit before you'll feel the effects."

I did not nod or even acknowledge him because in the heartbeat before this, I had glanced over at where the Third Century formed their part of the square and saw Gratianus staring at me suspiciously.

Instead, I took the cloth Alex offered to wipe the sweat from my face, muttering, "I remember."

I tossed the cloth to the ground so that I could put the felt liner back on, grimacing at the clammy, cold feeling even after Alex had wrung it out before taking my helmet, which Alex had checked once again to make sure the faceguard was still secure, then tied my chin thongs before bending down and snatching up my *rudis*. This, I knew, was the moment where Gratianus' suspicious nature posed the greatest danger, and I twisted my body slightly, not much but just enough that I saw him glaring at me, yet when my hand closed around the handle of the normally weighted *rudis*, to my intense relief, he did not say anything, nor did he give any indication that he noticed. Just as it does when we switch from *rudis* to *gladius*, the wooden blade in my hand felt absurdly light, and I had to fight the urge to make a couple of practice thrusts and slashes to enjoy the feeling, but I managed to refrain, then for the first time, I looked across the square at my brother. This would be our third bout, and in that moment, I could understand why there were men who were willing to wager on him, because he had improved each time. I do not know why, but despite this being the third time we had faced each other, this was the first occasion where I was struck, with an almost palpable force, by the thought; is this what men feel when they're facing me in the square? What I realized in that moment was that I had never given any thought to this question; I had always been my size, and while I had met larger men, none of them had been Roman, exclusively being Germans. Yet, here I was, standing there facing someone every bit as formidable, at least when it came to their size and strength, and over the previous two bouts, I had tasted the power that he was capable of producing with his thrusts, but what stuck in my mind more than anything was in how much he had improved between the first and second bout. Most crucially, when I tested him the second time by duplicating the moves I had made that had led to one of his mistakes in our first bout, something I do with every man I am teaching, he had not repeated them, and while he had erred in our second bout, they were not the same ones, and he did not make as many.

Truthfully, most of the men showed similar improvement; there were four or five who, in my private estimation, would be blessed by the gods to live through their first battle because they insisted on making the same mistakes, but there were only a couple of men who showed drastic improvement with every bout, and Corbulo was one of them, along with Scaurus and Diadematus. I was barely conscious that I was watching Nerva walking into the center of the square, holding his arms out for silence so that he could speak, and I suppose I noted that the noise was at a level I had not heard since the very beginning, but most of my attention was on Corbulo, his expression impossible to read because of the faceguard, though I did notice how he was rocking back and forth from one foot to another, yet what riveted my attention was how he was holding his *rudis*, point down as his wrist moved so that the tip was making tiny circles. How, I thought with something very close to dismay, and perhaps a bit of fear, does he know how to do that, my composure sufficiently shaken that the obvious answer did not occur to me. Then, the shrill blast of Prefect Nerva's whistle drowned out the shouting, and without any thought, my legs began moving me towards the center of the square, noticing how much more quickly Corbulo was doing the same, with an eagerness that he had not displayed the previous two bouts.

"You did well."

Corbulo's response to my statement was to look down at his cup, but I could see that, while he was pleased at the compliment, which was sincere on my part, he was still upset that he had lost.

"I should have known better than fall for that feint," he said finally. He shook his head, and even with the din of men in the throes of debauchery, I could hear the rueful quality. "Even as I did it, I *knew* it was a mistake."

We had been at the Faun for more than a third of a watch, but this was the first chance I had gotten to speak to Corbulo with any semblance of privacy, seated at a corner table in the new part of the *taverna*. Corbulo had been sitting there with Scaurus, their new Sergeant Spurius Bibulus, and Numerius Aelianus, and I enlisted Vinicius to draw the others away so that I could sit with my brother.

"Yes, it was a mistake," I agreed, amused at the flash of irritation that crossed his face, making me wonder if I pursed my lips in the same manner. "But we had been sparring for a long time, you were tired, and your mistake wasn't the same ones you made in our other bouts."

"I *was* tired," he admitted, then shook his head. "But that's no excuse, Centurion."

In that moment, I knew I had a choice to make, and perhaps it was because of the wine that had been flowing, I chose to let the dice fly.

"Corbulo, the reason I did that was because I was fucking exhausted," I said, enjoying seeing his jaw drop in astonishment, and surprise, which made me chuckle. "Well, I clearly hid it from you. But," I shook my head, "no, I had tried almost everything I could think of, and I was near the end of my tether."

"I couldn't tell," he admitted. "Every thrust was like getting kicked by a mule!"

"That's exactly what I was thinking." I laughed; this was when something occurred to me. "So now we *both* know what it's like facing an older, more experienced Pullus, eh?"

While I said it in a lighthearted way, I was being serious, but I was completely unprepared for his reaction, the grin on his face vanishing and replaced by an angry scowl, and he snarled, "Except I'm not a fucking Pullus, am I, Centurion?" So astonished was I that I could not think of what to say, which he clearly took as an acknowledgement. "Exactly! I'm not a fucking Pullus! He wanted nothing to do with me! He abandoned my mother…"

"Shut your mouth about things you don't know anything about, Corbulo."

Neither of us had seen Macer approach, standing just off my left shoulder and slightly behind me, but my concern was Corbulo, who did not react in the manner a freshly minted *Gregarius*, or a hoary veteran for that matter, should when his Primus Pilus tells him to shut his mouth.

In fact, he started to come to his feet, which was when I reached out and clamped my hand down on his forearm, pleased to see that he winced with pain, while at the same time, I was made uneasy by the feeling that I was grabbing a twisted iron bar.

"Sit down, *Gregarius*," I ordered, hiding my relief when he did so, though he still glared up at Macer.

Who, I saw with some concern, was on his way to being drunk himself, but he dropped down onto the bench next to me, snatching up the pitcher to refill the cup Scaurus had left behind.

"Now," he said after he drained half the cup, "you're going to sit there and shut up and listen." To my utter shock, he turned and said harshly, "And that means you too, Primus Hastatus Prior. Is that understood?"

"Y-yes, Primus Pilus," Corbulo responded, and I was relieved to see that the anger was gone, at least temporarily.

"I understand and will obey, Primus Pilus," I replied, through slightly clenched teeth, realizing later that my feelings had been somewhat hurt, but fairly quickly, I understood why.

Addressing Corbulo, Macer began, "When your Centurion showed up here, it was with a different name, but there were men," I saw him give me a sidelong look, "who saw the similarity between your father and the Centurion. And," I believe only I heard the slight quaver, "I was his best friend, so I tell you now that he had no idea that the Centurion was even alive, let alone his son. At least, not at first."

"What does this have to do with me?" Corbulo interrupted, and since I was looking at him, I know that he was not the one who gasped aloud at his unthinkable rudeness to our Primus Pilus.

Fortunately, Macer is not the type to punish men for transgressions like this, although he did snap, "If you'd keep your mouth shut, you'd find out."

Whether or not he truly felt badly or realized what a foolish error he had made, I do not know, but Corbulo did sound sincere when he mumbled, "I'm sorry, Primus Pilus. Forgive my rudeness. It won't happen again."

Ignoring this, Macer continued, "I'm not going to divulge any of the details about the situation with the Centurion here. That's up to him to tell you." He glanced over at me as he said this, and I nodded my understanding, that he expected me to tell Corbulo the story at some point in time. "What I'm telling you is that he didn't know about the Centurion. And," he leaned forward and tapped the table with a finger for emphasis, "he didn't know about you either. I know this without a doubt."

He paused then, and while he took a sip from his cup, I had the feeling that he was actually silently encouraging Corbulo to break the silence, which he did by asking, hesitantly, "How could you know this without a doubt?"

I was certain that Corbulo was not prepared for what was coming because *I* was not prepared for Macer to answer flatly, "Because Niobe told me she was pregnant with you, and she asked me for advice on whether or not to tell your father. And," now he did hesitate, "I told her not to."

Corbulo and I stared at each other, and I suspect that we were both thinking similar thoughts, that we must be looking in a mirror, our expressions being as close to identical as it is possible for two men to have.

"But...why?" I beat Corbulo to it. "Why would you do that?"

"Because I didn't think he could bear losing another woman, and another child," Macer replied sadly.

"But he didn't!" Corbulo exclaimed, pointing at me. "He's sitting right here, and so am I!"

This was when I understood the look Macer had given me, so that when he opened his mouth to answer, I put a hand on his forearm to stop him so that I could explain, and for the next few moments, I told my brother the rest of the story, of which I had only given the bare bones during his visit for the evening meal at my apartment. When I finished, the three of us sat there in silence, while I warned first Vinicius, then Glaxus off with a glare when they approached the table, clearly drawn by the sight of us engaged in an intense conversation.

Finally, Corbulo broke the silence, speaking in a musing tone, "So, he only knew about you after you were grown, and he never knew about me." He had been staring at a spot on the table, but when he looked up, it was not at me but at Macer. "Because *you* thought it was best for him not to know. Isn't that right, Primus Pilus?"

I was not liking where this was going, but since I was not the one being addressed, I remained silent, while Macer replied evenly, "I suppose that's one way of putting it, yes, Corbulo."

"But you were wrong," Corbulo said bitterly, then pointed at me first. "He's sitting here, and," he pointed at himself with his thumb, "so am I."

"He did what he thought was best, Corbulo," I interjected.

"For who?" he shot back, giving me a hard stare that I did not like at all. "For our father? Or for him?"

"For the Legion," Macer said flatly. He surprised me slightly then, because he turned so that he could look at me directly to ask, "You understand that at least, don't you, Gnaeus?"

"I do." I nodded, then decided it was time to stop this now, returning Corbulo's glare with one of my own. "You've been under the standard four fucking months, and you're not even a *Gregarius* until the lustration ceremony in two days, so I'll forgive you for your ignorance, but there's something you're going to need to learn. Any one of us with this," I picked up my *vitus* from where it was leaning against the table, "or who wears the white stripe, or carries a standard, all know one thing. The needs of the Legion come first…always. What the Primus Pilus did wasn't just to protect our father, it was to protect the Legion by making sure that the best fucking Centurion, not just in this Legion but the entire Army of the Rhenus was in the right frame of mind to march against the enemies of Rome."

I paused to take a breath, which was probably a mistake,

because it gave Corbulo an opportunity to cry out, "But at what cost, eh? Was he happy when he found out you were alive?"

"I…suppose so," I replied warily, then admitted, "although I honestly never thought about it."

"That's because you knew him!" Corbulo shot back, and even with the chatter going all around us, I heard the bitterness and the pain there, while I had to acknowledge that this certainly had much to do with it. "I never got the chance, and why? Because of the *Legion*?"

"Yes!" I snapped. "And for the next twenty fucking years, you better learn that's how things work!"

Corbulo's mouth dropped open, looking as shocked as if I had suddenly stood up and pissed into his wine.

"Twenty years?" he echoed in a manner that alarmed me, and a glance at Macer confirmed I was not alone. "You mean I enlisted for *twenty years*?"

"Are you really telling me that you didn't know that?" Macer asked. "That Centurion Volcacius didn't tell you?"

"Who?" Corbulo shook his head. "I never talked to that Centurion. My…Manius Corbulo did."

"And he didn't tell you that the enlistment term is twenty years?"

"No," Corbulo answered my question, then added, "at least, not that I remember. He just told me that he was done with me and that I needed the Legions just like he had when I was his age."

This is certainly a common enough story, one that I have heard related more times than I can count, around fires in marching camps, in section huts, and in *tavernae*, frustrated fathers handing their sons over in the hope that the Legions will succeed where they have failed in turning their boys into men.

"Corbulo, the Legion isn't some sort of magic spell or charm that will fix your problems," Macer explained. "And if you're looking at being under the standard that way, then you're going to be disappointed. And, as I'm sure Centurion Pullus will agree, disappointed men very quickly become angry men, and they blame the Legion for that disappointment and anger. Those men never do well. *But*," he reached across the table to grasp Corbulo's forearm to emphasize his words, "what the Legion *will* do is not only give you the tools to become whatever you want to be and rise however high you want to rise within our system, it will give you the best friends you will ever have in your life, men who will become closer than any brother, men you're willing to kill or die to protect…or lie to them."

Corbulo had lowered his gaze to Macer's hand, and his eyes stayed fixed on it for a couple of heartbeats, with what I thought was a thoughtful frown on his face, giving me the impression that he was considering what Macer had said.

Finally, he looked up, not at Macer but at me, asking bluntly, "Is what the Primus Pilus said true?"

"Every word," I answered immediately, easy to do since I believed the same thing that Macer had expressed.

"Well," he shrugged, "it's not like I had plans to do anything different for the next twenty years." I saw the lump in his throat bob up and down as he swallowed before he addressed Macer directly, looking him in the eye as he said, "Primus Pilus, I want to apologize for my words, but I can't lie and say that I agree with your decision…but I do understand it. Besides," he actually grinned, "it's not like there's anything I could do about it now."

I had to make an effort not to sag in relief, and I was certain Macer felt the same way. He made his excuses shortly after this, and by unspoken consent, Corbulo and I switched back to safer subjects, like our last sparring match and what he thought of his comrades in the Fifth Section, and I was both amused and impressed with some of his insights about his veteran comrades. Once Macer drifted off to visit another table, I signaled Vinicius that it was safe to approach again, and once he was there and rejoined by Bibulus, I made my own exit.

"I'm an old married man," I joked. "All of this debauchery isn't good for my health." While I said it as a jest, I was also honest when I added, "Besides, I'm tired and sore from all you young pups beating on me."

I found Macer now sitting with Clepsina and their Optios, but since there were others present, I did not mention what had just transpired with Corbulo, deciding that a discussion about that could wait. Repeating my intention to leave, I made my way towards the door, exchanging farewells and the barbed quips about my performance that day, but just as I reached it, I remembered that I had yet to speak to Turbo.

Signaling one of the girls who served drinks, when I asked her, she informed me in broken Latin, "Master Turbo went to Venus' Passion, Master Gnaeus. Mistress Pandora said it was emergency."

I was not particularly concerned; "emergencies" were an everyday occurrence with Pandora, so I used the private passageway to the brothel, where I learned that the emergency was actually a disagreement between husband and wife that, from what I could tell, had begun the night before and spilled over through the next day and into the night. With a few words, I ended their argument by informing Turbo that the night's celebration would be on the Faun, thereby uniting them against a common enemy in the form of an owner who was too free with his largesse and, as nearly as I could tell from her screeching, literally taking the last crust of bread from an old woman's mouth. Rather than be followed from the brothel back into the *taverna* with a harpy gnawing my bones, I decided to take the shortest route out of danger, which was the brothel entrance, despite the fact that it was actually farther from my apartment. By doing so, I set in motion a series of events that have yet to be fully resolved.

"I cheated."

Bronwen stared at me across the table, and I could tell that she was uncertain whether I was jesting or not, but I was deadly serious.

"How did you cheat?" she asked, but I had just spooned chickpeas into my mouth, so I did not reply immediately.

The children were asleep, despite Titus' declaration that he would stay up however long it took to hear his Tata regale him with the story of his victory, it not being in the realm of possibility in his young mind that his father was capable of losing. Alex and Algaia were in their apartment, where he undoubtedly had already informed his wife how my day had gone, and I confess I was a bit concerned when I entered my apartment that she had already visited and told Bronwen everything Alex told her but she had not, which I had torn feelings about, but this had not occurred.

Swallowing my food, I explained, "There are regulations against blows or thrusts above the neck. Everything else I had tried on Corbulo hadn't worked, and I was getting tired…"

"Did you not use the elixir?" Bronwen interrupted.

"Yes, I used the elixir," I answered more sharply than necessary, but I was irritated, not so much by her question but by the fact that the potion did not seem to work as well as it had when I faced the Praetorians. "But remember, I'd already faced thirty-four of these new bastards over the past week and a half-dozen today, so I was a little tired already. And," I blew out a breath as I recalled the bout with Corbulo, "he's strong, *meum mel*. Very, very strong. And fast."

I know I have said it before, but it bears repeating that my Parisii wife is a clever woman in her own right, and she showed it then by pointing out, "So now you know what it was like for your father when he sparred with you, neh? A younger version of himself."

Although it was not quite a perfect comparison; my father was seven years older than I was at that time, and the only thing I had taken seriously in my youth to that point was the exercises on the Campus Martius, it was certainly close enough that I took her point, because it had been quite unsettling.

I continued, "I knew I had to do something because the parries with my *vitus* were coming slower, but his thrusts didn't seem to be slowing down much, if at all. So, I feinted a thrust to his head, and he overreacted when he brought his shield up too high." I shrugged. "And I landed a first position thrust under his shield."

My hope that this would suffice lasted the length of time it took her to ask in puzzlement, "But if this is against the rules, why were you allowed to do it?"

The truth was that Nerva knew I was fatigued and needed to end this bout, by far the longest of the day, and he chose not to blow his whistle to interrupt the bout, although that was not what I said.

"I suppose Prefect Nerva just missed it," I replied, then more honestly, I added, "I'm just glad that he did, because if that hadn't worked, we might still be out there."

"He is that good?"

"He's very strong, and he's at least as fast as I am," I allowed, somewhat evasively since that was not the question. I also felt compelled to point out, "And he was fresh, while I wasn't. He's got a lot to learn still, but I think that he'll fit in with the boys."

We fell into a companionable silence then, finishing our late meal in a leisurely fashion before retiring to the bedroom, which for a brief period of time was ours once again now that Giulia was old enough to share the room with her brother. Bronwen was undeniably pregnant by this time, though she was not yet at what I called the waddling stage, which she never found as humorous as I do, but she was also still at the stage where the midwives say that it is perfectly safe to have sexual relations. I had consumed enough wine to be pleasantly lightheaded but not so much that I was unable to perform my husbandly duties, as Bronwen likes to call them, and after making love, we both fell into a deep, satisfied sleep, sometime before the midnight watch, which meant that the sudden banging on the door made for an extremely rude awakening.

"Centurion! Centurion! *Pullus*!"

I have no idea how many times the voice that I only recognized as belonging to Vinicius just as I reached the door called my name, though I paused long enough to snatch up Scrofa's *gladius*, hanging on the hook next to the door, despite recognizing the Optio's voice.

"Gnaeus, wait!" Bronwen called out urgently, stopping me from opening the door, and when I turned I saw the sparks flying as she was striking the flint to light the lamp that sat on the table. I was about to snap at her that this was unwise, but she proved me wrong by whispering, "I will stand behind you and hold the lamp up so it will be shining in his eyes."

"It's Vinicius," I began, but she cut me off.

"And who else?"

I remember the thought flashing through my mind that her time in Rome had made her think this way, not that I was complaining in the moment, and once she was in place, I opened the door while stepping to the side, immediately feeling foolish when I saw that it was only my Optio. The next emotion was alarm when the flickering light of the lamp caught the gleam of what turned out to be blood that covered both of Vinicius' arms up to the elbow.

"Centurion," he was panting heavily, his face shining from sweat despite the temperature, "you need to come with me immediately! There's been trouble!" I was reaching for my *sagum* as I demanded more detail, my hand freezing when Vinicius said, "It's Corbulo, Centurion!"

"Pluto's *cock*," I snarled. "Don't tell me he lost his fucking head again!" I actually began to hang the *sagum* back up with the intention of telling Vinicius to turn him over to the provosts, thinking that if I intervened this time, it would become something he expected, but Vinicius shook his head.

"It's not like that, Centurion. I mean," he amended quickly, "yes, I think he had a…well, you know, but it wasn't his fault, I swear it. He and Scaurus left the Faun and were heading back to camp when they were attacked by at least five men. One of them got away, while Corbulo put paid to the other four *cunni*, but not before Scaurus went down."

"How bad is Scaurus?" I asked, my heart sinking when he shook his head; fortunately, he must have seen my face because he said quickly, "He's alive, Centurion, but it's not good. He was stabbed in the gut. But," he suddenly leaned to look past me to where Bronwen was still standing, and when I glanced back at her, she was still holding the lamp, while the other hand was to her mouth, her eyes wide, and Vinicius lowered his voice, "I tried to question one of the bastards, but he died before I could get anything out of him."

I followed Vinicius at a run through the streets, reaching the spot a half-block from The Dancing Faun where several men, some of them now holding torches, were gathered around four bodies lying in the street, their congealing blood puddled around their corpses shining in the torchlight. Most of the onlookers were wearing the soldier's tunic, but my eyes were drawn to the one man who was neither standing nor supine, instead sitting with his back against the side of the building, arms around his knees with his head hanging, and I did not need to see his face to know who it was. Seeing that there was no ongoing emergency, I stopped and took a moment to take in the scene; four bodies were lying in that shapeless fashion that is the sign their spirit has fled their fleshly encasing, while there was a large pool of blood but with no body that would have been the source that I felt certain had come from Scaurus, who Vinicius had managed to communicate had been rushed to the *quaestorium* during our dash to this spot. Despite all that was going on in my mind, I remember thinking about the bitter irony of Lucius Scaurus dying in a street of Ubiorum on the night celebrating the completion of his training. It was when I reached Corbulo's side that I noticed Macer, whose back was turned to my brother while he was conferring with my *Tesseraurius* Hybrida, so I took the opportunity to drop to a crouch to examine Corbulo, instantly recognizing the expression on his face that told me it would be fruitless asking him what happened.

"Are you hurt?" I asked instead. "Is any of that blood yours?"

For a long heartbeat, he did not move before he slowly lifted his head to look at me with the kind of dull, disinterested expression I expected, shaking it first before he finally answered, "No, Centurion." He glanced down at his tunic. "I don't think so anyway."

Since I was focused on Corbulo, I only saw Macer reach us by the sight of his *bracae* suddenly appearing in my field of vision on the opposite side of my brother, and I looked up at him, seeing the grim expression that seemed a bit accusing.

"Your *Tesseraurius* was the first one outside," he began. "He was heading back to camp and saw the end of it. When he came outside, it was just as another man ran past, and he was bleeding, heading in that direction." He pointed down the street, past the entrance to the Faun, "He followed the blood trail to the next corner and saw where it was headed before he came back to check on Scaurus and your brother. We've done everything we can do here. I'll put Clepsina in charge for when the provosts show up. I think we need to follow that trail."

I could tell by his tone this was not a suggestion, but I was also the only one with a *gladius,* yet at the same time, we did not want whoever it was who escaped to have more time to make a plan, or even worse, summon reinforcements. Consequently, I stood and stepped around Corbulo, and when I did, my eyes naturally were on the street so I could avoid stepping in the blood from the nearest dead man, and it just happened to be at the moment that one of our men used his foot to roll the corpse over onto his back, and I immediately recognized the face of Tullus, his eyes partially open, making him look as if he was half-asleep, his chest soaked in the blood that had drained from his body thanks to what I could tell was a *pugio* thrust; more accurately, from several thrusts, as if whoever had done it was in some sort of frenzy.

Macer was clearly impatient, so I did not say anything and led the way, the trail easy to spot because the wounded man was using the walls of the building for support, and the blood he was spilling fell within the circles of light created by the torches placed in brackets to provide illumination. Setting the pace, I moved at a quick trot, slowing only when I reached a corner or alleyway, and while it was late, there were still enough people out, most of them men under the standard, that I kept the *gladius* sheathed, able to see by the reaction of several of the men heading in the opposite direction that they recognized us. I suppose it is a mark of my hubris that I felt certain that it was me they recognized and not the Primus Pilus of the Legion, something that I never mentioned until this moment. Our quarry seemed to be heading directly for some destination, but was clearly stopping at every corner, the evidence of this the larger pools of blood, and I slowed just long enough to try and recall where this street terminated, remembering after a heartbeat that it ran into the eastern wall, and the gate that led directly down to the wharfs was a few blocks to the south of this street. While the main gates are closed at dusk, there is a smaller postern gate that is open so that the masters and freedmen crews of the ships that are a constant presence at what is now the second largest inland port on the Rhenus next to Mogontiacum can enter the town to debauch or eat and sleep at one of the inns. This gate is manned by a pair of men from the city watch, which meant that a man who was still losing blood would want to avoid it, but this was not why I discarded it as a possibility for their escape.

Once I had seen that Tullus was one of the dead men, an idea had begun forming about who was behind this, although in that moment, what I believed was that our fleeing prey would lead us to the man I was now certain had given the order. This was why I barely even glanced in the direction of the wharf gate when we reached the end of the street, turning left instead, and as I did, I glanced over my shoulder to check on Macer, a couple paces behind me, his face a mask set in the kind of expression that told me he was as invested in running our quarry down as I was. I still worried that he only had a *pugio*, but I reminded myself that he was an experienced, and deadly, man in his own right, despite his unassuming demeanor most of the time. My decision not to spend any time contemplating the southern gate as a possibility paid off when, still moving at the brisk trot, I saw a flash of movement about two blocks ahead, my eyes seeing what it took my mind an eyeblink longer to identify as a figure ducking around the corner, and without thinking, I lengthened my stride, immediately going to a full run.

"Gnaeus! Slow down!" Macer panted this, but once I had seen our prey, I am afraid that I entered that place where I do not listen to anyone, even my Primus Pilus.

Additionally, I only realized in that moment that my mind had continued working on the larger meaning of Tullus being one of the would-be killers, though in this moment, I still thought that Corbulo had been the target. As odd as it might sound, another thing that fueled my accelerated speed was that I was curious, wanting to know from either this wounded man, or even better, from the individual to whom I was certain he was trying to reach, either to warn or to receive aid from him, about why they had decided to try and kill this new *Gregarius*, although it seemed as if the answer was obvious. Libo, I thought; that has to be who this bastard's trying to get to, this idea driving me to ignore the growing ache in my side and burning lungs as I used my longer legs to close the distance down to the point that he was exactly a block away when he once again changed directions, this time veering across the street from the left to the right side to make a wide turn down the cross street to the right. When he did so, I got a better look at him when he was away from the shadows of the buildings, and I could see that he was clutching his right side while stumbling every couple of strides, enabling me to close the distance even further, but while I did glance back over my shoulder to see that Macer was now more than two blocks behind me, I did not slow down to make sure that he saw me. I was too close to running our quarry down, but it was only after I was several paces down the cross street that I was jolted by the realization that, not only did I know exactly where we were, when the man made another turn, this time to the left and down an alley that was exactly midway between the two cross streets, I knew where he was going. I knew this because this alley is two blocks from where Bronwen was waiting, hopefully not overly worried, but more importantly, I knew this alley was a dead end that terminated at a place I knew very, very well indeed.

Now, I thought grimly as I turned the corner myself, what will this *cunnus* do when Latobius smells his master enter his stable right behind him? I did abruptly slow when I heard the sharp crack, followed by the sound of metal grating on metal that I assumed was created by my prey using his dagger to manipulate the latch to the door into the stables, while I paused only long enough to draw my *gladius*. Behind me, I faintly heard the footfall of someone running, knowing that it had to be Macer, yet I still did not call out to him, my argument later being that I did not want to alert the wounded man now inside the stables that I was right outside, preferring instead to take the risk of letting Macer run past the alley. I heard him do so, puffing mightily, but I kept my eyes on the doorway, relaxing slightly when I heard my Primus Pilus' footsteps receding off to my right rear, although even in that moment, there was a part of my mind that was chiding me for being so reckless and sure of myself that I did not want an experienced man at my side. I do not know why, but I approached the door as silently as I could, trying mightily to make my breathing less audible, seeing that the door was ajar because the latch mechanism was hanging askew from where it had been pried open. It was not enough of a crack for me to peer in, it naturally being as black as pitch inside, the only light source being the large openings at both ends of the building just under the peak of the roof. The large double doors were to my left, high enough that a mounted man could enter if he bent down, the alley leading directly to the building, and I had always wondered which had come first, the alley or the stables. There was another large door, the same size that would allow a mounted man to pass, but only a single one on the opposite side of the stable that led to the enclosure where the horses were allowed to spend time out in the open air, although stallions like Latobius had their own times where they were not with other stallions, or mares in season.

It was where Latobius' stall was located that gave me the idea, being at the far end, next to the opposite door, which is closed at night, and I stepped immediately next to the small door, hoping that my odor would reach my horse through the small gap. This did not happen even after a couple of heartbeats so, with my left hand, I pulled the door open wider, gritting my teeth as I prepared for the squeal of hinges, but the gods smiled on me because when they did protest, it was a fraction of an eyeblink after I heard what I will cross the river believing was my horse shouting a warning. Normally, when Latobius catches my scent, I am usually still a few paces away from the entrance to the stables because the doors are kept open during the day, and he will either issue a soft nicker or simply blow out a huge gust of air through his nostrils, accompanying it with a stamp or two of a hoof. On this night, however, he gave what could only be described as a horse version of a shout, in the form of a full-throated whinny, and I did not hesitate. Throwing the door open, I moved fast, counting on my eyes to spot my target because I was certain that Latobius' warning that shattered the quiet would elicit a reaction, either with the man inside the stable spinning about from facing the door or at the very least turning his head. I was right; I spotted the movement immediately, sensing as much as seeing that my foe had begun turning his body towards Latobius in an unconscious reaction, and by the time I slammed into him and sent him sprawling, he was only beginning to turn back to face me.

The collision was terrific, and satisfying, my left arm that I held out with my elbow bent and across my body striking him in the chest with enough force that it made my arm numb, wrenching a sharp, shrill scream of pain that was cut short when the breath was driven from his lungs by his body hitting the hard-packed dirt that was the stable floor. I could have ended him right then, and in fact, I felt my right arm drawing itself back in an unconscious reaction, the muscles remembering how taut they needed to be, with the point just a hand's width in front of my waist, and I probably should have followed through, but in the moment, I was proud of myself for staying my hand from driving forward and ending his life. There was enough light from the reflected moonlight of that half-moon that I could see the whites of his eyes immediately as he looked up at me in sheer terror, while it took perhaps an eyeblink longer for me to actually recognize the man in the gloom, and I heard a voice that sounded like my own, hoarse and breathless, utter it.

"*Libo!*"

At first, I thought he refused to answer out of obstinance, though I quickly realized it was because he had not regained his breath, and in that brief moment, I thought to call to Latobius, promising him a reward for his help in a soothing voice.

This elicited a sound from Libo that, while it sounded nothing like one, I decided was a bitter chuckle, then as if to himself, he muttered, "Of course this is where *your* horse is stabled." A bit louder, he said, with a hint of the kind of haughtiness that comes from a man who expects to be obeyed, "You know that you can't kill me, Pullus. Now, go get one of your *medici*. I'm badly wounded, and I've lost a lot of…"

"I don't answer to you," I cut him off. "And I'm not in the fucking Praetorian Guard anymore either, so I don't answer to your master, Libo. You don't give the orders here. *I* do."

"We'll see about that," he snarled. "But very well, if you're not clever enough to understand your situation, then help me find your Primus Pilus. He'll know when to do as he's told."

"No, he won't."

The only reason I felt safe to turn about to see Macer standing just inside the door was because Libo's attention was on him as well, but at that moment, his face was still obscured by the shadows. Macer took a couple of steps closer out into the relatively brighter light, and the expression he wore reminded me of one of our ancestor's death masks, devoid of any human feeling.

His voice was just as cold as he went on, "You and your men tried to kill one of my men, you *cunnus*. He was a *Tirone*! He's only been under the standard for four months! What could he *possibly* have done in that time for you to want him dead?"

Libo gave another mirthless chuckle, but he turned his attention from Macer to me, although he still addressed Macer, "Is that what you think? That we were after some…*nobody*?" He had pushed himself up to a point where he could support himself on his hands, and he shifted his weight so that he could point a finger at me. "We thought it was *you* coming out of The Dancing Faun, not some ranker!"

Macer and I looked at each other, and I could see he was similarly mystified, then I turned back to Libo, pointing to my face. "And not only did you not notice he wasn't carrying a *vitus*, but none of you saw *this*?"

Now, while it was difficult to tell, I had the sense that Libo was embarrassed, which he partially explained, "I was on the opposite side and a bit farther up the street, and I couldn't see his face. It," he said disgustedly, "was that idiot Tullus who initiated the attack."

"That didn't work out well for him," I commented, "or the other men for that matter."

"Your half-brother may only be a *Tirone,* as you call it," Libo shook his head, "but I know that I've never seen anything like that before, even at the arena. I," he heaved a sigh, "should have brought more men, but I thought four would be enough given the element of surprise and that the wine was flowing."

There were other questions I wanted to ask, like how he knew that Corbulo and I were related, although it was something that was obvious when we were standing side by side, but I could see that Libo was weakening, so instead, I asked simply, "But why?"

"Why?" His upper lip twisted into a sneer. "Are you honestly that thick?"

"I suppose I must be, because I have no idea why you'd want me dead."

He answered then, with a name.

"Marcus Sempronius." He pointed at me again, and I noticed that his hand was shaking even worse than it had been a moment earlier, prompting me to examine the ground he was sitting on, just able to see the growing darker stain as his bleeding continued, not clotting despite the cold, always a bad sign for the wounded. "You were warned there would be consequences for helping him, and yet you went ahead and did it anyway!"

"Because Marcus Sempronius serves our Imperator," I answered evenly, although I confess a part of me was marveling that this was a conversation at all. "And our Imperator is the supreme authority in Rome."

"He won't be much longer," Libo answered, and I do not believe there is any way that I can convey the magnitude of the shock at his reply, as much at the tone as the words themselves, his voice sounding matter-of-fact and, most chilling of all, as if it was foreordained.

"How could you know that?" Macer beat me to the question, and for the first time, Libo seemed, if not uncomfortable, then cautious.

He was also acutely aware of his lifeblood leaking out of him, or into his belly cavity, because he replied, "I'm not saying another word until you either take me to your camp, or you bring one of your *medici* to help me. Not," he added, "some new man who doesn't know which end of the probe to hold!" His head dropped, and I was afraid he had suddenly passed out, but he was trying to examine the wound, gasping when he used his fingers to explore it before muttering, "I think some of my tunic is inside me." When he looked back up, there was no mistaking the note of panic in his voice. "Well? Why are you both standing here, you fools?" Macer gestured with his head for me to follow him, and I braced myself to be told that I needed to run to the camp to fetch Philippos, but then Libo thought it wise to threaten, "I swear by Dis, and on Jupiter's black stone, that if I survive this without your aid, I'll destroy you both. And you, Pullus," I stopped walking to look over my shoulder, "I won't stop with just you. I'll make sure that your entire line is wiped from the earth like it should have been a long time ago. Prefect Sejanus told me that it was his biggest regret, that he hadn't handled you and your barbarian whore of a wife back when you were in Rome, but perhaps this is even better now that you have your two brats. Maybe I'll make them watch…"

He never finished, although I suspected that he was about to tell me that he was going to make Titus and Giulia watch as their mother was probably raped multiple times before she was slaughtered, and I barely even felt the impact of the sweeping blow that separated Libo's head from his shoulders, a reminder that, while it is not the same quality of my great-grandfather's Gallic *gladius*, it is close, because I could not even recall the last time I had sharpened the blade crafted by Scrofa. Judging from how high his head went spinning into the air; I heard it strike one of the rafters then fall to the ground with the kind of hollow, wet thudding noise that one never forgets once one hears it before it bounced directly towards Latobius' stall, clearly all of my strength was put into the effort. My horse reacted immediately with an alarmed bellow that in turn sent fear through the other animals, all of whom had already been nickering nervously while we interrogated Libo, but it was when the head went bouncing directly for him that he responded in more than a verbal manner, lashing out with one hoof. In a manner reminiscent of a game children play where one child rolls a ball on the ground towards their playmate, whereupon the second child then kicks the ball as hard as they can to see how far it will go, Libo's head went hurtling back in more or less the opposite direction from which it had been going, striking the wall of the opposite stall with enough force that we both heard the muted crunching sound that told us the skull was fractured before bouncing a foot or two off it back down onto the ground, where it rolled to a stop…less than a foot from the rest of Libo's remains, which had toppled over, in almost the identical position it would have been if his head had just fallen from his neck after being executed.

"Gnaeus," Macer's voice was calm, almost eerily so given the violence of a heartbeat earlier, "what have you done?"

At that moment, the truth was that I neither knew nor cared; he had threatened not just my wife, but my children, and it was with this thought in mind that, while it took effort, I turned to face Macer.

"Do you think that he was serious?"

I never asked, but it was clear that Macer was expecting something else from me, because when I asked this, he was obviously surprised, and it took him a moment before he answered slowly, "I don't know, Gnaeus."

"Neither did I," I said, and I was being honest. "But the one thing I do know now, and I knew it right before I took his head off was that I wasn't and I'm not willing to risk the lives of my family. As long as he," I pointed down at the head, noticing then how one side of it was a bit flatter than normal, "drew a breath, he posed a threat to not just me, but to Bronwen and my children. You heard him, Marcus." Shaking my head, I said flatly, "I'm sorry, but 'I don't know' isn't good enough."

I thought he would be angered by this, but instead, I heard him take a deep breath that came out as a sigh, then he said quietly, "I can't argue that, Gnaeus." He was standing too far away for me to see it, but I heard the grin as he said, "I just wish you could think of less...dramatic ways to solve a problem."

"So, what now?"

He considered my question, then decided, "He needs to disappear, but you and I can't have anything to do with it."

This I could not argue, but I braced myself for what I suspected was coming; I did not have to wait long for him to suggest, "What about Turbo? Does he have experience in...this?"

"You mean in how to feed a man to the pigs? And who owns pigs that have developed a taste for us instead of the other way around?" I said this in a joking manner, but I was serious.

"Yes, that's what I mean," he agreed, and I heard the anxiety. "Do you think he will?"

I nodded, then realized he could not see that in the darkness, so I assured him, "Yes, I think he will."

We left the stables then, though not before I went to Latobius, stroking his neck as I calmed him, his head tossing and blowing in great gusts, until finally he subsided, the sign he had calmed being how he thrust his nose into my midsection.

"I'll be back later in the morning," I promised him. "We'll go for a ride."

This was not just a reward for Latobius; I do much of my thinking while on horseback, and there was quite a bit to think about. When we returned to the Faun, the bodies were gone, and a pair of slaves from the brothel were on their hands and knees, scrubbing the blood from the paving stones. We entered to find Clepsina, Gratianus, and Caudex still present, though they informed Macer that they had all sent their men back to camp under the command of their Optios, but I was more interested in Glaxus' whereabouts.

"He went back to camp with his Century," Clepsina informed us.

"Did you tell him that I was likely to want to talk to all of you?" Macer asked, and when Clepsina nodded, he let loose a string of curses, then muttered, "I'll take care of that later."

On our way back to the *taverna*, which we had done at a much slower pace, Macer and I had discussed what to tell the others, so I was prepared when the Primus Pilus informed them that we had lost the fifth assailant, nor had we gotten a good look at the man, and I spent that time surreptitiously watching their expressions, especially Gratianus, but there was nothing in his demeanor, or the other two, that indicated they suspected anything different.

"I'm going to go talk to Turbo," I announced, which was prearranged as well. "I want to remind him to give those slaves out there a coin or two for being out there in the cold scrubbing."

"Why, that's kind of you, Pullus." Gratianus smirked, but I ignored him, knowing this was the last task before I returned to my apartment.

The rest departed, Clepsina heading to his own apartment, which thankfully was on the opposite side of town from mine so he would not wait for me, and I headed for the passageway, but Turbo emerged from it heading back to the Faun. Since a pair of girls were busy scooping up the cups from tables, I pulled him aside into a corner where we would not be heard. Keeping my voice low, I told him about Libo, where to find him, and what I was asking him to do, and if I made it sound as if they were not only coming from me but Macer was unaware of it, it was because that was my intent. Even as I gave him the extra instructions, I understood the implications and what it likely meant, yet what I had learned about myself, and reading my father's words, he was the same, that, even if I had not lost my head to a divine fit, there was an aspect of it that remained, and that was how little I cared about the consequences of my actions. In that moment, while my head agreed with Macer that the best way to deal with my admittedly spontaneous action with Libo was to make all of him disappear, my heart wanted to let the world know that this man and his minions had tried to kill a Pullus, and had failed.

I was not surprised to find Bronwen still up, nor was she surprised when I informed her almost as I came through the door that I would be going into camp to check on Scaurus. For the most part, she sat and listened impassively, although even in the lamplight, I could see how pale she was, which was why I decided not to go into details about what I had done to Libo. That, I thought, is a battle for tomorrow…or later. I did tell her that I had been the target, and that Corbulo had been mistaken for me, and this seemed to affect her more than anything else I told her, her eyes shimmering with tears.

"That poor boy," she whispered. "I cannot even imagine what that must have been like, to be attacked without any warning or any idea why."

Stung, I pointed out, "That's what would have happened to me!"

Blinking away the tears before she did so, she looked at me with a direct gaze as she said, "Only the first part, but my love, you know as well as I do that there are many men who would like nothing better than to strike you down. You," she tapped me lightly on the chest, "have done things that give other men reason to want to hurt you. But Corbulo?" She shook her head, and I knew she did it in a manner that I enjoyed because it made the light catch her red tresses in such a manner that it looked as if there were tendrils of fire around her head. "He has been in his training ever since he arrived in Ubiorum! He has not had any time to make an enemy." This was certainly true, yet I could not deny the spark of jealousy I felt at her obvious concern; whether she sensed this, or she understood how her words might be construed, she added, "He is your brother, Gnaeus, and you and he have just found each other. It would have been a tragedy if either of you died tonight."

It was with this thought in my mind that before I left for camp, I went and kissed my children, taking a moment to savor their smell by burying my nose in my daughter's thick curls, while Titus stirred a bit in his sleep murmuring a word that sounded like Latobius, reminding me that I had not taken him with me for a few days.

"Will you return tonight?" Bronwen asked as I walked to the door.

"No," I replied with a laugh. "It's only about a watch until first call as it is."

Remembering that I had not cleaned Scrofa's blade, I invented a lie about remembering it needed to be sharpened, but I saw that Bronwen was suspicious, though she thankfully did not say anything.

Reaching the *quaestorium*, I found Corbulo, Bibulus, and Hybrida seated on the bench where walking wounded or men with some sort of injury normally wait, and as *Tesseraurius*, it was Hybrida who told me what he knew.

"Philippos has to do some rummaging in Scaurus' insides," he informed me. "There's a scrap of tunic that he needs to find."

I knew that it was an accident, but it seemed as if this was the cue for an almost inhuman scream of pain to come from behind the wooden partition that had been dragged in front of one cot. After battle, this sort of kindness for the others around them is missing, but when it is a situation where there are only a handful of other patients, then some concessions are made for them. Steeling myself, I walked over and stepped around the partition, Philippos looking up from what was a gaping hole in Scaurus' side, which I could tell was larger than the original wound because it had been enlarged to enable the *medicus* to probe his insides.

"Centurion, please come here," he ordered peremptorily, pointing to a lamp that was sitting on a table a few feet away. "I need more light for this."

I did as he bade, swallowing down the bile that rose up at the sight of the glistening coil of Scaurus' intestines that were clearly visible once I held the lamp where Philippos directed. Whether he saw my eyes or it was a natural thing to say given what was visible I do not know, but he said, "The good news is that his bowel is not punctured, nor are his intestines." He paused to allow one of his two assistants to mop the sweat from his brow, which was odd given that, even with the braziers glowing, it was quite cool, almost cold. "The bad news is that I am having a difficult time pulling out this last scrap of his tunic." He resumed work without waiting for a response, not that I was in the mood to say anything, and I looked at Scaurus' face, my intention being to give him an encouraging grin, or perhaps a jest that might help take his mind off his agony for a heartbeat or two, but while his eyes were open, they were staring directly up at the wooden ceiling. I did see his lips moving, but he was inaudible, though it appeared by the cadence of his whispering that he was repeating a prayer to the gods over and over. My attention was still on Scaurus when Philippos suddenly exclaimed, "By the gods, yes! There it is! I found it. Now," his volume diminished, murmuring to himself as he used the pair of brass tweezers to delicately grasp something that I could not see, "if they are with me, the gods will help me as…I…do…"

He did not finish, but there was no need as he straightened up on his stool, holding the tweezers up so that I could see them, the jaws clamped on what I could see was a quite large scrap of fabric, dripping with blood. Out of the corner of my eye, I saw Scaurus' head move, and when I looked over at his face, I saw that he was conscious, and staring at the scrap.

"Normally, *Gregarius*," I deliberately used that term before the lustration ceremony instead of the proper title, and I saw the word register, his eyes widening slightly, "as your Centurion, I'd have to warn you that the cost for damaging your tunic outside of your normal duties means that a replacement would be deducted from your pay. But," I gave him as broad a smile as I could manage, "given the circumstances, I think we can scrape up a few coins to pay for it."

I did not expect much reaction if any, but he gave me a weak smile, and while it took him two times, he did manage to hoarsely whisper, "T-thank you, Centurion. I'll try not to fuck the new one up next time."

"See that you don't."

I made a half-hearted attempt to sound severe, but I could see he was not fooled, and I turned to Philippos.

"Thank you," I said quietly, which earned me an inclined head in response. Remembering the pain of my own wounds, I spoke a bit more loudly, "Given where his wound is, would a spoonful of poppy syrup be in order?"

"It would," Philippos agreed, and I turned back to Scaurus, winking as I said, "You can thank me later."

Telling Scaurus that I needed a moment with Philippos, I led the *medicus* far enough away that the *Gregarius* could not hear me ask bluntly, "What are his chances?" I saw him take a deep breath, and I held up a hand. "Yes, yes, I know. There are a number of things that could happen, but let's say none of them take place. Will he survive?"

"Yes," Philippos answered immediately, without any sign of hesitation. "As I said, none of his internal organs were pierced, nor were his intestines or his bowels, and I am as certain as I can be that I removed all of the foreign material from the wound. So, yes, barring the usual dangers, he should recover fully, although I am sure I do not have to remind you what it is like to have that kind of wound where it is located."

He did not; even now, if I make a sudden and unexpected twisting movement at the waist to the right, I experience a sharp stab of pain from the knot of scar tissue. Nevertheless, having that kind of discomfort is far better than the alternative of not having any pain because you are dead.

I realized that I had stopped listening when Philippos asked, "Did you not hear me, Centurion?"

"No, sorry," I answered, a bit embarrassed.

"Do you know what happened? Your man Scaurus was not

much help because he was in too much pain."

"Only in general terms," and I went on to tell him what I knew, though I was deliberately vague about who he was with, which Philippos noticed with some amusement.

"I see you are not naming any names." He did not smile, but I saw the amusement, then Philippos took a step away so that he was effectively beyond the partition, and I learned why when he raised his arm to point in the direction of the bench, although I was still standing at a spot where it and the three men sitting on it were obscured from my view. "But if I had to guess, I would say that at least that large *Tirone* had some sort of involvement in whatever happened."

"How do you know that?" I asked, hearing the defensive tone in my voice.

Now, Philippos did smile broadly as he looked back at me and said cheerfully, "Why, because he looks exactly like you, Centurion! And the number of men who want to kill you must be very large indeed."

"Oh, go piss on your boots."

It was all I could think to say, but the indirect mention of Corbulo did remind me I still had things to do, so after offering my arm to the *medicus*, then patting Scaurus on the shoulder as I told him I would be by to visit at some point the next day, I walked back to the bench.

"You can go visit him now," I said, then seeing how this did not assuage their concerns, I repeated what Philippos had told me, though I did think to add a warning. "That doesn't mean he's out of danger. You and your comrades are going to be busy making offerings to make sure nothing happens that sends him across the river."

"I'll make sure it happens," Hybrida assured me.

"Then, you can go see him," I told them, "but he just had a spoonful of poppy syrup, so I'd hurry if I were you."

They leapt to their feet, but it was with this in mind that I waved Corbulo off when it was clear he wanted to speak to me.

"We'll talk later. Although," I warned, "until we do, you don't answer *anyone's* questions, I don't care who it is, Corbulo. Tell them that I ordered you and that you'll only speak if I'm present. Understand?"

R.W. Peake

"I understand and will obey, Centurion," he answered, looking quite relieved, then moved at a trot towards Scaurus' cot.

Just as I was not surprised that Bronwen was awake, nor was I when I entered the outer office to find Alex seated at his desk, although there was only one lamp lit, and I could hear Euphemios snoring softly from behind the folding screen that gave him a modicum of privacy in the corner. Rather than trying to keep our voices to a whisper, I beckoned Alex to follow me into my quarters, and I confess that the sight of my cot was so alluring that it took an almost physical effort not to drop onto it. Over the next few moments, I apprised Alex of all that had transpired, leaving almost nothing out, though I did not make any mention of my extra instructions to Turbo, wondering if I had cut it too fine. While getting rid of Libo's body was a straightforward affair, especially once Turbo confirmed that he not only knew a man who kept pigs for this exact purpose but that he had availed himself of the man's services on more than one occasion during the tenure of my silent ownership of The Dancing Faun, which surprised and disturbed me in equal measure. Whether that gave him enough time to do the other thing I had given him to do before the sun rose and the townspeople along with it was certainly more of an open question at this moment than it had seemed when I was with Turbo. With an effort, I shoved that aside in my mind, focusing instead on the larger implications of the attack by Libo and his men.

"The fact that they're all dead is a good thing," Alex began, but as is his habit, he was not through, "in the short term. It will take weeks for Sejanus to finally accept that Libo is dead and not just missing, and that gives us time."

I almost blurted out why Alex's assessment about it taking a long time for Libo's death to be discovered was incorrect, but I did not, choosing instead to change the subject.

"I'm going to write a letter to Septimus," I began, and as I expected, whereas he had been slumped in his chair, the fatigue clearly affecting him, this got him to sit up straight, his manner suddenly alert.

"And?"

514

"I'm going to tell him that he has another nephew," I replied. I knew it was a bit cruel, but I paused then to rummage about for a fresh piece of vellum and a usable quill. Once I found what I was looking for, I laid them out in front of me before I said, as casually as I could, "And I'm going to ask him to formally adopt Corbulo into the Pullus family."

I suppose that one reason I relish moments such as this, when I catch Alex so completely by surprise that he is speechless for several heartbeats, is because it happens so rarely. However, I also knew him well enough to see that he was thinking furiously, his eyes suddenly narrowed and frowning in a manner that I recognized, so I cannot say that I was all that surprised that my moment of happiness was not destined to last all that long, the first sign the manner in which his eyes went suddenly wide, followed by a slow nod of approval.

"I see," he said at last, "or at least I think I do."

"Tell me what you're thinking and I'll tell you if you're right."

"But you'll be even happier to tell me if I'm wrong," Alex retorted, and I could not suppress a chuckle.

"There's only one way to find out. So," I extended my hand palm up in a gesture of invitation, "please proceed."

"By bringing Corbulo into the family, he'll be more protected than he would be on his own," he began, then paused, looking at me questioningly.

Pretending I did not want to, I nodded, though all I said was, "Go on."

"It also sends a message to certain other officers in the Legion, and the army. By acknowledging your kinship in such a public way, it lets men like Gratianus in this Cohort and a handful of others in the other Cohorts that there's essentially a second Pullus watching your back."

This was all true, but hearing it put aloud made me balk, and I felt compelled to point out, "I think given our respective positions, it's the other way around."

"Which I was about to say," Alex replied evenly. "My point being that it's mutually beneficial to the both of you." Suddenly, he got up and walked over to the table where I take my meals, bringing back the pitcher and two cups, pouring us both a liberal portion of wine. We were silent for a moment, both taking deep swallows of the unwatered wine, then he set the cup down. "What about you adopting him instead of Septimus?"

This was when I understood why he had gotten the wine for us, but the truth was that I was not surprised, which I explained.

"I actually thought about that," I answered, and I saw by his expression he had not expected this. "In fact, it was the first thing I considered. But," I shook my head, "that creates a whole other set of issues."

"He would have to be moved out of your Century at the very least, and probably the Cohort," Alex said immediately. "Although I'm guessing that Marcus would want him in one of the front-line Cohorts, and the obvious choice would be the Fourth."

"I would want him under Saloninus," I said, and this did not surprise him.

"But you clearly don't want to do that," Alex observed, and he was right, though I dreaded the next question, no matter how natural and obvious it might have been. "So I suppose the question is, why?"

"Actually," I admitted, "it's not moving him out of my Century that bothers me. In fact, in some ways, it might be better for both of us." I paused, thinking of something that compelled me to divert slightly. "You know that I'm going to ride him harder than anyone else, don't you?"

To my intense relief, Alex did not hesitate to answer, "I do. In fact, I worried about that, because he's so similar to you that I'm afraid that if both of you lost your temper at the same time…" He did not finish, only shaking his head, but there was no need for him to explain.

"That's certainly part of it," I acknowledged, while at the same moment, I was struggling about how honest I was willing to be before finally deciding. "But that's not the main reason. The main reason is because I already have a son, Alex. How do you think Bronwen would react if I just suddenly told her that I was adopting Corbulo as my son? She doesn't fully understand our system of adoptions or how we view them, but she knows enough that she would view it as a threat to our Titus. Besides," I said this jokingly, yet this was the real kernel of the nut, "how can I have a son who's only twelve years younger than me?"

This did elicit a chuckle, but it lasted only long enough for him to pick up his cup to take another sip, and when he set it back down on the desk, he was nodding.

"Yes, I see that, and I understand," he began. Then, after a heartbeat, he added, "And I agree. I should have thought it through better before I spoke."

I waved that off, thinking it unnecessary.

"So, I think that's what I'm going to do," I announced. "I'm writing Septimus to let him know he has a new nephew and we have a new member of the family, and ask him to consider adopting him legally, but also assure him that this is more about giving him his real name than any expectation that he would inherit anything."

We toasted each other then, draining our cups while I gave him leave to get sleep if he wanted to; I had resigned myself to this being a sleepless night, and while the moment was with me, I wanted to write this letter. Talking it over later, we both discovered that the other had never even considered the idea of Corbulo saying no to this offer.

My regret at not getting any more sleep aside from the perhaps third of a watch before Vinicius was banging on my door intensified with the *bucina* call that signaled the start of the day. Still, I was satisfied with the letter, and happy that I had changed my mind to write it out on tablet and not directly to vellum. Outside, the world seemed normal for the time of day; I could hear Vinicius bellowing at the Sergeants to speed our men up from the leisurely stroll they were taking to make their spot in the formation, while Sergeants bellowed at the men in their section because Vinicius was shouting at them, while the rankers bellowed at each other, blaming one of their comrades for being the cause of the delay. And, I thought with amusement, it's always the same names that are blamed as the cause for this uproar that is part of the morning routine in a

Legion of Rome. Judging matters in this fashion, nothing unusual had happened, but I suspected that I was not the only man who did not get much sleep the night before, imagining all the chatter that was taking place in the section huts as they talked about what had taken place the night before, although it did make me wonder how this would impact Corbulo and his integration into the Fifth Section and our Century. When I heard the rapping on the outer door, I shoved the last hunk of bread into my mouth, wiped the crumbs from my fingers and tunic, then walked to my *vitus* leaning next to the door leading out to the office, opening it to find that Vinicius was already there.

"They're all ready, Centurion," he announced, then grinned. "They look like *cac*, but they're all here. It looks like they didn't get a wink of sleep."

"I know the feeling," I assured my Optio, then we both wiped all signs of levity or humor from our faces as we exited the hut.

Because we were in the dead of winter and there was no inspection scheduled, the men were wearing their fur-lined *sagum*, and just as one can with tunics, it was easy to spot the new men in the ranks, between the bright red of the cloaks, and because none of them had had the time, or the money, to go into Ubiorum to purchase one. Once Vinicius called the Century to *intente*, the other way it was possible to tell was because they were the only men shivering, even Corbulo, but I suspected that his haggard demeanor had less to do with cold and lack of sleep than worrying about his close comrade in the hospital.

I stepped down into the street to face Vinicius, who barked, "Fifth Century of the First Cohort all accounted for, Primus Hastatus Prior! All sections are present save one man, in hospital at this time, sir!"

While he did not mention the name, I decided I needed to address the men, and once I returned Vinicius' salute, I waited until he trotted to his spot before I spoke, forced to raise my voice because of the hubbub going on around us as the other Centuries went through the same ritual.

"As I'm sure all of you know by now, there was an attack

on one of our own last night," I began. "And," I hardened my voice, "as you also undoubtedly know, four of the five men who initiated this cowardly attack are dead, and if there's any justice, their corpses are floating down the Rhenus right now." The men did not make any kind of overt demonstration at this, but I heard a low-pitched, barely audible rumble that might have been a collective growl of approval, which I ignored. Pointing directly at Corbulo with my *vitus*, I continued, "The fact that they're dead is because of *Gregarius* Corbulo here, but he was only able to do so because he had *Gregarius* Scaurus there with him, watching his back while he took care of those *cunni* who were mad or foolish enough to test him." This time, the sound was audible, and while not a growl, it was the kind of nonverbal form of approbation that men use occasionally when they are at *intente*, and since he was almost a head taller than anyone in front of him, I saw Corbulo flush. I was not done, however. "But right now, Scaurus is in the hospital, suffering from a serious wound to the gut. The chief *medicus* said that there is good news, that none of his internal organs or guts were pierced, and the wound is clean, so it's in the hands of the gods now. So, to that end, I'm...*suggesting* that you boys make offerings to Febris, to Dis, and to any other god you think will help his cause." Reaching down, I pulled my coin purse free, held it aloft then shook it so the sound of coins clinking together was audible, at least to the men in the front rank. "And just to prove I'm not a cheap bastard who tells his men to do something he won't do, I'm going to be buying a white kid goat in his name for the lustration ceremony."

The *bucina* sounded then, announcing the call for morning formation, which set the Centuries into motion, but I had essentially said everything I wanted to say, so I gave the facing command that got us ready to follow the Fourth Century to the forum. Everything was now part of the routine, performed more times than many men could count, whereas for a man like Corbulo, it was still relatively new for him since he had only been part of the Century for about a month, though it is still long enough to react automatically. I usually spent the interval only partially engaged, most of my mind occupied with other things, while a tiny sliver is in the present, barking out the command to turn at the proper time as we marched into the forum.

This was why I did not notice that Clepsina had stepped away from his Second Century and was standing there, obviously waiting since he let both the Third and Fourth Century march past, until I almost collided with him, but even if I had been fully engaged, I do not think I would have behaved any differently when, seemingly out of nowhere, he demanded, "Well? Did you do it?"

He had begun walking next to me as I drew abreast, but I was not feigning my bafflement, despite him obviously thinking so, asking, "Do what? What are you talking about?"

"As if you don't know," he snorted, but because his eyes were still on his own Century, he snapped, "Fine. If you don't want to tell me, that's up to you, but Macer isn't likely to take this innocent act very well."

Then, without another word, he broke into a trot, rushing to catch up to his Century for the moment when they entered the forum, leaving me grappling with what he meant. When it came our time to execute the turn, we did so, giving me my first view of Macer and his Century, but it was impossible to see his face from where I was marching. It was not until I gave the command that would put the Fifth into the right position to march into their spot immediately behind the Second Century that I remembered something. Clepsina, being a family man like me, had an apartment in Ubiorum, and because of where it was located, it meant that the most direct route from his apartment to our camp meant cutting directly across the town forum...the forum where the severed head of Marcus Curio Libo had been shoved onto one of the spikes that adorn the front of the small Rostra, although unlike its namesake in Rome, it is not made of the prows of ancient conquered ships, but was a simple wooden platform. Usually, these upturned spears were empty, and had been the last time I had had occasion to pass through the forum, but they were used on occasion to display the severed head of an executed criminal, depending on his notoriety, or the leader of a particularly pesky warband from one of the tribes across the Rhenus. I do not remember anything of that morning formation, my mind occupied with the question of what had possessed me to think this was a good idea, while my stomach began churning when, shortly before the formation was ended, I saw that Marcus Macer was looking over his shoulder at me, his face a cold mask, without the slightest hint of warmth.

Nerva, not being Camp Prefect long, clearly still remembered the days when he had been a Primus Pilus, wondering how long it would take for whoever was in command to relay that we would be doing the same thing we had done the day before, and would do tomorrow, meaning that his address was consequently brief, which is all I remember. Then, in the same manner as we had marched into the forum, but essentially in reverse, the 1st and 20th marched in opposite directions back to their sides of the camp. Returning to our street, the habit of years helped now, as I turned the command over to Vinicius, mouthing the same words as always, then entered my quarters, where I would normally go into my office and prepare the morning report. That would not be happening on this morning; I knew it immediately when I saw Lucco standing there next to Alex at his desk, although it was the expression on Alex's face that told me this.

"Primus Hastatus Prior Pullus," Lucco began, the use of my full rank another sign, "Primus Pilus Macer requires your presence in his quarters immediately. Optio Vinicius is in command until further notice."

Doing my best to behave as if this was a minor matter, I looked at Alex, but he beat me to it.

"I'll go inform the Optio immediately, Centurion."

Then, without waiting for me to give my permission, or even acknowledge him, he stood and walked past me, refusing to even glance at me as he did so, and I could almost feel the anger radiating from him. This was the first moment where I began thinking that I might have underestimated exactly how angry my actions would make the people around me whose opinion mattered, at least to me. Lucco just looked embarrassed, and a little afraid, leading me outside as the inevitable stragglers, almost always men who had a friend or relative in another Century, were the only men left outside, using this small period of relative freedom to interact with each other, which usually consisted of making plans for that night. I was relieved that neither Alex nor Vinicius were anywhere in sight, although Lentulus was standing at the door to the quarters he shared with Siculus and Hybrida, but when he glanced over at me, he seemed more curious than concerned. Very briefly, I debated asking Lucco what this was about, but decided I did not want to put him in a position that made him uncomfortable, worried that he would relay that to Alex, who was clearly angry enough as it was. Lucco reached the door, and while I was right behind him as he entered the Legion office, I did stop just outside to take a deep breath, and remind myself that losing my composure was about the worst thing I could do no matter what was coming.

"Please wait here, Centurion," Lucco said after I entered, but my mouth had suddenly gone so dry that I could only nod.

He disappeared into Macer's office and private quarters, which are as large as my entire hut, but for the first time, ever, in my association with Marcus Macer, he played the same game that is the favorite of insecure Tribunes and petty Legates by making me wait...and wait. Even more disconcerting was that, even after I tiptoed as close to the door as I dared, then leaned over and strained to listen, I did not hear one murmur of conversation between Macer and his chief clerk, their relationship being very similar to that between Alex and me, Lucco having been his clerk since Macer was a Centurion. I actually counted to a hundred in my head, then when there was still not a peep, I crept back to my original spot, standing there with my hands clutching my *vitus* behind my back while I stared at a spot on the wall above Lucco's desk. The absence of the other two clerks when we entered did not surprise me; at that time of morning, one of them was usually at the *Praetorium* delivering reports, while the other was busy preparing the Primus Pilus' break of his nightly fast. It was when they never returned over what was at least a third of a watch that I knew this was all part of a larger design; even worse, it gave me an idea just how enraged my Primus Pilus, and friend, was. Finally, when the *bucina* sounded the call that marked the beginning of the working period, I heard the first sounds from the office, a scuffing sound followed by the door opening, and Lucco appeared, his face pale.

"The Primus Pilus is ready to see you, Primus Hastatus Prior Pullus."

I had been standing so long I had lost the feeling in my legs, but I did my best to appear unruffled, and pretended not to notice how Lucco practically leapt out of the doorway to let me pass. There was no way for me to read Macer's expression, because I had my eye on the spot above his head as I marched, not walked, to his desk, stopping the required pace from it, which I had always wondered about as far as from where it came, crashing my heels together so hard that I felt a sharp pain, though the cracking sound of my leather soles meeting was satisfying.

Rendering my salute in the manner I had been instructed to during my time in the Praetorian Guard, I bit each word off, "Primus Hastatus Prior Gnaeus Volusenianus Pullus reporting to Primus Pilus Macer as ordered, sir!"

I had struck my chest hard enough that it hurt, and I now had two spots where I was experiencing some pain, in the hope that Macer would see that I was not taking this lightly.

I held my salute to a count of thirty; I know this because I was doing it in my head, before Macer, still seated, returned it, and the relief at being able to drop my arm was quite noticeable.

Since I was still staring above his head, I only heard Macer take a breath before he spoke, and when he began, there was not a hint of anything familiar in his tone, "There's one thing I need to know before we go any further with this." He paused long enough that I thought he might want some sort of reply first, though I had no idea what it might be, but then he asked, "Did you tell Turbo to do this or did he do it on his own? Or, did you do it yourself?"

I had already determined that stalling by asking what he meant would be foolish in the extreme, and I was about to tell him that I had done it myself when, as has happened before, I heard not my voice in my head but Alex's, asking, "How often have you seen Macer ask someone a question when he already knows the answer?"

This was the absolute truth; consequently, I said honestly,

"I told him to do it, Primus Pilus."

I saw him nod at the bottom of my vision, and I was struck by the thought that it seemed as if he had more gray in his hair than I remembered.

"And you told him to do it to achieve what end?"

Here it is, I thought. The moment where I have to choose between total honesty, or at least attempt to offer some rationalization; I chose honesty.

"I was angry," I replied. "And I want to send a message to that *cunnus* Sejanus that there's at least one man in this fucking Empire who doesn't fear him."

"*Well you should!*"

His verbal blast, accompanied by slamming an open palm down onto his desk as he leapt to his feet, made my ears ring, though the fact we were in a closed space helped.

It was when he pointed directly in my face that I knew what he was up to, yet it still was a struggle to keep my temper in check as he bellowed, "How many times is your pride, your damnable fucking *pride* going to make things worse?"

"Primus Pilus," I was determined to speak calmly as long as he was yelling, "while I understand what you're saying, it's also *my* life, and *my dignitas*!"

"Oh, fuck your *dignitas*!" He snarled, "And I wouldn't give a rotten fig if it was just your life! But not only do you have a family, who, I would remind you, have absolutely *nothing* to do with you and your feuds with men far more powerful than you, but you are part of *my* Legion! Everything you do reflects on the 1st, and if you end up like Libo feeding the pigs, that hurts *my* Legion! You're becoming a danger not just to yourself, but to the 1st, and I *will not stand for it*!"

If he had kicked me in the balls, I do not think it would have been as devastating. Never before had he spoken to me in this manner, nor had he ever been this cold, but more than anything, hearing it put so plainly, that his concern about my safety and well-being was based more in his concern for the Legion than for me personally was a turning point for both our relationships, and for how I viewed our world. So far to this point in time, we have never been as close as we were before this moment, yet what I have come to realize is that Marcus

Macer was not doing this just to punish me, because I can look back and mark this as the moment where I began the process of preparing to be a Primus Pilus, and while a Primus Pilus can be friendly with his men, and can even be friends with a very select few, the only way that friendship can succeed is if the subordinate man realizes that, if it comes to a moment where his friend the Primus Pilus has to choose between him or the Legion, the Legion will always win.

"What do you want me to do, Primus Pilus Macer?"

"Right now," he sighed, "I don't think there's anything we can do."

"Is it…the head, I mean. Is it still there?" I asked, and for the first time, he smiled, but it was mirthless.

"Yes, I knew what you were talking about," he said dryly, then shook his head. "No, it's not there."

For the briefest moment, my heart leapt as my mind ran away with itself. Yes! I told myself. Of course! Clepsina saw the head, recognized him, and took it. Macer's just trying to scare some sense into me, that's it! He doesn't want me to…

"Gnaeus," Macer's use of my *praenomen* was what yanked me back to the moment, and I saw in his expression that he must have figured out where my mind was going, "the reason it's not there is because it was taken…by Tribune Vitellius. He found it on his way to camp, and took it down. Clepsina saw it happen. And," he went on, "I just learned from Prefect Nerva that the Tribune has arranged passage on the first barge to Mogontiacum, and he's taking his baggage. Nerva feels certain that he's returning to Rome."

I was assailed by an almost overwhelming urge to vomit, but somehow I managed to maintain my composure enough to say, "I wonder what that means?"

"It means," Macer replied grimly, "that you're about to be at war with Praetorian Prefect Sejanus."

I opened my mouth to argue, then shut it, knowing that he was probably right.

Young Titus' prediction of a new baby brother turned out to be correct, which made him a bit insufferable for a few days, but his parents were too happy to be cross with him whenever he brought it up, which was whenever he opened his mouth. However, Marcus Parisius Pullus was born five days before his older brother's name day, arriving on the Ides of April in what, to my initial relief, was a comparatively easy labor when compared to the birth of our firstborn, despite both being the same gender. The reason for that has since become apparent; Marcus is much smaller than Titus was at the same age, and in fact is about the same size his sister Giulia was. What he lacks in size he makes up for in other ways, something that Bronwen is very quick to point out whenever the opportunity arises, which, like with my son, seems to be almost every day. Another difference is that he has my wife's coloring and complexion, with hair a deep red and blue eyes that are a stark contrast to his older brother, who has my hair and eye color, while Giulia is a beautiful mixture of her parents. I am as proud a father as any man, but I confess that matters between us have been strained, with Bronwen finding fault in my actions and attitude towards our youngest child when I swear upon the black stone there is no cause for her anger at me. It took almost a year before—after Marcus had begun walking almost a full month earlier than either of his siblings, but my display of pride was not sufficient for my wife—things came out into the open, resulting in one of our bitterest quarrels.

"You do not love him as much as you love Titus, or Giulia for that matter, and I know why!"

Bronwen had shouted this, though I was still a bit distracted because I had just ducked the bowl she had hurled at my head, and if her tactic had been to get me to freeze in my tracks and not keep dodging the objects she was hurling at me by shouting this, it worked.

Despite knowing it was unsound to do so, I stood there motionless as I stared at her and gasped, "*Gerrae*! What are you talking about? Of *course* I love him just as I love my other children!"

"Liar!" she spat, actually lapsing into her Parisii tongue, though she continued in Latin, "I see how you look at him! I see the disappointment in your eyes because he is small!"

Although I denied this vehemently, later when I was alone with my own thoughts, I began asking myself if it was true;

while I did not, nor do I now believe this is the case, I have tried very hard to not give my wife any cause to believe it. So far, this has not been altogether successful, but I suppose the fact that it is no longer something that gets thrown in my face on a weekly basis is a good thing. When it comes to his unusual *nomen*, I only have myself to blame, though not for the reasons that might seem obvious, and it serves as a reminder to me just how clever my wife is, because when she informed me that she wanted to honor her own roots by a Romanized version of her tribe as his *nomen*, I balked.

"But my love, is that not how you Romans do it? Your *nomen* is usually based in your tribe, is it not?"

"It is," I agreed, reluctantly, though I did think it important to add, "but it's not a requirement, and frankly, it's a custom that has fallen out of use over the years."

"That is what I have been told as well," She nodded, but while she seemed to be agreeing, I knew her too well to be lulled into a sense of security. "But is that also not one reason to do it? You Romans are very fond of your traditions and customs. It seems to me that it would be a good thing, that it proves you are a Roman who values the old ways, given...everything that is happening."

She did not expand, but she did not need to; despite the fact that up to that moment nothing had happened that might be blamed on my actions with Libo and his head, it was never far from our minds.

Still, I was not ready to give in, and I replied by acknowledging, "That's a good point, but our *nomen* is based on *Roman* tribes, and they're for the purpose of voting now more than anything else. They're not..." I caught myself before I said "barbarian," "...for non-Roman tribes."

This was when she sprang her trap, asking sweetly, "But what about Gaius Gallienus? His mother is not Roman either. And as your uncle Sextus told your father, is it really a battle worth fighting, knowing that it will make your wife happy?"

I was defeated, and I knew it, although I did groan, "I should have never taught you to read and use his account to do it."

"No," she laughed, "you should not have done that. But,"

her cheerfulness was particularly irksome, "you did!"

As far as my son's *praenomen*, I do not suppose it takes much explanation from where it came, although as Macer reminded me, just because I named my son after him, it did not mean that I would be treated any differently, though he said this with a smile. The naming of my son turned out to be less of an ordeal than convincing my brother to accept the offer of adoption from my uncle Septimus, which he immediately agreed to do after receiving my letter.

"Tell your, I mean, *our* uncle that I appreciate the offer, sir," Corbulo told me at The Dancing Faun, "but I don't know that I'm ready to change my name and abandon the one I've known my whole life. Manius Corbulo may not have been my father, but he was good to me. It," he shrugged, looking down into his cup, "just doesn't seem right somehow."

This was something I completely understood, and I said as much, pointing out, "My *nomen* is Volusenianus for that reason, Corbulo. And," I added before I thought it through, hearing the bitterness in my voice, "Quintus Volusenus wasn't all that good to me, truth be told. But," I shook my head, "it just didn't seem right, somehow."

He looked relieved, and when we parted, I thought I had convinced him, but that proved to be premature, and he remains Titus Corbulo for now. Otherwise, he has exceeded even my expectations, and best of all, he has managed to control his temper, and in fact, during a recent brawl out in town, he used his prodigious strength to restore the peace while managing to avoid the appearance of favoritism. He has become one of the most dependable men in my Century, and has never used our kinship as a pretext for special treatment, but best of all, he has responded to my treatment of him, which is harsher than all but the most recalcitrant troublemakers, with an equanimity and understanding that I do not believe I would have been capable of exhibiting. He is a guest at my apartment once a month, and it has become an occasion, one where not just young Titus and Giulia look forward to it, but Iras and Diocles are every bit as excited. For his part, despite my misgivings, Corbulo convinced me that he enjoys these times immensely, and does not feel put upon by the children.

"It reminds me of my sisters and brother," he explained once, forgetting that they were not really his siblings. "I always enjoyed spending time with them."

The other major event that has occurred with Titus Corbulo is that he has become a hero, not just in the Fifth Century and the First Cohort, but the entire 1st Legion because, as much as it pains me to admit it, I was finally defeated in a sparring session, and I still cannot decide whether it is better or worse that it was at the hands of Corbulo, although I can say this much; if I had to lose, I much preferred losing to him than to Glabius. As for the bout itself, I will make no excuses; he wore me down, relying on his youth and the seemingly inexhaustible energy that comes from being young, and he did not fall for any of the various feints and tricks that I tried. Finally, after what Macer assured me was the longest sparring bout in memory, when I tried to dodge his thrust, after he had managed to fool me into thinking that the one that had come an eyeblink earlier was not the feint it turned out to be, the wound to my calf betrayed me, my leg partially buckling, but even if it had not, I would have lasted at best a few more heartbeats. It is probably easy to imagine the joyous atmosphere, not just at The Dancing Faun, but as I was forced to endure hearing about, at every *taverna* catering to the 1st Legion, of which there are now almost twenty in Ubiorum. What I will say is that the loss spurred me to work harder than ever, and beyond that, forced me to accept that I would never have the same mobility I had enjoyed before I suffered that wound to my calf, which I still do not remember incurring. The result is that, so far, Corbulo has been unable to best me again, although he did achieve a draw once. For reasons that are probably obvious, the Primus Pilus has also expressly forbidden us from sparring against each other more often than would be normal in the rotation of training, though only after a month where we faced each other five times.

Although to this moment, nothing overt has happened that would substantiate Macer's prophecy about Sejanus being at war with me, I believe that it has more to do with a simple fact; I am not important enough to be anywhere near the top of

Praetorian Prefect Sejanus' list of enemies. Unfortunately, Gaius Silius is, and his travails are taking place now, here in the year of the Consulships of Servius Cornelius Cethegus...and one Lucius Visellius Varro. Yes, dear reader, just five years after he was forced to flee back to Rome after the debacle with Catualda, and three years after his inept performance during Sacrovir's Revolt, Varro's "punishment" for that ineptitude was being named Consul, and if what we heard here on the frontier is to be believed, it was a matter of days after he assumed the junior Consulship that he formally charged Gaius Silius with being complicit in Sacrovir's Revolt, and with misappropriating provincial funds for his own enrichment. The trial is currently taking place, while we are about to cross the Rhenus, our ostensible purpose to pursue some Sugambri raiders who crossed the river and attacked the outpost of Durnomagus (Dornhagen), but with the real aim of reminding the barbarians that Rome is here and always will be, so this is as good a time and place as any to stop, as I am joined for the first time with another man who, while still not carrying our name, marches with the blood of Titus Pullus in his veins, my brother.

Printed in Dunstable, United Kingdom